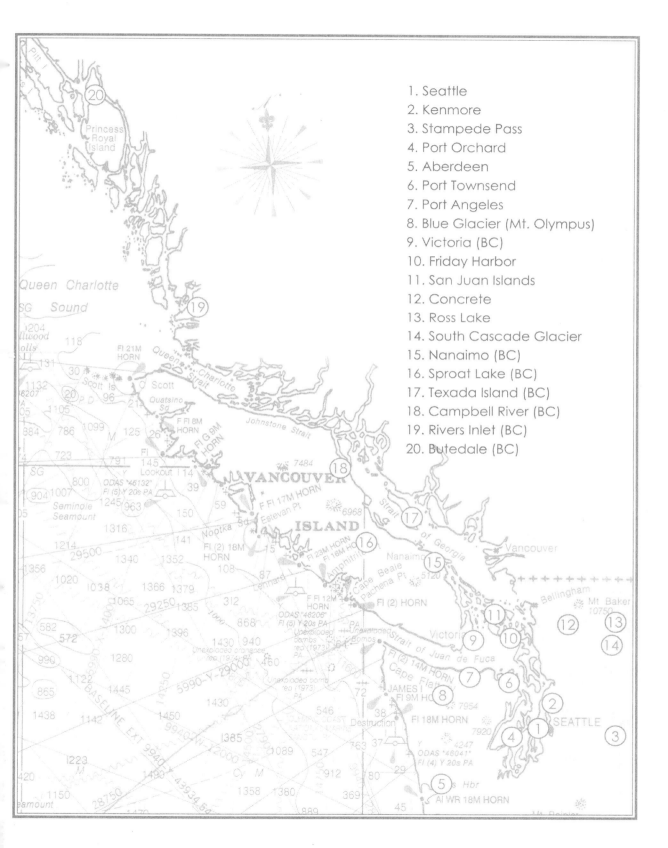

1. Seattle
2. Kenmore
3. Stampede Pass
4. Port Orchard
5. Aberdeen
6. Port Townsend
7. Port Angeles
8. Blue Glacier (Mt. Olympus)
9. Victoria (BC)
10. Friday Harbor
11. San Juan Islands
12. Concrete
13. Ross Lake
14. South Cascade Glacier
15. Nanaimo (BC)
16. Sproat Lake (BC)
17. Texada Island (BC)
18. Campbell River (BC)
19. Rivers Inlet (BC)
20. Butedale (BC)

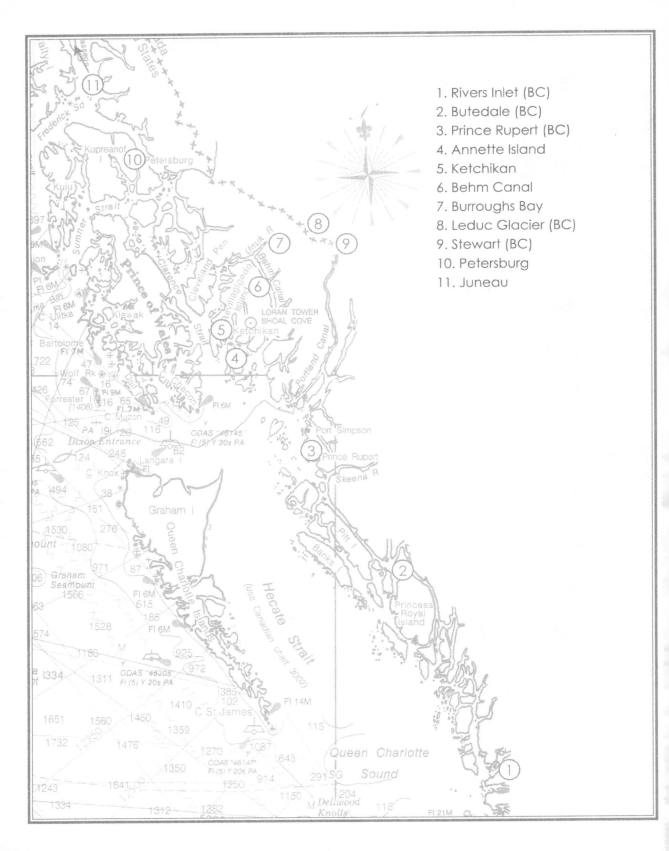

1. Rivers Inlet (BC)
2. Butedale (BC)
3. Prince Rupert (BC)
4. Annette Island
5. Ketchikan
6. Behm Canal
7. Burroughs Bay
8. Leduc Glacier (BC)
9. Stewart (BC)
10. Petersburg
11. Juneau

SUCCESS
on the
STEP

FLYING WITH KENMORE AIR

C. Marin Faure

EARMARK PUBLISHING

SUCCESS on the STEP

FLYING WITH KENMORE AIR

2004 © C. Marin Faure
All rights reserved.

Editing by Cliff Carle
Cover design by Beth Farrell
Text design and layout by Jenny Wilkson

Photographs not credited courtesy of Kenmore Air Harbor
Harrison Ford photograph by Neal Slavin
Cover photograph by Ed Turner

Published by Earmark Publishing
Seattle, Washington

In collaboration with
Elton-Wolf Publishing
Seattle, Washington

ISBN: 0-9760200-1-7
Library of Congress Card Catalogue Number: 2004110869

08 07 06 05 04   1 2 3 4 5

First Printing September 2004

Printed in the United States

EARMARK PUBLISHING
2013 Fourth Avenue Suite 402
Seattle, Washington 98121
206.441.4745

CONTENTS

FOREWORD

by Harrison Ford

BY ALL RIGHTS, MY DE HAVILLAND BEAVER probably should have been melted down for pop cans years ago. But they made tough planes in 1955. That's when de Havilland rolled my Beaver out of the factory and delivered it to the United States Army. I've got a letter and a bunch of photos from one of the guys who flew it in Vietnam, and the fact it survived the heat, humidity, dust, and bullets says a lot about the pilots as well as the people who built it.

The war couldn't kill it, but peace sure tried. The government gave it to a technical college where it sat with weeds growing up around it until it was traded off to a salvage company. The salvage company figured if they couldn't sell it they'd get what parts they could off of it and cut the rest up for scrap.

But they did sell it, to a company in Washington State called Kenmore Air. Kenmore sent their truck out and hauled the carcass back to their yard near Seattle, which is where it was sitting when I came along.

The first time I'd ever flown a Beaver was when I played a freight pilot in the movie *Six Days and Seven Nights*. I did most of the flying during the filming, and I fell in love with the plane, with its simplicity and its capacity for heavy loads and getting in and out of short fields. I was so impressed I decided I wanted one of my own.

They stopped making Beavers in 1967, so I knew the only way I'd ever get one was to find one to rebuild. When I started asking who did the best job of restoring old Beavers, I kept getting the same answer. Kenmore Air.

So that's where I went, and that's where they showed me this beat up, worn out, war veteran of an airplane they'd hauled out of the salvage yard. I asked them if they could turn it into the best example of a Beaver anyone had ever seen, and they said, "Just watch us."

It didn't take me long to realize I was dealing with a very special company. My plane was doing the phoenix thing out in the shop, rising from the ashes of years of mistreatment and neglect to become a stunning example of the breed. But there's a lot more to Kenmore than resurrecting de Havilland Beavers.

The Kenmore story is filled with fascinating characters, characters who in 1946 started with a wrecked, two-seat Aeronca Model K and built it into the world's most successful seaplane airline. Characters like Bob Munro, the incredibly competent mechanic and pilot who ran the company for its first fifty-four years. Bob didn't talk a lot, but he could do things with a floatplane the owner's manuals said couldn't be done.

Characters like the cranky, gruff, and superstitious Bill Fisk, the ex-bomber pilot who was known to turn around and go home if he saw a black cat on his way to work. Flying came as naturally to Bill as breathing, and in more than forty years of flying for Kenmore he never had an accident. Well, one, but it wasn't his fault as he was quick to point out.

I met Bob Munro during one of my visits, and it was hard to believe this quiet, self-effacing man was the same person who'd used a couple of old Noorduyn Norsemen and a Seabee to airlift an entire copper mine onto a glacier in Canada, launched float-equipped Beavers down a forty-five degree slope on top of Mt. Olympus in Washington, and rescued a critically ill scientist from a lake the size of a postage stamp in winds that even the Coast Guard refused to fly in.

Actually, everyone I met at Kenmore was like this. They go about their jobs with a quiet competence that belies the amazing work they do on a daily basis. Whether it's transforming a beat-up, Army-surplus Beaver into a magnificent flying machine or carrying a load of passengers on the flight of their lives up the spectacular coast of British Columbia, the people of Kenmore prove every day why they're the best.

I started taking flying lessons in 1962 while I was in college. I couldn't really afford it, though, so I had to give it up. It wasn't until forty years later that I was able resume my lessons and get my license. I've got a lot of hours now, and I've flown a lot of planes and helicopters. But I never get tired of it.

I love to challenge myself, to try new things. Every flight teaches you something new, no matter how experienced you are. So I can understand how Bob Munro and Bill Fisk lived for the moment when their planes broke free of the water and carried them off to their next adventure, their next challenge. I'm betting it's the same feeling Kenmore's pilots get today.

I'm lucky to have met a lot of interesting people in my life, and I've learned to appreciate the aspirations and achievements that make each one of us unique. The Kenmore story is the story of some truly unique and remarkable people. I'm glad it's being told.

HARRISON FORD

AUTHOR'S NOTE

THIS BOOK WAS WRITTEN FROM MEMORY. Not mine, but the memories of thirty-six people who helped bring Kenmore Air Harbor from a one-plane operation based in a mud bog to the turbine-powered airline it is today. I traveled to Anchorage to interview Tom Wardleigh, San Diego to talk to Mildred Hall, and Ketchikan to visit Stan Bishop. Bill Fisk and Walt Winseman came in from their retirement activities to talk to me. I spent more than fifteen hours in conversation with Kenmore founder Bob Munro alone. The transcriptions of over seventy hours of recorded memories form the backbone of the Air Harbor story.

I've tried to convey the events and personalities that make up Kenmore's remarkable history as accurately as possible, but I'll be the first to acknowledge there will be people who will remember things differently than I've described them. But while my descriptions of the incidents and events may differ in details from what others remember, I believe I've captured the essence of what has made Kenmore Air one of the most unique companies in aviation history.

At the start of this project, Bob Munro was adamant in telling me he didn't want the book to be about him. He wanted it to be about the company and the people who've made it a success. I've tried hard to do that, but there's no getting around the fact that the story of Kenmore is very much the story of Bob Munro. He and Ruth put their stamp on every aspect of the company, and it's virtually impossible to talk about Kenmore without talking about them. But to Bob and Ruth, the real heroes of the story have always been their employees and their customers. All of them. Without them, there would be no Kenmore Air.

But there are a few without whose help there would be no book. Bob Munro's good friend Dick Gee has been an enthusiastic supporter of the project from the beginning, and helped keep me going when I was convinced there was no light at the end of the tunnel. Jerry Rader reviewed what I wrote about the company's Beaver rebuild program, and then spent several hours patiently explaining how I'd gotten it all wrong. Thanks to his help, the story is not only more accurate, but it includes details I hadn't heard before. Bill Peters pointed out mistakes that would have had employees wondering what company I was writing about. Tim Brooks and Gregg Munro set me straight on the complex web of events that led up to the company's introduction of scheduled service to Victoria and the San Juan Islands. Bob Munro himself read each chapter as I finished it, making notes as he went. Then we would get together and he would point out where I'd gotten the facts mixed up, or elaborate on some point he felt needed more attention.

A lot of the credit has to go to my wife, also named Ruth. For more years than she cares to remember, she put up with my coming home from work only to disappear into my office to write. And fellow Boeing employee Jay Spenser deserves credit, too. A noted aviation author himself, he took time from his incredibly busy schedule to read the manuscript and give me the benefit of his objective, but encouraging observations.

You wouldn't be reading this story at all were it not for Mark Torrance's firm belief that Kenmore Air's unique blend of adventure and sound business practices is a tale worth telling. A lot of people told me they hoped my book would be published. Mark is the one who made it happen.

Finally, I'd like to extend my thanks to the individuals who took the time to tell me about the remarkable company they helped create. Not all of them are named or quoted in the text, but that in no way implies that their recollections and experiences did not contribute to this story. I couldn't have written a single page were it not for Durwood Alkire, Leslie (Munro) Banks, Todd Banks, Gordon Barnes, Stan Bishop, Tim Brooks, Norm Bullen, Jim Campbell, Paul Carlson, Mark Easterly, Bill Fisk, Jay Frey, Steve Gattis, Greg Gay, Dick Gee, Marnette Hall, Mildred Hall, Gordon Holbrook, Ted Huntley, Jim Kastner, Bob Munro, Gregg Munro, Ruth Munro, Bill Peters, Susan Peters, Jerry Rader, Brent Robinson, Lloyd Roundtree, Jerry Scudero, Bill Steadman, Wendell Tangborn, Tal Taylor, Tom Wardleigh, Bill Whitney, Tom Williams, and Walt Winseman.

From its first day in business in 1946, Kenmore Air Harbor has been a team effort. Including the whole team in this story would have resulted in a book too big to print. But the names that aren't here are just as important to the story as the names that are.

C. MARIN FAURE

INTRODUCTION

by Robert Munro

IF YOU STAY IN BUSINESS LONG ENOUGH, people will eventually start asking you if you would have done anything differently over the years. It's a question Marin asked me several times while he was researching this book. My answer is always no. Oh, there might have been things I'd have done differently on a particular flight had I known what was going to happen. But when Reg, Jack, and I put the company together in 1946, our only goal was to be our own bosses and be involved in aviation. There was no grand plan or anything. So I don't know that making some different decisions along the way would have changed things very much. We'd still have gone from day to day, dealing with things as they came up.

I think the fact the Air Harbor is still in business today proves the decisions we made were the right ones, which may say more about our employees than it does about me. My business philosophy is pretty simple: do the right thing. That might sound kind of naive in today's world of fancy finance and mega-mergers, but I've always felt that treating your customers honestly and conducting your business ethically will get you farther in the long run than anything else.

The one thing I regret was that I didn't spend more time with my family. They always seemed to come second. Ruthie and the kids have always been the most important things in my life, but I can see how they sometimes didn't think so. It's a dilemma every business person with a family has to face. You need to make sure the business succeeds so you can provide for your family, but your family needs your time, too.

Aviation isn't an easy business to be in. The competition is tough and the profits are small. There's always another flight to take or another airplane to fix. It's the kind of business where you start working at first light and often don't finish up until well after dark. You do whatever it takes to keep the customers happy, because without them, you'll be out of work in a week. So you end up choosing between delivering a customer's plane on time or taking your kids to the beach.

It's a hard decision, and I think I made the wrong one too many times. My family put up with a lot. I canceled picnics at the last minute, I missed school events that were important to them, I'd have a flight on someone's birthday. Looking back, there were probably times when I should have had someone else take the flight or fix the plane. But because we lived right here on the property, it seemed to make more sense for me to deal with the things that came up rather than call someone else back to work. So my family suffered. But their support never wavered.

Ruthie in particular made it possible for us to succeed. She'd been brought up in a nice house with lots of friends around. I moved her to an abandoned sawmill in a mud bog at the far end of nowhere. She had hardly any nearby friends, and a husband who was out flying most of the time, often in bad weather and usually over pretty rough country. She wasn't happy with a lot of the things I was doing, particularly the glacier flying, but she never stopped me from doing them. And when the wind and rain would whip in off the lake in the middle of the night, she'd be right out there with me making sure the planes were tied down. People who come to Kenmore and say, "Look what Bob Munro built," are only seeing half the picture. Every flight that leaves our dock, every airplane we rebuild, and every part we ship is a tribute to Ruthie's patience and support. I hope our employees will always remember that.

Since starting the company over fifty years ago, I can't recall a single day when I didn't look forward to going to work. Sometimes I'd be flying through the mountains or up along the coast of British Columbia, and I'd have a hard time believing I was being paid to do it. The beauty of the Pacific Northwest and southeast Alaska have to be seen to be believed. There's nothing I can say that can even begin to describe how it makes me feel to be in this country. I've never wanted to be anywhere else. Ruthie will tell you how frustrating it was because she likes to travel and see new places. I couldn't imagine anywhere nicer than the country I was flying through, so I was never very enthusiastic about going anywhere else.

Most people think about airplanes when they think about Kenmore. I can understand that, because we've had some unique ones in the fleet over the years: Seabees, Norsemen, Bellancas, Beavers, Otters, and now the turbines. But to me, Kenmore is all about people. I'd intended to list the ones I felt have contributed the most over the years, but I kept adding to the list until it included pretty much everyone who's ever worked here. We've had some wonderful customers, too, people that have become as much a part of the Kenmore family as the employees. Having customers like Terry Wills up in Ketchikan, Lloyd Roundtree of Alaska Island Air and Jerry Scudero of Taquan Air as friends is one of the best things about being in this business.

Would I have done anything differently than I did? No, I don't think so. But I sure wouldn't mind doing it all over again.

ROBERT B. MUNRO

THE CONVERGENCE ZONE

PREDICTING THE WEATHER IN SEATTLE is a risky business. If the wind is from the southwest, off the Pacific Ocean, it probably will be overcast. If the wind is from the northwest, out of the Gulf of Alaska, it probably will be clear. There are exceptions, of course, weather being what it is, but for the most part the southwest-cloudy, northwest-clear rule is pretty reliable. The trouble occurs when both weather systems are active at the same time.

When the wind blows into town from both directions at once, a dart board makes as good a prediction tool as any. The two armies of air collide in what local meteorologists call the "convergence zone," a seventy-mile stretch of Puget Sound that extends from Tacoma in the south to Everett in the north. Seattle lies almost at the center of the zone, her back to the Cascades and her feet in the water, facing west and the jumbled bulk of the Olympic Range which rises like a wall to shield Puget Sound from the ocean.

The outcome of the rolling, tumbling free-for-all of air in the convergence zone is anybody's guess. In a matter of hours, overnight fog burns off to blue sky which in turn is replaced by an overcast the color of old lead. The wind gusts fitfully back and forth and then vanishes altogether, only to come roaring back from an entirely new direction. Sometimes there's no wind at all in the zone as the two armies take stock of each other across a dull drizzle that's almost hypnotic in its persistence.

North of the zone, Whidbey Island points its forty-mile finger of summer homes, farms, and U.S. Navy runways toward the San Juan Islands and the Canadian border. Beyond, the San Juans, Vancouver Island, and the rainswept coast of British Columbia loom through the salt haze rising from the Strait of Juan de Fuca. Puget Sound would be an inland sea were it not for the Strait, a twenty-mile-wide channel of rip tides and whirlpools left behind when a shift in the earth's tectonic plates tore Vancouver Island from the Olympic Peninsula.

South of the convergence zone, the Sound dead-ends at Olympia in a tangle of tidal mudflats. Beyond the flats, a network of grassy valleys and timbered hills weaves down the Washington coast to the Columbia River and the Oregon border.

Seattle is a city dominated by water. Henry Yesler got the ball rolling in the mid-1850s by

1

building a steam sawmill on the shore of Elliott Bay. Half a century later, Yesler's mill had meta-morphosed into a bustling waterfront of warehouses and massive wooden piers. The piers were built into the bay at an angle to accommodate the railroad tracks that brought carloads of lumber, coal, and steel within reach of the derricks that bobbed and weaved among a forest of masts and funnels.

The city made the big time in 1898 when it became the jumping off point for virtually every-thing and everybody going north to the Klondike gold fields. It wasn't long before the docks were awash in a floodtide of miners, loggers, bums, prostitutes, wagonmasters, millhands, chandlery clerks, cardsharks, train crews, and stevedores that sloshed back and forth between the schooners and steam sloops lining the piers and Yesler Way, America's original Skid Road. The city's char-acter was defined by the harbor, although most of Seattle's more upstanding citizens weren't too happy with the definition.

Today, the Klondike gold rush has moved to Asia, and the only evidence of character on the docks is the graffiti adorning the endless walls of intermodal shipping containers. A handful of the great angled piers remain, their once-bustling warehouses given over to trendy restaurants, trinket stores, and the city aquarium. The lace-boomed derricks are gone, stomped into extinction by a herd of stiff-legged container cranes. The graceful schooners and steam sloops are gone, too, rel-egated to faded photo galleries on the walls of the Port Authority building. In their stead, slab-sided container ships and bulk carriers with bow thrusters and satellite navigation lie at anchor waiting their turn to unload. The average turnaround time is less than twenty-four hours. Even if the Skid Road saloons and bawdy houses were still intact, today's crews wouldn't have the time to visit them.

The water in Seattle isn't all salt. Mile-long Lake Union lies just north of the business district providing a sheltered location for yacht brokers, marine supply houses, and several neighborhoods of expensive floating homes. Immediately east of the city is Lake Washington, eighteen miles of million-dollar estates, windsurfers, and commuter-choked floating bridges. To the east again, be-yond the upscale neighborhoods of Bellevue, is Lake Sammamish. Although outside the city limits, Sammamish has become the eastside's playground, the occasional bass fisherman invisible behind a neon blur of chrome-powered speedboats and jetskis.

But the lakes weren't always like this. In the beginning, Lakes Union, Washington, and Sammamish had been little more than places to drop trees into, as the loggers who founded Seattle denuded the surrounding hills. Then early in the 20th Century and long before the advent of en-vironmental impact statements, Lake Union and Lake Washington were connected to each other and to Puget Sound by man-made waterways and a pair of immense locks. When the engineers opened the last of the gates they'd built to keep the water out of the cut, two things happened: the level of Lake Washington dropped nine feet, and Lake Union took on a commercial importance second only to the saltwater port in Elliott Bay.

The locks officially opened for business on July 4, 1917, and it wasn't long before Lake Union was ringed with the masts of steamers, tugs, and even an old square-rigger or two. Not to be left out, Lake Washington got into the act by playing host to a small whaling fleet. But before the ships came the airplanes.

Three years to the day before the locks opened, a pilot named Terah Maroney was over on Lake Washington selling rides in a Curtiss seaplane. Among his holiday passengers were a young timber baron-turned-aviation-enthusiast and his friend, an engineer in the employ of the U.S. Navy. The timber baron, whose name was William E. Boeing, and the engineer, Conrad Westervelt, decided they could build a better airplane than the one Maroney was flying. Their design, a conventional, twin-float biplane, was constructed in a boatyard south of the city. The completed wings and fuselage were hauled to Lake Union where they were assembled in a three-bay hangar Boeing had built to house his new flying club. On a warm, spring day in June, 1916, Boeing took his new airplane up for the first time. The plane's official name was *Bluebill* but history has named it the *B & W*, after the two men who created it. The *B & W* was not a commercial success, but it led to a design that was.

Bill Boeing's new airplane company soon abandoned Lake Union for an airfield south of the city, but seaplane activity on the lake continued. In 1920, a Boeing test pilot named Eddie Hubbard purchased a small Boeing flying boat and started a side business flying the mail from Seattle to Victoria, British Columbia. Then, in 1928, young Lana Kurtzer stuck an "Open for Business" sign in his window, and the man who was to become synonymous with seaplane service on Lake Union for nearly sixty years sat down to wait for his first customer.

Kurtzer's Flying Service was pretty much a one-man-band operation. He occasionally hired other pilots, but he was a hard man to work for. Fiercely independent, Kurtzer knew exactly how he wanted things done and he wasn't too interested in anyone else's opinion. Kurtzer's success was due in part to the diversity of the services he offered. He flew charters, of course, taking people to destinations on the Sound and in the San Juans, and he also offered scenic flights around the city. As the years went on, he began to specialize in seaplane instruction, and after World War II, his little fleet of red Taylorcrafts with "Kurtzer" spelled out in black letters on the floats became a fixture in the air around the lake. Kurtzer also offered seaplane storage, and it wasn't long before a variety of privately owned floatplanes were pulled up wingtip to wingtip on his floating ramp in the southwest corner of the lake.

One of the planes on Kurtzer's ramp in the early 1940s was a tiny, two-seat Aeronca Model K owned by a local flying club. By today's standards, the Model K wasn't much, but at the time it represented the state-of-the-art in affordable, personal aviation. With side-by-side seating, a wood-and-fabric wingspan of 36 feet, and powered by a 40-horsepower engine, the Model K had an advertised top speed of 93 miles per hour and a gross weight of 1,060 pounds. The fuel in the little tank behind the engine yielded a range of 250 miles, provided no strong headwinds were encountered along the way.

This particular Model K, registration NC18885, "Eight-Eight-Five" in pilot's parlance, was mounted on EDO Model D-1070 aluminum floats. The twin floats and their attachment gear reduced the plane's already-meager useful load by about 150 pounds. Getting two people off the water meant waiting for a stiff headwind; the engine needed all the help it could get.

There is no known record of how Eight-Eight-Five ended up on its back in the lake, and Lana

Kurtzer is no longer around to tell us. But when the wind gets squirrely in the convergence zone, the squirreliest place of all can be Lake Union. It's not uncommon to see windsocks at each end of the lake extended stiff as boards in totally opposite directions. It's easy to imagine what might have happened...

The turbulence over the city was rapidly taking the fun out of flying, so the pilot banked Eight-Eight-Five back toward Lake Union and the safety of Kurtzer's ramp. Takeoff had been to the north but the windsocks on Kurtzer's office and the old Boeing hangar across the lake indicated a south wind now. The pilot turned final over the gas plant at the north end of the lake and touched down in the southwest corner. The Aeronca skimmed along for a moment on the step, the break in the bottom of each float that reduces the water's drag at higher speeds, before settling down in a shower of spray to idle slowly toward Kurtzer's two-story wooden hangar. By the time the pilot powered the little plane onto the ramp, the wind was rocking the wings and shotgunning the raindrops against the fabric fuselage. The two-cylinder engine popped twice and quit and the pilot gingerly stepped out onto the slippery surface of the ramp. He'd already seen one club member lose his footing and scoot into the icy water and he didn't want to repeat the performance.

Shielding his eyes against the rain, the pilot ran tiedown lines from the bow cleats on the floats to one of the metal rings bolted to the top of the ramp. By now it was pouring, and after a quick tug on the lines to make sure they were secure, the pilot dashed for the office and Kurtzer's coffee pot.

The wind picked up after dark, but the planes on Kurtzer's ramp were somewhat protected in the lee of the high shoreline. Then the wind began to shift. Within minutes, the wind had backed around 180 degrees to blow with renewed fury directly into the southwest corner of Lake Union.

In the ten-plus years that Lana Kurtzer had been in business, he'd learned a lot. One of the things he'd learned early on was that the wind often blew into his corner of the lake. As a result, he always used three sets of lines on his ramped floatplanes. Lines to the bow and stern of each float kept the planes from pivoting, while a stout line to the underside of each wing kept the planes from blowing over.

The wood and metal and fabric floatplanes creaked and groaned as the gusts pushed against tails and lifted wings but Kurtzer's lines held fast. They would have held fast to Eight-Eight-Five, too, if only the pilot had remembered to fasten them. With a whoosh, the Model K lifted into the air, held only by the light bow lines. The metal tiedown ring jerked out of the ramp with a bang and the Aeronca blew over backwards into the water.

That's one theory. Another is that Eight-Eight-Five was blown over while it was taxiing out on the lake. We may never know the real cause of the accident, but we do know that Kurtzer salvaged the plane. Righting a waterlogged, fabric airplane is not an easy task, and by the time the Model

K was sitting on dry land, it needed a fair amount of repair work in addition to a thorough drying out. The flying club couldn't afford to have the plane fixed, so Kurtzer disassembled it and stacked the parts where they wouldn't be in his way.

The plane that got the company going. The Aeronca K on Lake Sammamish, 1946.

Any interest the club members may have had in restoring the little Aeronca vanished on December 7, 1941. As invasion fear gripped the west coast, priority was put on protecting the Boeing's B-17 assembly plant which was an easy target for the enemy carrier fleet everyone assumed was on the way. One of the first steps was to ban civilian flying within one hundred miles of Seattle, a ban which remained in place throughout the war. Even if the club could have fixed their airplane they wouldn't have been able to fly it. Kurtzer himself was spending most of his time flying in support of the Army's Alaska Highway project. The pile of parts that had been Eight-Eight-Five lay neglected, the wooden wing structure soaking up the winter drizzle. Only fate and the fact that Kurtzer was busy kept the Aeronca out of the scrap bin.

One of the club members had a cousin who was working as a mechanic for Pan American over on Boeing Field. The cousin had a friend, also a Pan Am mechanic, and the two of them were looking for a little airplane to rebuild in their spare time. They weren't interested in flying; neither of the men had a pilot's license. They just wanted a project that would give them a chance to use their skills, from overhauling the engine to stitching on new fabric. The club's Model K filled the bill perfectly. The agreed-on price was $300, and Eight-Eight-Five's new owners drove down to Lake Union to pick up their plane.

If Kurtzer had known the eyesore being carted off his property would cause the world's largest and most successful seaplane company to spring up only one lake over from his, he probably would have bought the Aeronca himself. As it was, he was glad just to see it go. The wings ended up in the cousin's garage in Wallingford, a residential neighborhood just north of Lake Union. The rest of the plane went to his friend's home on Haller Lake, a few miles farther north. The cousin's name was Reginald Collins. His friend was Robert Berquist Munro.

FISH GUTS, GOLD, AND THE MODEL K

2

OR THE FIRST TWENTY-TWO YEARS of his life, the man who would exert more quiet influence over the North American seaplane industry than anyone else expressed no interest in aviation whatsoever. The son of an accomplished, but irregularly employed meatcutter, Bob Munro wanted to be an automobile mechanic. He loved working with his hands on anything mechanical, especially engines. He took every machine shop course Roosevelt High School had to offer, and then wangled a waiver that let him substitute even more shop hours for study hall.

He also had an aptitude for music, playing first the trumpet and then the French horn. Munro's straight As in machining and music courses landed him on the senior honor roll, although he claims the only reason he got an A in Orchestra was because he volunteered to carry the harp up and down the stairs between the classroom and the auditorium. At home, his sister helped him buy an accordion, which he lugged along with him to his summer jobs in Alaska. In 1935, backyard microwave receivers and satellite TV were still forty years in the future; Munro's accordion became a major source of entertainment at the jobsites.

Munro's first exposure to Alaska was a smelly one. One of his three sisters had a boyfriend who'd been working as a game warden in southeast Alaska. He happened to be within earshot when Munro wondered aloud about the job prospects for high school graduates in the middle of the worst economic depression on record.

"Got any interest in working in a fish cannery?"

Munro allowed that he might.

"Well, I can probably get you a job in one, but you'll have to go to Wrangell to do it."

This sounded more like an adventure than a job!

"Sure, I'd love to go," and Munro soon found himself in the middle of the wondrous mosaic of islands and bays that is southeast Alaska, up to his elbows in fish guts.

The Diamond K Cannery operated at full throttle during the salmon run, twenty-four hours a day. They worked their employees hard, but young Munro wasn't afraid of hard work. His ability to get a job done was the one thing he knew he could depend on amid the wreckage of the nation's economy. Besides, what better place to sweat for your wages than southeast Alaska? The clear, green water; the dense forests of spruce and hemlock cloaking the slopes of the glacier-capped Coast Range; the massive cedar totem poles shrouding the islands in carved mystery. Just peering out at it all through the steam of the roaring, clanking cannery was exciting. When Munro came home in the fall, he was thoroughly hooked on the beauty and awesome isolation of the north.

Munro had managed to save enough from his cannery wages to pay the enrollment tuition at Washington State University in Pullman, over by the Idaho border, but by Christmas he was almost out of money. College itself wasn't expensive in those days, but the cost of room and board was more than his meager finances could stand. He moved back to Seattle where he at least could live at home while he attended classes at the University of Washington.

Living at home reduced his expenses but it didn't entitle him to a free ride. Like many of America's young men who were trying to help their families weather the Depression, Munro became an odd job specialist. He worked at Seattle's premier department store, Frederick & Nelson, during the Christmas rush, and for two dollars a day delivered coal and sawdust in an old truck owned by Frank Mason, a family friend. Lumber was king in 1936, and sawmills of every size and description dotted the waterfront and squatted on pilings in the Duwamish mudflats south of the city. The lumber coming out of the mills was a valuable commodity; the sawdust piling up out back was not.

Then someone got the idea of using a little sawdust burner to heat their home, and a new industry was born. Soon sawdust was rivaling coal in popularity as a home heating fuel. Munro could get all the sawdust he wanted from one of the Duwamish mills and there were several companies around town that sold coal. The truck driving job turned out to be a real gold mine because if he could deliver three loads a day instead of two, Mason paid him an extra dollar. Earning that third dollar meant getting up at four in the morning to beat the rush at the loading yard, but it was worth it.

Munro worked as much as his class schedule would allow, but odd jobs don't pay much and it was getting increasingly difficult to cover all his expenses. Then in April he got a phone call from the cannery.

"We need someone to come up here early and help get things ready for the season. The job's yours if you want it."

"Just tell me when to be there." Munro's college education had come to an end.

Munro's skill with his hands had not gone unnoticed at the Diamond K, and he was put to work on the rigging scow building fish traps. The traps were huge funnels of piling and nets that spiraled out hundreds of feet offshore. The migrating fish would swim into the wide mouth of the funnel and be forced through the curving channel to the center where they would mill about in confusion, unable to figure a way out. The fishermen simply had to scoop the fish into a barge.

Some days, the dip nets would pull over 60,000 salmon from a single trap. It was a slaughter; commercial trap fishing would be outlawed by the end of the decade.

The 1936 fishing season was pretty much over by October, so Munro went home to start the search for winter employment. He could have driven the coal and sawdust truck again, but he decided that fixing trucks promised a better future than driving them. His older brother Jack was working as a mechanic at a little garage on East 71st Street called Cook's Auto Repair. The owner, E. H. Cook, was more than happy to pay Bob Munro a commission for tinkering on the various jobs that came in the door. One of these jobs was brought in by a Mr. Max Hirschberg, who owned a small gold mine in Teller, Alaska, seventy-two miles north of Nome. Hirschberg practiced hydraulic mining, using a monitor firing a powerful jet of water to cut up a hillside and wash the dirt and gravel into a sluice box where the gold, if any, was separated out. Hirschberg had a Chrysler car engine he wanted rebuilt to power his monitor. E. H. Cook put Jack Munro in charge of the project, with Bob Munro as his assistant. As Hirschberg watched them work, he realized the Munro brothers could do more for him than just rebuild his engine.

"How'd you two like to go up and help me install this motor and then run my equipment all summer?"

To Bob Munro, it was an opportunity to see someplace new in the north country he'd come to love.

"Sure!"

First flight. Bob Munro (second from right) and his brother Jack (right) in front of Hans Mirrow's converted Bach on the airfield at Nome.

The Munros and the Chrysler pump engine left for Nome on the first ship of the 1937 season. The *Victoria* pushed her concrete-reinforced bow across the Gulf of Alaska, through the Aleutian Islands and into the ice-choked Bering Sea. Shouldering through the ice floes, she eventually reached Nome, where travelers going on to Teller could pick one of three ways to continue their journey. They could walk, they could hire a dog sled, or they could fly. The Munros got to fly.

Bob Munro's first experience with an airplane was memorable, to say the least. Waving his arms to augment his heavy German accent, pilot Hans Mirow stuffed his passengers up front in the big, high-wing Bach monoplane and filled the rest of the cabin with sacks of coal. The Bach originally had been built as a tri-motor, but somewhere along the way it had been converted by removing the two outboard engines and replacing the center engine with a more powerful Pratt & Whitney Hornet.

After taxiing to the end of Nome's crude runway, Mirow coaxed the rough-running radial up to full power and the Bach staggered into the air a few feet short of the end of the strip. Then it refused to climb. Mirow peered through the filthy windshield at the low range of hills in front of the Bach and decided to take the long route to Teller. Banking left, he headed out to the ocean where he skimmed the beach up the coast to the tiny village.

Bob Munro found the whole experience thrilling. Looking down on the world, even if only from the five hundred feet Mirow had managed to coax out of the Bach, was fascinating. Munro had no idea why the airplane flew or how Mirow controlled it, but he definitely liked the sensation of flight.

At Teller, the Munro boys got to experience another unique form of transportation: the dog sled. Unfortunately, the only things that actually *rode* on the sled were supplies and equipment. The Munros and the two laborers Hirschberg had hired walked the several miles to camp.

The work at the mine was hard and the hours, like the days themselves, were long. When Bob Munro wasn't helping his brother maintain the monitor engine and the two ancient International Harvester tractors, he worked alongside the rest of the crew moving dirt to and from the sluicebox. He enjoyed the work and was fascinated by the country, so he wasn't particularly suspicious when Mrs. Hirschberg suggested that he and his brother wait until her husband had cleaned the gold out of the sluicebox at the end of the season before collecting their pay. There wasn't anything to spend money on in Teller anyway. He still wasn't suspicious when Hirschberg paid off the crew at the end of the summer with hundred-dollar company bonds instead of cash.

"These bonds are *better* than cash," Hirschberg explained as he distributed the notes among his crew. "You'll probably be able to sell them for more than their face value."

The Munros began their journey home in style, flying back to Nome in Hans Mirow's sleek, green and white Lockheed Vega. The Vega was a much more suitable conveyance for a young man with five one-hundred dollar bonds in his pocket than the rickety old Bach. It wasn't until the Munros were back in Seattle that they learned Hirschberg had found almost no gold in the sluicebox when he'd cleaned it out. The bonds were completely worthless.

Bob Munro was not about to waste his time again, so the following summer he went back to the cannery in Wrangell. But while he was working the fish traps, major changes were occurring at the Teller gold mine. For starters, the Hirschbergs were out and there was a new owner, Frank Rice. Rice was positive the Teller mine contained gold; Hirschberg just hadn't known how to extract it properly. The operation had expanded, with a bulldozer working in conjunction with the tractors and the monitor. Rice knew Bob Munro was familiar with the mine's hydraulic equipment, so that winter he telephoned him and asked if he would come up and work the 1939 season. After making sure he would actually be paid this time, Munro signed on.

The trip north on the *Columbia* was almost as much of an adventure as Munro's first airplane ride. As the ship bashed her way across the Bering Sea, it quickly became obvious that the ice was much thicker than usual. Then a day or two out of Nome, the *Columbia* got stuck. The open water leads had disappeared; the ice floes stretched unbroken to the horizon. For five days, the *Columbia* sat trapped. Captain "Andy" Anderson became increasingly worried as his ship's water supply began running low. Then Hans Mirow's green and white Lockheed Vega appeared overhead, the same plane that had flown the Munro brothers back from Teller two years earlier. This time, the pilot was Jack Jefford. Using a crude radio mounted on a board in the back of the Vega, Jefford told Captain Anderson he would try to find the nearest open water. Jefford flew west, hoping the currents farther out at sea would have dispersed the ice, but they hadn't. He returned to Nome to refuel, and then flew back to the ship by a different route. To his amazement, there was open water only eight miles east of the *Columbia*.

From Bob Munro's vantage point on deck, fog had reduced the visibility to less than a quarter of a mile, but Jefford circling overhead could see everything. He began issuing steering instructions to the helmsman. The *Columbia* took quite a beating as she squeezed and scraped between the floes; Jefford could see long streaks of paint and rust staining the ice behind the ship. Finally, the hull couldn't take any more. Repeated contact with the ice had sprung some of the plates and the ship began to leak.

Captain Anderson was truly worried now, and he began to question the competence of the pilot circling overhead in the Vega. Jefford threatened to fly home and leave the ship to her fate. Finally, everyone calmed down and the harrowing journey continued. Five hours after she first began to move under Jefford's guidance, the *Columbia* broke through to open water. With the pumps easily keeping up with the water seeping in around the damaged plates, Captain Anderson rang for full speed ahead. Twenty-four hours later, Bob Munro stepped ashore in Nome. It had been a close call, but the airplane had saved the day. Munro was impressed.

The work at the Teller mine was even harder than it had been the first time around. The company's five employees were split into two crews, each of which worked a twelve-hour shift to keep the mine running twenty-four hours a day, seven days a week. Munro helped maintain the mine's equipment in addition to running one of the tractors and the dragline that had been set up to clear the tailings away from the sluice box. But despite the long, dusty hours and head-pounding racket, Munro loved the work. He proved especially adept at rigging, moving heavy equipment and freeing mired vehicles with ingenious arrangements of pulley blocks, lines, and winches. It was a skill that was to pay off many times over in the years to come. Unlike Max Hirschberg, Rice paid promptly and with real money, so when he offered to raise the base pay to seventy-four cents an hour for the 1940 season, Munro was happy to sign on.

Bob Munro's life was not all work, however. Back in Seattle he had joined a church-sponsored organization called the Triune Club. There were monthly dances and in December, hikes into the woods to cut Christmas trees. Another member of the club was a young man named Reginald Heber Collins. Collins, whose nickname "Bud" was the result of a dispute between the Reginald and Heber sides of his family, was as fascinated with mechanics as Munro, and the two became fast friends. One of their early projects was a car-top ski rack, which they assembled in the Munro family garage. It was the first such contraption of its kind in Seattle, and everyone who saw it wanted to know where they could get one. Years later Munro was still sorry they hadn't put the ski rack into production; he and Collins probably would have made a fortune.

One of the unofficial leaders of the Triune club was a tall, husky engineering graduate named John F. Mines; "Jack" to his friends. Mines came from a completely different background than Collins and Munro. While the two future ski-rack inventors were growing up in working-class Seattle, Jack Mines' family was living in England. The Mines children were well-educated and enjoyed the benefits of a well-to-do family that was managing to weather the Depression relatively unscathed.

Bob Munro got along okay with Jack Mines, but he always felt a little uneasy in the Mines family home. The fact that he ripped a hole in the felt top of their expensive pool table the first time he picked up a cue stick didn't help matters any. And he was always amazed when Jack Mines would come home from a shopping trip with three new pairs of shoes. Munro had never in his life been able to buy a white pair, a black pair, and a brown pair of shoes, all brand new, at the same time.

Jack Mines was an organizer. He had his own car and his own boat, a Columbia River double-ender, and together with his best friend and fellow club member Durwood Alkire, he organized sailing trips to Victoria and car trips to the ocean to dig for clams or set traps for crabs. Munro did the maintenance on the boat's little Graymarine engine, so he got to go along on some of the sailing trips, but it was one of the clamming expeditions that he remembers best. Mines wanted to take his girlfriend on a weekend trip to the beach. However, he was also developing an interest in one of the other girls in the club, a lovely young woman named Ruth Holden. The solution was obvious; take *both* girls to the beach. Taking them by himself was out of the question; it wouldn't have been considered proper. What he needed was someone to act the role of a date for Ruth. It was a good plan, but it was doomed to failure the moment he asked Bob Munro to come along as Ruth's phony date.

Munro and Ruth hit it off right away. From then on, when Munro headed north to his summer jobs Ruth was always there to see him off. Durwood Alkire figured it must have been pretty hard on Munro.

"He'd stand there on the deck as the ship pulled out, waving good-bye to Ruth and looking
at all the guys that had come down with her to see him off. Ruth was very popular, and I'm sure
Bob wondered if she'd be on the dock to greet him when he came home five or six months later."

DURWOOD ALKIRE

She always was and they were married in 1942.

Bob Munro had never declared dissatisfaction with his first name but his good friend, "Bud" Collins, had. Tired of being called "Reginald" by some people and "Bud" by everybody else, he finally decided to take matters into his own hands.

"That's it," he declared one day. "No more Reginald, no more Heber, and no more Bud. From now on it's just 'Reg.'"

And for the rest of his life, it was.

While Bob Munro had been dividing his time between Alaska and Cook's Auto Repair, Reg Collins had been holding down a job as a motorcycle driver at the Seattle Times, running errands for the newspaper's advertising department. So far, the two friends' mechanical interests had centered mainly around cars, or in the case of the ski rack, car accessories. But it was almost impossible to live in Seattle and not be aware of the exciting events occurring in aviation. After all, the Boeing Airplane Company was just down the street. Boeing had built the Navy's first truly successful carrier fighter, the hot little F4B and its Army cousin, the P-12. They had pioneered the all-metal monoplane with the Monomail, following it up with the revolutionary Model 247, the most modern airliner of its day.

Then there was the huge, luxurious Model 314 Clipper flying boat and the experimental XB-15, the largest landplane in the word. Most recently, Boeing had rolled out its Model 299. A local newspaper reporter had taken one look at the sleek, four-engined bomber and gasped, "She's a flying fortress!" The Army Air Corps was not given to such histrionics; they simply assigned it the number B-17.

Meanwhile, activity at the Sand Point Naval Air Station on Lake Washington was picking up. Almost every day saw formations of Navy fighters and trainers snarling over the city on practice flights. Add Bob Munro's exciting encounters with Hans Mirow's airplanes up north, and it's easy to see how two young men who were fascinated by machines might begin to wonder about the possibilities in aviation. Munro already knew he didn't want to spend the rest of his life being an auto mechanic. He was grateful for his winter job at Cook's Auto Repair, but skinning his knuckles on dirt-encrusted parts while standing in a pool of oily mud at the bottom of Cook's earth-walled grease pit didn't seem like much of a career. When he came home in October, 1940, after his second grueling summer in a row at the gold mine, he listened with mounting enthusiasm to Reg

Collins' proposal that they attend the Boeing School of Aeronautics in Oakland, California to get their aircraft mechanic licenses.

Collins had a six-cylinder Plymouth, and in December, he and Munro headed down the coast to California. They signed up for the Boeing School's twelve-month Airline Mechanic course on December 30, 1940. Tuition was sixty dollars a month; students were responsible for their own room and board. Neither Munro nor Collins had enough saved up to pay for the whole year, so they both got part-time jobs at a gas station to help cover expenses.

They couldn't have picked a better school. There were four hours of classroom instruction in the morning in subjects ranging from electricity and civil air regulations to algebra. The afternoons were spent in the shop learning the practical aspects of engine and propeller repair, welding, hydraulic system repair, sheet metal repair, and woodworking. Munro's grades ran mostly to A's and B's. His weakest subjects were blueprint reading and aircraft instrument theory, but when it came to engines and propellers, it was straight As all the way.

Bob Munro and Reg Collins headed for the Boeing School of Aeronautics in Oakland, California in 1940.

Ten months into the course, Munro's money ran out. The job at the gas station covered his room and board but not his tuition. An uncle in Tacoma agreed to lend Munro the $120 he needed for his last two months' tuition if Munro would sign a statement agreeing not to get married until the loan was paid back. Munro signed, and paying back that loan became his first priority after graduation.

Graduation came on December 12, 1941, five days after the bombing of Pearl Harbor. Munro was anxious to get home, but Collins was concerned about the amount of oil his car had been burning. He decided to fit new piston rings before they took off for Seattle. The next morning, Collins wriggled under the car to release the connecting rods from the crankshaft while an impatient Bob

Munro stayed up above to install the new rings. Everything went fine until one of the rings broke as Munro was slipping it onto a piston. Collins, under the car, didn't hear it snap. Munro held a quick debate with himself. It was Saturday. The stores were closed and he knew it would be impossible to get a new ring until Monday. He also knew that Collins, who was an absolute perfectionist as a mechanic, would insist on remaining in Oakland until they could get a new ring. Munro decided he didn't want to wait that long. He stuck the two halves of the ring on the piston and went on with the job. The broken ring didn't seem to make a bit of difference to the way the engine ran and Collins didn't suspect a thing. Munro never told him what he'd done, although it was years before he stopped feeling guilty about it.

The drive back to Seattle was an adventure in itself. The roads were jammed with traffic as invasion fear gripped the west coast. Bridge crossings at night were especially hazardous as all vehicles were being ordered to drive across with their headlights off to thwart enemy air attacks. The much-feared attacks finally came, but they weren't against the bridges. After a marathon voyage from Japan, the submarine *I-25* surfaced off the Oregon coast and launched a low-wing Yokosuka E14Y-1 floatplane into the night. The tiny plane buzzed in over the beach and dropped a pair of 167-pound bombs into the middle of a forest.

Hoping his attack would start a fire that would spread to engulf the entire west coast in flames, Warrant Officer Fujita flew back to the *I-25* where the Yokosuka was hurriedly stuffed into its waterproof hangar. By the time the sun came up, the sub was safely out of sight beneath the swells. Daylight failed to reveal any towering clouds of smoke to the anxious crewmen peering through the periscope, so the captain of the *I-25* decided to unleash Fujita and his diminutive airplane a second time.

Jack Mines in his Lockheed PV-2 Harpoon patrol bomber somewhere in the Pacific, 1945.

The next attack was no less successful than the first. Minutes after his bombs sent geysers of moss and rain-soaked evergreen needles harmlessly into the air, Fujita splashed down beside the submarine. The gnat-like Yokosuka was sealed into its hangar, and the *I-25* slipped away to the west, her mission completed. The first and last attacks by an enemy warplane against the mainland United States were over.

Bob Munro and Reg Collins arrived safely in Seattle and immediately registered for the draft. Munro was just short of his twenty-fourth birthday. Jack Mines figured it was just a matter of time before they all ended up in the military, so he and Durwood Alkire went down and joined the Navy.

"I'd rather do something interesting than get stuck with what the draft board hands out," Mines declared.

Being a pilot certainly sounded interesting, so he and Alkire applied for flight training. Alkire soloed at Sand Point a few weeks after Mines, but the Navy soon decided Alkire's administrative skills outweighed his flying abilities and he was transferred to the personnel department. Mines completed primary flight training and went on to multi-engine school, where he qualified in patrol bombers. He eventually was assigned to a PV-2 Harpoon squadron, flying the big, twin-engined Lockheed on anti-submarine patrols in the western Pacific.

Bob Munro's primary concern after returning from California was finding a place to stay. The incoming flood of factory workers and military personnel was rapidly exceeding Seattle's capacity to contain it and housing was almost impossible to come by. Fortunately, Reg Collins had an extra room in his downtown apartment and he was happy to let Munro use it. As soon as Munro was settled in, he began looking for work. He and Ruth had planned to marry as soon as he came home from the Boeing School, but his year in Oakland had left him broke, and he still had his uncle's loan to repay.

The Boeing Airplane Company was receiving orders for more B-17s almost daily now, and they were hiring anyone who could tell one end of a rivet gun from the other. Munro went down to the company's Plant 2 on Boeing Field and was hired immediately as an inspector. It didn't take him long to realize he was not cut out to be a cog in the huge Boeing wheel. His first assignment was in final assembly where he stood around and made sure the line workers remembered to torque the bolts that secured the engines to their mounts. Then he'd take a flashlight and peer up the exhaust stacks to make sure no one had accidentally left a tool inside.

After a few weeks, he was moved to the engine buildup line. All he had to do here was make sure each engine had its accessories bolted in place before it was sent out the door to final assembly. For someone who loved to work with his hands, this job was even more frustrating than the first one. Munro didn't want to just *look* at starters and magnetos; he wanted to work on them. After four months he'd had enough and he began looking for another job in his spare time. It didn't take him long to find one.

The first months of the war were hectic ones as the military scrambled to build up its strength and counter the enemy's advances at the same time. There was no way the government could cope with training the thousands of mechanics, electricians, welders, and heavy equipment operators that were needed to get the war effort underway. Fortunately, the country's civilian trade schools were able and willing to take up the slack. There was even a civilian pilot training program in which Air Corps and Navy cadets received their primary flight training from people like air racing legend Roscoe Turner and A. M. "Tex" Johnston, who later would become Boeing's chief test pilot on the B-52 and 707 programs.

Munro heard that the Edison Trade School in downtown Seattle was looking for someone to teach an engine mechanics class to military recruits. He applied for the position and was accepted. When the issue of salary was raised, Munro heard someone mention the number "thirty six."

"Fine," he said. "When do you want me to start."

He didn't care if "thirty six" meant $36 a week or $3,600 a year. He just wanted to get out of Boeing's big, impersonal factory and into a job he felt would make better use of his mechanical knowledge and skill. His last day at the B-17 plant was May 18, 1942.

Reg Collins, meanwhile, had braved Warrant Officer Fujita's bombing attacks to drive back to Oakland. The Boeing School of Aeronautics, like the Edison School in Seattle, was in desperate need of instructors to help train the military's new mechanics. Collins had been an excellent student and the Boeing School jumped at the chance to get him back as an instructor. He had also demonstrated an amazing talent in the shop.

"Reg could take a tube of toothpaste and make a cylinder out of it."

Bush pilots do not give out praise freely, but Lloyd Roundtree, who flew for Alaska Coastal in the 1960s and later owned Alaska Island Air in Petersburg, was impressed by Collins the first time he met him.

"He was a mechanic to beat mechanics."

Back in Seattle, Bob Munro became one-fourth of the Edison School's aviation department, sharing offices with another engine instructor, a parachute rigging instructor, and an airframe repair instructor. The school had a number of radial engines that the students learned to tear down and rebuild, as well as some ancient Curtiss OX-5 in-line engines Munro used to teach engine theory.

The year Collins and Munro had spent as students at the Boeing School of Aeronautics had resulted in both of them becoming licensed mechanics. The wartime trade school courses, on the other hand, were intended only to familiarize recruits with basic maintenance and repair procedures. Even so, Munro taught his students everything he could in the short time allotted to the engine course, and he found that he really enjoyed sharing his knowledge with people who were eager to learn.

He probably would have stayed at the Edison School for the duration of the war, but the decree banning all civilian flying within a 100-mile radius of Seattle brought with it the demise of the school's aviation department. The ban on flying was followed shortly by an Air Corps decision to concentrate all the state's civilian-taught aviation training programs in Yakima, 110 miles southeast of Seattle on the other side of the Cascade Mountains. This would put everything a safe distance away from the critical aircraft production and shipbuilding facilities in Puget Sound. Besides, the dry weather east of the mountains was much more conducive to flight training than the unpredictable murk in the convergence zone. The Edison School program closed down in September 1942.

In the few months he'd been at the Edison School, Bob Munro had become a valued instructor and he was invited to continue teaching his engine course in Yakima. But as much as he enjoyed instructing, Munro turned down the offer. He and Ruth had been married in February; if nothing else, the job at Boeing had enabled a quick repayment of his uncle's loan. After living first in a motel and then in a tiny apartment in the University District, the Munros had finally settled down in a small house on Haller Lake, north of Seattle. Neither of them relished the idea of moving again, this time clear across the mountains from their families and friends. But Munro would not be out of work for long.

In the pre-dawn hours of June 7, 1942, the long-feared Japanese invasion of the United States became a reality as 2,500 assault troops clambered out of their wooden whaleboats and stormed the beaches of Attu and Kiska, two barren, windswept islands at the western end of Alaska's Aleutian chain. Suddenly, the U.S. military's half-hearted campaign to beef up Alaska's defenses took on an unprecedented urgency. The Alaska Highway, already under construction, became a priority project. A string of new airbases stretching from Canada to the Bering Sea was rushed to completion, and the operation to evict the Japanese from their ice-choked beachheads swung ponderously into motion.

The Aleutian Campaign would drag on for a year, culminating in the vicious battle to retake Attu where the weather proved as fierce an enemy as the Japanese. Everything the military needed for its war in Alaska had to be shipped or flown in from the states. It was the Klondike gold rush all over again as Seattle became the major staging point for everything going north. Civilian tug and barge companies and commercial air services became strategic assets, and they were kept busy around the clock.

A number of commercial operators provided air service within the Territory of Alaska itself, but the vital air link to the "Outside" was dominated by a single carrier, Pan American. Their fleet of Lockheed Lodestars and DC-3s rumbled back and forth between Seattle, Anchorage, and Fairbanks with an intermediate stop in Prince George, British Columbia. Pan Am's Alaska service was based on Boeing Field, and as the demands on their airplanes increased, so did the demands on their mechanics.

The Civil Air Regulations of the day required commercial airlines to have one fully licensed mechanic for every five journeyman mechanics on their payroll. Bob Munro's year at the Boeing School paid off when Pan Am went looking for licensed mechanics to help staff their expanding Seattle base. And Munro not only had the requisite Airframe and Engine certificate, he had teaching experience, too, thanks to the Edison School. It was a combination Pan Am's base manager couldn't afford to pass up. The airline wanted to set up a maintenance training center in Seattle; with Munro on board they'd have someone who could do it.

The building the base manager told Munro to use for the training center wasn't much, about twenty by fifty feet, but the airline did get him free access to the salvage yard out at Sand Point Naval Air Station. Munro quickly filled his little training center with worn out engines and propellers and stocked the workbenches with magnetos, prop governors, fuel pumps, and anything else he thought Pan Am's mechanics should know how to fix.

Unlike the Edison Trade School courses, Munro's curriculum was designed to turn out licensed mechanics. The training center was right next to the Civil Aeronautics Board office on Boeing Field, and it didn't take long for the CAB licensing officials to realize that any mechanic who had learned his stuff under Bob Munro's tutelage was a cut above the rest.

One of the apprentice mechanics who enrolled in Munro's training center was a thoughtful young man named Tom Wardleigh. Wardleigh, who was just finishing high school, worked the swing shift at Pan Am from four-thirty in the afternoon to midnight. When the airline started offering free training classes to any employee willing to take them on their own time, Wardleigh signed up. He would arrive at the training center at one o'clock and attend classes until the beginning of his shift. He still values the education he received at the airline's expense.

> "It was a very high-quality school. Bob was the instructor, and it didn't cost us anything but our time. We worked on real parts. If you overhauled a carburetor, it went right on the shelf to go on an airplane. There was no make-believe about it. We learned to overhaul fuel pumps, vacuum pumps, carburetors, propeller governors and oil pumps, and every part we worked on went onto one of Pan Am's airplanes."
>
> **TOM WARDLEIGH**

For a young man like Wardleigh, working on real parts was more than good training. It also taught responsibility. The failure of a fuel pump or a prop governor on an airplane carrying passengers was serious business. Wardleigh and his fellow classmates paid close attention to Munro's instructions and learned to treat every aspect of an overhaul as though their own lives depended on it.

Mechanics weren't the only people to go through the Seattle training center. The airline had hired twenty apprentice engineers; college graduates with degrees in chemical, electrical, and structural engineering. They were well-versed in engineering theory, but most of them didn't have a clue when it came to how a radial engine worked. Pan Am wanted their new engineers to get a quick dose of aviation reality, and Bob Munro's training program looked like the perfect place for them to get it. Munro was a little intimidated at first. Lack of funds and the need to help support his family had kept his own college education from getting off the ground, and he wondered how much credibility he'd have in front of a bunch of graduate engineers.

He needn't have worried. The course was a smashing success. Munro used a cutaway engine he'd made to demonstrate the operation of valves and pistons and illustrate the radial engine's unique connecting rod arrangement. He then set up a rotating, six-week schedule to give each engineer hands-on experience in Pan Am's propeller, accessory, and engine overhaul shops.

Munro conducted many of his classes right out in the shops and concluded each one with a test. His efforts paid off for the airline for years. By learning what makes an airplane work and what it takes to *keep* it working, Pan Am's new engineers were equipped to make decisions based on operational reality, not just college theories.

Munro enjoyed running the training center, but he also enjoyed the fact that, when he wanted to, he could pick up a toolbox and put in some time in the base maintenance shops. He even managed to get up to his beloved north country a few times. Pan Am had small repair stations in Prince George and Fairbanks. The mechanics at the stations were competent enough, but few of them were licensed. In an effort to license as many of its mechanics as possible, the airline sent Munro north to help the local mechanics prepare for their licensing exams.

He was in Prince George when one of Pan Am's new DC-3s taxied in with a rough engine. The station manager asked Munro if he would help figure out what was causing the problem. This was something new for Munro. Usually he worked on parts someone else already had diagnosed as being faulty. Now he was being asked to help troubleshoot the engine itself. But it didn't take long to figure out the problem was in one of the engine's two magnetos. The bad mag was replaced and the DC-3 was sent on its way, and Munro discovered he enjoyed the challenge of tracking down a problem as much as he enjoyed fixing it.

Reg Collins drove home from California during a break in his teaching schedule and, after seeing what Munro was doing down at Pan Am, decided he preferred real airplanes to classroom mockups and hangar queens. Pan Am's Seattle base was still hiring licensed mechanics, so Collins signed on. Then he rushed back to Oakland and resigned his position at the Boeing School. His reason for returning to California was not to resign; he could have done that with a phone call. The real reason was a young woman named Margaret Otrich. Collins had met Margaret on an outing sponsored by the Dexioma Club, the Oakland equivalent of the Triune Club. The two were married on September 5, 1943. They spent the first night of their honeymoon in the Oakland airport, waiting for a flight back to Seattle.

The one thing neither Munro nor Collins had given much thought to was the draft. But Jack Mines had been right; it was just a matter of time before the military came knocking on their doors. Munro's invitation to go to war was mailed on January 1, 1943.

"Greetings: Having submitted yourself to a local board composed of your neighbors for the purpose of determining your availability for training and service in the armed forces of the United States, you are hereby notified that you have now been selected for training and service in the ARMY. You will, therefore, report to the local board named above... at 6:30 AM on the eleventh day of January, 1943."

Bob Munro packed his suitcase and got ready to go, but Pan Am was not happy about the situation at all. Reg Collins and several other mechanics had received similar letters and suddenly the entire core of the Seattle base was in jeopardy. The situation was made worse by the fact that Pan Am had recently landed a contract with the Navy to fly equipment and people to Alaska. How was the airline supposed to hold to the terms of the contract if it didn't have enough mechanics to keep the airplanes flying?

The weekend before Munro was supposed to report for induction into the Army he got a telegram from Pan Am telling him to go to the Navy induction center instead. He did, and the next thing he knew, he was an Aviation Chief Machinist Mate. The Navy then immediately transferred him to the reserves and assigned him to their contract with Pan American. Munro was back at work in his training center the next day.

The Navy did the same thing with Reg Collins and the other Pan Am mechanics who'd received orders to report for induction into the Army. After all, the Navy reasoned, why should they put one of their critical transportation links to Alaska at risk? A handful of airline mechanics wasn't going to make any difference one way or the other to the Army's war effort. Munro suspected that a fair amount of the Navy's reasoning had been supplied by Pan Am, but he didn't feel he was shirking his national duty by remaining at Boeing Field; Pan Am's DC-3s really *were* critical to the Navy's operations in Alaska.

When Pan Am decided to put stewardesses on its flights to Alaska, Munro was given the job of familiarizing the eight young women assigned to the Seattle base with the airplanes they would be flying on. Much of his instruction was practical: how to open and close the cabin doors and operate the oxygen system. However, he felt they would do a better job if they understood the airplane itself, so he taught them the theory of flight and showed them how the engines and flight controls worked.

Some of Pan Am's Alaska flights were over water so Munro arranged for the stewardesses to receive lifesaving instruction in the University of Washington swimming pool. One of the more useful things taught in the course was how to keep an injured or unconscious person's head above water using floatation devices made from jackets or other articles of clothing. The airline's new flight attendants weren't the only ones who had to get wet; the lifesaving course was made mandatory for the cockpit crews, too.

The airplane familiarization course was Bob Munro's last assignment at the training center. He'd made it clear he wanted to do more mechanical work, so he was assigned to the maintenance shop on a full time basis. He loved the job, but he didn't like the way the attitude at the airline was changing. It had been a matter of pride at the Seattle base that no matter what condition a plane was in when it arrived, it would be ready to go at eight o'clock the next morning. If that meant working late to replace a magneto or a prop governor, so be it. But a union had wormed its way into Pan Am's maintenance operations, and now everything was different. The new union contract specified who could do what and when. The base manager no longer could come out and help the mechanics remove engine cowls or perform system tests. Anyone who worked even a few minutes past the end of their shift had to be paid overtime, and there were strict regulations governing how much overtime mechanics could work and when they could work it. Any problems that arose between labor and management had to be settled by an arbitration board. The days of working out problems by discussing them in person with the base manager were over.

Some of the mechanics liked the new rules but Bob Munro wasn't one of them. The way he saw it, he'd been hired to maintain airplanes. If that meant working extra hours now and then, well, that was the nature of the job. No one had forced him to become a mechanic; if he didn't like the hours or the work, he could leave. The union said it was there to protect Pan Am's mechanics from being overworked and under-compensated. Munro had worked twelve and fourteen hours a day in the fish cannery and been cheated out of a summer's wages at the gold mine. He was no stranger to long hours, low pay, and unscrupulous employers, but they were issues he preferred to resolve on his own. He didn't want anyone fighting his battles for him.

Reg Collins didn't care much for the changes at Pan Am either, and he and Munro began to talk about going into business for themselves. It was an idea they'd kicked around before, but now they had a motive. The ideal situation, they decided, would be to have a little shop of their own where they could repair and rebuild small planes. Even though civilian flying had been banned in the vicinity of Seattle, they were sure that once the war was over there would be a resurgence of interest in private flying.

But first they had to find out if they even had the talent to put a small plane back together. Collins and Munro were engine specialists; outside of a few classes, neither one of them had done much airframe work. What they needed was a test project, a little airplane that required a total overhaul. They weren't concerned about rebuilding the engine; they could to do that in their sleep. But straightening and welding fuselage tubes, repairing wooden wing components, fitting and stitching new fabric; these were skills Collins and Munro had not had many opportunities to practice.

The subject of finding an airplane to overhaul came up in a conversation between Collins and one of his cousins, who was a member of a local flying club.

"I've got the perfect plane for you, Reg."

"Oh?"

"It's the club's old Aeronca floatplane."

"What's wrong with it?"

"It blew over a few years ago and Kurtzer salvaged it. It needs a little work to make it right again, that's all."

On an April weekend in 1944, Collins and Munro drove down to Lake Union to see the plane for themselves. It was a pathetic sight. Kurtzer's primary concern had been getting the remains of Eight-Eight-Five out of his way; he'd stacked the fuselage and wings on top of the floats and then jammed the whole thing up against the outside wall of his hangar. The fabric had fallen apart in the damp weather and it hung in tatters from the rusty tube fuselage. Dry rot had attacked some of the wooden wing structure, and the little two cylinder engine had rusted up solid.

"Your cousin has an interesting idea of what constitutes 'a little work,' " Munro said dryly as he picked through the skeletal remains of the Aeronca.

"Maybe," Collins replied, "but this is just what we've been looking for. Something we can rebuild from the ground up."

"We may have to start lower than that."

But Munro agreed the Model K would make a perfect project. With Collins' cousin acting as negotiator, a price of $300 was agreed upon, and the club signed over their former flagship to the two Pan Am mechanics. Kurtzer was delighted the day they showed up with a borrowed trailer to haul Eight-Eight-Five off his property; he was close to chucking the whole works into the lake except for a few fittings and the floats, which still had some value. The Aeronca's new owners stashed the wings in Collins' garage in Wallingford and took everything else out to Munro's house on Haller Lake.

Bob and Ruth Munro in 1943.

They worked on Eight-Eight-Five one or two evenings a week after work and almost every weekend for the next year. Ruth Munro found her husband's new hobby mildly interesting. She'd recently had their first child, a girl they'd named Leslie, but as long as Munro didn't ignore his family duties, Ruth didn't begrudge him the time he spent working on the plane.

Collins and Munro decided to start with what they regarded as the easiest part of the project; rebuilding the Aeronca's horizontally opposed, two-cylinder engine. They took it completely apart, cleaned off the rust, polished the cylinders and bearings, and fitted new piston rings. After overhauling the carburetor and ignition system, they put the whole thing back together and painted it black.

Next came the wings. They stripped off what was left of the fabric covering and knocked apart the wooden spars and ribs. Some of the ribs just needed re-gluing to make them serviceable, but the ones which had succumbed to dry rot had to be replaced. Munro cut out the new parts in Pan Am's maintenance shop and glued them together at home.

Then it was time to attack the fuselage. They ground the rust off the tubing and cut out the really bad sections. After welding in new tubing, they painted it and re-installed the brackets and pulleys for the control cables. Next came the motor mounts and the sheet-metal cowling around the engine. Eight-Eight-Five didn't have much of an instrument panel; the altimeter and airspeed indicator were augmented by an engine tachometer, an oil pressure gauge, and a turn coordinator. Collins and Munro cleaned the instruments and re-fitted them, and installed the side-by-side seats, control yokes, and rudder bars.

By August 1945, the only thing left to be done was to cover the fuselage and wings with new fabric. So far, Collins and Munro hadn't given much thought to what they would do with Eight-Eight-Five when they finished it. They certainly weren't going to fly it; neither one of them knew how to fly. Their interest in aviation was purely mechanical. Rebuilding the Aeronca had given them faith in their ability to perform whatever repair work might be needed on a small plane, so the next step was to find a location where they could set up shop. It was obvious they didn't have to be on an airport to rebuild airplanes; the only drawbacks to working on Eight-Eight-Five at home had been the cramped quarters in their respective garages and the lack of heat.

The two friends began searching the neighborhoods in the north end of Seattle for a commercial garage they could rent. Their plan was to work for themselves at night and on weekends while continuing to work for Pan Am during the day. Only when it looked like their own shop would be a success would they quit the airline. They found what they were looking for on Green Lake Way, a couple of miles north of Lake Union. The old garage was the right size, it was heated, and most important, the rent was reasonable. Then Jack Mines came home from the war and changed everything.

FIRST FLIGHT

THE WAR CHANGED AMERICA FOREVER. Teenagers whose world had been defined by the county line suddenly found themselves on intimate terms with places that previously had been mere blotches of color in a high school geography text. England, France, China, the Mariana Islands; farmboys and neighborhood rowdies became international travelers at the stroke of a pen. Clutching their official orders, they clambered on board the troopships and C-47s and headed for the horizon.

The ones who came back brought with them a new sense of mobility. They'd journeyed by jeep, tank, and half-track. They'd skimmed the waves in PT boats and flattened the swells in battleships. Hands that only months earlier had been changing gears on the family tractor now gripped the throttles of 2,000-horsepower fighters. America never turned back at the county line again.

Whatever plans Jack Mines had made for a career in engineering paled in comparison to the excitement of blasting his 4,000-horsepower Harpoon over the waves in search of enemy submarines. The Navy made him turn in the keys to the plane at the end of the war, but by then he was hooked. Aviation was where it was at, he decided, and he arrived home with little interest in pursuing a desk job. He wanted to fly.

One of the first things Mines did when he got home was look up Reg Collins and Bob Munro. They'd written back and forth a few times during the war, so Mines knew they were both working for Pan American. The airplane under restoration in Munro's garage at Haller Lake was something new, however, and he wasted little time in driving out to see it. As he walked slowly around the completed fuselage frame he listened without comment to his friends describe their plan to go into the airplane repair business. When they were through, he stopped and tapped the freshly painted tubing.

"How soon do you think you'll have this finished?"

"Hard to say," Collins replied. "We still have to cover it, dope it, and paint it. I'd say maybe a couple of months."

"What are you going to do with it when you're done?"

Munro shrugged. "We haven't thought much about that. Sell it, maybe, and get another one to fix up."

"Why don't you go into business with it? Offer flight instruction, charter flights, things like that?"

Collins and Munro exchanged glances. "Well, that'd be interesting, Jack," Collins said, "but neither one of us knows how to fly."

"No, but I do. We could start a company. You guys would do the mechanical work and I'd do the flying."

Collins and Munro were skeptical. They hadn't planned on getting into something as extensive as a full-blown flying service. All they wanted to do was work on airplanes and be their own bosses. But Mines kept after them and they eventually agreed to give it a shot. The company would be in the form of a partnership. Collins and Munro would be responsible for the mechanical end of the business, repairing customers' planes and keeping their own airplane operational. Mines would handle the flying, instructing, and promotional work.

"What about the financial aspect?" Munro asked. Conservative by nature, he'd learned early on that bills don't pay themselves. "Who's going to take care of the business side of the company?"

Mines had an answer for that, too. "I'll bet we can get Durwood Alkire to help us when he gets out of the service. He knows all about that kind of stuff."

The one aspect of the business that wasn't discussed was how the company would be divided up. Collins and Munro assumed they all would be equal partners, each with a one-third share of the business. Mines probably did, too, but their assumptions were never formalized. After all, the three had been friends for years; a legal agreement just didn't seem necessary. It was an omission that ultimately would change the direction of the company.

But for now, the challenge was to get the business off the ground, or in this case, the water. The partners hadn't decided to start a seaplane company because market surveys indicated the potential for water-based air service in the area. They decided to start a seaplane company because Eight-Eight-Five happened to be a seaplane. If Collin's cousin had found them a wheelplane to rebuild, they would have been looking for space on one of the local airports. Fortunately for aviation history and almost every bush pilot in North America, the Aeronca's wheels had disappeared long before Collins and Munro went poking around behind Kurtzer's hangar.

The new company would be called M-C-M, for Mines, Collins, and Munro. The plans to rent the commercial garage in north Seattle were scrapped immediately. Even though the building was close to Green Lake, the lake's small size and the residential neighborhoods crowding its shores ruled out seaplane operations of any kind. Lake Union was out of the question, too. Even by 1945 standards, the price of waterfront commercial property was exorbitant, and besides, the trio knew Lana Kurtzer would be gunning for them the moment they tried to set up shop on "his" lake.

Operating from Elliott Bay was not a viable solution, either. Boat wakes and wind chop rendered the harbor too rough for the tiny Aeronca on all but the calmest days, and Collins and Munro were well aware of what happens to a metal airframe in the vicinity of saltwater.

That left Lake Sammamish and Lake Washington. Sammamish was simply too far out in the country to be practical, although its size and protection from the wind would have made it ideal for seaplane operations. Lake Washington, on the other hand, offered definite possibilities. Most of the development on the lake had occurred between Boeing's huge B-29 assembly plant at the southern end and Sand Point Naval Air Station thirteen miles to the north. The five miles of lake north of Sand Point were still relatively remote, with only a scattering of homes and cottages piercing the screen of second-growth forest that lined the shore.

Collins and Munro were still spending their days at Pan Am, so Jack Mines started driving around the lake on his own, looking for a place to fly their plane. On a whim, he decided to check out the north end. There wasn't much there, he knew, but he hadn't come across anything suitable, or affordable, farther south. He soon found himself approaching the small community of Kenmore on the Bothell Highway, a two-lane brick road on top of the low bluff that years before had been the shoreline of the lake.

The opening of the Montlake Cut and the subsequent nine-foot drop in water level had created a ring of new real estate around Lake Washington, a big chunk of which was in the form of

The shingle mill site almost as Jack Mines found it. The Air Harbor has barely gotten started; the abandoned shingle mill and log deck beside the dredged channel are still in place.

a wide, alder-covered shelf below the Kenmore bluff. There were a couple of homes on the shelf, and a small shingle mill. The tracks of the Northern Pacific branch line from Seattle to Woodinville ran along the base of the bluff, with a siding that angled over to the head of a short channel that had been dredged back from the lake.

Mines swung his six-cylinder Nash off the highway, banged over the railroad tracks, and careened down the narrow dirt road that ran across the shelf out to the lake. He bounced to a stop in the shade of a big tree and switched off the engine. Except for the lap of the water against the piles supporting the mill and the occasional chirp of a bird, it was dead quiet. Mines waited until the dust settled and then he got out to do some exploring.

The first thing he checked out was the mill itself. It actually fronted on the hundred-foot-wide channel that had been dug out back to the railroad siding. Mines assumed the channel had been put in to enable the railroad to dump logs directly into the water where they were then rafted up and towed to the big mills at the south end of the lake. The shingle mill was too small to have been a customer of the railroad; Mines reasoned that most of their logs had come in by truck, which would explain the wide turnaround area in front of the mill.

Mines stepped up into what was left of the building and looked around. The remains of a jack slip curving up out of the water showed that at least some of the mill's logs had come by water, or perhaps the trucks simply dumped their loads into the lake. The rusty bull chain in the trough of the V-shaped jack slip had brought the logs up to a large, open-grid log deck where they were rolled into position for the saws. It was obvious the place hadn't been in operation for years. Most of the machinery was gone, and all that was left of the boiler was a massive concrete base. Whoever owned the mill clearly had no intention of starting it up again.

Mines climbed down off the log deck and crunched through the dry grass and wood shavings out to the lake itself. Three or four dilapidated boats lay alongside a sagging dock next to the mill. At the mouth of the channel, a row of creosoted piles marched out into the water, the underpinnings for what once must have been a substantial pier. There was a ramshackle house not far away and beside it, a dilapidated one-car garage. A small outhouse stood in mute testimony to the property's lack of indoor plumbing. Back toward the mill was a garage-sized shed that could have been a scale house but which looked to Mines more like a chicken coop. His assumption was reinforced by the appearance of several hens which proceeded to peck noisily around the base of the building.

A few yards to the west of the house was a nice dock that was not at all in keeping with the rundown appearance of the mill buildings. Mines assumed the dock belonged to the large home some thirty yards further on, which would place the mill's property line only a few feet beyond the ramshackle house. Still, it was a sizable piece of real estate with a fair amount of shoreline.

The lake itself was calm, with only a slight wind-ruffle marring its surface, ideal water conditions for a little plane like the Aeronca. The northernmost mile of Lake Washington is in the form of a gentle dogleg bending to the east. The inside angle of the dogleg is Arrowhead Point, which offers some protection from the waves stirred up by southerly winds, while the low hills that surround the lake somewhat diminish the impact of winds from the north. All in all, it looked like a great place to keep a floatplane.

Mines turned to walk back to his car and was startled to see his feet sinking out of sight beneath him. Too late he realized he'd been deceived by the trees and bushes growing out of what appeared to be solid ground. Except for the fill dirt that had been brought in for the road and the truck turnaround, the property was a quagmire of mud and shingle shavings. The muck oozing up over Mine's shoes was certainly a detriment, but it didn't offset his enthusiasm for the location. There was plenty of space, good access to the lake, and hardly any neighbors to complain about noise. He had no doubt that Collins and Munro could figure out how to deal with the swampy parts.

The jolting drive back to the highway revealed three other buildings Mines hadn't noticed on the way in. There was a second old house near the entrance to the property while across the driveway to the east stood a small barn and something that looked like a tool shed. Mines stopped at the railroad tracks and took one more look back at the mill site. Yes, he decided, it was perfect. The next step would be to find out who owned the property and try to get permission to bring Eight-Eight-Five out and fly it. He wheeled his car up onto the highway and headed home to break the good news to his partners.

Collins and Munro were enthusiastic about the site the first time Mines took them out to see it. As he had predicted, the two mechanics dismissed the problem of boggy ground with a wave of the hand; a little fill dirt would firm things up nicely. Had they known the effort that would ultimately go into stabilizing the ground, they probably would have gone home right then, but at the time the swampy nature of the site didn't seem like much of an obstacle.

Collins and Munro were more concerned about how they would get the plane in and out of the water. They'd need a ramp of some sort, so they spent most of that first visit tromping back and forth along the shoreline trying to decide on the best place to put one. Mines ruled out the channel, saying its width wouldn't provide enough maneuvering room. This left the lakeshore in front of the house and garage.

"We could use the garage as a shop," said Collins, "and maybe move that chicken coop over next to it for an office or something."

"We'll have to remove all that piling," said Munro, pointing offshore to the remains of the pier. "And the water here is awfully shallow. We'll have to dredge a channel out from the ramp."

But they all agreed it was the perfect spot for the fledgling M-C-M Company.

The mill was owned by a Mr. Gus Newburg. He had no objection when Mines, Collins, and Munro approached him about bringing their airplane out and launching it from his property. He'd been thinking about getting rid of the place, anyway. He'd shut down the mill when the war started and had since gone on to other ventures. There was still some machinery he wanted to salvage along with the big timbers that made up the log deck, but everything else would stay with the property.

Newburg's asking price was $30,000, which was about $29,000 more than M-C-M's partners could afford. But no one had been pounding on Newburg's door to buy the old mill, so he told Jack Mines he'd be willing to entertain the idea of a lease.

Mines was beginning to see more in M-C-M's future than just a flying service and repair fa-cility. Kenmore was still considered the country in 1945. Perhaps if they put a small hotel and restaurant on the property, more customers would be enticed to make the drive out from the city. He kept the hotel idea to himself for the time being, but his enthusiastic picture of the company's future was enough to convince his mother, Lillian Mines, to invest in the idea. Lillian agreed to sign a five-year lease for the mill property with an option to buy. She then leased the property back to M-C-M. Lillian also signed an agreement giving the company the right to purchase her option to buy. At the time, the agreement was regarded as little more than a formality. No one suspected it ultimately would decide the fate of the company.

Acquiring the mill site was easy compared to what came next. Even in 1945, there was plenty of red tape standing in the way of getting a little company like M-C-M off the ground. First, they would need authorization from the Civil Aeronautics Administration (CAA) to operate an airport at the north end of the lake. Then, before any new hangar, shop, or office buildings could be built, the mill site would have to be re-zoned for use as a commercial seaplane base. Re-zoning the prop-erty would require the blessing of the King County Planning Commission.

Collins and Munro didn't have the time to deal with the legalities of getting the company started. Such free time as they had after putting in a full day's work at Pan Am was taken up either by family responsibilities or the airplane nearing completion in Munro's garage. Fortunately, Jack Mines had both the time and the enthusiasm. He began collecting signatures on a petition to re-zone the property and initiated a letter-writing campaign to solicit community support for M-C-M.

Only it was no longer called M-C-M. Actually, no one was sure what to call it. For a company that ultimately would become the largest seaplane facility in North America, it is surprising how little planning went into its creation. There were no marketing studies or late-night strategy ses-sions. There were no letters of intent from potential customers. The company's assets consisted of an unfinished, underpowered airplane, a short-term lease on a mud bog, and some vague ideas about a hotel which two-thirds of the partnership didn't even know about.

Given the casual nature of the company's startup, the lack of concern over the company's name was not surprising. M-C-M had been an interesting idea, but no one was in love with it so Jack Mines tried out a few others. The letter of authorization from the CAA to operate an airport in Kenmore was addressed to the "Mines Service Airport." The letters Mines sent out to com-munity leaders to drum up support for his re-zoning petition referred to the company as "Mines Seaplane Service."

In January 1946, the King County Planning Commission voted against re-zoning the shingle mill site. Mines applied for a re-consideration of his petition and immediately began another letter-writing campaign. The first evidence of the partners' fourth attempt at naming their new company appears on a letter of support from the Washington State Advisory Commission. Perhaps the mot-ley collection of motorboats at the mill dock had gotten Mines thinking the planning commission would be more favorable toward a company tied to the boating community, at least in name. The letter, dated February 1, 1946, is addressed to Mr. John F. Mines, Manager, Kenmore Air Harbor. This time, the name stuck.

In the years immediately following World War II, aviation was heralded as the business of the future. Everyone wanted to climb aboard the aviation bandwagon, so it's not surprising that Jack Mines' letter-writing campaign elicited a positive response. The idea of a seaplane base at the north end of the lake was supported by the Boy Scouts of America, the Committee for Industrial Organization (CIO), and Lodge 751 of the Aeronautical Mechanics Union. There were letters of support from the Bothell and Lake City Lions Clubs, the Kenmore Businessmen's Association, and the Lake City Commercial Club. There was support from private homeowners in the area, too, including one letter which concluded:

> "It is a very interesting and beautiful sight to watch these planes land and take off on the water. I strongly recommend this operation."

Most of the objections to the establishment of a seaplane base in Kenmore came from the planning commission itself, which was worried about noise and safety. To answer the commission's concerns, Mines wrote a masterful letter which first listed the advantages of a north end seaplane base and then addressed the commission's concerns.

First Objection: Planes are noisy.

Answer: It is inconceivable how people surrounding the north end of Lake Washington could call a small plane of forty or sixty-five horsepower noisy when they have bought property faced with the noise of outboard motors, trucks from the highway around the lake, trains between the highway and the lake, and planes from 2,000 to 8,000 horsepower from nearby Sand Point.

Second Objection: Planes are dangerous.

Answer: There is room enough in this area to have our entire traffic pattern over water. The most dangerous time in flying is takeoff, because if your engine quits you usually do not have enough time to select a good landing area. This is eliminated in seaplane flying with a lake the size of Lake Washington.

Third Objection: Seaplanes will interfere with the fishing.

Answer: Mr. Hugo Petersen has rented the fishing boats from Kenmore for fourteen years and is in full accord with the seaplane base. He has signed the petition for approval and we have worked out plans to avoid any conflict with the fishermen. The planes only draw approximately six inches of water and there is nothing to snag fishing lines. They do not disturb the water as a boat propeller would. The peak season for fishing [in the lake] is at a different time than the peak season for flying.

Fourth Objection: We don't want to commercialize the district.

Answer: There is nothing to stop planes from other bases from coming to practice in Lake Washington. Many people along the lake will have planes to be serviced just as many boats will be serviced at the boat marina next to us. There has been no opposition to the establishment of this motor boat marina. The operation of seaplanes is no more a commercial operation than the operation of boats. Any commercial operation is usually associated with the word unsightly; however, anyone who has witnessed seaplane operation would vouch for the fact that seaplanes are graceful and very interesting to watch.

Conclusion: These objections have all come from people unfamiliar with small seaplane operation, and I feel that when they have a chance to observe our operation, their objections will seem unfounded.

Armed with his letter, the signed petition to re-zone the shingle mill site, and the letters of support from the community, Mines went back to the King County Planning Commission to plead his case for the second time. They agreed to reconsider their initial recommendation and promised to let him know the moment they reached a decision. It was a decision Jack Mines was never to hear.

In February 1946, while Mines was formulating his second attack on the King County Planning Commission, Reg Collins and Bob Munro finished Eight-Eight-Five. They had a devil of a time with the plane's fabric covering. Fitting and stitching the new linen in place had been a snap; it was the doping process that gave them so much trouble. The noxious-smelling dope performs two critical functions: it causes the fabric to shrink drumhead tight around the plane's fuselage and wing framework, and it fills in the pores, or weave, of the fabric, leaving an aerodynamically smooth surface that's ready for painting.

Collins and Munro dutifully doped the Aeronca's fabric skin and then rushed for the door to gulp in lungfulls of the crisp, fresh air outside. Behind them, the fabric tightened up nicely, but to their dismay, the dope refused to dry. The culprit turned out to be the damp, cold air in Munro's unheated garage. All they could do was wait. It was a cold winter; the plane stayed sticky for weeks.

King County's initial refusal to re-zone the shingle mill site placed certain restrictions on what the partners could do to the property but it didn't mean they couldn't build a ramp and fly their plane. Bob Munro's mining experience made him the natural choice to head up the construction project.

"What we need," he said, ticking off the items on his fingers as he named them, "is a tractor, some rope and cable, lumber for the ramp, and a basement scraper."

"A what?"

"A basement scraper. A heavy metal scoop used to dig basements. We'll use it to dredge the lake in front of the ramp. They used to pull them with horses," Munro added.

"Horses?" Jack Mines began to wonder if Munro maybe was taking this construction project a little too far. "You mean on top of everything else we have to find some horses?"

"Usually you only need one." Munro paused to let Mines ponder the idea of becoming a stableboy and then added, "but we'll pull ours with a tractor."

Mines brightened immediately. "I'll pay for the tractor," he announced. "After all, you two bought the airplane as well as all the tools we'll be using in the shop. I think it's only fair that I buy the tractor."

When a newspaper ad appeared announcing a sale of surplus Army equipment at Fort Lewis, south of Tacoma, Mines drove Munro and Durwood Alkire down to the base on the chance they might find a bargain. They came home with a four-wheel-drive, Dodge weapons carrier, the Army's version of a three-quarter ton pickup truck. The weapons carrier was noisy and slow, but it had three things going for it. It was rugged, it had an extremely powerful winch mounted up front, and it had cost exactly what Collins and Munro had paid for the Model K: three hundred dollars.

As they rattled north on Highway 99, Munro quizzed Alkire about the advisability of depreciating the company's new wheels.

"Well, it's a used truck," Alkire shouted above the roar of the wind whipping through the open cab, "so I'd suggest depreciating it over three years. Spread it out any more than that and the depreciation won't be worth the ink it takes to fill out the tax form."

Jack Mines, Reg Collins, and Bob Munro with the Aeronca Model K on the ramp at Kenmore. This is the only known photo of all three founders at the Kenmore Air Harbor site. The photo was probably taken by Ted Huntley, possibly on the day of the plane's first flight.

Munro nodded thoughtfully and drove on. His business education had begun.

The dope finally dried on the Aeronca and Collins and Munro spent a weekend painting it yellow with a black stripe. The next step was to see if all the major assemblies fit the way they were supposed to. They positioned the floats on Munro's front lawn and attached the float struts and spreader bars. The fuselage came next, bolted atop the float struts. Finally the wing struts were bolted in place and the wings attached to the fuselage. All that remained was to hook up the control surfaces and Kenmore Air Harbor's flagship would be ready to take to the air.

But not from where it was sitting. Eight-Eight-Five would be little more than a yard decoration until they had a way of getting it in and out of the water at the millsite.

Jack Mines had found the property in the fall, when things were still relatively dry. By mid-winter, the rain had turned the fill dirt on entrance road into a rutted, muddy mess. It was bad enough at times to defeat even the four-wheel-drive weapons carrier, and the partners became quite proficient in the operation of its front-mounted winch. Nevertheless, by early March they'd managed to clear off a patch of ground next to the lake and construct a simple ramp just west of the entrance to the channel.

While Reg Collins and Bob Munro had been rebuilding Eight-Eight-Five, they'd had an eager helper in the form of Munro's fifteen-year-old first cousin, Ted Huntley. Huntley was fascinated by airplanes and he made sure he was there the day they took the Aeronca to the lake.

> "They took the plane apart and hauled it over from Bob's place on a trailer. Then they put it back together right next to the water. I remember standing in the back of the 3/4-ton truck to help put the wings on. They weren't very heavy, so we just climbed into the truck and held them up while Reg put the bolts in."
>
> TED HUNTLEY

On March 21, 1946, Jack Mines eased his tall frame into Eight-Eight-Five's pilot's seat and closed the door. The plane was tailed up onto the ramp, its nose pointing down the lake toward Arrowhead Point, one mile away. Bob Munro stepped cautiously forward on the right float until he could reach the propeller. On the ground behind the plane, Reg Collins and Ted Huntley got a firm grip on the tail. Mines opened the throttle and primed the engine. Then he switched on the magneto ignition and nodded at Munro.

"Here we go!" With one hand on the wing strut for leverage, Munro grasped the end of the wooden propeller and pulled it sharply downward.

"Pop........ pop.....pop, pop, pop, pop, pop." The two-cylinder engine banged into life and Munro retreated off the tail of the float.

Mines let the engine idle for a few moments and then he waved his left hand out the window. Collins and Huntley let go of the tail and stepped out of the prop blast. Mines eased the throttle forward and the pops blended together into a harsh buzz. Eight-Eight-Five began to vibrate, but it stayed firmly glued to the top of the ramp. The buzz got louder. The wingtips started to tremble, but still the plane stayed put. The buzz became a rasping snarl as Mines eased the throttle up even more. There was a lurch, and then the Aeronca was in the water, the wake from its floats flashing in the brittle, spring sunlight as Mines maneuvered the plane clear of the line of piles.

Collins, Munro, and young Ted Huntley sat down on the tailgate of the weapons carrier to watch as Mines ran through the Aeronca's simple check list. He rotated the control yoke from side to side and then pulled it all the way back to make sure the ailerons and elevator were free and moved in the right direction. Pushing down on first one and then the other side of the rudder bar swung the nose back and forth and confirmed the rudder system was working properly. Finally, he checked the engine's single magneto by switching it off and on to make sure it was grounded properly. It was.

The two mechanics sitting on the truck tailgate saw nothing historic in what was about to happen, nor did the man in the cockpit. This wasn't the *Wright Flyer* on the catapult at Kill Devil Hill or the *Spirit of St. Louis* poised at the far end of Curtiss Field on Long Island. Had Bob Munro known what the airplane clattering around on the lake would lead to, that someday the mud bog behind him would be crowded with hangars and maintenance shops, that someday the rattle of pistons would fade under the rising whine of gas turbines, he probably would have regarded the event differently. As it was, he just wanted to see if Eight-Eight-Five would fly.

Jack Mines pointed the blunt nose of the Model K a little to the right of Arrowhead Point and eased the throttle all the way in. Aided by full up-elevator, the front of the plane rose dramatically as its forward speed increased the hydrodynamic pressure under the forebody of the floats. Mines eased off on the elevator as the speed increased until the plane was skimming the surface in an almost level attitude, its weight supported by the water pressure just ahead of the steps in the float bottoms.

As the speed increased, so did the flow of air around the wing. When Mines sensed the wing was developing enough lift to fly, he eased back on the yoke, and the yellow Aeronca rose gracefully from the water, twin streamers of spray sparkling off the back of the floats. Kenmore Air Harbor was officially in business.

HOME IMPROVEMENTS 4

Jack Mines banked Eight-Eight-Five into a tight, 180-degree turn and clattered back up the lake toward Kenmore. The forty-horsepower two-banger in front of him was a far cry from the 2,000 horsepower, eighteen-cylinder radials he was used to, but it felt good to be back in the air again. He rocked his wings in response to the waves from the three figures perched on the back of the truck five hundred feet below.

Young Ted Huntley hopped off the tailgate of the weapons carrier to get a better view of the Aeronca as it buzzed around in a circle over the property.

"Boy, it flies great," he exclaimed, "and that yellow paint job really looks sharp."

Reg Collins and Bob Munro shaded their eyes and watched as Mines rolled out of his turn and headed north on the downwind leg of his landing pattern. The Model K certainly wasn't the most sophisticated machine in the sky, but after devoting most of their free time to it for the better part of two years, they had to agree with Huntley that it looked pretty darn good up there.

Mines eased the power back and banked around over the tiny town of Kenmore until he was headed back toward the lake. Mindful of the shallow water and debris near the shore, he picked a touchdown spot safely out in deep water and adjusted his final approach accordingly. He landed in a shower of spray and taxied back to the ramp.

"C'mon, Bob, it's your turn!"

"Oh, I don't know." Munro shook his head. "I just work on 'em."

But it didn't take much prodding to get Munro to climb into the cockpit.

"I probably shouldn't do this," he said as Mines slid over into the right seat, "but it will be kind of fun to see the place from the air."

"This isn't a sightseeing trip," said Mines, "it's a lesson. I'm going to teach you and Reg to fly."

Munro flew two-tenths of an hour that day, twelve minutes that were duly noted in the little black logbook he purchased a few days later. Collins got a quick lesson, too. But the most significant event occurred later, as they were pulling the plane out of the water. A car drove down from the highway and a young man got out. He'd seen the plane flying around over the lake and he wanted to know if they were going to be selling lessons to the public. Kenmore Air Harbor had its first customer.

Actually, Kenmore's bright yellow Aeronca had been noticed by a number of people. One of them was a nearby Lake Forest Park resident named George Yeaman, who owned a couple of seaplanes, a Savoia-Marchetti S-56 amphibian and an Aeronca C-3. The C-3, nicknamed "The Bathtub" because of its shape, was the even-more-underpowered forerunner to Kenmore's Model K. The Savoia-Marchetti, on the other hand, was a work of art. The delicately streamlined, three-place biplane had its small radial engine elevated on a pair of struts just forward of the open cockpit. The struts also helped support the upper wing. Yeaman liked the idea of being able to keep his planes close to his home and he'd been a vocal supporter of the seaplane base from the very beginning. It wasn't long before he was down negotiating storage and maintenance fees with Jack Mines.

With their own plane in operation and a growing list of real and potential customers, it was obvious that Reg Collins and Bob Munro were going to have to give up their jobs at Pan American. Not that they didn't want to, but the idea of walking away from a secure job was a little scary, especially for the Munros, who were expecting their second child.

Ruth's parents were especially upset. To them, the ideal situation was a government job with good security and a guaranteed pension. The next best thing was to work for a big, stable company like Pan American. The absolute worst thing was to head out independently and start something risky like a flying service.

"Even if the business succeeds," they warned, "everyone knows that flying leads to accidents, accidents lead to lawsuits, and lawsuits lead to financial ruin."

Bob Munro didn't see it that way. As a mechanic, he had an advantage over most people in that he understood how an airplane worked. And, like most mechanics, he knew that understanding a machine is the key to operating it safely. As for the risk of starting a new business, Munro truly believed he could accomplish anything he felt was worth accomplishing. His experiences in Alaska and at Pan Am had given him confidence in his ability to get a job done. And the little yellow plane sitting on the ramp at Kenmore was proof he could get the job done *right*. Still, he admits, they were all a little naive about the realities of starting a company from scratch.

> "Other than Jack's ideas about a hotel we didn't have much of a plan other than Reg and I would fix planes and Jack would give flying lessons. We just assumed it was going to work."
>
> **BOB MUNRO**

Ruth Munro supported her husband's decision to leave Pan Am, but even she found herself wondering if they were doing the right thing.

> "It was really rather overwhelming. It was difficult having him come home and say, 'I've quit my job and we're going to start this new business.' A lot of our friends wondered if we knew

what we were doing. But anyone who has a dream and feels strongly about it should be able to pursue it."

RUTH MUNRO

Their friends might have wondered if Mines, Collins, and Munro knew what they were doing, but the partners themselves didn't have the time to worry about it. It wasn't a question of "what do we do now?" but "what do we do first?" Their orderly list of home improvements disintegrated in a flood of overlapping necessities. If customers like George Yeaman were going to keep their planes on the property, someone would have to keep an eye on them which meant living in the house by the lake. Reg and Margaret Collins were the obvious choice, but Margaret understandably wouldn't set foot in the place until it had indoor plumbing.

They were going to need a floating dock of some sort; the ramp wasn't very practical for flight instruction and it could only accommodate one airplane. But before they could build a dock, they'd have to pull out the old piles and dredge the lake.

Then there was the mud. A rainy day turned the place into a challenge for the weapons carrier; a customer's car wouldn't stand a chance. The company needed fill dirt and it needed it fast.

And they needed a shop. A good chunk of Kenmore's business was supposed to come from Collins' and Munro's repair work, but they couldn't very well rebuild engines, weld tubing, and paint fabric out in the rain.

Fifteen-year-old Ted Huntley desperately wanted to learn to fly, so Jack Mines put him to work cutting trees and clearing brush for forty cents an hour. Ten hours' work got him a twenty minute flight with Mines, who charged $12 an hour for lessons. Huntley worked every weekend until school let out for the summer, riding buses for two and half hours each morning to be at work by 8:15.

The piling out in the water became the next priority. Huntley, whacking away at the brush while standing ankle-deep in mud and cedar shavings, figured Mines would hand him a saw and point him in the direction of the lake, but Bob Munro had a better idea. After maneuvering the weapons carrier until it was facing the lake and the row of piles, he grabbed the free end of the winch cable and sloshed out into the water as Mines freewheeled the winch from the cab. Munro secured the cable to the top of the closest pile and got out of the way.

"Okay," he called to Mines, "put the winch in gear and pull. The pile should break off at the base."

It should have but it didn't. As the weapons carrier slid, wheels locked, toward the water, Munro waved at Mines to stop.

"We'll have to block the wheels," he shouted over the idling engine, "or you're just going to pull yourself into the lake."

There was plenty of scrap lumber lying around so it wasn't long before Collins and Munro had the front wheels of the weapons carrier solidly braced.

"Okay, try again."

Mines put the winch in gear and the cable rose, dripping, from the water to become a taut, black line drawn across the blur of trees on the far shore. The pile didn't budge. The cable began to vibrate and the weapons carrier groaned forward against the blocks under the wheels. The pile remained motionless, a creosote-covered monolith rising from the lakebed. Mines had a sudden vision of the cable shrieking through the air, its jagged, broken end wrapping itself around his head in the open cab. He was about to duck below the dashboard when he felt the back of the truck lift off the ground. This was more than he had bargained for! He was frantically trying to decide if he'd be safer in the truck or out of it when the decision was made for him. There was a bang from out in the lake and the rear of the truck crashed to the ground, its laboring engine settling back into a smooth idle. Mines peered over the dash and saw the pile drifting toward shore, the bright wood of a clean break showing well below the waterline.

To young Huntley's relief, Munro's plan worked perfectly. Flying lessons or not, the teenager had regarded the notion of squatting in frigid water up to his chin while sawing through a log the size of a phone pole with something less than enthusiasm. Bob Munro's method certainly put the frame of the weapons carrier to the test, but they had the piles out in no time; some of them even snapped off *below* the bottom of the lake.

The next step was to dredge the area in front of the millsite. Munro had come up with a basement scraper, but his plan to use it was somewhat more labor-intensive than simply dragging it back and forth with a horse. Once again, the weapons carrier was parked facing the lake and Jack Mines took his place in the cab. The winch cable was yoked to the rings on the front of the scraper while a long rope was attached to the back. Taking the free end of the rope, Collins and Munro waded as far as they could out into the lake. When they were in position, Mines paid out the winch cable and the two mechanics pulled the scraper backwards off the shore and out to where they were standing. Then Mines changed gears and winched the first scoopfull of mud up out of the lake and onto the bank. Collins and Munro trudged along behind the scraper to empty it and then the whole process was repeated again.

Munro lost count of how many times he and Collins waded back and forth through the sucking muck at the bottom of the lake, but he never forgot the incredible variety of junk they hauled out.

"There was rusty wire, broken glass, pieces of pipe, metal spikes, old chunks of machinery, tin cans, you name it. Plus all the mud and cedar shavings. We dumped it in the low spots for fill."

BOB MUNRO

Mines left most of the grunt work to Collins and Munro. Other than his stints in the cab of the weapons carrier, the pilot spent his days drumming up support for his re-zoning petition and practicing for his flight instructor's test with the CAA. It didn't take him long to realize that Eight-Eight-Five wasn't going to make it as a training airplane. It took a stiff breeze to help the forty-horsepower engine lift two people off the water. Anything less, and the plane simply plowed along on the surface. One of the first demonstrations of the Model K's inadequacy occurred when one of the company's secondhand parachutes came due for repacking. The parachutes were required for spin training, which the CAA insisted student pilots receive before soloing. The closest rigging loft was on Boeing Field, so Mines handed Huntley the parachute and enough bus fare to get him into town and back.

"Wait a minute," said Huntley, who had yet to experience his first airplane ride. "Why don't you fly me over to Lake Union instead? I can catch a bus from there right to Boeing Field and I won't have to transfer. It'll save a lot of time."

Mines shrugged. "Okay, hop in."

Huntley scrambled into the plane and shoved the heavy parachute into the little baggage hammock behind the seats. Mines propped the engine and they taxied out onto the lake. After checking the controls and running up the engine, Mines pointed the Aeronca toward Arrowhead Point and opened the throttle. The nose of the plane rose obediently but it refused to tip forward onto the step. Mines horsed the yoke back and forth as he tried to force Eight-Eight-Five to start planing. Huntley, fascinated with everything that was going on, looked down out of the side window at the floats. After a moment he looked up and tapped Mines.

"Are the floats supposed to be going in and out of the water like that?"

"Don't worry about it, kid," shouted Mines as he continued to shove the yoke around. "This is the way we got flying boats off the water in the Navy."

But as the plane continued to porpoise along without gaining any speed, Mines took a look out the window himself. He was shoving the yoke forward at the time and he was treated to the sight of the float diving under the surface of the lake like a submerging submarine. Horrified, he yanked back on the yoke and jerked the throttle to idle. Like a broaching whale, the float broke slowly back up into the sunlight, water pouring from the deck.

"Well," Mines said as he gingerly turned the plane back toward the ramp, "maybe you'd better take the bus after all."

The wind was stronger a few days later and Huntley finally got his first airplane ride, but the search was on for a more powerful machine. They found what they wanted in Aberdeen, out by the coast.

The float-equipped Taylorcraft, or what was left of it, was owned by Issaquah Flying Service. It had been the victim of a "chain of events," that aviation bug-a-boo in which a seemingly insignificant problem cascades into a major disaster. Kenmore Air Harbor got the Taylorcraft cheap because someone in Aberdeen had tried to be helpful by tossing a rope to the Issaquah pilot as the plane approached the dock. Unfortunately, the descending rope had punched a hole in the top of the wing. This was an inconvenience, but it wasn't long before a local mechanic had scrounged up some fabric and dope and effected a temporary repair.

It was raining that day in Aberdeen and the dope wasn't drying fast enough to suit the pilot. Anxious to get home, he decided to help the process along by applying some heat to the patch with a blowtorch. Dope is volatile stuff and within minutes all that was left of the Taylorcraft was a charred frame, an engine, and a pair of floats. Collins and Munro carted the skeleton out to the shingle mill and began rebuilding the plane in the makeshift shop they'd fashioned from the one-car garage next to the house.

With its four-cylinder, sixty-five horsepower Lycoming engine, Taylorcraft NC29560 would give Mines the trainer he needed to get the flying school going. The only other thing he needed was his instructor's license. On the appointed day, Inspector Clayborne showed up at the property to administer the official CAA flight instructor examination. The inspector looked at Jack Mines' six-foot-three-inch, two-hundred-plus pound frame and then at Eight-Eight-Five's two-cylinder, forty horsepower engine.

"Okay," he ordered, "go up and show me a couple of stalls." Clayborne pointed to a chair leaning against the shop. "I'll watch from over there."

Mines fired up the Aeronca and took off. Circling to altitude, he flew in over the mill site and performed a couple of power off stalls. Not knowing what else to do, he closed the throttle and circled back down for a landing. As he taxied in he saw Clayborne get out of his chair and walk to the ramp, scribbling furiously on his clipboard. Mines' heart sank. I must have forgotten to do something, he thought, and he's going to fail me.

Mines powered Eight-Eight-Five onto the ramp and killed the engine. Clayborne finished writing and tore the sheet from his clipboard.

"That was fine," he said, handing the paper up to Mines. "Here's your license."

Shortly after Collins and Munro had doubled the size of Kenmore's fleet by rebuilding Five-Six-Zero, the company was given the opportunity to buy a second Taylorcraft. People were signing up for lessons almost every day and the plane was sorely needed, but Kenmore's bank account fell considerably short of the purchase price. Reg Collins managed to convince his sister Jean to loan him the difference, and the size of the company fleet increased to three.

Up near the back of the property, Ted Huntley continued to clear brush and cut down the scrawny alder trees that had grown up out of the bog. The trees were firmer than the ground they landed on so they were left to lie where they fell. But trees and bushes and dredgings from the lake weren't going to do much for the stability of the ground. The company needed dirt. Commercial fill didn't come cheap, so for the time being Munro put Huntley to work shifting dirt from the back of the property to the access road. For the remainder of that spring, whenever Huntley didn't have a plane to wash or floats to pump out Munro sent him to the back of the property with a wheelbarrow. It was hot, dusty work and only the thought of the flying lessons he was earning kept him at it.

"Bob said it took me longer and longer between loads as the day went on. I'd get the first load moved in a half an hour and the last load in an hour and a half."

TED HUNTLEY

Huntley must have found the process depressing. The ground was so spongy that his efforts often disappeared completely under the weight of customers' cars as they mashed the fill dirt deep into the bog. But Huntley kept at it and by mid-summer the road into the property was level and firm.

Somehow during those first busy weeks, Collins and Munro found time to install indoor plumbing in the house next to the shop. There was still a lot of work to be done, including plugging the gaps in the walls that provided convenient access for the rats living in the mill, but once the spectre of stumbling at night through the mud and sawdust that surrounded the outhouse was gone, Margaret Collins agreed to move into the house. With the Collins family living on the property full-time, the partners felt they could now offer secure tie-down accommodations to the private seaplane owners in the area.

One of the first tie-down customers was George Yeaman, the Lake Forest Park resident with the Aeronca C-3 floatplane and Savoia-Marchetti amphibious flying boat. The delicate streamlining of the Savoia-Marchetti lent a certain sophisticated air to Kenmore's rough-and-tumble sawmill atmosphere, but the plane was not without its indelicate moments.

The Savoia had no brakes; it relied on a tail skid to slow it down after a runway landing. The air rudder was effective at higher throttle settings, but the only way to steer the plane at idle speeds was to have a person walk beside each of the lower wingtips ready to physically manhandle the plane in the direction the pilot wanted to go. Ted Huntley often was assigned to be part of Yeaman's steering system as he taxied to or from the water. One day Yeaman powered up the ramp a little too fast, and as he rolled off into the parking area it was all Huntley could do to maintain his grip on the right wingtip.

"I was digging my feet into the ground trying to get the plane to turn but it just kept chugging along straight ahead. I finally got it to start turning but just about the time I figured we were home free the upper left wingtip whacked into the roof of the little shop building and knocked off half the shingles."

TED HUNTLEY

Huntley had more than his share of misadventures during those first hectic months as the fledgling Kenmore Air Harbor found its wings. His first flight was courtesy of Jack Mines, but it was not in an airplane. The partners had decided the chicken coop over by the mill would make a good office. The building's foundation consisted of a pair of logs so it was an easy matter to skid it over next to the maintenance shop using the winch on the front of the weapons carrier. Unfortunately, the company's new front office took on a decided list in its new location, which was not surprising, the ground being what it was.

"If we jack up the corner of the building," said Collins. "we can put some supports under it to hold it level."

Open for business. Kenmore Air Harbor shortly after the chicken coop was dragged over beside the garage to serve as the corporate headquarters.

"We'll lever it up," said Munro, and he and Collins rummaged around in the remains of the mill until they came up with a huge plank, one end of which they wedged under the corner of the chicken coop. Then they stuck a log under the plank for a fulcrum.

"Walk out to the end there, Jack," said Munro. "The corner should lift right up."

Jack took his two-hundred-plus pounds out to the far end of the plank. The building came up but not quite enough for the two mechanics to get the supports in place.

"Go on out there with him, Ted," said Collins.

Huntley obediently walked out to Mines' end of the teeter-totter and the building groaned up another few feet.

"How's that?" called Mines.

"Pretty good," answered Munro. He and Collins began pushing the supports into position. The supports were awkward and there wasn't much room to maneuver them. From his position on the end of the plank, Mines couldn't see what was going on. He stood there as long as his patience would allow but finally his curiosity got the better of him.

"What's the matter?" he asked. Collins and Munro were too busy to answer so Mines stepped off the plank to see for himself.

The two mechanics dove out of the way as the chicken coop crashed back to the ground. Mines heard a startled yelp behind him and turned around just in time to see Huntley begin his descent back to earth. He hit sitting down, and as he sat enveloped in the dust of his landing he must have wondered why a boy who wanted so much to fly seemed to be spending so much of his time in the dirt.

Huntley was apparently none the worse for wear, but Bob Munro felt bad about the accident and always believed he was partly, if not entirely responsible. Huntley, on the other hand, maintains that his skyward journey was due solely to Jack Mines' inability to stand still for more than about a minute.

As spring warmed into summer, the trickle of student pilots became a steady stream. The underpowered Model K had a lot of sentimental value but it was a lousy trainer, so the company sold it and used the proceeds to help purchase a third Taylorcraft. The fleet grew to four with the addition of a sixty-five-horsepower Aeronca Champ. Although the two planes were inexpensive even by 1946 standards, less than $1,000 each, the acquisitions left the tiny company nearly devoid of cash. None of the partners liked living on the financial edge, but there was no denying the value of the investment.

Bob Munro and Reg Collins working on an airframe in the Kenmore Air Harbor maintenance shop in 1946. The shop had started life as a one-car garage.

The post-war surge of interest in civilian flying was putting a lot of flying schools on the map. The key to *staying* on the map was having enough airplanes to go around.

The repair side of the business was growing, too. Word of Collins' and Munro's mechanical expertise was spreading and people fortunate enough to own their own seaplanes began bringing them to the little shop at the north end of the lake. Compared to the repair shops on Boeing Field and at Kurtzer's on Lake Union, Kenmore's shop was under-sized, under-equipped, and under-lit. But the converted garage contained something that was in short supply even at the largest maintenance facilities in the area, and that was the integrity Collins and Munro brought to the job. Their philosophy was simple: charge fairly for the work and do whatever is necessary to ensure customer satisfaction. The old shop building is long gone, but its foundation of integrity and customer satisfaction continues to support the company to this day.

Collins and Munro also shared an appreciation of what it meant to be a working man, something which Jack Mines found difficult to comprehend. Like many businessmen, Mines believed labor was something that should be obtained as cheaply as possible. When the maintenance and repair work piling up in the shop became more than Collins and Munro could handle by themselves, they decided to hire another mechanic to help out. Mines agreed and suggested a wage of twenty cents an hour, which even in those days was ridiculously low. Fifteen-year-old Ted Huntley was getting twice that for moving dirt. But with airplane mechanics a dime-a-dozen now that the war was over, Mines felt that twenty cents an hour was all the company should have to pay.

Collins and Munro flatly refused to go along with it. Mechanics were skilled individuals and they should be treated, and paid, accordingly. Granted, the company couldn't pay much, but it could pay more than twenty cents an hour. After a spirited debate, Mines gave in. There is no record of the wage they finally agreed on, but Durwood Alkire remembers the company's first professional employee was paid at least as much as Ted Huntley.

Most of the people who were signing up for Jack Mines' flight lessons were returning GIs, but as his flying school picked up speed in April, two of his first students were civilians: Reg Collins and Bob Munro. Mines must have assumed that anyone who worked on airplanes must know almost everything about flying them because he signed off his partners for solo flight after only three or four hours of instruction. He should have known better.

The first one of the pair to get into trouble was Munro, who received his endorsement for solo flight on June 8th. The next day, he took off in one of the Taylorcrafts for a short flight which was uneventful until he returned to the lake. As he lined up for his final approach, he failed to notice he was landing across the wind rather than into it. This was understandable, since Mines had never mentioned the possibility that the wind could come from any direction other than straight ahead. The Taylorcraft was drifting sideways at a pretty good clip when Munro touched down, and the resulting shock broke one of the brace wires between the floats.

As the plane bounced to a stop it sagged sideways until the wingtip contacted the surface of the lake. The weight of the water pouring into the fabric wing slowly rolled the Taylorcraft over until the only things visible from shore were the float keels. Munro scrambled out the door as the plane went over and swam around until things had stabilized to the point where he could climb up onto one of the upturned floats. Reg Collins rowed out in a skiff and towed the plane close enough to shore to get a line on it and turn it right side up before they hauled it out of the water.

Munro took the incident in stride. After all, no one had been hurt and airplanes were easy to fix. His wife, on the other hand, didn't share his pragmatic philosophy. She was at home with Leslie and their infant son, Gregg, when the telephone rang. She didn't recognize the man's voice on the other end.

"Is this Mrs. Bob Munro?" the voice asked.

"Yes, it is."

"I'm calling about the plane your husband crashed. Is the salvage for sale?"

"You must be mistaken. My husband hasn't crashed an airplane."

"Oh, yes," the voice said. "Just a little while ago."

Needless to say, Ruth experienced some anxious moments while she tried to get through to Kenmore on the phone. The news that her husband was wringing wet but otherwise okay relieved her immediate fear, but something new had moved into a remote corner of her mind, a hovering worry she would have to battle every time Bob Munro climbed into a cockpit. The battle is fought by every pilot's wife, but thanks to her faith in her own strength and in her husband's ability, it is a battle Ruth Munro never lost.

Reg Collins was nothing if not observant, and he quickly perceived that the way to avoid repeating Munro's mistake was to always land into the wind. His dedication to this concept almost cost the company another airplane. A few days after Munro's dunking, Collins was flying solo in one of the other Taylorcrafts when he noticed the wind had shifted west to blow across the lake rather than up its length. He altered his landing pattern accordingly and flew his final approach to touch down in front of the property, into the wind and parallel to the north shore. With only a few hours of flight under his belt, Collins' judgment was not what it should have been and he flew his approach much too high. He was still fifty feet up as he sailed past the mill site. He was twenty feet up as he passed the point of no return, the point beyond which there was not enough room to abort the landing. Collins was committed. He touched down a few feet from the curving shoreline and shot up out of the water onto the bank. After careening through an assortment of bushes the Taylorcraft slid to a stop inches from a substantial tree.

Munro and some of the students who were on the property dashed down the shore to find Collins unhurt and the plane undamaged except for some scratches in the paint. Recovery was simply a matter of pushing the Taylorcraft backwards into the water, where a sheepish Reg Collins propped the engine back to life and taxied over to the ramp. Jack Mines began to suspect that his theory about a mechanic's inherent ability to fly was in error, so he suspended his partners' solo endorsements until he had given them several more hours of dual instruction with special emphasis on landings.

July 19, 1946 started like any other day, with Collins and Munro in the shop working on a customer's airplane while Jack Mines was up flying with his students. But deep in the Cascades, events were unfolding that would ultimately end in tragedy; tragedy that would change Kenmore Air Harbor forever. It had all started nine days earlier with the disappearance of a four-place Stinson Voyager flown by Sidney Matz, vice-president of the Ex-Lax company. Matz had taken off from Ellensburg east of the Cascades for a flight to Seattle. He hadn't bothered to file a flight plan, so no one missed him until his associates in San Francisco became worried when they hadn't heard from him for several days. A check of all the airports within range failed to turn up any trace of the Stinson, and when someone said they had seen a red and blue plane similar to Matz's flying through a heavy overcast near Snoqualmie Pass on the 8th. Six Army search planes and several ground teams were sent out to comb the mountains along the plane's suspected route. Among the searchers was a small group of deputies from the King County sheriff's department.

George Yeamen, whose Savoia-Marchetti was responsible for Ted Huntley's newly-acquired ability to shingle a roof, had a twenty-three year old son, George Jr., who occasionally worked as a volunteer with the King County sheriff's department. When the deputies searching for Matz radioed from the Cascades on the 18th to say they were running out of food, the sheriff called the younger Yeaman to ask if he thought it would be possible to air-drop supplies to the men the next morning. Yeaman told the sheriff he'd get right back to him and called Jack Mines.

"Do you think we could go up there and drop some food to these guys?" Yeaman asked after explaining the situation to Mines.

"Sure, we can do that," Mines said. "Where are they exactly?"

"The sheriff said they were camped by Stirrup Lake. That's up near Stampede Pass."

"Okay, tell him to bring the food out here today. We'll take off at first light in the morning."

The supplies arrived in the late afternoon and Yeaman helped Mines wrap them up and then stash the parcels in the back of one of the Taylorcrafts.

"I'll meet you here at four in the morning," Mines said when they were finished. "I'll fly, and you can toss the stuff out to the guys on the ground."

"Hey, how 'bout if I bring my camera?" Yeaman said. "I can take pictures of the whole thing. Maybe we can sell them to the newspapers."

Mines climbed into his car to leave. "Sure, bring your camera. But don't be late. Four o'clock. That's a.m., not p.m."

Mines slammed the door closed and accelerated off toward the highway, his rear tires spraying a roostertail of Huntley's fill dirt into the air behind him. Yeaman followed at a more leisurely pace. He'd go home, have supper, and try to get to bed early. He decided to set his alarm for 3:30 a.m. That would give him ample time to get up, get dressed, and drive the couple of miles from Lake Forest Park to Kenmore. He made a mental note to make sure he had film for his camera. Tomorrow's flight promised to be an exciting one and he hoped he'd get some good pictures to show his friends.

TEN DOLLARS A SHARE

Jack Mines was late. George Yeaman Jr. opened the door of his car and swung his legs out to sit sideways with his feet on the running board. He sensed the lake in front of him more than saw it, liquid black against the dull black of the shoreline. Two tiny sparks, dock lights perhaps, glowed a mile or more away to the south. Yeaman tried to determine which side of the lake they were on but after a few moments he gave up. It was just too dark. He'd gotten a flash of the loaded Taylorcraft as he'd arced his car around to park facing the office but now even it was invisible in the gloom.

Where the heck was Mines? Yeaman switched on his headlights and moved his arm until he could read his watch in the glare reflecting from the office wall. Ten minutes after four. He could see the Taylorcraft now, glowing softly against the blackness behind it. This should be exciting, Yeaman thought. An official rescue flight! He checked to make sure his camera was still on the seat beside him and snapped off the car lights. He assumed Reg and Margaret Collins knew about the early morning flight but there wasn't any point in disturbing them any sooner than necessary.

There was a hum of tires on the highway and then an erratic flash of headlights as Jack Mines' big Nash bobbed and weaved down the dirt driveway. The car slid around George Yeaman, Sr.'s Savoia-Marchetti and bounced to a stop beside the office. Mines switched off the engine and pushed open his door.

"Ready to go?"

"You bet." Past experience had taught Yeaman there was nothing to be gained by bringing up Mines' tardiness.

Mines fished a ring of keys out of his pocket. "Turn on your headlights for a moment so I can see to unlock the office."

Once inside, Mines snapped on the light and spread a map across the top of the secondhand desk that occupied one corner of the tiny room.

"Stampede Pass is only about fifty miles away." Mines moved his finger across the map from Lake Washington southeast into the mountains. "Right here, just north of Lester."

Yeaman peered over Mines' shoulder. "There's Stirrup Lake." He pointed to a blue dot two miles east of Stampede Pass.

"Little bitty thing, isn't it," Mines said. "Well, it shouldn't be hard to find. We can use the road over the pass and the railroad tracks as reference points."

He re-folded the map and stuffed it into his jacket pocket. "As soon as it's light enough to see, I'll pre-flight the plane and we'll turn it around on the ramp. We'll take off as soon as the sun comes up, about five-thirty I should think. I'll follow the highway east through Snoqualmie Pass and then turn south to Stampede. Once we've found the deputies, I'll come in real slow right over the top of them. When I tell you, open your door and get ready to throw the food out. Throw it out just as we come up on them and make sure it goes out far enough to clear the float."

Yeaman didn't have time to take pictures while they were getting the plane ready but once they were airborne he reached around for the camera he'd stowed behind the seats.

"This will be a super sunrise shot," he yelled over the clatter of the sixty-five horsepower Lycoming. Mines nodded and scanned the mountain range looming in front of them. It looked like the timing was going to be perfect. Stampede Pass was still twenty minutes away; by then the sun would be plenty high enough to illuminate the lake.

The days start early in the summer and Bob Munro made it a practice to be at the Air Harbor by six-thirty. He and Reg Collins were already at work on a project in the shop when the phone rang shortly after seven. It was the sheriff's office.

"Your plane's gone in," said the caller. "They said on the radio that someone's been injured so you'd better get up there right away."

Stampede Pass is an easy, fifty mile flight in an airplane but it's a long, twisting drive in a truck. Munro drove the weapons carrier as fast as he dared on the narrow, two-lane highway that corkscrewed east into the mountains, but it was almost three hours before he and Collins reached the dirt road that climbed up over Stampede Pass to Lester, a coal and water stop on the Northern Pacific Railroad. They had only gone about four miles when a man ran out of the brush and flagged them down.

"Leave your truck here," the deputy said after ascertaining who they were. "The plane's a couple of miles up this trail at Stirrup Lake. The passenger's hurt pretty bad and they could probably use your help carrying him out. We radioed for an ambulance quite awhile ago. I heard your engine and thought maybe you were it."

"How's the pilot?" Collins asked.

"He's dead."

George Yeaman Jr. was still conscious and coherent when Collins and Munro reached the crash site. As they helped the deputies make a stretcher using wood and fabric from the plane, Yeaman did his best to describe the events leading up to the crash.

They found Stirrup Lake almost immediately. The deputies were camped in a clearing a short distance away. After circling the area a few times to get the lay of the land, Mines eased down to treetop height to begin his drop run. In order to minimize the risk of losing the food in the water or having it disappear into the woods, he slowed the Taylorcraft almost to its stalling speed.

"Open your door and get ready to throw the first package." Mines shouted over the engine.

Yeaman pushed his door open against the slipstream and maneuvered the first parcel onto his lap. Beside him, Mines rapidly scanned back and forth between the trees ahead to the clearing fast approaching below.

"Now!"

Yeaman shoved the package out and clear of the float. Mines, unable to resist seeing for himself where the food was going to land, opened his own door and was peering back at the drop zone.

The next thing Yeaman knew, the Plexiglas windshield was exploding in his face and the cockpit was full of branches. He remembered feeling the plane wrench violently sideways before pitching over to plunge toward the ground. He thought the engine had kept running all the way down, but he wasn't sure. All he knew was that when the noise stopped, he was lying on the ground next to the wreckage. The gasoline fumes were so strong he could hardly breathe, and he was terrified the plane would catch fire.

Mines hadn't moved or made a sound after the crash. So far as Yeaman could tell, he was still inside the plane.

"Jack! Hey Jack? You okay?"

No answer. Yeaman called a few more times, and then decided his friend must have been knocked unconscious by the impact. The gas fumes didn't seem so bad anymore, but his left leg and wrist were starting to throb. He tried to move them and the throb became a searing flash of pain.

"They're broken, I bet," he muttered to himself. He had a moment of panic when he realized he couldn't just get up and run out to the road for help, and then he remembered the deputies. He was about to yell for help when there was a crashing in the brush and two men burst, panting, onto the scene. Gordon and Dale Bennett had been fishing from a raft in the lake when they were stunned to see an airplane first zoom overhead and then plunge headlong into the trees. The brothers had paddled to shore as fast as they could and then beat their way through the underbrush in the direction the plane had disappeared.

"Jack's still in the plane," Yeaman said, pointing to the crumpled fuselage. "I'm okay. Get him out."

The deputies arrived a few minutes later, but there wasn't anything they could do to save Mines. He'd been killed instantly, they figured, crushed when the Taylorcraft slammed into the ground.

Bob Munro was surprised to find the wings missing from the plane. One of the deputies told him they'd come off and were back in the trees near the lake. Even with Munro's limited flying experience, it was becoming obvious to him what had happened. When Mines had twisted around in his seat to look out his door, he must have pulled back inadvertently on the control yoke. As the nose pitched up, the slow-moving wing had stalled and quit flying altogether.

A stall is not a dangerous maneuver; student pilots practice them all the time. But students practice stalls at altitudes of three thousand feet or more above the ground so they will have plenty of room to nose over and recover flying speed. Jack Mines had stalled a few feet above the treetops. Even if he had been concentrating on his flying instead of looking backwards out the door, recovery at that altitude would have been impossible.

But the crash should not have been fatal. At less than fifty miles an hour, with the floats and struts bearing the brunt of the impact, the fabric-covered Taylorcraft should have fluttered into the trees and hung there like some giant, crippled bird. Mines' greatest concern should have been how he was going to explain the whole thing to his partners after he and Yeaman had figured out a way to climb down to the ground. But any conjecture about what should have happened went out the window when the wings came off the plane as it tore through the branches. With little left to support it, the fuselage tipped forward and plummeted to the ground between the tree trunks.

It was late afternoon by the time George Yeaman Jr. was carried out of the woods and loaded into the ambulance that had finally arrived. His injuries were severe but they did not appear to be life-threatening, and he was in remarkably good spirits despite having been stuck at the crash site for six hours until enough people had arrived to carry him out. But shock and exposure had left him vulnerable. He contracted pneumonia, and early in the morning of July 22, almost to the minute when his alarm had rousted him out of bed to meet Mines three days earlier, he died.

One of the deputies had found Yeaman's camera in the wreckage of the plane. Thinking the film inside might help pinpoint the cause of the crash, he had it developed. The last exposed frame showed the sun just clearing the jagged peaks of the Cascades. It was Yeaman's "super sunrise shot."

The Taylorcraft was left to lie where it had crashed. A group of kids went up and stole the engine out of it a few days later, but the sheriff found out who did it and made them return it to Kenmore. Bob Munro paid the boys one hundred dollars for the effort of lugging the valuable engine out of the woods.

The accident was a terrible blow, especially to George, Jr.'s father, but there was no talk of abandoning the fledgling company Jack Mines had worked so hard to get started. Esther Mines announced her intention to maintain her husband's interest in the company and went to work in the office, answering the phone and keeping the simple account books up to date. New instructors were hired: Garth Smith was a test pilot at Boeing who loved to teach water flying in his spare time; Virginia Hill had ferried planes for the military during the war, and went on after her stint at Kenmore to become a bush pilot and resort owner in Alaska; Joe Tymczyszym saw Bob Munro and Ted Huntley through to their Private licenses before embarking on a much-honored career as a test pilot with the FAA.

The flight school had the potential to become Kenmore's biggest money maker, thanks to the GI Bill. Initially intended to help returning veterans continue their education, the GI Bill soon had been expanded to cover all types of vocational training. It didn't matter if a veteran wanted to be a lawyer or a welder; the government would pick up most of the tab either way. When flight training was added to the list of things the GI Bill would pay for, it ignited a flame in thousands of returning GI hearts. Now men who'd worked on planes, loaded bombs on planes, poured fuel into planes, or simply stood in the mud and watched planes, could learn to fly. GI Bill flight schools began popping up all over the country as anyone with an airplane and a desire to make a buck scrambled to take advantage of the country's growing love affair with flight.

Collins and Munro wanted to get in on the action but they knew they'd have to improve the company's facilities before the government would even consider adding them to the list of GI Bill flight schools. Moving the chicken coop and turning it into an office had already stretched the zoning regulations; building a hangar or a classroom building would violate them. Until the land was re-zoned, Kenmore would have to do the best it could with what it had.

On a calm afternoon almost two months after Jack Mines' accident, Collins and Munro were drawn outside by the sound of an engine they'd never heard before. As they watched, a strange-looking airplane snarled up the lake and banked into a tight circle north of the highway. The plane's engine was mounted backwards in a pod atop the bulbous, boat-tailed fuselage. The pusher propeller just cleared the top of a slender boom that curved back and up from the bottom of the fuselage to support the vertical tail. The underside of the fuselage was sculpted into a V-shape and pylon-mounted floats hung a few feet inboard of each wingtip.

"It's some kind of a flying boat," said Collins.

"It's got wheels on it," Munro observed. "See, tucked up next to the fuselage?"

"An amphibious flying boat, then." Collins watched as the plane rolled out of its turn and began a final approach to the lake. "It's got wing flaps, too. That's a nice feature. I wonder who owns it."

The plane splashed down in front of the shingle mill and idled in toward Kenmore's rudimentary dock. Collins and Munro walked out to help bring the plane to a stop but they began to worry when the pilot showed no sign of shutting down the engine. Seaplanes have no brakes so the only way a pilot can safely approach a dock is to shut down the engine and coast in. The trick is in judging the distance; shut down too soon and the plane will come to a stop before reaching the dock. Shut down too late, and the consequences are usually measured in dollars.

It was impossible to tell if the pilot of the bulbous amphibian relentlessly approaching Kenmore's dock had forgotten to shut off his engine or if he couldn't, but in either case a collision was imminent and Collins and Munro didn't want to be anywhere near it. They were backing hurriedly toward solid ground when the sound of the engine changed and the plane came to a smooth, quick stop beside the dock. The motor coughed and quit and the gray-haired pilot threw open the large bow door.

"Reversible-pitch propeller," he said in answer to the quizzical expressions on the faces of the two men in front of him. He stepped to the dock and tied the plane to a cleat. "Pretty slick-looking machine, isn't it?"

"Yeah," Collins said. "What is it?"

"Republic Seabee. This is the first one in Seattle."

The two mechanics may not have recognized the airplane but they certainly knew the pilot. Two years earlier, as manager of Pan American's Alaska Division, he had been their boss. His name was Joe Crosson, and he was considerably younger than his gray hair implied. In 1926, Crosson had turned an unpromising start as an Alaska bush pilot into an illustrious career. Nine years later he'd gained international recognition by flying the bodies of his friends, Wiley Post and Will Rogers, back to the States from the scene of their crash near Barrow. In 1937, he became Pan American's youngest division manager when he was appointed head of the airline's Alaskan subsidiary, Pacific Alaska Airlines. Crosson did much to bring scheduled air service to Alaska, but the job had been frustrating and was responsible, his friends claimed, for the streaks of gray that began appearing in his jet-black hair. In 1944, he'd had enough. He resigned his position with Pan American and took over the management of an aircraft parts business on Boeing Field.

The history behind the airplane Crosson had just tied to Kenmore's dock was almost as interesting as his own. The Seabee was the brainchild of a man named Percival H. Spencer; "Spence" for short. Spence was a direct descendent of Christopher M. Spencer who had invented, among other things, the Spencer Repeating Rifle used so effectively by the North during the American Civil War. Born with the same genius of invention, Spence designed and built his first successful flying boat in 1914, when he was only 17 years old. He started the first aircraft sales, training, and charter business in Hartford, Connecticut before turning his attention back to small flying boats as a partner in a seaplane design firm called Spencer-Larson. The company came up with an advanced concept for a single-engine amphibian, but World War II put an end to their plans to market the little plane, which flew quite well.

The end of the war meant an end to the huge government contracts that had been supporting the nation's aircraft industry for almost five years. Survival now depended on finding a niche in the civilian aviation market. Boeing, Douglas, and Lockheed set their sights on the airliner business. Bell began experimenting with helicopters while North American and Republic tried their hand at building general aviation airplanes. The North American entry was the Navion, a four-place landplane which used surplus P-51 parts to help keep the cost down. Republic thought an inexpensive amphibian would have a broad appeal so they purchased a design from Spence, replaced his twin-tail arrangement with a more easily manufactured single tail, and created the Seabee, which had a sticker price of $3,900.

Joe Crosson had been impressed with the Republic Seabee the first time he'd seen one and thought it would be perfect for the land and water environment of his Alaska bush pilot friends. With the help of a partner, he secured a dealership for the Seabee and decided that the Air Harbor would be the ideal place to keep his demonstrator. First, however, he wanted to take his Kenmore friends for a ride to show off the plane's attributes. Munro came away impressed with the plane, especially the rugged construction of its hull, which looked like it could withstand almost anything. Little did he know how often he would put that hull to the test.

Collins and Munro were enthusiastic over the prospect of having a Seabee dealership in Seattle. However, it was obvious the ramp they had built for the Model K would have to be replaced before the plane could be taxied safely up onto the property. The existing ramp was too narrow and it didn't extend far enough into the water. Unlike George Yeaman's Savoia-Marchetti which had a simple tailskid, the Seabee had a tailwheel, and there was danger of it catching on the submerged edge of the short ramp when the plane was taxied up out of the water. In return for building a larger ramp, Crosson promised to send his customers to Collins and Munro for any service or maintenance work they might need on their new Seabees.

Despite the tragic loss of Jack Mines and one of their airplanes, Kenmore's future was looking brighter with each passing day. The repair business was holding its own, there were several new students enrolled in the flight school, and Joe Crosson's Seabee dealership held the promise of even more maintenance work.

Things were not all rosy, however. Financially, the company was barely breaking even. Esther Mines received a small salary for her office work and Reg Collins and Bob Munro paid themselves only enough to cover their families' basic living expenses. Every other penny of profit went back into the company to pay for fuel, parts, tools, and the thousand-and-one other expenses involved in keeping a little fleet of airplanes in the air. The first victim of Kenmore's shoestring budget was Jack Mines' promotional scheme to build a hotel and restaurant complex at the mill site. Collins and Munro had never been more than lukewarm about the idea, anyway. From the beginning, all they'd wanted to do was work on airplanes. The sixteen-hours-a-day, seven-days-a-week struggle to keep the Air Harbor afloat left them little time to ponder the future, but when they did, it's a safe bet that room rates and lunch menus weren't on the agenda.

Shortly after Jack Mines' accident, a young man walked into the shop, introduced himself as a friend of the late pilot, and began asking Munro about the kind of new buildings the company might require in the future. Munro was noncommittal, explaining that the issue was academic until the county re-zoned the property. The man soon left and Munro forgot about the incident until several weeks later, when he received a set of plans in the mail. One sheet showed an expanded shop and office facility. The other sheet contained preliminary drawings for a small but modern hotel and restaurant complex. Munro looked inside the mailing envelope to see if there was anything else and pulled out a bill for $449.

Collins was as mystified by the arrival of the plans as Munro, but Esther Mines thought she knew the answer. The man that had come around inquiring about Kenmore's expansion plans had been an architect friend from her husband's engineering days. Perhaps Mines had asked his friend to draw up some plans for the hotel and restaurant he'd wanted to build on the mill site.

Munro called the young man and was informed that, yes, he and Mines had discussed the idea of drawing up plans for the buildings. They hadn't signed a formal contract, but the standard fee for such work was $4 an hour. What with inspecting the property and drawing up the plans, the architect had spent about 112 hours on the project.

Bob Munro always tried to avoid confrontation; he firmly believed that an argument always costs more than it gains. On the other hand, he had no fear of opposing what he believed was wrong.

"I don't know what kind of arrangement you had with Jack," Munro explained patiently to his late partner's architect friend, "but I do know that Kenmore Air Harbor didn't hire you to draw up these plans. I'm sorry you went to all this effort, but since we never authorized it, I don't think we should have to pay for it."

The architect didn't agree, claiming he'd had a verbal contract with Mines for the plans. He began sending Kenmore a monthly bill for the unwanted plans and refused to consider any compromise. Finally, two years later, he was persuaded to settle for $100 in cash and a few hours of flight instruction. Munro figured it was a bargain; the time saved by finally eliminating the issue from the monthly board of directors meetings more than made up for the $100 payment.

All the work Mines had done to drum up support for his re-zoning petition paid off early in the fall of 1946 when the King County Planning Commission reversed its earlier decision and voted to let the shingle mill site be used as a commercial seaplane base. The vote couldn't have been more timely for the flying school. The GI Bill had made flight instruction available to anyone who had served in the military, but it didn't say a thing about how good that instruction should be. In the beginning, anyone with a valid instructor's rating and an airplane that could get off the ground could declare themselves a flying school and collect government money for each student they managed to coerce into taking lessons. The situation had started to get downright dangerous, so Congress began amending the GI Bill to establish minimum standards for flying schools. The most recent target had been sloppy maintenance procedures due to poor or non-existent facilities. By the beginning of 1947, every GI Bill-approved flight school would have to have an enclosed, covered maintenance facility where their planes could be worked on regardless of the weather conditions outside.

Kenmore's shop was a one-car garage; the only way to fit an airplane inside was to take it apart. The Taylorcrafts and the Aeronca Champ were maintained outside, wherever they happened to be sitting at the time. Mines, Collins, and Munro had talked about the need for a hangar from day one, but until the land was re-zoned, they legally couldn't do any more than just talk. The Planning Commission's decision solved the problem. Finally, the Air Harbor was free to put up whatever buildings it needed to support its operations. Paying for them was another matter, but at least now they had official permission to build them.

The joy over the Planning Commission's decision was short-lived, however, as a growing rift between Reg Collins and Esther Mines began casting a shadow across the company's future. The problem stemmed from the fact that the company had never been formally divided among its founders. Collins and Munro had assumed each of the three partners would receive a one-third interest in the company. Jack Mines had agreed at first, but not on paper. Then, after his mother had underwritten the lease on the property and after he had gotten the CAA to designate the north end of Lake Washington as a landing site, Mines began to think that maybe he was entitled to more than just a one-third interest in the company. After all, he seemed to be doing all the work. True, Collins and Munro were pulling the piling and dredging the lake and fixing the plumbing, but he, Jack, was the one doing all the legwork and letter-writing. Besides, he was the pilot.

Bob Munro really didn't care if Mines got fifty percent of the company and he got twenty-five percent. He was happy just to be working for himself and not for some big, impersonal corporation where a union told him what he could and could not do. Collins, on the other hand, was more vocal with his objections, and he and Mines had several discussions on the subject. When Esther announced her intentions to maintain her husband's interest in the company after the crash at Stampede Pass, she stated that this included Mines' position on company ownership as well. She, Esther, should receive fifty percent of the company while Collins and Munro split the other fifty percent.

This was too much for Reg Collins. He liked Esther but she hadn't tromped back and forth in the muck during the dredging operation, she hadn't fixed the plumbing in the house, and she hadn't pulled the piling out of the lake. She didn't know how to fix a carburetor or weld an engine mount or dope new fabric onto a wing, and she certainly didn't know how to fly. As far as Collins was concerned, awarding Esther fifty percent of a company she'd played only a minor role in starting just wasn't right.

After Jack Mines' crash, and as the number of instructors and students increased through the summer, Collins and Munro, with the encouragement of Esther's father who was an attorney, decided to incorporate the company. Making Kenmore Air Harbor a corporation would have a number of legal and business advantages, not the least of which would be the shifting of liability from the partners to the corporation. If someone was killed or injured while flying in a Kenmore Air Harbor, Inc. airplane, any lawsuits that resulted would be directed at the corporation; the personal assets of the company's owners would be protected. Ownership in the company would be represented by shares, worth ten dollars apiece, that would be issued to each of the three partners. It was the division of the shares that brought the whole matter of company ownership to a boil.

Esther, with the active backing of her father, was adamant that she should receive fifty percent of the shares. Collins was equally adamant that she shouldn't. With nothing on paper to support either position, Collins figured it would just be a matter of time before the situation got so ugly it destroyed the company.

"I think I'd be better off out of here," he announced on a drizzly fall day as he and Munro were working in the shop.

"What will you do?" asked Munro, who was saddened by his friend's announcement but not terribly surprised.

Bob Munro on the ramp in front of a company Taylorcraft. The T-crafts were dwarfed by the planes that came later, but Munro and his pilots flew the tiny machines to every corner of the Pacific Northwest raincoast.

"I can always work for Margaret's father in California. I sure can't stay here, not with things the way they are."

Munro let his gaze wander around the inside of the shop for a moment while he tried to imagine the Air Harbor without Reg Collins. "It doesn't seem right," he said finally. "You've been behind this thing from the beginning, first with the plane and then the idea of starting a shop. It doesn't seem right you should be the one to leave now that we've finally got something going."

"I'll be okay. And you'll do fine."

The two men went back to work in silence, any thoughts of conversation overwhelmed by the realization that their great adventure together was about to come to an end.

The shares were divided up a few days later. With Collins already having made up his mind to leave and Munro not feeling the stock issue was worth arguing about, Esther received the fifty percent she'd wanted. Collins and Munro each received about twenty five percent and Durwood Alkire received a few shares for his assistance in setting up the company's financial structure.

Collins still owed his sister the money he'd borrowed to help the Air Harbor buy one of the Taylorcrafts. The company didn't have the cash to pay him back so he was given the best of the two remaining Taylorcrafts instead. He and Margaret spent the next few days packing their belongings into a borrowed trailer for the drive down the coast to California. The morning they were to leave, Collins made the short walk from the little house to the shop for the last time.

"I've got a going-away present for you," he said, handing Munro an envelope.

"You're the one going away. I should be giving something to you."

Collins shook his head. "I want you to have this. You deserve it."

Munro opened the envelope and pulled out a piece of paper. He recognized it immediately because he had one just like it. It was a certificate for 455 shares of Kenmore Air Harbor, Inc. stock.

"Now you have almost as many shares as Esther," Collins said. "You know Durwood will support you, so you should be able to run the company as you see fit."

It would have been easy for Munro to convince himself that he didn't have much of a company left to run. His most visionary partner had been killed and his best friend had just disappeared up the driveway headed for a new life in California. The Air Harbor was down to two planes, a Taylorcraft and the Aeronca Champ. The government had made GI Bill approval even more difficult to obtain by requiring a hangar that Munro didn't have the money to build. As it was, he was barely making enough to support his family; earlier in the summer he'd had to sell his beloved accordion just to put some food on the table. His friends were urging him to quit and go back to Pan Am.

But Bob Munro had no intention of quitting anything. Some people saw only obstacles when they looked around the old shingle mill property. The buildings were dilapidated, the ground was a bog, the ramp was too small, the dock was inadequate. Munro saw the same things, but he didn't see anything he couldn't fix. And he saw something else his friends seemed to have missed. He saw the freedom to succeed.

EXPANDING **6** HORIZONS

WHEN BOB AND RUTH MUNRO decided to move into the house the Collins' had just vacated, Ruth's mother was horrified. She took one look at the holes in the walls and the shafts of sunlight seeping in through the cracks in the ceiling and burst into tears.

"I didn't raise you to live like this," she sobbed as she watched the floor tremble under two-year old Leslie's scampering feet. Later, after she'd calmed down a bit, she filled a jar with water from the kitchen tap and took it into Seattle to have it analyzed by the Health Department. She just knew the well water at the mill site was contaminated and proof of it would provide the ammunition she needed to persuade her son-in-law to move his family back to Haller Lake. The Health Department tested the water and said it was fine, but Mrs. Holden remained skeptical.

The little book Esther Mines had been using to keep track of the Air Harbor's income and expenses soon ran out of pages, so on December 21, 1946, she started a new one. The first entry was for the balance carried over: $221.92. The next entry, dated three days later, was for check number 159, payable to mechanic Tom Wardleigh for one week's wages in the amount of $31.30.

Bob Munro always referred to Tom Wardleigh as "Tommy," possibly because when they first met at Pan American, Wardleigh was still in high school. Wardleigh had been raised by his grandmother, a unique person in her own right because as early as 1930, she foresaw the tremendous growth of aviation and encouraged her two sons and grandson to get involved with it. A few years later, as further encouragement, she bought a Curtiss Robin that had crashed on the beach at Birch Bay, near the Canadian border. Tom Wardleigh and his two uncles drove up to retrieve it and then spent the next year completely rebuilding the Robin in the basement of the family home. The plane was unique in that it was one of the few Robins built with a Curtiss-Wright Challenger engine. The six-cylinder, twin-row radial put out 185-horsepower but it had a reputation for being rough-running and short-lived. However, perhaps due to the careful rebuilding it received in the basement, Wardleigh remembers the engine as being quite smooth and trouble-free.

Wardleigh used his high school woodworking classes to repair some of the damaged wing ribs and make parts for a new stabilizer, but his age tended to relegate him to much less glamorous tasks.

"My uncles did most of the work. I was permitted to sandpaper. We put an eighteen-coat, hand-rubbed, dope finish on the plane and I put a lot of effort into the rubbing part of the hand-rubbed finish. This was in the old nitrate-dope era, and you got a finish like a grand piano if you really worked on it."

TOM WARDLEIGH

While the Robin was undergoing its restoration, one of Wardleigh's uncles learned to fly. After the plane was assembled, he landed a contract with the state to re-seed land that had been burned over by a forest fire. Wardleigh would help load bags of vetch, rye, and millet into the Robin and then pour them out of the plane as his uncle cruised back and forth over the burned areas. The fast-growing ground cover would help stabilize the soil and prepare the way for reforestation.

World War II and the ban on civilian flying put an end to the Robin's flying days; the plane was disassembled and Wardleigh's grandmother eventually sold it to a coyote hunter in Montana. But young Wardleigh wasn't about to let a minor irritant like a war interrupt his involvement with aviation. He applied for a job at Pan American and spent the rest of his senior year working as an apprentice mechanic on the night shift at Boeing Field. When the airline offered free training classes to its employees, Wardleigh signed up and was soon rebuilding carburetors and fuel pumps under the tutelage of Bob Munro.

Wardleigh was inducted into the Navy along with the rest of Pan Am's mechanics but it wasn't long before he was transferred to a naval base in Kodiak, Alaska. He spent the rest of the war as an Aviation Machinist Mate, moving from Kodiak to Hawaii to Guam, maintaining R-4Ds and R-5Ds, known to everyone outside the Navy as DC-3s and DC-4s.

When Wardleigh was discharged in 1946, he enrolled at the University of Washington where he planned to study dentistry. He signed up for GI benefits to help with the tuition but when he told his grandmother what he'd done, she would have none of it.

"Stand up and hold out your hands." Wardleigh did as he was told. "Now turn around." Wardleigh pivoted uncertainly on the carpet. "Well," his grandmother pronounced, "you don't appear to have been injured or shot or impaired in any way by your military service."

Wardleigh allowed that he hadn't.

"Our family doesn't take charity," his grandmother continued. "If you want to go to college, you earn your way. You go right over to that office and you cancel those papers that you signed."

With Fall classes about to start, Wardleigh needed a job fast. He'd heard that Bob Munro and a couple of partners had started a seaplane base at the north end of Lake Washington, so he dropped by to say hello and to find out if his former Pan Am instructor knew of any aviation outfits that needed a part-time mechanic. He found Munro working alone on a surplus Stinson L-5 a customer had asked him to rebuild. Munro remembered the quiet competence Wardleigh had demonstrated at Pan Am and offered him a job on the spot. Wardleigh's first assignment was the L-5, which he worked on whenever he wasn't in class.

Not counting the flight instructors, who worked when they were needed for four dollars an hour, Kenmore Air Harbor now had a grand total of four people on the payroll. Bob Munro and Esther Mines were the only ones working full-time; Tom Wardleigh and Ted Huntley worked part-time.

When Esther hung her new 1947 calendar on the wall, the most pressing problem the company faced was satisfying the GI Bill requirement for an enclosed maintenance hangar; the company didn't have a hope of cashing in on the stampede of student pilots until the hangar was in place. The only patch of firm ground near the lake large enough to support such a structure was under the shingle mill, so tearing the mill down went to the top of the "things-to-do" list. Munro saved some of the floor and wall timbers for the new ramp he'd promised to build for Joe Crosson's Seabees, but the rest of the building was knocked apart and burned. After the fire had burned itself out, and the ashes and bolts and nails and chunks of charred wood had been hauled off to the bog behind the house, there was only one obstacle left. Munro rented a jackhammer and Ted Huntley spent the next week enveloped in a cloud of concrete dust as he banged away at the massive foundation that had once supported the mill's boiler and stationary steam engine. When he was finished, a little pick-and-shovel work was all that was needed to level the ground and prepare it for the foundation of the hangar the company still couldn't afford to build.

Tom Wardleigh hand-propping an Aeronca Champ.

But Munro was undaunted. There were other ways of acquiring a hangar besides building one. During the war, the shipyards on Elliott Bay had constructed dozens of portable, wood-framed buildings that could be craned onto the deck of a ship to shelter welders and electricians from the weather. These deck buildings, which had no windows or floors, were built in a variety of sizes, the largest of which was about eighty by thirty feet, the perfect size in which to hangar a couple of small floatplanes.

Now that the war was over, the shipyards didn't need all their deck buildings so they sold off the ones they didn't want for next to nothing. Munro bought three of them for $500; a large one to use as a hangar and two smaller ones. He knew the sand and gravel company starting up next door would buy one of the small ones, and he figured it would be easy to find a buyer for the other one. The two buildings ultimately sold for $250 apiece, which meant Munro wound up getting his hangar for free. He couldn't recoup the shipping expenses, however; it cost more to barge the buildings up the lake than it did to buy them in the first place. Munro delayed the delivery of the deck building for a few days so he, Wardleigh, and Huntley could lay an asphalt pad to serve as the hangar floor. Then they rounded up some logs to use as rollers and a heavy-duty block and tackle and waited for the barge to arrive.

At mid-morning on the appointed day, the barge moved slowly into sight around Arrowhead Point, the diesel tug lashed to its side sending a muted rumble across the glassy water. The skipper of the tug maneuvered the barge into the mouth of the channel and up next to the bank. Munro and the rest of the Kenmore crew shoved some of the heavy timbers they'd salvaged from the mill across to the barge and under the edge of the deck building. While Munro rigged the block and tackle to the side of the building, Wardleigh maneuvered the weapons carrier into position for the first pull. When all was ready, Wardleigh engaged the winch and the deck building inched off the barge and across the planks to shore. As the building came off the makeshift ramp it was levered up onto the log rollers for its final positioning over the asphalt floor. It was not an easy job. The weapons carrier had to be repositioned constantly, and while it provided the strongest pull, much of the power to move the building came from the muscles of Munro and his employees. It took the rest of the day, but by evening the heavy building had been maneuvered into place, and Munro could honestly say he was in compliance with the government's GI Bill requirements. Kenmore Air Harbor had its hangar.

The first order of business after positioning the building was to cut a wide door in the south end so they could get the planes in and out. The next thing was to figure out how to move the floatplanes from the ramp into the building. Forklifts were out of the question; Kenmore couldn't afford one and the man who would eventually build the adjustable fork system the company uses today hadn't even been hired yet. Munro's solution to the transportation problem was simple and cheap, and as a side benefit, provided hours of entertainment for his children.

With Wardleigh's help, he constructed several two-wheel dollies, each one nothing more than a long plank with a wheel attached crosswise at each end. When a floatplane was to be hangared, it was driven up onto the ramp and one of the dollies was positioned between the floats, parallel to the fuselage. The plane was rocked backwards until it was sitting nose-high on the heels of the floats. A crossplank was set on top of the dolly and pushed aft until it wedged up against the float

Kenmore Air Harbor, 1947. The old shingle mill has been torn down and replaced with the surplus Navy deck building. The deck building was Kenmore's solution to a requirement that all GI-
bill flight schools have an enclosed building for airplane maintenance.

keels. Then Huntley or whoever was responsible for moving the plane into the hangar would lift
up on the tail of the plane and shove a crossplank in from the rear, sliding it forward until it was
directly under the float steps. The last step was to pull down on the tail of the plane to release the
front crossplank so it could be slid forward on the dolly to a position where it would share the load
evenly with the rear plank.

Moving the plane was simply a matter of grabbing the outer end of one of the wing struts,
pulling down until the plane was balancing level on the two-wheeled dolly between the floats, and
shoving against the plane to roll it sideways. It was rather like pushing a huge handcart. The
hangaring process was easier with two people, although Wardleigh remembers doing it by himself
on occasion.

When they weren't being used to move planes, the dollies provided personal transportation
for Leslie and Gregg Munro. At first, they just sat on them and scooted around in the parking area
but as their sense of balance improved, they began using them like giant skateboards. They were

careful to stay away from the ramp, however; Ruth Munro had made it clear that if either of them were caught playing anywhere near the water, they would regret it for a long, long time.

In February 1947, the CAA came out and inspected Kenmore's airplanes and maintenance facilities and the following month announced its approval for the company to teach flying under the GI Bill. A few days later, Bob Munro glanced up from the project he was working on to see a slim young man standing patiently outside the door to the shop. Thinking it might be a newly discharged GI with a question about flying lessons, Munro wiped off his hands and went out to see how he could help.

"I'm Bob Munro," he said. "What can I do for you?"

"Well, I was wondering if you needed a flight instructor," the young man replied. "I asked the lady in the office and she said I should talk to you. My name's Bill Fisk."

With the ink barely dry on the document permitting the Air Harbor to operate a GI Bill flight school, Munro was very definitely in need of a flight instructor. Virginia Hill had departed for Alaska, and the rest of the instructors, Joe Tymczyszym included, could only work part-time. Munro invited Fisk into the shop to talk about his qualifications.

Fisk had become interested in flying right about the time the government declared there wouldn't be any within one hundred miles of Seattle. Undaunted, the twenty-year-old drove across the mountains to Cle Elum, where a fellow was selling rides in a Piper J-3 Cub. Fisk was struck by the way the ground seemed to fall away from the plane as they climbed out over the pine forests surrounding the town. By the time the J-3 plopped back onto Cle Elum's grass runway, Fisk knew what he wanted to do with the rest of his life. He drove back to Seattle and enlisted in the Air Corps.

He soloed in an open-cockpit, helmet-and-goggles, Ryan PT-22. The Air Corps was desperate for bomber pilots so Fisk went on to multi-engine school, eventually finding himself high over Italy in the right seat of a Consolidated B-24. After 25 missions, he moved over to the left seat, finishing his 35-mission tour as a first pilot with the 15th Air Force. The end of the war brought an end to the ban on civilian flying in Seattle, so Fisk got a job as an instructor at a GI Bill flight school in Kent, a farming community fifteen miles south of the city. The school had thirteen Aeronca Champs; Fisk felt airplanes Seven and Eleven flew the best, so he made sure his students always signed up for them.

It was more than coincidence that Fisk's favorite planes were numbered seven and eleven. The war had left the B-24 pilot quite superstitious. It's easy to write off superstition as a personality quirk, but Fisk had good reasons for his beliefs. He flew 35 missions in a B-24 at the height of Germany's desperation. The Allies were working their way up through Italy and they had a solid foothold in northern Europe. The German fighter attacks against the bombers were vicious and the flak from the anti-aircraft fire looked solid enough to walk on. On more than one occasion, Fisk watched the B-24s in formation beside him blow apart in thundering explosions, yet in 35 missions, his own plane never received so much as a scratch.

"If you weren't religious when you went over there, you were by the time you got back. And superstitious, too. We lived in a row of tents. Right next to us there was a tent, and every time a crew moved in there they'd fly one mission and get shot down. This happened time after time. You couldn't have gotten us to move into that tent for anything. Then a crew showed up who'd heard this rumor about what happened to people who moved into that tent. The pilot of this crew decided to do something about it, so he changed the appearance of the tent. He put in a door with a window and he put painted bricks all around the outside. He was determined to break the spell. Then they took off on their first mission. We figured they wouldn't come back but they did. They flew the rest of their missions and never got hit once."

BILL FISK

Fisk didn't think his superstitions were relevant to his abilities as a flight instructor so he didn't bother mentioning them during his job interview with Munro. It probably wouldn't have made any difference if he had; the summers Munro had spent among the characters inhabiting the fish canneries and gold mines had taught him to judge people by their attitudes and abilities, not by their personal beliefs. In Fisk, Munro saw a young man who had racked up a lot of valuable experience in a very short time. In addition to his combat flying and GI Bill instructing, Fisk had learned to fly a seaplane with Lana Kurtzer and then had gone out and obtained an instrument rating. Early the following Monday, Munro called Fisk at home and told him he could have the job of running Kenmore's flight school if he wanted it. Fisk showed up for work at 8:00 a.m. and stayed for the next forty-two years.

One of the first things Fisk did was start a ground school. It was a government requirement but Fisk had a personal reason, too.

"I wanted to get up in front of people. I could talk to one guy easy, but with more than one person, I would really shy away. I wanted to get over that so I decided to teach ground school. I'd get up there and the ladies in the class would say, 'Speak up, we can't hear you!' Boy, that straightened me out pretty quick."

BILL FISK

To drum up business for Kenmore's flight school, Fisk would check the newspapers to see if a church or company picnic was scheduled to be held at one of the local lakes over the weekend. If there was, he'd show up in a company plane and offer rides. The charge was a penny a pound for a fifteen minute flight. Fisk's on-site advertising campaign was remarkably successful; dozens of veterans began showing up at the Air Harbor to take flying lessons.

Fisk was always on the lookout for ways to promote the company, so he was all ears when a young man burst into the office one Saturday and announced he wanted to jump out of one of Kenmore's airplanes.

"There's a big picnic down on the lake at Kirkland today," he explained excitedly, "and I want to parachute into the water in front of the beach but I need an airplane. Can I use one of yours?"

"Well..." Munro began slowly, wondering what they should charge for such a short but unusual flight.

"I'll make you a deal," the parachutist continued, pacing the floor and cranking up his sales pitch. "I'm flat broke. I can't pay you a dime. But I can pay you in something better than money." The parachutist paused for dramatic effect. "I can pay you in publicity. Everyone will know the plane I jumped out of was from..."

He stopped and swept his hand through the air as though indicating a huge, arched sign,. "Kenmore Air Harbor!"

The parachutist resumed his pacing. "All the people at the picnic will see your plane, and they'll tell all their friends. You couldn't *buy* better publicity. So how about it?" He whirled to face Munro who was staring at him from behind his desk. "Don't you think all that publicity's worth a quick flight down to Kirkland?"

Munro's idea of good publicity was a happy customer telling other people about Kenmore's great service and quality work. Off-the-wall stunts like this parachute jump didn't strike him as being a very reliable way of drumming up business. Fisk thought otherwise.

"This would be great," he said, barging into the conversation before Munro could turn down the parachutist's request. "Kirkland's only five minutes down the lake, and a lot of people would see our airplane. I could even land and sell rides."

"There you go," the parachutist said, thumping Munro's desk with a fist. "You could sell rides. And since you'll have to fly down there anyway to do that, you can drop me off on the way, so to speak."

Munro leaned back in his chair and shrugged. Fisk obviously wanted to take the flight, and the two gallons of gas it would take to fly the Aeronca to Kirkland and back weren't worth quibbling about. And if Fisk could sell some rides at the picnic, who knows, maybe they *would* get some good publicity out of it. "Fine," he said. "Just be careful."

"Let's go," Fisk said, bolting for the door before Munro could change his mind.

The young man pulled a battered parachute pack from the trunk of his car and walked over to where Fisk was readying the Aeronca.

"You sit in back," Fisk instructed. "When we get to where you want to jump, tell me and I'll slow down. Then when I tell you to, climb out this door onto the right float and jump."

"Got it." The parachutist wriggled around to settle the bulky chute in place and tightened the harness straps. When he was satisfied everything was secure, he backed awkwardly into the two-place plane and perched as best he could on the rear seat. Fisk turned the Aeronca out from the dock, propped the engine, and scrambled into the front seat.

The flight to Kirkland took less than five minutes. The picnic was in full swing on the beach, and Fisk began to circle as he climbed to three thousand feet.

"How's this?" he yelled over his shoulder when he leveled the plane. The parachutist, now sporting a leather helmet and a pair of goggles, nodded and flashed a thumbs-up. Fisk eased the power back and raised the nose until the plane was mushing along just above the stall speed.

"Okay," Fisk yelled again. "You can get out now and jump."

The parachutist leaned out the door and clamped both hands around the aft wing strut. Fisk could feel the plane shift as his passenger gingerly eased off the seat and out onto the right float. Fisk rolled in some left aileron to compensate for the parachutist's weight and began to circle slowly over the crowd. He'd expected the man to jump right away, but after a moment he realized the parachutist was still standing there. Thinking the man might be waiting for another command, Fisk yelled over his shoulder again.

"It's okay. Go ahead and jump."

Nothing. The man didn't move. Fisk turned around in his seat for a better look and found himself peering into a face white with fear, the eyes wide and staring behind the leather goggles. Fisk had seen that look before, on the faces peering out of the B-24s beside him, teenagers too terrified to move as their flaming plane slowly rolled into a death dive.

Bill Fisk fueling a company Taylorcraft for a flight on a blustery day.

"Hey!" Fisk hollered as loud as he could. The glazed eyes shifted slowly to focus on the pilot. "Either jump or get back in. I can't stay up here all day and I can't land with you out there."

The parachutist dropped his gaze to the beach and the lake sparkling 3,000 feet below.

"Are you going to jump or not?" Fisk was running out of patience. The parachutist looked back up and nodded. Swallowing hard, he took a deep breath, closed his eyes, and stepped off the float.

"Holy cow!" Fisk slammed the stick hard left as the right wing dropped violently. Looking wildly around in search of the problem, he was stunned to see the parachutist dangling from the aft wing strut, his fingers locked around the slender steel tube.

"Are you nuts?" Fisk bellowed. "Let go of that!"

The parachutist turned his face skyward, clamped his eyes shut, and locked his hands in a death grip around the strut as his body swayed back and forth in the slip stream. The Aeronca continued on its course for a moment, and then Fisk became aware he was having to put in more and more right aileron to keep the wings level.

"What the heck's going on?" he wondered out loud, and peered around for the cause. He found it an instant later, and his heart raced with fear. The aft right strut was beginning to bend under the weight of the dangling parachutist, and it was pulling the trailing edge of the wing down with it. The drooping wing was acting like a giant aileron, forcing the plane into a roll to the left. Fisk moved the stick to the right to compensate, but he knew it would be only a matter of moments before the sagging wing overpowered the ailerons. Then the roll would accelerate, and the Aeronca would enter a spiral descent from which recovery would be impossible. With no parachute, Fisk would have to ride it down, a 3,000 foot drop that would give him plenty of time to think about the impact. It just didn't seem right that he should survive dozens of bombing missions in that huge sitting-duck of a B-24 with the whole German army shooting at him only to die in a crummy little Aeronca. And all thanks to that chicken-hearted stuntman dangling from the strut beside him.

"Well, we'll just see about that," Fisk muttered as he shoved his door open. Keeping his left hand on the stick, he twisted his body sideways in the seat and stretched his right leg out as far as he could. Lifting his foot, he took careful aim and slammed his shoe down on the fingers curled around the buckling strut. The parachutist yelped in pain and stared unbelievingly as Fisk took aim for another blow.

"Let go, doggone it!" Wham! The leather sole of Fisk's shoe smacked down on the tingling fingers again. "Let go before the whole damn wing comes off!"

It took only seconds for the parachutist to decide that jumping into the lake was far more preferable to the rain of kicks being delivered by Kenmore's demented pilot. He released his grip on the wing strut and headed for Kirkland.

Fisk didn't wait to see if the man's chute opened or not, and frankly, he didn't care. Scrambling back into the cockpit, he slammed the stick all the way to the right in a desperate attempt to stop the roll. For a moment nothing happened, and he feared he'd been too late in kicking the parachutist free. But he'd seen no black cats that morning, and he'd been careful not to walk under any ladders. Slowly, the left wing began to come up, and he thanked Lady Luck for sticking by him one more time.

Making only the shallowest of turns, Fisk nursed the unstable plane back to Kenmore where he made a wobbly, but safe, landing.

"I'm not sure how much of this publicity we can afford," Munro said as he examined the Aeronca's bent strut and sagging wing. Fisk wisely said nothing.

The Depression had demonstrated graphically to Bob Munro what bad financial planning could do to individuals and even whole companies, and he early on had resolved never to let himself be caught in the trap of spending more than he was earning. But Kenmore desperately needed another plane if the flight school was going to take full advantage of its new GI Bill-approved status. Reluctantly, Munro applied for a short-term bank loan and Taylorcraft NC96344 was purchased to replace the plane Jack Mines had crashed. The Air Harbor fleet now totaled three, all of which could be hangared to the government's satisfaction.

One of Ted Huntley's many jobs as line boy and general helper was refueling airplanes. Refueling in the spring of 1947 meant manhandling a fifty gallon drum through the mud over to the airplane and filling the tank with a hand pump. As more and more students began signing up for lessons, Munro decided it was time to get into the gas business. He didn't have any trouble finding a supplier; everyone was predicting aviation would be the business of the future and the oil companies were competing fiercely to get in on the action. Munro settled on General Petroleum, partly because they offered to include a thousand-gallon tank and an electric fuel pump as part of the deal. They also offered to paint the name KENMORE in huge, block letters on the metal roof of the hangar. Munro liked the colors the painter used; each letter was sunflower yellow with a chocolate brown outline.

One-year-old Gregg Munro didn't care about the colors on the roof but he really liked the dirt General Petroleum used to cover the thousand-gallon tank. Most of the tank was above ground to keep it from rusting in the wet, boggy soil, and the mound of earth was General Petroleum's contribution to the Air Harbor's landscaping scheme. Bob Munro put some timbers around the base of the mound to keep it from migrating away from the tank and Ruth planted flowers, but it was Gregg who most appreciated the oil company's efforts. For the next several years, Ruth's flowers led a tortured existence as Kenmore's future Flight Operations Manager careened down the hill in his red wagon and carved out a network of roads for his toy trucks.

One of the items on the agenda for discussion at the March 1947 meeting of Kenmore's board of directors was Joe Crosson's request for a Seabee hangar. The new ramp Munro had promised to build was scheduled for completion the following month, but Crosson had started lobbying for a new hangar, as well. Munro thought the idea of a Seabee hangar was great, but it was taking every dime the company made just to keep the operation running. For the time being, Crosson would have to be content with the new ramp.

Kenmore's board of directors had been elected on January 6, 1947, at the first-ever stockholders' meeting. Present were Bob Munro with 910 shares, Esther Mines with 930 shares, Durwood

Alkire with 10 shares, and Neil McConnell, a seaplane enthusiast who worked part time at Kenmore as a mechanic and painter in return for 200 shares of company stock. Bob Munro was elected president of the board, Durwood Alkire was elected vice-president, and Esther Mines was voted secretary-treasurer. The stockholders meeting was adjourned, McConnell went home, and Munro called the first board meeting to order. Pay was the first item to be discussed; Munro's salary was set at $300 a month while Esther Mines would receive $75 a month for her work in the office.

The discussion at the March board meeting about Crosson's request for a Seabee hangar had been preceded by a decision to allow Island Airways to base their big Noorduyn Norseman at Kenmore for a one-week trial period. Island Airways was the latest addition to a flock of seaplane services that had been formed as the result of a state-wide ferry strike. The strike was making it difficult to get to the cross-sound towns of Bremerton, Port Townsend, and Port Angeles, to say nothing of destinations in the San Juan Islands, and the seaplane operators had moved quickly to fill the gap.

One of the first to get going was Albert Almosolino, who started Seattle-Bremerton Airlines a day or two before the crews walked off the ferries. He was doing a land-office business flying people to and from the huge naval shipyard that sprawled along the Bremerton waterfront until the day he took off from Lake Union with an empty wing tank. He was still climbing steeply to clear the Aurora Avenue Bridge when he hauled his Norseman around into a tight left turn to pick up his heading for Bremerton. With one tank empty and the fuel in the other one pulled away from the outlet pipe by the angle of the plane, the six-hundred-horsepower radial quit instantly. Overloaded and at a high angle of attack, the Norseman stalled before Almosolino could react. The plane fell into a cluster of floating boathouses, fortunately missing all of them to splash down in a small patch of open water. Everyone managed to get out relatively unscathed, but the Norseman was a mess. Bob Munro and Tom Wardleigh went down to help Almosolino pull it out of the lake.

"I'm going to have to rebuild this thing," Almosolino said as they stood looking at the pile of bent tubing and torn fabric sitting on the dock, "but I don't know where."

"We've got an old barn you can use if you like," offered Munro. "It's not big enough to hold your whole plane, but at least you can rebuild the fuselage and the wings inside, out of the weather. Then when you're ready, you can use the A-frame on our truck to put it together."

Almosolino accepted Munro's offer and spent the next several months restoring his plane in the barn at the back of the property. It was Munro's first experience with a Norseman, a plane he would come to know intimately over the next few years. With its powerful Pratt & Whitney R-1340 engine and cavernous fuselage, the Canadian-built Norseman was one of the first planes to be designed specifically for rugged use in the northern bush country.

While Almosolino was rebuilding his plane in the barn, his competition began parking theirs at the dock. Each evening, NC55555, the Island Airways Norseman, rumbled in after its final run and tied up for the night. The company had a couple of limousines, and one of them was always on hand to meet the big silver and red plane and shuttle the passengers into Seattle. Then Ted Huntley or one of the mechanics would scramble up onto the wing and fuel it, after which they topped off the oil and pumped out the floats. The next morning, one of the limousines would bounce down the driveway with a load of passengers, and the Norseman would roar off to the San Juans on its first flight of the day. The arrangement proved satisfactory, and Island Airways agreed to pay Kenmore $100 a month for nightly moorage.

Munro finished the new ramp in April, and Joe Crosson moved his Seabee from Boeing Field to Kenmore. Munro also managed to come up with a little money for fill dirt. For seventeen cents a cubic yard, a local contractor agreed to haul in enough dirt to fix the road and fill in the worst of the low spots in the tie-down area.

As the spring of 1947 prepared to give way to summer, Wardleigh approached Munro with a suggestion. Why didn't the two of them take one of the Taylorcrafts for a week or so and fly to Alaska? They both needed solo cross-country time, Wardleigh for his Private license and Munro for his Commercial. Munro, who hadn't been to Alaska since his last stint at the gold mine before the war, thought it would be a great way to cut down the cost of getting their licenses. They decided on Ketchikan as a destination, but then Munro remembered they had a customer in Petersburg, another hundred miles or so to the north.

"Are you sure we want to visit him?" Wardleigh asked when he heard what Munro had in mind. "You know how, well, *difficult* he can be sometimes."

The man Wardleigh was referring to was Jim Parks. Parks was a member of a well-to-do Seattle family who owned one of the canneries in Petersburg. A few years earlier he'd purchased a Taylorcraft which he used to fly back and forth between Seattle and his favorite resorts in the San Juan Islands. Munro welcomed Jim Parks' fuel and maintenance business, but he was disturbed by the man's habit of climbing into the cockpit while still under the influence of the liquor he'd consumed earlier. Wardleigh was uncomfortable about dropping in on such an unpredictable character, but Munro didn't think it would be a problem.

"Jim's not such a bad guy. Besides, we'll only be in Petersburg for a day or so."

The flight north was every bit the adventure Munro and Wardleigh had hoped for. The Taylorcraft with its twelve-gallon fuel tank didn't have much range, but there were a lot of canneries scattered along the coast where Munro knew they could get gas. The Taylorcraft's little baggage area was big enough for a couple of sleeping bags, an ax, a few cans of food, a change of clothes or two, fishing gear, and a box of matches.

Their first stop was Vancouver, where they cleared customs and topped off the little tank. Then it was on to the logging and fishing town of Campbell River, on Vancouver Island. They spent their first night on a lake outside of town, sleeping under a tree. Wardleigh had somehow managed to grow up in the Northwest without ever going fishing, so Munro showed him how to cast and they spent a pleasant evening fishing from shore beside the plane. Wardleigh hooked into a nice cutthroat trout which Munro cleaned and cooked for dinner. As they climbed into their sleeping bags, Wardleigh decided spending the rest of his life doing this sort of thing wouldn't be such a bad idea.

The islands along the Inside Passage are dotted with countless lakes, and Munro and Wardleigh had no trouble finding good places to camp and fish as they hopped between gas stops. Their most exciting moment came just outside Ketchikan.

"We landed at a little place called Luck Lake, on Prince of Wales Island. We saw some black bears in the stream as we flew over and landed. I'd never seen bears like that and I was somewhat apprehensive, but Bob said, 'Don't worry, they're more scared of you than you are of them.' We fished a little bit and caught some nice cutthroat trout, and then we made a little camp and lay down to sleep. It was a bright moonlit night. Bob stuck the ax in a tree beside us so we would know where it was if we needed it, and we went to sleep.

About one or two in the morning the ax fell out of the tree. I guess Bob must have been worrying about the bears because he jumped up right away. He couldn't find the zipper, or the zipper wouldn't work on his old, surplus, mummy sleeping bag, so he just tore it open. I woke up to this tearing sound and a huge cloud of chicken feathers in the moonlight. It looked to me like a bear was attacking Bob, so I started yelling and looking for the ax. It's probably a good thing I didn't find it. Between the two of us, I suspect we made enough of a racket to keep the bears away from Luck Lake for a week."

TOM WARDLEIGH

Early the next morning, the pair reached Petersburg only to be given a message that Munro was needed back at the Air Harbor. Reluctantly, they gassed up and flew back to Prince Rupert where they cleared customs and fueled up for the long trip back down the Passage. They flew the last leg of the flight into Kenmore in the moonlight, the calm air and shimmering water a fitting conclusion to their week-long aerial adventure.

Ironically, it was Jim Parks who was responsible for their next foray into southeast Alaska, this time on a flight both Munro and Wardleigh would just as soon forget. Parks had decided he wanted a bigger plane, so he sold his Taylorcraft and bought a 165-horsepower Stinson Model 108 on wheels. The 108 came in two versions: a four-seat model called the "Voyager," and a utility model with front seats only called the "Station Wagon." Both models had been certified on floats, but no such installation had ever been made in the northwest. The ideal float for the job was the EDO Corporation's Model 2425, so an order was placed for a pair of them along with a complete set of attachment drawings.

Fitting floats to the tube-and-fabric airplanes of the 1940s was not the simple, bolt-on process that came with the mass-produced airplanes of later years. Installing the attachment hardware was a tedious, time-consuming job involving a lot of cutting, fitting, and welding. EDO's drawings were a big help, but Wardleigh, who by now had been named shop foreman, relied as much on common sense as he did on the paper blueprints. Finally, the mechanics had everything welded into place, and a CAA inspector came out to look over the installation.

"Seems fine to me," he said after a careful examination.

Wardleigh's crew sewed patches over the holes they'd had to cut in the fabric skin, and Parks was on his way to Petersburg. He got as far as Alert Bay near the north end of Vancouver Island. After refueling both himself and his airplane, Parks taxied out into the harbor for takeoff. There was a swell running, and Parks apparently misjudged the conditions. Partway into his takeoff run the Stinson bounced off the top of a swell and slammed into the face of the next one. The force of the impact was so great it sheared off the float struts, and the fuselage dropped down onto the spreader bars. The wooden propeller bit into solid, green water and shattered, and Parks was left drifting in silence. Someone came out in a skiff and towed him to shore, whereupon he immediately began making arrangements to have the plane loaded on a boat and sent back to Kenmore. A few days later, the same mechanics who had been so clever in figuring out how to mount the plane on floats were picking the seaweed out of the fuselage and trying to figure out what to fix first. Parks took off again for Petersburg a few weeks later, and this time, he made it.

No one knows what the Stinson was subjected to that summer, but Parks refused to fly it home in the fall. He was too busy, he said, so he asked Munro to go up and bring it back for him. With the pleasant memory of his first flight to Alaska still fresh in his mind, Munro asked Wardleigh if he'd like to come along and share the flying.

"Sure," Wardleigh replied. "It should be fun."

It wasn't. The best part of the flight was the steamer trip north. Munro spent the three days in the lounge studying for the written portion of his Commercial flight exam. When the ship reached Juneau, Munro and Wardleigh found out why Parks had sent someone else to fly his plane home. The Stinson was a mess. To begin with, it wouldn't start. After trying everything they could think of, they finally removed the cowling and pulled the plugs. They were filthy, fouled with oil and corrosion. Corrosion had ruined some of the threads in the cylinder heads, too. Munro and Wardleigh borrowed some tools from Alaska Coastal Airlines and cleaned the plugs and re-cut the bad threads.

This would have been a routine job back at the Air Harbor, but they weren't *at* the Air Harbor. They were in Juneau standing on a dock in the most incredible wind either man had ever experienced. Munro had heard about Juneau's famous Taku wind, but he'd had no idea it was this bad. The frigid air roared down off the Taku glacier and literally beat the town into submission. The wind was so strong that the sidewalks were equipped with handrails so pedestrians could pull themselves along from building to building. A government-owned anemometer on the mountain behind the town had once recorded a gust of two-hundred miles an hour before it was ripped off its concrete base. The true strength of the wind was never known; two-hundred miles an hour was as high as the needle on the anemometer could go.

Munro re-installed the plugs in the Stinson's rusty and corroded Franklin engine while Wardleigh struggled to keep the cowling from being blown over the horizon. When they finally had everything back together, Munro climbed into the plane to try again. The battery was just about dead, so Wardleigh hand-propped the engine. After several attempts, it fired into life, albeit reluctantly. When they went to return the tools, Alex Holden, one of Alaska Coastal's most experienced pilots, had a few words of advice.

"Don't just taxi out in the harbor here and try to take off. The downdrafts spilling off the mountain will kill you. Go around to the right under the bridge and taxi up Gastineau Channel as far away from town as you can. Take off to the northwest and go clear out around the north end of Douglas Island before you head south. Whatever you do, stay away from town and the mountain."

It was good advice, especially since Munro and Wardleigh had, in fact, been planning to taxi out into the harbor and take off in front of the town. After all, it had looked like the most logical place to go. As Munro taxied under the bridge and up Gastineau Channel he added another lesson to the growing file in his mind: *always ask the local experts for advice; what they know could save your life.*

The Stinson's performance was pathetic. It missed and backfired and had hardly any power, but Munro managed to get it into the air before reaching the web of mudflats and sandbars that marked the end of the channel. Following Holden's advice, Munro banked left as soon as they were off and rounded the north end of Douglas Island before heading southeast. Bypassing Petersburg and Ketchikan, they landed at Prince Rupert to clear Canadian customs and refuel for the trip down the Inside Passage. The headwind seemed to be increasing as they flew south from Prince Rupert, so just to be on the safe side they decided to stop at the huge Butedale cannery complex for lunch and a few more gallons of fuel. This time when Munro went to take off, he couldn't get the Stinson into the air at all. The engine was just flat worn out.

"We're going to have to lighten the load," he told Wardleigh as they taxied back to the dock. "The battery's worthless, so we can throw that away, and anything else you can think of."

"The radio won't work if we take out the battery," Wardleigh cautioned.

"It doesn't work now," Munro said, snapping the radio's power switch on and off a couple of times.

Wardleigh pulled out the little sacks of potatoes and canned food they'd stashed behind the seats for emergencies and a few other odds and ends and piled them on the dock beside the cracked and corroded battery. "That's about it, " he said. "The only thing left is us."

"All right," Munro said. "Let's try it again."

Wardleigh propped the plane and scrambled into the right seat as Munro guided the sputtering Stinson out into the channel in front of the cannery. He turned the plane into the wind, retracted the water rudders, and shoved the throttle all the way in. For a moment nothing happened, and then the needle in the tachometer started a slow, wobbly climb up the dial. Butedale had long since disappeared astern by the time Munro managed to coax the plane onto the step. A half mile or so later, the asthmatic Franklin coughed up another hundred rpm and Munro eased the plane into the air.

Keeping their fingers crossed, Munro and Wardleigh guided the wheezing Stinson down the Passage, past Klemtu, Bella Bella, and Namu. After a quick refueling stop and another reluctant takeoff at Port Hardy, it became obvious they had a bigger problem than the questionable reliability of the plane they were flying. The weather to the south looked downright nasty. By the time they reached Campbell River it was obvious that the low, dark clouds were going to make visual navigation difficult.

"Why don't we go into Sproat Lake while this weather blows through?" Wardleigh suggested.

Munro nodded in agreement. It was already late in the day, and the gloomy, gray light beneath the cloud layers made it seem even later. Munro had been eager to get home to his family, even to the point of finishing the flight at night if necessary. Now that the weather had put an end to that plan he just wanted to land somewhere and get out of Parks' crummy airplane. Wardleigh's suggestion of Sproat Lake made sense. One of the summer cabins on the lake was owned by a Kenmore customer, and the idea of spending the night in a comfortable bed was much more appealing than the prospect of sleeping out on a beach somewhere.

In the end, they did neither. Munro and Wardleigh managed to find the cabin, but the owner had already boarded the place up for the winter.

"I guess we'll have to sleep on the porch," Munro said. "At least we'll have a roof over our heads."

They left the Stinson floating just offshore, held in position by lines they strung into the trees. Dinner was something they'd have to do without; the ingredients had been left sitting on the dock at the Butedale cannery. The two men spread their sleeping bags out on the porch and turned in.

They awoke to a pair of surprises. Several inches of snow had turned the world a frosty white, and Jim Parks' Stinson was sitting on the bottom of the lake. It didn't take long to figure out what had happened. The EDO floats had little vent holes in the inspection covers over each float compartment. As the heavy, wet snow built up on the airplane's horizontal stabilizer, the tails of the floats were forced lower and lower into the lake. Eventually, water began dribbling into the rear compartments through the vent holes. The water added more weight, and the floats sank even lower. Soon, the next compartment forward began to fill, and then the one in front of it. Once this aquatic domino process has been set in motion, the only way to halt it is to sweep off the offending snow and pump out whatever water has accumulated in the float compartments. In this case, the only people who could have saved the situation were sound asleep, and the Stinson slipped beneath the waves unnoticed.

Fortunately, it didn't slip far. The water in the cove was only a few feet deep. Munro and Wardleigh took turns lifting on the tail of the plane to expose the access covers while the other man pumped. It took hours, but the floats were finally pumped dry and the Stinson resumed its rightful position on top of the lake. For all the trouble it was giving them, the two men were probably sorry they hadn't moored the plane in water that was a few *hundred* feet deep, but at least their ride home was secure.

The weather showed no signs of improving. In fact, it was getting worse, so they rearranged the mooring lines and pulled the Stinson in until it was sitting on the beach. They'd still have to keep an eye on the plane to make sure any further accumulation of snow didn't damage the wings, but at least it couldn't sink.

As it turned out, they didn't have to spend another night on the cabin porch, either. The fishing and vacation lodges on the lake were closed for the winter, but one of them had a caretaker. Drawn to the shore by the sound of voices and splashing water, the old man invited the stranded pilots to move their bedrolls to the resort. The weather remained virtually unflyable for the next three days, so Munro and Wardleigh made themselves useful by helping the caretaker with his chores and repairing the phone lines that connected the lodge with the outside world.

The outside world was not a particularly happy place at the moment. Ruth Munro had expected to see her husband two days earlier. A delay of one day was not unreasonable, but when there was still no word after three days she decided to take action. She couldn't very well jump in a plane and go look for him herself, so she did the next best thing. She called the Royal Canadian Mounted Police. The RCMP couldn't go look for Munro either, the weather being what it was, but they did start a telephone search up and down the coast. It took awhile, but they eventually learned that an airplane with two men aboard had landed on Sproat Lake just ahead of the snowstorm. A few more phone calls confirmed that the plane was indeed the missing Stinson, and that both pilots were safely holed up at a fishing lodge. Ruth was relieved, but she decided it was time to put a stop to this business of flying off north somewhere and not checking in for the duration of the trip.

Back on Sproat Lake, Munro and Wardleigh were getting restless. They'd been stuck at the lake for four days, and while they'd appreciated the caretaker's hospitality and enjoyed the challenge of repairing the phone lines, they wanted to get home. On the fifth day, a tiny patch of blue sky appeared above the lake. It didn't matter that the rest of the sky remained just as dark as before; that patch of blue meant they could get home. They bid a hasty farewell to the caretaker and scampered down the beach to the Stinson.

"It's *always* clear over the San Juans," Wardleigh said as they yanked the mooring lines free of the trees. "All we have to do is get on top through that hole and head for the islands."

Wardleigh propped the plane, and Munro taxied out into the main body of the lake. Both men kept scanning the sky, anxiously hoping the hole would remain open long enough for them to take off and climb up through it. Sproat Lake is quite long, which was fortunate since the clapped-out Stinson needed a good part of it to get airborne. Munro coaxed every bit of power he could out of the engine as he spiraled up towards the hole. The last thing he wanted to have happen was for the hole to close while they were in it; the mountains rising steeply from the west shore of the lake had already snagged a fair number of airplanes, and Munro didn't want to add to the total.

They popped out of the hole at six thousand feet. It was hard to believe that clouds could be so dark underneath and so white up above. After four days of living in a gray gloom, the billowing, white cloud tops stretching unbroken to the horizon under a brilliant blue bowl seemed like a fairyland. Munro leveled the Stinson at 6,500 feet and picked up a compass heading for the San Juans. Both men peered eagerly ahead for the break in the undercast they knew was awaiting them just below the Canadian border. Wardleigh had estimated it would take thirty-five minutes to reach the San Juans from Sproat Lake, not counting the time it had taken to spiral up through the hole. When the time was up, both men scanned the cloud deck below for any sign of a break. Nothing. In fact, the undercast looked even more solid than it had back at Sproat Lake.

"Maybe we'd better go back and find that hole again," Wardleigh said. "This stuff looks like it goes all the way to California."

"Let's just hope the hole is still there." Munro banked the plane around until he was on the opposite heading. "We flew for thirty-five minutes, right?"

Wardleigh monitored his watch, and when the thirty-five minutes were up both men started looking for the hole over Sproat Lake. It wasn't there.

"Are you sure you held the right heading on the way back?" Wardleigh asked as he scanned the unbroken clouds below.

"Absolutely. Are *you* sure you counted off thirty-five minutes?"

"Absolutely," Wardleigh retorted.

For the first time in his life, Munro didn't know what to do. The Stinson had perhaps two hours of fuel left, but two hours wouldn't be any better than two minutes if they went in the wrong direction.

"Well," he asked Wardleigh, "what do you think?"

"I wonder if we should spiral down right here and hope we're over the lake."

Munro shook his head. "There are too many mountains and we wouldn't see them until we hit them." He circled the plane one more time hoping that maybe the hole would magically appear, but it didn't. "We've got about two hours of fuel. We're over Vancouver Island, but we don't know where. I think we should head southwest across the island and keep going until we see the ocean. There's always holes in the overcast over the ocean, so we should be able to pick our way down until we can see the beach."

"I suppose that's the best thing to do," Wardleigh said uncertainly, "but how will anyone know where to look for us?"

"Somebody will find us." Munro tried to sound optimistic as he banked the plane around to pick up a heading of 210 degrees. The sunny skies and puffy cloud tops that had been so beautiful a short time before were now menacing and cold. Munro and Wardleigh would have given anything to be back on the gloomy shore of Sproat Lake, but instead they were in the cockpit of Jim Parks' sick Stinson, powerless to do anything but measure the time remaining before fate took over the controls. For an hour they droned westward, a tiny speck against the vast sea of clouds. They discussed their options, although they both knew there weren't any. Spinning down through the clouds was dismissed as being too dangerous, as was setting up the plane for the slowest possible descent. As terrifying as it was, the image of drifting helplessly at sea was more palatable than the thought of smashing into the side of a mountain.

The conversation died away as they started their second, and last, hour of flight. The clouds were still unbroken, probably all the way to Japan, Wardleigh figured. Munro was sure they must be over the ocean by now. Another hour of flight could take them out of sight of land, perhaps clear beyond the shipping lanes. We should head down now, he thought. If we wait, we may never get picked up. He was about to pull the power off when he suddenly thought of something else. What if we *haven't* reached the ocean yet? What if we go down through the clouds and crash on the cliffs just a few hundred yards short of the water? No, he decided, we'd better keep going.

Suddenly, Munro caught a flash of something white below the plane. He banked the Stinson slightly so he could see better. There it was again. White spots and streaks through a thin spot in the undercast. For a moment he stared, puzzled. White streaks? And then he knew what he was looking at.

"Whitecaps! I see whitecaps!"

Whitecaps on gray-green water. They *were* over the ocean! Munro shoved the nose of the Stinson down and bored in on the tiny hole that had opened in the clouds. He wasn't about to let this opportunity disappear. The plane blew out of the bottom of the overcast and the two men found themselves looking at a rocky, windswept cliff. Neither one of them had ever flown along the west coast of Vancouver Island, so they weren't surprised that they didn't recognize the shoreline. They were just thankful to be so close to land. There was a small bay up ahead that looked like it might offer a good place to land, and Munro banked the Stinson toward it.

As they came around the point, Munro and Wardleigh were surprised to see a big log raft moored against the side of the bay next to a floating bunkhouse. Men were maneuvering logs into the raft with pike poles, and they looked up, startled at the sight and sound of the plane that had come buzzing unexpectedly into their remote corner of the world. Munro set the Stinson down on the calm water beside the raft and shut off the engine. As the plane drifted to a stop, he popped open his door and stepped onto the float. The loggers waited expectantly, leaning on their pike poles as they effortlessly rode the bobbing logs. The smell of fresh-cut timber hung in the air like perfume.

"Excuse me," Munro said politely. "We seem to have gotten a little turned around in this weather, and I'm not that familiar with the west coast of Vancouver Island. I wonder if you could tell us which bay this is?"

The loggers glanced at each other in amusement. "Vancouver Island you say?" The French-Canadian accent was unmistakable.

"Yes." Munro wondered what was so funny.

"I'm afraid you are more than a little turned around, my friend." The logger who had spoken jerked his head toward the rocky shoreline behind him. "This is Texada. Vancouver Island," he pointed out the bay with his pike pole, "is there. About twenty mile."

Munro was stunned. "This is Texada?"

The loggers nodded.

"Thank you." Munro hoped he didn't look as confused as he felt. He climbed back into the Stinson to be confronted by an equally confused Tom Wardleigh.

"How could this be Texada?" the younger man whispered. "We flew southwest from Sproat Lake for an hour, and they're saying we've ended up thirty miles northeast of where we started?"

Munro shrugged. "I don't understand it either, but they've got no reason to lie to us. Let's take off and find out for sure."

Wardleigh climbed out and propped the engine, and Munro coaxed the Stinson off the water one more time. The clouds had lifted a bit, and as Munro got some altitude under the plane, he and Wardleigh saw immediately that the loggers were right. There was Lasqueti Island, a few miles to the south just like it was supposed to be, while to the west the shoreline of Vancouver Island drew a dark line across the flat, gray canvas of water and cloud.

"It must have been the wind," Munro said as he pointed down at the whitecaps seething a hundred feet below the float keels. "We probably never got anywhere near the San Juans. The wind's been pushing us east ever since we took off from Sproat Lake."

The ceiling was still very low, but the visibility under the clouds was actually pretty good. The city of Vancouver lay about fifty miles to the south, and Wardleigh calculated they had just enough gas to reach it. After refueling, another hour would see them back at Kenmore.

Ruth Munro watched the Stinson taxi up to the dock with mixed emotions. Her husband was home safe, and for that she was tremendously thankful. On the other hand, she didn't want to repeat the ordeal of worrying and wondering where he was every time he took off on a trip. It was an issue they would never really resolve. Munro felt he was actually doing his family a favor by not calling in.

> "They wanted to hear from me every night. I knew I probably wouldn't be able to call every night, and I was afraid that if I promised to call and then couldn't, they'd start to worry about me. So I always told them, 'Don't expect to hear from me. I'll be back in four or five days.' That way, they wouldn't worry if they didn't hear from me, and I didn't have to worry about trying to get to a phone. I didn't use flight plans very often for the same reason. If I couldn't close it, there would be even more people worried about me. It was probably a foolish thing to do, but I didn't want to get everybody concerned if they didn't hear from me. Today, of course, I want to know exactly where everybody is all the time."
>
> **BOB MUNRO**

Munro and Wardleigh were none the worse for wear after their ordeal with Jim Parks' Stinson, although Munro did make himself a solemn promise. *Never again,* he vowed, *would he be caught on top of the clouds, out of sight of water or land.* And he never was.

NEW CUSTOMERS, NEW PLANES, AND A DUCK

THE STUDYING MUNRO HAD DONE on the ferry trip north to pick up Jim Parks' Stinson paid off when he successfully passed the written exam for his Commercial pilot's license. A short time later, he added up his logbook entries and discovered he'd accumulated just over two-hundred hours, the minimum required to qualify for a Commercial ticket. Bill Fisk was kept pretty busy as the Air Harbor's only full-time instructor, but Munro managed to squeeze in enough dual instruction time between GI Bill students to learn the maneuvers he'd be required to demonstrate during his flight test. When Munro felt he was ready, he scheduled a checkride with Joe Tymczysczm, who was still instructing part-time, and as a CAA-designated examiner, gave all the checkrides.

Munro passed his Commercial checkride with flying colors and Kenmore Air Harbor was in the charter business. One of Munro's first flights for hire was with a photographer who wanted to take aerial pictures of the troopships and Navy vessels that were coming home to Seattle and Bremerton from overseas. After being deposited back at the Kenmore dock, the photographer would rush home and develop the film so he could meet the ships when they docked and offer his pictures for sale to the crews and returning soldiers.

Munro learned the do's and don'ts of charter seaplane flying on his own; the only person around with experience in the field was Lana Kurtzer, and he wasn't about to teach his upstart competitor a thing. Munro had barely pocketed his commercial license when he received a dramatic demonstration of the importance of dockside safety. A family friend, Martin Packard, needed to make a quick business trip to Portland, Oregon. He called Kenmore from his office in Seattle thinking that Munro might be able to fly him down. The flight would cover more than 150 miles, but there didn't seem to be anything risky about the trip except perhaps the weather which was being reported as marginal south of Olympia.

"Okay," said Munro. "We'll give it a try. When do you want to go?"

"Right now," said Packard. "Pick me up at Seattle Seaplane Service on Lake Union."

Jack Pickle's Seattle Seaplane Service occupied a three-bay hangar that had earned its place in history the moment Bill Boeing shoved the *Bluebill* out the center door and down the ramp into the lake. Boeing had built the hangar to house the *Bluebill*, the *Mallard*, and the Martin floatplane they both were patterned after, and he continued to use it as a final assembly building for the improved floatplanes he was fabricating for the Navy. It wasn't long, however, before Boeing outgrew the Lake Union hangar and it was sold. The building underwent numerous modifications over the years, but the steep ramp, slippery with algae and duck droppings, remained unchanged.

Munro approached the old Boeing hangar and applied power to pull the Taylorcraft firmly onto the ramp. When he thought the plane was solidly on the boards, he pulled the throttle to idle and prepared to shut off the engine. To his dismay, the Taylorcraft began sliding backwards. This had happened occasionally at Kenmore, and was one reason Munro had developed an early dislike for ramps. He shoved the throttle back in, and the 65-horsepower Continental hauled the Taylorcraft back up the ramp. Once again, Munro pulled the throttle to idle and once again, the plane began sliding backwards into the water. Annoyed, Munro shoved the throttle back in and the Taylorcraft stopped, held in position by the thrust of the propeller.

At this point, Munro wasn't sure what to do. He couldn't leave the engine running while he got out to collect his passenger; if either of them slipped and fell into the propeller it would be the end of Kenmore Air Harbor. On the other hand, if he shut off the engine, he still wouldn't be able to board his passenger because the plane would slide back into the lake. He was glaring down at the slimy boards that were responsible for his predicament when out of the corner of his eye he saw someone climb onto the bow of the right float. Before Munro could react, Martin Packard walked nonchalantly past the whirling propeller, missing it by less than an inch, and stood by the passenger door waiting to be let in.

Stunned, Munro killed the engine, and the Taylorcraft slid back into the water and began drifting away from the ramp. Munro slid over into the right seat and opened the door.

"Hi," Packard said as the pilot climbed out to stand beside him on the float. "How does the weather look?"

"I don't know," Munro murmured, still shaken by what had just happened. He hadn't even noticed Packard leave the building and walk down the ramp towards the plane. If he had, he could have yelled at him to stop, but he'd been so concerned about sliding back into the lake that he hadn't noticed what his passenger was doing until it was too late. It was a miracle the man hadn't been killed, either by slipping and falling into the propeller or walking into it after he'd climbed onto the float. *From now on,* Munro told himself, *the safety of the passengers comes first. The plane comes second.*

As Munro stepped forward to prop the drifting plane back to life, he glanced over his shoulder at Packard, who was gawking at the fascinating variety of boats and buildings that lined the Lake Union waterfront.

"Do you know how close you came to being hit by the propeller when you climbed onto the float back there?"

Packard looked puzzled. "What propeller?"

Munro didn't get to Portland that day. The weather had worsened considerably by the time he got to Olympia, so he turned around and took Packard back to Kenmore; tackling the old Boeing ramp once in one day was enough.

Not long after the Martin Packard incident, a man called and asked if he could be flown to Anderson Island, a few miles south of Tacoma. A renter pilot had booked the company's Taylorcraft at ten o'clock the same morning, but Munro figured that as long as he was airborne for Anderson by eight he should have no problem getting the plane back to Kenmore by ten. Had he even suspected the bizarre chain of events that would surround the seemingly routine flight he probably would have left the Taylorcraft locked in the hangar.

The morning sky was clear when Munro eased NC29560 off Lake Washington, but when he clattered past Tacoma's huge Asarco copper smelter and rounded Point Defiance he found the south end of Puget Sound blanketed by dense, low fog. Trees sticking up through the mist marked Anderson's location, but the island itself was invisible. Circling, Munro noticed the fog ended abruptly about a mile away, and the water sparkled brilliantly under the cloudless sky. I'll land out there, he decided, and taxi to the island through the fog by compass. He lined up his final approach with the trees marking Anderson's location and noted the compass heading before touching down on the smooth water outside the fog bank. Moments later, the plane was enveloped in gray as Munro taxied slowly through the fog, one eye on the compass and the other on the water in front of the plane. It took a long time to reach the island, and still longer to taxi his way carefully along the shoreline to the proper dock.

The customer was delighted with Munro's ingenious solution to the fog problem, but by now it was almost ten o'clock. His mind filled with visions of the renter pilot angrily pacing the dock, Munro decided to save time by taking off in the fog rather than retrace his course all the way out to open water. After all, he reasoned, I only have to climb up as high as the trees, and I'll be out of it. How dangerous can that be?

Other than the engine instruments, only an altimeter and an airspeed indicator graced the Taylorcraft's simple panel. There was no artificial horizon, no directional gyro, no turn coordinator, and no rate of climb indicator. Not that it mattered; Munro didn't know how to use any of them anyway. His climb up through the fog would be under the sole guidance of the seat of his pants.

"I appreciate your giving us a call," Munro said as his disembarked passenger pushed the plane away from the dock. "Let us know if we can help you again."

"I'll do that," the man replied. He watched as Munro propped the engine, and then he cupped his hands around his mouth and yelled over the clatter. "Be careful in the fog!" Munro acknowledged the warning with a wave, and the Taylorcraft slipped from sight into the mist.

Munro held his heading until he was sure he'd taxied well clear of the shoreline. Then he turned the plane to the reciprocal of the heading he'd used to approach the island. Watching the compass carefully, he retracted the water rudders and applied full power. The Taylorcraft nosed to the left as it came up onto the step but Munro quickly straightened it out with the air rudder. A few moments later, the plane reached flying speed and Munro eased back on the yoke.

The water dropped from view almost instantly and Munro was in a world without form. He was careful not to move the yoke. The plane felt fine. He had no sensation of turning or diving, and he knew it would be only seconds before he broke out into the sunshine. He concentrated on not moving the yoke, delighted that it took so little effort to keep the plane on an even keel. But where was the sun? Time seemed to be slowing down, and he felt a nervous twinge in his gut. Surely he'd climbed as high as the trees by now. He had a sudden vision of gray-green water smashing through the windshield. Had he relaxed his grip on the yoke? He'd been trying hard not to move it, but had he let it slip just a bit? Instead of climbing, was he diving? Or had he leveled off and was only seconds away from hitting the next island? Which would be worse, crashing on land or hitting the water? He fought the impulse to pull the yoke back as tentacles of panic began to twist through his mind. *Why didn't I stay on the water? Why didn't I taxi out to where it was clear?* The knowledge that these choices were forever lost to him fueled the panic even more. The translucent whiteness offered no direction.

The Taylorcraft burst out into clear air in a seventy-degree bank. Munro's relief at seeing blue sky was instantly dashed by the realization that he was rapidly rolling into a dive. The horizon snapped into focus and he rolled the wings level. He pulled the power back and eased the nose up. The shock of seeing how far out of control he'd been made him afraid to do anything but fly the plane straight and level, but he quickly realized the foolishness of his fear. It was his impatience that had put him at risk, not the airplane. *I'll never do that again,* he vowed, and he banked the Taylorcraft back to the north and Kenmore. As he droned along over the jewel-like Sound, he marveled that the plane could have gotten into such a radical attitude in the fog without him feeling it. It was his first experience with vertigo, and he didn't like it one bit. *From now on,* he declared to himself, *I want to see where I'm going.* Years later, changing regulations required him to obtain an instrument rating, and while he passed the course with ease, he saw no reason to challenge the rule that kept the birds alive: *if you can't see, don't fly.*

As he'd feared, the renter pilot was furious. Munro apologized and tried to explain why he was late but the customer would have none of it. He had booked the plane for ten o'clock and the plane should have been ready. No excuses. As the pilot fumed and swore, Munro began to suspect the man was upset about more than just the delay of his flight. Maybe he should go flying later, Munro suggested, after he'd cooled down a bit. It was good advice, but all it did was add fuel to the fire. Munro listened to the tirade for another minute or two, and then he flatly told the renter there was no way he was going to fly the Taylorcraft or any other airplane on the premises in his present condition. Shouting a few final curses over his shoulder, the pilot stalked to his car and roared off. Munro waited to make sure the man got off the premises without hitting anything, and then he walked over to the office. He got there just as the phone began to ring. It was the renter's wife.

"Don't let him fly," she pleaded. "He left here threatening to commit suicide by crashing the plane."

Munro assured her that her husband had just driven off in his car, and there was no way he would be allowed into an airplane if he should happen to return. An hour later the telephone rang again. This time it was the sheriff's office. The renter pilot had shot himself to death in his car. His wife had mentioned the Air Harbor, and did anyone there have any information for their investigation? Munro felt terrible about the way the situation had ended, but he couldn't help wondering what might have happened if he'd returned from his flight on time and turned the Taylorcraft over to the waiting pilot. He, Wardleigh, and the rest of the mechanics may very well have been left wondering if the subsequent crash had been the pilot's fault or theirs.

Soon after Munro began flying charters, the Air Harbor received an unlikely customer in the person of Lana Kurtzer. Kurtzer had acquired the Taylorcraft distributorship for the Seattle area, but he wasn't equipped to put his customers' planes on floats. Unlike the planes that came later, the Taylorcrafts built in the 1940s did not have factory-installed fittings for the attachment of floats. The fittings had to be installed in the field, which meant performing major surgery on the airframe. It was a tricky job. The first step was to slice four holes in the brand new fabric to give access to the fuselage tubing. Then the lower longerons were cut so the front and rear float fittings could be welded into place on each side of the plane. After the fittings and surrounding tubing were painted to stave off corrosion, fabric patches were sewn over the holes and doped and painted to match the rest of the fuselage. Kurtzer ordered the necessary welding equipment, but until it arrived he was dependent on Kenmore to install his customers' floats.

Kurtzer had no reason to complain about the quality of Kenmore's work; when Munro and Wardleigh were finished, the attachment fittings looked like they'd been installed as original equipment at the factory. If Kurtzer was impressed he wasn't about to admit it, but he had no such qualms about expressing his opinion of Munro's chances of success in the seaplane business.

"You don't have a prayer," Kurtzer growled the first time he brought a Taylorcraft out to Kenmore for welding. "I'll run you out of business in no time." Presumably not until *after* Munro had finished installing Kurtzer's attachment fittings.

Bill Fisk's efforts with the flight school were paying off nicely. He'd been hired back in February 1947; four months later he was juggling thirty-five students. The shop business was picking up, too. By summer that same year, the company had three full-time and two part-time mechanics. As shop foreman, Tom Wardleigh received a dollar-fifty an hour. Ted Huntley, in his role as line boy and general helper, was at the bottom end of the scale at forty cents an hour. Bill Fisk had started out getting paid by the hour, too, but he talked Munro into changing his hourly pay into a salary. Munro agreed, and Fisk was guaranteed $250 a month plus an additional three dollars for every hour he flew over eighty hours. This proved to be a good deal for both parties; Fisk had the security of an income unaffected by the seasonal ups and downs of the flight school business, and Munro had an employee who was motivated by his bonus to go out and drum up more customers.

That June, a customer came in looking for a used Piper J-3 Cub to buy. Munro knew of a J-3 that was available for $900, so Kenmore bought the plane and sold it to the customer for $915. The new owner wanted a number of repairs made before he took delivery, so the Air Harbor's fifteen-dollar resale profit was augmented by $386 worth of shop work.

The significance of the J-3 transaction was not the money it represented; even in 1947 a fifteen-dollar profit on the sale of an airplane was nothing to write home about. The significance was in the pattern of the transaction, a pattern the Air Harbor continues to use to its advantage today. A worn out or damaged seaplane is purchased for a fraction of its original price, restored to better-than-new condition by the company's airframe, powerplant, and interior specialists, and then sold for a reasonable profit. Bob Munro never claimed to have invented this concept; people have been rebuilding and reselling machinery for centuries. But no other company has so perfected the art of resurrecting seaplanes as Kenmore Air Harbor.

At first, this provided a way for Kenmore's customers to obtain a nice seaplane at a cost considerably below that of a new plane. The subsequent withdrawal of de Havilland of Canada, and more recently Cessna, from the manufacture of single-engine airplanes has increased the value of used floatplanes to the point where many of them are worth more now as wrecks than they were when they were new. To this day, Kenmore continues what that J-3 Cub transaction began, and a worn out or war surplus de Havilland Beaver as rebuilt by the Air Harbor has become the world standard by which floatplanes are judged.

By the summer of 1947, Joe Crosson's prediction that the Republic Seabee would be a success had come true. A price tag of $3,900 put the rugged amphibian within reach of a lot of aviation enthusiasts, and the planes were being snapped up as fast as Republic could turn them out. Unfortunately, they didn't turn them out for long. Republic had put the Seabee into production in 1946 to help fill the void left by the cancellation of P-47 Thunderbolt orders after the war. One year later, the world was facing a new threat in the aggressive posturing of the Soviet Union and Communist China. Germany's twinjet Messerschmitt Me-262 had begun hammering the nails into the piston-engine airplane's coffin during the closing months of World War II, and the onset of the Cold War accelerated the process. Using captured German research data, Boeing developed the world's first sweptwing jet bomber, the B-47. Lockheed perfected America's first jet fighter, the P-80 Shooting Star. Not to be outdone, Republic developed the P-84 (later F-84) Thunderjet. The third member of the Air Force's first-generation jet fighter trio was a sweptwing beauty from North American called the F-86 Sabre.

Republic's Seabee assembly line was right next to the Thunderjet line. This arrangement worked fine for awhile, but as the Air Force began clamoring for more jet fighters, Republic began to run out of room in the factory. It wasn't a hard decision to make; Seabee number 1,060 would be the last one off the line. Scarcely a year after production had started, the Seabee tooling was dismantled and the floorspace was turned over to the fighter program.

Jim Campbell's new Seabee in 1947. He would own the plane for the next 17 years.

Kenmore's board of directors had a decision to make at their monthly meeting on August 15, 1947. After getting off to a promising start, Joe Crosson's Seabee dealership was in serious jeopardy. Not only had Republic terminated production of the airplane, but Crosson himself had passed away during the summer. The decision facing Bob Munro and the board was whether or not the Air Harbor should take over the dealership. The popularity of the Seabee seemed to be increasing every day, but unless someone put it back into production, the opportunity to make money from the sale of new Seabees was nonexistent. On the other hand, the Seabee was proving to be something of a high-maintenance machine, so the prospects for parts sales and service looked pretty good.

Munro thought a lot about the business pros and cons of taking over the dealership, and he also thought a lot about the four or five people who'd begun parking their new Seabees at Kenmore. While it was true the owners hadn't purchased their planes from Kenmore, they were paying tie-down fees to Kenmore, they were buying their gas from Kenmore, and they were having their engines serviced at Kenmore. They were loyal customers, and Munro wasn't about to turn his back on them just because Republic had decided to dump the Seabee program. At the end of the meeting, Kenmore's board of directors approved Munro's recommendation to take over the dealership.

That same August meeting brought a decision about the Seabee hangar Crosson had been pushing for. The increase in activity during the summer had underlined the company's need for more hangar space, so the board decided to explore the possibility of financing a new building with advance rental payments from the Seabee owners. One of the owners who welcomed the idea was Jim Campbell.

Campbell was the sales manager for University Chevrolet. He'd learned to fly in 1941 but he'd had to wait until after the war to get his seaplane rating. After Bill Fisk had shepherded Campbell through Kenmore's seaplane course, the Chevy sales manager was content to fly a friend's Aeronca until the day Joe Crosson showed up with a new Seabee for sale. One look at the tough little amphibian was all it took. Campbell became Crosson's first customer when University Chevrolet took delivery of a brand new Seabee in June 1947.

> "Jim brought the owner of University Chevrolet out to take him for a ride around Seattle. It was a beautiful day and they had a great flight. When Jim came back, he taxied up the ramp rather smartly and unlocked the tailwheel and spun the plane around like a fighter. Then to illustrate the backup characteristics of the Seabee, he slipped the prop into reverse and backed the plane straight into the only telephone pole on the property."
>
> TOM WARDLEIGH

The destruction of one of the Seabee's elevators did nothing to dampen Campbell's enthusiasm for the plane; he owned it for seventeen years, during which he put 2,200 hours on the airframe. It was unfortunate that Republic bailed out of the Seabee program after only a year. Had they stuck with it, it's probable that most of the plane's weaknesses would have been fixed. As it was, dedicated Seabee enthusiasts like Jim Campbell had to live with a number of chronic problems.

One thing that very definitely was not a problem was the hull. It was built like a battleship. As a result, a Seabee could take on far rougher water than a floatplane of similar size and capacity. Another benefit was the arrangement of the doors. The Seabee was nothing if not easy to get in and out of. A large door on each side of the cabin gave access to the front and rear seats. These doors alone would have been sufficient, but Spence's design also called for a bow door. The entire right half of the huge, curved windshield was hinged to the center post and opened to allow easy access when the plane was nosed up to a dock or a log along the shore of a lake.

Technically, the Seabee was a four-place airplane. It didn't take Bob Munro long, however, to discover that the Seabee easily could carry five adults if the heavy landing gear was removed. Removing the wheels also enhanced the plane's reliability. The gear was raised and lowered by pumping up and down on the lever of a small hydraulic pump. It was a reliable system in theory, but in reality it caused a lot of problems. Republic had designed key linkages in the system to sheer if someone landed in the water with the wheels down, either through negligence or as the result of a retraction system failure. The broken linkages were supposed to allow the wheels to kick back and up instead of digging in and flipping the plane.

Joe Crosson actually made use of this feature during a landing at Kenmore after a retraction system failure, and the landing gear kicked up as advertised. Crosson's experience was the exception, however; most of the time the linkages didn't break and the plane would somersault over onto its back. On other occasions, the linkages would sheer off during a normal wheel landing. Bill Fisk experienced this once during a routine landing on a grass runway, and the Seabee he was flying slid the whole length of the field on its belly.

Republic used the break-away theory on the wingtip floats, too. The wingtip floats on a flying boat are intended to keep the airplane upright on the water only while it is at rest or taxiing at very slow speeds. If the floats were to contact the water at high speed during takeoff or landing, the sudden drag on the ends of the wings could throw the plane completely out of control. To prevent this from happening, the wingtip floats do not extend down as far as the bottom of the airplane. This is why a flying boat, regardless of size, tilts to one side or the other when at rest.

Knowing some of their amphibians would end up in the hands of relatively inexperienced pilots, Republic deliberately weakened the Seabee's float struts by drilling a large hole through the strut close to its attachment point on the underside of the wing. Should a pilot accidentally let a wing drop low enough during takeoff or landing to dig a float into the water, the float and its strut would sheer cleanly away instead of throwing the plane into a violent water loop. The breakaway strut also helped protect the wing from stress damage if a pilot happened to ram a float into a dock. It was good planning on Republic's part; the Seabee's $3,900 price tag put it within reach of some fairly mediocre pilots, and for years Kenmore did a brisk business selling replacement wing float and strut sets, most of them as a result of docking accidents.

The Seabee's landing gear links and float struts were *designed* to break under stress. It's engine wasn't, but it unfortunately did. The six-cylinder, 215-horsepower Franklin mounted atop the fuselage simply wasn't up to the task of hauling around a bulky, 3,000-pound airplane. Actually, Republic had planned to use a 175-horsepower Franklin in the Seabee, but the performance of the prototype was awful. All the production planes came off the line with the larger engine.

The best thing that could be said about the Franklin was that it was easy to start. Like all piston engines designed for aircraft use, the Franklin had a dual ignition system, but instead of powering each of the two sparkplugs per cylinder from one of two identical magnetos, the Franklin powered one set of plugs from a magneto and the other set from an automotive-style coil and distributor. A magneto is like a little generator; as it turns it creates the electricity to fire the sparkplugs. The advantage of a magneto is its total separation from the airplane's electrical system; a dying battery or an electrical malfunction will not affect the operation of the engine. A distributor, on the other hand, depends on power from the plane's battery to fire the plugs. But because a distributor is not dependent upon engine RPM to generate a spark, it can send a full electrical charge to the plugs even at very low speeds. With one plug in each cylinder blasting away at full power, the Seabee's Franklin often fired up the moment the starter began to turn.

The Franklin was a lot easier to start than it was to keep running. The cylinders were prone to cracking and the engine had a penchant for swallowing valves. Six hundred hours was about all a Seabee owner could expect to get between top-end overhauls. At four hundred hours it was wise to start pulling the engine through by hand before firing it up. If a wheezing sound was heard, it meant a valve had stretched and was beginning to leak. Once a valve had stretched it was only a matter of time before it broke off altogether. When it did, the lower half of the valve would drop into the cylinder and break the piston in half, at which point the wildly thrashing connecting rod would punch the whole mess out the side of the engine case.

The Seabee's variable-pitch propeller was another example of an excellent theory frustrated by poor execution. A variable-pitch propeller performs the same function as the transmission in a car. In low gear, a car engine develops a lot of power and the vehicle can accelerate quickly. In high gear, the engine turns over relatively slowly; there's not enough power for rapid acceleration but the engine is operating much more efficiently. In an airplane, the propeller is set to fine pitch for maximum RPM and horsepower during takeoff and climb. Upon reaching cruise altitude, the propeller blades are moved into coarse pitch to take a bigger "bite" of air with each revolution and pull the plane along much more efficiently.

The propeller itself on the Seabee was fine; it was made by Hartzell and was unique in that the two blades were constructed of plastic fiber instead of metal. The headache was the pitch-change mechanism. A control in the cockpit allowed the pilot to change the pitch of the propeller blades in flight by adjusting the amount of oil pressure being sent to a large piston and cylinder arrangement bolted to the crankshaft. Higher oil pressure forced the piston out and moved the blades to fine pitch. Lower oil pressure allowed centrifugal force acting on a pair of counterweights attached to the propeller blades to push the piston in, which moved the blades to coarse pitch. There was a separate control for putting the propeller into reverse pitch. The reverse pitch feature was how Joe Crosson was able to baffle Bob Munro and Reg Collins with his quick stop alongside the dock at Kenmore. A reversible-pitch propeller is a handy thing to have on a seaplane, but Munro feels the Seabee's reversing system got more people into trouble than it helped.

> "The problem was that if you were carrying any power at all, the centrifugal force would keep the propeller from going into reverse, or if you had it in reverse and revved up the engine, the centrifugal force would take it back out. We'd be working in the shop and hear a Seabee taxiing in, and the next thing you know, we'd hear the engine rev up and then we'd hear a bang as the plane hit the dock. People would wait too long to put the propeller in reverse. Then they'd panic and rev up the engine trying to stop, and the prop would come out of reverse and actually drive them into the dock harder than if they'd done nothing at all."
>
> **BOB MUNRO**

Tom Wardleigh, who rebuilt more Seabee propeller mechanisms than he cares to remember, has little good to say about the system.

> "It had a number of different failure modes. Sometimes the [piston guide] pins would get so loose, the O-rings around the piston would grind themselves up and the oil would leak past

them. Or the pins would crystallize and break off and the whole works would start revolving and leaking oil. The thing failed in almost every combination possible. It was called a Hydroselective Propeller. You could get an infinite selection of pitch on the prop. The concept isn't really all that bad, but the execution was pretty terrible."

TOM WARDLEIGH

If the pins or the O-rings let go, it was often only a matter of minutes before all the oil in the engine was pumped overboard through the rear of the propeller hub. Unless the pilot happened to be looking at the oil pressure gauge at the time, his first indication of trouble would be a wrenching silence as the engine seized up. One of the first modifications Kenmore made to the Seabee was the installation of a little mirror out on the wing strut so the pilot could see the tail. As long as the tail was clean, everything was okay. If the tail began turning black, the pilot knew that oil was spraying back from the propeller hub and that he'd better get the plane down *now*.

Despite its mechanical drawbacks, the Seabee continued to gain popularity in the Seattle area. The growing number of owners who based their planes at Kenmore found they had a common bond that extended beyond the peculiarities and frustrations of their airplanes. Puget Sound offered countless destinations for picnicking, digging for oysters and clams, or just relaxing with the family. Seabee owners like Jim Campbell, Clarence Black, and Bob Dent began organizing social expeditions to Hood Canal, Coronet Bay, and the San Juan Islands. More than any other airplane before or since, the Seabee brought together a unique group of people who combined their love of the Northwest with their love of aviation and adventure.

The decision to start construction on a new, eight-bay, Seabee hangar was made at the board of directors meeting in September 1947. To keep the cost down, Bob Munro and his employees would do as much of the construction work as possible. The first job on the list was the driving of 140 creosote-covered piles to stabilize the ground and support the concrete floor of the building. Thanks to his experience building fish traps in southeast Alaska, Munro knew how to rig and operate a pile driver; it was procuring the piling that presented the challenge. Someone noticed an ad in the paper that said one of the mills at the south end of the lake was offering a good price on piling, so Munro drove down and bought enough for the hangar project. The only catch to the deal was that the mill's good price was for piles at the mill; it was up to the purchaser to figure out how to move the piles to the job site.

What they needed was a tugboat but Kenmore didn't have the funds for such an extravagance. Munro called around until he found someone who had an ancient launch he was willing to rent cheap. The mill said they'd raft up the piles, so early on the morning of the appointed day Munro and Wardleigh steered their rented, leaking boat down the lake and tied onto the cables that bound the piles together. Then they opened the throttle and waited for something to happen. For a long time it looked like nothing would, but they finally began to discern forward progress. The pull back up the lake took the entire day, and there were times when it was debatable which would fail first, the launch's sputtering, overheated engine or the men's patience as they tried to coax an extra rpm or two from the motor or stabbed with the bailing bucket at the water sloshing around their feet.

The next day Munro took the weapons carrier over to Star Machinery and rented a double-drum winch, a pile driver hammer, and a set of hammer cables. The log raft had included some extra-long poles to use as uprights, and it wasn't long before Kenmore's homemade pile driver was up and running. By the end of October, all 140 piles had been pounded into place and work had begun on the framing for the four-inch thick concrete floor.

The company couldn't afford to have the 220' by 35' slab poured at one time, so Munro decided to pour the floor in sections. He knew his "pay-as-you-pour" plan would delay the construction schedule, but he didn't see that he had any other choice. Total income in October had been just under $5,000. Expenses had come to almost $4,000, leaving barely $1,000 to put toward the new building. The floor alone was going to cost almost $2,000. Then there was the framing, siding, roof trusses, and roofing material, to say nothing of the all hardware that would be needed to hold everything together. One of the Seabee owners, Clarence Black, had paid $250 advance rent on a stall in the new building, but even if all the other Seabee owners chipped in, too, it looked like the hangar would be a long time in the making.

The company received an unexpected financial boost in December. Despite losing his son as a result of Jack Mines' air-drop accident in the Cascades, George Yeaman was still a strong supporter of the Air Harbor. Knowing Munro was skating on thin financial ice, Yeaman suggested an issue of two-hundred new shares of company stock for which he would pay $2,000 cash. The offer was gratefully accepted, and the hangar floor was poured later that month.

The Air Harbor had another staunch supporter in Harold Nicholas, a successful greenhouse owner and keen aviation enthusiast who lived in the tiny farming community of Hollywood, east of Kenmore. The flower business took Nicholas into Seattle several times a week, and from his vantage point on the highway along the top of the bluff, he observed with growing interest the seaplane activity at Gus Newburg's old mill site. One day he decided to find out first hand what was going on, and he turned off across the railroad tracks and down the dirt road that led to the Air Harbor office.

Nicholas and Munro hit it off right away. It wasn't long before the flower entrepreneur had purchased his own Seabee, but his interest in Munro's operation extended far beyond that of a normal customer. In Munro, Nicholas saw a man who approached his work from a position of total integrity; if Bob Munro said he was going to do something, you could bet everything you owned that he would do it. Nicholas also knew about banks. He had experienced first hand the skepticism with which they view a new business, and he could visualize the raised eyebrows over a new business involving seaplanes, an aviation oddity if there ever was one. A bank wants to loan money on a sure thing. Buying a half-rotten, clapped-out seaplane on the theory that it could be fixed up and sold for a profit wouldn't sound like a sure thing to a bank, but it did to Harold Nicholas.

Kenmore Air Harbor, 1947. Ted Huntley has succeeded in clearing a substantial portion of the property, and the foundation for the new Seabee hangar is slowly being poured.

Nicholas understood something else, too. A bargain deal has to be acted on right away. During the time it takes to apply for a loan and wait for a decision, someone else will probably show up with the cash and walk off with the bargain. Knowing that Munro would get little help from the banks, Nicholas began making short term loans to the Air Harbor for the purchase of an airplane, or a set of floats, or whatever was needed to keep the business going. The loans were short term because Munro didn't like owing money to anyone for very long, especially his friends. He also insisted on paying Nicholas the going interest rate. Nicholas is a modest man, and he is quick to downplay the importance of his contribution to Kenmore's success. Munro, however, firmly believed the Air Harbor may well have folded during those first few years had it not been for the assistance of the flower grower from Hollywood.

Nicholas's first loan to Kenmore was for $4,000. Part of the money went to help complete the hangar, and part of it went for dirt. The ground under the converted Navy deck building was relatively firm, and the driveway into the office was holding up all right, but the rest of the property was still a bog. The ground oozed water whenever the lake rose, customers' cars got stuck, and it was impossible to keep the mud and cedar shavings out of the shop. Munro decided it was time to deal with the mess once and for all. He learned that a property owner across the highway had contracted to have the hillside on her land excavated to make the lot more attractive to commercial developers. There were about twelve-thousand cubic yards of prime soil to be hauled off, but the contractor who took the job wanted only half of it. Munro walked across the road and made a deal for the other half. The agreed-on price was thirty cents a yard, delivered, and Munro finally saw the bog Jack Mines had discovered a year and a half earlier become a firm, level, and relatively dry piece of property.

On December 19, 1947, Esther Mines announced her resignation from the company. An intelligent woman, she had been quick to learn the ins and outs of the flying business after her husband's death. But while she had done an excellent job of running the office and keeping the books, she did not share her late husband's passion for aviation. A humanitarian organization in Gatlinburg, Tennessee, had advertised for a new director, and when Esther heard about it from some of her sorority friends, she applied for the position and was accepted. Her last day at the Air Harbor would be December 31. She would, however, retain her majority stock holding in the company. Neil McConnell was elected to the board to fill Esther's position of Secretary, while a long-time friend of the Munro's, Norman Jacobson, was elected Treasurer.

Yellow and brown did not become Kenmore Air Harbor's official colors by virtue of an official decision. Bob Munro liked the colors General Petroleum had used on the roof of the metal hangar and nobody else had an opinion, so yellow and brown it was. Earlier in the year, just before Munro and Wardleigh took their "solo" cross country flight to Alaska, a friend from Munro's high school days dropped by the Air Harbor to see how things were going. Munro showed Harold Higgins the airplanes and the new hangar that was under construction, and they were back chatting in the office when Higgins had his idea.

"You need a logo," he said. "Here you've got a growing company, and the only identification you have is your name painted on top of a roof. You need something you can use in ads and put on stationary and jacket patches."

"A logo would be nice," Munro admitted, "but I don't think we can afford it."

"I'll do it for free," said Higgins. "I've already got some ideas."

Higgins had done some cartooning in school, and the design he came up with had a definite Walt Disney feel to it, with a smiling yellow duck perched atop a silver seaplane float. Higgins showed it off around the Air Harbor, and the employees immediately began demanding duck patches for their coveralls and jackets. Munro liked the design, too, and Kenmore Air Harbor had an official logo. It was printed on the company's stationery, painted on the sides of the company's airplanes, and patches were made available to employees at seventy-five cents apiece.

The mechanics sewing duck patches onto their coveralls never knew how close the duck had come to taking a fatal dive into oblivion. Were it not for a half-forgotten clause buried in a mass of fine print, Esther Mines' departure from the Air Harbor at the end of 1947 probably would have killed the company. When Lillian Mines had leased the mill site from Gus Newburg the year before, the agreement had included an option to purchase the property at the end of five years. Lillian had immediately turned around and leased the land to Kenmore Air Harbor, but her option to buy still stood.

Now, with Jack Mines dead and his widow about to leave for Tennessee, Lillian no longer had any personal reasons to see the seaplane base succeed. The town of Kenmore was growing by leaps and bounds, and Lillian was well aware that the land under the Air Harbor would soon be worth far more than the struggling business on top of it. Years later, Bob Munro said he had always believed that Lillian Mines would have exercised her option to purchase the land, after which she would have terminated the Air Harbor's lease and sold the mill site to a commercial developer for a substantial profit. From a purely business point of view, it would have been a sensible decision.

Fortunately for the hundreds of employees who have called Kenmore home and the hundreds of thousands of customers who have benefited from the company's philosophy of putting their satisfaction first, Lillian never got the chance to decide one way or the other. The half-forgotten clause buried in the fine print of Lillian's lease agreement gave Kenmore Air Harbor, Inc., the right to buy Lillian's five-year purchase option on the property. Lillian may have forgotten the clause, but Bob Munro and Durwood Alkire hadn't. After a suitable payment plan was worked out, Lillian had no choice but to sign over her purchase option to the Air Harbor. It's doubtful that Munro slept any easier; if anything, the pressure to generate sufficient business to cover expenses had just been increased. But along with the pressure came the satisfaction of knowing that Harold Higgins' little yellow duck had a permanent home.

NEVER A DULL MOMENT

THE BOOKKEEPER WHO TOOK OVER from Esther Mines wrote out eight salary checks on the fifteenth of January, 1948. Check number 805 went to Bill Fisk in the amount of $105.95. Number 806 went to Neil McConnell in the amount of $59.40. Bob Munro rarely took all that was owed him; check 809 was for only $63.70. The preceding check in the series went to a new-hire, a young man who was about to demonstrate that rebuilding an engine is not a skill, it's an art form. Check number 808 was made out to Walter H. Winseman.

As a kid growing up in Seattle, Winseman was forever fixing bicycles. He was not, however, fixing them to hone his mechanical skills. He was fixing them so he could go fishing. Fishing is Winseman's life; his career as a mechanic he views as being merely a legal method of supporting his steelhead habit. His reaction to the mountains of praise heaped upon him by anyone fortunate enough to fly behind, or in the case of the Seabee, under one of his engines is a shrug of the shoulders.

"It paid for the fishing," he says.

By 1940, he had graduated from going fishing on a bicycle to going fishing in a car, although the car seemed to need every bit as much maintenance as the bike. The Army called him up in 1943 and sent him to Fresno, California for basic training, after which he was given a battery of tests to determine what he'd be good at.

> "I figured I'd be digging foxholes or something, but I told them a bunch of b.s. about changing transmissions and rear ends on my car and on other people's cars, so they decided I was a mechanic and they put me in the Air Corps."
>
> **WALT WINSEMAN**

The first thing the Air Corps told Winseman to do was to take the train to Texas and enroll in the Dallas Aviation Air College on Love Field. Like the Edison School back in Seattle, the civilian-run Aviation Air College was supporting the war effort by teaching basic engine maintenance to the military's new recruits. Winseman and aircraft engines got along right from the start. His classes covered a broad range of topics, and much to his surprise, he remembered everything he was taught. In high school he'd had a tendency to forget everything his teachers said within minutes of their saying it, but at the Air College there wasn't a fact or a procedure about engine maintenance that he didn't retain.

His newly-acquired knowledge stood him in good stead when he was assigned to the Central Flying Training Command in Liberal, Kansas. Liberal was a B-24 base, and Winseman was supposed to help keep the boxy, four-engine bombers airworthy. He made an impression his first day on the job. A Liberator had come in on three engines, and Private Winseman was in the crew that was supposed to fix it. After poking around the bad engine for awhile, the Master Sergeant in charge of the crew announced his verdict.

"One of the magnetos is shot. We'll pull the engine off and send it down to the depot for repair."

Private Winseman raised his hand. "I can put a new mag on it right here if you want."

The sergeant was skeptical. "You sure? It's a pretty complicated job."

Private Winseman was sure. He knew the sergeant was right; it was a complicated job requiring, among other things, the precise timing of a set of compensating gears; but in a couple of hours, Private Winseman had the B-24 ready for its next flight.

The Master Sergeant was impressed. It turned out that Winseman was the only one of his crew who actually had received formal maintenance training. Everyone else had been sent to the base straight from boot camp. Before long, whenever a B-24 needed engine work, be it a simple carburetor adjustment or an entire cylinder replacement, Private Winseman was the man to put on the job.

The Air Corps, true to form, transferred Winseman out of B-24 maintenance just about the time he became an expert at working on every system in the plane. He was sent instead to work on the B-29. In a way, this was understandable; the Air Corps was desperate to get the B-29 into action but was having nothing but trouble in the process. They needed every competent mechanic they could find just to get the planes ready to go overseas. The B-29 was the most complicated bomber in the world at the time it was built, and Winseman didn't care much for it.

> "It took only four men to work on a B-24, on the whole airplane. On the B-29, it took four men just to work on one engine. Everything on the B-24 was hydraulic. The B-29 was electric, and that caused all kinds of problems. They had gas tanks that went in the forward bomb bay to give the plane more range. The tanks would dribble gas once in a while, and the bomb bay would fill up with fumes. There was a big electric motor in there, I think it was a hydraulic pump for the brakes or something, and it would spark when it came on. If you had a bad gas leak, well, people on the ground would wonder why the plane blew up."
>
> **WALT WINSEMAN**

Despite his dislike of Boeing's new Superfortress, Winseman tackled his B-29 assignment with the same degree of professionalism he'd demonstrated on the B-24. On at least one occasion, his addiction to detail saved a B-29 and its eleven-man crew from probable destruction. After performing some routine maintenance on one of a B-29's Wright R-3350 engines, Winseman requested that the fuel system be pressurized before the cowling was replaced. Most people didn't bother with this test, but Winseman wanted it done. As he felt around behind the engine to check the fuel line one last time, his hand encountered a fine mist. A fitting had cracked, and high-octane fuel was spraying over the rear of the engine. The Wrights ran extremely hot; the turbo-superchargers mounted on either side of the 2,200-horsepower engine literally glowed red. If the fuel leak had gone undetected, there is no question that an engine fire would have been the result. Engine fires were the Achilles heel of the B-29; in the early days of the program an engine fire generally resulted in the loss of the plane.

When the B-29s at the base were up flying there wasn't much for Winseman and his fellow mechanics to do, so they were put to work picking up cigarette butts and scraps of paper and "moving rocks from one place to another." This was not Winseman's idea of how to spend an afternoon, so when the Operations Officer asked for volunteers to fly as observers on check-out and training flights, Winseman signed up. His position was usually in one of the gunsight blisters in the waist where he could monitor the flaps and landing gear and watch the rear of the engine cowlings for fuel and oil leaks. He may not have enjoyed working on the B-29, but he had no complaints about flying in them.

> "You'd just about freeze to death in a B-17 or a B-24. The B-29 was heated and pressurized and was just about the most comfortable airplane I ever rode in. It wasn't until later that we learned that the waist blisters we were sitting in sometimes blew out at 30,000 feet or so, and any nearby crewmembers would get sucked out the hole if they weren't tied down. Nobody told us about it, so we just sat in the blisters happy as you please with no harness or parachute or nothin'."

WALT WINSEMAN

When Winseman was discharged after the war he figured he'd apply for a mechanic's position at one of the airlines. But the airlines were hiring only licensed mechanics, so he decided to enroll in the Airframe and Engine course at the Edison Trade School, the same school at which Bob Munro had taught engine maintenance to raw recruits in 1942. Winseman wasn't particularly interested in sheet metal and wood repair or learning to splice control cables, so the airframe part of the course was a bit of a struggle. When it came to engines, however, it was a different story. Winseman found himself practically teaching the class thanks to his extensive, hands-on experience in the Air Corps.

One of his classmates was a young mechanic named Danny Marx. Marx knew that Winseman had his hopes set on an airline career, but he persuaded his friend to take a drive to the north end of Lake Washington and check out a place called Kenmore Air Harbor. Marx had been working at Kenmore since the previous June, and he knew Bob Munro was thinking about adding another mechanic. Marx had never met anyone who knew as much about engines as Winseman, and he thought the former B-29 mechanic would be exactly what Munro and Tom Wardleigh were looking for. He was right, and Winseman hired on at $200 a month.

Munro got him just in time. The number of Seabees on the property was growing rapidly. Word of the fun the owners were having with their rugged little amphibians was spreading, and more and more people wanted to get in on the action. Even though the plane had been out of production for months, they were still available. Friends of Jim Campbell, Bob Dent, and Clarence Black began buying Seabees out of state and flying them back. Campbell even bought a Seabee sight-unseen in North Dakota, and after Bob Munro had flown it home they sold it for a profit and split the proceeds. By the end of the year, there would be thirty-six privately owned Seabees based at the Air Harbor. Looked at one way, this meant thirty-six monthly tie down fees and fuel payments flowing into the Air Harbor's bank account. Looked at another way, it meant thirty-six temperamental Franklin engines and thirty-six unreliable propeller mechanisms that somehow had to be kept functioning.

By this time, Tom Wardleigh had a pretty good handle on repairing the Seabee's pitch-change mechanism, and Bill Fisk had become something of an expert at reconditioning the propeller itself. The fiber blades had a tendency to swell up over time to the point where they would no longer rotate in their bearings to change pitch. When he wasn't giving flying lessons, Fisk could be found at a little bench in the shop where he would turn down the base of each blade, fit new collars, recondition the bearings, dress and balance the blades, and set the proper pitch angles.

On the other hand, no one at the Air Harbor, or anywhere else in the country for that matter, was particularly eager to tackle the Seabee's Franklin engine. The Franklin was extremely intolerant of improper servicing; if everything wasn't set up just right, it would reward its owner by deciding suddenly to wear out and die.

Winseman had hired on as a general mechanic, which meant he was as likely to find himself pumping gas and washing windshields as he was to find himself working in the shop. It wasn't long, though, before it became obvious that Kenmore's new mechanic not only could work on engines, he actually *understood* them. The Franklin had met its match. Compared to the complicated, oil-guzzling Wrights on the B-29, the Seabee's engine was a walk in the park. Winseman didn't like the Franklin any more than he'd liked the Wright, but he took pride in his ability to make the quirky engine behave.

"The Franklin was a hard engine to get your hands into. Nobody really understood it. It was made different than most airplane engines. Things were pressed together and the tolerances had to be just right. There were two different models of engine cases and about four different models of camshafts. If you put the wrong cam in the wrong case, there would be a clearance problem. The engine had hydraulic valve followers and they had to be bled down just right before you could adjust the valves. The Franklin was full of little things like that that you just had to know."

WALT WINSEMAN

With a growing, active group of Seabee owners on the property, Munro and his mechanics were becoming more familiar with the Seabee every day, and it wasn't long before they began making improvements. One of the first changes they made was to the control cables. To help keep the Seabee's purchase price as low as possible, Republic had used regular steel cables to connect the yoke and rudder pedals to the control surfaces. This arrangement might have been satisfactory in Minnesota and the Great Lakes region, but in the harsh salt environment of Puget Sound, it didn't take long for the cables to rust. The rusting cables caused a lot of problems, but the last straw came during a flight Bill Fisk made to Friday Harbor in the San Juan Islands. Unknown to Fisk, the elevator cables in the Seabee he was flying had rusted almost completely through. As he climbed away from the harbor to start his return flight to Kenmore, there was a twang from somewhere back in the tail section, and the yoke flopped limply into his lap.

Quick thinking and the coordinated use of throttle and elevator trim were all that kept Fisk and his passengers from becoming statistics. Fisk has always prided himself on the smoothness of his landings, but with no direct elevator control, he had to be content with whatever landing he could manage to get. The touchdown was hard, but it wasn't anything the Seabee's hull couldn't handle, and Fisk taxied back to the dock to telephone Munro and wait for the rescue party. Examination of the other Seabees parked at the Air Harbor revealed that the plane Fisk had been flying was not the only one with disintegrating control cables.

The solution was obvious; replace the airplane's original cables with cables made of rust-resistant stainless steel. It wasn't long before every Seabee on the property had a set of Kenmore's new, stainless steel control cables, and as the word got out, orders began coming in from as far away as Florida and Alaska. Wardleigh was enthusiastic.

"This modification business could become a big thing for us," he told Munro. "Think of all the Seabee owners out there who could use our cable kits."

Munro was not quite as optimistic. He was too smart not to take advantage of every opportunity that presented itself, but at this point Kenmore's future seemed to lie more in the flight school and the maintenance shop.

"We'll sell a few of them," he agreed, "but I wouldn't bank on modifications becoming a big part of our business."

Seabee mod number two involved the wing. As built, the Seabee had a relatively short, stubby wing. A number of Seabee owners were positive the plane would perform better with a longer wing, so someone decided to find out. Building a new wing from scratch was economically out of the question, so an enterprising designer came up with a wingtip extension instead. The two-foot extensions would add a total of four feet to the Seabee's wingspan. Kenmore ordered a pair, and after Wardleigh and his mechanics installed them, Munro took the plane up for a test flight.

"How do they work?" Wardleigh asked after Munro and the modified Seabee had clattered back up the ramp into the parking area.

"It does everything better." Munro hopped to the ground and walked out to the end of the wing to see how the extension had fared during the flight. "It took off better, it climbed better, it was more stable in cruise. It didn't seem to affect the speed much. Republic should have built them this way in the first place."

A thorough examination of the extensions convinced Munro and Wardleigh that they were every bit as strong as the rest of the wing. The news spread quickly, and Kenmore's mechanics were soon installing wing extensions as fast as the manufacturer could turn them out. Eventually, every Seabee in the area had been modified, and like the Air Harbor's stainless steel cable kits, orders began coming in from all over the country. Munro began to think maybe there was something to this modification business after all.

Out in the shop, Walt Winseman was starting to see a lot of cracked oil coolers. The cooler, a square device mounted on top of the Seabee's engine, was subject to a tremendous amount of vibration. Eventually, the vibration and harmonics would take their toll, and the cooler would crack, covering the engine with oil and making a general mess under the cowling. Worse yet, a cooler occasionally broke off during flight, starving the engine of oil and giving the pilot an unwanted opportunity to polish his emergency landing technique.

Munro discovered the solution on a World War II basic trainer. The radial-engined BT-13, disparagingly referred to as the "Vultee Vibrator" by the students who had to endure it, had used a a much more robust cooler than the flimsy thing Republic had stuck on the Seabee. Munro brought one back to the Air Harbor, and Winseman engineered and built a mount for it. The BT-13 cooler showed no inclination to crack even after being subjected to hundreds of hours of vibration. Kenmore added the cooler and Winseman's new mount to their growing list of modification kits, and Seabee owners had one less problem to worry about.

Jim Campbell provided the solution to another Seabee design flaw. Knowing the Franklin engine's propensity to overheat, he enlisted the aid of some friends from the University of Washington's aeronautics department to help improve the air flow over the cylinders. Because there was no propeller up front to blow cooling air over the engine, the Seabee's Franklin was equipped with a cooling fan. Campbell's engineering buddies discovered that most of the air entering the front of the cowling slammed into the flat face of the flywheel and burbled around for awhile before eventually finding its way into the fan blades. Sending the air directly to the fan, they reasoned, would improve the flow of cooling air dramatically.

Campbell found the solution in a propeller spinner off a P-47. In what probably was just a happy coincidence, the spinner from the huge Republic fighter fit perfectly around the flywheel portion of the Seabee's cooling fan. Winseman figured out a way to attach it, and he also plugged up the weight reduction holes in the Franklin's engine mount. The holes had allowed cooling air to escape down around the bottom of the engine where it did absolutely no good whatsoever. Altogether, Campbell's modifications reduced the cylinder head temperatures of his engine by twenty degrees, and virtually eliminated the chance of valve problems caused by overheated and stretched cylinders.

By February 1948, the new Seabee hangar was well on its way to completion, but it was costing a lot more than had been anticipated. Once again, it was Harold Nicholas who came to the rescue, loaning Munro $8,000 to help finish the hangar. The winter was shaping up to be a harsh one, and the Seabee owners who had signed up for bays in the new hangar were anxious to get their planes inside. Munro knew the winter was going to be tough when he walked out of his house one morning to find that Lake Washington had frozen solid out to about a hundred yards offshore. He was down by the ramp trying to determine the thickness of the ice when Wardleigh and Fisk showed up for work. The winter sun was low in the sky and Wardleigh shielded his eyes against the glare.

"Doesn't look like there's going to be much flying today, does it?" he observed.

Fisk kicked at the ice encrusting the shoreline. "If it went farther out into the lake, I bet I could take off and land from it."

Munro shook his head. "It's not thick enough for that. I'm afraid if we put a plane out there the ice will shatter and rip up the floats. We'd better wait and see what happens. Maybe it will warm up and the ice will disappear."

It didn't. The temperature remained well below freezing and the ice continued to build up in front of the Air Harbor. The water remained open, however, off the mouth of the Sammamish Slough, a quarter of a mile away down the eastern shore. In its day, the slough had seen a lot of traffic as Lake Washington's little fleet of lake steamers ferried picnickers and summer cottage owners to and from Lake Sammamish. The steamer traffic halted abruptly on August 28, 1916, when the temporary gates keeping Lake Washington out of the newly-dug Montlake Cut were opened. The subsequent nine-foot drop in water level barred the slough to everything but salmon and the occasional canoeist, and the steamers were reduced to ferrying school children and commuters between Mercer Island and the trolley car stop at Leschi. The slough still flowed, however, and the sluggish current moving out into the lake was just enough to keep the water from freezing.

A day or two after the ice had appeared, Munro announced his decision. "We'll operate from the open water in front of the slough. The ice is thick enough for us to taxi the planes across in the morning and bring them back at night. Students and customers can drive around to the river mouth and we'll fly them from there."

The arrangement proved satisfactory, but Bill Fisk wanted to work a little closer to home. It was hard to stay warm over by the slough, and getting a hot cup of coffee from the pot brewing in the office meant a long, slippery trek across the ice. The ice was several inches thick by now and extended a good ways out into the lake. Fisk couldn't see any reason not to land on it, so at the end of his next flight, he did. Using the solidly frozen channel beside the property as a runway, he touched down as close to shore as the surrounding buildings would allow and scooted out toward the open lake. It was like being on a pair of skates. Fisk didn't think the plane was ever going to stop but he finally ran into some small snowdrifts and the Taylorcraft crunched to a halt.

The next step was to turn around and head back to base. The water rudders were useless, so Fisk pushed the air rudder clear to the stop and revved up the engine. The results were not what he'd hoped for. The plane began to turn, but it also began to skitter across the ice at an alarming rate of acceleration. It didn't take but a second for Fisk to realize he was going to run out of ice long before he got himself turned around. His only option was to shut down, get out, and aim the plane back toward the base by hand.

The lightweight Taylorcraft was easy enough to manhandle around on the slippery ice, and Fisk and his student scrambled back in for the short taxi back to the Air Harbor. Munro was concerned about damage to the floats, but they appeared to be no worse for wear after Fisk's smooth touchdown and slide across the frozen lake surface.

"I'm going to try a takeoff," Fisk announced after his student had disembarked. "If that works, we can start flying from here instead of taking the planes clear across to the slough."

Munro told him to be careful, but Fisk was too excited to pay much attention. A cautious pilot by nature, he nevertheless enjoyed doing things no one had attempted before. Flying off the ice was an accepted practice in Alaska, but no one at Kenmore had ever done it and Fisk was eager to be the first. He taxied the Taylorcraft as far up the channel as he could, shut off the engine, and turned the plane around with the help of one of the mechanics. The plane began to move almost as soon as the mechanic had propped the engine back to life. Fisk opened the throttle and the Taylorcraft zipped off across the ice toward the lake. With virtually no friction holding it back, the plane reached flying speed in seconds. Fisk eased back on the yoke and the Taylorcraft lifted smoothly off the ice and climbed briskly through the cold, dense air above the lake. The landing was just as smooth, and once again, examination showed no damage to the floats.

Munro tried it himself, but after landing he decreed that students could fly off the ice only when accompanied by an instructor.

"It's not difficult," he said after he'd taxied back to shore, "but you have to be careful to keep the plane going in a straight line after you land. If it gets at all sideways and you hit a patch of rough ice, it could bang up the float keels pretty bad."

Once they'd gotten used to it, Munro and Fisk didn't think flying off the ice was any big deal, but the local newspaper did. The editor of the *Seattle Times* heard about Kenmore's ice flights, and thinking there might be a good picture in it, sent photographer Harold Hill out to the Air Harbor. Hill trudged out onto the ice with his big press camera and waited while Bill Fisk maneuvered one of the company's Taylorcrafts into position. Fisk opened the throttle and zoomed across the ice toward Hill, who pressed the shutter release just as the Taylorcraft lifted into the air. The *Times* ran the picture the next day, and while it brought Kenmore some welcome publicity, it marked the beginning of a sequence of events that still brings a blush of embarrassment to Tom Wardleigh's cheeks.

Wardleigh had joined a flying club so he could build hours toward his commercial license. None of the members had much flying experience; like Wardleigh, they were looking for an inexpensive way to build time. The club owned one airplane, a seventy-five horsepower Luscombe 8A on floats. The little two-seater was economical to fly, but it met its end when one of the club members crashed it in the mountains while dropping supplies to a bunch of hikers. The circumstances were similar to the ones that had killed Jack Mines, but this time the culprit was a sack of supplies.

The pilot had wrapped the supplies in duffel bags and piled them on the passenger seat. Just as the pilot threw out the first bag the pile collapsed. One of the bags fell forward and wedged the control stick up against the instrument panel. With the stick jammed all the way forward, the plane nosed over immediately. Fortunately, the pilot had the presence of mind to pull the power off and jerk one of the duffel bags up in front of his face before the plane hit. The pilot walked away unharmed, but the sleek little Luscombe was totaled. Determined to get back into the air, the club members passed the hat and scraped together enough money to buy a used Taylorcraft.

Bill Fisk landing on the ice in front of the base in February 1948. Munro decreed that students could fly off the ice only in the company of an instructor. Note the lack of doors on the Navy deck building that served as the company's maintenance hangar. It was almost as cold working inside as it was outside.

Ralph Woodrig was a University of Washington student and a mountain climber who one day had decided it would be an interesting challenge to learn to fly. He got his Private license at Kenmore and then joined the flying club. Woodrig was an adventuresome sort, and shortly after the photograph of Fisk's frozen water takeoff appeared in the paper, Woodrig decided it would be fun to do the same thing. Without telling anyone what he was going to do he fired up the club's Taylorcraft and skittered out onto the ice. By the time Wardleigh realized what was going on it was too late; all he could do was watch as his fellow club member accelerated off through the snow drifts. It was one thing for an experienced pilot like Bill Fisk to fly off the ice, but it was something else entirely for a low-time rookie to try it, putting not only his life but the club's only airplane at risk. No one at Kenmore had ever seen Wardleigh so angry. The normally calm shop foreman paced up and down in front of the hangar as he waited for Woodrig to return.

Wardleigh stopped pacing long enough to watch the Taylorcraft make a tentative but safe landing on the ice in front of the Air Harbor. When it was apparent that Woodrig had the situation under control, Wardleigh turned and disappeared into the shop. He reappeared a few minutes later with a hammer. Without a word, he strode over to the Taylorcraft which by now had been taxied to the ramp and shut down. Jumping onto one of the floats, he raised the hammer and proceeded to bash the Plexiglas windshield to smithereens.

"There," he said when he was finished. "That'll stop it. There won't be any fools flying off the ice now, that's for sure."

Wardleigh regretted his outburst almost as soon as the sound of it died away across the lake. He had a deep concern for aviation safety, a concern that ultimately would lead to an impressive career with the FAA. But no amount of concern, in his opinion, could justify what he had just done. The next day he ordered a new windshield for the club's Taylorcraft, and when it arrived he paid for and installed it himself.

Dealing with icy runways become a way of life for Wardleigh when he moved to Alaska in 1951, but there was a moment early in his Kenmore career when it seemed frozen water literally was going to be the death of him. Flying off the open lake in front of the Sammamish Slough was better than not flying at all, but it was inconvenient. Flying off the ice next to the Air Harbor was exciting, but there was the risk of damaging the floats. The ideal situation was to have open water right up to the dock, and Munro knew how to get it. One day, after a spell of cold weather had iced up the lake again, Munro fired up the weapons carrier and rumbled off to visit a local construction company. He drove back down the driveway an hour later with a case of dynamite and a coil of fuse on the seat beside him.

"What's that for?" Wardleigh asked as Munro cradled the wooden box in his arms and began picking his way across the slippery parking area to the dock.

"We're going to make our own channel through the ice."

Wardleigh wasn't sure this was such a good idea. "Have you ever done this before?"

"We used dynamite all the time at the gold mine. If it'll move rock, it'll move ice."

Munro went on to explain his plan. Starting at the outside edge of the shelf of ice rimming the lake, he and Wardleigh would punch a hole in the ice with a couple of pry bars. Munro would cut a fuse long enough to give both men enough time to light it, shove the dynamite into the hole, and scamper to safety. The explosion would shatter the ice, and Munro and Wardleigh would go back out and repeat the process a little closer to shore. The ice would drift out into the lake, and before long Kenmore would have a nice, clear channel from the ramp out to deep water.

Wardleigh remained skeptical, although it was obvious Munro knew exactly what he was do-ing. The first explosion went off without a hitch, and Wardleigh trudged back onto the ice behind Munro to help prepare the next charge. It was spooky, standing out there bashing a hole with the pry bars while all around them the ice creaked and groaned in protest. Munro cut the fuse and stuck it into the top of the next charge.

"Here," he said, handing the dynamite to Wardleigh. "You can light it this time."

Wardleigh set the stick down on the ice and stretched the fuse out full length. The last thing he wanted to do was accidentally light the fuse at the halfway mark. Munro had picked up the pry bars and was almost to the dock when Wardleigh touched a match to the end of the fuse. As the thick, waxy string began to sputter and hiss evilly on the ice, Wardleigh gingerly picked up the stick and shoved it into the hole. He stood up, took two steps toward shore, and crashed through the ice up to his armpits. The shock of the icy water was like a hammer blow. He struggled to pull himself out but there was nothing to grab on to. He forced himself to relax for a moment to assess the situation but a whiff of acrid smoke reminded him that relaxation was a luxury he couldn't afford. A quick glance over his shoulder showed that the fuse had burned almost halfway to the dynamite. He resumed his frantic struggle to get out, but it was a futile effort; he couldn't get any leverage with his legs and there was nothing for his fingers to grip on the slick surface of the ice.

Munro had turned around just in time to see Wardleigh plunge through the ice beside the lit charge. His first instinct was to run out to help, but he immediately realized that if Wardleigh could break through the ice, he could, too. His eyes swept the dock and came to rest on the ladder Ted Huntley used to wash windshields and fuel airplanes. Munro threw the ladder onto the ice and shoved it out to where Wardleigh could get a grip on it. Digging his heels into the ice, Munro pulled as hard as he could on the ladder. For a moment nothing happened, and then two things happened at once. Wardleigh flipped out of the hole and skittered across the ice toward Munro, and the dynamite went off.

"Are you okay?" Munro asked as a rain of muddy water and ice particles crashed down on their heads.

"I think so," Wardleigh replied. He brushed the ice out of his hair. "I wouldn't care to repeat the performance, however. That was too close for comfort."

"Yes, it was," Munro agreed. "I'll add another ten seconds to the fuses."

By March 1948, there were thirty-two students enrolled in the flight school. Twenty were working toward their Private license while twelve had advanced to the Commercial course. The advent of the GI Bill Commercial course presented Munro with a bit of a problem: the company didn't have an advanced airplane for the students to fly. The simple Taylorcrafts and Pipers were sufficient for practicing maneuvers, but part of the Commercial requirement was flight time in a so-called advanced airplane. The opportunity to acquire one arose when Henry Serrie decided to sell his old Fairchild Model 24. In its day, the four-place Model 24 had been considered quite a performer. The most powerful version of the plane used an inverted, in-line Ranger engine that developed 175 horsepower. Other versions of the Model 24 came with Warner radials of either 165 or 145 horsepower. Serrie's airplane had the smaller radial.

Serrie wasn't asking a lot for his airplane and he was willing to carry the financing himself. The only drawback to the deal was that the airplane was on wheels; it wouldn't do Kenmore's Commercial students much good unless Munro could find a pair of floats to put under it. A telephone search turned up a pair of EDO Model 2880 floats in Maine. The seller swore they were in great shape, so Munro ordered them. After a lengthy and circuitous journey that had railroads sending tracers all over the country, the boxcar from Maine finally showed up on the siding behind the cement plant. Munro, Wardleigh, and Ted Huntley grabbed some pry bars and walked over to uncrate the Fairchild's new floats. As the boards screeched apart under the pry bars, it became obvious that the seller's idea of "great shape" was a lot different than Kenmore's. The floats were pretty beat up. Still, they seemed seaworthy, so they were hauled back to the shop where the worst of the wrinkles and dents were repaired. The Fairchild was hauled out to the Air Harbor on a trailer, and the flight school had its advanced airplane.

Munro also used the plane for charters, but in this service it had a major disadvantage. The Fairchild was comfortable and fast, but with a full load of four people and fuel the thing went nearly all the way to Sand Point before its little engine got it going fast enough to get off the water. Eventually Walt Winseman replaced the engine with a 165-hp radial from a Cessna Airmaster that had been caught in a hangar fire, and Munro's takeoff visits to Sand Point were over.

Island Air's Norseman, NC55555. The plane would eventually be acquired by Kenmore and used on the Leduc Glacier airlift.

Not so the Island Airways Norseman. Every day their big Dodge limousines would trundle down to the dock, and the passengers for Friday Harbor, Eastsound, and Roche Harbor would pile out and clamber up the ladder into the cavernous fuselage. When everyone was seated, Ted Huntley would tail the silver and red plane out from the dock, and the pilot would crank up the six-hundred horsepower radial. After taxiing around for awhile to bring the cylinder heads up to temperature, the pilot would point the Norseman south and open the throttle. A shattering roar would ricochet off the hills, and NC55555 would charge off toward Arrowhead Point, its propeller kicking up a monstrous roostertail of spray. The roostertail would disappear around the point, but Huntley could follow the plane's progress by the sound booming back up the lake.

Takeoff invariably occurred only a few hundred yards from Sand Point. The engine had a one-minute time limit on the use of full power, so Huntley always knew the moment the floats had left the water by the sound of the pilot's power reduction. A few minutes later, Five-Five would reappear, surprisingly low for the amount of time it had been gone. The Norseman would thunder up the lake, its pilot coaxing every possible inch of altitude out of the straining engine. Then came Huntley's most exciting moment as the huge machine roared past the Kenmore dock and disappeared over the hill behind the bluff.

What was exciting to young Ted Huntley was pretty nerve-wracking to everyone else, especially the Island Airways pilot. The Norseman's performance was terrible. The takeoff runs were so long passengers began to joke about *cruising* to the San Juans on Island Airways instead of flying. The climb rate was pathetic, so much so that it was questionable on each flight whether the plane would actually clear the hill behind the Air Harbor.

Tom Wardleigh and his mechanics checked everything and found nothing. The compression in each of the nine cylinders was within tolerance. The engine revved properly. The propeller settings were correct. The flaps worked perfectly. The rigging of the wings, tail surfaces, and floats matched the manufacturer's specifications. The floats weren't full of water; Huntley pumped them dry every morning. There was no reason for the plane not to perform as advertised. Yet day after day, it pounded its way clear to Sand Point on takeoff and barely missed the hill on the way back.

The only answer seemed to be that the Norseman was simply an overrated dog of an airplane, but Munro wasn't buying it. After all, Albert Almosolino had done very well with his Norseman until he'd crashed it into Lake Union. As Munro pondered the problems Island Airways was having with their plane, it occurred to him that no one had bothered to remove the float compartment access plates. He could understand why; the access plates on the big EDO Model 7170 floats were a pain in the neck to take off, and Huntley's daily workouts with the bilge pump had made it obvious that the floats weren't taking on much water. Still, Munro decided it wouldn't hurt to take a look.

Armed with the special tools needed for the job, Munro, Wardleigh, and Huntley set about removing the first plate. A few minutes later, they found themselves staring into a bathtub. The float compartment was at least half full of water. Munro and Wardleigh looked at Huntley. Huntley had seen that look before.

"I pumped this out this morning. Honest. I pumped out every compartment. I got maybe two squirts of water from each compartment and that's all."

Munro and Wardleigh moved to the next compartment and removed its access plate. If anything, there was more water in this compartment than in the previous one.

"I swear, I pumped this float out this morning." Huntley said defensively. "I got two squirts of water, maybe three, before the pump went dry."

Munro and Wardleigh moved down the float to the next plate. Huntley peered anxiously over their shoulders as they removed the last fastener and shoved the plate aside. The watery reflections visible through the open hatch showed this compartment to be at least half full, as well.

"Two or three squirts, that's all I ever get out of them," Huntley said miserably. "I don't know where all this water came from." They'd fire him for sure, he reckoned. He'd obviously been using the pump incorrectly for months. All those endless takeoff runs and near-collisions with the hill, they'd all been his fault. He watched dejectedly as Munro and Wardleigh systematically removed the remaining access plates. Every compartment in both floats was flooded with water. A couple of times one of the men would reach down through the access hatch and Huntley could hear his hand swishing around in the water which he, Huntley, was supposed to have pumped out.

When they were done, Munro and Wardleigh gathered up the access plates and stepped to the dock. Huntley figured he'd like at least to know the cause of his dismissal.

"How'd I miss pumping out all that water?"

"You didn't," Wardleigh answered. "You couldn't have pumped it out if you'd wanted to."

Huntley looked perplexed. "What do you mean, I couldn't have pumped it out?"

"The plane was probably sitting a long time before Island Airways bought it," Munro explained, "and the floats filled up with water. It could have leaked in or rainwater could have run in. Then in the winter, the water froze and cracked the aluminum pump-out tubes. Now you come along and put your pump in the top of the tube to suck out the water, but instead of pulling the water from the bottom of the float, you only get suction as far down as the crack."

"You'd pump out the little bit of water that had leaked in during the night and then you'd get air," Wardleigh added. "You'd think you were taking the water out of the bottom of the compartment but you weren't."

"I wouldn't be surprised if there's a ton of water in those floats," Munro said. "No wonder the darned thing can't climb."

Munro, Wardleigh, and a couple of the mechanics worked late into the evening to remove the water from each of the float compartments and install new pump-out tubes. It was a different airplane that took off for the San Juans the next morning. Freed of its burdensome load of stagnant water, the old Norseman fairly leapt into the air. Ted Huntley watched from the dock as the plane climbed out past Arrowhead Point and circled back to the north. He was glad they'd found the problem, and gladder still that it hadn't been his fault. Still, as he watched Five-Five drone high over the Air Harbor on its way to the islands, he found himself missing that thundering struggle for altitude that had brought the excitement and power of flight so low over his head every day.

SEABEE CENTRAL

I SLAND AIRWAYS DIDN'T ENJOY THEIR airplane's new-found performance for long. In a prelude to the chaos that would devastate the U.S. airline industry forty years later, mounting expenses and cutthroat competition took their toll, and Island Airways filed for bankruptcy in April 1948.

Munro was left holding $300 worth of unpaid maintenance bills. Big outfits like Pan American and United spilled that much in coffee on the carpet every day, but to Kenmore Air Harbor, $300 was a significant chunk of income. Munro attempted to put a lien on the Island Airways Norseman but he was thwarted by the bank, which declared that a lien could not be applied until the airplane's mortgage was paid off. Munro wasn't too worried; the plane was sitting on Kenmore's property and couldn't be moved without his consent. Still, it was an aggravating situation.

On the plus side of the balance sheet, April enrollment in the flying school climbed to forty-five students as the post-war fascination with flying reached its peak. Bill Fisk and the part-time instructors were in the air constantly, but it was a frustrating business. Few of the students who started flight training actually finished the course. Jobs, school, or family pulled them away, and it wasn't long before their abandoned and forgotten logbooks filled the shelves in Kenmore's tiny office to overflowing. Ruth Munro couldn't bring herself to throw them out, so she started packing them away in apple boxes on the outside chance a former student might show up and want to continue his lessons. She can't remember anyone ever coming back, but the apple boxes are still safely tucked away just in case.

April also saw the completion of the Seabee hangar, and eight happy owners promptly rolled their amphibians into the bays and began paying rent. Jim Campbell was one of them. For years his University Chevrolet Seabee occupied Stall Number 2 on the west side of the building. The Seabee gang had already started planning the first of their summer fly-ins, and it wasn't long before weekends at the Air Harbor took on the atmosphere of a county fair as planes full of kids and parents and picnic baskets waddled down the ramp and took off to explore the beaches of Hood Canal and the San Juan Islands.

The Island Airways situation finally resolved itself when the bank foreclosed on the company's mortgage and seized its assets. One of the first things they did was pay the $300 maintenance tab the airline had run up at the Air Harbor. The next thing they did was put the Norseman up for sale. It was purchased by a Mr. Ken Armstrong who was sure he could make money with it. Ted Huntley had enjoyed servicing a "real" airplane, and he was sorry to see the Norseman leave. Neither he nor anyone else at Kenmore had any idea that the NC55555 would one day return to become one of the most famous planes in the company's history.

Bob Munro fueling a company Taylorcraft.

Munro had watched the rise and fall of Island Airways with interest. It confirmed his feeling that the local seaplane market was pretty much limited to flight instruction and airplane repair, with a few dollars to be made from the occasional airplane sale and a smattering of charter flights. It's not surprising, then, that he was somewhat skeptical when Noel Wien, recently retired from his Alaskan aviation endeavors, presented Kenmore's board of directors with a proposal to start an aerial photography and charter service in partnership with the Air Harbor. Wien's plan was to purchase a Seabee which he would then turn over to the Air Harbor in exchange for Kenmore stock. Kenmore could keep any revenue generated by the plane, but the company would have to guarantee Wien $200 a month plus four dollars an hour for his services as the Seabee's pilot.

Munro was not at all convinced this was a practical idea, but he agreed to try it. After all, Wien's aviation exploits had made him a living legend, and you don't tell a living legend that his idea probably won't work. Wien found a Seabee in Fargo, North Dakota, and he flew it out to Kenmore in September. Over the next two months the plane generated barely $500 in revenue, and the prospects for additional work were looking as gloomy as the approaching winter weather.

Munro tactfully suggested that perhaps Wien's time and abilities were being wasted under the current arrangement. Wien agreed, and the Seabee was sold.

A slightly more successful arrangement was one involving an enterprising aviation enthusiast named Howard Raleigh. Raleigh believed there was money to be made in expediting newspapers and small packages by air. If he'd had greater vision and a whole lot more capital, Raleigh might have beaten Federal Express to the punch by decades. As it was, his Speedair Delivery Service consisted of a hub and a single spoke, from Seattle out through the saltwater communities of Bremerton, Poulsbo, and Port Townsend to Port Angeles.

Every weekday afternoon, Bill Fisk cranked up the Speedair Seabee and headed west with bundles of the *Seattle Times* and boxes of automobile and appliance parts. If the passenger seat wasn't piled with packages, and if there weren't any planes to gas or windshields to wash, seventeen year old Ted Huntley often went along for the ride. Huntley had put all his wages and most of his spare time into earning his Private license, and now he was trying to build time toward a Commercial. Fisk occasionally let the teenager take the controls, but of more value was the weather and navigation knowledge Huntley extracted from the former bomber pilot.

Despite a growing number of customers, Speedair Delivery was rapidly going broke. Raleigh was paying Kenmore $100 a month for Bill Fisk's services, but the real problem was the Seabee's voracious appetite for parts and service. The airplane's battery finally deteriorated to the point where it would no longer turn over the engine, but Raleigh couldn't afford a new one. The engine had to be hand-propped at Kenmore before each flight, and then left running throughout the flight. Fisk didn't dare shut it down during his stops, because once the plane was in the water it was almost impossible for someone to get into a position where they could safely pull the propeller through to restart it.

One day, while Raleigh was bemoaning the fact it was costing him more to deliver a package than he could reasonably charge, Munro suggested a solution.

"I know of several people who are looking for a Seabee to buy. Why don't you sell yours and use our Aeronca Champ instead? It's reliable and inexpensive to run, and I'll make sure we give you a rate you can afford."

"I'll still have the expense of a pilot," Raleigh said. "Bill Fisk is good and he's worth every penny, but I just can't afford him anymore."

Munro had the solution to that, too. "Ted Huntley can fly the route. He's trying to build time toward his Commercial license and I know he'd jump at the chance to fly for you. As long as he doesn't carry any paying passengers, it's perfectly legal. We gave him a raise the other week to seventy-five cents an hour for pumping gas and baby-sitting the kids, so that's all you'd have to pay for his time."

Raleigh agreed to the idea, and Ted Huntley realized his dream of becoming a bush pilot. The Champ had dual controls, so Munro built a wooden box to cover the second control stick and provide a shelf for Speedair's packages. Every afternoon Huntley dutifully chugged out to Port Angeles with his load of newspapers and car parts. On the return trip, he'd drop into Dabob Bay

Kenmore Air Harbor circa 1950.

on Hood Canal and pick up a load of fresh oysters from Canterbury Farms. The next stop was Lake Union, where Ivar Haglund would meet the plane and cart the oysters off to his soon-to-be-famous seafood restaurant. From Lake Union, Huntley flew east over the Montlake Cut to Lake Washington, and then north past the Sand Point Naval Air Station back to Kenmore. As far as Huntley was concerned, flying for Speedair Delivery was the best education a young pilot with his eyes on the horizon could hope for.

"It was a great experience because I flew every day at the same time, rain, shine, sleet, or snow. I learned very rapidly to assess a situation and then make a decision. If the weather was real bad, I wouldn't go, but lots of times I'd get halfway out there and get socked in. Then I'd have to make a decision. Should I figure out an alternate route and keep going? Should I land and wait it out? Or should I turn around and try to get back to Kenmore? There wasn't anybody I could ask. I had to figure it out for myself. It was a super experience."

TED HUNTLEY

By the end of the year, Kenmore was the undisputed center of Seabee activity in North America. Each week seemed to bring at least one order for stainless steel control cables or wing extensions. Word of Walt Winseman's expertise with the Franklin engine was getting around, and out-of-state Seabee owners began shipping their engines to the Air Harbor for overhaul. Some of the local Seabee owners like Jim Campbell and Harold Nicholas purchased used Seabees in other parts of the country and had Munro fly them back, after which the planes were fixed up and sold. Kenmore usually received a sales commission on top of its shop repair bill, but the company often shared in the profits, as well. Payment was not always in dollars. One of the overhauled Seabees was sold to a Mr. Harvey Barnhill. Kenmore's share of the deal was $267.98, part of which was in the form of a car which was then sold to an Air Harbor employee.

The Seabee era was a happy one at the north end of Lake Washington. It was a simpler time, free from the complex airspace controls and aviation security requirements that would usher in the next century. The doctors, dentists, and professional men that comprised the Seabee gang were a diverse bunch, all of them brought together by a shared love of the northwest and the unique personalities of their airplanes. There were fly-ins and picnics in the San Juans, and overnight camp-outs on Vancouver Island. The Air Harbor employees were often invited to participate in these activities, and the Munros came to regard the Seabee owners more as family members than as customers.

The north end of the lake offered little in the way of playmates for young Leslie and Gregg Munro. New homes in the area were bringing more children to the community, but none of the growing neighborhoods were in the vicinity of the Air Harbor down at the bottom of the bluff next to the cement plant. Leslie did have one close friend, a girl about her age who's parents lived half a mile away at a fuel yard.

"We used to walk up and down the railroad tracks to see each other. Nowadays you would never let a small child do that, but our parents would telephone back and forth to make sure we were okay. Those were the days when parents didn't just jump in the car and drive you wherever you wanted to go. When Gregg and I started going to school, we'd catch the bus up on the highway and go to school in Bothell. Most of our friends lived over there, and here we were, a pretty long bus ride away. So we felt pretty isolated, growing up with no neighbor kids to play with."

LESLIE BANKS

Leslie and Gregg learned early steer clear of the docks and keep their distances from moving airplanes or vehicles. Still, familiarity breeds contempt, and Leslie was no exception. Her parents warned her repeatedly about the dangers that could befall her belongings if she left them lying about the property, but the warning went unheeded until the day a lumbering Seabee mashed her shiny new tricycle flat as the unsuspecting pilot maneuvered past the office on his way to the ramp. Leslie was devastated but her parents were unmoved. Perhaps now you've learned your lesson, they said, and her tearful demands for an immediate replacement were turned down. She could earn a new tricycle by helping out in the office, she was told, but until then she'd just have to walk.

Out in the flimsy red barn near the entrance to the property, Albert Almosolino finally finished rebuilding his Norseman. He, too, had witnessed the demise of Island Airways, and he knew the prospects for his Seattle to Bremerton operation didn't look much better. When he heard that Albert Ball was looking for a Norseman to use that summer in western Alaska, Almosolino offered his plane up for lease. Ball accepted, and Munro and Fisk flew the Norseman up the coast to Alaska and then out to Ball's operation at Dillingham near Bristol Bay.

Moving Almosolino's Norseman out of the barn solved Munro's newest problem: what to do with the Seabee carcasses that were beginning to pile up on the property. The Air Harbor had been started with the idea of providing airplane maintenance and flying lessons. Selling parts had not been part of the plan. Then a windstorm piled four Seabees into a heap at the Bellingham airport, and Kenmore was in the parts business.

Kenmore Air Harbor, 1948. The Seabee hangar has been finished, and the sturdy amphibians have become the dominant airplane at the base.

By the early 1990s, the Parts Department was ringing up in excess of three million dollars a year in sales, and its computerized inventory system listed everything from lock washers to impeccably rebuilt 450-horsepower radial engines. It didn't start out that way, though. When Munro heard about the Seabee pileup at Bellingham, he, Wardleigh, and Winseman piled into the weapons carrier and headed north in a haze of blue exhaust smoke to check it out. After pawing through the mess for an hour or so, they determined there were enough unbent pieces left to make one flyable Seabee. Further investigation revealed that the insurance companies carrying the policies on the planes had decided to write them off as total losses. Any offer on the Seabees would be a bonus as far as they were concerned.

Munro bought the wrecks for a song and had them trucked back to the Air Harbor. As the "new" Seabee began taking shape in the shop, the rejected pieces of the other three planes began piling up outside. As Ted Huntley watched the pile grow higher he could pretty much guess what his next seventy-five-cents-an-hour project would be. Loading the unwieldy, jagged-edged chunks of busted-up Seabee into the back of the weapons carrier and hauling them off to the dump was not a job he was looking forward to.

Seaplanes live in a tough environment. Wings and tails are bashed into pilings, fuselages and floats are scraped against docks, hull bottoms are torn open on rocky beaches, and corrosion gets into everything. With the Seabee out of production, the availability of spare parts was limited, and it wasn't long before the amphibian owners at Kenmore were rummaging through the remains of the Bellingham wrecks and asking Munro how much he wanted for this particular wing float fitting or that particular aileron hinge. Munro knew he could charge an arm and a leg for the parts; many of the Seabee owners were well-to-do and besides, he wouldn't be doing anything that wasn't already being done by just about every other parts supplier. But that wasn't the way things were going to be done at the Air Harbor. In Munro's eyes, charging more than something was worth was flat out unethical. Besides, the Seabee owners were his friends, and their continued friendship was a lot more important to him than their dollars.

On the other hand, Munro knew a good business opportunity when he saw it. As the owners scavenged parts, and the five, ten, and fifteen dollar payments began mounting up in the account books, it soon became evident that Kenmore was going to earn more from the wrecks than from the sale of the planes being assembled in the shop. The low purchase price of a used Seabee put it within the financial grasp of some amazingly incompetent pilots. Gear-down water landings, grossly overloaded takeoff attempts, and of course the inevitable engine failures assured a steady supply of bashed-up Seabees. The rigging skills needed to recover a flipped or sunk seaplane were not unlike those needed to build a fish trap or put together a dragline, and it wasn't long before Munro had the reputation of being the man to call if you had a Seabee that needed salvaging. On the plus side, the wrecks accumulating on the property ensured a fine supply of spare parts. On the downside, the growing pile was something of an eyesore.

Then Almosolino moved his Norseman out of the barn and the problem was solved. Orange crates were set up around the inside walls of the barn to serve as parts bins. Scrap wood left over from building the Seabee hangar was used to make a sturdy set of shelves, while a couple of upright apple boxes and a board made a dandy table. The large chunks of salvaged Seabee, the wings, hulls, and tails, were stacked up against the side of the barn. The smaller parts went up on the shelves or into the orange crates. Huntley, assisted by the other mechanics when they had the time, spent many an hour unbolting control cable pulleys and landing gear legs and cockpit fittings from the wrecks as they were hauled in and dumped next to the barn. It was a messy job. The barn occupied the last, unfilled section of the property, and the activity associated with unloading, stripping, and storing the wrecks kept the ground around the building in a perpetual state of ooze. Bill Fisk was appointed manager of Kenmore's new parts department, and the first thing he did was lay a row of heavy planks across the muck up to the front door.

Fisk's title of manager referred primarily to his relationship with the parts. Other than Huntley, squatting in the mud with his toolbox, Fisk didn't have a staff. Customer orders came through the office and were filled by Fisk himself, who once or twice a day would pedal the fifty yards to the barn on a bicycle and rummage through the orange crates until he found what he wanted. If the required part wasn't in the barn, he'd have Huntley or a mechanic pull it off one of the hulks outside.

In May 1949, Kenmore put a Seabee into service for themselves. Charter requests were on the increase, and the rugged Seabee with its spacious cabin offered advantages over even the re-engined Fairchild 24. Seattle-area sportsmen were becoming increasingly interested in British Columbia. Vancouver Island and the southwest mainland were dotted with lakes and rivers rumored to be teeming with trophy-size trout and steelhead, while the interior of the province was reportedly a moose-hunter's paradise. Munro applied to the Canadian government for permission to operate commercially across the border. The permits were extremely difficult to get, and Munro figured a small operation like Kenmore didn't stand much of a chance, but it wouldn't hurt to try. Much to his surprise, a permit was granted the following month, one of only a handful to be given out by the government in Ottawa. Kenmore's service to British Columbia began that same month, and it continues to this day.

Virtually all of the charters were to water destinations, principally lakes in both Washington and British Columbia. Munro couldn't see any point in hauling around the Seabee's heavy landing gear if it wasn't needed, so he took it off. This added another hundred pounds or so to the useful load and made the plane ideal for the groups of hunters and fishermen who were eager to exploit the seemingly unlimited resources of the northwest backcountry.

Seabee activity continued hot and heavy through the summer. In addition to the numerous trips taken by the resident owners, there was a lively business in the buying, rebuilding, and selling of Seabees from out of state, with Kenmore often sharing in the profit from the sale. Of course, more Seabee activity meant more Seabee accidents, and by the end of the year, the Kenmore crew's salvage skills had been well honed. One Seabee recovery in particular stands out in Munro's mind, partly because of the challenge it represented, and partly because the whole thing was Kenmore's fault.

Bill Gilbert and his family loved their Seabee, and they used it almost every weekend during the summer. When the Navy announced it was turning its facilities at Coronet Bay on Whidbey Island over to the Parks Department, Gilbert was one of the Seabee owners who decided to fly up to attend the official ceremony. His airplane was at Kenmore at the time, undergoing its annual inspection, and Gilbert was concerned that it might not be ready in time. Munro assured him they'd get the inspection finished even if it meant working all night to do it. In fact, to make sure Gilbert and his family got to Coronet Bay in time for the ceremony, Munro volunteered to deliver the plane to Gilbert's Mercer Island home first thing the next morning.

Anything that sits in the water eventually gets water in it, and the Seabee was no exception. What with condensation running down the inside of the hull and spray seeping in around the seams and rivets on the outside, water was always accumulating in the airplane's bilges and wing floats. On Percival Spencer's advice, Republic designed several removable drain plugs in the bottom of the Seabee's hull and wing floats. Some owners went so far as to take the plugs out after a flight and keep them out until their next flight to give any water or condensation trapped in the hull plenty of time to drain out.

It was almost midnight when the mechanic assigned to Gilbert's plane finished his inspection. He was exhausted, but he forced himself to run a mental checklist to make sure he hadn't overlooked anything. He knew Munro would be taking the plane out early in the morning, and he vividly remembered crawling underneath the Seabee to replace the drain plugs. Everything else seemed in order, so he put away his tools and prepared to go home. After a last glance around the shop, he doused the lights and headed for his car. Behind him in the darkness the two small drain plugs for the wing floats remained where he'd placed them two days earlier, on the back of the workbench.

Munro ran the plane down the lake to Mercer Island the next morning and the Gilberts loaded up and took off for Coronet Bay. The dock was already crowded with seaplanes, and the Navy was instructing new arrivals to moor to a line of buoys anchored offshore. Bill Gilbert clipped his bow line to one of the buoys and flagged down the launch that was ferrying people to shore. When everyone was assembled, they boarded a bus for a tour of the Whidbey Island Naval Air Station a few miles away.

On the return trip, the talk on the bus was all about how some poor fellow's airplane had capsized in Coronet Bay. Gilbert felt a momentary pang of uneasiness, but he told himself not to worry. After all, his Seabee had just undergone a thorough scrutiny by the mechanics at Kenmore Air Harbor, and Bob Munro himself had flown it down the lake that morning. They must be talking about some other poor fellow's airplane, he told himself.

When the bus rounded the last curve, Gilbert's eyes shot to the line of moored seaplanes. His Seabee was gone. Why would someone move it, he wondered, and then he realized it was still there. It had been easy to overlook, with only its gently curving keel and a pair of wing floats showing above the water. Stunned, Gilbert walked out to the end of the dock to get a better look. He was bombarded with offers of help from the rest of the seaplane owners, but he wisely kept his wits about him and said he wanted to study the situation before he did anything that might damage the plane even more. He knew he'd need help getting the plane out of the water. What he didn't know was that expert help was already on the way.

Jim Campbell had arrived late at Coronet Bay, and as he circled to check out the situation on the water he noticed one of the moored Seabees had taken on a severe list to starboard. In fact, the right wingtip was almost in the water. It was obvious the plane was moments from capsizing, so he forgot about the Navy tour and opened his throttle for Kenmore. Campbell had recognized the sinking Seabee as Gilbert's, and he knew the future of the man's airplane depended on how fast it could be pulled out of the salt water. What was needed was a seaplane salvage expert, and the only person Campbell knew who qualified for that title was Bob Munro.

Campbell bounced his Seabee up the ramp at Kenmore and slid it to a stop in the parking area. He found Munro and Wardleigh working in the hangar and quickly explained the situation. Wardleigh ran off to round up some tools and as much rope as he could carry while Munro went down to the dock to give the company Seabee a quick preflight inspection.

"Call the Navy and tell them to get word to Bill that we're on the way," Munro instructed Campbell, "and tell them to be real careful if they move the airplane. Pulling it into shallow water won't make it any less wet, but it could bend it up pretty bad if they drag it over a rock."

Wardleigh tossed the tools and rope into the back seat and scrambled into the passenger seat beside Munro. Campbell turned the airplane out and Munro fired up the engine. When they reached open water Munro shoved the throttle all the way forward. The Franklin responded with a roar, and moments later the red and white Seabee lifted off the lake, the midmorning sun sparkling off the feather of spray trailing back from the keel. Munro eased the power back to climb and banked into a steep right turn to pick up the northwest heading for Whidbey Island.

Gilbert owned a marine construction company, and he was no slouch when it came to moving awkward objects around in the water. Under his direction, the Navy launch had carefully pulled the inverted Seabee over next to the dock. The news of Munro and Wardleigh's impending arrival reached Coronet Bay only minutes before their airplane, and Munro was relieved to see that although the plane had been moved, it was still floating on top of the water apparently undamaged. Gilbert had done an excellent job of getting the salvage operation underway, but it was obvious from his expression that he was not a happy man.

"I don't understand how this could have happened," he said testily as Munro arrived on the dock. "You just gave the plane a thorough inspection yesterday. There hasn't been enough wind this morning to flip it over. I didn't hit anything with the hull when I landed. I can't figure it out. What do you think?"

Munro had his suspicions, but he refrained from speculation.

"The first thing we've got to do is get the plane rightside up and on shore. Then we can try to figure out why it turned over."

The next step in the recovery process was to extend the landing gear. Munro figured he'd have to jump into the water, open the bow door, and reach in to pump the gear lever. With the plane nosed up to the dock, however, he could see that the Plexiglas windshield panel in the door was missing. Wardleigh noticed it, too, and speculated that the panel had probably popped out as a result of the fuselage flexing as the plane turned over.

The missing windshield made the job of extending the gear somewhat easier. By lying down on the dock and having Wardleigh hold his ankles, Munro was just able to reach into the cockpit and get hold of the gear lever. It was an awkward position, with the waves lapping over his head and shoulders, but he finally managed to pump the gear down, or in this case, up, until it locked into position in the air above the hull.

Gilbert had already asked the Navy for a truck with an A-frame derrick mounted to the front of the frame. When it arrived he and Munro guided the driver out onto the dock until the A-frame stuck out over the water above the upside-down Seabee. Gilbert fashioned a quick-release sling around the rear of the fuselage and attached it to the hook on the end of the derrick line. The men in the Navy launch maneuvered the inverted plane until its tail was pointed away from the beach, at which point Munro told the truck driver to engage the winch at the base of the A-frame. The derrick lined tightened, and the tail of Gilbert's plane began to rise into the air.

If the onlookers on shore thought the plan was to lift the Seabee out of the water with the derrick, they were mistaken. There was no way the tail could support the weight of the waterlogged plane, and Munro knew it. As the Seabee tipped up onto its nose, Munro signaled to Wardleigh on shore. Wardleigh and the men he'd enlisted to help him grabbed the long rope he'd attached to the tailwheel and began to pull. At the same time, Munro directed the truck driver to slack off on the winch. As soon as the weight came off the sling, Gilbert jerked it free. Wardleigh and his crew hauled on their line as hard as they could, and the Seabee sighed over onto its belly, upright, but full of water. The air that had been supporting the plane escaped through the windowless bow door with a whoosh, and the Seabee sank gently to land wheels down on the sandy bottom fifteen feet below the surface.

So far, so good. Munro directed the truck to the beach, and Wardleigh attached his tailwheel line to the towing rings on the front bumper. The driver shifted into reverse and eased up on the clutch pedal. Unseen, the Seabee began to inch backwards across the seabed toward the beach. A few minutes later, it crept on shore like some prehistoric sea creature, festooned with kelp and cascading water in all directions. Munro took one look at the solid stream squirting from the bottom of each wing float, and the capsizing mystery was solved.

"There's the problem," he said to Gilbert. "The drain plugs were left out of the wing floats."

"I don't see how that could cause the whole plane to go over."

Munro pointed to the other Seabees moored in the bay. Like all flying boats at rest, they sat tilted slightly to one side, with only one of the wing floats in the water. The other float was suspended clear of the surface by at least a foot.

"The float that was down on the water gradually filled up until it pulled the wingtip under. Once the wing started to fill, there was no stopping it. The only thing that kept it from sinking was the air trapped in the hull."

Munro knew what Gilbert's next question would be before he asked it. "Didn't you notice the plugs were missing before you brought the plane down to me this morning?"

Munro shook his head. "No. I should have, though. It's our fault this happened. We should have made sure the plugs were in, and I should have checked them again this morning."

Gilbert walked sadly around his dripping airplane. "I guess I'm out one airplane. I don't have the insurance to get this fixed."

"It's our responsibility," Munro said. "Don't worry about it."

"Well, that's very generous of you to say, but we don't really know for sure what happened. I suppose it's even possible the plugs could have vibrated loose during the flight up here."

"It doesn't matter if they were left out or if they fell out," Munro said firmly. "It was our responsibility to put the plugs in, and it was my responsibility to make sure they were in tight before I brought the plane down to you. Whatever the cause, it shouldn't have happened, and we'll make it right."

By now it was early afternoon. Munro wanted to get the plane back to Kenmore as quickly as possible so they could start flushing away the salt water. He was even considering submerging the plane's wings and tail surfaces in the fresh water of Lake Washington for a day or two.

"I suppose we should start with the wings," Wardleigh said as he walked up with his toolbox. After the first few seaplane salvages, a procedure had evolved: get the plane on shore with as little damage as possible, and then disassemble it into pieces small enough to be trucked back to the Air Harbor.

"No," Munro answered. "I'm going to fly it home."

"You're crazy," Gilbert exclaimed. "The engine's full of water, the gas is contaminated, and even if you could get the thing started, the instruments are ruined and half the windshield is missing."

Munro shrugged. "It doesn't have to run very long. Twenty or thirty minutes should be sufficient." He turned to Wardleigh. "Take our plane and go get one of the spare batteries and enough oil for two complete oil changes. I'll clean the spark plugs and the distributor while you're gone. And you'd better bring a couple of cans of gas back, too. We'll need to drain the fuel system."

Wardleigh was about to turn away when Munro thought of something else. "While you're at it, bring back a couple of drain plugs for the wing floats. We don't want to have to pull this thing off the bottom twice in one day."

Wardleigh departed in the company Seabee, and Munro set to work pulling the engine cowl off Gilbert's plane. He didn't bother to disassemble and clean the complicated magneto. The second spark plug in each of the Franklin's six cylinders was fired by a simple, automotive-style distributor, and Munro figured one ignition system would provide sufficient power to get the airplane home. Gilbert, meanwhile, mopped as much water and seaweed as he could out of the cockpit. Wardleigh swooped in ninety minutes later, and the oil change process began.

"Once we get it started, I'm going to let it run for a minute or two to pick up all the water, and then we'll change the oil again," Munro explained to Gilbert. "If there's any water in the oil when I fly it back, it'll ruin the bearings."

The first three starting attempts were duds, but Munro was confident he could get it running if the battery held out. Sure enough, there was a watery bang the next time he hit the starter, and the Franklin sputtered to life shooting clouds of spray and steam out the exhaust stacks. As soon at the engine settled into a relatively smooth idle, Munro pulled the mixture and the prop clanked to a stop. Wardleigh scrambled up and unscrewed the oil plug.

"How does it look?" Munro asked.

Wardleigh peered into the can he was holding under the oil sump. "It's a little milky, but it actually doesn't look too bad."

Munro handed the cans of fresh oil up to Wardleigh and then dumped the clean avgas Wardleigh had brought from Kenmore into the Seabee's fuel tank. Wardleigh replaced the engine cowl and slid off the wing onto the beach.

"You're sure you want to do this?' he asked, frowning at the bedraggled Seabee. "You know there's got to be at least *some* water still in the fuel, and it's going to be pretty drafty with that windshield missing."

"I think I'll be okay," Munro said as he lowered himself gingerly into the sopping wet pilot's seat. "If something happens, I'll try to put it down in the water and you can send a boat after me."

The Franklin fired on the first try.

"Good luck," Wardleigh shouted above the noise of the idling engine.

Munro waved and powered the Seabee into the water. He retracted the gear and idled out into the middle of the bay. There was no point in doing a run-up; he'd find out soon enough if the engine had enough power to get the plane off the water. He ruddered the amphibian around into the wind and eased the throttle all the way open. The engine was a little rough, but it spooled up reasonably close to maximum rpm. With only a pilot and a few gallons of gas on board, the Seabee should have fairly jumped into the air, but it didn't. The plane thudded across the wind chop, the needle in the airspeed indicator creeping up the dial with agonizing slowness. The other side of the bay was approaching fast, and Munro began to wonder if he'd have enough room to get airborne.

The problem was the missing windshield panel. The Seabee's gracefully curved nose performs two critical functions: it reduces drag by streamlining the fuselage, and it efficiently guides air back into the propeller. The gaping hole in the bow door not only created a huge amount of drag, it messed up the airflow into the prop. Munro was only seconds away from having to abort the take-off when the airspeed indicator finally quivered up to liftoff speed. Munro eased back on the yoke and the Seabee staggered into the air.

If he thought he was home free, he was wrong. As he lowered the right wing to bank south toward Kenmore, the engine began to sputter and miss terribly. It obviously was about to quit, so Munro quickly rolled the plane level in preparation for a straight-ahead emergency landing. The

Franklin began running smoothly almost immediately. Probably just water in the fuel line, Munro thought. Not surprising under the circumstances. He banked around toward Kenmore again. Bang! The engine coughed and began to miss even worse than before. Munro rolled the wings level and the engine settled down again. Okay, Munro thought calmly, if it doesn't want to bank to the right I'll do a 270-degree turn to the left. He turned the yoke, the left wing dropped, and the engine suddenly sounded like it was about to fall out of the plane. Wings level, and it smoothed right out.

Munro continued climbing straight ahead as he ran through a mental schematic of the Seabee's fuel system and tried to come up with a logical reason for the airplane's mysterious ailment. The only explanation that made any sense was water in the intake manifold. Banking the plane conceivably could cause the water to slosh around enough to partially block the intake ports. If this was the case, yawing the plane should have the same effect. Munro pushed on the left rudder pedal and the Seabee slewed sideways. The effect on the engine was instantaneous; the sputtering and missing was as bad as before.

Munro straightened out and then tried a very shallow bank, being careful to keep the turn perfectly coordinated. With the exception of a minor hiccup or two, the engine continued to run smoothly. This seemed to be the answer, and he continued the turn until he was pointed south towards Seattle. With his engine iffy at best, Munro decided to remain over water as long as possible. This meant making a few turns along the way, but as long as he kept them shallow and coordinated he had no trouble with the engine. In fact, the problem seemed to diminish with each passing minute, which he assumed was due to the water in the manifold being sucked gradually into the cylinders and blown out the exhaust.

On the other hand, the hurricane blowing though the empty windshield frame didn't diminish at all. Munro shielded his eyes from the blast as best he could, but he couldn't do anything about the sound. The noise and pressure pulsing against Munro's eardrums were almost painful. Earplugs and headsets were unheard of in general aviation in the 1940s; the flight from Coronet Bay took less than half an hour, but by the time he landed his ears were ringing.

The mechanics were ready when Munro taxied up the ramp. Armed with hoses they removed the Seabee's access plates and cabin bulkheads and began the long process of flushing out every nook and cranny of the airframe. They got to it just in time. Thanks to the fast salvage job at Coronet Bay and Munro's quick, albeit deafening, flight home, corrosion didn't get so much as a toehold on the aluminum. The engine fared almost as well. A couple of days in Walt Winseman's capable hands was all it took to return it to like-new condition, although in the case of a Franklin, that was a somewhat dubious distinction.

The interior was another story. The seats, carpet, and sidewall upholstery went in the trash along with the wiring, the radios, and most of the instruments. By now, of course, Kenmore had a pretty good selection of wrecked amphibians on hand, so Bill Fisk hopped on his bike, and after a few trips to the parts barn, the restoration of Bill Gilbert's Seabee was complete.

Time has blurred the details of what happened next. Munro's version ends with the plane being turned back over to Gilbert following its restoration, and Gilbert and his family continuing to it without incident. Tom Wardleigh's version of the story ends a little differently. According to Wardleigh, after Gilbert got his plane back, Munro noticed he wasn't using it very much. Gilbert and his family had used their Seabee constantly during the summer, but now their gleaming amphibian just sat on the property, seemingly forgotten. When Gilbert showed up one day to give his unused airplane a wash, Munro decided to find out what was going on. He walked over to where the man was hosing off the fuselage prior to soaping it down.

"I notice that you haven't been flying much. Is there something wrong with your plane? Whatever it is, we'll make it right for you."

'No, no." Gilbert shut off the spray and stuck the end of the hose into a bucket. "It's my wife, actually. She's just not comfortable flying anymore. She knows about corrosion and what it can do to aluminum. She's not questioning the quality of your work," he added hastily, "but she just doesn't trust the airplane anymore. Nothing I say seems to be able to change her mind."

"Oh." Munro looked around the tie-down area and then across to the dock. "What about that one?" He pointed to the Air Harbor's Seabee that was being fueled for its next flight. "Do your think your wife would feel better flying in our plane?"

"I'm sure she would," Gilbert replied. "She's not afraid of flying, she's just very worried about what being submerged in saltwater might have done to our plane."

"Well then, why don't you take our plane, and we'll take yours. You should be out flying on a nice day like this, not standing around with a hose and bucket."

So the deal was done. The company Seabee was signed over to the Gilberts, who immediately resumed their flying activities, and Gilbert's airplane joined the Air Harbor roster.

Whether or not Wardleigh got the story right, his memory was razor sharp about Munro's character. Swapping airplanes to see a customer happy and satisfied is just the sort of thing he would have done. He couldn't imagine anything better than the magical and sometimes mysterious world of islands, inlets, mountains, and lakes that comprise the northwest raincoast. Anyone with the same feelings had a friend in Bob Munro, and Munro would go to great and occasionally unexpected lengths to help his friends experience the same wonder and excitement he felt as he winged his way north.

Regardless of the exact fate of Gilbert's airplane, Munro was true to his word and picked up the tab for the entire recovery and restoration job. Some of his business acquaintances thought he was nuts. Yes, a pair of drain plugs had been found on the back of the workbench, and yes, the mechanic who'd worked on Gilbert's plane had admitted he could have forgotten to put them in, but nothing could be proven. The plugs *could* have fallen out accidentally during the flight. Kenmore at least should have tried for a fifty-fifty split on the repair bill.

Munro didn't see it that way. Whether the plugs were left out or fell out was irrelevant. Kenmore had promised to deliver a thoroughly inspected airplane, and as far as Munro was concerned, they'd failed. Gilbert deserved to get what he'd been promised, and Munro intended to see that he did. Satisfying a loyal customer, to say nothing of keeping a good friend, was far more important than the negative impact the repair job would have on the company's account books.

Not that Munro was unconcerned about Kenmore's financial health. For a while during the summer of 1949, the company's bank account contained exactly $25. During their forty-plus years with the company, neither Bill Fisk nor Walt Winseman could remember a single instance when their paychecks were delayed, but the lack of cash put off a lot of improvement projects. The Seabee hangar had been completed thanks to another loan from Harold Nicholas, but other projects like paving the parking and tie-down areas had to wait. Ted Huntley and the mechanics worked to level the dirt in their spare time, but the only surfacing the company could afford was road oil. It kept the dust down which was better than nothing, but a proper asphalt or concrete surface would have to wait.

Bob Munro had been flying for only three years and Tom Wardleigh even less than that, but both men had garnered enough experience to be amazed at the dumb things some pilots did to get themselves into trouble. "I can't believe this guy did this," was a common observation as Wardleigh and Munro worked to pull someone's airplane from a lake that was too small or a field that was too short. It never occurred to them that they were just as likely to make mistakes as everybody else. They found out just how likely the day Harold Nicholas invited them to go fishing with him east of the Coast Range in British Columbia.

Nicholas had two airplanes, a sleek Cessna 195 on wheels and a Seabee. The Seabee was up in Prince George, and Nicholas wanted to bring it back to Seattle. The plan was for all three men to fly to Prince George in the 195, at which point Munro and Wardleigh would take over the Seabee and follow Nicholas to his vacation home on Ootsa Lake, about 150 miles west in the rolling, pine-covered hills of central BC. After a day of fishing, the three would fly home in the Seabee, leaving the 195 behind for Nicholas to use later.

The first half of the flight went off without a hitch, but after departing Prince George, the speedy 195 soon left the Seabee wallowing in its wake. Munro and Wardleigh had some challenging moments as they navigated their way across unfamiliar territory to an unfamiliar destination, but after only a few minor deviations they plunked down on the little Ootsa Lake airstrip to find Nicholas pacing back and forth in front of his tied-down 195, anxious to get out on the water.

As promised, the fishing was fabulous, and the men had little trouble convincing themselves to extend their visit to two and then three days. Business called, however, and the time soon came when they couldn't put off returning to Seattle any longer. The first stop would be Prince George, where the Seabee would be refueled for the flight home. Nicholas couldn't bear to give up on the fishing, however, so rather than fly directly to town, he decided to visit a few more lakes on the way out.

There had been more than enough fuel to reach Prince George when they started, so gas consumption was the last of their worries as the men hopped from lake to lake, drinking in the beautiful scenery and chattering about the terrific fishing. Finally, Wardleigh thought to look at the fuel gauge.

"The gauge was way down, but it said we still had enough gas to get to Prince George. The question was, did we have enough to fly to another lake first? We debated about it for awhile, and then we decided to land and find out exactly how much gas we had by sticking the tank with the wooden dipstick that came with the airplane. We got a reading of a little over forty gallons, which was considerably more than we needed to get to Prince George. In fact, it was quite a bit more fuel than we thought we ought to have, considering the amount of flying we'd been doing. But you can't argue with a dipstick, and we were having too much of a good time to properly analyze the situation. We went on and fished this other lake, and then on the way in to Prince George we ran out of gas."

TOM WARDLEIGH

The sudden silence shocked the three into immobility, and for a moment they simply stared straight ahead out the windshield as the Seabee began a gentle glide toward the ground. Then Nicholas and Wardleigh up front and Munro in the back looked at the gas gauge. The needle was parked on Empty.

"What happened to our forty gallons?" Nicholas wondered aloud as the Seabee's blunt nose pitched farther down toward the trees. No one bothered to answer as they all began frantically searching the woods for someplace to land. It didn't look promising. The country around Prince George is thickly forested, and while the slender evergreens and willows of the interior are not nearly as intimidating as the massive trees studding the western slopes of the Coast Range, they are still stout enough to reduce an airplane to confetti.

"There!" cried Wardleigh, pointing to the right. "There's a spot over there."

"Spot" was an apt description. The clearing looked to be only a few feet wider than the Seabee's wingspan and no more than two hundred yards long. Still, it was better than nothing. Nicholas was a good pilot, and he soon had the Seabee lined up on final approach.

"I'm going to leave the wheels up," he announced. "I don't know if we'll stop before we hit the trees, but at least we won't flip over."

It was like being inside a drum. The metallic boom of the touchdown became a hollow rumble as the Seabee lurched through the grass and bushes. Nicholas did the best he could with the rudder pedals but they had little effect. The Seabee cut its own course across the clearing toward the trees at the far end.

"Hang on!" Nicholas shouted a final warning and threw his arms across his face as the Seabee thundered into the woods. Whether through blind luck or Nicholas's manipulations of the rudder pedals, the fuselage sliced neatly between two stout trees. There was a jerk as the wings sheared off, and then another as the trees added the horizontal stabilizers to their collection. The fuselage continued on by itself for another twenty yards and crunched to a stop.

The racket scared every living thing within a quarter mile into silence. Even the squirrels in the trees surrounding the clearing were struck dumb. Below them, the bulbous Seabee fuselage sat tilted to one side, a bizarre space vehicle come to rest. For a long moment, nothing moved. Then the side door fell open and Bob Munro eased his lanky frame out onto the pine needles. "Is everyone okay?"

Nicholas and Wardleigh slowly lowered their arms. "I think so," Wardleigh replied. Nicholas unfastened his seat belt and began moving toward the door Munro had just exited. The fuselage creaked and shifted suddenly on the forest floor.

"Be careful how you move around in there," Munro cautioned from outside. "The wings are gone and there's nothing holding the plane up. You don't want it to roll over on you."

Nicholas and Wardleigh gingerly climbed out the side door and walked over to stand beside Munro. "What a mess," sighed Nicholas as he looked back along the jagged furrow of raw earth to where the wings of his plane were bent around the trees.

"That was a good piece of flying," Munro offered in an attempt to make his friend feel better. "The important thing is that nobody was hurt."

Wardleigh was more upset over not knowing the cause of the accident than he was over the accident itself. "I don't understand it," he declared as he removed the gas cap and peered down the filler neck. "We had forty gallons of gas in here. You saw it the same as I did. The dipstick was wet to the forty-gallon mark."

Yes, Munro and Nicholas agreed, the dipstick had showed forty gallons. It was certainly a mystery, but right now it was more important for them to find their way out of the woods. Not only had they not filed a flight plan, they hadn't told anyone when to expect them home again. With no information other than a vague notion of where in British Columbia the three would be fishing, it would be days before anyone became worried enough to start a search. The men were on their own.

Wardleigh removed the magnetic compass from the plane while Nicholas and Munro dug out the sleeping bags and some of the fish they'd caught earlier. If they didn't make it out by nightfall they would at least be warm and have something to eat. Munro spread the chart they'd been using across the windshield. Nicholas, who knew the country best, studied it for a few moments before banging his finger down on a point southwest of Prince George.

"We're right around here. If we walk north, we'll eventually get to this road here."

Wardleigh held the compass in front of him and turned until he was facing north. "That way," he said, pointing. The three picked up the sleeping bags and the fish and, with a last look at the listing, wingless Seabee, struck off through the trees. It was not difficult going. Unlike the west side of the Coast Range with its dense and dripping undergrowth that makes passage all but impossible, the pine forests of the interior are relatively open. The only real obstacles were the occasional patches of boggy muskeg that forced the men to detour from their straight-line course.

An hour or so after leaving the Seabee, Wardleigh, who was in the lead with the compass, came across a trail. It was an old trail, but it was a trail just the same. The question was, which way should they go?

Wardleigh turned to Harold Nicholas. "Any suggestions?"

Nicholas had several, but when he opened his mouth to voice them, nothing came out. Wardleigh and Munro stared as their friend flapped his jaw and tried to speak. Finally he gave up and began massaging his throat.

"Are you hurt?" Munro peered at Nicholas anxiously.

Nicholas shook his head. No.

"Can you talk at all?" Wardleigh asked.

Nicholas tried. If anything came out, Wardleigh couldn't hear it.

"Maybe it's a delayed reaction from the accident," he told Munro. "A kind of shock or something."

"You're sure you're all right otherwise?" Munro asked again. Nicholas nodded. Munro dug out the map and unfolded it. "Okay then, which way do you think we should go?"

Nicholas studied the map for a moment and then pointed. "That way," he mouthed silently.

Munro agreed, and Wardleigh took a quick compass reading before stepping out down the trail in the direction Nicholas had pointed. The trail was old and overgrown but it didn't get any worse over the course of the next hour, which was encouraging. The trail widened gradually, and the men began to see signs of human activity. Old stumps showed where trees had been cut, and there were scattered piles of rotting logs. This was encouraging, indeed. The trail continued on until suddenly there were two trails running parallel, a couple of feet apart. The men tramped along for almost five minutes before they realized the significance of this second trail. They were tire tracks. The original trail had become a road.

The road wound through the woods, becoming more distinct with each passing mile. The knowledge that they were getting somewhere encouraged the three to pick up the pace. They crossed a stream on a crude log bridge, followed the tracks up a slight incline, passed through another logged-off area, and then stopped abruptly. The dirt road had come to an end, and Wardleigh, Nicholas, and Munro stood staring at the pavement of the highway that ran in to Prince George. They flagged down the next car that came along, and by dusk they were safely ensconced in one of the local hotels.

Nicholas was still voiceless the next morning when the three met in the lobby to decide what to do next. The Seabee was junk but its engine wasn't, so they decided to go back and get it. They would procure a vehicle, drive as far as they could down the dirt road, and then hike the rest of the way in, marking their path as they went. Wardleigh had jotted down their compass headings on the way out, so it should be an easy matter to reverse them to find their way back in. Once at the plane, Wardleigh and Munro would remove the engine and any other parts they felt were worth salvaging. Then they would return to town and hire someone to pack the engine out and ship it south to Kenmore.

It was a good plan, but it was based on their finding the plane again which, for the life of them, they were unable to do. After spending half the morning tromping around in the woods with no success, they came across an Indian guide who was working for the fish and game department. After listening to their story, the guide asked for a description of the place where Nicholas had landed.

"Okay," he said after the three had told him all they could about the clearing and what they had seen on the hike out. "Follow me." And he led them straight to the plane.

Wardleigh and Munro had borrowed some tools in Prince George, and as they set about removing the engine cowl Nicholas showed the Indian the sheered-off wings and tail surfaces. The guide was very interested in the control cables dangling from the wing roots, and when Munro told him they were stainless steel he became downright excited.

"Could I have these," he asked eagerly, running the shiny, smooth cables through his fingers.

"It's up to Harold," Munro said, pointing at Nicholas. "It's his plane."

Nicholas nodded his consent when the guide repeated his question.

"What do you want them for?" Munro asked.

"Bears," the guide replied.

"Bears?"

"All around Prince George is crawling with bears." From his perch atop the Seabee, Wardleigh looked up and peered around apprehensively at the surrounding woods. "More bears than anyone can remember," the Indian continued. "I trap them for the government, and I need strong wire for my snares. The wire I have now rusts quickly and breaks, but this wire will last a long time."

"You can have all you want," Munro said. "Besides the cable here in the wings, there's cable running through the fuselage."

Wardleigh and Munro had the engine off the Seabee in a couple of hours and the guide said he'd get someone to pack it out and ship it south. The next day, Nicholas, Munro, and Wardleigh caught a commercial flight to Vancouver and then on to Seattle. Ruth Munro and Jan Wardleigh met the three men at Boeing Field and gave the still-speechless Nicholas a ride home. When his voice returned three days later, he lost no time in hunting up Munro and Wardleigh to discuss the fuel mystery. How could they have run out of gas less than an hour after seeing with their own eyes a measurement of forty gallons on the dipstick? An inaccurate fuel gauge they could understand, but an inaccurate dipstick? It's either wet or it isn't.

Unless, as it turned out, it happens to be a Seabee dipstick. A few weeks after Nicholas had parked his plane in the trees, Wardleigh was working on a customer's airplane when he discovered yet another of the Seabee's quirky characteristics. It seemed that after the engine was switched off, the fuel trapped between the tank and the carburetor would dribble back to the tank through a return line. Wardleigh knew about the return line, but it wasn't until he happened to hear fuel gurgling inside the filler neck of his customer's airplane that he found out where it emptied back into the tank. He pondered his new discovery for a moment, and then he went and got the dipstick out of the cockpit. He had a pretty good idea of what he was about to find out. Sure enough, when he stuck the dipstick into the tank, the fuel dribbling from the return line splashed onto the stick at exactly the forty-gallon mark. It didn't matter how much fuel there was in the tank; the dipstick would always come out wet to the forty-gallon mark if it was inserted soon after the engine had been shut off. The fuel gauge in Nicholas's Seabee had been right all along. It had been an expensive lesson.

By Christmas 1949, Wardleigh had six mechanics and two helpers under him in the shop. Scribbled notes on scraps of paper and a casually-kept logbook were no longer adequate to keep track of everyone's time. Munro's experience with the union at Pan Am had done nothing to lessen his dislike of conformist regulations, but with the Air Harbor's financial solvency in continuous jeopardy, accurate timekeeping was becoming essential. Reluctantly, he bought a time clock and hung it just inside the door of the shop.

Money for tools was tight, but Wardleigh remembers the shop as being adequately equipped to work on the relatively simple airplanes of the day.

> "We had a good air compressor for riveting and sandblasting. And good welding equipment was absolutely essential, and Bob made sure we had it. We built a lot of seaplane fins in those days. Most of the smaller landplanes we put on floats required some sort of auxiliary fin, which we often built right there in the shop. The work required a lot of skill on the part of the mechanic, but the tools it required were pretty rudimentary."
>
> **TOM WARDLEIGH**

Munro was beginning to wish there were more hours in a day. When he wasn't out flying he could be found out in the shop working on an airplane, or in the office negotiating with a customer. Then there were docks to fix and buildings to paint and shelves to build and planes to salvage, to say nothing of finding the time to make sure Kenmore was keeping its financial head above water. The last thing he needed was a crisis, but he got one just the same when the Air Harbor's right to occupy the old mill site was suddenly thrown into jeopardy.

Questions were being raised about the option-to-purchase agreement Lillian Mines had supposedly worked out with mill's owner, Gus Newburg. The agreement gave Lillian the option to purchase the land after leasing it for five years, and it was this option that Mrs. Mines had agreed to sell to Kenmore Air Harbor. Now the legality of Lillian's agreement with Newburg was in question, and if Lillian didn't have the option of purchasing the land, neither did Kenmore Air Harbor. It's not clear why the agreement was called into question in the first place. Land around the north end of the lake was increasing in value as more people moved into the area, and perhaps someone felt they could make a lot more off the property if they used it for something other than a seaplane base. In any event, the questions posed a serious threat to the future of the Air Harbor, and Munro lost no time in trying to get the situation resolved.

Lillian turned the whole thing over to her attorney. Part of the problem stemmed from the fact that several of the parties who could help confirm the original agreement could not be located, and it took Munro several months to track all of them down.

Lillian's title to the land was finally cleared in December 1949, just in time to herald a new problem. Kenmore had been paying Mrs. Mines for her purchase option whenever there was money to spare, but the slim margin between the company's breaking even or going out of business had caused many of the payments to be deferred. The next payment was due in February 1950. Including past deferments, the total owed was $2,400, and Lillian made it clear that another deferment was out of the question. Munro was stuck. The company simply didn't have that kind of money. Fortunately, Harold Nicholas did. He was more than happy to loan Kenmore the $2,400, which Munro could repay in monthly installments of $100. A handshake sealed the agreement, and the Air Harbor's future was assured for at least another few months.

Anyone who thought Munro's lack of college education would make him easy prey when it came to legal and financial negotiations was soon sorely disappointed. Munro always claimed hayseed status when it came to business acumen, but in fact, exactly the opposite was true. The gut line at the Diamond K cannery, the sluice box in Teller, Alaska, and the grease pit in Cook's North Seattle garage offered a graduate degree most college students are hard pressed to earn. As he worked first to help support his family and then pay for his mechanic's training, Munro mastered the art of learning how to learn. Whether the subject was financial forecasting or land use ordinances or environmental regulations, Munro had the confidence of knowing he could learn whatever was necessary to deal intelligently with the issue.

Coupled with his willingness to learn was an unflagging devotion to honesty. Munro's principles were impossible to subvert, something a few of his competitors discovered the hard way over the years. The loans Harold Nicholas made to the Air Harbor were never drawn up on paper. There were no notarized and witnessed signatures, no copies filed away in lawyers' offices. But Nicholas didn't become a financial success by misjudging the people he dealt with. Every loan he made to Kenmore was paid back in full, on time, with interest, as he knew it would be.

Munro's forays into the snake pits of business finance and land titles were made somewhat more palatable in 1950 by the fascinating variety of flights he was being called upon to make to Vancouver Island. The sudden increase in charter requests could be traced to one man who, with a single telephone call, expanded the horizons of Seattle sportsmen forever. Enos Bradner wanted to go fishing. Actually, Bradner *always* wanted to go fishing, but as the outdoor editor of the *Seattle Times*, he was required to show at least a passing interest in other northwest activities as well, from hiking to elk hunting. As far as Bradner was concerned, however, there was only one topic truly worthy of discussion with his readers, and that was the religious experience sometimes referred to as *fly fishing*.

For some time, Bradner had been hearing about the huge steelhead trout that supposedly visited the rivers that drained the east slopes of the mountains on Vancouver Island. Every year the big, ocean-going rainbows battled the rapids to spawn in the headwater lakes before speeding back downstream to grow even larger for the next year's assault. Bradner decided to find out for himself if these fish were real, so he called Kenmore Air Harbor to arrange a charter.

Bob Munro (second from right) examines the results of a successful fishing charter.

Munro, who enjoyed fishing almost as much as Bradner, was more than happy to fly the columnist and a *Times* photographer up to the island in the Air Harbor Seabee. Based on his conversations with fishermen who claimed familiarity with the area, Bradner decided Nahmint Lake would be their destination on this first trip. The two-hour flight was uneventful, if a flight through a fascinating maze of islands, bays, and mountains can be considered that, and Munro parked the Seabee on a sandbar at the outlet of the lake. The photographer loaded his camera while Bradner and Munro assembled their fly rods. Bradner's plan was to fish around the outlet for awhile and then work his way down the first half mile of the river.

By late afternoon, when the three men met back at the Seabee for the return flight to Kenmore, Bradner had determined to his satisfaction that the rumors about the steelhead inhabiting Vancouver Island's rivers were false. The fish were not huge. They were monstrous. He probably came to regret writing it, but Bradner's next column detailed the fantastic fishing he had experienced at Nahmint, and the phone began to ring in the Air Harbor office. It wasn't long before the lakes on Vancouver Island were every bit as familiar to Bob Munro and Bill Fisk as the lake lapping their doorstep in Kenmore.

Enos Bradner (center) and Bob Munro (right) with the company Seabee on a fishing trip to Ross Lake. Bradner's newspaper articles about the superb fishing in the Cascades and on Vancouver Island gave a big boost to Kenmore's charter business.

Enos Bradner became a regular at Kenmore as he continued to fish the Nahmint as well as the streams flowing out of Sproat Lake near Port Alberni. He didn't ignore his home waters, either. Bradner and Munro were the first to make a fly-in fishing trip to newly-created Ross Lake. The lake was formed in 1949 when the gates were closed for the first time in Seattle City Light's third and newest dam on the Skagit River. The resulting reservoir wound from the dam back through the North Cascades to the Canadian border. When the new lake had stabilized, it was opened to the public, and Bradner and Munro flew up to sample the fishing. Considering the radical changes the dam had brought to the underwater habitat, Bradner was pleased to inform his readers that the trout fishing was actually quite good. As with Nahmint and Sproat Lakes on Vancouver Island, Bradner's description of the beauty and adventure he'd experienced on Ross Lake inspired numerous phone calls to the Air Harbor, and it wasn't long before the Kenmore Seabee was droning back and forth to the North Cascades several times a week.

Bradner's timing couldn't have been better. By late 1949, the post-war fascination with flying had begun to wither. The GI Bill would still pick up most of the training tab, but there weren't many job opportunities awaiting a young man with a freshly pocketed pilot's license. Airline growth was steady but slow, and there were more than enough experienced fighter and bomber pilots available to fill any vacant seats in the cockpits of the DC-7s and Lockheed Constellations. By the end of the year, the Air Harbor's flight school was down to eighteen students. Fortunately, the number of requests for fishing and hunting flights was on the increase, thanks in large part to Enos Bradner's newspaper columns.

The sale of Seabee parts continued to generate income, although Bill Fisk was no longer involved in the operation. As the chief, and often the only flight instructor, he was constantly looking for ways to bring in more students. He was also becoming more involved in the company's grow-ing charter business, taking any flights that were booked while Munro was away on another job. Probably to his relief, he simply didn't have the time to be pedaling up to the barn to retrieve a parts order or sort out the inventory. When young Leslie Munro began clamoring for a "two-wheeler," Fisk was more than happy to donate his parts bike to the cause. Leslie was delighted, and this time she made sure her new wheels remained well clear of the taxiing Seabees.

The shop was doing well, too, although it sometimes seemed the number of customers who defaulted on their repair bills exceeded the number who paid. Several Seabees came into the company's hands as a result of their owners signing them over in lieu of paying the repair bills. All of them were sold off for a small profit except one which was added to the Air Harbor fleet. Walt Winseman by now was the acknowledged expert on Franklin engines in the northwest if not in the entire country. Every day brought phone calls from owners or mechanics who were trying to troubleshoot their quirky engines. Winseman didn't like the Franklin any more than he had when he started, but at least now he understood it. When he heard that Franklin was about to stop pro-duction of the engine model used in the Seabee, he and Munro decided it would be a good idea to acquire as many new ones as the Air Harbor could afford.

Actually, the Air Harbor couldn't afford any, but once again Harold Nicholas saw the wisdom in Munro's plan. He loaned the company enough money to buy twelve new engines which were shipped by rail from New York. It was a timely purchase, and the new engines contributed greatly to Kenmore's ability to dominate the Seabee repair business for the next several years. If Munro had for some reason wanted to change the name of the company in 1950, "Seabee Central" would have been an appropriate alternative.

When Jim Campbell learned that Percival Spencer was living in Santa Monica, California, he promptly invited the Seabee's designer to Washington for a Seabee trip to the Campbell's va-cation home on Sproat Lake. Spence had envisioned a recreational airplane when he designed the Seabee, but other than a couple of test flights at Republic, he'd never gone anywhere in one himself. He was happy to accept Campbell's invitation, but his shaky financial situation dictated that he make the trip up the coast by bus. Campbell met him in Portland and flew him to Sproat Lake, where they were soon joined by Bob Dent and Bob Munro. The four men spent a delightful evening talking aviation in general and Seabees in particular, but the sun was beginning to set on the bulbous amphibian.

Seabees would populate the Air Harbor for years, but after 1950, attrition began to take its toll. The most active owners like Jim Campbell and Bob Dent continued to organize picnic and vacation flights to Sproat Lake or up the coast to the Malibu Club Resort on Jervis Inlet, but by 1960, most of the Seabees were gone, sold for parts or to pilots who had the time and dedication to keep them running.

Campbell, who'd been Joe Crosson's first Seabee customer in 1947, continued to fly his air-plane until 1962 when he moved to Chehalis, some sixty miles south of Seattle. Campbell had barely settled into his new home when a storm packing winds of 107 miles per hour tore his beloved Seabee from its tiedowns on the local airport and smashed it upside down into the tarmac. Campbell had the plane repaired, but it just didn't fly as well after the accident. A few months later, the last of the Kenmore Seabee owners traded up to a brand new Cessna.

PACEMAKER

FOR YEARS, THE ONLY AIRPORT in Cordova, Alaska, was back behind the town, chiseled into the base of a mountain that clawed skyward out of the jewel-like waters of Eyak Lake. Hangars hugged the base of the slope alongside the gravel runway that extended out into the water. Most of the time the runway was a few feet higher than the surface of the lake, but when winter rains poured off the sides of the mountains, this relationship often was reversed as the lake crept across the gravel to the very doorsills of the hangars. In 1941, construction was started on a new airport some thirteen miles down the coast, but Eyak Lake continued to be used by local pilots and floatplane operators.

The lake was up in the fall of 1949 when a huge, single-engine Bellanca Pacemaker rumbled slowly over the town and banked around for a landing on the lake. The Bellanca, which carried the registration N251M on its red fabric sides, was only twenty years old, but World War II had propelled aviation into the jet age, and the old Pacemaker looked like it belonged in a museum. Still, its broad wings could carry a remarkable load, and someone had replaced the trouble-prone Wright Whirlwind on the nose with a 450-horsepower Pratt & Whitney Wasp Jr. The EDO floats installed in place of the landing gear looked a little small for an airplane of this size, but so far they had proved to be adequate. Appearance to the contrary, Bellanca Five-One-Mike was still a rugged workhorse as long as speed was not part of the equation.

The pilot had never landed on Eyak Lake before. He'd heard about the cantankerous winds that could make a landing on the lake a challenge for even the best of pilots, and he'd spent enough time at the controls of the Bellanca to know its huge wings were especially susceptible to gusts. Carefully avoiding what looked like the most likely places for violent downdrafts, he lined up his final approach to touch down as close as possible to the buildings clustered along what he took to be the shoreline. Concentrating as he was on making a good landing, he failed to see the gravel runway lurking just below the surface. The Bellanca touched down in deep water with a thump and chattered across the wind chop toward the hangars.

Pleased that he'd pulled off a such smooth landing in a place with such a bad reputation, the pilot never noticed as the Pacemaker flashed across the edge of the runway into water that was barely two feet deep. The plane had just begun to drop off the step when the float keels screeched into the gravel. It sounded like the whole airplane was coming apart. The pilot had the presence of mind to yank the mixture off, but by the time the propeller had jerked to a stop, the damage had been done.

The Bellanca was loaded onto a dolly and pulled out of the water, where inspection showed that the bottoms of the floats were not nearly as ripped up as the noise had implied. Still, there were gashes and punctures that would have to be repaired before the pilot could continue his flight down the Inside Passage to Seattle, where the plane's new owner, Virgil Kay of McCall, Idaho, was waiting.

The next day was spent pounding out the dents in the floats and riveting aluminum patches over the holes. Anxious to take advantage of the good weather, the pilot took off early the following morning for the long haul down the coast. Prince Rupert was as far as he got before nightfall, and he fueled and oiled the plane and double-checked the mooring lines before catching a ride to his hotel. If the weather held, he would be in Seattle the next evening, and his days of flying the big, noisy antique would be over.

The weather continued to hold, but the patches on the bottoms of the floats didn't. The pilot arrived at the floatplane base the next morning to find a motley assortment of fishermen, mechanics, and pilots peering down into the water. His first thought was that his plane had been moved, as he didn't see it moored alongside the dock. Shouldering his way through the crowd, he found that Five-One-Mike had indeed moved, vertically, to a new position underneath the floating dock. The hasty efforts with the tin snips and rivet guns alongside Eyak Lake hadn't been enough. The patches leaked like sieves, and as the water dribbled into the floats, the Bellanca sank slowly until the only thing keeping it from disappearing completely were the mooring lines fastened to the dock cleats.

The local authorities were sympathetic to the pilot's plight, but his suggestion that they "just leave the damn thing where it is" was unacceptable. The plane had to be moved, the harbormaster insisted, if for no other reason that it was blocking access to the dock. A barge and crane were procured, and Five-One-Mike was lifted from the water nose-first by a line attached to the propeller hub. A call was placed to Virgil Kay to find out what he wanted done with his soggy airplane.

"Fix it," Kay ordered. "Fix it to the point where it can be flown down here to Lake Washington. I want Bob Munro and the boys out at Kenmore Air Harbor to look at it and determine what it will take to restore it. And don't worry about the bill. My insurance company will reimburse you for your work."

The seaplanes that supplied the fishing and logging communities along the coast and in the Queen Charlotte Islands had priority when it came to repairs, so it was well into December before the Pacemaker was fit for flight again. The pilot had disappeared a few days after the sinking, so Kay hired another one to fly the eight-hour leg from Prince Rupert to Kenmore. Bob Munro, Tom Wardleigh, Walt Winseman, and Bill Fisk watched from the dock as the big red plane droned over the hill north of the lake and circled around to land. It touched down gently on the glass-smooth water and idled in toward the ramp, the offbeat rumble of its nine-cylinder radial punching cleanly through the crisp, cold air.

Wardleigh had rounded up a set of beaching gear, and when the wheels were attached to the floats, Winseman pulled the plane up the ramp with the weapons carrier. It would be the biggest repair job ever undertaken by the Air Harbor, a job made even more challenging by the fact that most of the Bellanca's complicated wing structure was made of wood. As shop foreman, Wardleigh was in charge of the mechanics, but with such a small staff, he spent as much time working on the planes as anyone else.

> "There were about three of us who worked in the shop in those days. The others were a man named Danny, and Neil McConnell. Neil, Danny, and I, and of course, Bob, worked the whole winter rebuilding that Bellanca. It wasn't particularly hard to work on, it was just big. A lot of airplane for such a small crew. It consumed a tremendous amount of material. We took it clear to bare metal and sandblasted it and primed all the tubing. Then we rebuilt the woodwork and re-covered the entire airplane."
>
> **TOM WARDLEIGH**

After the fabric had been doped and shrunk onto the fuselage and wing framework, it was painted bright yellow with black registration numbers. The job was finished in March 1950, and Munro sent the bill, which totaled just over $8,000, to Virgil Kay out in Idaho. Kay promptly forwarded the bill to his insurance company who just as promptly sent it back. The work Kenmore Air Harbor had done, the insurance company said, had been necessitated by the sinking at Prince Rupert. The sinking at Prince Rupert had been the direct result of sloppy repair work on the part of the mechanic at Eyak Lake, a mechanic who, the insurance company claimed, was unlicensed. The unauthorized use of an unlicensed mechanic violated the terms of Kay's policy, so as far as the insurance company was concerned, they weren't liable for a penny's worth of repairs. Kay appealed the ruling, but to no avail. The insurance company flatly refused to pay.

Kay managed to pay for the repairs done in Prince Rupert, but the $8,000 Kenmore bill was beyond his means. Bob Munro and his board of directors were in a quandary. The value of the materials and labor the Air Harbor had invested in rebuilding the Bellanca exceeded the cash assets of the company plus a good share of its credit. Munro hated the idea of having to resort to legal action, but it looked like he wasn't going to have a choice; Kay's repair bill was just too big to write off. Fortunately, Kay himself came up with a solution.

The market value of a reconditioned 1929 Bellanca Pacemaker was almost identical to the total at the bottom of Kenmore's repair bill. What Kay suggested was an even swap; he would sign over the title to Five-One-Mike in return for cancellation of his bill. Munro agreed, and the Air Harbor added another plane to its fleet, which consisted of an Aeronca Champ, several Taylorcrafts, the Fairchild 24, a Seabee, and now the monstrous Pacemaker.

As soon as the Bellanca was signed over to Kenmore, Munro began trying to get rid of it. It

Bellanca Five-One-Mike. Left to right, Bob Munro, Walt Winseman, and Bill Lund.

wasn't that it was a bad airplane. It was simply too big. And too slow. There weren't many planes a Seabee could claim to outrun, but the Pacemaker was one of them. On the other hand, Munro doesn't remember any floatplane that could get out of the water as fast as the Bellanca.

> "It had a great big wing and no weight. It was a side-by-side cockpit, but it had a control stick instead of a yoke. A single, big control stick. With that 985 engine on it you could push full throttle and hold the stick right back in your lap and the thing would just come up out of the water and keep going. You didn't have to let it fall over onto the step. It was really uncanny. You could just push the throttle in and hold the stick back, and the nose would come up and it would just climb right on out of the water."

BOB MUNRO

Despite the Bellanca's load-carrying capabilities, Kenmore didn't have much use for a plane that traveled barely eighty miles in one hour and burned over twenty gallons of fuel to do it. Almost all of the Air Harbor's charter requests could be handled in the much more economical, albeit less reliable, Seabee. Munro let it be known that Five-One-Mike was for sale, but no one seemed particularly interested. Figuring that a partial return on their investment was better than nothing, Kenmore began sending out feelers to see if someone might want to lease the plane for the upcoming summer season. In the meantime, Munro and Fisk used it for charters whenever the Seabee was down for maintenance or out on another job.

If you asked either Bob Munro or Bill Fisk what they considered the most challenging aspect of flying the northwest raincoast, without hesitation they would inevitably answer, "The weather." Even a big airplane like the Bellanca could be bested by the unpredictable conditions often encountered in the Puget Sound convergence zone or under the climatic question mark that hangs over the San Juan Islands and the Strait of Georgia. It's one thing to take off on a flight knowing the weather is bad; at least you know what you're in for. But it's far more frustrating when the forecasters get it wrong, and you head out under blue skies only to have the whole thing fall in on you fifty miles north.

Sometimes, when the wind smashes into a current running the other way and the water is whipped to a frenzy, it's better to keep the plane on the beach than risk a takeoff in the seething waves. Munro and Fisk were caught this way once, on what had started out as a routine flight to the San Juans. The survival gear on board the Bellanca consisted of a book of matches Fisk happened to have in his pocket. The sun was going down, and while it wasn't particularly cold, the light clothes the men were wearing were not at all suited to spending a windy night on an exposed beach. The plane didn't offer much shelter, either; it's fabric fuselage was uninsulated and the cabin was drafty.

As soon as they were sure Five-One-Mike was in no danger of drifting away on the receding tide, Munro and Fisk jumped down and began combing the beach for anything that would burn. Fisk had the presence of mind to make sure they built their fire pit well clear of the Bellanca's fabric flanks, and by nightfall the two pilots were warming themselves around a roaring blaze. They took turns sleeping; someone had to keep the fire stoked, but even more important, the plane had to be tugged up higher on the beach whenever the returning tide threatened to float it away.

High tide and first light arrived together. The wind had died away and the channel was smooth as glass. The two men shoved the plane backwards off the beach, turned it around, and scrambled aboard. Munro got the engine going, and the Bellanca slid off the sand and into open water. By the time the cylinder head temperature was in the green, the eastern sky was a blaze of color. Munro eased the throttle open, and Five-One-Mike lifted itself effortlessly out of the water. The fire on the beach was probably still smoldering when Munro and Fisk sat down to breakfast forty-five minutes later and, between bites, explained to a relieved Ruth what had happened.

Ruth Munro's patience had been tried considerably during the past four years. Determined to do what she could to help the company succeed, she worked in the office part time, taking care of the account books. It wasn't long, though, before Leslie and Gregg discovered that the Air Harbor offered almost unlimited opportunities for getting into mischief, so Ruth decided she'd better work full time keeping them out of it. Then there was the house. The indoor plumbing Margaret Collins had demanded was a blessing that was offset somewhat by the homemade oil stove in the living room. It cranked out plenty of heat, but it was a low scorer when it came to appearance. And despite Ruth's best efforts to make their home as attractive and pleasant as possible, the shingle mill had left a legacy that was impossible to disguise.

The legacy put in an appearance one afternoon when Ruth and a friend were having a chat in the living room over tea. Suddenly, in mid-sentence, the friend's mouth dropped open, her face turned white as a sheet, and the teacup hit the rug.

"What's wrong?" Ruth asked in concern.

The friend pointed a trembling finger at the front door. "Look," she whispered.

Ruth turned around to see a monstrous rat taking a leisurely stroll up the outside of the screen door. "Shoo!" she yelled, stamping her feet on the floor. The rat hit the porch with a thump and dove for cover under the house. Ruth turned back to her still-horrified friend. "They live in the logs under the floor," she explained apologetically, "and there isn't much we can do to get them out. I think their numbers are dwindling, though. They haven't chewed their way into the house for months."

Bob Munro spent as much time with his family as he could, but working as he did in an industry whose hours are dictated by the customers, he found he had precious little time left. On weekends especially it often seemed to young Leslie and Gregg that Kenmore Air Harbor was surviving at their expense.

> "It really used to hurt when on a Sunday my dad would say, 'Hey, it's a nice day. Let's plan a picnic. Get the food and we'll fly over to Hood Canal.' So we'd get all ready to go and then he'd come in and say, 'A flight just came in for the islands. We won't be able to go on a picnic today.' We kids would cry but the business always came first. Service to the customers took priority. There were other times when we'd be closed for the evening, everyone would have gone home, and a private plane would come in just before dark and want fuel. It would have been easy just to stay in the house and not go over. Eventually, the people would have realized we were closed. But not my dad. He'd get his keys and put on his coat and go over and sell them gas."
>
> **GREGG MUNRO**

The canceled picnics and interrupted dinners were viewed with resentment by the Munro children, and at times even by their mother. But Bob Munro instinctively understood that the formula for success in business contains only one ingredient: satisfied customers. It's a simple formula, really, and it's amazing how many companies have forgotten it. Diversification, merger, takeover, buyout, down-sizing, right-sizing; without satisfied customers it's all just a big waste of time.

To Leslie and Gregg, tearfully helping their mother put away the picnic things, their father's willingness to drop everything to help a customer was unfathomable. But Bob Munro didn't go out of his way just to further the business. He accepted the last-minute charter requests and pumped gas for the after-hours customers because he genuinely enjoyed doing it.

> "He believed in people. That's a rare quality in business these days. Most businessmen you run into today believe that people are inherently wrong or dishonest or immoral. They believe that given half a chance, everyone, customers and business associates alike, will try to take advantage of them. Bob had quite the other opinion. He believed that all of us are good, honest, hardworking individuals, and should be treated accordingly. Any business, and especially a business like Kenmore, has to be people-oriented to be successful. How many times do we go into a store and the guy behind the counter doesn't know you, you don't know him, and it's obvious he doesn't care. Kenmore has grown up from a one-man company to eighty-plus people, but I think the message has come from Bob down to the staff to care about the customer, to deal with the customer on a one-to-one basis, to recognize and acknowledge each individual customer. What customer wouldn't appreciate that?"
>
> DICK GEE

Now, years later, as they assume increasingly responsible roles in charting the Air Harbor's course, it is often Leslie and Gregg who forego their weekend plans to make sure no Kenmore customer goes unserved.

> "I know I really resented those canceled picnics. I felt that my dad could have told those people 'no' just once. Why did someone else's last-minute plans have to mess up ours? But his attitude was if you're going to provide a service, provide the very best service you can to everyone who walks in the door, without exception. If I had to single out one thing that was responsible for the company's success, it would be that attitude.
>
> "When we started our scheduled service to the San Juans [in the late 1980s] we debated about what we would do if we had just one passenger booked for a flight. We'd lose money if we flew an airplane to Friday Harbor for just one passenger. So the debate was, should we go or should we cancel the flight? My dad said, 'If you advertise a service, either you provide it or you don't. You can't have people guessing if Kenmore is going to fly today or not.' So if someone books a flight and they're the only passenger, we'll go. We could say, 'I'm sorry, we've canceled that flight and we really feel bad,' and come up with a bunch of excuses, but we won't do that."
>
> GREGG MUNRO

Five-One-Mike spent most of the winter stored out of the way in the tie-down area. The Air Harbor continued to spread the word that the airplane was available for sale or lease, but no one was interested. Then in March 1951, a call came into the office from Fairbanks, Alaska. It seemed the U.S. government was planning to conduct an extensive survey of the country north of Fairbanks during the summer, and they were going to need air support. The caller had heard about Kenmore's big Bellanca and thought it might be just what the survey team was looking for. With Durwood Alkire's help, Munro and Wardleigh put together a bid for the contract and mailed it off. A few weeks later, Kenmore was notified that it had been awarded the job. The Bellanca finally was about to earn its keep.

The contract called for total air support for the survey team, not just for the lease of the Bellanca. This meant Kenmore was responsible for providing a pilot as well as an airplane. Munro, Fisk, and Wardleigh kicked around the idea of flying the contract themselves, but decided it would be smarter to hire a pilot who was familiar with the area being surveyed. The name that kept coming up was Sam White. White was an excellent pilot and a good friend of the Wien brothers. He'd been the first game warden in the Territory of Alaska to fly an airplane in support of his job, and he knew the country around Fairbanks as well as he knew his own front yard. As an added bonus, he'd flown in support of previous Coast and Geodetic surveys, so he knew the routine.

White was agreeable to the idea of flying for the Air Harbor during the summer, so the next task was to get Five-One-Mike up to Fairbanks. Kenmore's bid for the contract had been based on the assumption that the survey team wanted a floatplane, but a few days before Munro was scheduled to take the Bellanca north, the head of the survey team called and said they'd changed their minds; they wanted a wheelplane instead. The Pacemaker's original landing gear had long since disappeared, so Munro sent everyone out to comb the local airports for an undercarriage that could be modified to fit Five-One-Mike. Walt Winseman scrounged up some wheels and struts he thought might work, but by now they were out of time. Munro stuck the gear components in the back of the Bellanca, and with Winseman riding shotgun, took off for Alaska.

It was not a particularly pleasant trip. The snail-like cruising speed was no surprise to Munro, but the constant headache he suffered during the flight was. It was Winseman who finally figured out the cause. The Bellanca's engine mounts were not very good, and they passed the vibration of the nine-cylinder radial straight into the fuselage frame which shook the entire airplane and everything in it. The pounding was tolerable on a short flight, but as the hours dragged by on the flight up the Inside Passage, a headache was almost inevitable. To pass the time and take their minds off their throbbing skulls, Munro and Winseman tried to work out the best way to attach the landing gear struts to the Bellanca's fuselage, but the more they talked about it, the more skeptical they became.

"It's not going to be an easy job," Winseman shouted over the noise of the engine. "We're going to have to do some pretty fancy fabricating, and even at that I'm not convinced we can make the gear fit."

Munro didn't disagree, but he tried to remain optimistic. "All we can do is try. They used a lot of Bellancas up here before the war. Maybe we'll get lucky and find some Pacemaker struts in the back of somebody's hangar."

Two days after leaving Kenmore, Munro banked Five-One-Mike into final approach for Hood Lake on the outskirts of Anchorage. A telephone call to Sam White in Fairbanks yielded the welcome news that the survey team had decided they'd be better off with a floatplane after all. The decision eliminated the dilemma of fitting wheels to the Bellanca, but Munro and Winseman weren't out of the woods yet. The floats under Five-One-Mike had always been too small, and recently they had started to leak again. This hadn't been a concern back at the Air Harbor where the plane spent most of its time sitting on dry land, but the survey project would take the Bellanca to lakes hundreds of miles from the seaplane base at Fairbanks. White made it clear he had little interest in spending his summer struggling to keep Five-One-Mike afloat, so Munro said he'd try to solve the problem before they took off for Fairbanks.

"Walt and I poked around the seaplane base at Hood Lake and found an old set of EDO 6470 floats that had come off another airplane, probably a Norseman. The price was reasonable, and the owner was willing to take our smaller floats in trade.

"We taxied the Bellanca across the lake to an outfit that could hang it up in the air for us, and we started fitting the larger floats. It took us about three days. We just kept cutting and welding and bolting things together until we decided everything was balanced right and strong enough. I had every intention of getting the CAA to check the installation and sign it off, but they were closed for the weekend. I knew the Coast and Geodetic people were in a big hurry to get the plane, so Walt and I took off and flew it on up to Fairbanks and turned it over to Sam.

"Sam thought the installation looked great, and he flew the plane for us all that summer. In the meantime, the CAA wanted to put me in prison. They were threatening to do everything they could think of to me for flying an airplane with an unauthorized float installation. We went around and around on that until finally they went and looked at the plane. Back then, the inspectors really knew about airplanes, and they could see right away that Walt and I had put together a real good installation. Of course, Sam had a great reputation up there, and when he said it was a good installation, that pretty much ended it. Eventually, we got it all signed off and legal. Doing something like that today would be impossible."

BOB MUNRO

Kenmore Air Harbor had been smart to hire Sam White to fly the survey contract. His knowledge of the country and his flying and maintenance skills did much to make the project a success. White enjoyed flying Five-One-Mike despite its age, so it was with some sadness that he called Kenmore in the fall to announce that the surveyors had finished for the season, and it was time to ferry the Bellanca home.

The lakes were starting to freeze by the time Munro arrived in Fairbanks. The local seaplane operators based their machines on the Chena River, and while its current had thus far kept it open,

White cautioned that it could begin to ice over any day. Munro would be wise to get going while the going was still good.

Bidding his new friend good-bye, Munro took off for Anchorage. The low weather and scattered snow flurries made for poor visibility, but the tracks of the Alaska Railroad ensured a safe arrival in Anchorage. Munro intended his next stop to be Eyak Lake at Cordova, the same Eyak Lake where Virgil Kay's pilot had forged the first link in the chain of events that ultimately put the Bellanca in Kenmore's hands. The route from Anchorage to Cordova can be tricky, and the weather was coming down fast.

Landmark visibility was an essential requirement when flying a Bellanca Pacemaker because it was the only form of navigation that would work in the plane. There was so much steel tubing in the forward structure of the fuselage, a magnetic compass was rendered useless within a few days of installation. One of Alaska's first Bellanca pilots, Bill Lund, successfully solved the compass problem by mounting one in the rear of the cabin and reading it by means of a mirror strapped to one of the windshield supports. He said it took him awhile, but he eventually got pretty good at navigating with a backwards-reading compass. Unfortunately, Bob Munro was still years away from meeting Bill Lund, so Five-One-Mike did not sport one of the veteran bush pilot's nifty, rear-mounted compasses. All Munro had was a hand compass and a chart.

He managed to squeak through the mountains to Whittier, but as he headed out over Prince William Sound it began snowing hard enough to hide the islands he was using to guide him to Cordova. Using the water below him for a visual reference, he executed a 180-degree turn by his hand compass and headed back in what he hoped was the direction of Whittier. At eighty miles per hour, the snow streaked almost horizontally into the windshield, and he could barely see as far as the propeller arc. The visibility out the side was a little better, and it wasn't long before the islands blurred back into view again.

Encouraged, he tried for Cordova again, but again he was forced to turn back. Third time's a charm, he thought as he tried once more, but once again the islands faded away behind a veil of blowing snow. Frustrated, he returned to Whittier and landed. He'd hoped to get at least to Cordova on his first day, if not farther. Now he was stuck on the water in Whittier during a snowstorm which meant two things, both of them bad. His family would worry because he'd be at least a day late getting home and, if it continued to snow, he'd have to spend the whole night periodically sweeping the snow off the Bellanca's horizontal stabilizer to keep the weight from forcing the floats underwater.

He was off again at first light, hoping to get to Ketchikan or even Prince Rupert by the end of the day. The weather was still low, but the snow flurries were light and he was able to maintain visual contact with his landmarks as the Bellanca crept down the coast. The islands are close together in southeast Alaska, and there isn't much outside of fog that can prevent a pilot from threading through the narrow channels.

Munro got home at dusk on the third day after leaving Fairbanks. It had been the longest and most tiring flight he'd ever made. There was a set of Norseman beaching gear stowed behind the shop, and the mechanics dragged it over and attached it to the Bellanca. Tom Wardleigh fired up the weapons carrier, and Five-One-Mike was pulled out of the water and parked. It was the last time the big yellow airplane would move under Kenmore ownership. The following spring it was sold to Bob Hall, who planned to base the plane in Kodiak, Alaska.

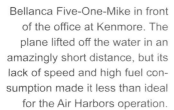

Bellanca Five-One-Mike in front of the office at Kenmore. The plane lifted off the water in an amazingly short distance, but its lack of speed and high fuel consumption made it less than ideal for the Air Harbors operation.

Munro watched with mixed emotions as Five-One-Mike rumbled off the surface of Lake Washington and headed west over the hill toward Puget Sound and the route north to Alaska. He was glad the Air Harbor had recovered the money it had poured into the Bellanca's restoration, but he was sorry to see such a unique and well-mannered airplane leave. Like a Duesenberg in a driveway, the old Pacemaker had attracted a lot of attention. It was almost impossible to visit the Air Harbor without making the dusty pilgrimage through the tie-downs to stand in the shadow of aviation's Golden Age and declare to anyone within earshot, "Now *this* is an airplane."

The broad-winged relic had provided the Air Harbor's pilots and mechanics with experiences they'd not soon forget, but there were even larger airplanes looming on Kenmore's horizon, and Munro's snowy flight home from Fairbanks would seem like a walk in the park compared to what was coming next.

11
THUNDERCHICKEN

WORLD WAR II BROUGHT AVIATION to Alaska in a big way. The Japanese landings on Kiska and Attu, two windswept, God-forsaken rocks near the western end of the Aleutian Chain, accomplished overnight what years of pleading and desk pounding on the part of the American officers assigned to the backwater Alaskan command had failed to do. The drone of obsolete B-18 bombers gave way to the rumble of B-24s, and ancient P-36 fighters were replaced by P-40s and twin-boom P-38s with tiger heads painted on their cowls. The chain of landing fields General Simon Buckner had managed through manipulation, coercion, and downright deceit to get built before the war were suddenly swarming with transports and attack planes heading north and west to the Aleutians.

Attu was retaken in May, 1943. What the invasion lacked in size was more than made up for by the miserable conditions under which it was carried out. Mud rendered mechanized vehicles useless within a few yards of the beach, and the gun crews had to haul their howitzers inland by brute force. The Japanese backed into the hills where snow and bitter cold reduced both sides to stumbling automatons. The only thing never in doubt was the outcome. The Japanese had been living on borrowed time almost from the moment they set foot on the island. Mounting pressures elsewhere in the Pacific required the attention of the Imperial Navy, and the handful of lumbering Kawanishi Type 97 ("Mavis") flying boats and Nakajima A6M2-N ("Rufe") floatplane fighters left behind at the hastily-constructed base on Kiska proved no match for the growing American air onslaught.

The battle to retake Attu lasted nineteen mind-numbing days. In proportion to the number of troops engaged, it was the second most-costly American battle in the Pacific, exceeded only by the invasion of Iwo Jima. And Attu was only the warm-up. Most of the Japanese were on Kiska, and the defenses there were much more formidable. But the Japanese knew a lost cause when they saw one. On the night of June 28, while demolition charges destroyed what little was left of their base, the island's 5,183 defenders scrambled up the sides of the eight ships that had been sent to evacuate them. When the Allied troops roared ashore on August 15, they were met only by a pack of pet dogs whose masters had been forced to leave them behind.

151

The successful end to the Aleutian Campaign did not signal a decrease in Alaskan air activity. If anything, it increased as the trickle of lend-lease bombers and fighters on their way to Russia became a flood. The North American B-25 Mitchell bomber and the mid-engined Bell P-39 Airacobra fighter were particular favorites, as their cannon were wonderfully effective against the mechanized German army. Photographs of Buckner's airfields with lines of Russia-bound planes stretching almost to the horizon were popular front-page evidence that victory was growing closer by the day.

The Japanese incursions onto U.S. soil did nothing to bolster the fortunes of wartime Japan, but they did serve to get the point across in Washington that Alaska was more than just a year-round refrigerator. The vast expanse of treeless tundra that swept west to the Bering Sea had tremendous strategic value, a value that appreciated greatly over the next few years with the outbreak of the Korean War and the disintegrating relationship with the Soviet Union. It was time to close the back door. Runways were blasted into the barren rock of the Aleutians. Foundations of hangars and mess halls and living quarters were poured. Radar stations were erected along the island chain and up the Bering coast. Squadrons of interceptors were sent north with orders to blow out of the sky any Soviet airplane foolish enough to try a sneak attack from the Siberian mainland. Alaska was a military backwater no longer.

Most of the construction projects were contracted out. Unlike their military counterparts, the civilian engineers and construction crews took vacations, quit, or were transferred to other jobs, and headed for town on weekends to stimulate the local economy by consuming vast quantities of alcohol. With only two days to complete a round trip to town from a remote construction site and still have enough time to get thoroughly blasted, the airplane was the obvious vehicle of choice. Between the comings and goings of the construction crews, the freighting in of essential equipment, and the ferrying of military personnel, business at the local and regional airlines serving western Alaska was booming by the late 1940s.

Construction continued year-round, which meant the airlines had to have planes that could operate off land or water in the summer and snow in the winter. There were lots of pre-war Stinsons, Bellancas, and Fairchilds around, but they were getting pretty tired. After cranking out Mosquito attack bombers during World War II, de Havilland Aircraft of Canada was marketing a design of its own, an all-metal, single-engine, utility plane called the Beaver, but it was too new to be widely available. There was one airplane, however, that was rugged, versatile, relatively cheap, and thanks to the end of the war, plentiful.

The Norseman had been the brainchild of Robert Noorduyn, a Dutch-born engineer who rose to become the manager of Tony Fokker's Atlantic Aircraft Corporation in the United States. The Fokker Universal, a single-engine, high-wing airplane, became quite popular among Canadian pilots during the early 1930s, and its sales convinced Noorduyn there was a market for a rugged plane designed specifically for the northern bush country. He tinkered with various design ideas for several years before moving to Montreal in 1934 and forming Noorduyn Aircraft, Ltd. One year later, on November 14, the prototype Norseman took to the air for the first time.

Noorduyn's design criteria had been rigid. The plane had to be equally at home on floats or skis. Noting that many of the lakes Canadian bush pilots were called upon to serve were small, Noorduyn fitted his plane with flaps, which permitted a touchdown speed of fifty-five miles per hour. A floatplane can't have too many doors, but most planes of the era had only one or two. The Norseman had four, one on each side of the cockpit and a larger one on each side of the main cabin. The two cabin doors were detachable to make it easier to load bulky fuel drums and machinery. The cabin was insulated with aluminum foil, and there were air scoops for ventilation in the summer and a cockpit-controlled heater for use during the winter. The air scoops were effective enough, but it wasn't long before the Norseman's heater acquired a nickname, the "Northwind," because as the pilots liked to say, "That's all we get out of it."

The engine cowl and fuselage panels forward of the cockpit were aluminum, while the cabin, wings, and tail surfaces were fabric-covered. The prototype was powered by a nine-cylinder, 420-horsepower Wright R-975 Whirlwind. The Mark II production model used a 450-horsepower Whirlwind, but performance was improved dramatically in 1936 with the introduction of the Mark IV which sported a 600-horsepower Pratt & Whitney R-1340. A fully loaded Norseman weighed 6,450 pounds, which after subtracting the plane's empty weight yielded a very respectable useful load of 2,775 pounds. Fitting a pair of floats to the plane reduced the useful load by about three-hundred pounds; floats are not nearly as heavy as they look. The airplane's cruise speed also was reduced by the installation of floats. One hundred miles per hour was about all a pilot could expect to see on the airspeed indicator.

The plane was an immediate success, and not only among Canada's bush country air carriers. The Royal Canadian Air Force was impressed with the big workhorse, and ultimately purchased 79 Mark IVs. The outbreak of World War II threatened to end Norseman production, at least temporarily, but the rugged plane had come to the attention of the U.S. Army Air Corps. Needing a large-capacity utility transport that could operate from short, unimproved fields, the Air Corps saw the Norseman as a ready-made solution. Of course, the Army wasn't about to set a precedent by ordering an off-the-shelf airplane and putting it into service as-is, so they asked for additional fuel tanks in the belly, a higher gross weight, and enough other modifications to warrant a new designation. Robert Noorduyn wanted to reserve the designation Mark V, "Vee" for Victory, to use on a model he planned to introduce after the war, so the Air Corps' Norseman was called the Mark VI. The Army called it a C-64 and bought 749 of them.

One of the hottest, most rugged fighters in the Air Corps' inventory was the Republic P-47 "Thunderbolt." It was also the largest fighter in the inventory, so perhaps it was the vague resemblance between two, radial-powered, jug-shaped airplanes that caused the pilots assigned to the infinitely slower Norseman to nickname it the "Thunderchicken." The name stuck and can be heard even today in eastern Canada where a handful of Norsemen are still earning their keep deep in the northern woods.

Noorduyn did introduce a Mark V immediately after the war, which was essentially the military Mark VI stripped of its extra equipment, but the market for the "new" airplane dried up almost instantly when the military on both sides of the border began mass-surplussing the Norsemen they'd bought before and during the war. Noorduyn's financial backers decided the future for Canadian-built aircraft was bleak at best, and in 1946 they sold the manufacturing and sales rights for the Norseman to Canadian Car & Foundry. The new owners continued producing the Mark V for a few years, but the heavy plane with its complicated wooden wing structure just wasn't competitive. The smaller De Havilland Beaver with its lightweight, monocoque fuselage and all-metal wing could outperform it, while the Beaver's bigger brother, the still-in-design Otter, would out-haul it. Norseman production finally dribbled to a halt after only fifty-five Mark Vs had been built.

The fact that the Thunderchicken was no longer in production had little effect on its popularity. What other plane offered solid, relatively modern construction, a reliable powerplant, a payload of well over a ton, and the flexibility to operate equally well on wheels, skis, or floats? The Norseman was still very much in demand in 1949, so when a man walked into the Kenmore Air Harbor office that September offering to trade a Mark VI and a surplus PT-26 for the company's Fairchild 24, Bob Munro listened attentively.

"The Norseman is a good airplane, but it's just too big for my business," the man explained. "Your Fairchild would be perfect."

"The Fairchild's a nice plane," Munro agreed. "What shape is your Norseman in?"

"Both airplanes are on wheels," the man answered somewhat evasively. "I know several people who are interested in the PT-26, so you shouldn't have any trouble selling it."

Munro didn't care about the low-wing, primary trainer. "What shape's the Norseman in?" he repeated.

"Uh, well, right now it's sort of upside down."

"Upside down?"

"There really isn't that much damage," the man hastened on reassuringly. "The propeller is bent and the tail's a little banged up, but otherwise it's okay."

Munro asked several more questions and said he'd make a decision within a few days. The Air Harbor itself had little use for an airplane the size of the Norseman, but Munro was sure if they fixed it up they'd have little trouble selling it. There was a board of directors meeting coming up, however, and he wanted to hear what his associates thought of the deal. The board met on the evening of September 20. Present were Bob Munro, president; Durwood Alkire, vice-president; Neil McConnell, secretary; and Norm Jacobson, treasurer. The first item on the agenda was the possible trade of the Fairchild for the upside-down Norseman. Munro relayed the gist of the offer and asked for comments.

"How'd he manage to flip the plane?" McConnell wanted to know.

"He had a load of flowers in the back," Munro explained. "Roses. No weight at all. He says he landed and when he went to put on the brakes it just went right up over its nose and onto its back.

A Norseman's pretty nose-heavy when its empty, and I suppose he might have put the brakes on too hard. Anyway, that's where it is, down in Oregon in Springfield, on its back."

"How much will it cost to repair it?" Alkire asked.

Munro shrugged. "It's hard to tell without having seen the plane, but it sounds like the damage isn't too bad. It's certainly within our ability to fix it, no matter how bad it is."

"What do you propose to do with the plane after it's repaired?" This was from Jacobson.

"Sell it. We should be able to get at least $7,000 for it, which is a lot more than we've put into the Fairchild."

"I should think it would be easier to sell if it was on floats," Alkire said.

Munro agreed. "It shouldn't be too difficult to come up with a set of used 6470s or 7170s. The 7170 would be better on a plane that size," he added.

McConnell pointed out the down side of the trade. "If we get rid of the Fairchild we won't have an advanced plane for the commercial students to fly."

This was something to consider. Munro suggested that perhaps commercial students could use the Seabee instead, and he made a note to discuss the matter with Bill Fisk the next day. The board kicked around the pros and cons of the deal awhile longer and then moved on to the next subject.

No firm decision was made that evening, although everyone agreed that the Norseman's resale potential was considerably greater than that of the Fairchild. For his own part, Munro hadn't been as concerned with reaching a decision as he had been interested in hearing all sides of the argument. By nature Munro was a cautious man, but what some people interpreted as a reluctance to act decisively was actually a determination not to act impulsively. His refusal to move on an issue until all the facts have been gathered and evaluated frustrated his employees and business associates more than once, but the undeniable fact remains that the Air Harbor has thrived in an arena where failure is the norm rather than the exception. Munro claimed he'd just been lucky. Luck may indeed have played a role, but all the luck in the world can't do much in the face of bad management decisions.

Munro's discussions with Fisk and Wardleigh the morning after the board meeting reinforced his conviction that the Norseman trade was a good idea. The Fairchild 24 would not be greatly missed, and the repaired Norseman could be sold for a decent profit. A telephone call closed the deal, and the Kenmore crew sat down to figure out how to retrieve their new acquisition from Oregon.

"You could do some field repairs and fly it back," one of the mechanics suggested.

Walt Winseman shook his head. "The engine was running when it flipped over. Depending on how hard the prop hit the ground the crank could be bent or cracked. I'd want to check it out pretty thoroughly before trying to run it."

"In addition to that," Wardleigh added, "we don't know how much repair the tail will need. We could end up spending quite a bit of time down there fixing things."

Fisk had another reason not to fly the Norseman back. "We'd have to land it at Renton and then pay someone to barge it up the lake. I think it'd be easier and cheaper just to drive down there and haul it back on a trailer."

"Maybe we should send Ted and Tommy," Munro offered with a wry smile, and the rest of the group burst into laughter. The incident at the root of the merriment had occurred a few months earlier when Huntley and Wardleigh had driven up to Orcas Island to pick up a Luscombe that had ground looped on the local airport. The owner had asked Kenmore to repair the plane, but damage to the tail and one of the wingtips had rendered it unflyable. Munro had sent Wardleigh out with the weapons carrier to haul the plane back to the Air Harbor, and young Huntley had gone along to assist. A two-place Luscombe is a small airplane, but there was no way to fit one into the back of the weapons carrier without first removing the wheels, wings, engine, and tail section. Not wanting to go to all this trouble, Wardleigh hit on an ingenious solution: they would tow the Luscombe back to Kenmore on its own landing gear.

> "We took the wings off and put the tail up inside the weapons carrier. The fuselage stuck out the back and rested on the main gear like a trailer. We tied the wings on top, and away we went. But as we drove out of the airport up there at Orcas we found we'd tied down the tail too far forward in the bed of the truck. The pivot point was too far forward, so when we turned the corner the side of the truck put a kink in the side of the plane. The Luscombe had an aluminum fuselage, it was harder to repair than a tube-and-fabric fuselage, so our little miscalculation took quite a bit of work to fix."
>
> TED HUNTLEY

The idea of towing the Norseman back from Oregon on its own landing gear was dismissed as being too risky. It was decided, instead, to borrow a flatbed trailer and tow it with the weapons carrier. The trailer was procured, and at 1:00 a.m. a few mornings later, Munro herded a sleepy Tom Wardleigh and Ted Huntley into the cab of the truck and headed south. Huntley's primary recollection of that day was that it was long.

> "That weapons carrier was a convertible, you know. There was no top on it or anything. It was really cold riding along in that truck early in the morning. We rode along, teeth chattering, mile after mile, and I kept waiting for Bob to go into a restaurant or something so we could get a hot chocolate and something to eat. Breakfast time went by and it got even colder, but Bob just kept driving. 'We've got to get this job done,' he said, and we just kept going. We pulled into Springfield about 9:00 in the morning. It was foggy, and we'd been freezing in that truck for close to eight hours. It wasn't very long before we had that Norseman apart and up on the trailer, and I thought, well, it must be lunchtime. But lunchtime never came. We took off for Kenmore and drove straight through."
>
> TED HUNTLEY

The interstate freeway system was still just a concept in General Dwight D. Eisenhower's mind in 1949. The principal north-south road threading Oregon and Washington together was Highway

99, a two-lane strip of patched-up blacktop that rambled through every milltown and farming community within reach. The trailer had done plenty of bobbing and weaving on the drive down, and the vision of the Norseman crashing sideways onto the pavement on the way home was not something Munro or Wardleigh cared to contemplate.

"It's too tall," Munro observed as he eyed the massive fuselage perched on the trailer. "It's too tippy sitting on its wheels like that, and I'm afraid that even with the tail off it might hit a bridge."

A quick sweep of the airport turned up some sturdy lengths of pipe and a heavy-duty chain hoist. Under Munro's direction, a makeshift A-frame was constructed over the forward part of the fuselage and the chain hoist attached to the lifting rings on top of the cockpit. The wingless plane was hoisted a few feet into the air, and Munro and Wardleigh removed the landing gear struts from the main undercarriage stub fairings. When the fuselage was eased back down onto the trailer, it sat a good three feet lower. The next challenge was to figure out how to keep the plane from being bounced off the trailer. They'd planned to secure the plane with rope, but then Wardleigh had a much better idea.

"Look," he said, pointing to one of the stub fairings, "the landing gear bolts to those square plates on the bottom of each stub fairing. Why don't we just run some long bolts up through the deck of the trailer and into the plates? I should think it would be impossible for the fuselage to fall off if we bolt it down like that."

A few minutes work with a drill was all it took to eliminate the spectre of the Norseman crashing off into a ditch on the drive back to Kenmore.

Years later, Munro did not recall being quite the taskmaster Huntley claimed; he distinctly remembered stopping for dinner on the drive home. All in all, it was quite an accomplishment for three people, driving hundreds of miles in the cold and fog, disassembling a large, heavy airplane and securing its components to a small truck and trailer, and then driving hundreds of miles home, all in a single day. Huntley may have gone hungry, but the job left him with a deep respect for the ingenuity of his two companions.

"Bob was very clever with rigging. He could figure out how to pick up anything in such a way that it didn't get hurt. We did that whole job in Springfield with nothing more than a chain fall and some pipe and the like. I remember another time going up with Bob and getting a Taylorcraft out of Lake Stevens. The plane was completely full of water. Most people try to lift a plane too fast and they tear it up. Break the wings, bend the frame. We did it with pulleys and rope and the diving tower at the swimming hole. The tower was high enough, and we just kept easing the plane up with the line a few inches at a time. Bob had us cut tiny 'L' shapes in the wing fabric to let the water out just in front of the spar. He has a tremendous finesse at this kind of thing. Tommy was real good at figuring out things like that, too. They were a good combination. Tommy's a very clever mechanic, but Bob is a rigger, too. He can always figure out the best way to hold something up."

TED HUNTLEY

It didn't take long to repair the Springfield Norseman, and Munro found a decent set of used floats to put under it. Much to everyone's surprise, the first offer for the plane didn't come from Alaska but from eastern Washington. Eddie Olsen needed a floatplane with a spacious cabin to haul passengers and freight up and down fifty-mile-long Lake Chelan, and he thought Kenmore's Mark VI would be perfect. The value of a Norseman was on the rise; Olsen paid $10,000 for the plane in twenty-four monthly installments at five percent interest.

The Kenmore office had become a busy place by 1950. Pilots on their way to or from Alaska would stop by for a cup of coffee and a chance to impress Ted Huntley and anyone else who would listen with their flying stories, while operators and would-be operators went in search of Bob Munro to talk up their latest schemes to make money with an airplane. For every sound idea there were a dozen dumb ones, but enough air services were actually getting off the ground to convince Munro that it might be a good idea to have a few sets of Norseman floats on hand just in case an operator called with a sudden need for another seaplane.

The Air Harbor in the early 1950s. The office has begun to sink into the underlying bog, but the deck chairs and Coke machine make it a fine place to sit and swap flying stories.

Someone heard that another set of EDO 7170s was for sale in the Seattle area and told Munro, who in turn mentioned it to Harold Nicholas. Nicholas agreed that anything connected with the Norseman would have a good resale value, and he offered to loan Kenmore the money to purchase the floats. The asking price was $4,000. Munro thought this was a bit steep, but considering the scarcity of good Norseman floats, he went ahead with the purchase.

Munro had discovered early on that government surplus could be a gold mine when it came to aviation equipment. First there had been the training center for mechanics at Pan Am which he had outfitted with surplus engines and tools from the Sand Point Naval Air Station. Then came the weapons carrier, which Munro claims played as significant a role in getting the Air Harbor off the ground as the airplanes. Later, when the lack of a proper hangar threatened to close down Kenmore's GI Bill flight school, it was military surplus to the rescue again in the form of the Navy deck building. No government sale bulletin went unread in the Air Harbor office, so it was no surprise that when the Air Force published a call for bids on two sets of EDO Model 7170 floats Munro was dialing the phone before the postman who'd delivered the catalog had left the driveway.

A few weeks later a large envelope with a U.S. government return address showed up in the mail. Munro ripped it open and discovered that Kenmore's bid of one thousand dollars for the two sets of EDO floats was the winner. The jubilation of obtaining two pairs of Norseman floats for one fourth of what they'd just paid for a single pair dimmed somewhat in the light of reality; the surplus floats were in Ogden, Utah, and the Air Harbor didn't have the thousand dollars.

The financial wherewithal to buy the floats was provided by the same Ralph Woodrig whose takeoff from the ice in front of the Air Harbor had inspired Tom Wardleigh to take a hammer to the windshield of Woodrig's plane. Woodrig's loan secured the huge floats but did nothing to move them any closer to the Air Harbor. Munro would have to go to Utah and get them himself.

The tandem-axle, wood-decked trailer Kenmore had used to retrieve the Norseman from Oregon was still on the property, but the round-trip drive to Utah in the dead of winter was too much to ask of the weapons carrier. While it may have been sound enough mechanically to make the trip, the survival chances of anyone riding in the open, unheated cab would have been marginal at best. With the deadline to remove the floats from the government depot in Ogden rapidly approaching, Wardleigh solved the transportation problem by offering to tow the trailer with his 1948 Chevrolet sedan. It was a nice car and Munro hated the idea of submitting it to a rugged towing job, but Wardleigh insisted, pointing out that they had no other choice.

The lousy weather and treacherous roads made for a tiring drive, but any plans Wardleigh and Munro might have had for a rest were dashed when they arrived at the depot. The floats had to be off the property by closing time, they were told, or they would forfeit their bid. Wardleigh took one look at the floats lined up neatly in the storage yard and figured their long drive had been in vain.

"I looked at them and told Bob there was no way. They were boxed up in huge military crates. We'd have to take out what appeared to be a million screws, and there were reinforcing straps all over. We wouldn't even be able to get the boxes open by the end of the day, let alone get the floats out. But Bob had a plan. We tore downtown and bought a chainsaw. Then we zoomed back out to the depot and sawed the ends off the crates and slid the floats out endwise. We'd haul one just outside the gate of the depot and then go back in and saw the next one out. We got the last float out about five minutes before closing time. They were all just lying on the ground outside in a ditch.

"The officials at the base, I remember, were furious when they saw the mess from those crates. Their view of the situation was that we were supposed to take everything, crates and all. We told them we would have been glad to if we'd had a reasonable time limit, but in light of their imposed deadline we did the best we could. We got all the floats outside the gate by closing time, but they were quite cross with us for leaving the crates."

TOM WARDLEIGH

The floats were not so much heavy as they were awkward and bulky. After much speculation and a little trial and error, Munro and Wardleigh settled on a stacking arrangement that put two floats on the trailer deck rightside up with the other two floats on top of them upside down. Wardleigh took it easy on the drive home, and they had no problems until they were descending the Blue Mountains in Oregon. It was dark, it was snowing, and the road was a solid sheet of ice. It was tricky driving, but Wardleigh was doing fine until they came around a curve and saw a pileup of cars at the bottom of the hill. With the brakes worse than useless on the icy road, it seemed inevitable that the pileup would soon include Wardleigh's nice little '48 Chevy and the four huge EDO floats.

Munro decided otherwise. Opening his door, he slid his feet to the right until he was crouching on the doorsill of the slow-moving car.

"Steer toward the shoulder on your side," he directed Wardleigh, "but not so sharp that you jackknife the trailer."

Keeping a firm grip on the door, Munro stepped to the icy pavement and began to trot alongside the car, pushing sideways against the body as he went. Slowly, the car began to ease over to the left shoulder, the trailer following obediently. Munro's plan was working, but they were running out of room. The accident at the bottom of the hill was less than fifty yards away. Munro shoved

Towing two sets of surplus Norseman floats home from Salt Lake City in the winter of 1950. Tom Wardleigh provided the car, Kenmore provided the trailer, and Bob Munro provided the brakes when he jumped out and dragged the whole rig to a stop while descending an icy grade in the Blue Mountains (photo by Tom Wardleigh)

as hard as he could against the car one more time and lost his footing. He was clinging to the door trying desperately to keep his feet out from under the rear wheel when he felt the Chevy's tires bite into the snow piled alongside the road. The car came to a stop almost immediately, tipping to the left as the wheels broke through the crusty surface and dropped into a drainage ditch. The trailer remained upright on the road, however, its fragile cargo in place and undamaged.

The big surprise came when they got home. After proudly unloading their prize, the Kenmore crew found that instead of two pairs of floats, the government had sold them three rights and a left. The floats themselves were identical; it was the placement of the attachment fittings that was the problem. After loudly proclaiming their disdain for government officials who couldn't tell what they had when they were looking at it, Wardleigh and Munro made a closer examination of the floats and found that the internal deck fittings that attached them to the struts had been designed to be mirror images of each other. By removing the fittings from one of the right hand floats and reversing them, they could be remounted on the opposite side, making it a left float and giving Kenmore the two pairs they'd thought they'd bought in the first place.

The decision to stockpile floats for the Norseman couldn't have been more timely. Finding a war-surplus Mark VI was easy, but locating a suitable set of floats to put under it was another matter. Kenmore was a name well known to Alaskan operators thanks to Bill Fisk's flight school and Walt Winseman's Seabee expertise, and when it was rumored that the Air Harbor had Norseman floats for sale, the phone began to ring in the chicken coop that still served as the company's headquarters.

One of the callers had just been awarded a seasonal contract to support a Coast and Geodetic survey, the same sort of job Sam White would soon be doing outside Fairbanks with the Air Harbor's Bellanca. The pilot on the phone had decided a Norseman would be the perfect plane for the job, and he'd found a decent one for sale in Marion, Ohio. Now he needed some floats. Munro informed him Kenmore had sold all the floats they'd had on hand, but he'd be happy to call around and see what he could find. One contact led to another, and in due course Munro discovered a pair of EDO 7170s for sale back east. The Alaska operator purchased them and ordered them shipped to Cleveland. The man selling the Norseman agreed to deliver the plane to the same city. Munro caught an airliner to Ohio and oversaw the installation of the floats before flying the Norseman back to Kenmore and then up the coast to Anchorage.

"I hadn't had a lot of time in a Norseman, so it was an interesting trip. The first thing that happened was right after I took off from the lake in Cleveland the whole cabin filled up with cotton stuffing. It turned out one of the seat cushions was ripped and there was a window open. There was cotton all over the place. I didn't know whether to try to deal with the stuffing or keep flying or what.

"My first stop was at Bemidji, Minnesota. I knew I could get gas there, but I hadn't realized how shallow the lake was. The owner had a little Stinson and he could taxi right on in, but the Norseman ran aground about a hundred yards out. I needed gas badly, so we ended up going to the fire department. They brought down a bunch of fire hoses and strung them together. I took one end and waded out to the airplane while they attached the other end to the gas pump on the dock. It wasn't fast, but it was a lot better than sloshing back and forth through the mud with a couple of five gallon cans."

BOB MUNRO

Munro's next stop was Great Falls, Montana. A call on the radio yielded the information that the best place to land was on the Missouri River next to the city park. There were plenty of places to tie up the plane for the night, he was told, and in the morning he could taxi across to the mouth of the Sun River where he could get gas at the marina. It was almost dark when Munro made his approach to the Missouri and landed without incident. As he was securing the plane, a man walked up and remarked that it must have been difficult avoiding the power lines that were strung across the river.

"Power lines?" Munro said, surprised. "I didn't see any power lines."

"Oh, they're all over the place." The man pointed to where Munro had made his final approach. "There's four of 'em right through where you landed."

"They told me on the radio this was the best place to land. They didn't say anything about power lines."

"Well, believe me, they're there."

Munro saw them the next morning, four heavy cables strung through the area where he'd made his final approach to the river. Each one was capable of tearing the undercarriage or wings off any airplane unlucky enough to tangle with it. Drawing a mental picture of his flight path, he realized he must have skimmed over the first two wires and then just squeaked by under the third one. He hadn't seen a thing.

Munro touched down in front of the Air Harbor late the following evening. He spent the next few days flying charters in the company Seabee while the Air Harbor's mechanics carried out some minor repair work on the Norseman. Reg Collins was in town for a visit, and Munro's brother Jack had declared an interest in visiting Alaska again, so there were three people on board when Munro powered the Norseman off Lake Washington and banked right toward Puget Sound and the route north. The weather was great, and the 600-horsepower Pratt & Whitney thundered away reassuringly in front of the firewall. There was no reason for any of the three men chattering happily away in the cockpit to suspect how close this trip was to become to being the last flight any of them ever made.

True to form, the weather that had been so nice in Seattle deteriorated as the Norseman droned up the east shore of Vancouver Island and then entered the maze of channels and islands that comprised the Inside Passage. By the time they reached Prince Rupert, the wind had increased to a near gale, and the spray from the waves marching in through Dixon Entrance had been whipped into a haze that hung like a light fog over the churning surface. The shortest route between Prince Rupert and Ketchikan is straight across the Entrance, but when Munro saw what was going on out in the channel he decided to play it safe and hug the shoreline instead. Attempting a landing in the open water of the Entrance would be tantamount to suicide; the convoluted, rocky coastline offered at least some protection from the waves in the unlikely event of an emergency. Even with the wind and the longer route, Munro estimated the flight would take no longer than an hour.

Earlier in the day, Jack Munro had placed a box between the front seats so he could sit between his brother and Reg Collins. This not only afforded a better view forward over the engine cowl, he didn't have to yell as loud to participate in the conversation. It also gave him a good view of the Norseman's somewhat rudimentary instrument panel. About twenty minutes out of Prince Rupert, Jack Munro noticed something that didn't look right.

"Isn't the oil pressure gauge working?" he shouted over the roar of the engine. "It's reading zero."

Munro looked and chopped the throttle. "We're losing oil," he announced to his suddenly nervous passengers. "I'm going to set down behind that little island."

Not knowing how close the engine was to seizing, Munro got the Norseman on the water as quickly as possible. A chain of small, rocky islands that lay a half mile off the mainland broke up the force of the wind and waves and created patches of relatively smooth water on their leeward sides. Munro thumped the Norseman down in one of the smooth areas and taxied into a small bay where he'd seen a moored log raft. The three men were surprised to find it just as noisy outside on the logs as it had been inside the airplane with the engine running. The wind roared like an express train through the bent and battered trees that clung to the rocky surface carrying with it the evil hiss of the waves breaking against the windward shore along with an occasional spattering of salt spray.

What moments earlier had been a routine flight to Alaska had just become a survival situation, and the odds didn't look good. The Norseman had no radio, and Munro hadn't filed a flight plan. They wouldn't be reported missing for days, and then it was anyone's guess how long it would be before someone thought to look for them so far off the preferred route. It was possible that whoever owned the log raft might show up to tow it somewhere, but there was just as good a chance he wouldn't, so that form of rescue wasn't worth dwelling on.

More to pass the time than anything else, Munro and Collins decided to inspect the airplane in search of the ailment that had caused the loss of oil pressure. It turned out to be an easy search; all they had to do was trace the long, wet smear of oil covering the bottom of the fuselage back to its source. Munro expected to find a broken hose or a blown seal, but the culprit turned out to be the oil tank which had split open and dumped most of its contents overboard. It was the sort of thing that normally took only an hour or so to repair back at the Air Harbor, but on this windswept island with no tools, no welding equipment, and no spare oil, the wings might as well have fallen off the airplane. There didn't seem to be anything to do but wait.

Forty-five minutes later, the unmistakable sound of airplane engines blew in on the wind. The sound was followed almost immediately by the airplane itself, a twin-engine Grumman Widgeon flying boat that zoomed over the cove, banked around, and splashed down in the lee of the island. The Widgeon belonged to the U.S. Fish & Wildlife Department, and it had departed Prince Rupert shortly after Munro had taken off in the Norseman. Just as the faster amphibian was about to pass the wallowing floatplane, the Fish & Wildlife pilot was surprised to see the Norseman bank steeply and dive down to land near one of the tiny islands that lay off the uninhabited mainland. The Widgeon pilot continued toward Ketchikan, but the sight of the floatplane ducking down to land in the face of the wind and waves blasting in from Dixon Entrance bothered him more with each passing mile. He was only a few minutes out of Ketchikan when his curiosity got the better of him and he hauled the Grumman around 180 degrees and headed back toward Prince Rupert.

Needless to say, Collins and the Munro brothers were glad to see him. After talking the situation over, the Widgeon pilot took off for Ketchikan to get a sufficient quantity of engine oil to fill the Norseman two or three times over. Meanwhile, Munro and Collins stuffed rags into the crack in the Norseman's oil tank and wrapped it tightly with a length of rope from the Widgeon's survival kit. The Fish & Wildlife pilot returned and the Norseman was topped off with oil. The tank still seeped lubricant, but Munro thought it would hold together long enough to reach Ketchikan.

Careful to remain over calm water in the event they had to land suddenly, and with the Widgeon trailing along just in case, Munro nursed the leaking Norseman up the coast. They droned past the entrance to Portland Canal and back into U.S. airspace over the invisible line that runs the length of the seventy-mile long fjord and delineates the border between British Columbia and southeast Alaska. The last piece of open water to be crossed was the entrance to Behm Canal, the broad channel that separates Revillagigedo Island from the mainland. The oil pressure was dropping again, but Munro knew he had it made as he guided the Norseman past Mountain Point and lined up for a landing in Ketchikan harbor.

With the Norseman safely ramped up out of harm's way on the waterfront, Munro and Collins drained the remaining oil into a bucket, removed the oil tank, and took it to Ketchikan Welders for repair.

"I'd have been scared to death," the welder said after Collins had described their misadventures on the rocky island. "Stuck out there without food or anything. If that other pilot hadn't seen you go down, you could have starved or died of exposure before anyone came looking for you."

"Oh, I don't know," Munro said. "A fisherman would have come along, or someone looking for drift logs. I wasn't too worried. Someone would have turned up."

Munro wasn't trying to put on a brave face for the benefit of the welder; he really hadn't been very worried out on the island.

> "I never let myself worry too much about what might happen in situations like that. I've seen people do that, and it just makes things worse. The important thing is to deal with things as they come up. If you do that, and don't get so worried about what might happen later that you can't function, you'll probably come out okay. In this case, the first thing we did was make sure the airplane was secure. Then we decided to look for the problem and try to think of ways to fix it. That's what we were doing when the Widgeon flew over and saw us."
>
> BOB MUNRO

One of the jobs undertaken by Kenmore during the summer of 1951 was the repair of a Seabee owned by the State of Washington. The plane had been involved in a minor accident, and the state had put the repair out to bid. Kenmore's bid was the lowest and it won them the job, but it was what happened after the repairs were complete that caused the project to be remembered even to this day. Tom Wardleigh and his mechanics had the Seabee back in the air much earlier than expected and for considerably less than the original bid. The state was prepared to pay the total bid amount, so they were stunned when the Air Harbor submitted a bill charging only for the work performed. A letter was sent to the Air Harbor stating they were welcome, in fact, expected to charge the full amount, but Munro refused, saying the job had come in so much under budget that he didn't feel it was right to collect money the company hadn't earned.

Tom Wardleigh's sense of integrity and quiet competence had greatly impressed the state's pilot, Bob Josephson, during his visits to Kenmore to check on the progress of the repair work. When the day came to collect the Seabee, Josephson took the Air Harbor's young shop foreman aside for a moment.

"Do you have a multi-engine rating?" the government pilot asked.

"Sure," Wardleigh replied. "I got my Multi-Engine Sea in a Widgeon and my Multi-Engine Land in a Bamboo Bomber at Paine Field."

Josephson smiled at Wardleigh's reference to the five-place, twin-engine transport Cessna had built during the war.

"I don't know how you like it here at Kenmore or what you want to do with the rest of your life, but a job opportunity's just come up that I think would be perfect for you."

"I'm listening."

"There's a man in town named Clarence Rhode," Josephson continued, "who's hiring for the U.S. Fish & Wildlife service in Alaska. They've got about thirty airplanes up there, everything from Stinson Gullwings to Grumman Widgeons, and they're looking for a pilot who can also work as a maintenance foreman. I think the job would be right up your alley. If you're interested, I'll put in a good word for you with Clarence."

Wardleigh was definitely interested. He enjoyed working at Kenmore, and he loved the camaraderie of a small company where everyone pitched in to get the job done. On the other hand, he'd just gotten married and he was getting tired of the seven-day work weeks and fourteen-hour days. In addition to his responsibilities as shop foreman, he also served as the night flying instructor, teaching ground school in the evenings and then taking advanced students up for their required night flying experience. A job with shorter hours and time off on the weekends sounded nice, and he'd liked what he'd seen of Alaska on the flights he'd made with Munro. His new wife was willing to give it a try, so Wardleigh made an appointment to see Rhode. It didn't take Rhode long to figure out he had a real gem in front of him, and he offered Wardleigh the maintenance foreman job on the spot. Wardleigh accepted, but now came the hard part; telling Bob Munro and the rest of his friends and co-workers at the Air Harbor he was leaving.

"It wasn't easy, leaving Kenmore. It had been a wonderful learning experience for me. I got my start as a pilot there, and certainly a huge enhancement of my mechanical abilities. I guess Bob Munro is very close to a father-figure in my life. A highly esteemed friend with whom I worked very closely during an important time for me. We were such a small group, it was more like everybody getting together in the morning to get the job done rather than a structured company with rules and job titles and so on. It was perhaps the happiest working period in my whole career, although I've had many fine jobs since then."

TOM WARDLEIGH

Bob Munro was sorry to see Wardleigh leave. His former Pan American student not only had developed into a talented pilot and mechanic, he'd become a good and close friend. But it was obvious that Wardleigh was ready to take on greater challenges, and Munro was not one to discourage anyone's ambitions. He'd never regretted for a moment his own decision to leave the security of Pan American, and he wasn't about to stand in the way of someone else's bold jump.

Wardleigh headed north in September 1951. He worked for the Fish & Game Department for seven years, building up the maintenance facilities in addition to flying. Then in 1958, Clarence Rhode disappeared while flying a Grumman Goose over the Brooks Range with his son Jack and an enforcement agent named Stan Frederickson on board. At first it was assumed Rhode was stuck somewhere with a dead battery, but when the Fish & Wildlife pilots that flew out to find him failed to locate the Goose anywhere along his route, the government launched the most extensive search ever flown in the history of Alaska. It went on for weeks, but it came up empty-handed. It was as though the Goose had disappeared off the face of the earth.

If there was ever a time the Fish & Wildlife Department needed Rhode's dynamic leadership, it was now, as Alaska approached statehood. Much to Wardleigh's dismay, it was announced that the airplanes and facilities he'd worked so hard to improve would be split up between separate but similar federal and state wildlife organizations. Saddened by the death of his friend and disappointed over the imminent breakup of the Fish & Wildlife air operation, Wardleigh began to think about leaving Alaska and government service for something different.

Fortunately for the future of pilots everywhere, he was offered a job with the CAA. It was an important time for aviation in Alaska. The old four-course radio ranges were being replaced with VOR stations that offered tremendous advancements in navigation accuracy. Airports were receiving instrument landing systems for the first time as well, and the CAA was busy designing approaches and establishing airways all over the state. Wardleigh was right in the middle of it all flying DC-3s and DC-4s as the CAA began positioning navaids and designing landing approaches to the newly-discovered oil fields. The need for helicopters to find and land on offshore drilling rigs no matter what the weather led to the development of airborne radar approaches, a procedure Wardleigh helped pioneer in Alaska that is now used routinely around the world.

In July 1951, a couple of months before Wardleigh's departure for Alaska, Kenmore decided to add a Norseman to their own fleet. On the surface, the deal to purchased Olympic Airways' sole asset appeared straightforward enough, but by the time the dust and legal papers had settled, Munro's faith in human nature had been sorely tried. Olympic Airways had been conceived four years earlier when Seattle attorney Stewart Nielsen decided he wanted to be an airline tycoon. Pan American, United, and Trans World Airlines had little cause for worry; Nielsen's financial resources were good for a single airplane, a surplus Norseman, and a single route, Seattle to Port Townsend.

Like the Sirens whose song would have charmed Odysseus' ship into the rocks had it not been for the wax in his crew's ears, the Port Townsend run suckered in pilot after pilot. The route was a loser. Always was, always would be. The town had blossomed in the late 1800s on the promise of becoming the Pacific terminus of a new transcontinental railroad, and the substantial brick buildings lining the waterfront had been erected in anticipation of the business boom that would ride the rails directly into the pocketbooks of the founding fathers. But the railroad went to Tacoma instead, and Port Townsend sank into the doldrums of a backwater mill town. The arrival of air service in the northwest did nothing to improve Port Townsend's fortunes, yet operator after operator became convinced that there were substantial numbers of people who wanted to go there. There weren't, and operator after operator went broke. Stewart Nielsen was no exception.

Belatedly realizing there was no connection between the romance of aviation and financial success, Nielsen put his airplane into dry storage out at the Air Harbor and went on to other endeavors. For three years the silver and green Norseman sat, gathering dust and bird droppings. Munro advised Nielsen to let the Air Harbor mechanics run the engine occasionally and keep the fabric cleaned off but the attorney wasn't interested. Finally, strapped for cash for some new venture, Nielsen decided to put his plane up for sale. Kenmore's own operations didn't require so large a machine, but Munro figured Kenmore wouldn't have any trouble leasing the plane once it was put back into shape. The agreed-upon price was $7,000 which, as usual, was more than the Air Harbor had in the bank. A short-term loan of $4,000 from one of the company's supporters made up the difference, and the lawyer happily signed N66540 over to the Air Harbor.

Then the lawyer turned nasty. Shortly after cashing the Air Harbor's check, he fired off a letter to Munro announcing that he was suing the company for neglecting to maintain his airplane while it was on the property. In fact, he went on to say, Kenmore had rendered his airplane inoperable by removing the bilge pump and the starting crank from the cockpit. As far as Nielsen was concerned, Bob Munro and Kenmore Air Harbor had been responsible for the failure of his air service to Port Townsend, and he was seeking damages in the amount of $16,000.

This was just nuts, but Nielsen's charges couldn't be ignored. Kenmore filed a countersuit, and the battle was on. Nielsen claimed the Air Harbor had allowed the fabric to rot off his airplane. Munro invited the local CAA inspector to come out look for himself. Three years of neglect had done nothing to improve the fabric's condition, but it was still airworthy. Nielsen claimed the Air Harbor had allowed his engine to seize up with rust. The inspector noted that while there was indeed a fair amount of surface rust on the cylinder fins and engine case, mechanic Walt Winseman had demonstrated to the CAA's satisfaction that the internal components were in good shape and moved freely. That left the claim of the missing bilge pump and starting handle.

Kenmore lost that one. No one remembered having seen a bilge pump in the plane to begin with, so it was impossible to prove the Air Harbor had or hadn't lost it. The starting crank was another matter. The Norseman's R-1340 had an electric starter, but if the battery was low Pratt & Whitney had installed an inertia starter which consisted of a flywheel and clutch assembly that could be turned manually with a crank. The Island Airways Norseman that had been based at Kenmore a few years earlier had arrived on the scene with a chronically weak battery and no hand crank. Nielsen's air service had long since gone belly up and his Norseman was just sitting there, so it seemed logical to borrow its starting handle whenever the battery in the Island Airways Norseman wasn't up to the task of starting the engine, which to Ted Huntley seemed to be virtually every morning.

Nielsen's crank handle wasn't missing; it was hanging on the hook in the shop where Huntley kept it. Everyone, including Nielsen, knew where it was, but the judge was forced to rule that due to the death of the plane's original battery, removal of the crank had, in fact, rendered Nielsen's engine inoperable. It was a technicality and the judge knew it. He fined the Air Harbor twenty-five dollars for "losing" Olympic's crank handle and bilge pump, and tossed the rest of Nielsen's claim out of court.

The whole affair had been a puzzlement to Munro, who couldn't conceive why anyone would want to behave so dishonorably. Kenmore's only role in Nielsen's business had been to store his airplane, and Munro's offers to perform minimal maintenance on the machine had been firmly declined every time. Financial desperation seemed to be the only explanation, but to a man who believed if you needed something you worked for it, this wasn't a valid excuse. The judge's decision had upheld Munro's adherence to principle, but it didn't ease the disappointment of discovering there were people around him with such low ethical standards. Hoping Nielsen would see the futility of pursuing a similar course in the future, Munro paid the twenty-five dollar fine and went back to the Air Harbor to begin the search for an operator who might be interested in leasing Kenmore's new Norseman.

It was too late in the year to land a contract for 1951, but Bristol Bay Airlines said they would take the plane for the following season. Then word came that another Alaskan survey contract was coming up for bid for the 1952 season. Another Norseman seemed to be the answer, and there just happened to be one for sale. It was Huntley's old nemesis, NC55555, the silver-with-red-trim Island Airways airplane. The CAA had since switched to a shorter registration system, so the plane was now lettered N55555. Other than that, it was the same beast Huntley had cranked into life each morning for the run north to the San Juan Islands.

Ken Armstrong had purchased the plane when Island Airways went broke, and after messing around with it for awhile, he put it up for sale for $17,500, a price that included a rebuilt engine worth at least $3,000 and a bunch of parts valued at $1,000. Kenmore bought it and Munro immediately submitted a bid for the survey contract. Based on the excellent job Sam White had just done for the government with the Air Harbor's Bellanca and the fact that Kenmore was offering an even better airplane this time, Munro figured the contract was as good as won. It wasn't. The contract went to an operator whose bid was based on using an old Travelaire. Munro was surprised; he wouldn't have thought a Travelaire would be up to the job.

Like the Bellanca, the Norseman was way oversize for Kenmore's own requirements. The last thing Munro wanted was to be placed in the same position that had driven so many other operators out of business: too little business to support too expensive an airplane. Then Ray Petersen, who a few years earlier had combined his own air service in Alaska with two others to form Northern Consolidated Airlines, called to say he needed a big floatplane to haul supplies out to a string of fishing camps he was setting up. Did Kenmore know of anything he could use? Five-Five, as Kenmore's second Norseman was nicknamed, would fill the bill perfectly.

Now Munro could breathe a little easier; both airplanes would be earning their keep the following summer. Five-Four-Zero, the ex-Olympic Airways plane would generate $8,000 flying for Bristol Bay, while Five-Five would bring in $3,500 from Northern Consolidated. In the meantime, there wasn't much Kenmore could do other than set the big planes on wooden blocks out in the parking area. Occasions did arise, however, when a job would require the Norseman's tremendous load-carrying ability, and one of them, usually Five-Five, would be trundled down the ramp and into the water.

Munro found the Norseman quite easy to fly, although these attributes were often overpowered by the airplane's awkward flap system.

> "It had a real bum deal on the flaps. There was a great big handle up on the ceiling connected to a Teleflex cable that went to the flaps. You'd get ready to land and you'd have to reach up there and crank and crank and crank as hard as you could to get the flaps to move. On the other hand, you could land in almost any kind of water and it would just sit there. There wasn't any bang or anything on rough water. It was an extremely sturdy airplane."
>
> **BOB MUNRO**

It also was an extremely noisy airplane. The fabric fuselage did nothing to dampen the thunder of the nine-cylinder engine. In the early 1950s, earplugs were something swimmers wore, and comfortable, sound-deadening headsets were years in the future. Munro racked up hundreds of hours of Norseman time, much of it with the doors off and the engine at high power. His ears simply couldn't take it. The golden age of bush flying wasn't all radial-powered romance; its down side was evidenced in later years by the tiny, flesh-colored amplifiers nestled in the ears of Munro and most of his peers.

The Norseman had another drawback. If there is one thing that all radial aircraft engines have in common, it is their propensity to seep oil. It oozes from under rocker covers and dribbles from pipe fittings and eventually coats everything from the firewall forward. When the airplane is stationary, gravity is the ruling force, and the oil puddles on the ground beneath the cowling.

Gravity loses out in flight, however, when the air roaring through the engine compartment takes over and forces the oil aft where it emerges through gaps and seams in the skin to finish its rear-ward journey as a series of gritty, brown streaks. This is an eyesore when it occurs on a metal airplane, but it has little consequence except to the line boys who have to clean it off. In the case of the fabric-skinned Norseman, however, the oil streaming back from the engine compartment created a serious fire hazard.

The cylinders of the R-1340 exhausted into a collector ring that dumped overboard through a large stack projecting from the left side of the engine cowl. Most Norsemen had extensions that piped the exhaust several feet aft of the cowling. The extensions had advantages: they muffled the sound of the engine, although not by much, and they helped keep the exhaust fumes away from the cockpit. As far as Munro was concerned, however, these advantages were far outweighed by the fact that the extension ended right where the fabric fuselage skin began, a skin that soaked up every drop of engine oil that blew its way.

"That was one thing you had to be very, very cautious about. It was fabric right up to the en-gine, and it was always oily and sopped up. One little backfire and you'd have a fire on the front end. We usually had someone with an extinguisher standing by when we'd start up in the morn-ing, it was so easy to get a fire started with all that oil-soaked fabric right there by the engine."

BOB MUNRO

Kenmore took the stack extensions off their Norsemen which reduced the fire danger, but a healthy backfire could still send a tongue of flame squirting back to ignite the fabric under the cockpit. They also installed a three-bladed propeller on Five-Four-Zero to see how it would per-form against Five-Five's two-bladed prop. The balance of a three-bladed prop generates less vibra-tion, and its shorter blades are less susceptible to spray erosion during takeoff. Some pilots argue that a two-bladed propeller generates more thrust at high rpm, but there's no arguing the fact that the three-bladed prop is quieter.

If the Wright brothers had conducted their first flight near a residential neighborhood, some-one would have complained about the noise. Even in the early 1950s, airplane noise was an issue, especially in the growing lakeside communities under the Sand Point Naval Air Station traffic pat-terns. A considerate man to begin with, Munro knew that the future of his company depended to a great degree on maintaining good relationships with the homeowners who were moving in ever-increasing numbers to the communities around the north end of the lake. The fact that Five-Four-Zero was noticeably quieter during takeoff than Five-Five was not lost on Munro, and was largely responsible for the company's noise reduction policy that continues even today.

Munro flew two hunting parties into British Columbia during the fall of 1951. The customer on the first trip was Buzz Fiorini. He and his hunting buddies had been talking about trophy hunting in British Columbia for years. Finally in the fall of '51, they decided to do it; so Fiorini, who was famous among his friends for his negotiation skills, drove out to Kenmore to arrange a ten-day charter.

"There's five of us," Fiorini said in answer to Munro's query. "And we'll need you and the plane to stay with us because we're going to move camp every couple of days to a different lake."

"Where is it you're going to start?" Munro asked as he spread a large chart of British Columbia across his desk.

"The guide's main camp is on Joe Irwin Lake." Fiorini searched around the chart with his finger and then banged it down near the town of Dease Lake. "Here. This is where we need to go first."

"That's quite a haul," Munro observed as he mentally calculated the distance from the hunting camp back to the coast and then southeast to Seattle. "The five of you plus the pilot means we'll have to take one of the Norsemen, so the flight up will take about a day and a half. We can spend the night at Wrangell and then fly up the Stikine River the next morning. I can get gas at Dease Lake before we go on to the lake."

"We've booked a six day hunt."

"Plus two days up and two days back for a total of ten days," Munro said.

"Right," Fiorini settled back in his chair. "We've been dreaming about this trip for a long time," he said pointedly, "but the guide was awfully expensive. I just hope we have enough left for the flight."

The Norseman had a voracious appetite for fuel. Munro figured he could burn five-hundred gallons easily on a trip like this and probably more, depending on how much flying he had to do once he got up there. Then there was oil. Between burning it and leaking it, an R-1340 could consume up to a gallon an hour. Then he had to figure the value of his own time. He couldn't be in two places at once, so Kenmore would have to turn away at least a few customers while he was gone. Plus Munro was pretty sure he'd be called upon to help set up and strike the camps as they moved from lake to lake, and he wasn't about to give away his labor for free. On the other hand, he wanted to satisfy his customers, which at this point meant pricing the trip so they could afford it.

"I can do it for four thousand dollars," he said finally.

Fiorini shook his head and looked depressed. "I was afraid of that. We just don't have that kind of money."

"How much did you have in mind?" Munro asked.

"We could probably afford $2,000."

This time it was Munro who shook his head. "I'd lose money if I took the job for $2,000. We kind of live day by day out here. If I lost money on this trip I might not be able to make the payroll, and I won't do that to my employees."

"We could possibly come up with $3,000," Fiorini conceded.

Munro scribbled some calculations on a piece of paper. "Okay," he said at last, "I can do it for that." Kenmore's profit would be marginal at best, but at least it was ten days' worth of work for the airplane.

The group departed for Canada a few weeks later. It was autumn, which on the northwest coast means fog. The weather was fine through the San Juans and along the east coast of Vancouver Island, but north of Campbell River lacy fingers of fog began creeping through the mosaic of channels and islands. Munro got as far as Sullivan Bay, and then the fog closed in completely.

"This is as far as we go today," Munro announced as he led his passengers down the floating dock toward the white frame buildings clustered against the rocky shore. "We'll stay here tonight and hope the fog lifts in the morning."

The situation was no better in the morning. It was made even worse, in fact, by the tantalizing patch of blue sky that appeared directly over the bay. The hole was too small to climb through but it did show that the tops of the fog banks were only a few hundred feet above the water. Munro was tempted to try it, but the scare he'd received while attempting his fog-bound takeoff at Andersen Island a few years earlier kept him pacing on the dock beside the Norseman. But the hole kept getting bigger until he couldn't stand it anymore. The Pratt & Whitney was reluctant to start in the damp cold, but after a bit of coaxing with the primer, the nine cylinders sputtered to life. As soon as the engine settled down to a steady rumble, Munro scrambled out of the cockpit and trotted back to the clapboard cabin where his passengers sat staring glumly at the mist shrouding the tops of the trees across the bay.

"Let's go," Munro said banging open the door. "There's a clear hole right above us. Once we're north of Cape Caution we shouldn't have any more problems with fog."

By the time Fiorini and his partners had strapped themselves into the cabin, the engine was up to temperature. Munro studied the sky above the bay; the patch of blue was definitely larger. Leaning into the cockpit, he shut off the engine before dropping back onto the float to untie the mooring lines. A quick shove against the dock and Five-Five was drifting out into the current. The engine fired back to life at the first turn of the starter and the Norseman moved out smoothly through the dark green water. Lining up into what little wind there was, Munro retracted the water rudders and eased the throttle up to full power. As the plane climbed ponderously up onto the step, Munro had a sudden feeling of dèjá vu. It was the Anderson Island incident all over again. The heavily laden Norseman was accelerating so slowly, it would fly into a fog bank almost as soon as it left the water. The best he'd be able to do was start a turn back to the hole immediately after liftoff and minimize his time in the fog.

A slight surge in acceleration signaled the Norseman's departure from the water, and Munro cranked the flaps up and rolled into his climbing turn. The altimeter was approaching three-hundred feet when he began slipping in and out of the edge of the fog bank. At least he was better prepared this time. Keeping his eyes on the airplane's gyro horizon and rate of climb indicator, Munro held the plane in the turn. He also held his breath. He was positive he was well clear of the surrounding terrain, but as the seconds dragged on with only sporadic glimpses of where he was, he began to wonder. Where was that high, tree-covered island that sat just off the north end of the bay? He was sure he was nowhere near it, but what if he was wrong? He'd almost convinced himself he was headed directly for it when the plane burst back into the sunlight. A quick glance around and Munro could breathe again. There were the tiny white buildings of Sullivan Bay and there, half in the fog, was the tree-covered island. It was at least a mile away.

The fog banks were patchy enough so that, once on top, Munro had no problem picking his way north along the coast. As he had predicted, the fog thinned out as they rounded Cape Caution and left Vancouver Island behind. It was gone completely by the time they reached Rivers Inlet. The flight up the Passage to Wrangell was long, almost five hours, but Munro's passengers found the scenery so dramatic they hardly noticed the time. From Wrangell, Munro headed east up the spectacular Stikine River, past glaciers oozing from the black, brooding peaks of the Coast Range, to Telegraph Creek. From there it was a straight shot across the wind-swept eastern slopes to Dease Lake where Munro refueled before the short shop to Joe Irwin Lake.

Bob Munro and Norseman Five-Five during a hunting charter in 1951. The hunters only wanted the antlers, but Munro couldn't stand to see so much good venison go to waste. Each day while his customers were out hunting, he butchered the carcasses and stowed the best cuts of meat in the floats.

After what by now had been almost eight hours in the airplane, everyone was ready for a good rest at the hunting camp, but it was not to be. They had no trouble finding the lake and the cabin, but when they landed, the camp was completely deserted. It was the guide's first year, but Fiorini and his friends had been assured everything needed for a six-day trophy hunt would be on hand: horses, a cook, supplies, everything. Instead there was an empty cabin. The six men stood around in the failing light, swatting mosquitoes and wondering what to do. They rechecked the map countless times, but there was no doubt they were at the right place. They'd just about made up their minds to load up and try to make it back to Dease Lake before nightfall when they heard the snarl of an outboard motor. The boat it was attached to appeared a few minutes later, a large river skiff loaded to the gunwales with beds and boxes of supplies. The guide had finally arrived, but instead of the relaxing evening everyone had been anticipating, most of it was spent unloading supplies and setting up the guide's furniture.

The horses arrived the next day along with a second guide who also functioned as a cook, and the hunt got underway. As Munro had suspected while he was negotiating the price of the charter with Fiorini, he and his Norseman were soon pressed into service as elements of the guide's overall plan. After a day of hunting near the base camp, the party started on a two-day ride to another lake, hunting and camping out as they went. The cook, with Munro assisting, packed food and other camp essentials into the Norseman, and then directed the pilot to the second lake. The hunting party arrived late the next day, replenished their supplies, and headed out in the morning for yet another lake while Munro and the cook leapfrogged them in the airplane.

The guide may have been late, but he knew what he was doing. The party got several nice caribou and a couple of moose. Fiorini and his friends had really wanted a grizzly, but blacks were the only bears they managed to bag. It was a successful hunt, but Munro was distressed by what he viewed as a senseless waste of meat.

> "They'd get a beautiful animal, but all they wanted were the heads. In those days people weren't so concerned with conservation. They'd bring in a beautiful big caribou or a moose and they'd take the heads and just leave the rest of the animal lying outside. Nobody wanted to bring any meat home. They just wanted the trophies. It bothered me to see the animals wasted like that. I started going out when no one was around, and I'd take my knife and cut off some nice big chunks of meat and hide them in the floats or in the back of the fuselage. It was cold up there, lots of snow around, so the meat stayed good. I just couldn't let it lie around to spoil."
>
> **BOB MUNRO**

Munro didn't participate in the hunt, but he did get himself a trophy of sorts. He and the cook had just finished setting up camp at a new lake when they saw a caribou break from the brush and start swimming across the lake. Munro fired up the Norseman and taxied alongside the swimming animal. The cook got a line around the caribou's antlers and they towed it slowly to shore where they tethered it to a tree and gave it some of the feed they'd flown in for the horses.

"I don't understand you guys," Munro chided when the rest of the party showed up. "You spend all kinds of money on guides and fancy rifles when all you really need to catch a caribou is an airplane and a rope."

The caribou wasn't very big, but Munro let it go before one of the hunters decided he wanted a small set of antlers to make his other ones look that much more impressive.

The route the guide had mapped out brought the party in a big circle back to the base camp. By this time, the group had amassed quite a collection of moose and caribou antlers as well as the black bear hides, and Munro was beginning to have serious doubts about the Norseman's ability to get himself, his passengers, their heavy rifles and trophies, and the meat he'd surreptitiously stowed away, off the water in time to clear the trees. A look at the chart showed a much larger lake a few miles away, so he decided to ferry the hunters out in pairs to this second lake where he could then load everyone and have enough room to get the grossly overloaded plane into the air for the flight home. The plan worked to perfection, other than the fact his passengers had to spend the next day and a half fending off the sharp points of the antlers they held in their laps.

Ruth was delighted to see the stash of fresh caribou and moose meat her husband pulled from the plane after the hunters had driven off with their trophies. A quick trip to the butcher up the road to add beef suet for flavor and the Munro family had a month's worth of dinners free of charge. It wasn't much, but it helped offset the fact that the Air Harbor had barely broken even on the charter.

Five-Five was looking a little shabby when it came time to ferry it to Northern Consolidated in the spring of 1952, so the Air Harbor decided to spruce it up with a quick paint job. Naturally it began to rain, and it kept raining until the day before Munro was due to depart. There were enough breaks in the weather to get everything painted except the registration numbers on top of the wing. Wing numbers were a CAA requirement. As far as the government was concerned, it was illegal to fly an airplane without them.

Kenmore happened to be out of aviation fuel, so Munro decided to fly the Norseman down the lake to Renton and gas up for the next day's flight. Fully aware of the CAA's wing number requirement, the mechanics hastily marked out the numbers with masking tape, figuring they should be sufficient for the quick trip to Renton and back. They weren't. By the time Munro landed, most of the tape had blown off the wing.

Of course this was the moment one of the CAA inspectors chose to amble down to the Renton seaplane dock to see what there was to see. What he saw was a silver and red Norseman sitting there big as life with no wing numbers, clearly a blatant violation of the law.

"Just what do you think you're doing?" the inspector demanded as he marched up the dock to the airplane.

"I just came down here to buy some fuel," Munro replied politely from his perch atop the wing.

"Your airplane has no registration numbers."

Munro peered back at the tail where the registration stood out boldly in white block letters against the red surface. 'November-five-five-five-five-five," he read out helpfully to the inspector.

"I mean on the wing. The registration isn't painted on the wing."

"Oh," Munro said, and he proceeded to explain about the paint and the rain and the masking tape numbers that had just blown off on the flight down from Kenmore.

"That's no excuse," the inspector barked when Munro had finished. "This airplane is grounded until the registration number is clearly marked on the wing."

Munro didn't have any masking tape with him, so he tried once more to persuade the inspector to let him fly back up the lake to Kenmore where he promised the numbers would be painted on before the airplane flew again.

"No." The inspector crossed his arms to reinforce the finality of his declaration. "This airplane is grounded."

Grounded seemed to be the operative word. "Okay," Munro said, maintaining his polite demeanor, "can I taxi it?"

"To where?"

"Back to Kenmore."

The inspector thought about this for a moment. The law said an airplane couldn't fly without a number on the wing. It didn't say anything about taxiing. "Okay, but don't you dare fly it."

"Thank you." Munro finished fueling and then, under the watchful glare of the inspector, dutifully idled away from the dock and up the lake. This is crazy, he thought. I don't have any passengers, and the inspector knows we're going to paint the numbers on the wing as soon as I get back. I can't believe he's being so obstinate. But Munro knew better than to get on the wrong side of the CAA, so he plowed along down the lake, glancing back now and then to see if the inspector was still there. At this rate, it would take him a couple of hours to get back to Kenmore, but he was more concerned about the cylinder head temperatures. The poor flow of cooling air through the cowling was pushing the temperature needle steadily up the gauge.

The inspector stood there until the Norseman disappeared from view around the first point. By then the temperature needle was quivering just outside the red danger zone, and Munro decided he'd had enough. The inspector couldn't see him, and even if he claimed he'd heard the Norseman take off he'd never be able to prove it. Munro eased the throttle lever forward in its quadrant and powered the plane into the air. He throttled back immediately until he had the plane just skimming the wavetops. With a decent volume of air flowing around the cylinders it didn't take long for the temperature gauge to drop back into the green. Fifteen minutes later the Norseman was moored to the Kenmore dock and a mechanic was outlining the wing numbers in tape in preparation for their final painting.

Munro went to Anchorage to ferry Five-Five home at the end of the season. The plane was down on power thanks to Northern Consolidated's somewhat casual approach to maintenance, and Munro had a hard time getting it off the surface of Lake Hood, which isn't all that big a lake to begin with. As he staggered along a dozen or so feet above the homes of the surrounding neighborhoods he thought seriously about returning to the lake to check out the engine, but it was cold and getting colder and he wanted to get home. The engine was running smoothly enough and he decided it would hold together another couple of days. It did, but the weather didn't.

It was one of the toughest trips he'd made yet. Between worrying about the steadily weakening engine and straining to pick his way through the deteriorating visibility, he was exhausted by the second day. But the fog was relentless, depriving him finally of even a glimpse of the shoreline and forcing him to land when he was halfway down the Inside Passage. Butedale cannery, the largest salmon processing plant on the west coast, lay several miles ahead, and he figured if he idle-taxied by compass, he'd eventually come to it.

For two hours the Norseman rumbled through fog so dense it hid the water in front of the plane. There were times when Munro became convinced he was heading in the wrong direction, out to sea or up a blind channel, and it took all the willpower he possessed to trust the compass screwed to the windscreen frame. At least he didn't have to worry about the engine overheating; the cold, wet fog seemed to be keeping the cylinder head temperatures under control.

Suddenly a wall of sheer rock appeared in front of him and he jammed the left rudder pedal to the floor in panic. The Norseman responded with agonizing slowness, turning back into the fog as the wingtip came within inches of striking the cliff.

Munro was just plain scared now. He couldn't imagine where he could be, to encounter a cliff head-on like that. He certainly wasn't where he thought he was. He was about to shut down the engine altogether and drift when he got a glimmer of something off the right wing. The fog was thinning, and within moments he could see the shoreline clearly enough to determine his location. He was within half a mile of Butedale. A few minutes more and the visibility was good enough to return to the air, although the ceiling restricted him to less than a hundred feet of altitude. Then it was back to worrying about the engine while he strained to pick out the next landmark through the mist.

He probably should have called it a day and tied up at Butedale, Klemtu, or one of the other canneries scattered along the Passage. They were always ready with a meal and place to sleep, and he could have continued the flight the next day in a better frame of mind, but by now he was determined to get home.

It was almost dark by the time he droned south out of the San Juan Islands. All he could think about was how he'd be home in thirty minutes. The visibility was still terrible, but there was a dull sheen on the water and he could see the lights on Whidbey Island. Then the lights went out and the water disappeared. He'd flown into another fog bank. As much as he wanted the flight to be over, Munro knew better than to attempt to continue. He cranked on some flap and eased off on the power. As the Norseman began to settle he raised the nose slightly into the touchdown altitude. He'd been less than a hundred feet up, so seconds later he felt the plane thump onto the glass-smooth water. He couldn't see a thing, but he knew the compass heading for the nearest point of land. Thoroughly fed up with northwest weather in general and fog in particular, he taxied slowly through the gloom, and prayed there wasn't a ship coming the other way.

He motored along for half an hour and then he killed the engine to listen for waves. Thinking he'd hear better outside the cockpit, he opened the door and slid down to the float. A sudden rip of fabric sounded like a shotgun blast in the eerie silence, and he reached around to discover the door latch had torn open his brand new Eddie Bauer goose-down jacket. At that point, he figured the trip couldn't get any worse.

Just as he began to wonder if he'd find a suitable spot to beach the plane before darkness closed in completely, he saw lights off to the south. He'd drifted out of the fog. Pulling himself wearily back into the cockpit he coaxed the engine back to life and opened the throttle. The radial had little left to offer. After a seemingly endless takeoff run, the plane finally lifted into the air. Fifteen minutes later he touched down on the still, dark water in front of the Air Harbor and taxied up the shimmering path of golden light beaming from the front windows of his home. His long flight was over.

Munro had flown Norsemen clear across the continental United States, he'd flown them up the coast and across the tundra to western Alaska, and he'd flown them deep into the Canadian interior. He'd flown them empty and he'd flown them so loaded down that the float decks were awash. He'd been marooned by mechanical failure and forced out of the sky by fog. But if he figured he'd done just about everything there was to do in a Norseman he was wrong, for his greatest adventure was just about to begin.

ABOVE: Bob Munro relaxes beside a company Taylorcraft at Luck Lake in southeast Alaska. The plane is painted in Kenmore's new scheme of yellow and brown, and sports the duck logo on the fuselage. (photo by Tom Wardleigh)

ABOVE: The floating camp, or wannigan, in Burroughs Bay, Alaska. For two months, this was home for the Leduc Glacier airlift crew. (photo by Bob Munro)

OPPOSITE, ABOVE: Kenmore's future office manager and flight operations manager. Leslie and Gregg Munro strike a pose in front of the company hangar. Leslie's tricycle would soon be the loser in an encounter with a taxiing Seabee. (photo by Bob Munro)

BELOW: Bob Munro with a King salmon that's almost as big as his son Gregg. Fish this size were common when the photo was taken in the early 1950s. Today, they've become as rare as the Republic Seabees and Noorduyn Norsemen that once called Kenmore home.

ABOVE: Low tide, Burroughs Bay, Alaska. The homemade wooden ramp kept the heavy fuel drums from hitting the floats as they were rolled out the door.

BELOW: A rare jacket patch featuring the company's original duck logo and letterhead.

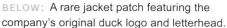

OPPOSITE, ABOVE: A custom beaver fresh from the rebuild shop rolls down the ram for a test flight. Sporting amphibious floats and a pink, putple and white paint job, the plane had been built for a customer in Las Vegas. (photo by C. Marin Faure)

RIGHT: C. Norseman Five-Five and the Seabee on the snow on the Leduc

ABOVE: Unloading supplies on the Blue Glacier.
The spectacular surroundings made every trip a thrill.

ABOVE LEFT: The company Seabee bogged down in
the snow after Bob Munro's first landing on the Leduc
Glacier in February, 1953. The plane's rudder was damaged in Ketchikan, so Munro borrowed a rudder from a
local operator. (photo by Bob Munro)

BELOW LEFT: Bob Munro standing in the Leduc snow
in front of Norseman Five-Five.

ABOVE: Bob Munro and his beloved Six-Six-Zulu on top of the Blue Glacier. This was the kind of flying Munro lived for.

ABOVE: Blue Glacier takeoff. There wasn't enough room on top of the glacier for the plane to accelerate to flying speed, but once the plane pitched over the edge of the icefall, gravity proved to be a far more effective accelerator than Pratt & Whitney. BELOW: Beaver Seven-Two-Zulu on the South Cascade Glacier. Munro always tried to steer the plane into a turn after touchdown to make it easier to turn the plane downslope for takeoff. (photo by Bob Munro)

ABOVE: Bill Whiltney putting Five-Five-Tango, the first Super Turbine, through its paces. (photo by C. Marin Faure)

ABOVE: Otter Two-Five-Sierra after it's conversion to turbine power. The experimental fold and black trim was eventually replaced with Kenmore's traditional yellow and brown. (photo by C. Marin Faure)

ABOVE: A Kenmore line boy removes the protective intake and exhaust covers from one of the company's turbine Otters at the start of another busy day. (photo by C. Marin Faure)

ABOVE: Kemore Air's first Cessna Caravan on a run through the Cascade Mountains. (photo by Ed Turner)

ABOVE: Kenmore goes back to its roots. The company's Top Cub is the 21st Century version of the original Piper Super Cub. Manufactured by Cub Crafters in Yakima, Washington, the Top Cub boasts a host of improvements over the original, including a 180 horsepower engine and stronger construction. Kenmore Air figured that what had been popular with student plots in the 1950s would be just as popular today. They were right. (photo by C. Marin Faure)

ABOVE: Kenmore Beaver N17598 shows off its impressive takeoff performance from a glacier lake deep in the Canadian Coast Range. (photo by C. Marin Faure)

ABOVE: Harrison Ford's Beaver was little more than a carcass when Kenmore started work on it. When they were done, the plane that had once served the U.S. Army in Vietnam had been transformed into a machine more perfect than even her designers could have imagined. (photo by Neal Slavin)

COPPER FEVER 12

THE MINUTES OF THE MAY 1952 meeting of the board of directors recorded both good and bad news. The bad news was that flight school activity had fallen to the point where it was almost nonexistent. It was not a problem exclusive to the Air Harbor. The government's decision to terminate the GI Bill was causing schools all over the country to close their doors. Reluctantly, Bill Fisk shut down his little ground school; there simply weren't enough students coming in to make the classes worthwhile.

The good news was that shop sales were on the increase. Word of Kenmore's high quality work and reasonable prices was getting around, and more and more customers were bringing their seaplanes to the north end of the lake for maintenance. Engines, particularly the quirky Franklins, were arriving for overhaul from as far away as Florida, crated up in boxcars or tied down in the beds of pickup trucks, all bearing explicit instructions to have Walt Winseman do the job. Most of Kenmore's customers were able to pay. Those who couldn't, or wouldn't, usually ended up signing over their airplanes to the Air Harbor in lieu of payment. Kenmore would then put the planes up for sale in an effort to recoup their labor and parts costs. Numerous Seabees had passed through the company's hands in this manner as well as the occasional Taylorcraft or Aeronca.

Back on the down side, the May minutes noted that parts sales were dropping off due to the gradual decline in the number of Seabees in the area. Some had been wrecked, some had been sold or traded as their owners moved up to faster and more modern airplanes, and some had simply been left to corrode in their tiedowns. The Seabee's glory days were over, and there was no more poignant evidence than the growing collection of bent and battered hulks that lay mired in the ooze surrounding the Kenmore parts barn. The board decided that Munro should explore the possibility of stocking parts for newer airplanes in order to bolster sales.

The company now owned five planes: two Taylorcraft trainers, the two Norsemen on lease in Alaska, and a single Seabee. Two years earlier, Kenmore had boasted six airplanes: two Seabees, two Taylorcrafts, an Aeronca, and a brand new Taylorcraft factory-equipped with a self-starter, a feature Bill Fisk thought would help encourage student flying. With the exception of the Seabees, the company's 1950 fleet had been geared toward instruction. Now, just two years later, the planes on the Air Harbor's roster were used almost exclusively for charter and commercial work.

The self-starting Taylorcraft purchased in June 1950, had been financed in large part by the insurance claim for Taylorcraft NC29560, which had been destroyed in a bizarre accident on the Strait of Juan de Fuca. Bill Fisk had been conducting a cross-country training flight in the older plane, and had instructed his student to make a refueling stop at Clallam Bay on the Washington side of the Strait. The Taylorcraft's fuel capacity was only twelve gallons, so the practice on long flights was to carry a pair of five-gallon gas cans behind the seats. Midway through the flight the pilot would land, pour the fuel from the cans into the almost empty tank, and be on his way.

Clallam Bay was surprisingly smooth this day, exposed as it was to the rolling swells out in the Strait, and the student executed a perfect landing. As he turned and began taxiing toward the beach, Fisk glanced back just in time to see a huge wave materialize out of nowhere and race in toward the shore. There was no time to do anything. Like a surfboard, the Taylorcraft was lifted and catapulted down the face of the wave, but unlike a surfboard, there was no quick way to move the center of gravity rearward to stay on the wave. The bows of the floats dug deep, and the next thing Fisk knew, he and his student were upside down in a cockpit full of water and swirling sand. Neither man was injured, but the plane was reduced to a tangle of twisted tubing, splintered wood, and shredded fabric.

Five-Six-Zero had already undergone one rebuild at the hands of the Air Harbor; it was the same plane that had been set ablaze in Aberdeen by an over-zealous pilot with a blowtorch. The damage was too extensive this time, however, and only the floats, engine, and propeller were deemed worth saving. The floats had survived the rogue wave surprisingly well, and they were installed under the new, self-starting Taylorcraft when it arrived two months later. As Fisk had predicted, the new plane, numbered N6618N, was an immediate hit with his students, and it was almost constantly in the air.

The luxury of starting an engine from the comfort of the pilot's seat lasted barely two months. That August, a renter took the plane up with the intention of practicing landings. He made several in Lake Sammamish and then returned to Lake Washington. If the Taylorcraft had any design flaw, it was the fact that the push-pull rods that applied carburetor heat and adjusted the fuel mixture were placed side-by-side and were capped with identical black knobs.

Pulling out the heat control to prevent ice from building up and blocking the carburetor throat is standard procedure in most single-engined airplanes when the power is reduced for landing. Perhaps the pilot was distracted by boat traffic entering his chosen landing area, or maybe he was scanning the sky for other airplanes. Whatever the cause, he pulled out the mixture control by mistake. Starved of fuel, the engine quit instantly. If he'd checked the controls and seen his mistake he could have shoved the mixture back in and the windmilling engine would have re-fired immediately. Failing that, he could have simply glided down to land on the lake; he was near Sand Point and there was water all around him.

The only logical conclusion that could be reached after the crash was that the shock of having no throttle response overcame the pilot's training and he panicked. Witnesses watched as he yanked the plane around in a tight turn toward the lake, but with no power and too much bank and too much up-elevator, the plane's response was inevitable. It stalled and spun down to slam into the shoreline just ten feet from the water's edge.

Other than the crash that killed Jack Mines and George Yeaman Jr., this was the first fatality the Air Harbor had experienced. Technically, the pilot had been at fault, but that didn't prevent Munro and the rest of the staff from taking the accident hard. For his entire career, Munro's first reaction on hearing of an accident was to ask if everyone was okay. The fate of the airplane was irrelevant as far as he was concerned. Some people were puzzled by his apparent lack of concern for the plane, especially in the light of the company's eventual fleet of million-dollar turbines. But once a mechanic, always a mechanic. In Munro's eyes, an airplane was just a bunch of parts that could be fixed or replaced. People, on the other hand, have a value that cannot be calculated. Munro would rather have seen one of his turbine Otters sink to the bottom of the lake than have any of his pilots or passengers receive so much as a scratch.

Unlike his wheelbound counterpart, the seaplane pilot operates in a world of variables. Currents, winds, and waves are in constant conspiracy against him. Accidents are inevitable, and Kenmore has had its share, but as long as no one was injured, there would be Bob Munro, calmly surveying the damage and guiding the recovery with little more stress than if he were taking a walk in the park. Of course, if the accident was caused by stupidity or neglect on an employee's part, Munro didn't hesitate to express his opinion, but as far as the airplane was concerned, it was just a concoction of metal, rubber, and plastic. "Drag it into the shop and let's see what we have to do to fix it."

While it never could make up for the loss of a life, one good thing did come out of the Sand Point crash. Taylorcraft began installing a clip on the mixture control that had to be released before the control could be moved. This not only prevented the knob from being pulled out accidentally, but it forced the pilot into making a conscious decision to adjust or shut off the mixture.

The Sand Point crash had a sobering effect on everyone, not the least of whom was Esther Mines. Esther hadn't been involved in the operation of the Air Harbor since her departure at the end of 1947, but she'd held onto her 1,003 shares of company stock in the hopes that they might increase in value. So far, they hadn't. Bob Munro maintained his position as majority stockholder, although his 1,016 shares didn't give him much of an edge. But Esther seemed perfectly content with her role as silent partner until October 1952, when she suddenly announced she wanted out. While there were other factors influencing her decision, it was based in part on advise from friends who insisted that her shares made her as liable for the company's actions as Bob Munro.

"You were lucky this time," they said. "The Sand Point crash didn't generate any lawsuits, but as a partner, you could be placed in financial jeopardy if the Air Harbor is ever proven to be at fault in a future accident."

The letter from Esther's attorney stating her desire to liquidate her interest in the company was the subject of much discussion at the October board of directors meeting, but no one was sure what to do about it. Munro would have been delighted to buy her out, but at ten dollars a share he would have to come up with $10,030. He was already plowing most of his $800-per-month salary back into the company as it was. Even with short term loans from friends like Harold Nicholas, Kenmore was barely keeping its financial head above water. Still, the opportunity to buy Esther out could not be ignored. Munro said he'd study the matter; perhaps there was some sort of time-payment agreement that could be reached.

As the Kenmore staff struggled to keep up with the demands of their shop customers while doing all they could to encourage the few flight students they had left, exciting things were happening hundreds of miles up the coast in British Columbia. Gold had been drawing prospectors north for over sixty years. To the miners on their way to the sluiceboxes set up alongside the Klondike River and across the gold-flecked beaches of Nome, the Coast Range had been an obstacle, something to traverse as quickly as possible. They'd tackled the mountains in every manner imaginable: on foot up the near-vertical slopes of Chilkoot Pass, on snorting sternwheelers that struggled to beat the swift-running Fraser and Stikine rivers into submission, and finally by rails laid along a narrow-gauge shelf blasted into the rock between Skagway on the coast and Whitehorse in the interior. Most of the prospectors were so busy getting *through* the mountains it never occurred to them that there might be something of value actually *in* the mountains.

But the value was there, and not everyone who went north succumbed to Klondike fever. The prospectors who stayed to poke around southeast Alaska eventually found their reward, and by the early 1900s, Juneau was on its way to becoming one of the top gold producing areas in the world. The boom lasted until April 9, 1944 when wartime labor shortages and government-mandated wage increases forced the owners of the monstrous Alaska-Juneau Mine to pull the plug. But gold wasn't all the mountains had to offer. Farther south, in British Columbia, it was copper than was setting prospectors' pulses to racing.

By global standards, the Coast Range isn't all that long, tall, or wide, but few places on earth have as much rugged wilderness packed into as small an area. The pine forests of the interior plateau are barely ninety miles from the coast, but the distance seems ten times that. To the west, heavy rainfall fertilizes a forest floor rendered almost impenetrable by moss-shrouded trees, clinging vines, dripping undergrowth, and intimidating slopes. The spine of the range is a hogback of granite slabs, sheer-sided and brutally sharp, rising from the white, featureless plains of the snowfields. Glaciers ooze from the fields like tentacles—rivers of ice and rock grinding ever downward between the sawtooth peaks. The eastern slopes are more forgiving, but the pine-covered foothills are guarded by moats of muskeg and swamp grass patrolled by vast armadas of mosquitoes and biting flies. The Coast Range is pierced by three rivers, a half-dozen roads, and four railroads. Most of the roads and three of the railroads follow the rivers. The rest of the range is accessible only on foot.

The copper, like the gold, is in the western half of the range. For years, prospectors had been stalking the slopes, dodging grizzlies, avalanches, and each other as they chipped off samples and pondered over the ground contours. Among them was a man named Thomas McQuillan. McQuillan had suspected for years there was a big copper deposit in the Coast Range, and by the autumn of 1952 he was sure of it. He'd even pinpointed the spot, a wall of rock bordering the Leduc Glacier in British Columbia. Seventy-five air miles northeast of Ketchikan, the icy finger of the Leduc points west from the edge of a massive snowfield. Hemmed in by upthrust slabs of rock topping eight-thousand feet, the snowfield generates its own weather, and the spectacular scenery of a clear morning can be blotted out in an instant as screaming winds push clouds of snow and ice fog down the glacier valleys. Into this monochrome world of black rock and blinding ice came Tom McQuillan, and after tromping over almost every inch of it, he knew where he wanted to dig.

Unfortunately, he hadn't been tromping alone. The signs were there in the rock for all to read, and several other people had read them. The rumors began to fly, and pretty soon copper speculators could be spotted climbing off the trains in Prince Rupert and hiring boats for the day-long ride up Portland Canal. The Alaska-BC border runs up the center of the seventy-mile fjord and separates the ramshackle mining towns of Hyder and Stewart at the head, which was as close to the rumored copper deposits one could get without actually expending any physical effort.

By Canadian law, staking a claim means just that; someone has to go out and pound marked stakes into the ground delineating the boundaries of the claim before it can be registered with the government. Whoever gets their stakes in the ground first gets the claim. McQuillan knew he had to get the Leduc staked and he had to get it staked soon. At least the weather was on his side. The country surrounding the glacier was foreboding enough in summer, but in winter it turned downright vicious. The first day of 1953 arrived on the leading edge of a Pacific storm, and the copper speculators played cards and shouted lies over the roar of the rain before skulking off to their rooms to pore over lab reports and dog-eared contour maps. There was no reason to hurry; no one in his right mind would try staking anything for months.

They hadn't reckoned on Tom McQuillan. Backed by Granby Consolidated, which was short for Granby Mining, Smelting, and Power Company, McQuillan decided to charter a plane and take his stakes in by air. His first attempts to reach the Leduc in late January ended in failure as low ceilings rendered the wall of mountains separating Stewart from the snowfield virtually impenetrable. It was probably just as well; there was fifteen feet of new powder on the Leduc and his chartered skiplane would have sunk out of sight the moment it touched down. Thinking the weather might permit an approach from the coast, McQuillan went to Ketchikan.

The situation there was just as frustrating. The airport serving Ketchikan was on nearby Annette Island, but no one there had a skiplane. What fell as snow in the mountains fell as rain out on the coast, and the few wheelplane operators in southeast Alaska had little use for skis. Wheelskis, a new type of cutaway ski that attached to the regular landing gear and permitted landings on both pavement and snow, were a relative rarity in the interior; out on the coast they were unheard of.

McQuillan caught the Grumman Goose that ferried passengers between Annette Island and Ketchikan's downtown waterfront to see if he could find a seaplane pilot that might be willing to try a landing on snow. No one was interested.

"Too many risks," they said. "We could get stuck, and if the weather turned nasty we'd be gonners. You'd be better off waiting for good weather in the spring and then hiking in on foot."

McQuillan was getting desperate. Waiting until spring was out of the question; he'd be in the same boat with all the other prospectors and there was no guarantee he'd get his stakes to the Leduc first. He had to mark his claim now. For all he knew the weather could have broken back at Stewart and someone else might already be winging their way over the snowfield to mark out the treasure trove he knew was buried there. He decided to return to Stewart, but there was one more operator in Ketchikan to talk to.

"No, we won't fly you onto the glacier," said the owners of Ketchikan Air Service. McQuillan turned to leave. "But we know someone who might."

McQuillan turned back. "Who?"

"A fellow named Bob Munro. He owns an air service in Seattle. He's got a Seabee, and he might get a real kick out of trying this."

"Why? Is he some kind of daredevil?" Prospecting was dangerous enough as it was; McQuillan didn't need some hotshot pilot running up the odds of an accident.

"Oh, no. Bob's got a real cool head on his shoulders. But he's a helluva pilot and he's the kind of guy who enjoys doing something different. He's also not the kind of guy who'll panic if something unexpected happens."

McQuillan figured if anything upped the odds that something unexpected would happen, it was flying onto a glacier in the middle of winter. "Okay, let's give this fellow a call," he said.

Munro was in the office when the call from Ketchikan came in. "I've never landed on snow before," he said after listening to the description of the job, "but I'd like to try it. I'd want a few guarantees, however."

"Like what?" McQuillan asked.

"If we get stuck, I want a guarantee that someone will come in right away and get us. I don't want to get stranded up there."

"That's fair enough. What else?"

"If the airplane gets damaged in the landing, or if for some other reason we can't fly it out, Kenmore has to be reimbursed for its value."

"I'll have to talk that over with Granby Consolidated," McQuillan replied, "How much is the plane worth?"

"About twenty-five hundred dollars. Maybe three thousand."

"I don't think that will be a problem."

Munro had a question. "How are you going to get out after I fly you in?"

"I'm making arrangements to have planes fly in from Stewart with supplies. If they can't get in because of the weather, I'll hike out."

If Munro had any doubts about the sanity of someone contemplating a hike through the trackless Coast Range in the winter he kept them to himself. But as a safety precaution, he decided to take another pilot with him. Tom Wardleigh would have been his first choice, but Wardleigh was gone, flying for Clarence Rhodes in Alaska. That left Bill Fisk and Paul Garner. Garner was the complete antitheses of the independent and opinionated Fisk. Garner's hitch in the Army during World War II had been spent as an infantryman in New Guinea. It had been a terrible campaign; the bad water, bad food, and putrid jungle had been as debilitating an enemy as the Japanese. Whatever boyhood exuberance Garner had taken with him to the Pacific was gone by the time he came he came home. He was a quiet young man, slim, almost frail in appearance.

Perhaps as a result of the horrors he'd witnessed on the ground, Garner decided he wanted to spend the rest of his life in the air. He went out to the Air Harbor and signed up for flying lessons under the GI Bill. He proved to be an excellent pilot, and in 1950, after earning his Commercial ticket, he hired on to fly a Super Cub in Alaska for a bush pilot named Nat Brown. Brown had just landed a contract to conduct a comprehensive survey operation for the U.S. government, and he was putting together a fleet of sixteen Super Cubs and a roster of pilots to do the job.

The gray and maroon Cubs would be operating from rivers in western Alaska, so he contracted with the Air Harbor to install floats on the planes that didn't already have them. Garner was one of the first pilots penciled onto Nat Brown's list. Twenty year-old Ted Huntley was the last, replacing a pilot who'd dropped out at the last minute.

> "Nat walked over to Bob and asked, 'Do you think this kid can fly up there?' That was really putting Bob on the hot seat, as he was kind of responsible for me. He could have said, 'I don't think he has enough experience' or almost anything and I wouldn't have gotten the job. But he told Nat he thought I was ready for it, and Nat hired me on the spot. I flew up there for two summers. It was an incredible experience, and it was all because Bob believed I could do it."
>
> **TED HUNTLEY**

Paul Garner flew those two summers for Brown, too. The next year, 1952, he flew a Norseman for Alaska Airlines. When the season ended, he headed back to Seattle and out to the Air Harbor where Munro agreed to take him on. When the McQuillan job came up, Munro's first impulse was to take the loyal Bill Fisk along to share in the adventure, but the fact of the matter was that Fisk was the only one of his pilots who understood the day-to-day operation of the Air Harbor. Munro didn't have much choice; he called Garner into the office after his telephone conversation with McQuillan and instructed the soft-spoken infantry vet to report for work early the next morning with the warmest clothes he could find.

The two men left for Ketchikan in N6295K at first light. As with all the Seabees that had flown under the Kenmore name, Nine-Five-Kilo's landing gear had been removed to permit carrying a heavier load in the cabin. Judging from his telephone conversation with McQuillan, Munro figured he'd need all the carrying capacity he could get. The two Kenmore pilots would occupy the front seats while the rear seat would be taken up by McQuillan and a man he'd hired to help drive the stakes. The rest of the cabin would be filled with the stakes themselves, some tools, and enough food and survival gear to keep the two prospectors alive until planes could begin bringing in supplies from Stewart.

McQuillan had no intention of simply driving in a bunch of stakes and then hightailing it home to register the claim. He was going to start mining. At Granby Consolidated's request he'd drawn up plans for a small, exploratory mine, and the power company was already lining up a mining crew and purchasing the equipment they'd need on the glacier. From diesel generators and tractors to air compressors and cookstoves, the intention was to have the operation up and running by summer.

The days were short and darkness had fallen when Munro pulled off the power and eased the lumbering Seabee down to land in the glare of the lights from the canneries and boatyards lining Ketchikan's waterfront. The wind was already kicking up a nasty chop in the channel in front of the town. If they'd still had the wheels, they could have landed at Annette and tied the plane down for the night, but with no landing gear, Nine-Five-Kilo would have to spend the night in the water. Wind gusts yowled through the propeller and rattled spray against the windshield as Munro guided the wallowing plane over to the Ketchikan Air Service dock. He wasn't happy with the situation but there wasn't much he could do about it now.

The Seabee whacked into the heaving boards and Munro and Garner tumbled out into a world alive with motion and sound. Hissing waves and moaning wind underscored the clang and clatter of trolling gear as the fishing boats around them surged and jerked against their moorings. Thin tinkles of music blew down from the bars perched high above the docks on rickety towers of piling while the hoots and catcalls of cannery workers going off shift were snatched short by the icy blasts that ripped between the buildings and tore off down the street. Ducking their heads against the needlepoints of spray lashing in off the channel, the two pilots tied Nine-Five-Kilo off as best they could before scrambling up the steep gangway to the street in search of a place to spend the night. McQuillan had said he'd meet them at the dock in the morning.

As the Seabee pitched and rolled beside its equally active dock, the lines Garner and Munro had fastened began to slip. Inch by inch the plane began to move backward toward one of the massive piles that held the dock in place against the seventeen-foot tides. The outcome was inevitable. There was a grinding crunch and Nine-Five-Kilo's rudder began to twist and wrinkle against the barnacle-encrusted pillar. It was totally destroyed by the time Munro and Garner arrived at the dock the next morning. They were lucky it was only the rudder. Had the movement been more violent, or had the wind not died down when it did, they might have lost the whole empennage. The owners of Ketchikan Air Service generously offered the use of the rudder from their own Seabee, and helped Munro install it on the Air Harbor's plane. Ketchikan Air's black and red paint scheme didn't match Kenmore's white and red fuselage, but at least Munro would be able to make the flight.

McQuillan wanted to land on the Leduc in the morning. On his earlier trips to the area he'd observed that the wind generally kicked up in the early afternoon unless there was a storm brewing, in which case it blew all day. A morning flight also would give him and his partner a chance to set up a decent camp before nightfall. Munro's first morning in Ketchikan was occupied with changing the rudder on the plane, so the Leduc flight was set for the following day. The owners of Ketchikan Air Service had volunteered to fly cover for Munro in their Grumman Widgeon. They weren't about to land the heavy twin-engined amphibian in the snow, but they would circle overhead until the smaller plane was safely off the glacier and on its way back to Ketchikan.

Four people plus food, survival gear, and mining equipment made for a long takeoff run, but Nine-Five-Kilo finally clawed its way into the air, and Munro headed southeast to Prince Rupert to clear Canadian customs. From there it was back north again, past the entrance to Portland Canal and up Behm Canal to Burroughs Bay and the mouth of the Unuk River. With the faster Widgeon carving lazy S-turns high above him, Munro flew up the Unuk for ten miles and then begin working his way southeast between the six-thousand foot peaks to the Leduc River. Another twenty miles deeper into the mountains, a sharp turn to the right, and the four men were face to face with the front slope of the glacier itself.

> "The weather was good, blue sky and clear, but very cold. I went in high and circled for awhile trying to get the lay of the land. The face of the glacier was steep but then it rolled over into what looked like a fairly flat surface that ran back to the surrounding mountains. I decided to drop down lower to get a good look at the surface, to see if it was hummocks or if it was smooth. I dropped down to the lower edge of the glacier, about 3,500 feet above sea level, and started flying up the slope. It looked pretty smooth, but then I realized the glacier was climbing faster than I was. I put in full throttle but I couldn't outclimb the glacier. I didn't have much choice so I just went straight in. It was so quiet and soft I didn't even know I'd touched down until snow started flying past the windows."
>
> **BOB MUNRO**

As soon as he realized they were down, Munro pulled off the power. Soft as it was, the snow exerted a tremendous drag on the bottom of the hull and the Seabee came to a stop almost immediately. A skiplane, with its weight on a pair of narrow runners, would have been swallowed instantly by the soft powder on the surface of the glacier, but the Seabee's hull spread the weight across a relatively broad footprint, and it remained safely on top of the snow. Munro didn't dare shut off the engine; he had visions of the oil cooling to the consistency of molasses, and he wasn't sure if the battery had enough punch for a restart. Warning everyone to stay forward of the wing and away from the idling propeller, he opened the door and got out.

His first step was a long one, almost three feet straight down as he broke through the thin crust on the surface and sank to his waist in the powder.

"You'd better put your snowshoes on," he said to the prospectors in the cabin behind him. "You won't be able to walk without them."

McQuillan and his assistant pulled their snowshoes out from under the pile of gear and set them on the snow outside the main doors. Then they stepped out onto them and laced them up. Garner began handing out the sacks of supplies, and the two prospectors carried them clear of the plane. Munro, meanwhile, bulldozed his way through the powder until he was far enough away to get the plane and the sunlit mountains behind it in the viewfinder of his 35mm camera. He took a few pictures and then looked around. He felt like an ant on a wedding cake. Everything was white, a white made even more brilliant by the blue sky above. The low February sun threw sharp shadows across the ridges and onto the surface of the glacier. Munro noticed the sky was not as clear as it had been earlier; thin wisps of cloud were warning of an imminent change.

The takeoff should be easy, he thought. We'll just point the plane downslope and go. If we're not going fast enough to fly when we reach the edge we will be after we go over it. A distant buzz penetrated the rattle of the idling Seabee, and Munro remembered his aerial guardian. He looked up and found the circling Widgeon. Its pilot certainly wasn't taking any chances; Munro judged the Grumman to be up around ten thousand feet. Munro waded back to the Seabee and climbed in beside Garner.

"Thanks a lot." McQuillan reached into the cockpit and shook each pilot's hand. "I was beginning to think I'd never get this claim staked. That was an impressive piece of flying."

Munro shook his head. "The plane pretty much flew itself onto the glacier. Anyway, you're the ones who have to stay here and work. All I have to do is give it some gas and go home."

McQuillan banged the door shut and snowshoed back out of the way. The two miners waved as Munro revved up the engine. Munro waved back and added some more power. Garner started to wave, too, and then decided against it when he realized Nine-Five-Kilo wasn't going anywhere. Munro shoved the throttle all the way forward and jerked the yoke back and forth in an effort to rock the plane free but it wouldn't budge. After a minute or so of fruitless manipulation of the controls he throttled back to idle and got out.

"We're going to need some help getting turned around," he said to McQuillan.

The prospectors had a shovel, so Munro and Garner took turns digging the snow away from the hull while McQuillan and his assistant packed it down with their snowshoes. When they had stomped a level pad around the plane, Munro climbed back in and firewalled the engine while the others pushed the wingfloats in opposite directions. It took a lot of huffing and puffing and falling face-down in the snow, but they eventually managed to pivot the Seabee around until it was facing downslope. Munro had hoped that once broken free of the snow, the plane would move forward under its own power, but it didn't. They'd have to push it.

Several hours had elapsed since they'd taken off from Prince Rupert, and the engine had been running the whole time. Garner stuck his head in the cockpit and was shocked to see the fuel gauge nearing empty. All that revving of the engine had used up a lot of gas. He showed the gauge to Munro, adding that while they probably had enough fuel to get back to Ketchikan, it wouldn't be long before they didn't. The four redoubled their efforts and soon had a twenty-yard stretch of snow packed down in front of the plane.

The men took their positions on each side of the plane, Munro and Garner at the open side doors and McQuillan and his assistant at the outer ends of the wing struts. Munro leaned in and shoved the throttle up to full power. The Franklin roared over their heads, while a few feet behind them the propeller started to yowl in the frigid air.

"Now!" Munro yelled over the din, and the men began to push.

With a screech that was lost almost completely in the racket of the engine, the Seabee began to inch through the snow.

"Harder!" Munro shouted.

The bulbous plane crept ponderously onto the strip of packed snow and began to pick up speed.

"Faster!" The four men were in good physical shape, but the muscles in their legs began to burn as they strained against the freezing metal and struggled to keep their footing in the soft snow. Then the entire keel slid onto the packed snow and with a lurch, the plane began to pick up speed. Garner stumbled but he kept a desperate grip on the door frame as the image of what the propeller would do if it overtook him flashed through his mind.

Suddenly Munro felt the fuselage begin to rise.

"Now!" he screamed across to Garner, and the two men vaulted into the cockpit. They were just in time. The Seabee climbed onto the surface of the snow and began to skim down the slope. The prospectors were left behind as Munro felt the controls stiffen in the solid airflow rushing over the wing and tail surfaces. In seconds they were at flying speed, and Munro eased the yoke back. There was a jerk of acceleration, and Nine-Five-Kilo was in the air, climbing smoothly away from the glacier which steepened then dropped off almost vertically into the valley below.

Seven thousand feet higher, the pilot of the Widgeon watched as the tiny white shape that was the Seabee crept away from the massive face of the glacier and turned to fly down the river valley. Everything seemed normal, so the pilot turned the twin-engine amphibian toward its home base on Annette Island. From time to time he checked on the Seabee's progress by banking slightly so he could look back, but the faster Grumman soon outdistanced the plodding Seabee, and after awhile he didn't bother to check. The pilot made a smooth touchdown on Annette Island, taxied the plane to its tiedowns, and went home.

Thirty miles to the north, as the setting winter sun washed a copper glow across the hillsides and plunged the valleys into shadow, Munro ran out of gas. It was more an annoyance than a problem. The sea was smooth and the shore was close. The trick was getting the powerless plane to the beach once it was on the water. Kenmore's floatplanes each had a canoe paddle clipped to one of the floats for just such an occasion, but no one had thought to put one in the Seabee. Garner and Munro drifted around for awhile in the hopes that someone would come along in a boat, but February in southeast Alaska is not considered prime sailing weather and no boats appeared.

Then Munro remembered the battery. It was mounted in a box in the bow, and the box had a cover about two feet square. Removing the cover was simple enough, and the two men took turns leaning out the bow door and paddling the plane toward shore. It was an awkward and inefficient process, but it worked. While Garner stood in the frigid water and held the plane off the rocks, Munro walked through the woods to the road and flagged down a car for the short ride into Ketchikan. He was back in less than thirty minutes, picking his way through the seaweed with two five-gallon cans of aviation fuel.

Munro was not one to hold a grudge, but he was, in his words, "a little put out," that the Widgeon pilot didn't bother to make sure the Seabee made it back safely. Granted, the pilot had no way of knowing the seriousness of the fuel situation down on the glacier, but it would have taken little effort to fly cover for the smaller plane all the way back to town. It's what Munro would have done had the roles been reversed.

The two Kenmore pilots headed south the next morning. McQuillan's flight had been an exciting adventure, but not something either man expected ever to repeat. There are few glaciers in Washington, and even fewer reasons to land on them. They guard no mineral secrets. Their principal value lies in the fact that they melt, thus helping to ensure an adequate water supply for the communities bordering Puget Sound. No, the McQuillan flight was a once-in-a-lifetime experience; the only task remaining was to return the borrowed Seabee rudder to Ketchikan Air Service and install a replacement from the Air Harbor's own stock. Then it would be back to flying charters, repairing airplanes, and giving the occasional flight lesson. They had no inkling of the job they'd be called on to perform only a few short weeks later.

FLOATS IN THE SNOW 13

T OM MCQUILLAN'S PLAN TO FLY in equipment and miners from Stewart went awry almost immediately. The huge, single-engine Junkers that had been brought in for the job spent most of its time stuck in town or stranded on the glacier while its crew waited for the weather to break. At least the Junkers was tough enough to take the punishment; the smaller planes McQuillan hired generally broke a ski in the soft snow. Sometimes they broke both skis, and on one occasion an entire airplane disappeared down a crevasse. McQuillan managed to get a handful of men and some stoves and wall tents flown in, but the compressors and drills and tractors they needed to start mining were buried in the growing inventory of equipment that was piling up on the dock at Stewart.

Faced with mounting pressure from Granby's directors who were demanding evidence of their promised profits and from the miners who were demanding something better than the Junkers' random deliveries of food and stove oil, McQuillan decided it was time to try something different. Kenmore Air Harbor had flown him onto the glacier when no one else could or would; maybe they could repeat the performance with his vitally needed supplies.

Munro was cautious but optimistic. "A Norseman will haul just about everything you've got," he assured McQuillan on the phone, "but I'd like to try an airdrop instead of landing on the glacier. Don't forget how much trouble it was to get the Seabee off again."

"If you can airdrop successfully, that's fine," McQuillan replied. "Just get the stuff in there."

Supplying the miners would be a major operation with multiple flights and a lot more at stake than simply flying a couple of guys onto the ice. This time, Kenmore wanted a contract, and Granby Consolidated was more than willing to sign one. Munro drew it up and mailed it off to Vancouver on March 10, 1953.

The airlift would commence on or about March 15, the contract stated, and conclude no later than May 30, when surface conditions on the glacier would make it increasingly dangerous for the floatplanes to land. Staging would be at the mouth of the Unuk River on Burroughs Bay, and Kenmore would deliver the airplanes to that site at their expense. Room and board would be supplied by the mining company, but Kenmore would pay a share of the board based on the number of Air Harbor employees staying at the site. The contract covered the carriage of freight only; the Air Harbor would not carry any liability insurance or assume responsibility for anyone injured while riding as a passenger in their aircraft.

The equipment and supplies would be crossing two borders on their way to the Leduc Glacier; first the U.S. border as the material was barged from Stewart to Burroughs Bay, and then the Canadian border as Kenmore flew the material back into British Columbia. Munro knew that customs officials from both countries would want to keep a close eye on the proceedings, so he made sure the contract stipulated that any fees or overtime payments be picked up by Granby Consolidated.

As the power company's representative, the contract went on to say, Tom McQuillan would keep track of the tonnage figures and flying hours. The freight rate would be $135 per ton if the total weight airlifted to the glacier was less than one hundred tons. If the total weight exceeded one hundred tons, the rate would be reduced in increments until a total of two hundred tons was reached, at which point the rate would drop to, and remain at, $101 per ton. Granby Consolidated signed the contract, and the airlift to supply the Granduc Mine, as it was now officially named, was on.

Munro decided to take only one Norseman to start with. He wanted to test his airdrop theory and size up the volume of freight to be flown in before deciding if it would be worth bringing up a second plane. Leaving Fisk to hold down the fort, Munro and Garner headed north in Five-Five. McQuillan had promised to have a base camp ready in time for Munro's arrival, so the pilots scanned ahead for signs of life as Munro banked the silver and red Norseman around the point separating Burroughs Bay from the broader Behm Canal.

"There," Garner shouted over the engine. "In that inlet over to the right. See it?"

Munro peered through the shimmering blur of the propeller and found what Garner had spotted. What would be their home for the next several weeks looked like something out of the 1930s. Three frame buildings and a shed of some sort were clustered together on what appeared to be a small barge. From the air, the shiny tin roofs contrasted sharply with the faded red and green siding and white-painted window frames.

"It's a wannigan," Munro said. "A floating camp. There used to be whole towns made up rafts like that in the islands north of Campbell River. They'd tow them from place to place depending on where they were logging. They're pretty much all gone now."

Garner pulled out the map he'd been using. "Klahini River," he announced after a moment's study. "That's the name of the creek at the head of the inlet."

Munro circled the wannigan a few times to check out the landing conditions. The inlet seemed clear of rocks and other debris, but it was narrow, and the heavily forested hills rising steeply from the water's edge offered no escape route if he had to go around. The best bet, he decided, was to touch down out in the open water of Burroughs Bay and taxi in.

"Where's the stuff we're supposed to fly up to the glacier?" Garner wondered as the Norseman idled through the clear, green water. "All I see are the houses."

"Tom said the first bargeload of supplies would be leaving from Stewart today," Munro replied as he evaluated the best way to bring the Norseman alongside the raft. "They have to go to Ketchikan to clear customs, and then they'll come here. If they run all night I expect they'll be here in the morning."

As they drew closer, the pilots could see that what they'd thought was a barge was actually a pair of planked-over log rafts chained end to end and held about thirty feet off the shoreline by a pair of boomsticks, slender logs that angled out from the rafts to tie-downs set among the rocks on the beach. Two red-painted buildings occupied the raft on the left, while the shed and the green building were perched on the right-hand raft. The buildings took up almost all the deck space; there was very little room left to walk around on.

A smudge of dirty brown smoke drifted from the spindly stovepipe angling up from the steeply pitched roof of the larger red house. Garner was about to ask what they were supposed to do for drinking water when he noticed a hose snaking across one of the boomsticks to shore, where it disappeared into the woods in the general direction of the creek. Then the door to the red house swung open, and Tom McQuillan stepped out onto the cedar planks and waved. Another figure appeared behind him, a wiry young man dressed in tan work pants and a wool shirt.

"There's Tom." Garner said. McQuillan stepped to the edge of the raft and waved the plane in with both arms.

"We'll have to tie up nose first," Munro said, reaching for the mixture control.

Garner opened his door and peered down. "The water's not very deep. I wouldn't be surprised if it goes dry at low tide."

"Is it rocky?"

"No. It looks flat. Probably mud."

The engine clanked to a stop and the Norseman glided the last few yards to the raft in silence. McQuillan and the wiry young man knelt down and cushioned the bows of the floats as they thudded into the heavy boards.

"This is Stan Bishop," McQuillan said as Munro and Garner stepped off the plane. The young man nodded a curt hello. "Stan lives around the corner on the Unuk and knows this country as well as anyone. He'll be our bullcook."

The men shook hands all around.

"What's a bullcook?" Garner whispered to Munro as they strung lines from the float cleats to a pair of heavy metal rings spiked to the deck of the raft.

"It's what loggers call someone who can do everything around a camp. Carpenter, rigger, mechanic, whatever needs to be done."

When the plane was securely moored, McQuillan ushered the pilots into the green building.

"This is the bunkhouse," McQuillan explained. "We got six bunks in here for sleeping and some cabinets for clothes."

Garner looked around the ten by twenty foot room and decided he'd take the bunk farthest from the door and closest to the oil stove if he could get it. "What about electricity and water?" he asked.

"No power," McQuillan answered, "but I've run a hose down from the creek for water." The prospector studied Garner for a moment. On their first flight to the glacier, McQuillan had been too preoccupied to pay much attention to the man, but now he noticed how thin and frail the young pilot was, especially when compared to the trim and fit Bob Munro. He wondered if Garner would be up to the strenuous job ahead. Munro must think so, he decided, or he wouldn't have brought him. It was obvious Kenmore's owner was intrigued with the idea of living in a floating home; in fact, he seemed pretty excited about every aspect of the airlift. Garner, on the other hand, didn't look at all enthusiastic at the prospect of living in such crude quarters.

"We've got plenty of lanterns," McQuillan volunteered, trying to make the place sound a little more habitable, "and the roof's sound. No leaks. The stove keeps the place real warm, and we've got a big kettle to heat bath water with."

"Where's the kitchen?" Munro asked.

"Next door." McQuillan led the way back outside and across to the other raft. "That," he said, pointing to the shed-like structure with the curved roof, "is the bathroom. The small building behind there is the storeroom." He stepped up to the red building and pushed open the door. "This is the mess hall."

Munro leaned in and peered around at the rough table and benches and at the oil-fired, cast iron cookstove in the corner.

"Who's the cook?"

"I plan on doing most of it," said McQuillan, "since you guys will be busy loading and flying all day. I might ask you to pitch in sometimes, though."

"Sounds fine to me," Munro said.

"Stan here will help with the fueling and loading."

"Where is the fuel, by the way?" Garner asked.

"On the barges that will be coming out from Stewart." He turned to Munro. "You said you had a barrel pump you'd bring up from Seattle."

Munro nodded. "It's in the plane. It's a lever pump with thirty feet of inch-and-a-half hose."

"Good. The first thing I want to send up to the glacier is stove oil and diesel fuel. Do you still plan on trying an airdrop?"

Munro nodded again. "We mounted a wooden ramp on the right side of the plane from the rear door down to the outside edge of the float. We'll fly with the door off, and when we're over the mine we'll roll the barrels out the hole and down the ramp. We tried it at home with an empty barrel and it works pretty good."

McQuillan looked at Bishop. "What do you think?"

Bishop shrugged. "Depends on the snow. If it's real soft the drums shouldn't break, although they might bury themselves so deep the guys won't be able to find them. But my guess is the drums will break open when they hit. Most of them, anyway."

"I'd still like to try it," Munro said. "If it does work, it will be a lot faster than landing on the glacier every time."

It was dark by four o'clock, and after they'd helped McQuillan clean up the dinner dishes there wasn't much else to do but go to bed. Garner curled up in his sleeping bag and was asleep in minutes, but Munro lay awake listening to the lap of water and feeling the gentle sway of the raft as it rode the seventeen-foot tide. Challenging flights were not something he was afraid of, but he'd had enough experience to know if something unexpected could happen, it would. The only way to beat the odds was to have a well thought-out game plan. Then, if an unexpected problem did arise, any deviations he might be forced to make would be based on a solid foundation.

If he just "headed out" like some of his peers were wont to do, the flight could be in trouble from the beginning. Spur-of-the-moment reactions to changing conditions could lead to an accelerating series of bad decisions which, in this terrain, could put a plane into the rocks in short order. So while the wannigan jerked against the restraint of its mooring lines and the oil stove muttered and hissed in the corner, Munro pulled his sleeping bag up to his chin and flew the airdrop over and over in his mind. The last image he had was of Garner shoving a barrel out the door of the Norseman. He was fast asleep before the barrel hit the snow.

At nine o'clock in the morning on Thursday, March 19, the throb of a diesel engine and the rattle of anchor chains announced the arrival of the barge from Ketchikan. The men on the wannigan had been up for several hours eating breakfast and preparing the Norseman for the airdrop. The temperature wasn't much above freezing, but the effort of moving around in their heavy tin pants soon had them sweating.

"Tin pants were used by loggers and people like that in the woods who wanted protection from the wires and devil's club, and also wanted to be dry at the end of the day. They were a pair of pants with three layers. There was a layer of canvas on one side, a layer of oiled silk in the middle, and a layer of heavy canvas on the other side. They were impervious to water, but they were so stiff that a lot of guys used to stand them up on their own legs next to the bunk-bed, and then they could jump off the top bunk into their pants in the morning. Even in warm weather they hardly got limber enough to bend much. They were hard to walk in because they didn't slide good on your legs. The loggers could get along with them because of the type of work they were doing, but they were too stiff to use in the back country. We used heavy wool for that."

STAN BISHOP

The right rear door of the plane was removed and stowed in the little round-roofed shed Garner had remarked on the previous day, which turned out to be the wannigan's storeroom. McQuillan had stashed away a couple of weeks' worth of food in the shed along with barrels of stove oil and an assortment of tools. Garner checked the oil in the Norseman while Munro showed Bishop how to walk the propeller through before starting.

"After the plane sits all night in this cold we have to walk the propeller through by hand for about five minutes to limber up the engine and get a bit of oil distributed around in there. It also tells us if we have a hydraulic lock," he added.

"Hydraulic lock?"

"These engines can have pretty sloppy tolerances," Munro explained. "When they aren't running, oil can sometimes seep past the rings of the lower pistons and collect in the compression chambers. If there's oil down there and you hit the starter, the piston will act just like a hydraulic ram. It'll hit all that oil and tear the cylinder right off the case. Turning the engine over by hand will let you feel if there's a hydraulic lock without damaging anything."

The endless job of refueling during the Leduc Glacier airlift. Paul Garner is manning the barrel pump.

"What do you do if there is a lock?" Bishop asked.

"Remove one of the sparkplugs and let the oil drain out."

It took a fair amount of cranking and priming and jiggling of the throttle, but Munro finally got the engine started. He and Garner sat in the cockpit blowing on their hands as they waited for the engine to come up to temperature; the Norseman was equipped with a rudimentary heater that was ineffective under the best of circumstances and totally worthless with the door off. Bishop stood on the dock and stared in fascination at the little waterspout that danced and twisted between the float bows, sucked up by the low pressure air whirling off the prop tips. The plane was still moored nose-first to the wannigan; Munro had explained that putting any strain on the engine before the cylinder heads were up to temperature could crack a cylinder wall or even blow a head out through the cowling.

The needles were in the green after about fifteen minutes of idling, and Munro pulled the mixture and killed the engine. McQuillan and Bishop untied the lines and turned the plane away from the raft. The engine fired at the first turn of the starter, and the Norseman idled smoothly away toward the barge anchored out in the bay. The other two men followed in Bishop's outboard powered skiff. As soon as the Norseman was securely moored alongside the barge, Bishop wrestled one of the drums of aviation fuel as close to the plane as he could get it and attached the barrel pump and hose. Garner scrambled onto the wing with the other end of the hose and pushed a funnel fitted with a chamois-skin filter into the filler neck. Sticking the hose nozzle into the funnel, he nodded to Bishop, and the young man began working the pump handle. It was a routine that would occupy a good part of Bishop's days for the next six weeks.

A Canadian customs agent had ridden the tug all the way from Stewart to clear the mine's equipment back into British Columbia and to make sure no unauthorized materials were added to the loads. Because the plane would be flying every day, the Canadian government had agreed to McQuillan's request for an agent to be stationed at the wannigan for the duration of the airlift. Known to the men simply as "Jacques," the agent immediately tried to introduce an atmosphere of pompous officialdom to the operation, but the others soon put a stop to that. It wasn't that they didn't respect the law; they just didn't have the time or patience to put up with Jacques' official shenanigans. Something was said about dunking the agent in the bay, and Jacques eased off.

As far as the tugboat crew was concerned, their job was done. The barge was anchored where they'd been told to anchor it, so they retrieved their towline and headed back to Stewart. McQuillan and airlift crew could figure out how to load the stuff into the plane on their own. It took about twenty minutes to refuel the Norseman during which time McQuillan and Munro rigged a makeshift ramp from the deck of the barge to the plywood floor of the cabin. They'd already figured out the load factors; a Norseman could carry five drums of gasoline but only four drums of the heavier diesel and stove oil.

When the refueling was complete, Bishop and Garner helped roll four drums of diesel across the barge deck and up the ramp into the plane, where they were stood up on end. Bishop wove a network of rope around the barrels which he snugged down to the exposed fuselage tubing.

"That should keep them from sliding aft when you take off," he said, twanging the lines with his fingers to make sure he'd removed all the slack.

McQuillan wanted to check Munro's route of flight again, so Garner retrieved the chart he'd stashed behind the right seat.

"We'll take off heading out the bay," Munro began, tracing his course on the map. "Then we'll turn around and fly up the Unuk for thirty-five miles to where the South Unuk comes in to join the main stream. Then we'll turn left and follow the South Unuk eighteen miles to the glacier."

"How long to you think it will take?"

"Once we're airborne, about sixty minutes round trip, not counting the time we spend dropping the barrels."

With 1,500 pounds of diesel fuel and steel barrels aboard plus the weight of the fuel in the wing tanks, Five-Five was loaded to capacity. There was no wind to speak of, so the takeoff run took up a good portion of Burroughs Bay. When the plane was finally off the water Munro began his 180-degree turn back toward the Unuk. He figured he'd need at least three thousand feet of altitude to make it through the mountains to the glacier, the lower edge of which was at 3,500 feet. He'd have to use climb power the whole way in. The noise inside the cabin was deafening. The Norseman was a loud plane to begin with, and removing the back door made it even worse. The only way he could communicate with Garner was through hand signals.

Thirty minutes after takeoff, Five-Five was at 3,800 feet and boring in on the Leduc glacier. Garner unfastened his seatbelt and squeezed back between the front seats into the main cabin. After loosening Bishop's tie-down lines, he tipped the rearmost barrel onto its side and manhandled it into position to be pushed out the door. Up front at the controls, Munro could feel the center of gravity shift as Garner clambered around the cabin and he compensated as best he could with the trim. He could see the rudimentary mining camp that had been set up out in the middle of the glacier; the trick was to drop the heavy barrels as close as possible to the wall tents without hitting them. He turned around in his seat and yelled and waved at Garner to get ready. Garner inched the first barrel up to the door and waited for the signal to push it out.

Munro eased the throttle back, and the straining engine dropped back to its normal thunder. Pulling the power back even more and winding in some flap, Munro let the plane drift down until it was only a hundred feet above the surface. This time he was careful to align himself so he was flying in a gentle turn across the slope and not trying to outclimb it as he'd done in the Seabee. When he'd gotten as close as he dared to the camp, he waved over his shoulder and Garner kicked the first drum over the door sill.

There was a muted boom as the barrel ricocheted off the ramp and tumbled out into space. Munro leveled the wings and headed away from the glacier while Garner maneuvered the next drum into the doorway. As he approached the drop zone for the second time, Munro was disappointed to see that the first drum had broken open; the stain of diesel fuel was clearly visible against the snow.

The next drum broke open, too. The last two seemed to hold together, however, so Munro headed back to Burroughs Bay for another load. The second flight was a repeat of the first one; two barrels broke and two didn't. Around the dinner table that evening, Munro conceded that his airdrop plan wasn't going to work.

"Tomorrow I'll try landing on the glacier. That seems to be the only way to make sure everything gets up there in one piece. It shouldn't be any different than the landing we made with the Seabee, but with the Norseman's power it should be a lot easier to get off again."

He also decided to send Paul back to Kenmore for the second Norseman at the first opportunity. "The flights will take longer because of the landings and takeoffs on the glacier. With two planes, we'll be able to ferry the stuff up almost as fast as airdropping it."

The next day, March 20, the loads were similar; four drums of diesel fuel on the first flight and three drums of gasoline and one drum of stove oil on the second one. In his bunk the night before Munro had tried to anticipate how landing on floats in the snow would differ from landing on the hull as he had in the Seabee. He decided the biggest difference would be the floatplane's tendency to nose over. The bulk of the plane sat high off the ground on the float struts, and with the snow dragging on two surfaces instead of just one, Munro could visualize the plane rocking forward quite violently the moment it touched down. It would be like landing on glassy water only worse. He'd have to be ready to put in full up-elevator the instant the floats contacted the snow to counter the sudden pitch-over.

He also decided to repeat his Seabee approach; fly in over the lip of the glacier and touch down going uphill. This would bring him to a controlled stop, and the slight upslope might even reduce the plane's desire to nose over. With six hundred horsepower at his command, he didn't anticipate any problems getting the plane turned around for the downslope takeoff. After all, the Norseman's Pratt & Whitney radial was a far cry from the Seabee's wimpy Franklin.

With a plan of action seated firmly in his mind, Munro rolled in on his approach the next morning with confidence. The landing went exactly as he'd anticipated. The Norseman began to rock forward as soon as the floats touched down, but the immediate application of up-elevator brought the plane back to an even keel. Like the smaller flying boat, the floatplane came to a quick stop in the deep snow. Leaving the engine running, Munro climbed into the back to help Garner roll the barrels out the door and down the ramp. The miners snowshoed over and wrestled the awkward drums away from the plane to keep them from piling up and falling over into the thin-skinned float.

Unloading took less than ten minutes. Munro and Garner climbed back into the front seats, and Munro eased the throttle open. The big radial responded with a roar but the plane didn't move. Munro shoved the throttle all the way up. The propeller blew a cloud of snow high into the air behind the plane, but the only movement was a sullen lurching as the Norseman inched forward in a series of jerks. Munro stood on the right rudder pedal, but the blast of air from the prop wasn't enough to overcome the grip of the snow. The best he could do was rock the plane back and forth with the elevator until the floats worked themselves sufficiently free to slide forward another foot or two.

Even in the freezing cold the cylinder temperatures were getting dangerously high, so Munro throttled back to idle and tried to figure out what to do. It was the Seabee flight all over again. The plane would have to be manhandled around 180 degrees, but the Norseman was a lot bigger and heavier than the Seabee. It was Garner who came up with the solution.

"We could tie a real long line to the tail and the miners could all pull straight out to the side while you rock the plane back and forth with the elevator." He held his left hand out flat and waggled it up and down while rotating it right with his wrist. "With constant pressure on the tail the plane should pivot a little bit every time you rock it."

It made sense to Munro, and he climbed down from the cockpit to explain what was needed to the miners. A stout rope was procured from the camp and fastened securely to the fittings that had once supported the tailwheel. Five of the miners walked the free end of the line ninety degrees out to the left of the plane and took up the slack. Munro revved the engine back to full power and waved to the miners to pull. At the same time, he began to shove the yoke back and forth the full extent of its travel.

Garner's idea worked. Engine roaring, the big plane swung to the right in increments until the red-painted cowl was pointing back downslope. Munro throttled back while one of the miners moved in and released the line from the tail. When he was clear, Munro pushed the throttle to its stop and hauled the heavy yoke back to his stomach. Helped by the downward tilt of the glacier, the plane surged up on top of the snow and began to skim down the slope. Munro eased the yoke to neutral to take the pressure off the tails of the floats. They were at flying speed in seconds. The Norseman thundered into the air, snow crystals streaming back from the floats and tail surfaces as the plane soared over the lip of the glacier and banked to follow the Leduc River back to salt water.

The second flight of the day was a repeat of the first. Garner's rope idea was working fine, but it took too long. In the time it took to fasten the line to the tail, rock and tug the plane around, and unfasten the line, the plane could have flown back to the barge and started taking on fuel and cargo for the next flight. That evening at dinner, Munro sketched the layout of the glacier and its surrounding mountains on a piece of paper.

"I think the solution is to swing the approach wide and land across the glacier. As soon as it touches down, I'll try putting in some rudder and swinging the plane to the right so it stops heading a little bit downslope. After unloading we should be able to put in takeoff power and the plane should start moving on its own. We shouldn't need the rope at all."

Munro tested his theory the next morning. Again, the load was four barrels of diesel fuel. The weather was good, clear skies and light winds, and they got off to an early start, lifting off from Burroughs Bay shortly before nine o'clock. As planned, Munro swung wide on his final approach and landed across the slope instead directly up it. As soon as he felt the floats touch, he added a bit of power to keep the Norseman moving and put in some right rudder. Sure enough, the plane eased into a right turn. When he figured it was heading sufficiently downslope to ensure getting it moving again under its own power, Munro pulled the throttle and let the plane sag to a stop in the snow. The four barrels were out the door in a matter of minutes, and Munro put the power back in. The plane immediately began to slide forward. The speed continued to build until suddenly the floats surged up to ride on top of the snow. The drag fell away fast now, and the Norseman sped forward. As the airspeed passed fifty miles per hour, Munro eased back on the yoke, and the silver and red plane rose into the air, the thunder of the Pratt & Whitney reverberating off the mountains and triggering a scattering of tiny avalanches among the rocky crags above the camp. As he looked at the spectacular scenery moving past the cockpit windows, Munro was exhilarated. The airlift was going to work!

The drums of fuel were easy to unload, and with Bishop and the pilots taking turns pumping as fast as they could on the hand pump and McQuillan helping with the loading, Munro and

Garner managed to cram in eight round trips to the glacier before darkness fell at four o'clock and put an end to the flying. Munro switched seats with Garner on some of the flights to give the younger man a chance to experience the glacier landings first hand. Early in the afternoon McQuillan motored back to the wannigan and put together a portable lunch of sandwiches and crackers which the pilots ate in the air on their next trip.

The four men were exhausted by the end of the day. Once the barge had arrived, they'd decided to leave the plane moored alongside it at night, using Bishop's skiff to get back and forth to the wannigan. The wisdom of this decision became evident at low tide, when the wannigan often ended up sitting solidly on the mud.

As they sat slumped in the skiff after refueling and securing the Norseman for the night, Munro announced a change in plans.

"We need a second plane up here now, " he said to McQuillan. "The barrels are easy, but once we start loading pipe and lumber and air compressors and all that other stuff you've got, each flight is going to take a lot longer. I want to fly Paul to Ketchikan tomorrow so he can take the airline back to Seattle and bring up the other Norseman."

The weather that had been so cooperative during the first flights to the glacier departed during the night. March 22 arrived with gusty winds, rain, and a solid cloud cover that shrouded even the relatively low mountains around the bay. Munro managed to take off and slither under the overcast around Bell and Hassler islands into the northern arm of Behm Canal. Following the shoreline of Revillagigedo Island into Ketchikan was easy even in the misty rain, and it wasn't long before Garner was on board the Alaska Coastal Goose for the short flight to Annette Island and the airline flight south to Seattle. Munro and McQuillan spent the rest of the day in Ketchikan purchasing supplies for the wannigan and visiting some of Kenmore's customers. Munro called home and talked to Ruth and the kids for a few minutes before calling the office and leaving instructions to prepare Five-Four-Zero, the silver and green Norseman, for the flight north.

The weather showed no signs of improving. Garner showed up in the second Norseman, but the weather remained relentless until March 27, when Munro managed to make one flight to the Leduc with a load of stove oil and some food. The tug crew arrived with another bargeload of equipment, but rather than simply leave the new one in place of the old one, McQuillan and his men were informed they would have to transfer the incoming cargo to the anchored barge. As soon as the transfer was complete the tug would haul the empty barge back to Stewart for another load.

Halfway through the strenuous task of manhandling the drums of fuel, boxes of food, and stacks of pipe, lumber, and tram rail from one barge to the other, Munro decided to bring up a third plane.

"A lot of this small stuff, food and parts and so on, could be flown up in a Seabee" he told McQuillan. "That would free up the two Norsemen for the heavy loads and we'd get the job done faster."

There was a brief respite in the weather on April Fools Day, and Munro and Garner managed two trips each. The cargo was stove oil. After seeing the living conditions on the glacier, the two pilots could understand why they were flying in so much of the stuff. The tents that comprised the camp were set up on the flat plain of the glacier, and there was no escaping the wind and blowing snow that soon piled up around them. Even on a nice day the temperature was well below freezing, and the stoves in the camp burned twenty-four hours a day. The camp was moved eventually, back against the base of the mountain in an attempt to seek protection from the weather. The new location offered some respite from the wind, but it set the stage for one of the worst mining disasters in Canadian history when in February 1965, a huge avalanche roared down off the mountain and buried the camp, killing twenty-six men outright and injuring dozens of others.

A snowy day at Burroughs. Paul Garner is examining the day's airlift load of fuel drums.

But in 1953, as Kenmore improvised its way through McQuillan's airlift, Granduc's big camp and ten-mile long railroad tunnel that carried the copper ore under the mountains to the trucks coming up from Stewart were still years in the future. On April 2, the weather closed in again and McQuillan, Munro, and Garner took Five-Five and went to Ketchikan for a day. Munro called Bill Fisk and told him to head to Burroughs Bay with the Seabee.

Munro made two trips to the glacier and Garner flew one on April 6. All three flights carried diesel fuel. Garner expressed surprise that they were taking up so much gasoline and diesel fuel when there wasn't anything that needed it on the glacier.

"There will be," McQuillan said. "You'll be taking up a generator, an air compressor, and a small tractor."

"A tractor!" Garner exclaimed. "We can't fit a tractor into a Norseman."

"You can if it's in pieces."

Bill Fisk and Nine-Five-Kilo arrived on April 7. The first good weather in weeks arrived two days later, and by four in the afternoon McQuillan had recorded an incredible thirteen flights on his tally sheet. Munro flew six, Garner five, and Fisk hauled two loads of groceries in the Seabee. In addition to the ubiquitous drums of diesel fuel, the Norsemen lugged seventy-nine heavy core boards and a large sleigh up to the glacier.

The next day's loads were even more diverse. Time after time, the Norsemen thundered off the bay and banked around toward the mountains, their engines straining against the weight of fuel drums, coils of rope, bundles of one-inch pipe, boxes of pipe fittings, an ore car and ninety sections of rail for it to run on, crates of fish-plates and rail spikes, twenty-eight cases of blasting powder, and finally, three sections of the tractor chassis.

While Garner and Munro were lugging the heavy stuff in the Norsemen, Fisk hauled more groceries in the Seabee. It wasn't all cases of canned goods, either. Miners ate well on McQuillan's jobs. There were steaks and chops and slabs of ham, eggs and potatoes and onions, and huge wheels of cheese. Spoilage wasn't a problem, Fisk soon discovered; the miners simply stuck the perishables in the snow where it froze solid in minutes. Fisk hauled nineteen cases of food that day, stuffing the spaces between the boxes with tools and bales of twine.

Norseman Five-Four-Zero moored to the supply barge in Burroughs Bay, Alaska in April, 1953. The lumber and barrels of oil represent only a fraction of the supplies and equipment the Air Harbor pilots ferried up to the Leduc Glacier.

The landing zone soon took on the appearance of a giant ski slope as the maze of tracks left by the arriving and departing planes spread across the surface. Sets of closely spaced, parallel grooves marked Garner's and Munro's landings while Fisk's visits to the glacier were evidenced by single grooves. The tracks were deep, and running across them could be even more dangerous than hitting a boat wake. Skiplanes are equipped with shock absorbers to soak up the punishment of a rough landing, but floatplanes have no such protection. Every bump, every jolt is transmitted full force through the float struts into the airframe. Hitting a set of ruts on the glacier could crack a float fitting, bend a strut, or even throw a plane onto its back. By the end of the day, finding a smooth patch of snow to land on and still slide to a stop reasonably close to the unloading zone was almost impossible.

The pilots ran out of daylight long before they ran out of things to carry. McQuillan's log for April 10 showed a total of twelve flights, one less than the previous day but still remarkable in light of the challenges they'd faced in loading the airplanes. The oil drums were easy, but the long lengths of pipe and rail, to say nothing of the heavy steel ore car and palletized chunks of tractor chassis, took some head scratching and discussion to figure out how to get them into the plane. McQuillan and Bishop had spent years in the bush, and they were experts at moving heavy equipment around without the benefit of forklifts and motorized winches.

On approach to the Leduc Glacier. The twin tracks in the snow were made by the Norsemen, while the single tracks were made by the Seabee. The pilots had to be careful not to hit any of their earlier tracks at high speed, as the jolt could easily break a strut or worse.

"We had an old-fashioned come-along [hand winch] but most of our power was block and tackle, two double blocks. If we couldn't move something with that, we'd put a luff [additional block for more leverage] on the end of the pulling line. If we still couldn't move it, we'd put a luff on the luff. We had all kinds of ways to move things. We had pry bars, too. But with skids and rollers and block and tackle it's amazing how much weight you can move around."

STAN BISHOP

With the possible exception of Paul Garner, the men enjoyed life at their floating camp. McQuillan, like most bachelors who live life on their own in the back country, proved to be an excellent cook. He'd stocked the wannigan well, but unlike the miners camped 3,700 feet above him, he had no way to freeze food. Many of his meals came from cans, but each new barge from Ketchikan would bring enough steaks and roasts and fresh vegetables for a few days at least. One McQuillan specialty that sat in particular favor with Munro was hooligan. A fish more commonly known as smelt, hooligan schooled in abundance in Burroughs Bay, and McQuillan and Bishop were quite adept at catching them. There were crabs, too, big, sweet Dungeness. The men would set pots on the way out to the planes in the morning and pull them up on their way back in the evening.

A rise and fall of seventeen feet left enough water under the equipment barge to keep it afloat, but as the month wore on the occasional minus tide put it on the mud along with the wannigan. This was of no consequence at night, but the first time the barge hit bottom during the day it brought the airlift to a screeching halt.

"I guess we're not going anywhere for awhile," Fisk said as the men stared down at the widening band of glacial silt separating the barge from the rest of Burroughs Bay.

"I think we can still fly," Munro countered. "This mud's not much different than snow. It's so slick and wet I bet we can taxi right through it."

"There aren't any rocks in it," Bishop pointed out helpfully. "It's all just silt that's come down the Unuk and the Klahini."

The Norsemen were docked parallel to the barge so they could be loaded. Five-Five happened to be the first plane in line that day with nothing but mud between it and the receding expanse of water. After checking to make sure his water rudders were up and locked, Munro started the engine and waited at fast idle for the cylinder and oil temperature needles to reach the green. Meanwhile, the men on the barge made sure there was nothing stacked on deck that could get in the way of the inboard wing when the plane moved forward. When all was ready, Munro gave a wave and eased the throttle lever forward in its slot. The propeller began to yowl and throw bits of mud and muck into the air where it pelted down on the heads of the rest of the crew.

The pelting grew heavier as Munro inched the throttle up to full power, and then suddenly the plane was moving. Munro had to back the throttle off right away; as he'd predicted, the Norseman slid quite easily once it got going, and at full power it was accelerating far too quickly. The V-shaped float keels knifed through the mud and kept the heavily-laden Norseman moving in a straight line, although Munro found that he could coax it into a gradual turn by shoving the appropriate rudder pedal all the way to the floor and sending quick blasts of air over the rudder by blipping the throttle.

The plane was at the water's edge in moments, and as soon as Munro felt the plane float free of the mud's suction he shoved the power all the way up and began his takeoff run. Garner waited thirty minutes and then followed in Five-Four-Zero. The pilots had discovered early on that staggering their flights minimized the time each man had to wait while the plane ahead of him was loaded or unloaded.

The weather remained flyable through April 17, and while landing overloaded floatplanes on a glacier was anything but routine, the day's activities soon fell into a pattern. McQuillan usually got up about five a.m. to fire up the big oil stove in the kitchen. There were no radio communications

Stan Bishop loading a diesel engine into Norseman Five-Four-Zero during the Leduc Glacier airlift. The engine would eventually be connected to an air compressor to power the Granduc Mine's rock drills.

between the wannigan and the glacier, so unless it was actually raining or snowing outside the men had to assume the weather would be good enough to fly in. The only way to determine if they could get through to the Leduc was to take off and try.

Breakfast was at six. By six-thirty the dishes had been cleaned and put away and the men were filling their coffee thermoses. Sunrise was still two hours away, but the shape of the barge was discernible out in the bay. Bishop would warm up his outboard and then ferry the crew out to the planes.

McQuillan determined which items were to be flown up each day based on the needs of the miners, and as Jacques stood by with his clipboard and customs forms, the first loads were pushed and levered into the Norsemen. Some items fit in easily and some didn't. The longer lengths of lumber were strapped to the spreader bars between the floats. The shorter pieces went into the cabin crosswise where they stuck out through the open doors on each side of the plane. McQuillan had some reservations the first time he saw Munro loading this way.

"Won't that stuff sticking out from the sides interfere with the airflow over the tail?"

Munro studied the pile of two-by-fours he and Bishop had wedged through the cabin. "It shouldn't. We'll find out in a few minutes, though, won't we?"

It was light enough to fly by eight-thirty, so as soon as the planes were loaded the pilots checked their engine oil levels and turned their machines nose-in to the barge so the propellers could be walked through. Once the oil was loosened up, Bishop and McQuillan stood by with fire extinguishers while the engines were started.

The first starts were the hardest, as the starter motors groaned against the gluey oil and the magnetos struggled to ignite the wet, frosty tips of the spark plugs. The pilots juggled their throttles, hunting for the just the right mix of air and fuel in the cylinders. Too much air and BLAM! a white-orange tongue of fire would lick back against the fuselage and bathe the barge in a flaring red glow. McQuillan and Bishop would nervously finger the triggers of their extinguishers and wait for the smoky whoosh that meant the oil and dope-soaked fabric was going up. Fortunately, Munro and Garner were pretty adept at starting the big radials, and the extinguishers never had to be put into play. Morning starts were always nerve wracking, though, because no matter how many times they were carried out without incident, everyone knew a flaming disaster was never more than one backfire away.

Sometimes an engine would hiccup and spit burning fuel back through the carburetor into the engine compartment. The inside of the cowl would flicker and dance in the glow of the flames, and the men on the barge would pray the pilot had the sense to keep the engine turning over to give the moving pistons a chance to suck the fire back into the intake manifold.

The water in Burroughs Bay tended to be glass smooth in the morning which was bad news for the pilots. With no ripples to induce air under the floats, the heavily-laden Norsemen often refused to break free of the water's suction and climb onto the step. Accelerating on the step was the only way to achieve flying speed;

The Leduc crew. From left to right, Paul Garner, Canadian Customs agent Jaques, Bill Fisk, Bob Munro.

plowing around at full power off the step would succeed only in burning up the engine. On those mornings when Mother Nature refused to provide ripples on her own, Stan Bishop did the job himself. Hopping into his skiff, Bishop would run up and down the bay ahead of the taxiing planes, crisscrossing his wake and making as much of a disturbance in the water as he could. Then, as each pilot went to full power to begin his takeoff run, Bishop would dart in to run directly ahead of the thundering Norseman, plowing the water and glancing back over his shoulder to make sure he dodged out of the way before being overtaken by the whirling propeller.

In a more civilized setting Bishop's maneuvering would have thrown the local police, the Coast Guard, and the CAA into a violent argument over who would get to arrest him first, but in the get-the-job-done atmosphere of southeast Alaska, it was seen as the logical thing to do. Bishop's calculated dash into the path of the departing Norsemen required him to have total faith in his outboard motor, but it got the planes into the air.

Bishop wasn't the only one trusting his life to a set of thrashing pistons. The Norseman's engine was equipped with a mechanical supercharger for improved performance at higher altitudes. Because they're designed to maintain sea level manifold pressures to altitudes of five thousand or more feet above sea level, it stands to reason that when they're actually at sea level, they can develop much higher pressures than the engine can stand. Shove the throttle up too far, and the supercharger will cram so much air through the carburetor and into the combustion chambers that the resulting ignition pressures can easily exceed the strength of the cylinder walls.

The engine's maximum pressure is marked on the manifold pressure gauge, and the pilot must be careful not to exceed this pressure as the throttle is opened for takeoff. It's an extremely important rule of operation, and it went right out the window as Munro and Garner struggled to break their heavy airplanes free of the surface of Burroughs Bay.

> "I always used full throttle to get it on the step, always. I didn't pay any attention to the manifold pressure. I flew the whole job that way. I suppose it was kind of foolish when you think about it because you just don't do that to a radial engine. But it held up, and it ran fine. It's funny, because the R-1340 is the same engine that's in the Otter. But they put a great big propeller on the Otter, and it puts too much of a load on the engine. It's not a very reliable engine on the Otter, but on the Norseman, that engine just ran and ran and ran.
>
> **BOB MUNRO**

The takeoffs might have been risky, but there could be treachery in the sky, too. One afternoon early in the airlift, Garner horsed Five-Four-Zero off the sparkling surface of Burroughs Bay and banked around to begin the straining climb up the Unuk River valley. The morning's landings had been routine in calm air and good visibility, but Garner had enough experience to know that the plumes of snow streaming off the sawtooth peaks to the east meant conditions were changing rapidly.

As Garner turned the corner to fly up the South Unuk, he was surprised to see Munro heading the other way. Munro had taken off twenty minutes before Garner, and while Garner readily acknowledged that his boss had the stamina of a horse and did everything at what seemed to be a breakneck pace, there was no way he could have landed, unloaded, taken off, and flown almost halfway home with a lead of only twenty minutes.

There was something odd about the approaching Norseman, and it was several seconds before Garner realized what it was. The red and silver plane was still loaded. There was the stack of lumber Bishop had tied down between the floats, and he could see the ends of the ore car rails sticking out through the door opening in the side of the fuselage. Maybe he's having engine trouble, Garner thought.

The planes were closing on each other at a combined speed of almost 180 miles per hour. Five-Five was about half a mile away when Munro began rocking his wings. Garner rocked his own wings in reply as the other plane flashed past. So far as he could tell, Munro's plane appeared normal. Probably an electrical problem, Garner decided. They weren't uncommon given the Norseman's propensity for vibration.

As Garner approached the Leduc, he noticed the glacier seemed harder to see than usual. Glancing up, he saw the sky had taken on a whitish pallor. He felt a moment's unease before deciding the pallor was probably the snow blowing off the peaks. The green and silver plane roared up over the lip of the glacier and Garner was surprised that he couldn't pick out the mass of tracks that marked their earlier landings. He couldn't even see the black smudge on the snow that was the miners' haphazard camp. Still, the surrounding peaks stood out clearly enough, and Garner knew precisely where he was. If I don't see the tracks and the camp when I'm on final, he decided, I'll abort and head back down the valley.

Still climbing, Garner swung wide toward the ridge on his left and then banked hard right to line up a final approach across the slope. He pulled the power back and glanced up at the ceiling as his hand reached for the flap crank. When he looked back out the windshield seconds later, everything was gone. Sky, mountains, glacier, everything was the same dead shade of white. There was no up, there was no down, there was no left or right. Garner began to panic, his mind seizing and rejecting options faster than he could act on them. Unable to make a decision, he froze, clinging tightly to the controls he was too terrified to move. Unguided, the Norseman wallowed through the downdrafts, yawing violently as it settled toward the invisible surface below.

Anyone else would have crashed. The plane was only a hundred feet above the glacier and closing fast on the opposite ridge. But Garner had seen panic before, had seen what it did to men under fire in New Guinea, men driven mad by fear and dysentery and jungle rot. He'd seen men die for no other reason than they'd given up control of their own minds. He'd gone down that road himself, and escaping the fatal bullet, had resolved never to let it happen again. You weren't dead until you were dead.

"Where are you?" a small voice from the sane corner of his brain asked. The Norseman had a pretty rudimentary instrument panel, but it did include a gyroscopic horizon.

"I'm in a right bank," Garner answered himself.

"Roll the wings level," the voice commanded, and the hands followed. The white bar in the instrument rotated to the horizontal.

"Where's the nose?"

"Down."

"Raise it." The hands eased the yoke back and the white bar slid up the face of the instrument to the nose-level markers.

"What's your power setting?"

"Fifteen inches."

"Increase it," and the hands responded, pushing the throttle up until the needle in the manifold pressure gauge quivered over the thirty-six inch mark.

Garner had no idea where he was in relation to the glacier below him and the mountains around him. All he knew for sure was that his wings were level and he had reversed his descent.

"Where's the valley?"

"To my right."

With the bulk of his brain screaming in paralysis at the specter of the Norseman smashing into a wall of ice and rock at full throttle, the small, sane voice coaxed the hands into a gentle right bank and forced the eyes to count the degree markers sliding past the window in the magnetic compass. When the count reached ninety Garner rolled the wings level again and held his climb.

Salvation did not come as a burst of sunlight or a brilliant swath of blue sky. It was only a mountain, a single pyramid of white snow and black rock against an ivory sky, but it was real, it was rightside up, and Garner recognized it. Suddenly the whole range snapped into view, and Garner eased the nose down and reduced power. He'd always regarded the bleak and foreboding peaks as the enemy, something to get away from as soon as possible, but after the featureless terror of the whiteout, the tangible, stable bulk of the mountains seemed as friendly and comfortable as a favorite armchair. He eased the Norseman into a curving turn to follow the South Unuk away from the glacier. He'd been airborne for less than thirty minutes.

> "It could be just like flying in a milk bottle. You headed in there and if you didn't see that snow you just didn't dare try for it. Visibility was extremely important. You had to see the surface. Even on nice days, the shadow from the surrounding peaks would hide the surface. We had to be out of there when the sun would start to set because the shadows would come across and we'd lose the surface. Of course, the more we flew in, the more stuff was on the glacier and the more visible the surface became. But on days when the wind was blowing snow off the peaks and everything was white, you just didn't dare go in there."
>
> **BOB MUNRO**

It wasn't until Garner had returned to Burroughs Bay that he learned the reason for Munro's wing rocking; he'd just been through the same terrifying experience and was trying desperately to signal the inbound pilot to turn around. Neither Norseman was equipped with a radio, a deficiency Munro now admits was foolish.

> "We should have had radios in the planes, especially for a job like that. We had no way of warning each other if conditions were bad up ahead, and if one of us had gotten into trouble he wouldn't have been able to call for help. But we didn't think about things like that back then. We were just eager to get the job done, and it never occurred to us that we could get into a situation where we'd need to call for help."
>
> **BOB MUNRO**

Bishop listened without comment as the pilots talked about the difficulties of landing when poor lighting conditions made it almost impossible to pick out the surface. That afternoon he motored his skiff a short distance up the creek and returned with several dozen small evergreens, each about five feet high and with its lower branches cut off.

"What are those for," Fisk asked as Bishop began off-loading the little trees.

"Stick 'em upright in the snow across the end of your landing area and down the length of it. They'll stand out dark against the white surface, and you'll be able to judge your height even in a whiteout."

It was a good idea and the pilots were quick to carry it out, flying the trees up on the first flight the next morning. The miners "planted" them around the landing area, and danger of becoming disoriented in a whiteout was somewhat alleviated. Conditions could still prevent the planes from landing, however, especially when the problem was blowing snow which concealed even the evergreen markers.

The engines were always left running while the planes were on the glacier. It was anybody's guess how the batteries would perform in the freezing temperatures, and none of the pilots were willing to find out. Concern for the electrical systems grew even greater when Garner's plane developed a generator problem. Munro performed a makeshift rebuild and expressed confidence that it would continue to charge the battery, but Garner wasn't taking any chances. The miners were warned to stay alert and away from the propellers when they were working around the planes, and the throttles were kept at a fast idle. As it turned out, Garner's intermittent generator was the only mechanical problem suffered by any of the planes during the entire airlift, a remarkable record considering the beating all three machines were subjected to on a daily basis for a month and a half.

Shutting down the engines on the glacier wouldn't have saved much in any event. In most instances, unloading took only a few minutes. Some items like the diesel engine and radiator for the tractor and the cases of blasting powder had to be handled carefully, but lumber and pipe and railroad iron were tossed unceremoniously out onto the snow. The miners would drag everything clear of the plane while the pilot clambered back into his seat and got ready for the takeoff. Most of the time this involved simply opening the throttle and careening off down the slope, but if snow conditions or ruts had prevented the pilot from turning the plane sufficiently downslope for an easy getaway the miners would trudge back and haul the plane around by the long rope attached to the tail.

The cases of blasting powder were unquestionably the most dangerous items flown in. The prize for the most unlikely item went to an upright washing machine complete with motorized roller wringer. But the most challenging piece of cargo had to be the huge air compressor tank. It was much too large to fit into an airplane, so McQuillan had it torched in half lengthwise before it was barged out to Burroughs Bay. Each half would fit, barely, through the rear door of a Norseman, but they were too long and bulky to be turned and slid forward into the cabin. The only solution was to carry them crosswise with the ends sticking out several feet on either side of the fuselage.

By all appearances, the tank halves should have done hideous things to the airflow over the horizontal tail surfaces, but they didn't. Bishop and the pilots were careful to secure them with their curved outer surfaces facing forward. This offered a modicum of streamlining; faced the other way, each section would have acted as a giant airscoop and it's doubtful if the planes could have built up enough airspeed to get off the water.

The tank was flown in on April 11. The two pieces weren't particularly heavy, just awkward,

High tide in Burroughs Bay. Norseman Five-Five is nosed up to the wannigan for some routine engine maintenance.

and loaded as they were, there was plenty of room in the planes for additional cargo. McQuillan recorded eleven flights that day; in addition to the compressor tank, the pilots carried ninety cases of blasting powder, sixty-five lengths of two-inch pipe, forty pieces of one-inch pipe, thirty sections of rail, several oxygen tanks, the radiator for the tractor, a radiator fan pulley, and a bunch of dishes. The oxygen tanks were part of a rig that the miners used to weld the tank halves back together. The compressor was a critical piece of equipment; it would soon be powering the mine's big rock drills.

The fact that no one fell in the water during the entire operation was somewhat remarkable in light of the fact that the men spent their days manhandling heavy and awkward items into bobbing floatplanes while balancing on precarious, makeshift ramps. Jacques almost went in the bay once when the rope he was pulling on broke, but the only person actually to go for a swim was Bishop, and he did it deliberately.

"One time we lost a fifteen-gallon drum of lube oil. Usually the gas drums will float, but that heavy, damn lube oil went right to the bottom. It was in about fifteen feet of water. Once when I wasn't real busy I went out there to try and get it back. I put a rope handle on an old storage battery, and then I stripped down and jumped in the water. I used the battery to pull me down. I could get my hands on the drum, but I kept floating away from it. I didn't have anything to hold me up tight against it to get a good grip. Pretty soon I ran out of wind. The water is almost thirty-two degrees, almost freezing, and I lost my wind and my nerve both. I had to come back up. I only had a one-shot deal at it. That water was so cold it was hard to breathe even when you were just swimming around on the surface. I was shivering so bad I had to get out. I'd have liked to have gotten that drum back. It was the only piece of gear we lost the whole time, but I just couldn't do it. McQuillan had to write that one off."

STAN BISHOP

Bishop wasn't overly impressed with the youngest Kenmore pilot, finding Bill Fisk a little too brash and cocky for his taste. In actuality, Fisk was a careful and conservative pilot, a fact few people suspected when first subjected to his opinionated demeanor. If he had any shortcoming, it was his desire to be different, to do something nobody else had thought, or dared, to do. The fact that his outbursts of independence never damaged anything or anybody in a career spanning over forty years says a lot for his flying abilities, but his boss and fellow employees didn't always see it that way. The only time Bishop saw Munro get truly mad was the day Fisk decided to land on another glacier just for the fun of it.

"There was one little glacier on the way back in there that I had my eye on. It was a nice, rounded glacier in a saddle. And I thought, I don't see how I can go wrong. Come in one way and take off out the other way. So I went in there one day on the way back from the Leduc, and I was just sailing through there, and I thought, jeez, this has got to be downwind. So I went all the way through and turned around and came back in. It looked a lot more normal this time, so I landed on that bugger, skidded along a little bit, and then gave her the throttle to get out of there before something happened."

BILL FISK

None of McQuillan's maps indicated that the glacier had a name, so Fisk decided to name it after himself.

"Fisk Glacier," he said proudly to Bishop and McQuillan back on the barge. "That's what it's called now. I bet I'm the first person that was ever on it."

Munro hadn't witnessed the landing, but on his next flight he noticed a new track in the snow, a single line going up one side of the little glacier and down the other. It didn't take but a second for him to figure out what had happened, and his suspicions were confirmed when he got back to the barge. Fisk had just taken off on another flight, which was unfortunate because it gave Munro that much more time to stew about what he felt had been a dangerous stunt.

"When Fisk got back to camp, Bob just stood there square-legged and dressed him down pretty good. He said 'Do you realize what you did? You could have had engine trouble or something on that glacier and we would have never known where you were. We wouldn't have known where to start looking for you.' The kid was pretty quiet after that, but I think he realized what he'd done after Bob explained it to him. A lot of people do things without knowing what the consequences will be. But that was a Seabee he did that with, and a Seabee isn't too trustworthy any time."

STAN BISHOP

Fisk put a few more gray hairs on his employer's head a couple of days later, but this time it was the younger pilot's sense of duty that did it. Munro had seen Fisk approaching the glacier as he'd taken off after delivering his last load of the day, and he expected to see the Seabee splash down in the bay no more than thirty minutes after his own arrival. When Fisk didn't show up, the men on the barge began to be concerned. If Nine-Five-Kilo had conked out while it was on the glacier, the miners would put Fisk up for the night, but if the problem had occurred on the way home, there was no telling where he might be. The pilots all dressed warmly, but even their long underwear, tin pants, wool shirts, and heavy jackets weren't enough to guarantee surviving a night in the mountains, especially if they were in shock or injured after an accident.

By now, Fisk was over an hour late, and the light was almost gone. Munro was truly worried now, a worry compounded by frustration because he couldn't do anything until morning. The men were preparing to climb into Bishop's skiff for the short ride back to the wannigan when they suddenly heard the buzz of an engine over in the Unuk valley. Moments later, the red and white amphibian curved in over the bay and did a neat touchdown in the dark water beside the barge.

Fisk's explanation was simple enough. The floats on the Norsemen could be pumped dry every day, but the Seabee had to be taken out of the water before the drain plugs could be removed from the hull. Since its arrival on April 7, the Seabee hadn't been out of the water except to fly, and Fisk had been growing increasingly worried about the amount and weight of water he might be lugging around in the bilges. His concern grew to the point where he decided to do something about it, so he borrowed a shovel from the miners and dug trenches underneath the hull large enough to let him reach in and remove the plugs. His efforts were rewarded as he watched gallons of trapped saltwater pour out onto the snow from each hull compartment.

Wriggling around on his back in the wet snow removing and replacing the drain plugs took forty-five minutes. It was almost dark by the time he took off, but the white snow reflected the waning light, and he had no trouble threading back through the valleys to Burroughs Bay. After hearing his story, Munro declared that, while he found Fisk's desire to keep his plane in top shape commendable, it was imperative that the pilots keep each other informed of their intentions at all times. The weather and overloaded planes were pushing the safety limits as it was; Munro didn't need the added burden of worrying about the whereabouts of his employees.

The last supply flight from Burroughs Bay took place on April 29. For the first time since March 19, the barge deck was clear except for the barrels of aviation fuel for the planes and several large packages of meat. Fisk had headed south with the Seabee four days earlier, so the meat would be flown up in Five-Five. The weather had been getting nastier by the day; Garner and Munro had managed only one flight each on the 28th. At first light the next morning, Garner knelt in the open cabin door and took the packages Bishop handed up from the barge while Munro got the plane ready to go. Wind gusts rattled over the deck and blew slanting streaks of rain across the face of the surrounding hills.

"It doesn't look very promising," McQuillan observed as he watched the mist swirling around the ridgetops.

"We'll go have a look," Munro said. "Paul's going with me, so we can airdrop the meat if we can't land."

"Just be careful, whatever you do."

The low ceiling and drifting rainshowers didn't make for easy navigation, but there were enough breaks in the clouds for Munro to pick his way through the mountains to the glacier. But once there, it was obvious to both men that a landing was out of the question. The flat light had plunged the entire glacial bowl into a whiteout. The surrounding peaks were still visible, however, white shapes against the overcast, so Munro decided to use them as references for an airdrop. Motioning Garner into the rear of the plane, he cranked down the flaps and circled as low as he dared before leveling his wings for a straight run across the still-invisible surface. Keeping his eyes on the peaks and ridges above the camp, he guided the wallowing Norseman through the milky air, making tiny corrections to bring the plane into line with the landing area.

"Now," he shouted, and Garner began throwing the packages of meat out the door as fast as he could. They dropped away behind the plane, dark specks that disappeared almost instantly into the immense whiteness below.

The miners on the surface saw the plane, watched as the packages tumbled out, and set stakes to mark the direction to the landing zone. The whiteout persisted, however, and it took the men almost two days of stumbling around in near-blindness to find the first package. Two more hours

Planning the day. Bob Munro, Paul Garner, and Bill Fisk discuss the day's flights.

of searching uncovered the second package, and then it was easy, a matter of simply following the drop line established by the first two packages.

Munro and Garner spent the rest of their last day getting the planes ready for the long flight south. Bishop filled the Norsemen's tanks for the final time, shook hands, and climbed into his skiff for the trip home.

"Hang on a minute," Munro called down from the barge deck. Puzzled, Bishop looked up from the motor he'd been about to start. Munro strode across the deck to the empty fuel drums and unscrewed the barrel pump.

"Here," he said, handing the pump and its valuable hose down to the man who's hard work had helped ensure the operation's success. "You spent so much time with this thing I think you should have it."

The pump was a significant gift in a world where elevating a heavy drum into position for gravity fueling often proved impossible. Bishop thanked the pilot whose quiet competence and gentle leadership had earned his respect. The pump would be put to good use, he promised. It was, and Bishop was still using it forty years later.

Garner and Munro headed home the next day. Their first stop was Stewart, where they dropped off Jacques and McQuillan. The weather along the Inside Passage was murky but fly-able, and the two Norsemen skimmed onto the calm surface of Lake Washington just before dark. McQuillan sent a tug out to retrieve the wannigan and the empty barge, and Burroughs Bay slipped back into a silence broken only by the liquid whisper of the tides against the rocks.

Up on the Leduc, the miners were proving McQuillan's predictions correct. The copper deposits were huge, and plans were being drawn up for a road and tunnel system to get supplies and equipment in and ore out. In the meantime, the airlift would continue, but from Stewart this time. Granby Consolidated purchased an airplane, a brand new de Havilland Beaver complete with wheelskis, and hired an experienced pilot to fly it. Skiplanes had proven worthless in the first Leduc flights because of their tendency to dig into the soft, unpacked snow on the glacier's surface. The snowfall tapered off in the spring, however, and it wasn't long before the surface was hard and crusty.

The first load to be flown off the Stewart airstrip was dynamite fuse. The unpredictable weather that had so frustrated the Kenmore pilots had given way to warm, clear days, and the pilot had no problems negotiating the formidable rock barriers that lay across the twenty-five-mile route from Stewart to the Granduc mine. The Beaver's 450-horsepower Pratt & Whitney R-985 engine was not as powerful as the Norseman's R-1340, but the newer plane was lighter and far more agile. As the pilot circled down over the glacier, he decided to land uphill. It made sense to him; the slope would help bring him to a quick stop, and the plane's steerable tailski would make it easy to turn around for the takeoff. He flew out over the valley and then turned to make his final approach in over the lip of the Leduc.

The Beaver smashed into the ice just short of the top of the glacier. Whether the pilot misjudged his approach or the plane was caught in an unexpected downdraft will never be known. The Beaver carries its fuel in its belly, and when it hit, the gasoline from the ruptured tanks sprayed forward onto the hot engine. The fire was instantaneous, and when it reached the boxes of dynamite fuse, it became an inferno. The only thing left on the ice when the flames died down were the wingtips and a tiny piece of the tail.

The mining company gave up the idea of supplying the Granduc by air; the only pilots to have done it successfully were Kenmore's, and their floatplanes couldn't operate on the glacier's hard, uneven, summer surface. From now on, the supplies would be hauled in through the mountains by cat train: huge caterpillar tractors hauling giant sleds.

Munro and Fisk would return briefly to the Leduc in the fall, and there were glacier operations in Kenmore's future that would make McQuillan's airlift seem tame in comparison, but the six weeks the men spent at the floating camp on Burroughs Bay provided memories they would never forget. For Bill Fisk, it was the glacier that, as far as he was concerned, still bears his name. For Stan Bishop, it was the knowledge that his skill helped make a remarkable operation a success. But Bob Munro's most vivid memory of the Leduc airlift had nothing to do with flying, or airplanes, or the challenge of landing a floatplane where few people would think it possible.

"I came up around the corner to where I was going to land and, and I thought, 'Uh oh, who's that out in the middle of the glacier?' I got closer, and then I could see that whatever it was, it was really moving across the snow. I was getting down pretty low by then, and I saw that it was a wolf. A big gray wolf. Right out in the middle. I went right by it as I flared into the landing. It was a beautiful animal, and I've always been grateful I had the chance to see it."

BOB MUNRO

WRONG PLANE, WRONG PLACE, WRONG TIME

K ENMORE MADE $13,500 ON THE Leduc airlift. The forty-second meeting of the Air Harbor's board of directors was held in May, 1953, and it was recorded that the company had taken in $21,892 during the first four months of the year. These were the highest earnings in the Air Harbor's eight-year history, but to forestall any overly-enthusiastic celebrations the treasurer pointed out that expenses during the same period had come to $18,869, while depreciation on the buildings and equipment totaled $3,895. Kenmore had, in fact, lost money during the first quarter, $872 to be exact.

The public's interest in flight instruction continued to plummet, but as spring gave way to summer, the Air Harbor was called upon for more and more charter flights into the Cascade Mountains and across the border to Vancouver Island. Ted Huntley was no longer available as a pilot; he'd graduated from college and was serving in the Air Force as a maintenance officer. Paul Garner's health continued to deteriorate as his personal life dissolved in anxiety and frustration over a girlfriend. He drifted away from the Air Harbor not long after the conclusion of the Leduc airlift, leaving Bill Fisk and Bob Munro to bear the brunt of the flying alone.

Five-Four-Zero, the silver and green Norseman Garner had flown onto the Leduc, went into the shop for a much-needed overhaul. Five-Five and the Seabee remained on the line along with a Taylorcraft for the few students who were left. Walt Winseman was as busy as ever, rebuilding Franklins from all over the country in addition to maintaining the two smaller planes in the Air Harbor's fleet. The Norsemen were a different story, however. Rebuilding a Pratt & Whitney R-1340 required tools that Kenmore didn't have, and Winseman didn't think they'd ever have enough radial business to warrant their purchase. Changing a cylinder or installing a new set of piston rings was as far as he was willing to go. Anything more sophisticated was farmed out to shops who had the right equipment and the know-how to use it properly.

One morning in the middle of the summer, Munro came into the shop and walked over to where Winseman was sitting on the floor under a customer's engine.

"I just got a call from D & D Flying Service," Munro announced as he squatted down beside the mechanic. "The engine in their Seabee's not right. They don't think they're getting enough power, and they want us to take a look at it."

"Can it come to us, or do we have to go to it?" Winseman asked.

"The owner will pick us up at the Bothell airstrip in another airplane. The Seabee's over at Port Orchard."

The short flight across the Sound gave Winseman a chance to pump D & D's owner for information on the company's ailing amphibian. The engine's weak performance was puzzling, the man said, because it had just undergone a thorough overhaul at the hands of a competent mechanic.

"Who was that?" Winseman asked, thinking it might be someone he knew, but he didn't recognize the name.

N6372K started readily enough, but Winseman immediately began noticing problems. To begin with, the mixture was wrong and the timing was off. That much was obvious, but he sensed there was something wrong with the propeller as well, although he wasn't quite sure what. Warning the others to stand clear, he shoved the throttle up until the bulbous amphibian was bucking and pitching against its wheelchocks. With allowances for the incorrect mixture and timing, the engine rasping over his head didn't sound too bad. The propeller, on the other hand, sounded downright weird. He stared at the instrument panel hoping to find the answer to the mystery there, but the tachometer and manifold pressure readings seemed fine.

Winseman throttled back to idle and then pulled the mixture control to kill the engine. As soon as the propeller jerked to a stop, he shut off the master and ignition switches and climbed out to confront Munro and the waiting owner.

"The mixture and timing are off, but the rpm's okay and the manifold pressure was right up there at thirty inches. The propeller sounds funny, but I can't tell you why until I take it apart."

Munro walked slowly around the airplane to get a feel for its general condition. Some discoloration on the lower end of one of the wing struts caught his eye, and he moved in for a closer look.

"You've got some corrosion started here." Munro pointed out the blistering and flaking paint. "I wouldn't let this go too much longer, or you could lose the whole fitting."

The owner pondered his airplane for a moment and then made a decision. "Okay, I'll tell you what. Fly the plane back to your shop and fix whatever's wrong with it, corrosion, engine, propeller, everything. That way I won't have to fly you back to Bothell."

Munro turned to Winseman. "What do you think?"

"Do you mean do I think it's a good idea, or do you mean do I think this thing can make it back to Kenmore?"

"Both."

"Like I said, the only way I'm gonna find out what's wrong is to take it apart and look. As far as making it back to the base," the mechanic shrugged, "it seems to be running well enough for that. It's only a fifteen minute flight."

Munro nodded his agreement. "Let's go."

Winseman pulled the chocks out from under the wheels and opened the passenger door to get in.

"Hey, wait a minute!"

Winseman turned around to see a young man dressed in mechanics overalls loping toward the plane with a propeller in his arms.

"Here," the young man panted as he came to a stop in front of Winseman. "This is the propeller that actually belongs on this thing. We couldn't get any rpm out of it, so we put on a different prop."

Winseman narrowed his eyes and stared skeptically at the D & D mechanic. "What do you mean, 'different'?"

"That one," the young man pointed to the prop attached to the Seabee's engine, "has a flatter pitch."

That explained the strange sound Winseman had heard as he'd revved up the engine earlier. He took the two-bladed propeller from the mechanic and tied it down between the front seats with a little piece of quarter-inch rope he found in the bow compartment. Munro fired up the engine and taxied Seven-Two-Kilo to the edge of Port Orchard's narrow runway. There was hardly any wind, but the fitful stirrings of the windsock showed it to be coming from the south. Munro dutifully trundled the Seabee to the north end of the field where he stepped hard on the left brake to pivot the plane back around to face the runway. One last check of the controls, and he eased the throttle up to full power.

The Seabee started forward with a lurch. Munro glanced down at the instruments and noted that the rpm was correct and the manifold pressure was a solid thirty inches. Satisfied that the engine was performing reasonably well, he shifted his attention to the challenge of keeping the lumbering plane on the centerline of the bumpy strip of asphalt.

Everything felt more or less normal during the takeoff run. The plane wasn't accelerating as fast as Munro would have liked, especially considering the light load on board, but he had 2,400 feet of runway in front of him so he wasn't concerned about running out of room. About halfway down the runway Munro eased the yoke forward, and Seven-Two-Kilo's tailwheel reluctantly left the ground.

"This thing doesn't have much soup, does it?" Winseman yelled above the thrashing engine and yowling propeller.

Munro shrugged. The Seabee's performance was definitely off, but the engine sounded smooth enough and the readings on the tachometer and the manifold pressure gauge were about right. They'd be at rotation speed in another couple of seconds, and there was still plenty of runway left in front of them if something unexpected happened.

The needle in the airspeed indicator hit sixty, and Munro eased back on the yoke. The Seabee delivered a parting thump to the runway and lifted smoothly into the air. The airspeed continued to build, and Munro pulled the nose up to climb over the tall fir trees that bordered the airfield. The needle in the rate of climb indicator swung into the positive quadrant, and Winseman began to breathe a little easier.

Munro was reaching for the gear lever when the Franklin began to miss. Winseman's practiced ear instantly diagnosed the sound; their six-cylinder engine had just dropped to five cylinders. Munro played the yoke expertly, staying barely on the safe side of a stall as he kept the plane clawing for altitude. Five seconds later the missing grew worse as another cylinder dropped off line.

The second cylinder took with it the Seabee's ability to climb. Gripping the controls of their expiring airplane, Munro had only seconds to make the decisions that would determine if he and Winseman lived or died. The first thing to go was the notion of raising the landing gear. Pivoted upward, the raised gear permitted water landings but did little to reduce drag. It was more important to concentrate on controlling the airplane.

The thought of turning around flashed through Munro's mind, but he dismissed it just as quickly. The plane barely had enough power to maintain altitude going straight ahead. Putting the plane into a bank steep enough to turn back to the runway would require power they simply didn't have. A crash would be inevitable, and if they lost another cylinder the consequences could well be fatal.

Clearing the eighty-foot trees looming dead ahead was out of the question, but there was a break in the forest off to the left where a grove of younger trees had filled in a logging site. If they could clear the grove, Munro knew they could make it to the saltwater expanse of Carr Inlet even if the sputtering engine quit altogether. He eased the Seabee into a gentle turn, straining upwards against his seatbelt in an instinctive attempt to bodily lift the plane to safety. The first trees in the grove disappeared under the nose, and Winseman could hear the uppermost branches bang against the bottom of the fuselage.

The two men held their breath. The ground ahead was already dropping away toward the inlet. All the Franklin had to do was run another fifteen seconds, and they'd be home free. Winseman heard another branch hit the fuselage, and then the view out the windshield exploded in a blur of color as he was thrown violently against the cabin wall beside him. The loggers hadn't cut down all the big trees in the grove. The Seabee's left wing slammed into solid wood, and the plane hooked around to face back the way it had come. The Seabee paused, suspended eerily as though for some diabolical camera, and then the left wing extension tore off with a screech. Free of the tree that had snared it, the plane plunged forward to smash, nose first, into the hard shoulder of a logging road.

As the plane went down, Winseman grabbed the propeller lying between the seats and lifted it in an attempt to guide it out the windshield. The prop shot forward upon impact, but instead of slicing neatly out through the Plexiglas, it twisted sideways to smash like an ax into Winseman's back. The bow door was wrenched open on impact, and the mechanic was ejected onto the ground beside the plane. For a moment, he lay still. His face was in the dirt, yet he felt like he was still flying. Try as he might, he couldn't get the sound of the engine out of his head. Suddenly he smelled gas, and at the same instant he realized the sound of the engine wasn't imaginary. It was still running at full throttle above his head.

Crawling as fast as his injured back would allow, Winseman scuttled across the road to a tree he thought might offer some protection in case the airplane blew up. He heard the engine cut out behind him, and a moment later Munro limped across the road to join him. The pilot was bleeding from a gash in his forehead, and there was blood oozing from his right eye. Winseman pulled himself erect, holding onto the tree for support. The pain in his back was excruciating, but he was pleased to see he could move everything.

"You're bleeding," he said to Munro, who was holding onto the same tree.

"I think the throttle went into my eye when we hit. This," Munro pointed to the cut on his forehead, "happened as I was trying to get out after I killed the engine. I smelled gas and was afraid the whole thing was about to go up."

He was about to ask how Winseman was feeling when several men came running up the road.

"We saw you go in," one of them shouted. "What happened?"

"The engine lost power," Munro answered.

The men crowded in close to gawk at the up-ended Seabee.

"There's fuel leaking from somewhere," Winseman warned. "Don't anybody go lightin' a cigarette or anything."

"Well, that's odd," Munro said, looking down at his feet. "I don't have my shoes on." He pushed himself away from the tree and limped over to the silent airplane. He peered through the twisted side door and saw his shoes lying in the bottom of the bashed-in nose. He leaned down and picked them up and walked back to sit beside Winseman. They were the last steps he would take for two months.

The men who'd run up the road sent one of their number back to call an ambulance. It arrived thirty minutes later, sliding to a stop in front of the wreck. Munro and Winseman were loaded into the back, and the driver careened back to the highway and headed for the local hospital. By now the shock of the accident was wearing off. When the doctors asked where it hurt, Winseman replied that it would save time if he just told them where it *didn't* hurt.

The first order of business was to take X-rays. Winseman was battered and bruised, but the real damage was in his back, where the impact of the propeller he'd been holding had crushed two vertebrae.

Munro's injuries were no less severe. The plane had hit so hard his feet had snapped the heavy rudder pedal castings in half. One of his ankles was broken, and the other was severely sprained. He'd broken a finger, either on the yoke or against the instrument panel as his hands smashed forward at the moment of impact. The gash in his forehead had stopped bleeding, but his right eye was swollen almost completely shut. The doctors wanted to admit both men into the hospital on the spot, but Munro would have none of it.

"We want to go back to Seattle. Give me a telephone so I can call my wife."

The doctors tried to talk him out of it, but Munro was adamant.

"We're going back to Seattle," he declared firmly as he hung up the phone. "My wife is coming to get us in the station wagon. Don't worry," he added reassuringly, "we'll go straight to the hospital."

It was a half-truth. Winseman went, and was promptly put into a body cast. You'll be in bed for at least six weeks, the doctors told him. Winseman nodded submissively; he was afraid they might not let him leave if he argued. The moment he got home, however, the doctors' orders went out the window. Winseman was up and walking in three days, and back to work in three more. He was supposed to wear the body cast for three months, but occasionally, as he pounded and pried the bushings from a customer's worn out engine, a tool would slip or he'd miss with the hammer, and another chunk of plaster would hit the floor. By the time the doctors pronounced him fit, there was little of the cast left to remove.

Munro, who had little faith in the medical profession's ability to do much more than run up a big bill, didn't go to the hospital at all. Ruth drove her husband home and helped him to the sofa where he spent the next eight weeks impatiently waiting for his ankle to heal.

The cause of it all, D & D's smashed Seabee, was loaded onto a trailer and hauled the long way around the Sound to join the hulks stacked beside Kenmore's parts barn. The Air Harbor mechanics removed the engine, and Winseman tore it down in an attempt to find out what had gone wrong.

"The kid that had done the rebuild was an automobile mechanic, and he'd never worked on an airplane engine before. The cylinders of an airplane engine expand as they heat up, they get longer, so they use hydraulic lifters on the valve pushrods to take up the slack as the cylinder stretches. Instead of bleeding the lifters down before setting the clearances, the kid just gave the pushrods forty thousandths clearance from the top as though it was a solid lifter. When we started running the engine, the cylinders started expanding. As they got longer, the valves began opening less and less because the lifters couldn't compensate for the expansion. Pretty soon there was so much clearance that the pushrods began jumping out from under the rockers. That's how we lost the power in those two cylinders.

"There's supposed to be an O-ring around the base of each cylinder. This kid didn't understand that there were two types of cylinders made for a Franklin. One took a thin O-ring and the other took a fat one. The kid didn't know which one to use, so he put them *both* on. Then, when he tightened down the cylinder bolts, the double O-rings forced the cylinder liners to crimp and crack. That made it real hard for the pistons to go up and down, which was another reason the engine wasn't developing enough power.

"The thing that really annoyed me, though, because I should have caught it, was that there was a hole in the manifold pressure line. There was sea-level air going in there that was thirty inches, and that was why I got the reading of thirty inches of pressure when I ran the engine up. When it was idling, the reading should have gone down to fifteen inches, but evidently I was looking at something else when it was idling, so I didn't see that it was staying at thirty inches. That's why the engine readings were correct when we took off. That hole in the line made it look like the engine was running fine, when in fact it was pretty sick."

WALT WINSEMAN

The owner of D & D Flying Service was convinced Munro and Winseman were responsible for the demise of his Seabee, so he filed a lawsuit demanding that Kenmore replace the plane or at least compensate him for its loss. For awhile things looked pretty bleak for the Air Harbor, as the company's only defense was the description of what had happened from the two men who'd been in the plane. Then Winseman tore down the engine, and Kenmore had hard evidence of the incompetence that had made their crash inevitable.

When the Air Harbor threatened to file a countersuit based Winseman's discovery, D & D's owner wisely decided to forget the whole thing. He'd placed his faith in an unqualified mechanic, and Munro and Winseman had suffered the consequences. His Seabee wasn't worth rebuilding, so he told Munro to sell off what parts he could and cut the rest up for scrap.

15 STAGGERWING

A S THE SUMMER OF 1953 faded into fall, Munro was asked to fly one of Granby Consolidated's executives up to the Leduc Glacier so he could see firsthand how the company's investment was shaping up. Munro was delighted to get the job, but he was somewhat apprehensive of his physical ability to carry it out. He'd only recently vacated the sofa to which he'd retired after the D & D crash, and his ankle was still weak and painful. He was sure he could fly, however, so he agreed to meet the executive in Ketchikan. Once again, the plane would be the Air Harbor's Seabee, N6295K.

The Granduc mining camp had grown during the summer. Wooden platforms supported six big wall tents on the rocky slope above the glacier. The two GMC diesels and belt-driven air compressors Kenmore had flown in were set up and running at the base of the hill where they fed pressure to the huge compressor tank. The loads of one-inch pipe Munro remembered from the airlift had been spliced together into air lines that snaked up the hill to power the miner's pneumatic drills. The noise was mind-numbing. The unmuffled diesels thundered away at full song, while up the hill the scream of escaping air and the metallic roar of the rock drills set Munro's ears to ringing. It was worse than flying a Norseman with the doors off.

Fascinated as usual by anything he hadn't experienced before, Munro prowled around the camp taking pictures and talking to the miners. He had to be careful where he stepped. The environmental movement had few disciples in 1953, and none of them worked at the Granduc. The site was littered with bits of machinery, rusty lengths of pipe, broken tools, and dozens of fuel drums. The hammering diesels alone consumed at least two barrels a day, and then there were the generators, the tractor, and the stoves in the tents. As each barrel was emptied, it was simply tossed aside and a full one set up in its place. Some of the barrels lay where they fell, while others boomed off down the rocks and ricocheted out onto the glacier.

Apart from the noise, it was quite pleasant on the Leduc; sunny and warm with a bright blue sky overhead. On the rare occasions when the machinery fell silent, the air filled with the sound of water as snow on the upper slopes melted and poured down through the rocks to the edge of the glacier. There it mysteriously disappeared only to reappear a mile away and a thousand feet lower as the headwaters of the Leduc River.

The company Seabee on the Leduc glacier in August, 1953. The snow was melting fast, and the rough surface put the Seabee's hull to the test on take-off. (photo by Bob Munro).

Continuing problems with the cat trains led Granby Consolidated to call on Kenmore several more times that fall, mostly for inspection trips or to fly in a critically needed part. Munro and Bill Fisk divided the flights up between them, using the company's newly-acquired Piper Super Cub. The mining company toyed with the idea of having Kenmore conduct another full-scale airlift the following spring, but the mine apparently got the bugs out of its cat train operation because a contract never materialized.

Airplane sales continued into 1954 with the refitting and sale of a Norseman to Wheeler Airlines in Quebec for $16,000. Another well-used Seabee appeared on the market, and the Air Harbor bought it with a loan from Bothell State Bank for $2,300. After making $500 worth of repairs, Kenmore sold the plane for $3,400, netting $600 in the process. The next big job into the shop was a Beech 17. The float-equipped biplane needed a lot of work, but the mechanics were only about half finished when the owners announced they'd run out of money. They did have a proposal, however. For a mere $3,200, Kenmore could buy the Beechcraft and the floats that went with it, if Munro would tear up the repair bill.

Beechcraft had introduced the wood-and-fabric Model 17 in 1932. The press took one look at the unique positioning of the Model 17's wings, which placed the lower airfoil out ahead of the upper one and dubbed it a "staggerwing." It was a name that rolled off the tongue and captured the imagination, and as the sleek biplane zoomed toward its rightful position as one of the great planes of all time, it's official designation departed just as rapidly in the opposite direction. By the time production ended in 1948 in favor of the all-metal, V-tail Bonanza, the Model 17 designation had been all but forgotten. The plane would live in history as the Staggerwing Beech.

While Bob Munro's attitude toward aviation was more pragmatic than romantic, he was not immune to the aura surrounding the legendary Staggerwing. He didn't think it was worth as much as a Norseman, but the Staggerwing was fast and comfortable and conveyed a considerable degree of status to its owner. Munro knew once the Air Harbor finished fixing it up, they could sell the plane for a lot more than $3,200. Its floats alone were worth at least twice that.

Munro told the Staggerwing's owners he'd consider their offer. Had he known what effect the airplane ultimately would have on his company he probably would have ordered it destroyed on the spot, but without the benefit of a crystal ball he simply viewed the deal as another opportunity to get some positive numbers in the account books.

Of more immediate concern was the company's bid for the 1954 Coast and Geodetic Survey in Alaska. Hoping the government's love affair with ancient airplanes was over, Kenmore submitted a bid based once again on a Norseman. While not the most up-to-date plane in the sky, the Norseman was certainly more modern and reliable than the creaking old Bellancas and Travelaires that had been winning the contract year after year. The bid was typed up and mailed, and Munro spent an anxious couple of weeks waiting for the formal announcement. By now it had become obvious there would be no follow-up contract with the Granduc Mine, so the survey was considered a must-win; the Air Harbor couldn't afford to keep two Norsemen sitting around doing nothing.

At last the envelope arrived, and Munro eagerly tore it open. Kenmore had lost again, this time to a man with a Travelaire even older and creakier than the venerable Five-One-Mike. More disturbing than the loss, however, was the fact that the Travelaire's owner was reputed to be a "good friend" of several key officials in the CAA. Although there was nothing to prove that the man's relationship with the officials had influenced the contract decision, the fact that a process based on price and capability could be influenced dishonestly rubbed Munro the wrong way. As far as he was concerned, no contract, no matter how lucrative, was worth the abandonment of the principles of honesty and integrity.

The loss of the survey contract was a disappointment, but the season didn't turn out to be a total bust. Norseman Five-Four-Zero was leased to Alaska Airlines for the summer season with an option to buy, while Five-Five was booked for three charter flights into British Columbia.

Running a small business is no easy job. Munro would have been delighted if the only thing occupying his time was fixing and flying airplanes. But there were plenty of frustrations to make sure he didn't start enjoying himself too much. One of them was Pioneer Towing. The tug and barge company had a contract to haul sand, gravel, and lime to the cement plant growing up next door to the Air Harbor. On several occasions the wash from their tugs had caused minor damage to floatplanes moored in the channel, but Pioneer refused to accept any liability. They were operating within their rights, they claimed, and there wasn't anything the Air Harbor could do about it.

After several attempts to reason with the towboat company ended in frustration, Munro turned to his employees for suggestions.

"Tell 'em if they don't knock it off we'll drive a row of pilings across the entrance to the channel," growled Fisk. "That ought to get their attention."

Munro had no desire for confrontational action, but Fisk's blustery threat gave him an idea. Anyone intending to build a dock or otherwise intrude upon the body of water that is Lake Washington has to submit their plans to the Army Corps of Engineers for approval. Munro dutifully telephoned the Corps and informed them that Kenmore Air Harbor, Inc. was considering the construction of a dock just inside of, and parallel to, their property line down the center of the Kenmore channel. The purpose of the dock would be to protect their airplanes from the damaging propeller washes kicked up by the tugboats delivering material to the cement plant next door. As soon as the plans were drawn up, the Air Harbor would forward a copy to the Corps for examination.

Munro was banking on human nature. The marine community is a close-knit group, and it wasn't long before someone from the Corps informed Pioneer Towing of the Air Harbor's intentions. Pioneer immediately realized their tugboats' ability to maneuver in the channel would be severely restricted if Kenmore put a dock down the middle. Thirty years later, the issue probably would have been resolved in a courtroom. But things were different in 1954, especially in the northwest where taking personal responsibility was considered a duty rather than a penalty. Pioneer Towing put the word out, and from then on their tugboat captains stirred up barely a ripple as they moved their barges in and out of the channel.

That May, the Air Harbor decided to accept the deal for the Staggerwing that was undergoing restoration at the hands of the company's mechanics. It was actually the second time N1256N had been worked on by the company. Twelve months earlier, the plane's owners had called Kenmore wanting to know if their Staggerwing could be put on floats. They had some sort of business venture they wanted to undertake in Panama, but it required them to have access to a seaplane.

Munro had thumbed through the EDO catalog and found that a Staggerwing powered by the 450-hp Pratt & Whitney Wasp Jr. required Model 4665 floats. As this was the same float that had been used on the single-engine Lockheed Vega and the popular Stinson SR-9 Gullwing, Munro knew a used pair in reasonably good condition would be easy to find. He was right; three or four phone calls later, a set of 4665s was on it's way to the Renton airport. When they arrived, Munro sent a couple of mechanics down to install them on the underside of Five-Six-November.

The business scheme the partners had cooked up in Panama remained a mystery forever, but one look at their plane a year later made it obvious their plans hadn't worked out. For reasons which were never explained, saboteurs had slashed dozens of holes into the fabric, and the once-proud Staggerwing limped back to Kenmore covered with tape and crude patches. The ruined skin was the most dramatic damage, but the months of tropical heat and humidity had taken their toll on the plane's woodwork and metal fittings as well. Kenmore was instructed to fix everything that needed fixing, and the work was almost complete when the owners broke the news that they were broke. Then came the offer to sign over the plane in lieu of paying the bill.

Beech Staggerwing Five-Six-November. Bob Munro is standing on the nose of the float Beside him is Bill Fisk, and then Vern Wilson, the young pilot who would be at the controls during the fatal landing on Lake Shannon.

Munro accepted the offer with the intention of selling the plane and its valuable floats as soon as the mechanics finished their work. But the more he looked at the Staggerwing, resplendent in a new coat of glossy yellow paint and dark blue trim, the more he thought how nice it would look tied to the Air Harbor's dock. On wheels, its cruise speed approached two-hundred miles per hour. Even with a set of floats slung underneath it should run circles around the Seabee, and it certainly looked a whole lot snazzier than a Norseman. It could be just the ticket to pump some more life into the company's charter business.

Also on the plus side was the fact that the Beech 17 was no stranger to the company's mechanics. In addition to the work they'd just completed on Five-Six-November, they'd also performed an engine swap for a Canadian customer, replacing the original Wright engine on his pre-war Staggerwing with a Pratt & Whitney Wasp Jr. So the fateful die was cast, and Five-Six-November joined the Kenmore fleet.

It was a beautiful machine, and passengers loved it. The interior was more like a car than a plane, with plush seats and automotive-style chrome fittings. Young Gregg Munro was particularly intrigued by the glove box, which featured the first four-tumbler combination lock he'd ever seen. But appearances can be deceiving, and it didn't take Bob Munro long to discover that, as a floatplane, the Staggerwing was a dud. The floats reduced its blistering cruise speed to a mere 120 miles per hour. The Wasp Jr. was a terrific engine, but it was powerless to shorten Five-Six-November's interminable takeoff run, a fault Munro attributed to the aerodynamic characteristics of the plane's small, negatively-staggered wings.

Even tied to the dock, the Staggerwing was a disappointment. The only true door was on the right, next to the three-place rear seat. The pilot had to enter the rear of the cabin and then squeeze forward between the individual front seats to reach the cockpit. Docking could be a real challenge; if there were no rear seat passengers available to step out and pull the plane to a stop, the pilot had to do it, scrambling aft between the front seats and diving out the cabin door onto the lower wing as the plane coasted, unguided, toward the dock. Docking the plane on the left was almost impossible. At some point in its life, Five-Six-November had been fitted with a small door beside the pilot, but it was designed for emergency use only. Wriggling through it quickly enough to effect a successful docking was out of the question.

> "The Staggerwing had some unique traits that you had to be real careful about. Most important was that when you taxied in, you were going to sweep everyone right off the dock if they didn't get out of the way. I saw people get knocked right into the drink trying to stop it. It was a fairly heavy airplane, and that lower wing would just sweep the dock clean. Being a lineboy at Kenmore could be a dangerous job when the Staggerwing came in."
>
> TED HUNTLEY

Munro was not the only one to become disenchanted with the legendary Staggerwing. Like everyone else, Walt Winseman had been awed by the plane's racy lines, snazzy interior, and spiffy finish. Then one day he found himself walking behind the Staggerwing in the tie-down area, and on a whim he reached up and shook the tail. To his amazement, the entire plane began to wiggle and wobble on its float struts. He shook the tail again and was rewarded with the same performance. Winseman knew the float installation had been approved by the CAA, and he knew for a fact that the work on Five-Six-November had been carried out correctly, but there was just too much flexibility in the rigging for his taste. He shook his head and walked on, convinced the Staggerwing's future at Kenmore would be a short one.

Bill Fisk flew the plane a few times, and while it didn't live up to his expectations either, he tried to maintain at least a modicum of optimism.

> "It worked. Probably better than a Howard DGA. Neither one had very long wings, but the Beech at least had four of them. We felt like we were flying a classy airplane."
>
> BILL FISK

While the plane had been restored to good physical condition, the abuse it had suffered at the hands of its previous owners had taken its toll on the engine. The 450-horsepower radial started readily enough, but when the throttle was advanced for takeoff, the engine would belch smoke and backfire as it came up to speed. They were the classic symptoms of a worn out supercharger, but because the engine ran smoothly enough once it got going, it was easy to keep putting off its repair.

Several weeks into the summer of 1954, a customer called the office and booked a charter to survey some property along the shore of Nootka Sound on the west coast of Vancouver Island. It would be a long flight, at least 250 miles each way, and as the customer was bringing some friends, Munro decided to take the Staggerwing. While not the world's hottest floatplane, the Beech still could outrun the Seabee by a measurable degree. Munro figured the flight would take six hours: three up and three down plus or minus whatever the winds were doing along the route.

The takeoff was accompanied by the usual pyrotechnics from the exhaust, but once airborne the engine settled into a smooth drone. The weather was good, and for the first hundred miles the flight held all the promise of being totally routine. Then, as the last of the Gulf Islands drifted out of sight under the floats and the plane headed out over the unprotected waters of the Strait of Georgia, something began to go wrong. It wasn't that the engine quit or even began to misfire. The tachometer indicated a steady 1,900 rpm and the manifold pressure gauge showed a solid nineteen inches of mercury. The engine just didn't sound right anymore. Munro couldn't put his finger on it, but there was definitely something amiss under the cowl.

Forward progress takes on the characteristics of cold molasses to a pilot at the controls of a sick airplane. Lasqueti and Texada islands oozed past the right wing as Munro strained to pick out any anomalies in the thunder of the engine. Has that whine always been there? Was that rasping sound new, or had he been hearing it all along? Has the exhaust always barked like that?

Cape Mudge on the south tip of Quadra Island swam into view, with the mill town of Campbell River just across the channel. Munro eased the power back and started a curving descent toward the Campbell River seaplane base. With the Staggerwing tied safely to the dock, Munro gathered his passengers together.

"I just don't feel good about taking you across the island today. It's all mountains between here and Nootka Sound, and it's not the sort of place you want to be if you're going to have an engine failure. I'm going to charter an airplane here to fly you across, and when you get back we'll fly home over the water."

"If you don't think your plane will make it back, I'd rather go home some other way," the man who'd set up the trip said. His companions nodded their agreement.

"I think we'll be fine," Munro assured them. "I just don't want to risk having a problem in the mountains."

It took only a few minutes to make the necessary arrangements, and the men were on their way. Alone on the dock, Munro carefully checked the Staggerwing for any indication of trouble. Aside from the smudgy streak extending aft from the exhaust stack, Munro could find no evidence of any malfunction.

His passengers were back from Nootka Sound by mid-afternoon. Munro had refueled the Beech, so as soon as everyone was aboard, he untied the plane and shoved off. The engine fired immediately, and he idled out toward open water while he waited for the oil and cylinder-head temperatures to stabilize. When all was ready, he pointed the bright yellow Staggerwing into the wind and eased the throttle up to takeoff power. The backfiring didn't seem so bad this time, and Munro began to regret spending the company's money to hire another airplane for the flight to Nootka Sound.

Twenty seconds after takeoff, the Staggerwing's engine exploded. Examination later would show that the worn out bearings in the supercharger had finally seized, stopping its rotation instantly. The tremendous shock snapped the drive gears like eggshells and shattered the spinning impeller. Chunks of the disintegrating blower ricocheted through the engine compartment, slicing through oil and fuel lines and igniting the volatile avgas. As the supercharger came apart, the sudden imbalance was more than the rest of the engine could tolerate. Connecting rods began snapping like dry twigs, their jagged ends flailing the inside of the case and smashing against the thrashing pistons.

For an instant, Munro sat stunned as greasy black smoke and tongues of orange flame began licking out from under the cowling. Catastrophic engine failure is something every pilot is trained to react to, but no one ever expects it to actually happen. Then Munro's instincts took over. Ignoring the shouted questions of his white-faced passengers, he shoved the nose over with his left hand to preserve airspeed while his right hand flashed between the mixture control and the emergency shut-off lever to staunch the flow of fuel to the engine compartment. He flipped off the magneto and electrical switches just as the forest of flailing connecting rods locked up and slammed the propeller to a stop.

There was no time to wonder if his actions had done anything to smother the fire under the cowl. The Staggerwing was settling fast, and he had to concentrate on the landing. At least he didn't have to make a turn. The plane was still heading into the wind, and there was plenty of open water in front of him. Playing the yoke expertly, Munro slowed the plane's descent and raised the nose to keep the floats from digging in when they hit. To someone outside the plane, Munro's landing would have looked perfectly normal, although an observer might have wondered at the motionless propeller and wisps of smoke drifting out from under the engine cowl.

Munro's quick action on the fuel controls saved the day. The heavy lube oil continued to smolder and smoke as it dribbled over the shattered engine, but the flames had disappeared. The four-knot tidal current racing between Campbell River and Quadra Island precluded any possibility of paddling to shore, but the explosion and forced landing had attracted the attention of a number of people in the harbor. A motor launch arrived and took the Staggerwing in tow, hauling it against the fierce current back to the seaplane dock in the mouth of the river.

After tying the plane to the end of the dock where it would be out of the way, Munro set about arranging transportation back to Kenmore. Hiring a plane to take everyone home wiped out the Air Harbor's remaining profit from the flight and then some, but at least everyone had come through the incident unscathed.

Munro considered hiring a Canadian company to replace the Staggerwing's ruined engine, but he couldn't bring himself to pay someone else to do what the Air Harbor was capable of doing themselves. One week after the forced landing, Munro and Winseman loaded a used but operable Wasp Jr. into the back of the weapons carrier and headed north in the pre-dawn darkness. The Canadian customs official at the border crossing looked at the two mechanics in their work clothes and at their battered truck and decided their story was most likely a ruse to get them across the border where they could then sell the valuable engine free of taxes or import duties. It took almost an hour of frustrating discussion to convince the man that they really were going to drive all the way to Campbell River and install the engine in a U.S. registered airplane.

Released at last from the border crossing, the two men drove to Vancouver where they caught the ferry across the Strait of Georgia to Nanaimo. Two hours later, they rattled down the gravel road to the Campbell River seaplane base. The Staggerwing was still where Munro had left it, but it would be impossible to change the engine on the narrow, floating dock. The sandspit at the mouth of the river looked much more promising, although they'd have to be mindful of the tide.

Winseman poked around behind the buildings and came up with a couple of heavy timbers, each about twenty feet long. Munro chained the timbers together at one end while Winseman dug two holes out on the sandspit close to the water's edge and about ten feet apart. After dragging the timbers onto the sand, the two men split the legs apart to lock the chained ends together and hauled the whole thing into the air with the truck, guiding the feet of the timbers into the holes as the chained ends went up. When they were done, they had a sturdy A-frame that could be tilted toward the water or back over the bed of the weapons carrier.

"We're in luck," Munro commented, pointing at the high-water line on the sand. "The tide's still going out, so we should have several hours before it comes back in far enough to be a problem."

Using a pair of long ropes, Munro and Winseman moved the Staggerwing over to the sand-spit and nosed it up against the shoreline in front of the A-frame. Now came the hard part. The Staggerwing's engine was mounted tightly against the firewall, and it was a real struggle to maneuver hands and tools through the confined spaces around the Wasp's accessories to the motor mounts. More than one wrench clinked down through the engine compartment and into the water between the floats before the mangled radial was hanging free from the chain hoist Munro had hooked to the top of the A-frame.

With Munro holding a rope on the water side to act as a brake, Winseman swung the A-frame inland until the engine was suspended over the bed of the truck. The damaged engine was lowered into place and Winseman transferred the chain hoist to the replacement engine. Three hours and countless dropped tools later, the Staggerwing had a new engine. The only real snag occurred as they were replacing the propeller. The crankshaft on the replacement engine didn't mate properly with the old propeller. The prop itself was secure, but the pitch-change mechanism wouldn't work, which meant Munro wouldn't be able to get the blades out of fine, or takeoff, pitch.

"The heck with it," he growled. "I'll fly it like this. It won't be very efficient, but it'll get me home."

Before they replaced the cowl, Munro fired up the new engine to make sure everything was functioning properly. Winseman checked all the hose and pipe connections but could find no evidence of oil or fuel leaks.

By now, the tide was coming in fast, and the two men raced to replace the cowl and knock apart their makeshift A-frame. Then they turned the plane around and tailed it back up onto the beach. Munro climbed through the door and squeezed between the front seats into the cockpit. The engine barked back to life instantly, and Munro inched the throttle up until the radial was idling at six-hundred rpm. Everything looked fine on the instrument panel, so he shoved the throttle up and powered the Staggerwing off the beach.

Once he was clear of the river mouth, Munro turned the sleek yellow biplane into the wind and slowly eased the throttle up to full power. Several hundred yards away on shore, Winseman listened carefully as the engine rumble swelled to a throaty roar. It sounded fine to him, but he waited anyway until the plane left the water and accelerated into the sky, the long plumes of spray off the floats shimmering gold in the late afternoon sun.

Winseman checked the beach for anything they might have overlooked and vaulted into the driver's seat of the weapons carrier. Cranking the tired engine to life, he coaxed the truck out of the soft sand and back to the road that led to the highway. Once on the pavement, he pulled his coat collar up against the wind whipping through the open cab and began to look for a coffee shop. Munro would be home in two hours. Winseman would be lucky to be home by the next morning.

While the Staggerwing had lost its patina of class as far as Munro was concerned, it was still the greatest plane in the world in the eyes of Kenmore's line boy. While Vern Wilson's schoolmates vacillated through their dreams of becoming firemen, race car drivers, and big-league baseball stars, Wilson wanted only to be a pilot. The center of the aviation universe was a long way from Lake Forest Park, but Kenmore Air Harbor was just down the road, and that suited young Wilson just fine. He managed to secure a part time job as a line boy, washing and fueling planes, lugging baggage around for customers, and doing the thousand and one other things no one else wanted to do.

It didn't take long for the enthusiastic and hardworking Wilson to become a popular member of the Kenmore family, and he was especially close to the Munro kids, who finally had someone nearer their own age to hang around with. He put all his earnings into flying lessons, and by the time the Staggerwing arrived on the scene, he'd earned his commercial license. As 1954 drew to a close, Wilson approached Munro about becoming one of the company's full-time pilots. Munro liked the young man, and respected the fact that Wilson had stuck to it, doing every demeaning task that came along without complaint. He'd demonstrated a real ability in the air, too, earning his Private and Commercial ratings with high marks from his instructors. But he didn't have enough experience, and experience was a requirement in the unpredictable world of water flying.

No, Munro told the nineteen-year-old, he'd have to have a lot more hours in his logbook before he could assume the responsibility for a planeload of passengers.

While Wilson was trying to figure out how to build his hours, Munro was trying to figure out how to buy his property. He hated the fact that the Air Harbor's future depended on a lease. The fact that leases expired and could be denied renewal was bad enough, but even more disturbing was the knowledge that his ability to succeed was under someone else's control. The issue was brought up before the board, and everyone agreed it was time to contact Mrs. Mines' attorneys and begin purchase negotiations. The Air Harbor would propose a down payment of $3,500 with subsequent fixed monthly payments to run until the agreed-on price was paid off.

The company's earnings in 1954 totaled $47,141. Expenses for the same year totaled $39,288. When the depreciation on airplanes, facilities, and equipment was figured in, the bottom line was a net loss of $3,165. On the other hand, the outlook for 1955 was optimistic. There was another government survey coming up for bid, along with a potential contract from Puget Sound Dredge and Barge Company to support the Western Electric installations under construction near Point Barrow, Alaska. A mining consortium had contacted the Air Harbor about conducting an aerial survey of the Ketchikan area, and the company had already booked numerous private charters for fishing and hunting trips.

The new year got off to a promising start. The Air Harbor finally won a survey contract, subleasing their old Bellanca, Five-One-Mike, from its current owner and subleasing it to the government for the sum of $13,500. Norseman Five-Four-Zero was leased to Alaska Airlines for the summer, and the airline was making noises about eventually buying the plane for $16,000. Someone made an offer on the company Seabee; its troublesome engine and high maintenance costs were a growing liability, so it didn't take much to persuade Munro to sell it. The Staggerwing and Norseman Five-Five were kept busy flying hunters and fishermen into the Cascades and across the border into British Columbia, while the Piper Cub and two Taylorcrafts took care of local flights and flight instruction.

The summer of '55 was good to Vern Wilson, too. When the Air Harbor sold a new Super Cub to a logging company in Ketchikan, Wilson got the nod for the delivery flight. The timing couldn't have been better. The logging company hadn't gotten around to hiring a pilot yet, so when Wilson taxied in after an exhilarating flight up the Inside Passage, the foreman decided to save himself the hassle of finding and interviewing applicants.

"How'd you like to fly this thing for us this summer?" he asked as Wilson handed over the paperwork for the new plane. "The pay's not bad and you can bunk and eat with the crew for free."

Wilson didn't have to be asked twice. By the end of the season he'd added over two-hundred hours of floatplane time to his logbook. As he boarded the Grumman Goose for the short flight to Annette Island and the airline ride home, he felt confident he could handle the big stuff.

By big stuff, he meant the Staggerwing. He'd fallen in love with the sleek plane the moment it showed up on the property, and Munro's increasingly dim view of its performance did nothing to dampen Wilson's desperate desire to fly it. As for Walt Winseman's concerns about the plane's shaky float system, Wilson wrote it off as the prejudiced opinion of a grouchy mechanic. After all, it was common knowledge that the pessimistic Winseman didn't like *anything*.

Munro spent most of his days in the air as cooler weather brought scores of fishermen to the Air Harbor for flights out to their favorite lakes and rivers, but Wilson managed to corner him long enough to get a checkout in the Beechcraft. The magic had long since worn off the big biplane as far as Munro and Fisk were concerned, but Wilson was enthralled. Flying the Staggerwing was pure delight, and he managed to log several hours in the plane over the next few weeks.

One afternoon early in October, Wilson checked the flight schedule and noticed a fishing charter to Ross Lake had been penciled in for the following morning. Backed up behind a tall hydroelectric dam, the narrow, deep lake curved north through the Cascades to the Canadian border, and was known for its population of large, hungry trout. According to the schedule, Kenmore was supposed to fly the four passengers to a specific spot on the shoreline early in the morning and return for them at the end of the day. Shifting his gaze to the top of the page, Wilson saw the charter had been booked in the Staggerwing's column. This could be his big chance.

As luck would have it, Munro was at his desk, trying to bring some semblance of order to the unruly pile of paperwork that seemed to grow larger each day.

"How 'bout I take the flight to Ross Lake in the morning?" Wilson asked, trying to keep the eagerness out of his voice.

Munro paused in mid-sort. "How much time do you have in the Beech now?"

"Oh, four or five hours, plus the time you spent checking me out."

Munro thought for a moment. On the one hand, he didn't want to discourage the young man who'd worked so hard in pursuit of his dream. On the other hand, he had the safety of his passengers to consider. Flying in the mountains could be tricky, especially on a cool, fall morning, when fog could ooze up out of the river valleys without warning and blanket the surrounding terrain.

"I'll tell you what," he said at last. "I'll take them in. If the weather's good in the afternoon, you can go up and bring them home."

One flight was better than none. "You got a deal," Wilson agreed happily.

The next morning brought a fog so dense the planes tied to the dock were barely visible from the office one hundred feet away. The four physicians who had booked the flight to Ross Lake stood around impatiently, sipping coffee and staring out the windows at the mist swirling around the planes in the tiedown area. Nine o'clock, ten, eleven; the fog brightened as the sun climbed higher but it refused to burn off. Then suddenly at noon, it was gone. The lake sparkled in the fresh breeze that blew the last threads of mist out of the trees, while overhead the sky deepened to that alluring shade of crystal blue that makes ground-bound pilots ache to become airborne.

Munro and Fisk hustled to get a local flight underway in one of the Taylorcrafts, and then Munro turned his attention to the doctors. "This darn fog has really cut into your day. Do you still want to go?"

"You bet. Half a day's fishing is better than none, and who knows when we'll all be able to take time off together again."

Munro made sure the Staggerwing was moored securely to the dock before climbing in and starting the engine. When it was idling smoothly, he climbed out and rejoined the four fishermen.

"As soon as the cylinder and oil temperatures are up we'll load you up and go," he explained. He saw Wilson watching from the office and waved the young pilot over.

"It's too late in the day to go into the lake twice," Munro announced over the offbeat rumble of the nine-cylinder radial. "I'm going to have Vern here fly you up and stay with you until it's time to come home. You need to be off the lake by six. I don't want you flying around out there in the dark, and the fog sometimes comes back in the evening. So at five-thirty you load up and take off."

As the doctors made a last-minute check of their fishing gear, Munro led Vern away from the idling Staggerwing. "I mean it now," Munro said sternly. "I don't care what those guys tell you when you're up there, I want you off that lake by six. If you're not off by six, no matter what the reason is, you stay there and camp until morning."

"Yes, sir," Wilson replied, "but don't worry, I'll have them out of there by six."

"Okay," Munro patted Wilson on the shoulder. "You'll enjoy it up there. It's beautiful country."

Wilson shut down the engine and helped the doctors stow their equipment. When everyone was on board and belted in, Munro untied the mooring lines and turned the Staggerwing out from the dock. The warm engine fired right away, and Wilson taxied out to the main body of the lake. Turning into the southerly wind, he checked the flight controls and ran up the engine. Everything was in order, so he retracted the water rudders and shoved the throttle up to full power. The Staggerwing lurched forward, its nose rising as it struggled onto the step and accelerated down the lake toward Arrowhead Point. The takeoff run seemed to take forever, but Wilson wasn't surprised; the Beech always went halfway to Sand Point before becoming airborne.

Forty minutes later, Wilson banked the Staggerwing around to land parallel to the heavily wooded shore of Ross Lake. The doctors had a selected a spot near a creek mouth where a small beach provided a good place to secure the plane, and where the inflow of fast-flowing, food-bearing water ensured an exciting afternoon's fishing.

The doctors assembled their fishing rods and tromped off down the lake shore in search of the legendary Lake Ross trout, leaving Wilson alone with the big yellow biplane. After running a line from the stern cleat of each float to a nearby tree, Wilson polished the windows and then started cleaning the oil streaks off the underside of the fuselage. He paused frequently in his work to stare up at the sleek lines of the Staggerwing. It was an indescribable feeling, breathing the crisp, pine-scented air, hearing the gentle slap of water against aluminum, and knowing that the magnificent machine towering over him was his to control. He'd made it. He was a professional pilot! Life just didn't get any better than this.

After what seemed like only minutes, Wilson's watch read five-thirty. Stowing his cleaning rags in the baggage compartment, he dutifully set off up the shore to round up his passengers.

"Five-thirty, guys," he announced. "Time to load up and head back."

The doctors looked at each other and then up at the blue, cloudless bowl that arched over the lake. "The weather's perfect and the fishing's picking up. We've got at least another two and a half hours of daylight left. How 'bout we fish until six-thirty. That will give us plenty of time to get back before dark."

Bill Fisk would have told the doctors to haul their butts back to the plane or he was taking off without them. But young Wilson didn't have the experience or the confidence to realize that as the pilot, he held all the cards. The best he could do was remind his passengers of the orders he'd received back at the Air Harbor.

"Mr. Munro told me specifically to be off the lake by six. We need to get back to the plane and load up now."

"I'm sure he said that because he was concerned about the weather. But look at it. I don't think he'd have any problem with us staying another hour in weather like this."

Young Wilson was torn. He'd received a direct order to be off the lake by six. On the other hand, his four passengers, all respected doctors who certainly knew what they were doing, had a point. Kenmore was only a half-hour away, and there was no denying the weather couldn't be any more perfect.

"C'mon, Vern. Only an hour more. The weather's not gonna change that much in an hour."

"All right," Wilson agreed at last. "You can fish to six-thirty. But then we've *got* to go. And you better make sure you tell Mr. Munro why we're late. I don't want him thinking it was my idea."

"Don't worry, kid. And don't forget, we're the ones payin' the bill."

Wilson checked his watch repeatedly as he nervously paced the shoreline between the plane and the four fishermen. The doctors were having a great time, but the fun had gone out of the trip for their pilot. He'd finally managed to win Mr. Munro's confidence, and then what happens? The first time he's given a real flight in the Staggerwing, he disobeys a direct order. I'll be lucky if they let me go back to pumping gas, he thought miserably.

True to the doctor's prediction, the sky remained cloudless. As Wilson urged his reluctant passengers aboard the plane at six-thirty, he took some comfort in the knowledge that at least the flight home would be an easy one. Maybe Mr. Munro would see the doctor's point of view and agree that, under the circumstances, delaying the departure had been okay.

Wilson tossed the mooring lines into the baggage compartment, and squeezed between the passengers into the pilot's seat. That's the one bad thing about the Staggerwing, he thought. There's only one door, and it's in the back on the wrong side.

The engine fired on the first try, and Wilson blipped the throttle to pull the plane off the beach. As soon as the floats were clear of the shore, he lowered the water rudders and steered the plane out to the middle of the lake. Turning into the wind, he let the plane idle slowly forward as he waited for the engine to come up to temperature. He felt his worries draining away as he taxied across the clear, sparkling water. The Staggerwing was running beautifully, and home was only a half hour away.

The temperature needles reached the green, and Wilson did a quick check of the controls. Everything felt fine. He ran the engine up to 1,500 rpm, and as the Staggerwing lifted its nose to plow through the water, he cycled the magneto switch; right mag, left mag, and back to both. The engine never missed a beat, and the rpm drop was within limits. Moving his right hand to the prop control, he pulled it back until he heard the propeller pitch begin to change. He shoved the prop control back up and retarded the throttle to idle. The Staggerwing settled back to glide smoothly through the blue-green water as Wilson made a final check around the cabin. The door was closed and latched, and everyone had their seatbelts on.

"Okay," he announced loudly over the rumbling engine, "here we go."

He retracted the water rudders, pulled the yoke all the way back and opened the throttle. The engine responded with a roar, and the yellow Beechcraft lifted its nose high in the air as the water began to pile up under the bows of the floats. As the speed increased, Vern eased the yoke forward until the plane was skimming across the water on the step. As usual, the takeoff run seemed to go on forever, but the plane was finally moving fast enough for the wings to develop sufficient lift, and it rose smoothly from the surface of the lake. Seconds later, the gray concrete wall of the power dam swept by, and then the Staggerwing was climbing out through the Skagit River valley, the sun almost touching the horizon ahead.

There was no sun at all on Lake Washington. The fog had rolled back in at four, and Munro watched with increasing concern as the visibility on the lake sank to less than a mile. Then at five, it began to rain. Even the ducks looked miserable as they splashed halfheartedly in the puddles under the parked planes; the weather had grounded them, too.

Fisk swooped down out of the murk and greased the Taylorcraft onto the rain-dimpled water. Munro watched him tie up and pick his way around the worst of the puddles to the office. "It's pretty bad out there," Fisk said, reading the question in Munro's eyes, "but it's flyable. If Vern got off he could still make it back if he's careful."

Six-thirty came and went with no sight or sound of the Staggerwing. At ten minutes to seven, Munro decided it was time to do something. There was no point in trying to reach Vern by radio. Aircraft radios were expensive luxuries in the 1950s, and most commercial seaplane operators couldn't afford them. Even the operators that installed them didn't find them very useful. VHF signals are line-of-sight only; a radio on the ground at Kenmore wouldn't have had a chance of contacting a plane as far away as the Skagit River.

Striding into the office, Munro picked up the phone and dialed the power station at the Ross Lake dam. Yes, he was told, a yellow floatplane had departed the lake a few minutes earlier. The generator operator was surprised to hear the weather had collapsed over Seattle; it was beautiful at the lake.

Relieved that the plane was on its way, but annoyed that Wilson had disobeyed his instructions,

Munro went back outside to wait. It was almost dark, and his greatest concern now was whether or not Wilson would be able to pick his way through the rain and fog back to Kenmore.

At that same moment, less than fifty miles away, Vern Wilson was realizing he'd made a big mistake. At first, the flight down the Skagit Valley had been easy, but as he approached the flat farmland of the Skagit River delta, he began to get worried. The fog had returned with a vengeance, and within minutes, the ground was completely obliterated from sight.

"I think we'd better turn around," he yelled to his passengers over the thunder of the Staggerwing's engine.

"It's always foggy up here this time of year," one of the doctors shouted back. "Just stay on top of it and head toward Seattle. It'll be wide open down there."

Wilson now faced one of the hardest decisions a pilot has to make. Should he continue the flight into uncertain weather conditions or should he turn back, annoying the passengers and prolonging an experience he would just as soon end quickly. Wilson hesitated for a moment, and then made up his mind. Easing the Staggerwing into a left bank, he let the nose track along the horizon until it was pointing south toward Seattle. Leveling the wings, he inched the power up and adjusted the trim. It was time to go home.

Five minutes later he knew he'd made the wrong decision. The doctor's prediction of good weather over Seattle was a myth. The fog obscuring the ground was as dense as ever, while up ahead, dark masses of clouds loomed high in the waning light. The first ticks of rain against the Staggerwing's sharply raked windscreen resounded in Wilson's ears like gunshots.

"I'm going back," he announced as he jerked the plane into a left turn. "There's no way we're going to get through that stuff up ahead."

His passengers were silent, perhaps realizing for the first time that their situation was getting dangerous. The sun had set, leaving Wilson only a dim afterglow with which to pick his way back through the jagged mountains to Ross Lake.

Halfway up the Skagit River valley, he knew he wasn't going to make it. He could barely see the mountains; the farms and woodlots lining the river had disappeared completely. The odds of a safe landing on the black, featureless surface of Ross Lake were almost nil.

Wilson fought the panic that rose like bitter gall in his throat as he tried to think of what he could do. Confronted by the same situation, Munro or Fisk might have elected to climb over the mountains and land into the reflection of the lights at the southern end of Lake Chelan. Or they may have decided to fly north to the busy and well-lit harbor at Vancouver; the Staggerwing had plenty of fuel on board and the fog seemed to be confined to the convergence zone. But Wilson didn't have the benefit of their experience, and he couldn't expand his thinking beyond the valley below him.

Suddenly, a tiny cluster of lights appeared in the murky darkness ahead. It was a straw of salvation in the swirling maelstrom of panic that filled Wilson's mind, and he grabbed it. The sparks of light marked the town of Concrete, where the Baker River flowed in from the north to join the much larger Skagit. In the 1920s, Puget Power had erected two dams in the narrow confines of the heavily wooded Baker River canyon, one a mile or so upstream of the huge silos that stored the product which had given the town its name, and the other about twelve miles in. The long, skinny lake behind the dam at Concrete was called Shannon, while the upper lake was given the name Baker.

The surface of Lake Shannon was as black as everything else in the valley, but the town lights immediately in front of it and the curved necklace of worklights along the top of the dam would provide good references with which to judge his alignment and height on final approach. Wilson chopped the power and angled the Staggerwing down toward the town. This is going to work, he told himself excitedly as the plane bored in on the short string of lights that marked the top of the dam. The lights swept under the floats, and then Wilson was staring into total darkness. Now came the hardest part of a night landing; waiting as the plane descends toward the invisible, ink-black water below, and praying that the floats touch down before the plane runs out of lake.

Wham! The Staggerwing slammed hard into the water, throwing Wilson and the doctors first forward and then back as the plane bounced viciously back into the air. Instinctively, Wilson shoved the throttle forward and jerked the yoke back to keep the nose up. Wham! The plane hit again, harder this time, and the men whipped forward and back like rag dolls as the plane again bounced high into the air.

With the engine roaring at full throttle, Wilson hauled the yoke back even farther.

"It's okay," he shouted over the engine. "We've got her this time!"

The third impact didn't seem to be as hard, but Wilson sensed immediately it was different. It was almost as though the Staggerwing was pausing, taking a moment to decide what it wanted to do. Then there was a loud crack, and the plane jerked forward and down. The engine stopped suddenly, and Wilson felt a tug at his arm. A blackness even darker than before enveloped the plane, while all around them the men heard the quiet sound of trickling water.

The shrill ring of the office phone pierced the hiss of the now-steady rain and sent Munro scurrying back into the office. It was the generator operator from the Lake Shannon dam.

"I heard you were asking about one of your planes. I think it just flew over us and went up the lake. I expect the pilot landed and put into shore for the night. I thought I ought to let you know in case you were starting to worry."

Munro thanked the man and started closing up the office. Wilson and his passengers would be cold, but at least they were safe. He, Ruth, and the kids had a cozy dinner as the rain drummed steadily on the wings of the planes in the tie down area. After the children were in bed, Munro and Ruth read for awhile and then turned in. Munro wondered how severely he should reprimand

Wilson the next morning for disobeying instructions, but he decided not to dwell on it until he'd heard the young man's side of the story.

The phone rang again at two in the morning. It was the generator operator again.

"You'd better get up here," he said soberly. "Your plane's had an accident."

Munro felt as though he'd been slugged in the stomach. "Is everyone okay?"

The line was silent for a moment before the man spoke again. "It doesn't look like it."

Munro struggled to ask the inevitable question, but the man saved him the agony.

"There's two guys made it for sure. They're on the way to the hospital now."

"There should have been five people in the plane," Munro said quietly. "Vern Wilson, he's our pilot, and four passengers. They'd been up at Ross Lake fishing."

"The two we found said something about other people. We shouted and shined our lights around, but we didn't see or hear anyone else."

"Where's the plane?"

"Upside down in the lake. The two guys we picked up were sitting on the bottom of the pontoons. It's black as hell out there. As soon as it's light we'll take the boat and search the whole lake. Maybe the others swam to shore."

Munro didn't want to hear the answer, but he had to ask the question. "The two people you picked up, who were they?"

"I don't know their names. They were just about froze and could hardly talk."

Munro thanked the man and hung up the phone. Ruth had heard only one side of the conversation, but she knew her husband well enough to know something terrible had happened. Munro told her what he knew, and then added a request.

"Don't tell the kids yet. We don't know if Vern made it or not, and I don't want them to spend the whole day worrying about it. I'll call Bill and Walt, and we'll go up there and find out what happened."

It's a long drive from Seattle north to the Skagit River and then east up Highway 20 to Concrete. By the time Munro, Bill Fisk, and Walt Winseman arrived at the dam, the sun was up and the power company had its boat out scouring the lake. News of the crash had spread, and several residents from Concrete showed up and volunteered their own boats for the search. While the three men from Kenmore waited for the power company boat, the generator operator Munro had spoken to on the phone filled them in on what had transpired the evening before.

"A couple of hours after the plane flew over I started wondering if they were okay. There's a lot of stumps and deadheads around the edge of the lake, and I was worried they might have had a hard time getting to shore in the dark, so I decided to take a boat out and make sure they were all right. Partway up the lake I thought I heard a strange sound, so I cut the engine and just drifted. After a moment I began hearing this weird scraping noise coming from somewhere up ahead. I got out the oars and started rowing toward it.

"What I found was two guys sitting on the bottom of the pontoons banging on them with a piece of metal. They were so cold and hoarse they could hardly talk, but they said the plane had flipped over and they'd gotten out. They'd hollered for help until their voices gave out, and then they broke off this piece of metal and started banging on the pontoons hoping someone would hear. That's when I came along."

A distant hum caught the men's attention and they turned to watch as a boat accelerated out from behind a point and began to plane across the shimmering surface toward the dam.

"That's our boat," the generator operator continued, shading his eyes against the sudden glare as the sun gleamed through a gap in the clouds. "They'll take you out to see for yourselves. Funny thing, though. The pontoons are there, but there's no sign of the plane."

"Isn't the plane attached to the floats?" Winseman asked.

"Nope. The pontoons are just floating by themselves. I was going to tow them to shore, but man those things are heavy! I'd have thought they'd be easy to tow, but it took all the power I had just to get them turned in the right direction. I finally just left them where they were." It was a significant statement, but the three Kenmore men were too preoccupied with their own thoughts to really hear it.

Lake Shannon is just over six miles long and half a mile across at its widest point. It didn't take long to run a boat the length of the lake and back, but no matter how many times they did it, the searchers were unable to find any trace of the airplane other than the pair of overturned floats. There was no wreckage floating about, and no sign of the plane in shallow water. Worse, there was no indication along the muddy shoreline that anyone had climbed out of the lake. Munro and Winseman had just about decided the plane must have sheared off the floats and sunk out in deep water when Fisk suddenly remembered what the power company man had said.

"That guy said the floats were real hard to move," he shouted to the others above the buzz of the outboard. "He said he needed full throttle just to turn them around."

Munro and Winseman nodded, half-remembering the conversation with the generator operator. Fisk turned and stared across to where the silver floats floated sullenly in the middle of the lake. "Take us over there again."

The skiff nosed up against the battered hulls and Fisk leaned as far as he dared over the side to peer down into the dark water. The sun slipped out from behind a cloud, and Fisk saw a sudden shimmer of yellow in the blackness beneath the floats.

"Gimme that oar," he barked to the boat driver, and moments later as he swept the oar back and forth under the upturned floats he'd solved the puzzle. "The plane's been right here the whole time. It's down there hangin' by its tail from the floats. The floats sheared off but the water rudder cables didn't break. That's why the floats were so hard to move."

A diver was sent down, and he confirmed what Munro had feared from the beginning. There were three bodies left in the plane. One of them was Vern Wilson. One of the young pilot's arms was nearly severed from his body, but the diver said Wilson's position in the plane left no doubt that he'd been trying to help his passengers out the airplane's single, aft-mounted door.

When Munro was able to get to a telephone, he called Ruth and told her what they'd discovered.

"I'm going to go get the kids out of school," Ruth said. "I think we should be the ones to tell them what happened, not someone who didn't know Vern and who doesn't know all the facts." Munro agreed.

The day after the bodies were removed from the plane a pair of salvage divers brought in a boat with a winch and removed Five-Six-November's Pratt & Whitney Wasp Jr. engine. Kenmore bought it back for $500. The floats were relatively undamaged, so Munro, Winseman, and a couple of the shop mechanics went back up to Concrete with a trailer to get them. As they motored slowly across the mirror-like surface of Lake Shannon, they debated whether or not to save the airplane itself, but in the end Munro decided he didn't want anything more to do with it.

Casting off the long line the power company had run out from shore to keep the wreck from drifting down the lake into the dam, the men slowly hauled the floats to the deepest part of the lake. The divers who'd recovered the engine hadn't trusted the water rudder cables, so they'd attached their own cable between the plane and the floats. Munro maneuvered the boat around while one of the mechanics severed the water rudder cables with a pair of long-handled bolt cutters. Then the mechanic moved the cutters into position on the salvage cable.

"Okay?" he asked.

Munro nodded. "Go ahead."

The mechanic took a deep breath and then levered the handles together as hard as he could. There was a sharp pop, and the floats bobbed up to ride higher in the water. Munro and Winseman peered over the side of the boat and watched as the shimmering yellow shape below them wavered for a moment and then drifted away into the darkness.

Kenmore Air Harbor had a $7,000 dollar insurance policy, which was all the company could afford. When the Kenmore board of directors heard that the widows of the two doctors lost in the accident had decided to sue, they quickly transferred the titles of the company's most valuable assets, the two Noorduyn Norsemen, to Bob Munro. This, they thought, would protect them in the event of a court decision against the Air Harbor. While the Navy deck building and the Seabee hangar were essential to the company's activities, they weren't worth much on the open market. The only other assets the company had were its assortment of tools and airplane parts, and of course, the document leasing the property from Jack Mines' mother.

Fortunately, the lawsuits didn't get very far. In statements about the accident, both survivors placed the blame squarely on the shoulders of themselves and their two companions. We were the ones, they said, who insisted on staying late at Ross Lake, and we were the ones who persuaded Vern Wilson there would be clear weather over Seattle. Young Wilson had done his best, but his passengers had placed him in a situation that would have challenged even the most seasoned pilot.

The design of the Staggerwing had done the rest. The airplane's light tube, wood, and fabric fuselage was noticeably nose-heavy with the 450-hp Pratt & Whitney engine installed, and required more back-pressure on the control yoke to raise the nose than an inexperienced pilot might expect.

With darkness obliterating any visual references to the surface of Lake Shannon, the Staggerwing's nose-heavy tendencies caused Wilson to slam the bows of the floats repeatedly into the lake until the attachment bolts could take no more and the floats simply sheared away from the airframe.

As the cabin slowly nosed over and filled with water, the confusion and panic that must have seized the passengers can only be imagined. The two men in the back seat closest to the airplane's only usable door were able to struggle free, but as the plane sank deeper in the inky darkness, the disorientation of the others became complete. Wilson did the best he could to help the front seat passenger climb into the back, but with the use of only one arm and not knowing for sure where the door was, his efforts were in vain.

The accident was a terrible blow to the Air Harbor. Not since Jack Mines' plunge to death on the shore of Stirrup Lake had an accident in a company plane claimed the life of a Kenmore employee. Munro couldn't help thinking that things would have turned out differently if he hadn't succumbed to Vern Wilson's eager plea to take the flight. On the other hand, the young man had been a competent pilot who's only fault was not having the experience or self-confidence to stand up to his passengers. And Munro knew the only way to get that experience and self-confidence was to go up and fly.

For the first time, he began to wonder if the flying business was really what he wanted to be doing. The loss of Five-Six-November itself was irrelevant; airplanes could be replaced or repaired. It was the loss of the people that was so devastating. Yet it was a constant possibility. Munro couldn't fly every flight, or guarantee every life. He had to trust his pilots, and now the Staggerwing accident had rocked the very foundation of this trust. Who was to say that Bill Fisk wouldn't be next? Or one of the part-time pilots the company employed? The fishermen and hunters and businessmen that chartered the company's airplanes climbed into them with the utmost faith that the Air Harbor would see them safely through Puget Sound's unpredictable weather to their destination. But did Munro still have that faith?

It was the lowest point in the company's history. Kenmore's fleet had dwindled to just three planes including the pair of outdated Norsemen, one of which was in dire need of a paint job and an interior overhaul. The happy, family atmosphere that had characterized the Seabee years had all but disappeared as the bulbous amphibians wore out and the owners moved on. The flying craze of the post-war years had faded, and only a handful of students continued to show up at Bill Fisk's little flight school.

Munro began to think about diversifying, exploring other business opportunities while de-emphasizing the company's involvement with aviation. Boating seemed an obvious choice, given the company's location. Munro had always liked boats, and the demand for marine sales and service was skyrocketing as recreational boating took the Seattle area by storm.

With the threat of lawsuits behind him and the prospect of developing a new business before him, Munro hoped the self-imposed burden of the Staggerwing accident would begin to slip from his shoulders. But it was not to be. The accident had been a personal tragedy for every Air Harbor employee and every member of the Munro family, but that did not change the fact that it had been

Vern Wilson's fault. When Munro explained the events leading up to the crash to Wilson's father, he fully intended to downplay the young pilot's mistakes in the hope that Mr. Wilson would not try to take some of the blame for his son's actions upon himself.

Mr. Wilson's reaction was exactly the opposite. Furiously lashing out at what he felt had been total irresponsibility on the part of the Air Harbor, he placed the blame for his son's death squarely on Munro. Vern should never have been allowed to take the flight, Mr. Wilson shouted accusingly, and by letting him go Munro sealed the fate of everyone on board the airplane. Stunned and hurt, Munro was perceptive enough to know that any attempt to set the record straight would simply enrage Mr. Wilson further, so he let the matter drop.

Helping a young man realize his dream did not make Bob Munro responsible for the terrible accident on the pitch black waters of Lake Shannon. But the knowledge that somebody, regardless of the facts, *did* hold him responsible would haunt him for years.

MASTER BUILDER 16

THE MAN WHO'S IMPACT ON the Air Harbor came close to exceeding even Bob Munro's actually had his heart set on becoming a gardener. During World War II, while Munro was fixing Pan American's DC-3s and teaching the finer points of engine repair, Bill Peters was plowing his way through high school and the one-acre field he'd purchased with his weekend job earnings. His goal was to create a Victory Garden, but the first thing he had to do was break up the dirt. Gas rationing was in full swing, which precluded the use of a tractor. Not that it really mattered, since young Peters didn't have a tractor.

What he did have was a neighbor who raised horses. Peters helped feed and water them, and in return was allowed to use a matched team of roans to plow his vegetable garden. There was an old harness hanging in the barn, and another neighbor supplied a single moldboard plow. It made quite a sight, and more than one passing motorist hit the brakes to watch the lanky teenager, reins over his shoulder, stride along behind his glistening horses, the antique plow carving a dark furrow through the rich Washington soil.

When he wasn't in school or working his acre of vegetables, Peters usually could be found helping his father. From erecting a shed to putting a new roof on the barn, the boy proved to have a real talent for carpentry. But growing things was his real love, so in 1947 he headed off across the mountains to Pullman near the Idaho border to join the freshman class at Washington State University where he majored in horticulture.

A lot of the students at Washington State were war vets attending classes on the GI Bill, but there were plenty of kids Peters' age, too. College life became even more fun when he persuaded a childhood friend to transfer over from the University of Washington. The friend was Ted Huntley. Peters' interest in horticulture was matched by Huntley's fascination for flying. Huntley was always messing around with an airplane, his own or somebody else's, and Peters became a willing helper. He particularly liked the challenge of making and installing interior components. Sidewalls, head-liners, seats, and floor coverings all required a precise fit, and he enjoyed experimenting with different fasteners and materials.

In return for working on the planes, Huntley took Peters flying. During school breaks when they were both back home in Seattle, Huntley would invite Peters out to the Air Harbor and they would borrow a plane and head up to the San Juans or over to Hood Canal. Peters had little interest in learning to fly, but he enjoyed these aerial expeditions immensely. He particularly liked the view, for only from the air could a person see the pattern of forests and farms that ringed the Sound.

Peters graduated from college in 1952. With no immediate job prospects and a draft notice in his hand, he decided to enlist in the Army in the hope that volunteering would land him a better assignment than he'd get as a draftee. He was assigned to Morse Code Intercept school and given a high security clearance. He was with an Army security group in Japan when he was abruptly sent to the Signal Corps in Kyoto for reassignment. Positive that he was about to be sent to some uninteresting, backwater unit, Peters was none too enthusiastic as he sat waiting for the assignment officer to finish reading his file.

"I see you've got a degree in horticulture," the officer said, tapping the file with his pen.

"Yes, but it doesn't seem to be particularly useful in the Army."

"You'd be surprised," the officer replied as he began rummaging through the papers scattered across his desk. "There's a farm just down the road from here. We've got some people down there helping to run it. If I can find my damn phone list, I'll give the major a call and see what they might need for personnel."

The call was made, and Peters soon found himself assigned to the small laboratory on the twenty-five acre farm testing chemical fertilizers and other solutions. He was surprised to see the Japanese field laborers still doing almost all their work by hand even though the farm had a couple of nice tractors. Never one to leave things the way they are if an improvement can be made, Peters designed and built a variety of attachments that could be pulled by the tractors to speed up the harvesting process. It wasn't long before Peters' homemade implements had increased the farm's output by an impressive amount.

Peters' farming days in Kyoto ended with his discharge from the Army in September 1955. It had been a thoroughly enjoyable two years, but now it was time to go home and find a job. His Army experience came in handy when he applied for a job in a nursery in Pasco, a small town near the confluence of the Snake and Columbia Rivers in south-central Washington. His fiancée, Carolyn, had a job with General Electric at the sprawling nuclear research facility at Hanford. They were married in December. Peters was doing what he loved, working with plants, but eastern Washington was not his idea of the perfect place to live. The summers could be blistering, and his years at Washington State had already exposed him to the bleak, freezing cold of winter. He missed the mild, moist climate of western Washington and the ever-changing moods of Puget Sound.

Ted Huntley got out of the Air Force early in the spring of 1956. After going out and taking a look at what was going on at the Air Harbor, he telephoned Peters in Pasco.

"Bob could use some help out there," he said after describing Vern Wilson's accident in the Staggerwing. "He's starting up a marina business, and they have a new building for it but there's a lot that has to be done to make it usable. It's the kind of work that'd be right up your alley."

"What about you?" Peters asked. "What are you going to do?"

"The only pilots Bob's got are himself and Bill Fisk. I figure they can use another pilot. When I'm not flying, I can help fix up the planes."

Peters and his wife liked the idea of returning to western Washington, so in early May he took a day off from the nursery and drove across the mountains to see if Bob Munro was interested in hiring him. He'd met Munro before, but asking the man for a job was a little different than simply exchanging pleasantries about the weather.

"Ted tells me you're looking for someone to run the marina," Peters began hesitantly.

"Yes, yes," Munro replied, looking around at the motley collection of buildings that comprised the Air Harbor. Across the drive from the Seabee hangar, cannibalized Seabee hulks and rotting logs threatened to obscure the sagging parts barn. The garage-and-chicken-coop office complex had been repainted, but there was no hiding the fact that the buildings had been cast-offs to start with. In contrast, the company's newest structure, an all-metal Butler building, gleamed brightly behind the weather-beaten Navy deck building. The Butler building had been erected to house the Bell Boy boats and Evinrude outboard motors Munro had acquired the franchises to sell. But the building was nothing more than a shell, and the docks, boat ramp, and outboard motor repair shop existed only as sketches on scraps of paper.

"There's a lot to do," Munro murmured quietly. He turned abruptly back to Peters. "Ted tells me you're good at fixing airplane interiors."

Peters shrugged. "I helped him with several planes when we were in college. I enjoyed doing the interior work."

Munro nodded toward Norseman Five-Four-Zero squatting in the tiedown area. "Alaska Airlines is interested in buying that plane over there, but it needs painting and the interior is pretty rough. Maybe you and Ted can get it fixed up."

It took Peters a moment or two to realize he'd just been hired.

Peters' job title might have been marina manager, but at first it didn't seem like he'd ever be given the time to do the job. Likewise, Ted Huntley was supposed to head up the flight department under the direct supervision of Bill Fisk, but his first assignment had nothing to do with flying. He and Peters found themselves out in the tie down area, removing the faded paint from Five-Four-Zero's metal cowling and ripping out the plane's battered floorboards and torn sidewall coverings. Then after Peters had fabricated and installed a new interior, they painted the plane inside and out. It was a mammoth undertaking for just two people, but the big plane fairly gleamed at the end of it. Munro was impressed, and so was Alaska Airlines, who bought Paul Garner's old Leduc Glacier war-horse that summer for the agreed-upon $16,000. The Air Harbor also sold a set of Norseman floats to Wheeler Airlines in Canada for $4,000.

If Peters thought he could now assume his duties as marina manager he was wrong. His next assignment was to deal with the mess up at the barn. What he wanted to do was hook a cable to the ridge beam and pull the whole thing down into a pile and burn it, but there was the matter of the

Kenmore parts department. Stacked on homemade shelves and improvised tables across the back of the barn, the salvaged and rebuilt parts provided the Air Harbor with a modest but steady income.

Peters persuaded Munro to let him build a little extension onto the south end of the Seabee hangar where the parts could be stored in a clean and dry environment. For someone with Peters' carpentry skills, it didn't take long to erect the extension and transfer the parts from the barn. From then on the project involved more brute force than skill.

> "I tore the barn building down, pulled all the logs out of the mud with the old Dodge, and pulled the aluminum out. We found a scrap dealer who wanted the metal, and he hauled off all the Seabee hulls. Then we piled the wood from the barn on top of the rotten logs and burned it. Everything that was left, nails and little pieces of metal and charred wood, we shoveled into the back of the Dodge and hauled it away. When we were done, we had a nice, clean area and a lot more usable room."
>
> **BILL PETERS**

Finally, Peters could begin work on the marina. In addition to the Butler building, which would house the showroom for the boats and motors as well as a small repair shop, the plans called for a set of docks, a boat ramp, and a gas pump. He put up shelving in the Butler building and built a desk for himself. He brought in a local contractor to drive the piles for the three new docks which he constructed himself in the channel near the back of the Air Harbor hangar. After he finished the docks, he set up the forms for the boat ramp and mixed and poured the concrete. He installed the marina's fuel tank and dockside pump.

The parts barn just before Bill Peters tore it down. The tangle of scrap surrounding the barn is all that's left of the salvaged Seabees. (photo by Bill Peters)

Then, while he was almost single-handedly putting Kenmore Marina together, he decided he wanted to learn to fly. His instructor was Ted Huntley. Peters proved to be almost as good a pilot as he was a builder. He quickly earned his Private license, and then using the GI Bill, he started on his Commercial. His only anxious moments came during check rides, but they weren't because he lacked the necessary flying skills. He just didn't see eye to eye with Bill Fisk.

> "Bill is a nice guy, and he's one of the steadiest, most reliable pilots that's ever lived. I'd fly anywhere with him. But I was used to college and people who knew how to teach. Bill would take it away from you too much. Instead of talking you through something, he'd say, 'Here's how you're supposed to do it,' and he'd grab the plane away from you. He wants you to do things a certain way, and if you don't he can get kind of upset.
>
> "I remember one time I taxied in after a solo flight and I was going to tie up to the front dock, which can be kind of tricky if there are other airplanes around. I had the docking all figured out, but here came Bill running out of the office waving his arms. I thought, my God, I must be about to hit something. Bill stood there waving his arms and waving his arms, and he so distracted me that I ran the wingtip into another airplane. I was trying so hard to figure out what Bill was trying to tell me that I stopped concentrating on what I was doing. That's when I made myself a promise to always watch out for myself and never let another person distract me."
>
> **BILL PETERS**

There was a very real possibility that civil lawsuits stemming from the Staggerwing accident would wipe Kenmore Air Harbor off the map entirely. The company had hardly any money in the bank. The only assets were the aircraft, buildings, tools, and equipment. All of it could be seized and sold if the Air Harbor lost in court. Anticipation of a negative decision was one of the main reasons for Munro's new undertaking, Kenmore Marina, Inc., which Bill Peters was busy putting together. Even if the Air Harbor was stripped away from him, Munro would still have a business to fall back on.

At least he didn't have to worry about losing the property. At the January 1956 meeting of the board of directors, it was announced that the Air Harbor had finally made arrangements to purchase the shingle mill site from Mrs. Mines for $30,000, with payments of $150 a month at five percent interest. As soon as the papers were signed, Kenmore Air Harbor, Inc. sold the property to Bob and Ruth Munro for $40,000, with payments of $200 a month at five percent interest. This gave the Air Harbor the $10,000 option profit which had been carried on the books since the company's inception in 1946. And like the two Norsemen, the property would be protected from any lawsuits since it belonged to the Munros and not to the Air Harbor.

Despite the gloomy outlook for the company's future, Munro continued to improve the Air Harbor's operation any way he could. By May the company fleet had grown to include two Super

Cubs, two Taylorcrafts, an Aeronca Champ, and of course, the two Norsemen. But Five-Four-Zero would soon be on its way to Alaska Airlines, and Munro was thinking seriously of selling Five-Five, as well. The huge machine was simply too much airplane for the two and three-person flights that made up the bulk of Kenmore's charter business. The Norseman was slow, and it's 600-horsepower engine consumed fuel at a prodigious rate. It was time for something better.

Cessna had introduced a new plane in 1953, the all-metal Model 180. Although the 180 was advertised as a six-seater, it was really a four-plus-two, with room in the baggage compartment for a couple of child-size jump seats. The plane was an immediate success, and it wasn't long before the sleek taildragger was approved for use on floats and skis. With its 230-horsepower Continental engine and cruise speed of 130-mph on floats, the Model 180 represented a big step up from the Aeroncas, Taylorcrafts, Seabees, and Super Cubs that most operators had in their fleets. Munro began thinking that a 180 might be the perfect airplane for the Air Harbor, but he wasn't about to make that large an investment in the company until he knew there would still be a company after the legal dust had settled.

Munro was getting tired of finding letters from lawyers on his desk every time he walked in, but then one arrived that he liked. Under the advice of her father, Esther Mines had decided that she wanted to sell her shares of Kenmore stock. Her father was concerned that, as one of the company's two major stockholders, her personal assets might be vulnerable in the event of a court ruling against the Air Harbor. The company immediately agreed to purchase the stock at par value: ten dollars a share. Esther's stock would be held in escrow by Bothell State Bank until the total amount of $10,030 had been paid. Payments would be $50 a month with no interest.

Bob Munro wasn't sure how to feel. On the one hand, the company had suffered a devastating loss when Vern Wilson slammed the Staggerwing onto the black surface of Lake Shannon. But now as a direct result of that accident, the threat of someday being kicked off the property was gone, and Esther's stock sale had left him totally free to run the company as he saw fit. Esther had never opposed any of Munro's decisions in the past, but knowing that there could someday be another confrontation like the one that drove Reg Collins to California was a bit like waiting for the second shoe to drop. Everyone at the Air Harbor was glad the uncertainty was over.

The legal and financial maneuverings that swirled around the company throughout 1956 were of no consequence to Bill Peters. He was too busy to worry about it. By the end of the year, the marina was up and running. The showroom featured a sampling of Bell Boy's fiberglass runabouts and fishing boats, while the adjacent parking area held trailered boats awaiting delivery. The summer of 1957 saw a steady flow of boats motoring up the lake to the fuel dock, and young Gregg Munro earned enough money pumping gas and doing odd jobs at Kenmore Marina to buy a little Bell Boy runabout of his own.

Bill Peters may have been hired to run the marina, but it wasn't long before he was spending most of his time working on projects for the aviation side of the house. The day-to-day responsibility for the marina was gradually turned over to George Sylvester, who had been hired to run the outboard engine shop. No one had a job title at Kenmore; Munro put more stock in performance than position. But if Peters had wanted a title, Facilities Director would have been a good one. Munro was no slouch when it came to carpentry, plumbing, or electrical work, but he was usually off flying when a problem cropped up. It wasn't long before the employees learned to go in search of Bill Peters when they needed something fixed.

One such person was George Grant, Kenmore's chief shop mechanic. Grant didn't have a problem with the maintenance hangar's plumbing or electrical wiring, he had a problem with the whole hangar. It was too low, it was too narrow, it was too dark, and in the winter it was too cold. Most of the airplanes that were brought to Kenmore for maintenance or repair work wouldn't fit through the doors, so Grant and his mechanics ended up doing a lot of their work outside in the rain.

Bill Peters did almost every job there was to do at the Air Harbor, including washing planes. (photo courtesy Bill Peters)

Grant began dropping hints that a new hangar would improve the quality of the company's work, to say nothing of improving the mechanics' working conditions. He found a ready supporter in Bill Peters, who agreed to take up the cause with Bob Munro. Munro agreed that the arguments for a new hangar were sound, but until the company was out from under the Staggerwing lawsuits and was in better financial shape, any new buildings were out of the question. It was a reasonable position, but Grant and Peters decided to continue their campaign for a new hangar anyway.

Even though the Air Harbor's net profit for 1956 totaled a mere three hundred dollars, the next year's business prospects looked promising. Kenmore Marina was doing well, and there were a few more students coming out to take flying lessons.

The next twelve months were relatively uneventful. Ted Huntley caused something of a stir when he decided to resign his position as chief pilot and start a floatplane service of his own. Some of his former colleagues were appalled that he would stoop so low as to go into direct competition with the company that practically had been his second home for over ten years, but they needn't have worried. Huntley's air service posed more of a threat to its investors than it did to the Air Harbor. Huntley was an excellent pilot and he had boundless enthusiasm, but he never managed to learn what Munro instinctively knew; that it takes more than just technical ability to succeed in running a business.

Down to his last $120 and with a new baby to feed, Huntley and his wife moved into a one-room cabin on the outskirts of Kansas City where he'd been promised a co-pilot's job with TWA. The pilot's job didn't materialize, so he was given a position with the airline's engineering department instead. Two years of that was enough, and in 1959 he moved back to Seattle where Pacific Northern Airlines hired him on as a flight engineer. When PNA and their fleet of Lockheed Constellations was taken over by Western Airlines, Huntley was given a choice: he could be furloughed or he could move to Anchorage and co-pilot a DC-3. He opted for the Anchorage job.

Arriving flat broke, he took any work he could find to bolster his meager DC-3 pay, all of which he sent back to his wife in Seattle. Driving an old car Tom Wardleigh had loaned him, Huntley survived on about one hundred dollars a month until Western moved him back to Seattle to resume his old post as flight engineer. He stayed with Western, eventually working his way up to the first officer's seat in a Boeing 727. By the time Western was taken over by Delta, Huntley was a captain. Two years after the takeover he turned sixty, the mandatory retirement age. When he stepped off his 727 for the last time, the boy who'd watched in awe as Jack Mines swooped and banked Kenmore's yellow Aeronca K over Lake Washington in 1946 could look back on a string of aviation experiences not even his wildest teenage dreams could have conjured up.

Most people would have been content with an airline career, but Huntley desperately wanted to do what Bob Munro had done; start a business from scratch and make it succeed. Even while he was flying for the airlines, Huntley involved himself in all sorts of enterprises from a gold mining venture with Tom McQuillan to a deep-water salvage operation. Most of them went the way of his ill-fated floatplane service, but the same optimism that had buoyed Huntley's spirits when he was washing planes and filling Kenmore's bottomless bog with dirt never left him. His friends might have questioned his business acumen, but no one could say Ted Huntley ever ran out of ideas.

Kenmore Air Harbor made $9,306 in 1957. One of the charter flights that year had been to Sproat Lake on Vancouver Island. *Life Magazine* wanted some pictures of people in the northwest using a seaplane for recreation. When they heard that Jim Campbell and his friend, Bob Dent, used a pair of Seabees to travel to their Sproat Lake vacation homes on Vancouver Island, they decided this would be the perfect setting for some pictures. Bob Munro agreed to fly the three-man crew from *Life* up to the island, but he wanted to use a nicer and faster airplane than the ones currently in his own fleet.

Dick White had started a seaplane base on American Lake near Tacoma, and he had a brand new Cessna 180. Munro called him up and asked if he could rent the plane for a few days.

"Sure," White replied. "Come on down and we'll go for a ride."

Munro drove down to American Lake, and White gave him a quick checkout. Munro loved the plane from the moment he took off, and the people from *Life* loved it, too. The visibility out the windows was great and the plane was fast enough to maneuver around the Seabees so the photographer could get air-to-air shots of Campbell and Dent flying over the San Juan Islands. They spent three days at Sproat Lake shooting pictures of picnics and fishing trips, and then it was time to head back to Kenmore. After dropping off his passengers, Munro returned the 180 to American Lake and with some reluctance handed the keys back to Dick White. As he drove back to Lake Washington, Munro resolved to buy one of the new Cessnas for the Air Harbor.

Not long after the *Life Magazine* job, Kenmore sold its last Norseman, the ever-faithful Five-Five, and ordered a brand new 180. At $17,500, it was the most expensive plane the company had ever purchased. In February, 1958, Munro went down to Boeing Field where Bill Blake, the local Cessna dealer, checked him out in a 180 on wheels. Despite the thousands of hours Munro had amassed since 1946, it was the first time he'd ever flown a landplane other than the one takeoff he'd made in the D & D Seabee at Port Orchard.

After two or three landings Blake pronounced him ready, and Munro caught an airliner back to Wichita to pick up his new Cessna at the factory. By the time he landed at Renton where the Air Harbor mechanics were waiting to put the plane on floats, he knew the decision to buy it had been the right one. It was fast, it was quiet, and it was comfortable. The paint spelling out the name "Kenmore" on the sides of the new EDO floats was barely dry when Munro began thinking about adding more 180s to the fleet.

The next few months saw a chain of events unfold that would have a significant impact on the company's future, even though they didn't seem particularly noteworthy at the time. The property immediately to the west of the shingle mill site was owned by Dr. Philip Nelson. He and his family occupied a substantial house facing the lake, and in the late 1940s he erected a large boathouse adjacent to the Air Harbor's office.

The boathouse posed no problem to the Air Harbor except for the time three-year-old Gregg Munro tumbled down the stairs leading to the small apartment built into the upper half of the structure. Fortunately, the young man renting the apartment was home and heard the thump and subsequent splash, and raced down to pull the youngster out of the lake. Ruth Munro was horrified when the man walked into the Air Harbor office carrying her soaked and sobbing son. She hadn't even realized Gregg had wandered off. From then on the docks, the boathouse, and even the lakeshore itself were strictly off-limits to the Munro children, a rule that was enforced with vigor.

The Nelsons were very active in their church, and when they were invited to go to India as medical missionaries in 1958, they decided to accept. Not wanting to give up their lakefront property, they worked out a lease arrangement with the Air Harbor. The house and yard had to remain intact, but the rest of the property could be used any way Kenmore saw fit.

It was the opportunity Bill Peters and George Grant had been waiting for, and they lost no time in presenting their concept to Bob Munro.

"Now that we have all this extra space," Peters began, glancing around to make sure Grant was ready to jump in with his support, "we should start thinking about a proper hangar and office building. There's no reason we should have to keep using these old buildings."

"What do you have in mind?" Munro asked cautiously. He didn't like the fact that his company was headquartered in a chicken coop any more than Peters did, but he wasn't going to rush into spending money the company didn't have just for the sake of appearances.

A Beaver on the way to the railcar supported by one of Bill Peters' adjustable, hydraulic forklift extensions. (photo by C. Marin Faure)

"I was thinking of one building. " Peters picked up a pencil and sketched out a rectangular building. "Two stories high. The main part of the building would be a hangar large enough to hold three or four 180s on floats. This end of the building will be walled off from the hangar and will contain the office and the parts department."

Munro looked at Peters' sketch and tried to envision the completed building. Although he'd spent most of the last twelve years in the air, the mechanic in him had never been far in the background. If there was one thing he loved, it was a clean, neat, well-lit, and organized shop. The surplus Navy deck building had solved an immediate problem, but Munro had never seen it as anything but a compromise.

"Where would you put the new building?"

Grant pointed out the door toward the deck building. "I think it should be where the other hangar is now," he said. "It's close to the ramp and we won't lose any tie-down space."

Peters shook his head. "There's not enough room over there for what I have in mind. The Butler building and the marina won't let us build the size of building we need."

Munro looked at the sketch again. The thought of a large, well-lit shop was very appealing. He looked up at Peters. "Where do you think it should go?"

"Right where we're standing," came the immediate reply. "I think we should tear down these old buildings and your house and put the building up right here."

"Tear down my house?" Munro said incredulously. "You want to tear down my house so you can put up a hangar? Let me know when you're going to tell this to Ruthie so I can be there to watch."

Peters stoically stood his ground. "I know there are some problems to work out, but I believe this is the best location for the building. The office would be on the end next to the lake which the customers will like, and the shop will be convenient to the ramp and tie-down area."

"You're probably right," Munro admitted. "I want to talk to Bill Fisk about this, too. And Ruthie," he added with a smile. Then he turned serious. "This is a good idea, and I wish we could do something about it now. But we just don't have the money." He picked up the sketch and handed it to Peters. "Keep thinking about how the building should be laid out, and figure out as close as you can what it will cost and how much of the work we can do ourselves."

With the new building tentatively approved but in a holding pattern, Peters set about solving a smaller but no less important problem: moving the company's airplanes around on the property. The Cessna 180 was too heavy for the homemade wooden dollies, and its floats were too small for the huge sets of beaching gear the Air Harbor had accumulated as a result of its Norseman experience. The immediate solution was to build a heavier dolly to fit the 180's EDO floats, but Peters was convinced there was a better way, one that would work for every floatplane on the property and eliminate the need to struggle with dollies and beaching gear once and for all. The answer, Peters decided, was a forklift.

He decided to test his theory using a machine borrowed from Fred Skyler, who owned a nearby manufacturing company.

"It won't work," Skyler assured Peters when he walked over to pick up the forklift, "The weight will pull the machine over onto its nose and you'll wreck your plane. But you're welcome to try it," he added cheerfully.

Ignoring Skyler's skepticism, Peters lashed a pair of heavy timbers to the fork tines to get the length he needed and drove up to the front of the 180.

"It's not going to work," Skyler called over the cough of the forklift's exhaust. He'd come down to witness the big experiment and the subsequent destruction of the Air Harbor's new Cessna.

Peters looked at him for a moment, and then he carefully eased the machine forward until the hoist was only a few inches from the 180's prop spinner. With his intuitive feel for machinery, Peters eased the fork up until the timbers just kissed the underside of the plane's spreader bars. He paused for a moment, and then inched back on the hoist control. The forklift leaned forward as it took the weight of the plane, but all four wheels stayed firmly on the ground as the Cessna rose smoothly into the air.

"I'll be damned," Skyler grunted as Peters eased out the clutch and backed the forklift with its precious cargo slowly around the parking area. The Cessna showed no propensity to fall off, so Skyler stomped back to his car and drove home.

Skyler's machine had provided the proof-of-concept, so Kenmore shelled out $2,950 for a ten-ton, war-surplus forklift to modify into a floatplane transport. Instead of simply strapping timbers to the fork tines, however, Peters designed a steel framework that supported a pair of long, padded arms. A hydraulic cylinder acting on a set of ingenious linkages moved the arms together or apart to accommodate any size of plane. The tines on the forklift fit inside the framework, and the controls for the hydraulic cylinder were mounted where the driver could reach them.

Peters hired Proctor Welding to fabricate his floatplane lift, and it worked great from the first day. What didn't always work great was the forklift itself. To remove a plane from the water, the pilot would first power it up onto the wooden ramp that occupied the shoreline between the office and the hangar. Then Peters or one of the mechanics would drive the forklift down the ramp until the lifting arms were under the plane's spreader bars. After adjusting the arms so they would contact the spreader bars as close as possible to the floats, the forklift driver would pick up the plane and back off the ramp. Launching a floatplane was just as easy; the process was simply reversed.

Like many early forklifts, Kenmore's machine didn't have any brakes on the rear wheels. A forklift carries most of its weight over the front wheels near the lift, and the manufacturers figured that installing brakes on the rear wheels would make little or no difference in the machine's stopping ability. What the manufacturers hadn't figured on, however, was that someone would want to drive their vehicle down a slippery wooden ramp.

"What would happen was that someone would drive down to launch a plane, and they'd get on that slick ramp and hit the brakes and nothing would happen. The front wheels would lock up but they wouldn't have any grip. The rear wheels would have traction but no brakes, so the whole machine would just slide down the ramp into the water. They'd slide right into the muck out there and go clean under. We'd have a hell of a time getting them out. This happened at least three times that I remember."

WALT WINSEMAN

No one seems to recall any airplanes getting damaged as the forklift did its slow slide into the drink, but Peters decided that unless he wanted "Forklift Recovery" added permanently to his job description he'd better figure out a less risky way of getting the planes in and out of the lake. That the Air Harbor has rarely had a problem with the machine's hydraulic lift mechanism itself is a tribute to the soundness of Bill Peters' mechanical abilities.

He made small improvements to his lift mechanism over the years and eventually had more of them made, but the basic design remained the same. Today, first-time passengers waiting to fly on one of the Air Harbor's scheduled flights stare in wonder as a heavy-duty forklift rumbles out into the tie-down area and smoothly lifts a massive de Havilland Turbo-Beaver high over the wings and tails of the surrounding planes and carries it to the lake. The company's current forklift fleet is a far cry from the war-surplus machine with the dubious brakes, but the Turbo-Beaver could very well be riding on a piece of history; Bill Peters' first lift mechanism is still in use today.

In 1959, Munro announced that the Air Harbor finally was in a financial position to proceed with the erection of a new office and shop building. The plans were unveiled during the March 1960 board of directors meeting, and the cost was estimated to be $25,000. There was a lengthy discussion about the best location for the new building, but in the end Bill Peters' original suggestion was adapted. The new shop and office facility would be built near the waterfront. The first step would be to demolish the old garage and shed that adjoined the chicken coop office. The chicken coop would remain in place until the new building was finished, and then it, too would be torn down.

The next step would be to tear down the white frame house the Munros had called home for almost fifteen years. Ruth was not upset in the least. Her husband had made arrangements to rent the Nelson's house next door, and while it had been a long time since Ruth had watched rats run up her screen doors, she was looking forward to the chance to live in a larger and nicer home.

The old buildings came down with a crash and a cloud of dust. The ground was far too unstable to support the weight of the planned building, so Weldon Gwim, who'd been contracted to build the foundation and put up the post-and-beam frame, brought in a piledriver and began hammering piles. There were eighty-four of them in all, and as they were pounded home through the gelatinous soil, the Air Harbor employees watched with mixed emotions. Bill Peters and George Grant were ecstatic as every blow of the hammer brought them that much closer to the new shop they'd been dreaming of for years. Bob Munro was less enthusiastic. It wasn't that he didn't want his mechanics to have a proper hangar. He was concerned about the cost. Like most of Kenmore's major airplane purchases and home improvements, the new shop and office building was being built with borrowed money, a situation that always made Munro nervous. So as the air reverberated to the harsh bark of the steam cylinder and the ground shook under the heavy thud of the hammer, Munro paced back and forth, hoping aloud that they were doing the right thing.

When the pile driver was done, it was Bill Peters' turn. Knowing that wood lasts almost indefinitely in the oxygen-free mud of a lake bottom, his primary concern was to protect the piles from rot that might attack from the top. With George Grant's son for a helper, Peters dug down around each pile with a borrowed backhoe until he hit water, which wasn't very far considering that the property was only a couple of feet higher than the lake. Manhandling chainsaws into the holes, Peters and young Grant cut off each pile even with the waterline. Finally, using the holes they'd dug as forms, they poured eighty-four concrete caps, and the piles were cut off from the rotting effects of the atmosphere forever.

With the ground sufficiently reinforced, the next step was to pour the floor. What Munro wanted for his mechanics was no less than perfection, and he was adamant that the shop floor be glass-smooth. A smooth floor painted white would ensure that the hangar would be a bright, pleasant place to work, especially when compared to the dark, damp confines of the old Navy deck building. It wasn't to be.

The floor forms were hammered together and the date set for the arrival of the concrete trucks. The pour went without a hitch, and the workmen began the final finish work that would give Munro the floor he'd always wanted. At about three o'clock in the afternoon, just as the floor was beginning to look really good, it began to rain. As fast as one section of concrete was smoothed off, the rain would rough it up. The contractor's crew stayed all night trying to save it, but in the end the rain won. The floor was strong and level, but it didn't have the smooth, friction-free surface Munro had longed for.

Peters said he would look into fixing the floor as soon as the building was up, but the moment the shop opened for business the demand on it was so great there never seemed to be enough time to clear everything out so the floor could be refinished. The company even bought gallons of a special white paint designed to smooth and seal concrete floors, but the shop was so busy the expensive paint went bad in the cans before any time could be found to apply it, and Peters had to throw it out.

It would be almost thirty years before Bob Munro finally got what he wanted. In 1992, service manager Mark Easterly waited until the Munros left town on their annual boating vacation, and then he had the hangar completely cleared out and steam cleaned. The walls were painted refrigerator white, and a coat of white sealer was applied to the floor. When Munro got back to the office, Easterly asked him out to the shop on the pretense of checking a repair to a customer's plane. Munro was stunned, if not blinded, by the glare. It wasn't a shop, it was a showroom, and the Beaver and Cessna floatplanes being worked on were bathed in a brilliance that highlighted the smallest detail.

Munro gazed around the gleaming shop and nodded in approval. "This is the way it should have been all along."

December 1961 saw the contractor's role in the erection of the Air Harbor's new building come to a close. The post-and-beam framework was up and the roof was in place. From then on, the building would be Bill Peters' personal project. He installed the siding and doors and windows. He designed and built the stairway connecting the office to the second floor and installed the decorative rockwork on the wall behind it. He laid down the two-inch-thick upper floor. He put in the plumbing, ran the wires, and built the interior partitions. He installed the baseboards and the trim around the windows. He had help, of course, from Bob Munro and the rest of the staff who lent a hand whenever they could to hammer nails or lift a window into place, but for the most part, Peters was on his own.

It was a big building for one man to put together, and Peters had other projects to attend to as well. But by the middle of 1963 it was finished, at least for the time being. Actually, the building has never really been finished; as business increased over the years, the office, flight dispatch, and passenger check-in sections of the building have been redesigned and rebuilt numerous times.

In the midst of the construction and improvement frenzy that gripped the company in the late 1950s and early '60s, Walt Winseman had begun to feel like the official Air Harbor orphan. Engine tune-ups and minor repairs were carried out on the airplanes where they sat, but major overhauls had to be done inside. At first, overhauls had been carried out wherever there was room; sometimes in the shed attached to the company's chicken-coop office complex and sometimes in the old barn. When the Navy deck building appeared Winseman set up shop in one end. It was cramped and gloomy, but at least it was permanent.

Ten years later when the metal Butler building went up Winseman was not shy about telling people he thought it would make a terrific engine shop, but of course it was earmarked for the marina. Then Bill Peters started work on the new office and hangar building. Winseman looked over the plans, but he didn't see any provision for his engine operation. I'm going to spend the rest of my life in that crummy deck building, he thought, and he began to think seriously about applying for a job at Boeing.

Fortunately for Kenmore and hundreds of bush pilots whose lives depend on their engines, Bob Munro decided it was time Winseman had a proper engine shop. Figuring that it made sense to have the engine facility as close as possible to the airframe shop, Peters built a one-story extension against the north wall of the new hangar. He installed a non-absorbent tile floor to make it easy to clean up grease and engine oil, and he put heavy-duty workbenches along the walls. Overhead, a track-mounted chain hoist made it easy to move engines around the shop, and transparent roof panels brightened the room even on the gloomiest winter days. Winseman moved his tools over from the deck building and Boeing's chances of getting one of the best engine mechanics in the business evaporated.

Peters would have been busy enough if his only responsibility had been to oversee the expansion of the company's facilities. But in the early 1960s, even as he was hammering together the company's new headquarters, another line was added to his job description: Charter Pilot.

He'd found the time to finish earning his Commercial certificate, so Munro began using him to fill in on last-minute charters when no one else was available to take the flight.

"All of a sudden the phone would ring and we'd have a customer and an airplane but no pilot. So Bob would say, 'Can you take the Cub and go pick up this person?' I'd have my overalls on and cement and paint all over me, so I'd rush in and pull off my overalls and brush my hair and wipe the stuff off my shoes. Then I'd jump into the Cub and off I'd go. After we got the building done the flights started to increase. I'd be flying pretty much all summer and even spotty during the winter. Whenever we ran short of a pilot, I'd go."

BILL PETERS

Munro initially restricted Peters to flights that could be made using the Air Harbor's Super Cub or Aeronca Champ. The faster, less forgiving Cessna 180 was reserved for the company's more experienced pilots. On a Saturday not long after Peters had started his fill-in flying career, Munro walked into the new hangar where Peters was doing some finish work.

"We've got four people who want to go to Big Heart Lake. I can take three of them in the 180, and maybe you could take the other one."

"Which plane do you want me to fly," Peters asked from his perch on top of a ladder.

"Bill has the Cub so you'll have to take the Champ."

Peters frowned at the thought of taking an eighty-five-horsepower airplane into a high mountain lake. Actually, he wasn't worried so much about taking it in as he was about getting it back out.

"Can the Champ make it out of Big Heart?" he asked skeptically.

""Oh, sure. You won't have any trouble."

Peters climbed down, took off his overalls, and did the best he could to wipe the paint off his shoes. Both planes took off together, but the faster 180 was on the lake long before Peters droned into sight in the Champ. The landing was easy enough, and the four fishermen were busily setting up camp as the two Kenmore planes slid off the beach and prepared to take off. Big Heart Lake is heart-shaped but it isn't big, at least not to a floatplane pilot. Peters figured the Champ would need every foot of available water to get airborne. The good news was that he only had to clear the rocks at the outlet end, about eight feet, and he'd be over the broad valley down below.

Munro idled the powerful 180 around in circles while Peters taxied into the farthest corner of the lake and turned to take off. Opening the throttle all the way, he held his breath as the eighty-five-horsepower Continental snarled up to full power and the plane began to accelerate. Actually, Peters was rather impressed by the Champ's performance as the little plane broke free of Big Heart's smooth surface well before the rocks. He cleared the shoreline by a comfortable margin and was soaring out over the valley when a sudden roar overwhelmed the clatter of his own engine.

He knew instantly what it was. It was Munro, thundering up behind the Champ in the 180. The yellow and white Cessna blew by under the Champ and then zoomed into a steep climb. Peters might as well have been standing still. Well, he thought, Bob might have the better plane, but I have a trick or two up my sleeve, too.

Knowing that Munro would be looking back to see the effect of his blast past the Champ,

Peters yanked the power off and pulled his plane into a steep climb until it stalled and fell off on a wing. He recovered and then stalled the plane again, forcing it to fall off on the other wing this time. He recovered, and then stalled again.

Munro was stunned to see the Champ fluttering out of control lower and lower into the valley. His high-speed pass had just been in fun. It had never dawned on him that it might startle Peters into losing control of his plane. Even more disturbing was the thought that his pass might have somehow wrenched the Champ from Peters' control to the point where the relatively low-time pilot was unable to recover. His heart was in his mouth as he banked the 180 around so he could watch the Champ's slow tumble toward the dark forest thousands of feet below. He suddenly found himself wondering what he would tell Peters' wife.

Munro was an exceptional pilot but he had never let it go to his head. Every flight, whether onto the frozen surface of a glacier or through the treacherous downdrafts surrounding a tiny mountain lake, was always carefully calculated. But now, the one time in his flying career he'd given in to the boyish desire to show off his more powerful machine, he'd sent a good friend spiraling to his death. Helpless and sickened, he watched as the Champ stalled again and fell into its final plunge toward the trees.

It never reached them. With an almost military precision the Champ's wings suddenly snapped level, the nose came up, and the little plane was climbing smoothly away from the valley floor under perfect control. For a moment, Munro felt an incredible wave of relief flow over him. Then he began to wonder. Peters' recovery had been a bit too precise for someone who had been so obviously out of control. By the time he was halfway back to Kenmore, Munro was convinced he'd been duped.

For his part, Peters began to wonder if he'd carried his joke a bit too far. I'll probably be in for a good chewing out when I get back, he thought. But it was worth it, he decided.

Sure enough, Munro was waiting for him when he got back. Peters secured the Champ and started walking up the dock, trying and then failing to keep a straight face. Munro glared at him for a moment.

"Peters..." he began, and then he shook his head in frustration. "Peters..." he tried again, and then he gave up. Turning on his heel, he stalked off to the shop. A practical joker himself, Munro wasn't used to having the tables turned on him. So for the next day or so, all he could do when he bumped into his master builder was shake his head and mutter, "Peters..." and walk on.

When a property speculator named Bob Hunter called and wanted to charter a plane to look at some lots on Vancouver Island, Peters got the nod for the trip. The first flight was so successful Hunter became a regular customer, always requesting Peters to be his pilot.

"Bob Hunter was real interested in the old native Indian sights. We'd be flying along and he'd say, 'Look at that point. That was an Indian campsite.' You can always tell them because the points are covered with deciduous trees instead of conifers. The Indians would clear the land for their camp, and then as they used the site over the years it would gradually be covered over with a layer of clamshells from their meals. Eventually the trees would grow back but the soil would be too alkaline from the clamshells to support conifers.

"Bob would see one of these sites and say, 'Can we land there?' We visited several of these sites, and we even found a couple of totem poles on the west side of Vancouver Island that nobody knew about. It was pretty exciting to come across these huge totem poles lying on their sides in the brush and realize we were the first people to see them since the Indians had left. It was an awesome feeling to stand there in the silence of the forest looking at the gigantic figures carved into the logs and wonder what they had meant to the people who had carved them."

BILL PETERS

One of Bob Hunter's later flights provided a level of excitement Peters could have done without. The land Hunter wanted to inspect was on the rugged west coast of Vancouver Island, this time at windswept Estevan Point. Peters wasn't sure a landing at Estevan was such a good idea, as it was totally exposed to the Pacific Ocean. But Munro had landed out there once or twice, and he assured Peters that if he went in at low tide, the rock reefs surrounding the point would act as breakwaters to form a sort of lagoon behind them where he could land perfectly safely. Hunter had a couple of people he wanted to take with him, so Peters got to take the 180 instead of his usual Super Cub.

He flew first to Neah Bay at the northern tip of the Olympic Peninsula to wait until he knew the water was dropping along the west coast of Vancouver Island. The flight across the Strait of Juan de Fuca and up the island was spectacular with the huge Pacific swells rolling in to smash against the sheer rock bluffs and sending ponderous geysers of gray-green water and spray shooting up at the floats of Peters' airplane.

Munro, as usual, had been right about the low-tide lagoons at Estevan, and Peters pulled the 180 up onto a small sandy beach at the base of the bluff. Hunter and his friends scrambled out and disappeared up the hill to check out the property while Peters stayed with the plane to make sure it didn't float away. The 180 had a High Frequency radio, and for want of anything else to do, Peters turned it on. There was a burst of static and then a voice came on announcing a tsunami warning.

Peters was suddenly all ears. A tidal wave? Well that's good news, he thought. Here I am less than a hundred yards from the open ocean with nothing but a little rock reef between me and the swells and there's a tidal wave coming. Terrific.

The voice on the radio continued. The tsunami was expected to arrive at such and such an hour Zulu time. Zulu time? What the heck is Zulu time, Peters wondered. He tried to raise the Neah Bay station on the radio but all he got was static. As he sat fiddling with the radio he began stealing glances out the windshield at the endless procession of waves that rose one by one to accelerate in toward the reef. Gee, that's a big wave there, he'd say to himself every time an extra-large swell would mound up and tip forward into a breaker that thundered onto the rocks. I wonder if that's it?

Just as he was about to give up on the radio Neah Bay answered his call. Yes, they confirmed through bursts of static, a tidal wave was on its way and was expected to hit the coast in ninety minutes. The static cut off any further conversation, but Peters had heard enough. It was time to get the hell out of Dodge.

Hunter and his buddies were still scrambling around in the brush up on the point. Every time Peters got a glimpse of them he yelled and waved at them to return, but they would just wave back and disappear again. This went on for almost an hour. Peters watched the minute hand of his watch creep slowly toward the moment of doom. The imminent arrival of a giant wave plus the fact the tide was coming in and rendering his reef breakwater less effective by the minute had put Peters in a real quandary. He didn't want to lose the plane or his life, but he didn't want to leave his passengers to be swept off the point, either.

Finally, Hunter and his friends began ambling back toward the beach. As soon as Peters saw them, he started shouting and waving. Sensing something was amiss, the men broke into a trot.

"Get in, get in," Peters ordered. "There's a tidal wave coming. We've got to get out of here."

Now it was Hunter's turn to be worried. "Will we make it?" he asked as he shoved his friends through the door and into the back seat.

Peters glanced at the waves that were now foaming through the gaps in the rapidly disappearing reef and washing into the lagoon. "I hope so."

He vaulted into the pilot's seat and fired up the engine. The 180 slid off the sand and immediately began rocking and bobbing in the swells that now covered the once-smooth lagoon. "You ready," he shouted over his shoulder at the men in the back seat. They nodded and stared wide-eyed at the thundering waves that were breaking less than twenty yards from the wingtip. Peters swung the plane as close into the wind as he could and opened the throttle. The engine's roar filled the cockpit as the nose came up. An instant later, Peters knew they were in for a rough ride. The waves spilling across the lagoon weren't big, but they were enough to start the 180 pitching up and down as the floats bashed across the confused pattern of swells. At fifty miles an hour water takes on the consistency of concrete, and it seemed that every part of the airplane was vibrating. The instruments were unreadable, the seats clattered in their tracks, and Hunter and his friends clung with death grips to anything they could get hold of.

As the airspeed approached sixty, Peters yanked back on the yoke and the 180 lurched out of the water. Peters kept the plane staggering along in ground-effect, an aerodynamic phenomenon that dramatically reduces the drag of a wing when it's within half its span of the ground. A few feet higher, and the plane would stall instantly. Peters skillfully kept the mushing airplane from sinking back onto the bone-jarring waves while the airspeed needle crept up the dial. By the time it hit eighty, the Cessna had flown itself out of ground effect and was climbing smoothly away from Estevan Point.

Back at Kenmore, Peters learned that Zulu time is aviation shorthand for Greenwich Mean Time. And the tidal wave never did show up.

As the weather began to cool in the fall of 1963, the company's desks, chairs, and filing cabinets were moved out of the chicken coop and set up in bright, airy office at the south end of the new building next door. The chicken coop was knocked apart and hauled off to the dump. No one was particularly sorry to see it go.

With the new building essentially complete, Peters turned his attention to solving the forklift problem before the machine took another header into the lake. Peters first thought about building an elevator to move the planes in and out of the water. Seaplane elevators were nothing new; Lana Kurtzer had one outside his hangar over on Lake Union, and Alaska Coastal had elevators built into their docks in Ketchikan and Juneau. The Alaska Coastal rigs were real monsters, lifting the airline's 20,000-pound Consolidated PBY flying boats up to the maintenance hangars, a vertical distance of almost thirty feet if the tide was out.

But even the simplest elevator requires a fair amount of machinery, which means maintenance. Peters wanted something that was utterly reliable and virtually maintenance-free. The little boat-yards scattered along the shores of Puget Sound all used slipways; hull cradles on wheels running on rails that sloped across the beach into the water. Gravity pulled the cradles down the rails; an electric winch pulled them back up.

Peters couldn't think of anything more reliable or maintenance-free than gravity, and a heavy-duty, industrial-grade electric motor was a close second. Grabbing a pencil, he sketched out a square, flat-surfaced car running on a pair of rails that sloped from the tie-down area into the lake. An electric winch mounted off to the side would raise and lower the car by means of a cable running through a snatch block mounted on the bulkhead between the rails. It was simple, reliable, and would be strong enough to lift any plane the Air Harbor would be likely to own in the foresee-able future. He was right on the first two.

The most logical place to put the railcar was to the west of the new hangar. The company would still need the ramp on the east side of the building for amphibious seaplanes and any plane that might prove too large or heavy for the railcar. Before construction on the railcar could begin, however, the Nelson's big boathouse would have to come down. The old Dodge weapons carrier was called upon once more, first to pull down the boathouse itself and then to break out the piles that had held it up.

With the boathouse out of the way, the next step was to drive the two rows of piles that would support the rails. The last step was to install the rail assembly, which was sixty feet long and had been assembled on land ahead of time. It was not an easy task, and one of the rails broke when the pile driver operator hit his winch brake too hard. Peters welded the rail back together and the tricky job continued.

> "We finally got the rails in, and they've been there ever since. I don't even want to think about ever having to change them. Fortunately, we've been able to fool around and get them bent back and usable again and again."

BILL PETERS

The first railcar was constructed of wood, but as the company began acquiring heavier air-planes it simply wasn't up to the task. Peters designed a railcar built entirely of steel, with a heavy grate of vertical bars for the platform. It lasted almost fifteen years, but eventually it, too, had to be replaced. But while the railcars have needed occasional replacing, the basic system has lived up to Peters' requirements for simplicity and reliability. During the busy summer months, the car is in almost constant use, whining smoothly up and down the rails as many as a hundred times a day, reaffirming with every trip the soundness of Peters' design. And best of all, no one can even remember the last time a forklift fell into the lake.

In 1965, two years after the completion of the new shop and office building, Munro decided it was time to do something about the Navy deck building. Peters had run his builder's eye over the improvised shop the first time he'd visited the Air Harbor and had been surprised that anyone would choose to use such a low building for an airplane hangar. But then he hadn't been around during the hardscrabble years when the Air Harbor was struggling to make it one day at a time, so he didn't realize what a triumph in survival the deck building represented. But now its log founda-tion was beginning to rot, and it's low roof had rendered it all but useless.

"It would be a shame to tear it apart if we can still use it," Munro said one day as he and Peters sat discussing future building projects.

"We could raise it," Peters offered. "Double the height, put on a larger door."

Munro considered Peters' suggestion for a moment. "If we moved it to the rear corner of the Nelson property behind the house, it would give us more clear space around the front of the shop."

Peters agreed.

"I think it would be a good idea," Munro said decisively, and Peters had another project. He set up forms for a cement foundation and floor and set eight-foot studs around the perimeter. As soon as the floor was poured and ready, he borrowed a big front-end loader from the cement plant next door and carried the old deck building across the property and set it on top of the studs. While he held it in position with the loader, Munro scabbed the studs to the deck building frame with lengths of 2 x 6. Peters spent the next several days framing in the lower studs, nailing on new metal siding, and replacing the roof panels. When he was done, Kenmore had a nice, high-ceilinged hangar that could accommodate any of the smaller floatplanes with plenty of room left over for the mechanics to work on complete wing, tail, or float assemblies. It's still in use today.

Each morning when Bill Peters came to work he could see his handiwork everywhere he looked. Thanks in large part to his ingenuity, skill, and sweat, the company had a big new shop and office building, it was easier to launch and recover planes and move them around the property, and the old Navy deck building had been turned into something useful. But there was one legacy of the early days that was as irritating to Munro as it was to Peters. Much of the ground around the buildings was still the same fill dirt that young Ted Huntley had shoveled so laboriously back in the

Kenmore Air Harbor in the late 1960s. The Bill Peters-designed office and maintenance hangar is in the center of the photo. Behind it is the Seabee hangar. Immediately to the east is the new long hangar with the paint shop at the south end. Beyond it, backed up against the cement plant, is the metal Butler building that first housed Kenmore Marina and then Walt Winseman's engine shop. The original Navy deck building has been moved to the northwest corner of the property and doubled in height.

1940s. During the summer, the dust stirred up by the forklift and by the revving of airplanes undergoing engine tests covered everything in a fine layer of grit, while in the winter the tie-down area was an obstacle course of icy puddles and muddy wheel ruts, and the office and shop floors became a maze of muddy footprints.

No one remembers who came up with the solution, or how they got the idea. It might have been the result of an idle conversation with one of the drivers from the cement plant next door or from watching what went on when the trucks returned at the end of the day. But regardless of who got the idea and how, it was a good one. Each day saw the cement trucks head out with loads of pre-mixed cement for the foundations, sidewalks, and driveways of the homes and businesses springing up around the north end of the lake. Not all the trucks came back empty, and what to do with the leftover cement was becoming a real problem.

The Air Harbor solved it. After a pleasant chat with the plant manager one morning, Peters came back and hammered together a bunch of square forms which he set up in a row along the back of the property. That afternoon, trucks returning with partial loads of cement went first to the Air Harbor where the driver dumped the load into one of the forms. It usually took a week or so to fill one form, but when the last of the concrete had hardened Peters knocked the boards apart and set them up again in a new spot. It took several years for the concrete paving to creep all the way to the lake, but the day finally came when the last square of shingle mill mud disappeared forever.

There were more building projects in Bill Peters' future. The extension on the south end of the Seabee hangar would be enlarged and turned into the permanent home of Kenmore's fully-staffed parts department. A brand new building east of the Seabee hangar would house a paint shop, sheet metal and airframe shops, and covered airplane storage. And Walt Winseman would finally get his wish. The phase-out of the Kenmore Marina would see the Butler building converted into a large, modern aircraft engine shop. But Bill Peters' most challenging job would have nothing to do with buildings. It came about as a result of a government contract that Bob Munro wanted to win. It wasn't a survey contract this time, but a transportation contract.

The deep, cold waters of Puget Sound offer an ideal environment for testing torpedoes, a fact that was not lost on the U.S. Navy. In a program run by the Applied Physics Laboratory at the University of Washington, the Navy began testing torpedoes in the deep, calm waters of Hood Canal. The easiest way to get from the university to the canal was by floatplane, and it wasn't long before the APL was one of the Air Harbor's best customers.

When the scientists decided they needed a larger test range they hired the Air Harbor to fly them in search of a better site. They found it in a little group of islands just north of Nanaimo on Vancouver Island. The closest shipping lane was miles away, and the local tidal currents were minimal. The only problem was that the new range was about 130 miles north of the Navy's torpedo research facility at Keyport.

The obvious solution was to do what the APL had done: fly people back and forth from the laboratories to the range. But the Navy hadn't been in the seaplane business for years. With their PBY Catalinas sold off and their PBM Mariners cut up for scrap, the Navy had no choice but to hire a civilian seaplane operator. Munro really wanted that contract; by 1965 the Cold War had made torpedo development a top priority, and supporting the Keyport test facility would provide a steady source of income for the Air Harbor for years.

Munro sent for a copy of the contract and realized he didn't have a chance. The Navy wanted planes that could carry six people plus the pilot. The Air Harbor's Cessna 180s could carry three plus the pilot. Munro submitted a bid anyway, and was awarded a limited contract based on their excellent support of the Applied Physics Lab. This was better than nothing, but most of the work went to a Canadian operator who'd submitted a bid based around his new, seven-place, DHC-2.

Like the Noorduyn Norseman, the DHC-2 had been designed and built in Canada. But instead of the Norseman's heavy, steel-tube construction, the DHC-2 featured a lightweight, aluminum monocoque fuselage and an all-metal wing. It got off the water in a heartbeat and handled like a dream. It was powered by one of the most reliable engines ever built, and it could lift over a ton of fuel, passengers, and cargo into the air. It was the second product off the manufacturer's drawing board, hence the uninspiring name. But its designers had given it another name, one that was meant to convey in a single word what their remarkable new machine was all about. The plane Bob Munro was up against, the plane that was stealing the Navy business away from the Air Harbor, was a de Havilland Beaver.

Munro had no intention of standing by while a lucrative contract disappeared over the horizon, especially when it was the Canadian horizon. The Navy contract would come up for grabs again in 1966, so Munro started thinking about what it would take to win. What it would take, he decided, was a larger airplane. The Cessna 180 was fast and it was efficient, but it just wasn't big enough for some of the loads the Navy wanted to carry. The Canadian operator was having great success with the Beaver. Maybe the Air Harbor should think about acquiring a similar plane. Munro decided to keep an eye out in case a used Beaver became available at a reasonable price.

It's tempting to look at this decision and marvel at the foresight it must have taken to embark on a program that would ultimately redefine the Air Harbor to its very core and ensure its success into the next millennium. But foresight had nothing to do with it. Munro was the first person to admit he worked without a game plan. The Air Harbor's success was not the result of adhering to carefully constructed, long-term strategies, but was instead an example of what can happen when day-to-day decisions are based on ethics, honesty, and logic. Kenmore was losing business because it didn't have a Beaver. The solution couldn't have been more obvious: buy a Beaver and get the business back.

It made sense to Bill Peters. Little did he know that Munro's decision would one day send him halfway around the world on a quest for de Havilland's remarkable machines.

ENTER THE BEAVER

I N 1934, WHEN ROBERT NOORDUYN perceived a need in Canada for a rugged airborne workhorse, he met it with the plane he called the Norseman. The Norseman was a marvel to the pre-war bush operators, but it was a short-lived marvel. Noorduyn's airplane was an antique in five years as the war that gripped Europe and Asia propelled aviation from the craftsmanship of wood, tubing, and fabric to the assembly line of mass-produced metal. Wood and fabric didn't die easily; the Norseman Mark V and the Staggerwing Beech continued in production for a short time after the war, and tube and fabric planes like the Piper Super Cub would continue to be built into the next century. But by the time low-budget operators like Kenmore got their hands on a Norseman, the plane was hopelessly out of date.

Not that the Norseman didn't do a good job for pilots like Bob Munro. But it was heavy, slow, and noisy, and it required a roomful of craftsmen to build. The parts of an all-metal airplane could be whacked out of aluminum sheets by machines and riveted together by almost anyone. In 1946, another Canadian company was preparing to do just that.

De Havilland of Canada had been manufacturing other people's designs for years. From 1928 to 1939, the planes assembled at the company's Downsview, Ontario plant were put together using parts shipped over from de Havilland of England, that country's oldest and most prestigious aviation firm. But the Canadian division's engineers dreamed of someday putting their own designs into production, and they lost no opportunity to put their ideas on paper, even if for the time being they flew no farther than the nearest filing cabinet.

Any possibility that the company's original concepts might soon see the light of day was dashed with Germany's invasion of Poland in 1939. The Downsview plant had all it could do producing Tiger Moth trainers and twin-engine Mosquito fighter-bombers for the Royal Air Force.

The war raging around the world seemed at times as though it would go on forever, but DHC managing director Phil Garratt knew it had to end sometime. With an eye on his company's post-war future, he authorized a "back of the envelope" design study for a utility plane, a machine which would fill the niche then occupied by Mr. Noorduyn's Norseman. The design was drawn up by the Polish designer Wsiewolod "Jaki" Jakimiuk. A brilliant engineer, Jaki had escaped to the west just ahead of the German invasion of his country. He eventually wound up in Canada where DHC hired him to head up the Tiger Moth program.

Jakimiuk's utility plane concept incorporated an all-metal airframe with a high-mounted, cantilever wing and a slim, pointed nose which would house a 330-horsepower, air-cooled, in-line engine then under development in England. But as long as war production demanded every resource the company could scrape together, pursuing the project was out of the question, and Jakimiuk's plans joined the others in the filing cabinet.

The end of the war brought the same stunned silence to de Havilland's little Downsview plant as it did to the giant factories of Boeing, Douglas, and Consolidated. Scores of huge military contracts were canceled virtually overnight, and DHC suddenly found itself with nothing to build. But the same post-war enthusiasm for aviation that sent returning veterans out to Bill Fisk's flight school in droves fed a similar demand north of the border. Everyone wanted to get into aviation, and de Havilland was determined to help them do it.

The first original design they put into production was for a two-seat trainer they named the DHC-1 Chipmunk. The low-wing, all-metal Chipmunk was an instant success, and its military and civilian career eventually outshone the Tiger Moth's. Then the Ontario Provincial Air Service announced it intended to purchase as many as thirty new planes to replace the aging Stinson Reliants it had been flying for years. With the potential of a guaranteed volume sale, de Havilland pulled Jakimiuk's "flying pickup" plans out of the file cabinet and created a team to finalize the design. The project was given an added degree of urgency when Fairchild announced they, too, were designing a plane to compete for the OPAS contract.

The Fairchild competitor was the Husky, an all-metal, high-wing machine with a rather odd, stepped-up rear fuselage. Powered by Pratt & Whitney's ubiquitous R-985 Wasp Jr., the Husky prototype flew in June 1946. If de Havilland wanted any chance of winning the OPAS contract, they'd have to get cracking.

"Jaki" Jakimiuk was busy with the Chipmunk, so the utility plane project was turned over to engineers Fred Buller and Dick Hiscocks. Hiscocks, an aerodynamicist by training, didn't bother trying to design any speed into de Havilland's new utility plane. Instead, he concentrated on generating enough lift to get two tons off the water with a 250-horsepower engine. The 330-horsepower engine Jakimiuk had planned for was still under development in England and couldn't be counted on; the smaller engine was a sure thing. Rejecting existing and proven airfoil designs, Hiscocks created his own airfoil by applying principals that were the exact opposite to what had been done on fighters like the P-51. Instead of a wing that performed best at high speeds, he designed an airfoil that worked best at low speeds. He took quite a gamble, flying in the face of established aerodynamic theory, but it was a gamble that paid off handsomely.

With the airfoil established, Hiscocks and Buller set about changing the other features of Jakimiuk's design they felt were less than ideal. Jaki's cantilever wing meant less drag, but it also meant that a large, heavy wing spar would pass through the cockpit and restrict the pilot's headroom. Hiscocks knew that, cantilevered or not, his wing design wasn't going to set any speed records, so he decided to add a pair of conventional lift struts. The struts made it possible to use a much smaller wing spar which reduced the overall weight of the plane and increased the headroom inside the cabin.

Hiscocks and Buller knew that in the bush pilot's world planes are loaded to the gills, lakes are always too short, and the trees around them are always too tall. In an effort to give pilots the optimum takeoff and landing performance, Hiscocks recommended that de Havilland's new plane be equipped with drooping ailerons. Moving the ailerons down with the flaps would allow the wing to generate even more lift at low airspeeds. Some of the plane's potential buyers were vehemently opposed to this idea. The Norseman had drooping ailerons, too, but they didn't always deploy properly and sometimes ended up creating more problems than they solved. Hiscocks persisted, however, and the doubters were eventually won over when Buller designed an aileron deployment mechanism that was absolutely foolproof.

While the Norseman's aileron mechanism wasn't so great, its door arrangement was. Floatplanes don't have brakes; the only way to stop them is to scramble out of the cockpit, snatch up a mooring line, and jump to the dock where the line can be used to physically drag the plane to a halt. Hiscocks and Buller knew that winds and currents often make it impossible to dock a plane on the left side, so they put a pair of doors on each side of the cabin, a smaller one up front for the pilot and a larger cargo door behind it. No matter which side of the plane ended up next to the dock, the pilot and passengers would be able to get in and out quickly. And because the lifeblood of the north flows in fifty-five-gallon drums, Buller shaped the two cargo doors to accommodate a drum rolled in on its side or manhandled in on end.

From the moment self-starting engines had been introduced to the north country, pilots flying during the winter had gotten into the habit of removing their plane's battery at the end of the day and taking it inside to keep it warm. This could be a real struggle as pilots wearing bulky gloves tried to manipulate small tools in tight spaces. The DHC design team made the whole process a lot easier by mounting their new plane's battery on rails in a compartment behind the rear cabin. All a pilot had to do was open a door in the side of the fuselage, slide the battery out on its tracks, and disconnect the cables.

De Havilland's utility plane had a wing and a fuselage; what it didn't have was an engine. The 330-horsepower Gypsy Queen engine was still having developmental problems, and in March, 1947, DHC finally dispatched two engineers to England to see for themselves what was going on. While they were enroute, Phil Garratt, who was now in charge of the company's strategic planning, had lunch with Jim Young, president of Pratt & Whitney of Canada. Young was eager to tell Garratt that Pratt & Whitney had obtained certification of war-surplus R-985 Wasp Jr. engines for civilian use. The stipulation was that the surplus engines, used or not, had to be thoroughly overhauled by Pratt & Whitney itself.

"You're really making a mistake, Phil," Young said. "You've got the makings of a fine plane. You're going to power it with an untried engine. Why not put the R-985 in? Put the Wasp in, and you'll have a reserve of power. There were thousands built during the war and you can get them dirt cheap."

Young was right about the cost; surplus Wasps in their original packing cases were selling for thirty-five dollars, although the required Pratt & Whitney overhaul brought the total cost up to about $9,000. And the Wasp's reliability was legendary. When word came from England that the Gypsy Queen had broken down once again on the test stand, Garratt made his decision. De Havilland's new plane would be powered by the R-985, and Hiscocks was put to work redesigning the fuselage to accommodate it.

The engine switch ensured the plane's success. Hiscocks squared off the fuselage cross-section to accommodate the round engine, thus creating even more room in the cabin. The gross weight of the original design had been targeted at four-thousand pounds; the Wasp's additional horsepower allowed the gross weight to be increased by a thousand pounds.

The DHC-1 Chipmunk had been named by Phil Garratt after the perky little creatures he'd seen scampering about the woods near his home. He decided to continue the practice of naming DHC's products after Canadian wildlife. As the new utility plane took shape in the Downsview plant, its stubby, powerful nose and sturdy fuselage had "hard-worker" written all over them. One look and there was only one name that made sense. Officially it was the DHC-2, but the name everyone would use, the name that would be painted neatly in loping script on the cockpit doors of the production planes, was "Beaver."

The Beaver's first flight took place on August 16, 1947. Dick Hiscocks had designed his wing to perform well with 250 horsepower. It's performance with 450 horsepower was little short of phenomenal. Add in the effect of the drooping ailerons, and the Beaver was an impressive STOL (Short Takeoff and Landing) airplane from the outset.

Despite its flying more than a year after the Fairchild Husky, the Beaver was the overwhelming winner in the OPAS competition, and de Havilland put it into full production. Full production in this case consisted of three airplanes a month, hardly the frantic assembly pace that had character-ized the company's war effort. But with the high-volume Chipmunk program going full-bore, the Beaver was viewed more as a supplementary project than a primary one. De Havilland knew the Beaver was a winner, but because it was a fairly specialized airplane it was assumed its market would be fairly specialized as well.

Then in May, 1949, Russ Bannock, chief pilot of the Beaver program, happened to pick up an issue of *Aviation Week* magazine in Edmonton, Alberta while he was killing time between demon-stration flights. As he paged through the magazine, a little article caught his eye, and the fortunes of both de Havilland of Canada and the tiny seaplane base emerging from the mud in Kenmore, Washington were changed forever.

According to the *AvWeek* article, the U.S. Air Force's 10th Search and Rescue Group in Alaska was looking for a STOL airplane with a five-hundred mile range that could operate on floats and skis and lift half a ton into the air. Their requirements described the Beaver to a "T", and Bannock lost no time getting himself and his airplane to Anchorage for a demonstration. The formal demonstration flights were impressive enough, but the clincher came when Bannock volunteered to fly some of the brass to the small river where they regularly went fishing. This real-world demonstration of the Beaver's dramatic STOL capabilities did the trick. The officers landed some nice fish, and Bannock landed an order for twelve Beavers. After conducting more demonstrations back in the Lower Forty-Eight, the original order was increased by two-hundred planes. The Air Force Beavers were given the designation L-20A, the "L" standing for Liaison.

The Air Force may have been the first service to order Beavers, but in 1951 after several grueling competitions, the U.S. Army decided the Beaver's STOL performance, easy flying characteristics, and rugged construction made it the perfect plane for supply and liaison work into forward combat areas. They eventually acquired 976 L-20s, including the ones ordered originally by the Air Force. Many of them were sent immediately to Korea. Fifteen years later, the Army's Beavers were back in Asia and back at war, this time in Vietnam.

But while the Beaver was soaring to success in the military, it didn't generate much interest among civilian operators in the United States. In Alaska, pilots stuck with their Stinson Gullwings, Piper Super Cubs, and Cessna 180s. If a larger plane was needed, the Norseman was still the aircraft of choice, or the twin-engine Grumman Goose. Part of the reluctance to try the Beaver might have been price; there were few used Beavers around and the cost of a new one was about $30,000.

Bob Munro was certainly aware of the Beaver prior to 1966, but he felt it was too big for the Air Harbor's needs. He'd gotten rid of the company's two Norsemen for that very reason. There was the money issue as well; the price of one new Beaver would just about cover the cost of two new Cessnas. In fact, Munro had been so impressed with the Cessna 180 that in 1964, Kenmore Air Harbor had become a bona fide Cessna dealer. By June, 1965, the company had sold ten new Cessnas which helped boost the company's gross income for the year to a record high of $358,704.

Then came the Navy torpedo range contract, and Munro realized the Air Harbor needed a big plane again. Fortunately there was someone in the Seattle area who was eager to sell one. Harold Hansen had acquired a used Beaver and was in the process of fixing it up. Looking for a buyer, he called Munro and talked glowingly of the plane's abilities and handling characteristics. Munro had never flown a Beaver, but it had to be an improvement over the truck-like Norseman, so he agreed to try it out.

"Great," Hansen said. "I'll have it together in a few days and I'll bring it up to you."

A few days became a week which became two weeks which became a month. Munro was about to give up and go in search of something else when Hansen called and said the plane was finally ready. It was a windless day, and as Hansen taxied the Beaver across the glassy water toward the Kenmore dock, it was immediately obvious to everyone watching that "ready" was a relative term. The exterior surfaces were a blend of bare aluminum and blotchy primer, and much of the interior seemed to be missing. The registration number was stenciled unevenly in black down the side of the cabin: N9764Z. The engine clanked to a stop, and the plane coasted the last few yards to the dock in silence.

"I know it looks a little rough," Hansen said cheerfully as he scrambled down from the cockpit and snatched up a mooring line, "but I guarantee you'll love it after just one flight."

Bill Fisk stepped onto a float and peered into the cabin.

"It looks like you had a tornado in here," he growled.

Hansen was undaunted. "The engine's in great shape, the float installation is solid, and I can vouch for the condition of the airframe. That's what's important."

Fisk grunted. "You can't fly passengers in something that looks like—"

"I really appreciate your bringing the plane up here, Harold," Munro interrupted, hoping to forestall any more of Fisk's disparaging remarks. "We're all looking forward to a chance to try it out."

Hansen may have misled the Air Harbor a little on the condition of his plane, but he hadn't exaggerated its flying qualities one bit. Munro took the first demo flight, and he was impressed from the outset. The sturdy plane felt right from the moment he swung himself in through the pilot's door and plopped down in the seat. The engine controls were laid out logically, and he liked the simple hydraulic flap system with its big actuating lever just below his right hand. The rudder and elevator trim system was equally handy with its two rubber wheels mounted on the ceiling. Radial engines were nothing new, but after years of pounding halfway to Sand Point in the Norsemen, and even farther in the Staggerwing, Munro found the Beaver's takeoff performance exhilarating.

It got even better in the air. The flight controls were light, but not too light. The plane responded immediately to the smallest pitch change, and while the long wings made for a relatively slow roll rate, the control feel was positive and predictable. The recommended power setting of twenty-eight inches of manifold pressure and 1,850 rpm yielded a cruise speed of 110 miles per hour, noticeably slower than the company's Cessna 180s. But what the Beaver lacked in speed it more than made up in stability and roominess.

In short, Six-Four-Zulu was the best plane Munro had ever flown, and when he got back from his first flight, the decision had been made. The minutes of the sixty-third Kenmore board of directors meeting held on December 7, 1966, listed the following planes on the company roster: one Cessna 185, four Cessna 180s, one Cessna 172, one Cessna 170, three Piper Super Cubs, and one de Havilland DHC-2 Beaver. Six-Four-Zulu's lack of paint had been rectified by the Air Harbor mechanics, who applied a base coat of white with a tasteful, two-tone trim scheme using Kenmore's official colors of yellow and brown. When they were finished, Bill Peters tackled the interior. The hours he'd spent fixing up Ted Huntley's college planes paid off as he cut, stitched, and fitted new sidewall and headliner panels and re-upholstered the seats. When he was finished, the plane boasted an interior that impressed even the skeptical Bill Fisk.

Actually, Kenmore's first Beaver had been put to work long before the December 7th meeting. Earlier in the year the company had submitted the winning bid for the Navy's torpedo test range contract, and this time they had the plane to do it. The Navy simply wanted transportation, but Kenmore gave them a lot more than that. The test torpedoes fired at the range in Canada were the same diameter as a standard torpedo but were considerably shorter and lighter. After firing, they were recovered and taken by boat to the Canadian naval base at Ranch Point on Vancouver Island. There the spent torpedoes were loaded onto trucks. What with two ferry rides, a border crossing, and close to three hundred miles of road, it often took two days to get a torpedo back to Keyport for analysis.

Bob Munro had a better idea. He'd carried enough rowboats and canoes on the float struts of various airplanes to know that it worked, and he didn't see any reason he couldn't do the same thing with a torpedo. With the help of the Navy personnel at Keyport, he and Bill Peters designed and fabricated a pair of racks that mounted to the Beaver's float decks. Each rack could hold one practice torpedo. That took care of carrying them, but now they had to figure out how to load them. They were too heavy and awkward to be loaded by hand and the Beaver's wings prevented them from being swung into position by crane. Peters pondered the situation for a moment and then came up with another one of his "better ideas." He designed a lifting device shaped like the letter "C." The crane was hooked to the top of the "C" while the torpedo was attached to the bottom. The curved part of the "C" fit around the leading edge of the wing and provided enough clearance to maneuver the torpedo into position on the rack.

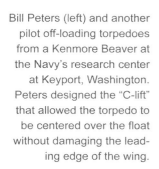

Bill Peters (left) and another pilot off-loading torpedoes from a Kenmore Beaver at the Navy's research center at Keyport, Washington. Peters designed the "C-lift" that allowed the torpedo to be centered over the float without damaging the leading edge of the wing.

The torpedoes were mounted on the Beaver facing backwards to minimize the buffeting effect of the air tumbling off the torpedoes' guidance fins and propellers. Peters had two "C" lifts fabricated, one for Ranch Point and one for Keyport, and the one or two-day wait between firing a torpedo and delivering it to the lab was reduced to a couple of hours.

By now, the Air Harbor had two Beavers in service. Even the ever-skeptical Bill Fisk had been won over by Six-Four-Zulu's easy handling and impressive payload, so when Harold Hansen offered to sell a second airplane in 1967, Kenmore jumped at the chance. There was something about N9766Z that struck a chord in Bob Munro, and after the plane had been run through the shop, he flew it almost exclusively for the next fifteen years. That's not to say it wasn't flown by other pilots, too, but whenever Munro was scheduled for a Beaver flight, the dispatcher made sure Six-Six-Zulu was penciled in next to his name.

For a while, it looked as though the torpedo transportation operation would go big-time. The Navy was so impressed with Kenmore's air-shipment scheme that they began thinking about the feasibility of shipping four, or six, or even eight practice torpedoes on each flight, or maybe even a couple of full-size torpedoes. The standard-size weapons were much too large and heavy for a plane like the Beaver, but the Navy felt a Consolidated PBY "Catalina" flying boat could handle them with ease. Munro and Peters had several meetings at Keyport to discuss the feasibility of the idea, and they even began negotiations with a California company to purchase a surplus PBY.

The thought of operating a huge seaplane like the Catalina was pretty exciting to a company who's largest plane to date had been a 1929 Bellanca. Munro flew to Los Angeles to inspect the twin-engine amphibian and discovered its wings still held the wartime external bomb racks. A closer look convinced Munro that the racks could easily be modified to accept practice torpedoes in place of bombs. He reported his findings to the officials at Keyport, who assured him that the PBY operation would soon be added to the Air Harbor's existing contract. Then someone let the Catalina out of the bag.

"The Navy said they still intended to go forward with the project but that they'd been ordered to put it out as a separate bid instead of just attaching it to our existing contract. So they opened it up, and pretty soon they had everybody in the country wanting to bid on flying torpedoes with a PBY. It turned into a big hassle. Then other people began arguing that it couldn't be done, and eventually it got so fouled up that the whole idea was dropped and they decided to use big trucks instead. It's too bad. I know we could have made it work, and it would have been an interesting experience for us."

BOB MUNRO

While the turmoil over the PBY contract built to a head, Kenmore continued hauling torpedoes with a Beaver. For two years the two Zulus, Six-Four and Six-Six, plodded back and forth between Keyport and Ranch Point without a hitch, saving the Navy hundreds of hours and thousands of dollars in transportation costs. The day the new trucks took over was a sad one, not only at Kenmore but across the sound at the test labs where the scientists had gotten used to the rapid delivery of their lethal experiments.

The worst thing about the Beaver as far as Kenmore was concerned was that by 1970, the company had managed to acquire only four of them. There was another Zulu, N9772Z, and N17598, which had come to Kenmore by way of the Falkland Islands. The Cessnas still provided fast, efficient service, but if the loads were heavy or the number of passengers exceeded three, the Beavers were the only plane that could do the job.

In total, de Havilland built 1,676 radial-engined Beavers. The company had undergone a lot of changes since the Beaver's first flight in 1947, not the least of which was a takeover by UK-based Hawker-Siddeley. The UK-based executives knew virtually nothing about bush planes, and didn't

Loading surplus Beavers in Austria. The fuselage is resting on a set of the stub landing gear Bill Peters had made up in Singapore. (photo by Bill Peters)

appear interested in learning. Then in the mid-1960s, Pratt & Whitney of Canada announced they were terminating their radial engine overhaul and re-certification program, and de Havilland realized the days of piston Beaver production were numbered.

The plane proved difficult to kill off. The turbine-powered Turbo Beaver had been developed as a replacement, but the turboprop was expensive and its reliability wasn't up to bush-operator standards. De Havilland continued to build piston Beavers as the orders came in, squeezing in a Turbo Beaver whenever they could, but everyone knew the program was living on borrowed time.

Hawker-Siddeley's marketing know-it-alls studied the situation, and in 1967 they decided the era of the single-engine bushplane was over. Anyone who knew anything about back-country flying knew they were wrong, but the Hawker-Siddeley executives in England didn't. They read the marketing reports and unceremoniously pulled the plug on the Beaver assembly line. A number of de Havilland employees quit in protest but it made no difference. The Beaver was dead.

It wasn't, of course. The factory may have stopped production, but there was another source on the horizon. Some of the Army Beavers being used in Vietnam were approaching twenty years of age. This and the fact that Vietnam was becoming more and more of a helicopter war prompted the Army to begin unloading their fixed-wing fleet. What started as a trickle soon became a flood as hundreds of military Beavers were sold off to other countries or put on the auction block.

Some of the Alaska operators who had dealt with the Air Harbor over the years for planes, parts, and floats had taken notice when Munro, Peters, and Fisk began singing the praises of Six-

Four-Zulu. Pilots and operators who found themselves in Seattle during the off-season went out to Kenmore to experience the Beaver's capabilities for themselves. Almost to a man, they went home determined to add a Beaver to their fleets of Cessna 180s and Piper Super Cubs. The problem was getting one at a reasonable price.

Munro was not so enthralled with flying Six-Six-Zulu that he overlooked the business opportunity taking shape up north. It was the Seabee deal all over again. The Seabee assembly line had run for barely a year before Republic shut it down to gain floor space for jet fighter production, yet the demand for the fat little amphibian had continued for almost a decade. Munro, Tom Wardleigh, and Walt Winseman had become experts at the art of salvaging and rebuilding wrecked or sunk Seabees and selling them for a tidy profit. It was good business then, and Munro couldn't think of any reason why it shouldn't be good business now.

The opportunity to put theory into practice arrived in mid-1972 with an auction notice for twelve surplus Army Beavers. Munro's visit to the Bothell State Bank was followed a few weeks later by a letter announcing that Kenmore had submitted the winning bid. The company was the proud owner of twelve de Havilland Beavers in "varying conditions." They could come pick up their planes anytime… in Singapore.

Twelve airplanes parked in a storage yard more than 8,000 miles away. Even if the war-battered planes been capable of getting off the ground under their own power only a complete idiot would be fool enough to attempt to fly one back across the Pacific. The Air Harbor would have their Beavers shipped home in a box.

Seven boxes, actually. Kenmore would have to send someone to Singapore to figure out how to pack the airplanes for shipping, and Munro knew there was only one "someone" qualified for the job. If Bill Peters could build hangars and railcars, figuring out how to ship a few airplanes ought to be a snap. It wasn't, as it turned out, but Peters approached the job with his usual degree of competence and ingenuity.

"I made some little scale outlines of a Beaver fuselage. Then I drew a shipping container to the same scale as my fuselage cutouts, and I started experimenting to see how I could fit the planes in. I finally figured out I could get two planes in one container if I took off the landing gear. But I still had to be able to roll the planes around, so I designed a real short stub gear that I could bolt on in place of the main gear. Rather than make up twelve sets of these things at Kenmore and then haul them down to Singapore I made up a cardboard pattern. I figured I'd be able to find someone down there who could weld them up for me.

"When I got to Singapore, the surplus yard brought in a man who could weld and I gave him my cardboard pattern. The pattern was for a right-hand stub gear, so I told him to make twelve units just like the pattern. Then I showed him how to bend the cardboard to make a left-hand pattern and told him I needed twelve of those. He came back about a day later and unloaded these things, and they fit perfectly. We're still using them today, in fact."

BILL PETERS

The twelve Beavers had been partly dismantled. All the wings were off, and some of the tails. The surplus yard assigned two local men to help, but while they appeared willing to work they didn't have enough mechanical knowledge between them to drive a nail. Peters had shipped over a few tools, but he hadn't anticipated having to work with people who not only didn't have tools but wouldn't have known how to use them if they'd had them. Fortunately, Peters' two years on the farm in Japan had taught him patience, and he figured it wouldn't take him long to teach his two assistants the basics.

He was wrong. It wasn't that the men were stupid; they were just lazy. Time after time Peters assigned them a task, showed them how to use the tools, and then went off to do something else only to look back and see his assistants doing nothing. Yelling at them did little good; a few minutes of lackluster work was all it produced. This was a lot different than Japan. There, the farmers may not have been familiar with modern methods, but they worked like there was no tomorrow. These guys worked like there was nothing but tomorrow.

But there wasn't. Everything had been pre-arranged with U.S. President Lines, and Peters had given himself two weeks to prepare the planes and pack them in the containers. There was no way he could do it all alone, but he couldn't figure out how to motivate his assistants to help him.

Then the rubber mattresses arrived. He'd asked for padding to use around the airplanes' wings and tails, and the surplus yard had suggested rubber mattresses. When they showed up, Peters' two assistants were dumbstruck. They'd never seen rubber mattresses before. They pulled two off the pile and sat on them. Then they lay on them. They tried every position they could think of on them. The mattresses were the most incredible things they'd ever seen.

Watching them cavort on his padding, Peters suddenly realized he was looking at his labor solution.

"I'll tell you what," he announced to his giggling assistants. "If we get all these planes disassembled and packed in the containers by the end of next week, you can each have one of these mattresses for your own."

That did it. The men leaped to their feet and simultaneously asked what they could do next. For the next week and a half, Peters had never seen two men work so hard or with so much enthusiasm.

A truck showed up with the first container, and it was time to find out if Peters' calculations were correct. The surplus yard had a loader that lifted the fuselages up to where they could be slid into the container. The first Beaver went in nose first and the second one tail first. Then Peters climbed up into the container with them and drilled holes into the floor for tie-downs to hold the fuselages firmly in position.

When the first two fuselages were loaded, he sketched out a design for a sturdy wooden frame that would hold the wings up against the roof of the container. Once the frame was firmly in place, the two wings were slid in and padded with mattresses. When everything was securely fastened, Peters realized there was room for one more wing between the fuselages. This would leave him with only six wings left over, and these would fit easily into the seventh container.

With the experience of loading one container under their belts, the job started to go faster.

When one container was ready to go a truck would come get it and leave an empty one in its place. The yard's loader would drive over whenever Peters had a pair of fuselages ready to load, but when it came time to install the wing frames he and his assistants were on their own. Pushing the fuselages and wing frames into place in the tight, airless confines of shipping container was a backbreaking struggle.

The wooden frame in the seventh container held the remaining six wings, tip tanks, landing gear, and all the other stuff Peters hadn't been able to fit in with the fuselages. When everything was packed to his satisfaction, Peters jumped down, tossed his coveralls into the container, and slammed the doors. He'd worn the coveralls for two weeks, and they'd gotten so saturated with salt they chafed and burned every time they touched his skin. He'd tried washing them once in the tub at the hotel, but the black, greasy ring they'd left had defied every attempt to remove it. Rather than risk the wrath of the housecleaning staff he decided to live with the coveralls the way they were, although the last few days had been agony.

As the last container disappeared down the road toward the docks, Peters presented his assistants with their mattresses. They'd certainly earned them. The wooden wing frames were so well built that when the loader accidentally slammed into a packed container hard enough to knock it out of alignment, nothing so much as budged on the inside. Not only that, but his assistants had worked so fast Peters had beaten his calculated schedule by a day. The last image he had of his airplane crating experience was the sight of his two assistants proudly carting their rubber mattresses away down the dirt road that led to their homes.

Kenmore's seven containers were all loaded on the same ship. It was the Air Harbor's first experience with ocean shipping, and there were several things they failed to find out until it was too late. One was that if a ship sinks, everyone who has cargo on that ship shares the cost of the loss. That's what shipping insurance is for; it covers not only the value of the shipper's cargo but also the shipper's share of the total loss in the event of a sinking. Kenmore assumed that because their cargo was on a U.S. President Lines ship, it was covered by the President Lines' insurance. There didn't seem to be any reason for the Air Harbor to purchase additional insurance, so they didn't.

The ship left Singapore in January. Peters and Munro, who by now had discovered their mistake with the insurance, called the President Lines at least once a day to check on the ship's progress. The first few days were uneventful and the ship stayed right on schedule. But it was winter, and the weather in the northern Pacific was getting worse. Peters and Munro tracked the ship's progress on a map, and as every mile brought it closer and closer to the storm region, the anxiety level at the Air Harbor increased accordingly. The seven containers on that ship represented not only the net worth of the Air Harbor itself, but the balance due on a sizable bank loan as well. If the Beavers went down with the ship, Kenmore Air Harbor would go down right along with them.

The situation went from bad to worse when Peters was informed that the ship had fallen behind schedule. It had run into a severe storm and the captain had elected to slow down. Then came word that the six-hundred-foot ship was in trouble. Sixty-foot seas driven by hundred mile-an-hour winds were breaking over the deck and pile-driving solid water against the sides of the containers.

High in the pilothouse, the terrified crew listened to the tortured shriek of bending metal and the rumble of shifting containers, and they stood by with plywood sheets and power drills in case a wave took the bridge windows out. Down on the main deck, the container tie-down chains were starting to break, but no one on board was fool enough to suggest replacing them. Anyone venturing outside the pilothouse would be almost instantly crushed, if not by a lurching container then by the huge seas cannoning in over the railings.

Within a few hours the ship had become almost impossible to steer. The captain radioed that he was abandoning any attempts to stay on course and was simply going to head into the seas in an effort to keep from rolling over. His decision may have saved the ship, but it sealed the fate of the containers stacked up forward. With each huge wave, the bow plunged down off the crest and into the trough, burying itself in the face of the next wave. Cargo chains and ring-bolts were no match for hundreds of tons of green water. One by one, the forward containers were beaten in on their contents until with a bang and whiz of breaking chains and a screech of twisting metal they pivoted sideways and toppled over the rail. The crew watched them go with mixed emotions. They were losing their cargo, but every container that went over lightened the bow.

Twenty-four hours later the captain radioed that he had resumed course and that as long as nothing else happened, he should be entering Puget Sound in about forty-eight hours. He also asked that a repair crew be standing by.

It was a nerve-racking two days. Finally Kenmore got a call saying the ship would be docking within the hour. Peters and Munro jumped in a car and headed for Seattle. The forward part of the ship was a mess. Many containers had vanished completely while others were hanging over the side, twisted and ripped apart. The few containers that were still in place had been bashed in almost beyond recognition. Many of the aft containers were damaged, too, although none of them had actually fallen off. Even if Kenmore's containers were still on board, the beating would have reduced their contents to scrap.

Peters and Munro strode up and down the dock beside the ship trying to find someone who could tell them where their containers had been loaded. When one person told them he was pretty sure their containers had been up forward, Munro figured it was all over. He was already trying to devise a way to keep the Air Harbor financially afloat when a heavyset man in a brown business suit hurried up to them.

"Are you from Kenmore Air Harbor?" the man asked between gasps for breath. Peters nodded grimly.

"Great," the man continued. "They told me you were here asking about your shipment." He flipped some pages on his clipboard and ran a stubby finger down a list. "You had seven containers, right?"

Peters nodded even more grimly. The use of the word "had" had not escaped him.

"Yes, here we are. Seven." The man flipped some more pages until he was looking at a pink form. "Your containers..." his voice trailed off as he bent his head to study the form intently. "Ah," he said suddenly. "Here we are. Your containers were all loaded aft and down below. They're fine."

He beamed up at Peters. "They'll be unloaded sometime tomorrow." The agent started to rush away but he thought of something and turned around. "You must have gotten your shipment to the dock early in Singapore," he said. "According to this," he tapped the pink form, "your containers were supposed to be loaded up there." He pointed to the wreckage on the forward deck and hurried off, leaving Munro and Peters staring at each other in stunned relief.

THE PLANE THAT MADE KENMORE FAMOUS

18

CLARENCE RADER WAS A CARPENTER by trade. He was also keenly interested in airplanes. The appearance of the seaplane operation at the old shingle mill site in Kenmore intrigued him, so in 1948 when he noticed they were pouring the foundation for a new building he turned off the highway and braved the Air Harbor's muddy, rutted driveway on the chance they might be looking for a professional builder. Yes, owner Bob Munro told him, the Air Harbor needed help but they couldn't pay much. Perhaps Rader would be interested in taking his wages out in flight instruction instead? This was just fine as far as Clarence Rader was concerned, and he worked enough on the Seabee hangar and other projects to get a fair number of hours recorded in his logbook. He never did get his license, but he thoroughly enjoyed his time in the air.

Rader's son Jerry, on the other hand, had little interest in airplanes until after he'd enlisted in the Air Force in the late 1950s. He'd joined to avoid the draft which he was convinced would land him in a ground-pounding Army outfit, but after being trained as a hydraulics technician and assigned to the Strategic Air Command base in Lake Charles, Louisiana, he began to take a real interest in aviation.

But not "heavy iron" aviation. Even though he was working on the most sophisticated machine in the sky, the Boeing B-47 jet bomber, Rader found he was far more interested in the Cessnas and Super Cubs that belonged to the base flying club. He started taking flying lessons and eventually flew the club's Cessna 175 from Lake Charles to Seattle and back to visit the World's Fair in 1962.

When his Air Force tour was over, Rader returned to Seattle and the job he'd had as a telegraph operator for the Great Northern Railroad. It didn't take him long to realize that unless he got some more education, telegraph operator was about as far as he'd ever go. So he said good-bye to the Great Northern and enrolled in the University of Washington. He enjoyed his classes, but he ran out of money after one quarter and had to quit. He didn't want to go back to the railroad, so when he read one day that TWA was hiring specialists for their airplane overhaul facility in Kansas City, he applied for the job. His Air Force experience virtually guaranteed him a position, and he soon found himself working on the airline's Lockheed Constellations and Boeing 707s. He was back in aviation, but it didn't take him long to decide that working on big civilian airplanes was no more satisfying than working on big military airplanes.

> "When you do something with a small plane, you put your personal touch on that plane, and when it goes out the door you see your work take off and fly. When I was working for TWA I had to fill out job cards day after day, and I never did see an airplane fly that I could point to and say, 'Yes, I worked on that particular plane and this is what I did.' That's where the satisfaction is for me, working on small planes. You get to see the results of what you do."
>
> **JERRY RADER**

He also didn't care for the union he was forced to join at TWA. When he was bawled out by a shop steward for going to the bathroom during a mid-morning break ("You go to the bathroom on the company's time, not during one of our breaks.") he decided the sooner his days at TWA came to an end the better.

Knowing his employment opportunities in general aviation would be far greater if he had an Airframe and Powerplant certificate, Rader enrolled at a local aeromechanics school. He didn't have a day off for two years. He spent his weekdays in school and his weeknights and weekends at TWA. It was a grueling schedule but Rader stuck with it and got his license. Then in 1966, at the end of the summer, TWA was hit by a mechanics strike. Faced with the choice of walking the picket line or crossing it, Rader decided it was time to go on vacation. After his nonstop school and work schedule he figured he deserved some.

He drove back to Washington State, through the Cascades, and out to the north end of Lake Washington and Kenmore Air Harbor where his dad had enjoyed working almost twenty years earlier. But Bob Munro was sorry, he just didn't have any openings. Maybe later in the year.

Disappointed but not discouraged, Rader drove on down to Boeing Field where he was offered a job at Washington Aircraft, the region's largest Cessna distributor. Rader returned to TWA and turned in his notice, but he wasn't thrilled with the idea of fighting the traffic to and from Boeing Field every day. The day before he was to report to Washington Aircraft he decided to give Kenmore one more try. Munro remembered Clarence Rader's conscientious attitude and his enthusiasm for flying, and he was impressed with his son's perseverance.

"Okay," he said. "Bring your tools in tomorrow and we'll put you to work."

The timing was perfect. Rader got a job with exactly the kind of company he'd had in mind all along, and Kenmore acquired a mechanic who proved to have a real talent for engineering airplane modifications. Better yet, and as much to his own surprise as anyone else's, Rader soon demonstrated an ability to maneuver Kenmore's airplane modifications through the FAA's rapidly growing paperwork jungle.

Munro and his pilots agreed the Beaver was a fabulous airplane, but as they racked up more and more hours carrying fishermen to the mountains, boaters to the San Juan Islands, and torpedoes to Keyport, it became apparent there was room for improvement. But the program that would eventually add a new name to the aviation lexicon didn't start with anything dramatic like a new, quieter propeller or bigger cabin windows or nicer seats or hundreds of pounds of weight savings. These things came later. The first step in the creation of what would one day be known as a Kenmore Beaver was a simple little square of sheet metal.

Installing floats on an airplane is a lot like putting feathers on the front of an arrow as well as the back. The deep forward sections of the floats add a fair amount of vertical surface ahead of the plane's yaw axis. This isn't a problem if the plane always flies in the direction it's pointed, but planes rarely do. Turbulence and sloppy piloting conspire to make an airplane slew sideways every now and then, sometimes rather severely. It's the vertical tail's job to straighten things out, a job it does very nicely until the plane is put on floats. With all that added vertical surface up front it becomes harder and harder for the tail to do its job. On some airplanes the addition of floats so destabilizes the situation that the plane can become downright dangerous to fly.

The Beaver was one of these planes. When de Havilland increased the gross weight of the DHC-2 soon after it entered production, it soon became apparent that the plane's directional stability on floats wasn't as good as it was when the plane was on wheels or skis. De Havilland's solution was to provide a large, rounded fin that could be mounted under the tail. In other words, they put even bigger feathers on the back of the arrow. This fixed the stability problem, but it wasn't long before pilots began complaining that the seaplane fin made the Beaver hard to taxi in a crosswind, to say nothing of getting in the way at docks and snagging in the brush when the plane was tailed up on shore. Kenmore tried the ventral fin, but when Munro found he couldn't turn Six-Six-Zulu out of the wind in an even moderate breeze, he ordered them removed from the company's planes.

Then the Beaver was certified for use on the larger floats that had been developed for the Turbo Beaver. The big EDO 4930 floats improved the plane's rough water performance, but they made the directional stability problem even worse; the feathers on the front of the arrow had gotten almost as big as the feathers on the back. In Canada, the hated seaplane fin was made a requirement when the plane was mounted on 4930s. South of the border, the Federal Aviation Agency, which had superseded the old CAA in 1958, went one step farther and declared that a float-equipped Beaver had to have auxiliary fins no matter what size floats were fitted to it. While most of the operators who switched to the larger floats grudgingly installed de Havilland's awkward ventral fin, a former Boeing test pilot named Clayton Scott thought there was a better way.

Scott developed a tall, narrow fin that sat on top of the Beaver's horizontal stabilizer. Nicknamed the "shark fin," a pair of them provided the required directional stability without the crosswind handling penalty of the ventral fin. The downside was that they were complicated to build and install. The more Bill Peters looked at them, the more he became convinced Kenmore could do better.

He got together with Jerry Rader, and the two of them drew up a list of what they wanted to accomplish. Crosswind controllability was an absolute must. Munro had made that very clear. Whatever the fin ended up looking like, it shouldn't make the plane difficult to handle in a crosswind. Keeping the fin clear of docks and shoreline brush was another requirement. The fin had to be easy to make and easy to install. And of course, it had to satisfy the FAA's directional stability requirements.

Rader doodled around on a piece of paper for awhile in an attempt to make a ventral fin work, but he soon realized it was a futile effort. Hanging anything below the Beaver's tail would defeat the first two requirements no matter how it was shaped. Scott had put his fins on top of the stabilizer for these very reasons. Frustrated, Rader walked outside to take another look at the back end of one of the company Beavers. As he walked slowly around the tail, he took a closer look at the horizontal stabilizers. Some airplanes, including the Cessna 180, have angled stabilizer ends. But not the Beaver, Rader noticed. The ends of the Beaver's stabilizer align perfectly with the direction of flight.

What if, he wondered, we mount a fin on the end of each stabilizer instead of on top of it as Scott had done? Scott's shark fins had already demonstrated that two smaller fins could do the same job as one big fin, and that mounting them on the stabilizer placed them within the profile of the vertical tail, so there was no additional surface for a crosswind to act against. But mounting a fin on the end of the stabilizer would be a lot easier than attaching one to the top.

Turning back to his pencil and paper, Rader sketched a simple, square fin projecting equally above and below the stabilizer. To make sure the fin wouldn't interfere with docking or beaching maneuvers he drew the lower edge of the fin slightly higher than the bottom of the fuselage.

No one at Kenmore was an aerodynamicist; they figured out how large Rader's seaplane fins should be by cutting a pair out of sheet aluminum, bolting them to an airplane, and trying them out. The first set vibrated badly at cruise speed so they tried a smaller pair. This cured the vibration problem, but now the fins were too small to meet the FAA's stability requirements. It was time to get some outside help.

The Air Harbor had created a number of airplane modifications over the years, from propeller spinners for Seabees to a remarkable 150-horsepower engine conversion for the Piper PA-12 Super Cruiser. In each case, Bob Munro had hired John Edson to do the engineering calculations and confirm that the modifications were structurally sound. Edson worked for Boeing, but his first love was seaplanes, and he was delighted to lend his expertise to the Air Harbor whenever they needed it.

After pondering Rader's seaplane fin design for awhile, he made two modifications he thought would make the fins more effective. He extended the leading edges forward of the stabilizer to add surface area, and he swept the fins back to move the center of pressure aft. The new fins were fitted to one of the Beavers and Peters and Edson took off to test them. Thirty minutes later they came back and proclaimed them a success. Edson then worked up the structural and aerodynamic data proving the fins met all the structural and stability requirements, and the design was submitted to the FAA for approval. The FAA approved, and Kenmore was granted a Supplemental Type Certificate for Rader's fin design.

The STC meant two things: Kenmore could legally fly with Rader's fins on their own Beavers, and they could sell them to anyone else who might want a pair for their own plane. As it turned out, this included almost everybody who had a Beaver. As word of Kenmore's new, low-profile fins spread, the phone began to ring with orders until today almost every Beaver in service around the world sports a pair of Kenmore seaplane fins.

Rader had been with the Air Harbor for five years when the seven container-loads of Beavers from Singapore arrived on the property. They were undamaged on the outside, but it was anybody's guess what might have come loose or broken on the inside during their rough ride across the Pacific. One by one, the containers were opened, and each time the condition of the contents confirmed the wisdom of sending Bill Peters down to do the packing. The dust on the fuselages and wings hadn't even shifted. In fact, Peters' sweat-stained overalls lay right where he'd tossed them inside the door of the seventh container.

The plan was to rebuild all twelve Beavers, keeping some for the Air Harbor's fleet and offering the others for sale. But if anyone thought this was going to be easy, they soon found out otherwise. Most of the engines were worn out and needed rebuilding or replacing. Front-line war duty hadn't done the airframes any favors, either, and there wasn't one of the twelve that didn't need damaged skin panels replaced. Dents and creases weren't the only things that needed fixing; several of the planes sported bullet holes as well.

The Southeast Asian humidity had done almost as much damage as the war. Corroded fasteners and rusty bolts had to be replaced. The interiors were a mess with mildewed fabric and sagging seats. Half the instruments didn't work or were missing altogether. And it was doubtful that any of the new owners would want to retain the peeling, olive drab paint and blacked-out military markings.

Repairing, rebuilding, and repainting the Beavers was only half the battle. From Aeroncas, Bellancas, and Pipers, to Seabees, Norsemen, and Staggerwings, Kenmore had been salvaging and remanufacturing airplanes for almost two decades. But so far, everything that had entered the shop had come in with a civil airworthiness certificate. The twelve Beavers from Singapore were a different matter. They had been built for the military from the outset, and as far as the FAA was concerned, they didn't exist.

Structurally, there were no differences between military Beavers and their civilian counterparts, but the FAA managed to find something they didn't like anyway. The military planes had been built with four square windows in the ceiling above the pilots' seats. This let more light into the cockpit and gave the pilots upward visibility, a handy feature during a steep, twisting approach to a war zone airstrip. The FAA, on the other hand, felt the overhead windows might compromise the structural integrity of the fuselage and required them to be removed.

Reskinning the top of the cockpit to eliminate the windows was no big deal, but the volume of paperwork the government required for a civilian airworthiness certificate was another matter. The number of forms seemed endless. Compared to the paperwork nightmares the company would experience twenty years later with its turboprop conversions, getting the Singapore Beavers certificated for civilian use was child's play, but at the time it seemed an intimidating process.

Paragraph 1.1 in the civilian Beaver's flight manual describes the airplane as "...an all metal, high-wing monoplane, designed to carry a pilot and seven passengers." One passenger sat in the co-pilot's seat up forward while the other six were accommodated on a center bench seat and a full-width sling seat in the rear of the cabin. The seating arrangement in the military Beavers was different. The center bench seat was replaced by a pair of individual seats, and there were hammock seats in the rear of the cabin that could be folded out to accommodate two more passengers.

The twelve Singapore Beavers were all ex-military planes and so carried two less passengers than the civilian Beaver. Bill Peters came up with a design for a three-place center seat that combined the lower frames from the military seats with a custom-made cushion and back frame. A copy of the civilian Beaver's three-place aft sling seat replaced the two folding hammock seats. Years later, when the supply of military seat bases dried up, Peters had John Edson engineer a complete three-place center seat frame the Air Harbor could make from scratch. Kenmore's center seat design was given an STC by the FAA, and is the seat used on all the rebuilds today.

The door, sidewall, and headliner panels of the Singapore Beavers ranged from mildewed and torn to missing altogether. Peters made patterns for all the interior panels and then purchased bolts of hard-wearing carpet and fabric to make new ones.

Eighteen miles away Boeing was cranking out 707s, 727s, and 737s. It's hard to imagine any similarity between the shiny jetliners lined up at the south end of Lake Washington and the battered Beavers being rebuilt at the north end, but there was. Bill Peters had learned that Boeing made their cabin sidewalls and bulkheads by gluing fabric onto precut plastic panels. The completed panels were then screwed or clipped to the interior structure of the fuselage. Peters didn't see any reason why this same technique wouldn't work in a Beaver. He called the company that supplied the plastic panel material to Boeing and ordered a small quantity for Kenmore.

Using his paper patterns, Peters marked and cut out all the sidewall, door, and headliner panels he'd need to complete the interior of a Beaver. Then working with a second-hand, heavy-duty Pfaff sewing machine, he bound the edges of the fabric linings. The last step was to glue the linings to the plastic panels. The end result was a set of handsome interior components that gave the utilitarian Beaver a feeling of luxury and comfort its original designers never would have thought possible.

Although no one at the company consciously made the connection, Kenmore was doing with the Beaver exactly what they'd done with the Seabee almost thirty years earlier. As designed, the Beaver was a fine plane. But Rader, Peters, and Munro were constantly finding ways of making it even better. Like the Seabee improvements, it was a team approach. Someone would have an idea, it would be kicked around for awhile, and then everyone would pitch in to make it happen.

After the seaplane fins and interior, the next thing to catch the eye of the Air Harbor improvement squad was the water rudder system. Like most floatplanes, the Beaver utilizes a pair of retractable water rudders on the float sterns to improve the plane's water handling. As built, the rudders were operated by long cables attached to metal stubs on the underside of the rudder bar in the cockpit. Not only did this arrangement make for sloppy steering control on the water, but the stubs were notorious for breaking off.

> "I looked at other floatplanes that used the tailwheel steering mechanism for water rudder control and thought, 'Why can't we do that on a Beaver?' So we did. We put an arm back there and attached the water rudder cables to it. This transmitted more pivot action to the rudders, and the long cables to the cockpit were eliminated which took a lot of the slop out of the system. The first time we took the plane out, wow, did it ever steer! That Beaver would turn on a dime."
>
> JERRY RADER

Rader then turned his attention to the huge, rail-mounted battery in the back of the cabin. Two massive cables running under the cabin floor connected the battery to the starter up forward. When Rader stacked all the pieces on a scale he found that de Havilland's method of supplying electricity to the starter added almost one hundred pounds to the weight of the plane.

He took some measurements and found that a modern, lightweight battery would fit between the engine and the firewall. While the lightweight battery didn't have the amperage of the monster in the back of the cabin, the R-985's low compression ratio and the extremely short cable run ensured there would be plenty of power for starting. Rader fashioned a battery bracket and secured it to the firewall along with a pair of short, lightweight connecting cables. The airplane's original battery, battery mount, and underfloor cables were pulled out and consigned to the scrap heap.

> "The battery conversion is probably the finest modification you can do to a Beaver because it does so many things for you. It gets rid of a whole bunch of weight, it moves the center of gravity forward, and it doubles the size of the baggage compartment."
>
> JERRY RADER

Having improved half of the airplane's electrical system, Rader figured he might as well improve the other half, so he replaced the R-985's generator with an alternator. This helped compensate for the lower power of the new battery by ensuring it would receive a charge even when the engine was idling at the dock or taxiing slowly on the water.

Beaver passengers are often as distinctive as the airplane itself. Loggers and commercial fishermen show up at the docks with all sorts of strange baggage, from bedrolls to bait buckets. Charter pilots often find themselves trying to stuff two or three hunters and eight or twelve moose quarters into the cabin. Sportfishermen show up for the flight home with gunny sacks full of smelly, dripping salmon. Small wonder that the ambiance in a working Beaver can get pretty rank.

In the course of doing some routine maintenance work on a Beaver float one day, Rader removed the small inspection panels in the top of each watertight compartment. He was peering down into the third compartment from the bow when it dawned on him that he was looking at a fabulous storage space. The third compartment encompasses the deepest part of the float, the section just forward of the step in the bottom of the hull, and Rader figured there was enough room in there for all sorts of stuff. Mooring lines, fenders, fuel cans, jugs of engine oil, tackle boxes, hip waders, moose meat, and stinky bags of fish would fit in the third compartment beautifully. All that was needed was a way to get them in there.

It didn't take him long to design a hinged, watertight hatch that covered most of the top of the compartment. Two quick-release fasteners would hold the hatch closed. The next step was to get the float hatch approved by the FAA. Fortunately, the EDO Corporation was more than happy to assist by providing the necessary engineering data. Taking into account the structural strength of the float and the position of the compartment relative to the airplane's center of gravity, EDO determined that the maximum safe weight that could be carried inside the float was one hundred pounds. With the float manufacturer itself declaring Rader's hatch design to be structurally sound, the FAA had no qualms about awarding Rader's float hatch an STC, and the atmosphere in many working Beavers become noticeably fresher.

The Beaver is a not a small airplane, and it's a bit of climb to get into the cabin. Entering and exiting the cabin is made easier by steps fastened to the float struts. The original steps were nothing more than lengths of steel tubing bolted to the struts. It was a simple solution, and probably looked great on paper. In practice, it was an accident waiting to happen. More than a few rifles, tackle boxes, cameras, fishing rods, and tool boxes clattered off the floats and disappeared with a splash as passengers and pilots alike lost their footing on the smooth round tubes. And in the floatplane's wet environment, particularly a wet, salty environment, the tubing would start to rust the moment it was bolted in place.

After probably slipping one too many times himself on the tubing, Bill Peters came up with the idea of making the steps out of V-bar. The V-bar would be just as strong as the tubing, but it didn't have any hidden inside surfaces to collect salt and moisture. John Edson helped Peters and Rader formalize the design and draw up the engineering data to satisfy the FAA's STC process.

As designed, the Beaver had only two windows on each side of the cabin, one in the pilot's door and one in the main cabin door. After the prototype was flown, a small porthole was added behind the main door to let light into the aft cabin. This was fine for cargo haulers and the Army, neither of whom cared if the cabin had any windows or not. But passengers who ended up in the middle of the back seat of Kenmore's Beavers began complaining loudly about the non-existent view, particularly when everyone else on board was exclaiming over a pod of whales or having contests over who could spot the most bald eagles.

Rader decided a larger window in place of the porthole would be a nice improvement. Cutting a larger hole in the side of the cabin and fitting a new piece of Plexiglas wasn't going to do it, however. The Beaver has a monocoque fuselage, which means the skin of the airplane also provides structural strength. Cutting a bigger hole in the skin would compromise the integrity of the entire fuselage. Not only that, but the ideal position for a larger rear window put it right smack in the middle of one of the fuselage stiffening frames.

Rader, Peters, and Munro studied the inside of one of Kenmore's disassembled Army Beavers and decided that a box-like structure constructed around the new window would carry the loads formerly carried by the stiffening frame. Rader then sketched out a streamlined, rectangular window with rounded corners. He also designed a smooth, fiberglass surround to provide a finished look on the inside where the sidewall panels met the new window frame.

Building the frames and installing the windows was the easy part of the job. Once again, it was the volumes of certification paperwork that proved to be the real chore. But with John Edson's help, Rader stuck with it, and in the end the Kenmore window joined the seaplane fins, the water rudder steering system, the new battery and enlarged baggage compartment, and the V-bar steps in being awarded an STC.

Word of Kenmore's Beaver modifications spread fast, and it wasn't long before orders for battery brackets, strut steps, water rudder steering arms, and rear window kits began pouring in from operators all over the world.

"We ask ourselves what we can do to improve an airplane. We find out from our pilots or our passengers that there's a problem or something could stand improvement, and we look for ways to accomplish that improvement.

"We do everything as simply as possible. We don't aim at putting a modification on a plane that requires a tremendous amount of engineering. All these things we've done are simple. If there is any engineering involved, it's a simple thing to draw up and write a spec for. That's why our Beaver mods have been so successful. You get a substantial improvement to the airplane, but the modifications themselves are relatively inexpensive and easy to install.

"We actually don't look as much at the potential market as you might think. We look at the modification in terms of what it will do to improve our airplanes in our operation. If a market does develop, that's great, but at least we know we have the best airplanes with the best modifications in the business."

JERRY RADER

When Bob Munro, Reg Collins, and Jack Mines trucked their Aeronca Model K out to Gus Newburg's mill site in 1946, the north end of Lake Washington truly could be considered the boondocks. Summer cabins peeked from the woods lining the shore, but larger homes like Dr. Nelson's beside the shingle mill were few and far between. By the 1960s, all that had changed. Neighborhoods flowed over the hills from north Seattle and Lake City and spilled down the slopes toward the lake. One by one the summer cabins were torn down to make room for expensive homes with broad lawns and whitewashed speedboat docks. Lakefront property became *the* status symbol in the greater Seattle area, and what had once been considered too far away now became the preferred place to live.

One thing hadn't changed at the north end of the lake, and that was the noise. The floatplanes based at Kenmore still hammered down the lake and into the air, the yowl of their propellers reverberating off the hills and rattling the picture windows in the expensive new homes. People began to complain. Not a lot of people, but enough to make Munro acutely aware of his position in the neighborhood. Like Lana Kurtzer who was facing the same situation over on Lake Union, it didn't matter that the Air Harbor predated the fancy homes by twenty years. Money and status talks, and they were starting to say they didn't like the racket.

The problem wasn't so much the engines as it was the propellers. Seaplanes need a lot of power to overcome the water's drag. The propellers of many seaplanes are set to a very flat pitch which makes it easier for the engine to spin them at the highest possible speed, which yields the highest power. The limiting factor is tip speed. If the tips of a rotating propeller equal or exceed the speed of sound, the shock wave can tear the blades apart. By juggling the pitch and length of the blades, the manufacturers can create an engine-propeller combination that at takeoff will spin the prop as fast as possible while keeping the tip speed just below the speed of sound. The result is the maximum possible power and the maximum possible noise as the whirling propeller tips approach Mach 1.

As built, the Beaver was equipped with a long, two-bladed propeller made by Hamilton-Standard. It was efficient, but it was incredibly noisy. Substituting a three-bladed propeller with shorter blades would provide several advantages. A three-bladed propeller has a different harmonic pattern, which is a fancy way of saying that less vibration would be transmitted to the airframe and into the posteriors of the passengers. At takeoff power, the tips of the shorter blades would be moving slower and would generate less noise. And the tips of the shorter blades would be higher off the water which would reduce spray erosion. Spray kicked up by the floats and hitting a fast-spinning propeller has the same effect as shot-peening; over time it will erode the leading edge, causing pits which, if they are not dressed out, will grow into cracks that can eventually cause the blade to fail.

Muting the Beaver's takeoff racket was the subject of several informal meetings in Munro's office. He was well aware of the advantages of three-bladed propellers, but so far as anyone knew, there was no approved propeller conversion for the Beaver. It wasn't that the R-985 had never been equipped with a three-bladed propeller; both the Grumman Goose and the Twin Beech used three-bladed props made by Hartzell. But these were twin-engine airplanes, and they used fully-feathering propellers to make them easier to fly on one engine. A single-engine airplane goes in one direction only if the engine quits, and that's down. So instead of a propeller that feathers and stops, single-engine airplanes need a prop that will keep turning after an engine failure, as it might make it easier to get the engine started again.

Not sure how complicated it would be to re-engineer Hartzell's feathering propeller hub to make it suitable for use on a Beaver, Bill Peters decided to start by calling the company. It turned out that making a non-feathering hub for a three-bladed propeller would be extremely easy because Hartzell had already done it. No one at Kenmore ever did find out what airplane had prompted Hartzell to design the hub, but it wasn't the Beaver. The Air Harbor would have to get the propeller and hub certificated for that airplane themselves. Munro approved the purchase of a non-feathering propeller and hub from Hartzell, and Rader began organizing the paperwork he knew he'd need to get FAA approval for its installation on a Beaver.

One of the Beavers in the shop when the new propeller and hub arrived was N616W. Part of Lloyd Roundtree's Alaska Island Air fleet, One-Six-Whiskey had been ferried south from Petersburg for a much-needed overhaul. Half-torn apart already, Roundtree's plane seemed the perfect choice for Kenmore's propeller conversion experiment. The vocal and opinionated Roundtree had been flying in southeast Alaska his whole life, and while he considered Bob Munro a good friend, he wasn't about to overlook a good business opportunity.

"Sure," he said when Munro called him about letting Rader use One-Six-Whiskey, "he can use my plane to get your propeller approval. But I want something in return."

What he wanted was FAA approval to fit One-Six-Whiskey with the same Hartzell propeller used on the Grumman Goose. He wanted this approval because he happened to own a Grumman Goose. Constant-speed propellers are expensive, and if Roundtree could use the same prop on both airplanes, he'd only have to buy one to keep as a spare. Munro promised to get the needed approval.

With Hartzell's help, Rader had little trouble obtaining a Supplemental Type Certificate for the three-bladed propeller. The difference was apparent to the people on shore the first time Munro took One-Six-Whiskey on its first test flight. The plane still made plenty of noise, but the ear-splitting howl that prompted people to run for the phone and complain was gone.

The change inside was just as dramatic. Flying a two-bladed Beaver for five or six hours is an exhausting experience. The unrelenting noise and vibration drain the body of energy, and pilots often find themselves nodding off to sleep during the drive home at the end of the day. Not so with the three-blade. There's still plenty of noise; nine cylinders, a supercharger, and a boxy fuselage don't bore through the air in silence. But the bone-numbing vibration and fatiguing propeller frequencies are gone. Add a pair of earplugs or comfortable radio headsets, and the Beaver becomes a downright pleasant plane to fly.

The Hartzell propeller with its shiny aluminum spinner was added to the growing list of Kenmore modifications, and its reduced noise and low susceptibility to spray erosion made it a popular seller. Rader didn't forget Munro's promise to Lloyd Roundtree, either. It turned out Hartzell had created a non-feathering version of its feathering propeller by inserting a mechanical stop that prevented the blades from twisting to full-feather if the engine quit. Removing the stop would restore the prop's feathering action. Rader got the installation approved by the FAA, and when One-Six-Whiskey headed north in the spring, it sported a propeller than Roundtree could use on either his Beaver or Goose, just as he'd requested.

By the mid-1970s, the Alaska operators' initial resistance to the Beaver had disappeared completely. Beavers were considered required equipment for every seaplane service and resort operator from Ketchikan to Fairbanks. While Beavers with porthole windows and ventral seaplane fins can still be seen in Canada today, virtually every Beaver that went to Alaska had most, if not all, of Kenmore's modifications. In fact, it wasn't long before the very name of the plane had changed. Canadian operators still talked about their de Havilland Beavers, but in Alaska the planes became known as *Kenmore Beavers*.

Kenmore continued to buy surplus Beavers when they came across one they could afford. Then in 1976 came the announcement the U.S. Army had decided to get rid all its remaining Beavers. Any federal, state, county, or city agency who wanted one could buy it for a dollar. The leftovers would be auctioned off to the public. When the dust settled after the feeding frenzy of fish and game departments, parks services, and law enforcement agencies, there were 104 Beavers left.

The Army set a date for the auction, and posted the rules. The planes themselves had been mothballed in foam cocoons; the only thing the bidders had to go on was a list of specifications and conditions. The auction would be a one-day-only affair, and every item would be sold, regardless of price. The auction would be live. Anyone who wanted to bid would have to do so in person, so Munro and Peters packed their bags and headed for Tucson.

The Army had allotted eight hours for the auction. It was over in three. Harold Hansen, the man who'd talked Kenmore into buying its first Beaver, was there, as was a friend of his from Idaho.

"That's a great one, bid on that one," he'd whisper to his friend. Caught up in Hansen's excitement, his friend would wave his paddle until the plane was his.

"This is a good one, too," Hansen would whisper a few minutes later. "Bid on this one." And his friend would add another plane to his growing collection.

He had no idea what he was buying, but Hansen did, and when the dust had settled the man from Idaho owned the twenty best Beavers of the bunch.

Munro didn't have that kind of money. The airplanes circled on the list Peters clutched in his hand were in much worse condition. But by now the Air Harbor had enough experience with the plane to know that they could create a first-class machine out of a Beaver in almost any condition. Walk into Kenmore with a bolt that fell off a Beaver, people were starting to say, and they'll build you a new Beaver around it.

When the auction banged to a stop just before noon, the Air Harbor owned ten of the twelve Beavers they'd circled on their list. Munro volunteered to fly the first one home after it had been checked out, but it turned out to be a less than enjoyable trip. The Beavers had been sitting in the desert long enough to become home to all sorts of bugs, and as Munro coaxed the clattering plane north he watched an unending parade of spiders and other multi-legged creatures meander across the windscreen and in and out of the gaping holes in the instrument panel.

From watching the very real spiders crawling around in front of him it didn't take much to imagine scorpions creeping up behind him. Munro began to think an engine failure might be a good idea. While a forced landing might bang up the plane a bit, it would at least give him a chance to escape before something nasty fell out of the headliner and bit him. The remaining nine airplanes came home on a truck.

The demand for rebuilt Beavers continued unabated. Even though it takes about 3,500 man-hours to bring a worn-out airplane up to Kenmore standards, it wasn't long before the row of surplus hulks in the tie-down area was almost depleted. Acquiring Beavers in ones and twos was better than nothing, but what Munro really wanted was another windfall like the twelve from Singapore and the ten from Arizona.

He got his chance two years later, in 1978. A Canadian company had obtained twelve surplus Beavers in Germany and had them shipped to Quebec. By now, Kenmore's reputation as a Beaver-rebuilder had spread coast-to-coast, so the company contacted Munro and asked him if he'd be interested in buying their twelve planes. This time there was no question of them being flown back. Kenmore had acquired its own tractor-trailer and they had their own long-haul driver, parts department manager Tal Taylor.

> "The Beavers were all sitting there in a yard. We had to tear all twelve of them down. We had a height limit of thirteen feet six inches. Bill made stands for the engines and fuselages. Then we tore down the first four airplanes and started loading. We hung engines off the side of the tractor on the frame. We put the wings across the top of the cab. We put all four fuselages on the trailer. Then we just started stuffing things. The stabilizers, landing gear, propellers, we put them wherever they would fit. When we were done, we were exactly half an inch below the height limit."
>
> **TAL TAYLOR**

Three round trips later, and the twelve Quebec Beavers were safely stored in Kenmore's tie-down area ready for rebuilding.

Five years after the Beaver auction in Arizona, Harold Hansen's friend over in Idaho was fed up with de Havilland Beavers. By 1981 he'd overhauled and sold only eight of the twenty airplanes he'd successfully bid on, and he'd had enough. He called Munro and offered to sell the remaining twelve for what he'd paid at the auction. It was too good an offer to pass up. Not only were the company's finances in better shape, but the accelerating demand for Beavers was driving their prices ever higher. Even if Munro had to get a loan from the bank, the twelve Idaho Beavers would pay for themselves and then some in the years to come.

Unlike the wheezing, bug-infested airplane Munro had flown home after the auction, the twenty Idaho planes had been in reasonably good condition. In fact, all of them had been flown to Lewiston with no problems. Five years spent sitting in a field hadn't done them any good, but Munro figured if they'd been sound enough to fly all the way from Arizona to Lewiston under their own steam, they ought to be able to make it across Washington state to Seattle. Tal Taylor and his sixty-foot semi wouldn't be needed this time.

In 1971, ten years before the Beaver sell-off in Lewiston, a new name had started appearing on the pages of the Kenmore pay book. As a boy growing up near Spokane, Washington, Bill Whitney had been fascinated by airplanes. He was still in high school when he decided that hanging around the local airport and watching planes from the ground wasn't enough. He scraped up enough money to start taking lessons in an old Aeronca Champ, and earned his Private certificate in 1965. He followed that up with a Commercial certificate, and then it was off to Moses Lake and Big Bend Community College where Whitney had heard they'd started a flying program.

Moses Lake was nothing to write home about. In the summer it was hot, dusty, and flat. It was different in the winter, when it was cold, dusty, and flat, except when it was snowing, which kept the

The Kenmore float transporter. The truck could carry up to nineteen pairs of floats or four disassembled Beavers. (photo by Bill Peters)

dust down. True to its tradition of never locating a base anywhere that was actually nice, the Air Force took one look at the bleak and barren ground surrounding Moses Lake and decided it was the perfect place for the Strategic Air Command. They rolled a pair of huge, intersecting runways across the prairie, built some hangars and barracks, and assigned a hapless group of bomber crews to live there.

While Moses Lake was, and still is by some accounts, a questionable place to live, it's a wonderful place to fly. Free from the fog and drizzling overcast that can keep pilots ground-bound for days west of the Cascades, central Washington enjoys ideal flying conditions most of the year. Pilots like Bill Whitney are not the only ones to benefit from Moses Lake's featureless landscape and drizzle-free weather. The Air Force left years ago, but when they moved out The Boeing Company and Japan Airlines moved in.

Boeing uses the base for testing everything from commercial jetliners to experimental un-manned observation aircraft. Japan Airlines, on the other hand, soon discovered that it was far cheaper to train 747 crews in the United States than it was in Japan with its high fuel costs and jam-packed airspace. Day in and day out at least one JAL 747 can be seen droning endlessly around the Moses Lake traffic pattern as the company's pilots take turns shooting landings.

The only thing that's ever been able to stop the JAL merry-go-round is Mt. St. Helens. When the dormant volcano blew its top on May 18, 1980, most of eastern Washington was ankle-deep in gray, abrasive ash within hours. A volcano's silicon-based ash can reduce a turbofan engine to junk in a matter of seconds, so as the boiling gray cloud advanced on Moses Lake, Boeing and JAL scrambled to move their equipment to safety. For a while it was thought the airport was doomed to permanent abandonment, but within a year the ash had dispersed or been absorbed into the soil, so the jet jockeys came back.

After earning his Instrument and Flight Instructor ratings at Big Bend, Whitney flew for a couple of small companies in Montana, Idaho, and eastern Washington before deciding to join the Air Force Reserve. It was while he was working as an electronics technician at McChord Air Force Base south of Tacoma that he decided it would be fun to add a seaplane rating to his growing list of aviation accomplishments. Someone told him about Kenmore Air Harbor, so he drove north one day to check it out. He liked what he saw, and signed up for lessons on the spot.

Adding a seaplane rating to an existing Private or Commercial certificate usually requires about ten hours of instruction. Given the constantly changing wind and water challenges facing seaplane pilots, a rating earned after only eight to ten hours of instruction simply means that the holder is now qualified to sink or severely damage a seaplane on their own. But Whitney showed a real aptitude for dealing with the inconsistent world of seaplane flying, a talent that did not go unnoticed by Bob Munro. When Bill Fisk recommended hiring a part-time flight instructor to help out during the busy summer season, Whitney was the obvious first choice.

What started out as a summer job eventually became a full-time position. When it was time to go collect the surplus Beavers from Idaho in 1981, Whitney was one of the pilots picked to help fly them back.

"We sent three mechanics over there and they spent about a week working on them, and then we went over and flew them back. Damage-wise and corrosion-wise the planes were beautiful, but the paint wasn't any good, the interiors weren't any good, and the instruments weren't any good. I don't think we'd ever run an ex-military engine that had sat in storage for so long, but they only had to run for about three or four hours. The guys who went over ahead of us cleaned the oil and fuel screens and changed the oil and pulled all the dead birds out from under the cowl. Whatever it took to get them to run for a few hours. I don't think the planes even had batteries in them. We propped them by hand, and then we ran them up to see if the mags worked. We figured that if they worked then they'd probably keep working for another three hours or so."

BILL WHITNEY

Pilots Whitney, Bob Munro, Bill Fisk, and ex-Alaska bush pilot Bill Lund made three round trips each to Idaho to ferry the Beavers to Harvey Field, a private airport a few miles north of Kenmore near the town of Snohomish. The fence-sitters at Harvey probably thought the Kenmore people were nuts when they heard that Munro's intention was to move the planes to the Air Harbor under their own power.

"How are they gonna land a bunch of wheelplanes at a seaplane base?" was the question most often voiced by the Harvey Field regulars as they wandered between the rows of ragged Beavers. "What're they gonna do, land 'em in the parking lot? If it was me, I'd take these suckers apart right here and truck 'em down."

But the Harvey Field pilots hadn't watched Munro and Fisk work planes in and out of tiny lakes and on and off glaciers. Nor had they been in Alaska before the war when Bill Lund was plunking down huge, ponderous Bellancas onto gravel bars and beaches. The newest guy on the team was Bill Whitney, and while he didn't have the bush experience of the other three, he'd landed on his share of small strips in Idaho and Montana.

All they needed was a flat space long enough to get a Beaver down and stopped, and this they had across the channel from the Air Harbor. While the Air Harbor and the cement plant had grown up on the west side of the narrow channel that had been dug years earlier between the lake and the railroad tracks, nothing much had happened over on the east side. But broad, flat pieces of ground were rare along the shore of Lake Washington, and the area had eventually been taken over by a barge company that specialized in shipping equipment and vehicles to the oil fields in Alaska. When they were getting ready to load the barges, the lot was jammed with containers of machinery, trucks, and even mobile homes. At other times it was totally empty. Munro talked to the owners of the barge company and received permission to use it as a landing strip whenever there was enough open space to do so.

"Sometimes it was just like a strip with all kinds of equipment parked along each side. You landed right down the middle. Other times the whole area was open. We'd call them up and find out when the area was available and we'd schedule our flights for those times. There's a bridge over the Samamish Slough at the east end of the lot. You could land either way, toward the lake or toward the bridge. It wasn't too rough a surface, but the surface wasn't as much a concern as how much of it would be available. At most, you might have a thousand feet, but lots of times it was less. The barge company didn't maintain it as a runway. It was just an area we could use when they didn't have a bunch of equipment parked on it."

BILL WHITNEY

Kenmore's mechanics went over the twelve Beavers again at Harvey Field to make sure nothing had come loose or broken during the flight from Idaho. They paid particular attention to the brakes. Harvey had a long enough runway for even bad brakes to do their job, but a brake failure at the shipping yard would destroy the airplane.

One by one, the tired radials were coaxed into life and the Beavers were taxied to the far end of Harvey Field's narrow strip. As the onlookers leaning against the T-hangars made bets on each plane's chances of getting into the air, the pilot would ease the throttle forward and accelerate down the centerline of Harvey's bumpy runway. Light and with minimum fuel, each Beaver lifted into the air almost immediately, much to the disappointment of the bettors over by the hangars. Fifteen minutes later the plane was down at Kenmore, the pilot gagging on the cloud of dust that swirled around the cockpit and drifted slowly off between the stacks of barge freight. Each plane was parked off to the side of the landing zone and the pilot was whisked back to Harvey by car to do it again.

The last Beavers thumped down on the freight lot to find the police waiting. A nearby resident, after watching an olive drab plane rumble over her house for the seventh or eighth time, had called the Kenmore police to complain that someone kept buzzing her home. The cops drove out, saw the offending plane making yet another pass, and headed for the lakeside. They got there just as the plane was being pushed into a lineup of nine identical suspects. Bob Munro explained the situation, that it hadn't been one airplane continuously buzzing the area, but a bunch of similar airplanes making their landing approaches to the field. The police watched as the last two Beavers curved in over the trees and dropped down into the freight yard. The whole operation looked unnatural to them, so they called the FAA.

"As far as we're concerned, anyone can land a plane wherever they want," the FAA said, "as long as they don't violate any Federal Aviation Regulations."

The police refused to believe they couldn't charge the Kenmore pilots with something. "Don't they have to have some sort of permission or paperwork to do what they're doing?"

"If the planes don't have airworthiness certificates, the pilots have to have ferry permits to fly them. The permits will be very specific as to what the pilots can do with the airplanes."

Greatly encouraged, the officers hurried over to where the pilots and mechanics were pushing the last plane into line and demanded to see the ferry permits. Much to their disappointment, the pilots produced them.

The planes still had to be moved around the head of the channel past the cement plant to the Air Harbor. A two-lane road runs along the lake below the bluff, but it's lined with utility poles

A surplus Beaver undergoing a rebuild. The Rader Rectangle has already been installed in place of the plane's original porthole window (photo by C. Marin Faure)

and fences. Someone suggested that since the Beaver carried its fuel in its belly, why not take off the wings and taxi the planes around on the road under their own power. It made sense at the time, so the shop mechanics lugged their tools over to the barge lot and removed the wings from the first plane. History has not recorded who actually drove the plane down the road to the Air Harbor, but based on his propensity for doing bizarre things, Bill Fisk is the most likely candidate.

The road is pretty narrow so it's possible the spectre of a collision between the front end of a running Beaver and a car made Munro nervous. In any event, none of the other Beavers finished its journey from Idaho under its own power. A sling was rigged from one of the forklifts, and the remaining eleven Beavers were carried down the road one at a time, suspended under the raised forks with mechanics guiding the wings and tail around the fences and phone poles.

The twelve Idaho Beavers made up the last big windfall of surplus airplanes the company would experience. Bill Peters continued to roam the world, shipping home three airplanes from Austria, two from England, and one from Australia. The company bought a big collection of Beaver parts in Thailand; the political red tape and 110-degree heat made Peters wish he was back in Singapore shoving Beavers into containers. But even though Beavers don't come in olive-drab twelve-packs anymore, the Air Harbor continues to pick them up whenever they can. Today, they are mostly worn out commercial airplanes or wrecks. One thing hasn't changed, though. You can still walk into the office with a bolt that fell off a Beaver, and the company can put a new airplane together around it.

A lot of mechanics have contributed to the Beaver Rebuild Program, as it came to be called. Steve Wenberg and Rick Erickson worked on the first overhauls. They were soon joined by Richard

"Ollie" Oliver. There have been others, as well, but the two that have been with it the longest are Gordon Barnes and Greg Gay. Barnes got his start in aviation as an aircraft electrician in the U.S. Coast Guard, working on HH-52 helicopters and HU-16E Albatross amphibians. His search for a civilian aviation job after his Coast Guard experience led him to a placement agency in Lake Forest Park. They recommended he try "the flying company" just up the road in Kenmore, and in April 1971, Munro took him on full time.

Gay had opted for the Navy where he ultimately became an aviation structural mechanic working on F-4J Phantom fighters. Not long after his discharge, he heard someone say Kenmore Air Harbor had just acquired a pile of old Beavers and they might need some help rebuilding them. Gay drove out to the Air Harbor and Munro hired him on the spot.

With orders from commercial operators piling up, Ollie, Barnes, and Gay began pulling apart the first of the Idaho Beavers. Kenmore had been rebuilding planes from the day Collins and Munro had started work on the Aeronca K back in 1944, so the Beaver Rebuild Program represented more of an evolution than a revolution. The basic process the Air Harbor mechanics developed for rebuilding the first one is still in use today.

> "We disassemble the plane completely, take everything out until all we're left with is the basic fuselage shell. We strip the paint and primer and dirt off everything and clean every single part. Then we overhaul all the components, and believe me there are a lot of them. The fuel system, the hydraulic flap system, the flight controls, the electrical system, the instruments, you name it, it gets overhauled or replaced.
>
> "While the airplane's apart we make whatever modifications the customer ordered, put in the larger back window, move the battery up forward, stuff like that. If there's a damaged skin panel we either cut out the damaged part and rivet a patch over the hole, or we replace the entire panel with a new one we make in the sheet metal shop. The commercial operators who used to buy most of our Beavers were perfectly happy with patches because they were a lot less expensive to make. The wealthy businessmen and celebrities who buy our Beavers today usually want the entire panel replaced because it looks better.
>
> "Then everything that needs painting before it's put back in gets painted or corrosion-proofed. Then we put the plane back together and paint it. It all sounds pretty simple when you describe it this way but it takes 3,500 man-hours or more to turn out an airplane with the kind of quality we want in it."
>
> **GORDON BARNES**

Restoring the existing interiors would have been a waste of time; not only would it have required a tremendous amount of work, but a fully-restored military interior wouldn't have been that much nicer than a ruined one. Bill Peters had crafted the interiors for Kenmore's first Beavers, and he continued building interior components for the Singapore Beavers. But he couldn't do everything.

He was busy enough as it was with flying and maintaining the company's facilities and equipment. Fortunately for Kenmore and its customers, Peters' daughter Susan proved even more adept at working with fabrics that her father.

It started out as a part-time job in 1974, something to earn her a little money during the summer before she went to college. Sitting at the big Pfaff machine, Susan sewed together the patterns her father cut out. She'd discovered she enjoyed sewing while she was in high school, and while the heavy fabric airplane panels and seat covers Peters had her putting together weren't exactly high fashion, they presented their own challenges.

When she graduated four years later from the University of Washington with a degree in textiles, she could have gone in any number of directions. But she was intrigued with the idea of using her knowledge of fabrics to create even better looking and harder wearing interiors that her father had been turning out. When she inquired about the possibility of working full-time at the Air Harbor, Munro was delighted to put her on.

Almost all the Beavers Kenmore was turning out were headed for a working life. The buyers were commercial operators and lodge owners, and their planes would have to earn their keep hauling fishermen and loggers and hunters and freight. The Beaver's days as a rich man's toy were years in the future. What Susan wanted were fabrics that would stand up under muddy boots and dirty oil barrels and still look good enough to make a favorable impression on passengers.

"Function has a big effect on the design of an airplane interior. We use a lot of different fabrics: polyester, nylon, wool, cotton, whatever has proved to work best for each application. We have carpet down low on the sidewall panels, for example, and we've found that a dark, non-loop carpet works best. Up in Alaska, having a dark color on the bottom of the panel has really worked well because they haul so much cargo. I went to a non-looped carpet because if you snag looped carpet on the side of a crate or something you get a big run. After you do that a few times it looks like heck.

"A non-looped carpet is cut pile, kind of like shag but much shorter. There are no loops to catch on people's boots or boxes of freight, so it stays looking decent a lot longer. That's real important to commercial operators because their passengers want to ride in a nice-looking plane but the owners can't afford to be replacing their interiors all the time. But when there's more duct tape than fabric inside the plane they usually start thinking about a new interior."

SUSAN PETERS

Cutting out patterns and sewing fabric is not something you want to do on the floor of a hangar, so Bill Peters fixed up a room on the second floor of the main building. On the plus side, Susan had her own workspace that she could arrange however she saw fit. The downside was there weren't any windows. Not only did this make for a somewhat gloomy atmosphere, but the hot air from the offices down below and the hangar next door had no way to get out. Add the heat radiating down from the tar-covered roof a few feet overhead and it wasn't uncommon for the temperature in the interior shop to reach one hundred and ten degrees during the summer. Susan put up with it for awhile and then she persuaded someone to take a saw to the wall and put in a window.

Making the seats, headliners, sidewall panels, and baggage compartment liners was only half the job. Susan had to install them, too. This meant drilling holes in the proper places and coaxing sometimes reluctant fasteners into position. It meant learning to be a contortionist as she maneuvered the panels and headliners in through the doors and fitted them into place. It meant learning how to work with air tools and torque wrenches. It meant getting used to working in wet pants and shoes on rainy days as she reached into the cabin to install sidewalls and baggage compartments. She still remembers the way she felt when she finished making and installing her first Beaver interior.

> "Girls don't have to turn screws and bolts when they're in high school. They aren't working on their cars. So I felt I'd really accomplished something when I could do all that and not have to ask for help when something didn't want to fit right. Sometimes the baggage compartments don't want to pop in, and you have to know a lot of little tricks to get them to slip into place. The day I realized I could take my car apart and pull the whole interior out, change it, and put it back in again, that really meant something to me."
>
> **SUSAN PETERS**

While the mechanics were rebuilding and modifying the fuselages and Susan was fabricating the interiors, the engines were undergoing a complete overhaul. Walt Winseman may have been brilliant when he worked on Franklins, but he was an absolute genius when it came to radials. As he took them apart on his bench, a sort of sixth sense seemed to tell him immediately which cylinders had microscopic cracks and which crankshafts had worn down past the point of no return. Naturally, he backed up his instincts with more scientific methods like magnafluxing and dye penetration, but time after time the tests merely confirmed what he'd known already.

But nobody's perfect. Winseman's sensitivity to steel and aluminum didn't always extend to his fellow employees. By 1960 there was enough engine work to keep two or three mechanics busy full time, but Winseman couldn't keep an assistant. Young mechanics would apply for the job and be hired, but within weeks the position would be vacant again. Winseman had extremely high standards, which was fine, but he also had little tolerance for people who's mechanical ability was less than his own.

> "I just loved doing all the engine work. I'd run them up, take them out of the plane, disassemble them, clean them, overhaul them, inspect them, reassemble them, put them back in, and run them up again, all by myself. I was a one-man operation for years. Finally I started getting help. I didn't like the idea of somebody else tearing the engines down, though, because

when I tore them down I could see what the problems were. When somebody else tears them down for you, you can't see firsthand what's wrong. I didn't like that at all, but it had to be done because we were getting too busy for me to do it all by myself.

"So we started hiring trainees. I had a couple that I practically threw out of the shop. I had one guy, he was two weeks with me and he said, 'Well, when do I get to put them together and sign them off?' He wanted to do it all right then. I don't think he even had a license, or maybe he had a license but had never worked on engines. Anyway, I let him put a couple together but both engines were messed up, so I kicked him out the door. I don't have much patience. Finally I got Gordy."

WALT WINSEMAN

Gordon Holbrook had been intrigued by engines from day one. When he was three, his parents moved north from Seattle to Edmonds, the small waterfront town that steps neatly up the hill from the ferry terminal and the main line of what was then the Great Northern Railway. By the time Holbrook entered high school in 1969, his love of mechanical things in general and engines in particular was well established. He became a fixture in his school's auto shop, and graduated with the intention of entering the automotive program at Everett Community College. The college accepted him, and then informed him that the waiting list for their highly acclaimed auto program was so long he wouldn't have a chance of getting in for at least two years. This wasn't what Holbrook wanted to hear. Thinking fast, the college advisor came up with an alternative.

"If you like airplanes, we can put you in the two-year Airframe and Powerplant program right away."

Holbrook said he'd think about it, and went home with the literature on the A&P course. If the brochures were to be believed, he'd be learning lots of interesting things about engines, things he wouldn't have been exposed to in the automotive program. His reluctance to sign up faded as he read more about the A&P course, and it went away altogether when he discussed the situation with his parents. They listened patiently, and then gave him a simple choice: go to college or get a full-time job. Holbrook chose college.

Two years later he had his A&P license. He'd started with the intention of enrolling in the automotive course after he got his A&P, but he was getting tired of classrooms. He decided to take his new license and see if he could earn a living with it. It proved to be a disappointing search. A friendship with three brothers who sold mobile homes got him a job installing awnings and aluminum skirting with the understanding that he could quit without advance notice if an aviation job came up.

Holbrook was beginning to regret his decision to get into aviation when he got a telephone call from the college. An overhaul shop called Precision Airmotive was looking for someone to do magnaflux and zyglow testing on the radial engines they were rebuilding. The college offered to give Holbrook a day of refresher training after which he could go to work for Precision. The rebuild company was agreeable so Holbrook spent that Friday in school and reported to work the following Monday. He'd broken into aviation at last.

> "This was in 1974, and I worked for Precision for three and a half months. Then in December the gas crisis hit. A lot of Precision's business was rebuilding engines for the car-part haulers out of Detroit. These guys were flying DC-4s, DC-6s, and some converted WWII bombers. When the gas crunch and recession hit, the demand for car-part haulers dropped off fast, which meant Precision's business dropped off fast. They called six of us from the engine teardown department into the office and told us they had to lay us off. So I went back to installing awnings and skirtings on mobile homes again."
>
> **GORDON HOLBROOK**

Holbrook spent the first few months of 1975 wandering from airport to airport on his days off in search of a job but there weren't any. It was April, after yet another fruitless visit to Boeing Field, that he remembered Kenmore Air Harbor. His A & P class had visited the place during a field trip, but he'd soon forgotten about the little seaplane base at the north end of the lake. Figuring that anything was better than working on mobile homes, Holbrook turned his car toward Kenmore to see if the Air Harbor might need an extra mechanic.

It was a lucky turn. The mechanic who'd been doing all of Kenmore's magnaflux and zyglow work had resigned to work for a building contractor. He'd agreed to work at Kenmore in the evenings if they had a part that needed testing, but it was an inefficient arrangement that often held up progress on a customer's airplane. The situation was becoming increasingly frustrating to Jerry Rader and Norm Raddick, the shop foreman, but they didn't see any solution until Holbrook walked through the door with three and a half month's experience doing magnaflux and zyglow work. They hired him on the spot.

There wasn't enough testing to keep Holbrook busy all day, so Rader and Raddick decided he could help out with engine teardown and cleaning. This sounded fine to Holbrook as he preferred doing a bunch of jobs instead of being stuck with only one. On the other hand, he'd never met Walt Winseman.

"Do you like to hunt and fish?" Raddick asked after describing what he expected from Holbrook out in the engine shop.

"No, not really," Holbrook replied.

"Too bad," Rader murmured. "It'd work to your advantage if you did."

"Why's that?" Holbrook asked.

"Oh, no reason," Raddick answered quickly. He didn't want to scare their new magnaflux expert off the premises before he'd even started work. "Come one, I'll introduce you to our engine guy."

"I ain't a teacher," Winseman barked at Holbrook as soon as Raddick was out of earshot, "and I don't like people pesking me to do stuff they don't know how to do. The bosses want you to tear down engines, fine, you can tear down engines. But you ain't gonna put 'em back together again, so don't ask."

Holbrook shrugged. "That's okay by me."

"We'll see." Winseman led Holbrook over to a stand supporting a filthy Pratt & Whitney Wasp Jr. "Think you can take this apart?"

Holbrook looked at the grimy blob on the stand and nodded. Compared to the huge, twin-row radials he'd helped tear down at Precision Airmotive, the R-985 was a toy, although he was careful not to say so.

"Okay," growled Winseman. "Throw all the hardware in a can. When the can's full, clean all the stuff in it and dump it in that box." Winseman pointed to a large wooden crate on casters.

Holbrook did as he was told, although he was perplexed at Winseman's order to dump everything in the wooden box. There are dozens of different bolt sizes in a radial engine, some almost identical. How could Winseman possibly know where everything went after the parts were all jumbled up together?

> "At first I thought Walt was crazy for mixing everything up but over time I learned that after you've taken apart a lot of engines, if you've paid attention to what you take out and where it came from, pretty soon you can dump a box of bolts onto the bench and you'll know where each one goes. Or in the case of a 985, that a screw can go here, here, or here. There may be a half-dozen places where a particular screw can go, and you can name every one of them."
>
> **GORDON HOLBROOK**

Much to everyone's amazement, Holbrook and Winseman got along fine. Holbrook was never in a rush to do anything beyond what Winseman told him to do, and he didn't push his temperamental boss to teach him things Winseman didn't think he was ready to learn. The engine shop was small, which meant they worked side by side. Tearing down an engine doesn't take the same degree of concentration as building it back up, so Holbrook had plenty of opportunities to observe as Winseman carefully reassembled a radial engine for a Beaver or a horizontally-opposed engine for a Cessna.

Not long after Holbrook was hired, the engine shop was moved across the property to the Butler building which had finally shed itself of the last vestiges of Kenmore Marina. Maybe it was the joy of actually having enough room to work or maybe he genuinely felt his young assistant was up to the task, but regardless of the reason, Winseman decided it was time Holbrook began putting engines back together. The first ones were flat engines, Continentals and Lycomings. Winseman kept a close eye on the proceedings, pointing out tricks of the trade when the part Holbrook was struggling to install refused to slip into place. But between learning from his own mistakes and Winseman's advice, it wasn't long before Holbrook was almost as good at engine re-assembly as his boss.

Like the Beaver itself, the Pratt & Whitney R-985 had long been out of production when Holbrook showed up on the Air Harbor's doorstep in search of a job. But thousands of the engines had been manufactured between 1929 and the end of WWII and used in a variety of airplanes from the Grumman Goose and Twin Beech to the infamous Gee Bee R-2 racer. Between the vast numbers of airplanes equipped with the Wasp Jr. and the hundreds of zero-time spares languishing in crates, the supply of R-985s was ensured well into the next century. And while complete engines were no longer being made, most of its critical parts were. Valves, valve seats, and piston rings could be purchased new, as could many of the bearings and bushings used throughout the engine. Cylinders could be chromed back up to tolerance as could all the bearing surfaces.

In fact, just about everything in the engine could be replaced or rebuilt except the crankshaft. Wear on the crank splines and bearing surfaces could be chromed back into tolerance, but if the crank was cracked or had been bent by a propeller strike, the engine was good only for parts.

If there is one thing that will arouse the ire of an engine mechanic it is the sound of a backfire. Radial engines can be tricky to start, particularly when they're cold. Every pilot has his own technique to get a cold engine going, but the fact that every engine is unique pretty much ensures that most pilots will get a backfire at least once in their careers.

The R-985 has a mechanical supercharger which uses a crankshaft-driven impeller spinning at high speed to compress the air going to the carburetor. As the engine starts to turn, the impeller begins to rotate fast. If the pilot mis-manages the throttle and gets a backfire, the engine momentarily kicks backwards. This puts a tremendous shock on the spinning impeller, which is forced to instantly reverse direction. It only takes a few backfires to damage the impeller bearings and ruin the oil seal.

Holbrook, having a fairly even temper, merely cringes when he hears the fat bang characteristic of a radial backfire. Winseman, on the other hand, was not above running out of the shop and yelling at the departing airplane. Bob Munro, who was every bit as aware as his mechanics of the damaging effects of a backfire, simply stood up from his desk and glared out the window at the offending pilot, a condemnation far more effective than anything he could have said.

The engines leaving Winseman's shop bore little resemblance to the black, oily lumps that went in. Shiny gray engine cases, stainless steel pushrod tubes, and gleaming silver cylinders combined to form a mechanical sculpture worthy of display in an art museum. For someone who insisted he wasn't a teacher, Winseman taught his assistant well. The flat engines and radials Gordon Holbrook puts together today are every bit as reliable and immaculate as the engines his old boss used to turn out.

> "I learned a lot from just observing and watching him. There were times when he and I would be working in the same room and we'd say hi in the morning and then we'd each get off in our little corner and concentrate on what we were doing. We'd hardly talk to each other all day. There were other times when something would come up during a break and we might stand there for forty-five minutes talking about engines or fishing trips or something. Those conversations are where I learned a lot from him."
>
> **GORDON HOLBROOK**

The Butler building was a vast improvement over the old engine shop in every way but one. Climate control inside the metal building was chancy at best thanks to an old-fashioned oil heater that refused to work most of the time. The combination of freezing weather outside and ice-cold tools and engine parts inside made for pretty miserable working conditions. On those occasions when the combined abilities of the two mechanics failed to fire up the heater, Holbrook was sent over to the office to complain to the management. Management's solution was to send someone over from the main shop to bang on the heater's innards until it started or until Winseman got tired of the noise and ordered the man out of the building.

Finally, on a particularly cold day when he couldn't even feel the tools he was trying to work with, Winseman's patience ran out. Trailing clouds of angry breath behind him, he strode across the ice-covered parking area to the warm, toasty office where Bill Peters sat in his shirtsleeves working on a stack of paperwork. Without a word Winseman walked up behind the Air Harbor's facilities manager and shoved his frozen hands down the back of his shirt. Peters let out a shriek and leapt out of his chair, his papers flying in all directions.

"How'd you like to work in a shop that cold?" Winseman asked flatly. "We're tryin' to overhaul engines out there and we can't even feel our fingers."

Peters ordered a new heater for the engine shop the next day. He ordered an air conditioner, too, just to be on the safe side.

Winseman likes to tell people the only reason he showed up for work all those years was to pay for his fishing trips. There's no question he enjoys his time on the rivers; the world-record steelhead he caught in 1959 still adorns the Air Harbor's office. But on the river or in the shop, Winseman has a sense of ethics and responsibility that's become all-too rare these days.

> "I had a C-4 Renault, one of those French cars with the engine in the back. We had a big, heavy boom pole supported by a couple of guywires that we used for putting engines in airplanes. One day something hit one of the guywires and the pole fell over. My little car was parked right there and it got flattened. It looked like a stepped-on pop can. I had just bought a newer C-4 to use for parts in the one that got squashed. So instead I put parts from the squashed one into the newer one. I never said nothing. I just lost the car and that was that. Nowadays, you'd sue everyone in the country."
>
> **WALT WINSEMAN**

When Kenmore began improving and then rebuilding Beavers, the customers were all commercial operators. Outfits like Alaska Island Air, Ketchum Flying Service, and Ward Air quickly realized that a Beaver, especially one of Kenmore's Beavers, was a real money-maker. Rugged and reliable, a Kenmore Beaver soon became required equipment for anyone wanting to start a flying service or open a fishing lodge in Alaska.

Then in the 1980s, the nature of Kenmore's Beaver customers began to change. Where the plane had once been viewed simply as an airborne pickup truck for ferrying people, mail, and supplies to logging camps, fish canneries, or sportsman's lodges, movies like *Never Cry Wolf* and *Mother Lode* turned the Beaver into a romantic icon. People who could afford it could achieve instant "bush pilot" status simply by writing a check to Kenmore Air Harbor and picking out a color scheme. Like Range Rovers and lakefront homes, de Havilland Beavers became *the* thing to own.

Greg Gay and Gordon Barnes rebuilt Beavers for attorneys and CEOs with vacation homes in the San Juans. They rebuilt them for Las Vegas entrepreneurs and Texas oilmen. They rebuilt them for musicians and movie stars. And occasionally, buried in the schedule between the celebrity Beavers, they rebuilt one for somebody who was actually going to put it to work.

Before the advent of GPS navigation, a pilot flying a Beaver for a living up north was lucky to have a communications radio installed. He was even luckier if it worked. A bush pilot's navigation system generally consisted of the pilot looking out the window and comparing what he saw down below to where he thought he was on his chart. If they matched, he was in the right place. While this system is pretty foolproof and requires no moving parts or electricity, it wasn't good enough for the new generation of Beaver owners.

A Beaver on floats cruises at 110 miles per hour. If the three fuel tanks in the belly are augmented by wingtip tanks, the plane can fly about 550 miles before it runs out of gas. A high-speed, high-altitude, long-range airplane it is not. But the celebrity Beavers leaving Kenmore today are equipped with GPS, VOR, DME, ADF, ILS, R-NAV, autopilots, moving map displays, multiple VHF radios, and sometimes even Stormscopes.

> "A Stormscope is a strike finder. It senses lightning bolts and displays their location on a screen. It's a little like having weather radar in that it shows you where the lightning is, which is generally where the worst weather is. The first time we installed one in a Beaver, someone—I don't remember who it was—said we ought to face it backwards so the pilot could see the storms overtaking him."
>
> **GORDON BARNES**

About the only things Gay and Barnes haven't installed in a Beaver are Doppler radar and inertial navigation. As it is, there's not a whole lot of difference between the instrument panel of a movie star's Beaver and the panels in the 737s rolling out of the Boeing plant at the other end of the lake.

With radio and navigation packages costing in excess of one hundred thousand dollars, it's not surprising that some of the private Beavers have pretty fancy interiors as well. Leather seats are not uncommon, and often the sidewall panels and headliner are covered in exotic fabrics, as well. One customer wanted a headliner made of white mohair to accentuate the blue leather he'd chosen for the seats and sidewall panels. Sue Peters managed to locate twelve yards of the stuff, which was just enough to make the headliner. The only problem was the mohair wasn't completely white. The fabric, which is made from Angora goat hair, was liberally sprinkled with black hairs, which from a distance made it look like it was covered with tiny oil spatters. So Sue spent fifteen hours plucking out each and every black hair with the tweezers from her Swiss Army knife. The end result was stunning to look at, but it took a lot of time, and it cost the owner a bundle.

While each celebrity Beaver the shop turns out seems to be fancier and more luxurious than the last, the Beaver Gay and Barnes are most fond of is the second one they ever put together for a private owner. Marco Vituli flew jets in the Air Force, but when he got out he only wanted to fly seaplanes. After getting his rating he had Bill Fisk check him out in the Cessna 180 and then the Beaver. The slim, olive-complexioned Vituli was a financier by trade, and an extremely successful one, but he still found the time and energy to become a first-rate floatplane pilot. He was so good that Kenmore would call on him to fill in if they ran short of charter pilots on weekends. Talkative and bubbling with enthusiasm for flying in general and the Beaver in particular, Vituli became one of Kenmore's most requested pilots even though he was rarely on the schedule. Passengers never forgot a flight with Vituli, who believed in flying low so they could see the fishermen and clam diggers and whales and seals.

Eventually Vituli was able to buy a Beaver of his own. Compared to the celebrity Beavers that came almost two decades later, Vituli's plane was pretty basic. But Gay and Barnes remember it fondly.

> "It was one of those jobs where everything goes right. The sheet metal work was perfect, the interior was perfect, the wings and floats were rigged perfect. It wasn't fancy and it didn't have a hundred-thousand-dollar panel in it, but it was, I think, the cleanest, slickest airplane we've ever turned out. Marco named it 'Night Train.' It had the same paint scheme as our planes, but where ours have a yellow speed stripe, his has a kind of coppery-gold stripe. He keeps it hangared down in Renton now, so we don't see it much anymore. It's a gorgeous airplane, and Greg and I are really proud of it."
>
> **GORDON BARNES**

When de Havilland shut down the Beaver assembly line in 1966, the tooling used to fabricate the airplane's parts was crated up and stored in a warehouse along with the tooling used for the Beaver's big brother, the Otter. In the early 1980s, de Havilland decided the stuff had to go. A deal was struck with McKinnon Enterprises, later to be renamed Viking Air. One by one, the heavy forming dies and assembly jigs were loaded into semi-trailers and sent west to their new home near Victoria on Vancouver Island.

Viking so far has elected not to put either of the de Havilland bush planes back into production. What they have done is produce parts and modifications, primarily for the Beaver. Parts that have been difficult if not impossible to find for years like cowlings are available once again, although for a stiff price. Viking also converts piston Beavers into turbine Beavers, complete with the fuselage and nose extensions, additional doors, and rectangular tail of the original Turbo Beavers produced by de Havilland in the mid-1960s. This would be an almost impossible task for Kenmore. But it's easy for Viking; they have the Turbo Beaver's original tooling.

Viking is a big company with upwards of seventy employees. But a few smaller companies scattered along the BC coast have gotten into the Beaver modification business, too. Extended cabin interiors and oversize baggage doors are the most popular modifications offered by the one-man shops. Other companies have tried to improve on the Beaver's wing, adding drooped wingtips to reduce drag or in at least one case, redesigning the airfoil altogether. Some of the new wings work quite well, but their cost has so far kept them from being widely applied.

Beaver row, 1984. Some of the company Beavers lined up in the tiedown area. (photo by Marin Faure)

There's another problem besides cost. Most of the wing modifications are designed to allow the Beaver to take off and land at even slower speeds than the original wing. While in most cases the wing mods deliver what they advertise, they can't prevent pilots from exceeding their own limitations and getting into trouble. There have been several accidents when pilots attempted to fly off lakes that were too short with loads that were too heavy because they thought the modified wings on their Beavers were up to the task. Kenmore has paid close attention to the development of the various wing modifications, and has so far decided that Dick Hiscocks original airfoil works just fine. Some of Kenmore's customers have requested wing modifications for their Beavers, but the wings of the company's own fleet remain unmodified.

Competitors may have grabbed a bit of Kenmore's Beaver rebuild business but they haven't changed the Air Harbor's reputation. "It's as good as a Kenmore Beaver" is the phrase often uttered by the competition as they tout their own modifications to a potential customer. One only has to take a stroll down "Beaver Row," the tiedown lane that holds Kenmore's own Beavers as well as the occasional private airplane, to see why the Kenmore Beaver still reigns supreme. Each of the immaculate de Havillands on the line is evidence that the Air Harbor's mechanics, interior fabricators, and painters are the best in the business.

The Beavers lined up in the tiedown area may all look the same to the passers-by outside the fence. But to the people who transform them from battered hulks into reliable, beautifully functioning flying machines, each plane they work on takes on a personality of its own.

"We had one rebuild, a beautiful plane that they took up north and crashed two days after delivery. It was like, 'You killed it!' It's hard to see them come back with dents in the panels and the interiors all beat up, but you know they've been working hard. I've climbed into airplanes that have come back and gotten flea bites all over because they've been hauling moose or caribou out of the hunting camps. Sometimes you look at the condition of a plane and wonder just what the heck they're doing with them up there."

SUSAN PETERS

19
SOUTH CASCADE

SEATTLE RESIDENTS GO TO GREAT lengths to promote the notion that their city is under a more or less permanent rain cloud. If Seattle had an official color, they say, it would be gray. A national talk-show host whose program originates in Seattle begins each broadcast with a description of the downpour currently drenching the city, even if the sky outside the studio is completely cloud-free. The object is to discourage people from moving to the area, particularly people from California. The Golden State's alleged party lifestyle and insatiable greed for water, electricity, and gasoline makes it easy for Seattleites, most of them recent arrivals themselves, to blame Californians for just about everything. Pollution, unaffordable housing, gangs: it's all "their" fault, they say, ignoring the fact that there are more license plates from Montana and Oregon cruising Seattle's streets than there are from California.

The "it's raining so don't come here" campaign is popular but futile, as evidenced by the suburban sprawl that has spread, amoebae-like, through the once-forested hills and valleys surrounding the city. Traffic is the first or third worst in the nation, depending on who you talk to, and provides a far more persuasive reason to stay away than the rain. If the people moving up from California brought their freeway designs with them, they probably would be met with less hostility.

It actually does rain a fair amount in Seattle, but if the city depended on rain to meet its water needs, there would be a lot of very thirsty people walking the streets. Push the button on a downtown drinking fountain and what comes out most likely started as snow falling in the Cascade Range, not rain falling on the city. And not snow that fell last winter, but snow that fell a thousand or more winters earlier. There are over 750 glaciers in the North Cascades, not huge ones like the massive rivers of ice in Alaska, but glaciers nevertheless. They cling to the upper slopes of the state's two biggest volcanoes, Mt. Baker and Mt. Rainier. Aptly named Glacier Peak sports a few, and the rest are scattered throughout hundreds of square miles of knife-edged peaks and hanging valleys. While each winter's snowfall sends a much-needed rush of water into the reservoirs come spring, it's the slow, steady runoff from the glaciers that keeps the region's toilets flushing year round.

From drinking water to the generation of electricity, the Cascade glaciers play a critical role, so it stands to reason that their health is of great interest to a large number of people. If you know how fast a glacier is advancing or receding, and if you know how much snow accumulates in the winter and how much water runs off in the summer, you can tell a lot about that glacier's long-range impact on the water supply.

Glaciers tell you something else, too. They are very sensitive climate indicators. By studying and measuring how a glacier is behaving in today's climate, it's possible to determine what the climate was like ten thousand years ago, and what it might be like decades in the future. Each summer, airborne dust and pollen drift down to the surface until by fall what had been a pristine, white snowscape has turned a dirty gray. Then comes the first snowfall of autumn, and the layer of dust and pollen is forever trapped beneath the surface. As year after year of snow accumulates, the increasing weight compacts the snow into ice. But the thin layers of dirt and pollen remain, marking each year like the growth rings of a tree. By counting the layers, measuring the thickness and density of the ice between them, and analyzing the dust and pollen it's possible to paint a picture of the climate thousands of years in the past.

And so it was that in 1957 a little glacier called South Cascade came under the scrutiny of the U.S. Geological Survey. Seventy-five miles northeast of Seattle, the South Cascade Glacier is one of the lowest glaciers in the range. Compared to the glaciers hanging off the steep slopes of Glacier Peak and Mt. Rainier, South Cascade is a pussycat. Its compact size and mild slopes make it relatively easy to walk around on. Only two miles long and half a mile wide, it starts against a ridge of rock 7,200 feet above sea level and steps down almost due north through a valley of its own making to end at a kidney-shaped lake that's not quite a mile high at 5,200 feet.

The South Cascade is receding fast. An aerial photo shot in 1928 shows no lake at all at the foot, while the head of the glacier is even with the top of the rock ridge. Twenty-five years later, the head of the glacier had dropped well below the ridge and the ice had receded enough to allow the formation of a tiny lake at its foot. Eight more years was all it took for the glacier to recede another quarter mile, and for the kidney-shaped lake to grow to a half mile in length.

The glacier itself may be a pussycat, but the surrounding terrain is not. Rows of razorback ridges surround South Cascade on all sides. The eastern wall of its narrow, north-south valley is dominated by Mt. LeConte (7,762 feet) and Sentinel Peak (8,261 feet). Just south of the glacier is The Lizard, a serrated pyramid of rock that tops out at 7,339 feet. The lake at the foot of the glacier bends around the foot of a ridge and escapes down a tiny stream optimistically named the South Fork of the Cascade River. The stream drops off steeply into a narrow valley heading west and is soon lost from sight below the treeline.

The weather at South Cascade can be just as intimidating as the geography. On clear days, the warm air lifting over the sun-baked ridges meets the cold air spilling down the slope of the glacier, and the result is the airborne equivalent of gang warfare. With no clouds to mark the battle, the only evidence is sound, an express-train roaring that fills the valley and knocks rocks off the surrounding slopes. The little lake is a frequent victim; the screaming winds need only seconds to whip the placid surface into a frothing maelstrom.

That's in the summer. In the winter it gets worse. Fog cuts the visibility to mere feet for days. Winter storms hammer clouds against the peaks and fill the air with horizontal snow so dense it becomes hard to breathe. Or perhaps the worst of all, the air can turn dead still. Clouds the color of lead hover close over the featureless snowfield. Distances become impossible to judge as the heavy underbelly of cloud sags down imperceptibly, until suddenly the glacier is smothered by an icy, impenetrable gloom.

You can't find out what a glacier is doing by studying it from afar. You have to go up and ride on it, preferably for a decade or two. The person picked to ride the South Cascade was Mark Meier. His planned as-

South Cascade Glacier. The gauging station was beside the outlet stream at the west end of the lake. The research cabin was at the top of the ridge in the center of the photo.

sault on the little glacier was nothing if not thorough. A gauging station would be erected at the outlet of the lake to measure its level and to record the volume of water flowing out of it. Recording thermometers would be set up to measure the temperature of the air at strategic locations on the glacier's surface. Humidity would be measured by hygrometers, windspeeds would be measured by anemometers, and the cloud cover would be measured by people looking up and writing down what they saw.

Core samples taken from all over the glacier's surface would yield the volume of snow that accumulated during the winter, and the amount that melted off during the summer. Pits would be dug at various locations to let the scientists examine the snow's density, crystal structure, hardness, and grain size. Holes would be bored all the way down to the bottom of the glacier to measure the water pressure underneath. Hundreds of stakes would be driven into the glacier and surrounding slopes to measure the loss of snow and ice from the surface. Other stakes would be surveyed periodically with theodolites to determine the glacier's speed.

To store and protect all the equipment as well as provide a shelter for the people who would be planting stakes, boring holes, fixing instruments, and watching clouds over the next several years, Meier decided to have a small hut constructed near the top of the ridge that formed the glacier's western "shore." What the hut lacked in size it would make up for in strength; Meier specified it be able to hold up under twenty-five feet of snow and withstand 150 mile-per-hour winds.

The installation of scientific instruments began in 1957. The hut was erected in 1959, and by 1961, everything was in place. It hadn't been easy. The nearest road was nine miles away down a rough and sometimes impassable trail. It was not the sort of hike relished by scientists, particularly scientists who would be lugging heavy and awkward cases of delicate instruments. One of Meier's first decisions was to support the South Cascade project as much as possible by air.

A helicopter would seem to be the obvious choice, but the machines available in the 1950s weren't very big or very powerful. Meier hired one when he had to, a three-seat Bell 47, but its payload was severely limited. Everything had to be weighed, and the pilots would not take off with even one pound more than the limit. So most of the flights to the glacier were by airplane, which was not only faster, but cheaper.

For the first ten years of the project, the pilot employed was Bill Fairchild. Fairchild had a two-place Aeronca Champ equipped with wheel-skis. If the conditions were right, he could land on the glacier itself, below the ridge where the cabin was being constructed. The Champ's carrying capacity was limited, but much of what couldn't be carried on the inside could be strapped to the outside, including the lumber and plywood needed for the cabin. In the summer, when the surface of the glacier was dimpled with suncups and criss-crossed with crevasses, Fairchild had a tougher time of it, and Meier would have to rely more on the helicopter.

In 1960, a new name appeared on the South Cascade project roster when Wendell Tangborn took over management of the activities on the glacier.

"I generally had two other people with me. We'd stay in the cabin up on the ridge for weeks at a time. We had a radio, so we could at least communicate with the outside world. Other than that, we were on our own. The cabin was ten feet by ten feet, and positioned halfway along the trail that ran from the outflow of the lake up over the ridge and down to the surface of the glacier. From the stream to the cabin was about three quarters of a mile, during which the trail climbed eight-hundred feet. You really felt like you'd done something when you got to the top. We worked more out on the glacier than down at the stream. We put a lot of wood stakes in the ice and snow and we had to measure each one of them every couple of weeks.

"Sometimes we'd be flown to or from the glacier, but lots of times we had to walk. It was nine miles and the trail was pretty rough, so we couldn't carry very much with us. All our supplies, food, propane, batteries, whatever we needed, came in by plane or helicopter."

WENDELL TANGBORN

Then in 1966, Bill Fairchild was killed in a crash at Port Angeles out on the Olympic Peninsula. The pilot who'd made hundreds of successful landings and takeoffs on snow and ice died in a plane he probably hadn't even been flying. A friend of his owned a Twin Beech, and he invited Fairchild to go for a ride. Moments after takeoff an engine quit, and the plane stalled, rolled over, and dove into the ground.

After Fairchild's death, Wendell Tangborn and his glacier team tried carrying more equipment and supplies in on foot, using the expensive helicopter only when it was absolutely necessary. After a season of this, it became obvious to Tangborn that they needed an airplane again. He wanted to increase the size of the research cabin, and the gauging station on the lake needed repairs. Carting lumber and plywood up the nine-mile trail from the road was out of the question, and having the helicopter carry it in one piece at a time was out of the budget.

In early 1968, Tangborn got on the phone and began calling every seaplane owner in Seattle to see if they'd be willing, once the ice melted, to land on the lake with a load of supplies. Every seaplane owner in the city turned him down. No way, they said. The lake's too short to take off from, the wind's too strong, the downdrafts will push us right into the rock. After a day or two of this, Tangborn figured he'd heard every reason in the world why landing on the kidney-shaped lake was an impossibility. Finally, there was only one seaplane company left to call. Heaving a sigh of resignation, Tangborn dialed the number for Kenmore Air Harbor and explained to the woman who answered the phone what he needed. Then he waited to hear another reason why it couldn't be done.

The woman who took Tangborn's call was Mildred Hall, and she wasn't one to tell anybody that something couldn't be done. Mildred had joined Kenmore in 1957, and she'd learned enough about Bob Munro, Bill Peters, and Bill Fisk to know that they never dismissed a potential customer's request with a brusque "we can't do that."

In a prelude to the commuter madness that would grip the Puget Sound area thirty years later, Mildred had grown tired of her daily journey to and from her job as a private secretary with American President Lines.

"I lived clear out in Kenmore and would commute back and forth to Seattle. It was wintertime, and I used to have to walk up a long hill. It was windy and wet as only a November can be, and I was very discouraged. I thought, 'Why am I up here plodding up this hill day after day?' So that evening after dinner I looked in the local newspaper, the *Bothell Citizen*, and there was an ad that said 'Wanted: Girl Friday for Kenmore business'. Well, I thought, I'll go ahead and answer it but there's nothing in Kenmore that's going to intrigue me because it's just a wide spot in the road between Seattle and Bothell. I answered the ad and then forgot about it.

"Two weeks later I got a phone call from Mr. Munro, who said he'd like to interview me. I went to the interview, and the job sounded real good to me because I lived right up the hill, I had three children who were in school, and my husband traveled a great deal. At Kenmore, I could be near home in case the children needed me, and I wouldn't waste an hour each day commuting back and forth to Seattle."

MILDRED HALL

Mildred, who had an accounting degree, was hired on the spot. She started out as the Air Harbor's bookkeeper, with a little desk in the converted chicken coop that served as company headquarters. Unlike the pile-supported buildings that came later, the chicken coop sat on a foundation of logs, which in turn sat on the thin layer of dirt that covered the soupy muck underneath. It wasn't long before sticking doors, jammed windows, and groaning floorboards served notice that the building was sinking. The company's newly-hired building expert, Bill Peters, examined the foundation and determined that the sink rate wasn't overly alarming.

"It's got a few years left before the situation becomes serious," he assured the building's occupants.

"We can always shore it up again if we have to," Munro said. "Meanwhile we should at least fix the doors and windows."

He and Peters re-cut the tops and bottoms of the doors to match the new angles of the doorframes, and planed down the edges of the sticking windows. When the slant began rolling Mildred's pencils off her desk onto the floor, Peters nailed a strip of wood to the desktop to hold them in place.

Mildred's interest in aviation and her ability to get along with even the most demanding customer soon got her promoted from bookkeeper to dispatcher. Her new job was much more demanding than the name implied. Until the advent of scheduled service in the 1980s with its staff of reservation agents, Kenmore's passenger requests, airplane scheduling, and pilot assignments all funneled through one person: the dispatcher. Mildred's fascination with weather and the geographic intricacies of Puget Sound and the BC coast gave her a real appreciation of the challenges the pilots faced on a daily basis. A depth perception problem precluded her from getting a pilot's license of her own, but she went through Bill Fisk's ground school, and she made it a point to learn everything she could about each airplane in Kenmore's fleet.

Mildred's grasp of the flying side of the business made her a good dispatcher, but her flair for customer relations made her a great one. She made sure that every passenger that entered the office left it feeling that their flight was the most important one ever undertaken by the company. With Mildred in the front office, the number of Kenmore's repeat charter customers began to skyrocket.

Enos Bradner's newspaper columns about the fabulous steelhead fishing on Vancouver Island had gotten the charter ball rolling, but the really big boom was sparked by boaters. Wealthy yacht owners had been taking their boats north to British Columbia's enchanting maze of islands and inlets for decades, but picking up invited guests or attending an important business meeting meant running the boat all the way back to Seattle, a voyage of at least two days. It was inconvenient, it was time consuming, and it was expensive.

Mildred has forgotten who it was that kicked off the revolution, but whoever it was, he was tight on time. Out of options, he hired Kenmore to fly his guests to his yacht in Desolation Sound. The flight took two hours, and the cost was surprisingly low, especially when compared to the value of the owner's time. The word spread, and soon Mildred was fielding calls from some of the biggest names in Seattle business. The Nordstrom family, developers Howard Wright, Herman Sarkowski, and Ned Skinner, restaurateur Peter Canlis, the Weyerhaeuser's, the Boeings, a prominent lawyer named William Gates, Jr. with his wife Mary and young son Bill, and dozens of others became frequent visitors to Kenmore's pastel green docks at the north end of the lake. Most were traveling to or from their boats, but some, like the Gates family, wanted to be flown to their summer homes in the San Juans or on Hood Canal. There were the occasional odd requests, too.

> "There was a young professor at one of the universities in Massachusetts. He would charter an airplane every spring and we'd fly him way up into the interior of British Columbia. We'd drop him off at a lake, and he would spend the next couple of months in the mountains studying the goats. He would literally lie on his belly and watch the goats for hours and hours each day, writing down everything he saw. He would come back so enthusiastic about his studies, and he'd always have funny stories to tell us about what had happened to him or the goats that summer.
>
> "I always assigned Bill Fisk as his pilot because the lake where we dropped him off and picked him up was very remote and in very rugged country. It was the sort of place where if you had a problem, you needed a level-headed and experienced pilot who wouldn't panic. If Bill landed on a lake and a Bigfoot came out of the woods and climbed into the plane, I don't think Bill would even blink. He'd just ask the Bigfoot where he wanted to go and if he had the money to pay for the flight."
>
> **MILDRED HALL**

When Tangborn called with his notion of using a floatplane to fly supplies to the South Cascade Glacier, Mildred didn't blink either. She wrote down the relevant details—the length of the lake, its altitude, the kinds of weather that could be encountered, and the nature of the loads Tangborn wanted to take in—and then said that while it certainly sounded feasible to her, she would have to run the idea past Bob Munro, who was out flying at the moment. He was due back shortly, however, so Tangborn could expect an answer within the day.

When Munro returned, Mildred told him about Tangborn's call and showed him the details she'd written down. Munro studied the paper for a moment and then set it down on his desk.

"Sounds interesting," he said. "Let's give it a try."

The last thing Tangborn wanted to do was mislead anyone into thinking the job would be easy, so when Munro called him back, the scientist listed all the reasons the other pilots had given why operating a floatplane at South Cascade ranged from impossible to suicidal. When he was done there was silence at the end of the line. I bet I've scared him off, Tangborn thought.

"Some of those fellows you talked to are real good pilots," Munro said tactfully, "and I don't want to say anything against their abilities. But I don't think we'll have any problems. Just to make sure, though, I'll do some takeoff tests down here. Then we'll make a trial flight up to the lake."

Tangborn promised to mail a detailed topographical map of the glacier to Kenmore that afternoon, and a date was set for the trial flight. Then Tangborn returned to his things-to-do list, and Munro began rummaging through his desk for a copy of the Beaver's operating manual. He wasn't too concerned about landing on the lake; floatplanes slow down and stop fairly quickly once they're on the water. What worried him was the takeoff. He found the manual and set it beside Mildred's page of notes. Then he unfolded his aeronautical chart of Washington State, found the Cascade River, and backtracked upstream with his finger to the junction of the north and south forks, and then up the south fork to the foot of the South Cascade Glacier.

The glacier was roughly seventy miles from Kenmore, a flight that would take less than an hour. The Beaver's R-985 radial burns between twenty and twenty-five gallons of fuel an hour in cruise. Accounting for the extra gas he'd use during takeoff and climb, Munro figured he could fly up to the glacier on the fuel in the center tank and then fly home on the fuel in the front tank. He wouldn't need to put anything in the rear tank at all which meant the plane would weigh that much less at takeoff.

Another factor in his favor was the Beaver's supercharger. Mechanically driven, it could ram enough air down the throat of the carburetor to fool the engine into thinking it was still at sea level when in fact the plane could be as high as 5,000 feet. Above 5,000 feet, the supercharger's ability to generate pressure fell off, but at 5,200 feet, the altitude of the glacier lake, Munro would have most of the engine's four hundred and fifty horsepower available for takeoff.

An empty Beaver on floats weighs about three-thousand pounds. To this Munro added everything else that would affect the weight of the plane when he took off at South Cascade: thirty-five gallons of fuel in the front tank, six gallons of oil in the engine, the radio in the panel, the yellow, white, and brown paint that comprised Kenmore's color scheme, and himself. All told, he figured his plane would weigh 3,400 pounds at takeoff. Munro flipped to the back of the Beaver's operating manual to the section titled Operating Data Charts.

Chart IV was what he was after, a complex, multi-part graph that if used correctly would yield the linear distance a float-equipped Beaver would require to take off and then clear a fifty-foot obstacle. The business about clearing a fifty-foot obstacle is not unique to the Beaver; virtually every general aviation airplane made since WWII has the equivalent of a Chart IV in its operating manual. The chart is based on the assumption that airports are generally surrounded by stuff that sticks up: buildings and trees mostly. A chart telling a pilot that a particular runway is long enough for his plane to become airborne is of little value if immediately after takeoff he finds his plane can't climb fast enough to avoid the grain silo on the other side of the fence.

Over the years, enough airplanes ran into trees and other obstacles to warrant the creation of the takeoff clearance chart. The rulemakers decided that fifty feet, the height of a five-story building or an average-size tree, was representative of the sorts of obstacles one might find surrounding an airport, so it became the standard parameter for takeoff performance.

Munro worked his way through Chart IV, which required the plotting of the pressure altitude of the lake, the airplane's gross weight, the temperature, and the headwind component. Munro had no idea what sort of winds he might encounter, so he assumed a headwind component of zero. When he was finished, his pencil was parked on the line representing a total takeoff distance of 1,390 feet.

Tangborn had said the maximum shore-to-shore length of the lake was 2,600 feet, but that was following the curve of the lake. The longest straight line down the lake would be considerably shorter. On the other hand, Munro wouldn't have to worry about clearing any fifty-foot obstacles after becoming airborne. The only way out of the lake was to the west, past the gauging station and then north down the valley of the South Fork of the Cascade River. According to Tangborn, the ground around the outflow was flat and it dropped away fast into the valley. The only obstacles Munro would have to clear were the gauging station itself, some scrubby bushes, and a scattering of boulders. If he reached the shoreline with only five feet of altitude he'd be fine.

The numbers on Munro's piece of paper indicated he'd have no trouble taking off from South Cascade's tiny lake, but he wasn't about to risk his airplane, let alone his life, on paper calculations.

"What I did was scale the glacier lake out real carefully on the map Wendell sent me, and then I marked out the same distance from Kenmore down along the shore toward Arrowhead Point. I got the airplane out in front of the dock with the same amount of fuel on board that I'd have up on the glacier, and I put in the same amount of power I figured I'd have at 5,200 feet. I made several takeoffs here at Kenmore first, and determined exactly how many feet it would take me to get airborne up at the glacier.

"The lake at South Cascade was so small that I knew once I'd pushed the throttle up to take off I'd have to keep going. There really wasn't enough room to back off the power and stop once the plane was on the step.

"When I was finally convinced I could get off in the distance I'd have up there, I went up and tried it."

BOB MUNRO

Tangborn was apprehensive the morning he and Munro made their trial flight to the glacier, but even though he barely knew the pilot, there was something about the slender, quiet man at the controls that inspired confidence.

"I had the utmost faith in Bob. I just couldn't believe he would do anything that was foolish or unreasonable. I always felt like he knew what he was doing. He was very calm. You just felt extremely safe when you were riding with him."

WENDELL TANGBORN

Of course, Munro was flying his favorite, N9766Z. He knew every one of its quirks and how it would handle in virtually any situation. The engine and flight instruments in the panel simply confirmed what he felt through the seat, saw out the windshield, and heard in the rush of air past the fuselage and in the thunder of the engine. He had no qualms about flying any of the company's other airplanes, of course, and frequently did so. But Mildred Hall knew about the special bond that can develop between a person and the supposedly inanimate machine upon which his life depends. She'd seen Munro give Six-Six-Zulu a pat on the cowl after a difficult trip. So she made sure as she made up each day's schedule that Munro had Six-Six-Zulu on any flight that had even the potential to be troublesome. A flight to a tiny mountain lake culminating in a do-or-die landing certainly qualified as potentially troublesome, so there was no question as to which airplane the line crew would be putting in the water that morning.

The clouds were white, high, and broken over Kenmore with plenty of patches of blue showing through, but the closer Munro and Tangborn got to the mountains, the denser and darker the clouds became. Finally, they weren't individual clouds anymore but a single sheet of gray overcast stretching unbroken to the east. Fortunately, it was fairly high, and Munro was able to climb up to almost seven thousand feet. There were peaks higher than this near the glacier, but the visibility below the overcast was excellent, so Munro wasn't worried about running into something he couldn't see.

As he'd learned to do on the Leduc Glacier airlift, Munro took advantage of the river valleys in plotting the best route to the South Cascade Glacier. From Kenmore he headed northeast to the little logging town of Darrington, then north down the Sauk River to its junction with the Skagit River at Rockport. From there a right turn took him up the Skagit to Marblemount where the Cascade River came in from the east. The mountains were beginning to get serious here, the steep, heavily wooded slopes rising to ice-mantled crags scarred by rockslides and pockmarked with eerie blue pools of half-frozen water.

The only tricky part of the route came at the very end. Ten miles up the Cascade the first of three narrow valleys runs in from the south. The last one was the one Munro wanted, the one which lead to the foot of the South Cascade Glacier. Munro never did learn the names of the streams that occupied the first two valleys, but when the weather was low and the visibility was poor, the second valley had a nasty way of looking convincingly like the third one, an illusion that would fool him into heading up the wrong valley on at least one occasion.

But that day was in the future. Today the good visibility showed the three valleys for what they were, and Munro guided Six-Six-Zulu unerringly up the last valley to the glacier itself. Two thousand feet above the dull white surface, he rolled the Beaver to the left and began circling the area while he studied the lay of the land.

Most of it lay pretty vertical. Although he was here to land on the lake, Munro couldn't resist a quick examination of the glacier itself to see what sort of a landing spot it might offer. Even from two thousand feet up, it was immediately obvious that the lower third of the glacier was unusable. As the river of ice dropped off into the valley, its surface was ripped open by a network of gaping crevasses. The upper third of the glacier looked too steep, although the snow was smooth. That left the middle third. Here the surface reminded Munro of the Leduc. It was relatively level and the snow appeared free of crevasses. Best of all, it was not too far from the trail that led up to the research cabin.

But unlike the Leduc, the South Cascade offered no escape route for a botched landing. The only approach was straight up the narrow glacier, with a slope too steep to outclimb in front and sheer rock walls on either side. Munro knew all about Bill Fairchild's landings on the glacier, but the Port Angeles pilot had used a light, two-place skiplane. Landing a two-ton floatplane on the same patch of snow would be a little different. It could be done, Munro decided, but it would be risky.

Not that his current undertaking was any less risky. As he peered down at the tiny, mud-colored lake cowering at the foot of the glacier, he began to wonder if his calculations and practice runs back on Lake Washington had been in vain. It was one thing to measure out half a mile along the shoreline of a twenty-three mile long lake, and quite another to look at a half-mile strip of dirty water surrounded on three sides by slabs of rock and ice. Through the window of the circling Beaver, the kidney-shaped lake looked like a puddle. There didn't appear to be enough room to land, let alone takeoff again.

But Munro had been flying too long to be intimidated by doubts inspired by nasty-looking scenery. He knew his calculations had been correct, and he knew his practice takeoffs had duplicated the conditions that now lay below him. The only thing left to do was figure out the best way to get down.

Flying his Norseman onto Leduc Glacier and his Seabee in and out of countless mountain lakes had taught Munro that it was critical to maintain the ability to judge altitude all the way down to the surface. As he studied the terrain surrounding the South Cascade glacier, it quickly became obvious there was only one approach that made any sense, and that was to come in over the top of the ridge to the west and follow the slope right down to the edge of the lake.

"The thing is," Munro hollered to Tangborn over the roar of the engine, "once we've crossed the ridge and the valley and are final approach for the lake we have to land. There's not enough room to turn around once we've started in there."

Tangborn nodded. Bill Fairchild had told him the same thing about landing up on the glacier itself: once you'd started your final approach you were committed.

"Are you ready?" Munro looked over Tangborn. The scientist smiled, pointed down at the lake, and nodded vigorously.

"Okay then," Munro said, more to himself than his passenger. He rolled the plane out of its orbit over the glacier and headed west, away from the lake. Pulling the power back, he waited until the airspeed began to bleed off and then he pumped in some flap. The racket from the engine died away and Tangborn felt the plane decelerate and start to descend. Munro kept glancing back through the side window until he figured he'd gone west far enough. He smoothly banked the Beaver into a tight left turn, pulled off a little more power, and swung the plane back around toward the lake.

From this angle, the lake looked even smaller, and for the first time, Tangborn felt a twinge of apprehension. Glancing around him, he was suddenly aware of how big the Beaver really was, much too large to land on the tiny smear of dirty water that lay ahead of them. He looked over at

Munro, but the pilot seemed unperturbed as he peered out through the windscreen. His left hand manipulated the yoke in gentle but positive movements to keep the plane precisely on track while his right hand made continuous, tiny adjustments with the throttle to maintain a constant rate of descent. He's like a musician, Tangborn thought. A musician who no longer has to think about how to play his instrument, but can concentrate instead on the feel and mood of the music knowing his hands will instinctively find the correct notes.

Munro felt he was a little high, so he pumped in some more flap and eased the throttle back an inch or two. The plane was dropping fast, although Munro was holding the airspeed at a steady eighty miles per hour. Dick Hiscock's effective flap system was proving its worth, allowing Munro to accurately follow the steeply sloping terrain down to the near shore of the lake without increasing his airspeed.

The lake was growing in size, and Tangborn began to feel more confident about their ability to land on it. He felt like a gnat, peering up at the massive ridges surrounding the lake. He'd been coming to the glacier for several years now, but he'd never lost the feeling of awe as he looked up at the surrounding mountains. Whenever you get the feeling that man is all-powerful, he'd tell his friends back in Seattle, go up and stand on a glacier. That's when you realize who's got the power on this planet, and believe me, it isn't us.

The Beaver crossed the bottom of the valley, and the ground started coming up fast as the plane continued to angle downwards. Suddenly Tangborn realized they were losing altitude much too quickly. The tumbling waters of the outflow stream were no longer below the plane, they were in front of it. His concerns about the lake being too short were rapidly being replaced by a fear that they weren't even going to make the shoreline before they hit the ground. But Munro had learned long ago not to be fooled by optical illusions. His attention was focused on what mattered: the surface of the lake ahead of him. Judging his approach perfectly, he skimmed Six-Six-Zulu past the gauging station and touched down gently on the water just a few yards offshore.

The big floatplane skated along on the step for a moment and then settled its full weight onto the water with a hiss. Munro lowered the water rudders and pumped the flaps up as he steered the plane around toward the gauging station. The offbeat rumble of the idling radial reverberated off the cliffs, and the floats sent twin vees of ripples widening out toward the rocky shores.

There was only one place to beach the plane, and that was just to the right of the gauging station. Everywhere else the shoreline was unapproachable, but the open area around the stream offered plenty of room for the plane. Tangborn had assured Munro that the bottom was smooth, covered as it was by tons of finely ground rock particles that had settled out of the meltwater coming off the glacier. Munro had to take Tangborn's word for it; the suspended particles in the water gave it the appearance and clarity of pea soup.

When the plane was a hundred feet from shore, Munro pulled the mixture control all the way back. The engine rumbled on for a few seconds and then clanked to a stop. Regardless of Tangborn's assurances, Munro wanted to be going as slow as possible when the floats contacted the bottom. He flipped off the master and magneto switches, and then opened his door and leaned out for a better view of what lay in front of the coasting plane. The first thing he became aware of was the sound of water. It filled the basin and seemed to be coming from every direction at once. He was tempted to look around to see what was causing it, but he knew better than to let his attention wander at this critical point.

The floats hit the bottom at almost the same instant Munro saw it, but the Beaver was traveling so slowly that the grounding was little more than a gentle nudge. Munro reached down by his left foot and pulled up on the D-ring attached to the water rudder retraction cable. Back on the tails of the floats, the big, spade-shaped rudders pivoted up into their retracted position where they would be out of harm's way.

Munro, who had made the flight wearing lightweight hip boots, swung himself out the door and onto the float. He walked to the bow and eased himself down into the water. The cold was a shock even through the rubberized fabric of the boots and his heavy cotton trousers. Shoving the plane backwards off the bottom, he manhandled it around until it was facing out toward the lake. Then he positioned himself under the horizontal stabilizer, and lifting up on it, pushed the plane backwards until the tails of the floats were sitting firmly on the bottom.

"Okay," he called to Tangborn. "We're here."

The scientist walked to the back of the float and stepped ashore.

"Quite a place," Munro said, looking around at the massive basin. With the plane safely beached, he could take a moment to study his surroundings. The roar of water was constant, and it was immediately obvious why. There were waterfalls everywhere. Thin streams squirted from cracks, clear sheets poured over ledges, and lacy ribbons snaked across angled slabs of rock the size of football fields. High above the lake, the snow was melting, and the glass of water that would one day appear next to the silverware and breadsticks in the dining room of Seattle's Edgewater Hotel ("Where You Can Fish From Your Room!") was on its way.

"Impressive landing," Tangborn remarked.

Munro acknowledged the compliment with a self-deprecating wave. "Oh, anyone could do it really, if you set it up right."

Two figures came into sight around the base of the rock ridge across the lake.

"Good," Tangborn said, "I won't have to carry the supplies up to the cabin myself."

He was referring to the small boxes of fresh food in the back of the airplane. This first flight was intended to confirm Munro's calculations that he could safely land and take off from the lake, but as long as we're were going up there anyway, he'd said, we might as well take some stuff with us. Tangborn had spent the afternoon before the flight at the store, buying fresh fruit and vegetables for the two researchers at the glacier. They'd been up there for weeks, huddled each night in the vibrating cabin, listening to roar of the wind as it tore at the roof and pounded against the walls. That was bad enough, but Tangborn knew that when the high point of each meal was guessing which label would be on the can that came out of the food box in the corner, patience went out the window and petty differences quickly became insurmountable grievances. So that evening Tangborn packed his apples and tomatoes and hoped that Munro knew what he was doing.

It didn't take long to unload the boxes into the arms of the delighted research assistants. Munro was understandably anxious to try a takeoff, and he'd noticed that the overcast had started to come down. It was time to go. Tangborn had business back in Seattle, so he would be riding in the plane on the way back. This was fine with Munro, who knew there would be times when he would be taking people and equipment off the glacier as well as up to it. His Chart IV calculations and takeoff tests had indicated he'd have plenty of room to take off plus a fair margin of safety, so having a bit of a load on the first takeoff would be a more realistic simulation of the conditions he'd be encountering in the future.

He and Tangborn climbed back aboard and Munro fired up the engine. He made a quick check of the flight controls, looked to make sure the oil temperature was in the green, and then fed in some power with the throttle. The Beaver hesitated, and then the floats slid off the mud. Munro lifted the D-ring out of its bracket and lowered it to the floor. Behind him, the water rudders pivoted down like a pair of huge cleavers and disappeared soundlessly beneath the gray-green surface. Pushing on the left rudder pedal, Munro turned the plane until it was tracking down the centerline of the lake.

The lake bent sharply to the right, around the base of the rocky ridge and up to the foot of the glacier. Munro could put a bit of a curve into his takeoff run, but not a sharp one. Besides, the water around the base of the glacier had little chunks of ice floating in it, and he didn't want to run the risk of hitting one as he picked up speed. He taxied Six-Six-Zulu as close as he dared to the massive rock wall that formed the eastern shore of the lake. When he swung the plane around, he had a momentary twinge of anxiety: the lake simply didn't look long enough. The two research assistants standing by the gauging station didn't look that much smaller than they'd been when he and Tangborn had been standing next to them.

But Munro didn't hesitate. He'd already lowered the flaps to their takeoff position, so all he had to do was retract the water rudders and push the throttle up to full power. The engine responded with a roar that boomed off the cliffs and sent showers of rocks tumbling down the slopes into the water, but Munro was too busy to notice. He hauled back on the yoke to help the plane climb up onto the step as quickly as possible. A glance at the manifold pressure gauge told him the engine was developing exactly the amount of power he'd calculated it should. Returning his attention to the view out the windshield, Munro eased off on the yoke, and the big plane pitched smoothly forward onto the step. With only a tiny portion of the float bottoms actually touching the surface, the drag from the water was reduced to almost nothing, and the Beaver surged forward.

Thirty miles per hour, forty, fifty. But Munro wasn't looking at the instruments. He'd know when the plane was ready to fly by sound and feel, not by watching a needle creep up a dial. The gauging station seemed impossibly close, but still Munro kept the plane on the water. Tangborn was watching the gauging station, too, unaware that he was instinctively straining upwards against his seat belt, trying to make himself as light as possible in an effort to help the plane off the water.

Suddenly they were airborne. The Beaver blasted out over the valley and the waving research assistants disappeared from view. Tangborn sank back in worried relief. So far as he could tell, they'd barely made it off with just two people on board. What would happen when it came time to fly out several people at once, or heavy boxes of data or damaged instruments? Beside him, Munro was thinking about the same thing, only he wasn't worried. Tangborn wasn't a pilot, so he had no way of knowing that Munro had actually kept the airplane on the water much longer than necessary. The Beaver had been ready to fly even before reaching the rocky ridge midway down the lake, but Munro had wanted to get a feel for just how much takeoff distance he really had. Confident now that he could not only get off the lake, but he could get off with a fairly heavy load if he had to, Munro slipped under the lowering overcast and guided his plane down the Cascade River, down the Skagit, up the Sauk, and then home.

Regular flights to the glacier with full payloads began the following week. Supporting Tangborn's teams of researchers on the South Cascade Glacier was not nearly as intense an operation as the airlift that had moved Tom McQuillan's copper mine to the surface of the Leduc Glacier fifteen years earlier.

> "We flew up to the South Cascade about once a week. They kept a little crew up there, four or five people, so they needed quite a bit of food flown in, and people would go in and out. We flew in propane bottles, big ones, 180 pounds each, for their stoves and heaters. Snowshoes and skis, sometimes, and a lot of scientific instruments. I went up there at least once with a whole bunch of stuff tied on the outside of the plane. Plywood and two-by-fours and some bigger stuff. They were working on the cabin, and they had a lot of lumber they needed brought in."
>
> **BOB MUNRO**

It made sense to have more than one pilot able to support Tangborn's operation, so Munro took Bill Peters along on a couple of flights so he could see how it all worked. As long as the weather cooperated, there was nothing particularly difficult about the flight other than the fact that a pilot was committed to land once he'd started his approach into the basin.

"There's no changing your mind," Munro cautioned Peters on their first flight to the lake together. "Once you've started in there, you have to land. There's no room to turn around."

Peters, who'd made his own share of flights to tiny lakes in the Cascades, was not unfamiliar with the concept. He adopted the same approach favored by Munro, descending over the west ridge and across the valley to the shoreline by the gauging station. Occasionally, if the cloud cover

Bob Munro taxiing Seven-Two-Zulu on the lake at the South Cascade Glacier. The usable part of the lake was less than half a mile long.

was too low to permit an approach over the ridge, the pilots would fly up the valley, make a sharp left turn at the end, and plop down onto the lake. The valley approach worked, but neither man liked it.

"The problem was that you couldn't see the lake until just before you made your turn. And when you finally did see the lake, you had very little time to set up your approach. Plus, instead of descending down to the lake you were sort of flying over to it, which meant if you had an engine problem, you had no margin of safety. On our normal approach, even if the engine quit you could always reach the lake. On this other approach, if you had a problem you'd probably be too low to make the lake."

BILL PETERS

Mildred Hall always put the glacier flights first on the day's schedule to avoid the winds that could turn the basin into an almost unflyable cauldron of swirling air by afternoon. The research assistants used their radio link to the Forest Service to pass the word to the Air Harbor whenever the winds were bad on the day of a flight, but the word didn't always get through. Peters and Munro would occasionally arrive over the basin to find the lake whipped into whitecaps by screaming winds that ricocheted off the cliff faces and slammed into the Beavers circling thousands of feet above. On those days, the pilots simply turned around and went home.

Most pilots would have regarded the challenge of flying a Beaver onto a tiny, glacier lake as job enough, but Bob Munro was not most pilots. As on the Leduc Glacier years earlier, Munro took a genuine interest in the activities that were taking place on the frozen surface above the lake. One of the scientists assigned to the South Cascade project was Tom Williams, who had worked for Tangborn when he was a graduate student.

> "A very interesting thing about being with Bob up on the South Cascade was that he had an intense scientific interest in what we were doing. He wasn't merely taking us in and out in a very safe manner. Quite often he'd have time to walk with us on the ridge or visit a bit out on the glacier, and he was always asking us questions about what we were doing and what did something mean. Not just about the glacier, but about the flowers that were coming in on the ridge or the rock that the ridge was made of. He's got a strong interest in natural and geological processes, and I think that was part of the enjoyment for him in going in there.
>
> "He'd bring things in to us, sometimes, that we weren't expecting. I remember once in the summer he brought in some watermelon for us. We hadn't had fresh fruit in weeks, and he landed in the lake and carried this big watermelon up to the cabin on the ridge."
>
> **TOM WILLIAMS**

Munro also insisted on doing what he regarded as his fair share of the work when it came to carting the supplies up to the cabin. If there were more armloads of supplies than there were researchers, Munro would grab a load and lug it up the steep trail himself rather than see someone have to make a second trip.

> "Bob brought his interest in what was going on at the glacier back to the office. He'd come back from a flight and tell us what the researchers were finding out about the movement of the glacier, and how much water was melting off of it. Once he brought back a jar of ice worms, tiny worms that live in the glacier and feed off the nutrients that get trapped in the ice. Other times he'd bring back little rocks that he'd found interesting. He'd always tell us about the birds he'd seen or heard, or how big the waterfalls were, or what the weather had been like. Bob loves that kind of country, and hearing him describe what he'd seen after he got back from a flight was the next best thing to going up there yourself."
>
> **MILDRED HALL**

The lake froze in October. While the activity at the glacier wasn't as intense as it was during the summer months, there was still work to be done. Tangborn had pretty much resigned himself to using the expensive and load-limited helicopter, but Munro had other ideas. He'd studied the glacier during the summer, both from the air and from the top of the ridge, and he was convinced he could land and take off from the relatively flat portion below the cabin. He showed Tangborn the pictures he'd taken during the Leduc airlift, and then on a big aerial photo of the South Cascade glacier he showed the scientist how he proposed to repeat the performance.

"I'll come in over the lake and then head right up the glacier. I'll touch down where the surface is pretty level, a little farther up than the trail to the cabin. That's where we'll turn the plane around."

"How are you going to do that?" Tangborn asked. "Won't the floats dig down into the snow?"

"They won't sink in as much as you'd think," Munro replied, searching for the photos Bill Fisk had taken on the Leduc of the Norsemen sitting high on the snow despite their heavy loads. "I'll attach a long rope to the tail, and if I can't taxi the plane all the way around after I land, we'll pull the tail around with the rope."

Tangborn pointed to the aerial photo. "Do you think you'll have enough room to get off before you get into these crevasses? Some of them are big enough to swallow your entire plane."

Munro nodded. "We'll have to keep the loads going out pretty light, but as long as the snow and wind conditions are right we'll be in the air before we get to the bad section."

A few months earlier Tangborn would have had serious doubts about the mental stability of anyone who suggested landing a five-thousand-pound floatplane on the surface of the South Cascade Glacier. But after a season of watching Munro and Peters make landing after flawless landing on the glacier's postage-stamp of a lake, Tangborn had no reason to doubt Munro could operate just as successfully from the snow up above. Besides, it wasn't totally unprecedented; Bill Fairchild had done it, albeit with a much smaller plane on skis.

So Tangborn agreed to let Munro give it a shot. As with his first lake landing, Munro elected to keep the plane as light as possible for the first glacier landing. He'd be landing higher up, over six thousand feet above sea level as opposed to the lake's 5,200 feet. The Beaver's supercharger could ram air at sea-level pressure down the carburetor throat at five thousand feet, but not at six thousand. Compared to the lake takeoffs, Munro would have less horsepower with which to overcome more drag.

In one respect the glacier landing would be the same as landing on the lake. Once Munro was on final approach, he would be committed to land. There was no room to turn around, and the Beaver would not be able to outclimb the glacier sloping up in front of it. But unlike the lake, it would be critical that Munro touch down in exactly the right spot. Too soon, and the plane would be torn apart in the rough snow near the crevasse field. Too late, and Munro would find himself trying to land on a surface that was climbing faster than he could.

It was absolutely critical that he be able to precisely judge his altitude and descent rate all the way through the approach, so Munro abandoned the landing pattern he'd used for the lake. Instead, he decided to start out over the glacier itself. After looking over the surface for any possible problems, he would head west directly over the top of the researchers' cabin on the ridge. As soon as he'd cleared the ridge, he would then start a sweeping 270-degree right turn that would carry him around the foot of the ridge and over the lake until he was heading straight for the glacier.

"I always did it the same way. I set up a procedure so I'd always know where I was relative to where I had to touch down. I wanted a certain altitude when I went over the cabin. If I was at the right altitude, I would start my turn. Then I would cut my throttle and keep turning until I was heading straight for the glacier. The first time would be a little tricky because I'd never done it before. But if I paid close attention to my altitude, my rate of descent, and my position, I'd be able to duplicate the approach the next time. I knew that if I did everything at exactly the same place on every trip, I'd touch down at the same spot every time."

BOB MUNRO

It was several days before the researchers at the glacier radioed in the weather report Munro wanted: clear skies and no wind. Flying alone this time, he took off in Six-Six-Zulu with a few boxes of groceries and headed for the glacier. His life hadn't exactly been dull since his last flight to the Leduc fifteen years earlier, but McQuillan's glacier airlift had been a high point, a job that had challenged him like no other. The fact that he, Bill Fisk, and Paul Garner had made it look

Unloading lumber at the South Cascade glacier. The boards have been bundled together and flown to the lake strapped to the float struts.

easy hadn't diminished the excitement he still felt when he thought about it. And now he was off to do it again, on an even tougher glacier than the Leduc.

He was apprehensive, but he wasn't nervous. His destination was no stranger; he'd been flying on and off the lake all season, and he knew every contour of the glacier above it. The big difference, of course, was the commitment to land once he was on final approach. On the Leduc, the pilots could put in power and fly away even at the last minute. Not so on the South Cascade. But the very real risks imposed by the landing were overshadowed by the sheer joy of doing something new in an environment he loved.

He flew the approach exactly as he'd planned it. As he swung around over the glacier he could see the five researchers scrambling down the trail toward the pristine white surface. The Beaver felt like it was on rails, the air was so smooth. He knew it wouldn't always be this way, but he couldn't have asked for better conditions for his first landing.

It wasn't until he rolled out on final approach that he began to wonder if he'd been foolish in suggesting this mission. The little patch of smooth snow he was aiming for appeared even smaller than the lake. The glacier seemed much steeper than he'd remembered, and the peaks and ridges surrounding the little river of ice seemed much more massive. And as challenging as the lake landings had been at times, the planes had at least been in the correct environment. Now he'd just flown a seaplane past the point of no return on its way to a touchdown on dry land. Well, it wasn't really dry, and it wasn't really land. But technicalities aside, he was about to force a pair of floats to do something the designers at EDO had never intended them to do. As he peered up at the ice-draped wall of rock looming ahead of him, Munro felt a sudden twinge of fear.

It was gone as quickly as it came. Munro had too much faith in his own skill and in the integrity of his airplane to question the outcome. He knew it would work because he'd answered every question and solved every problem beforehand. There was nothing left to chance. Luck wasn't part of the equation.

The floats slid across the snow with the same hollow hiss Munro remembered from the Leduc. The plane had pitched forward the instant the floats touched, but fifteen years had not lessened Munro's reflexes. His Norseman had done exactly the same thing on the Leduc, and he'd anticipated the need for full up-elevator to counter the nose-over tendency. One thing was unexpected, however. From the air, the middle section of the South Cascade had looked quite smooth. But as the floats touched down, Munro was surprised to find that the surface wasn't nearly as smooth as it had looked. There were lots of little dips and rises, and the plane nosed up and down like a boat in a gentle sea.

Within seconds of the floats contacting the snow, Munro put in full right rudder. Despite the high friction between the float keels and the surface of the glacier, Six-Six-Zulu began turning in a wide arc to the right. It made it about halfway around before the lumpy surface dragged the floats to a stop. Munro pulled the mixture control to idle-cut-off, and the engine clanked to a stop. On the Leduc, they'd left the engines running because they didn't trust the Norseman's electrical system, but Six-Six-Zulu was a much more reliable machine, and Munro wasn't worried about a re-start.

He opened the door and stepped out onto the float. This was the first time he'd been out in the middle of the glacier's surface, and he was struck by the silence. Down on the lake, the air had been filled with the sound of water tumbling down the stream and cascading off the surrounding cliffs. Up on the glacier, everything was frozen into immobility. But then Munro realized there was a sound. At first he tried to pinpoint the source, but then he realized it didn't really have one. It was the sound of vastness, the sound of rock and ice. It was a presence more than a sound, and it made Munro feel very small as he stood beside his yellow and white plane in the middle of a black and white landscape that measured time in centuries instead of seconds.

Beaver Six-Six-Zulu on the South Cascade Glacier. The glacier was tricky to land on, and there was no going around once the plane was on final approach. Munro didn't feel comfortable exposing his employees to the risk, so he flew all the winter flights himself. (photo by Bob Munro).

A sudden crunching startled him and he turned as the first of the researchers trudged up to the plane.

"Great landing," the young man said.

"Oh, it wasn't that difficult," Munro answered. "I've done a few of them before."

"Wendell told us. He also told us that once you start in here you have to land no matter what. There's no going around."

"Well," Munro said with a smile, "I try not to think about that."

He handed the boxes of food down to the researchers and then pulled a coil of rope out from under the rear seat.

"I'm going to need your help getting turned around."

The researchers put down their boxes and gathered under the tail where Munro was fastening one end of the line to the tailwheel steering post.

"What I need you to do is to pull the tail around when I get the plane moving forward. I'm going to turn this way," Munro pointed off to the right, "so you need to pull the tail the other way."

"Do you want us to untie the rope when we get you turned around?"

"No, leave it tied on. It will just flop around back there out of the way. I'll give you a signal when I want you to start pulling."

The five men grabbed the end of the thirty foot line and pulled it out at a right angle to the tail. Munro started toward the front of the plane, but then he remembered there was something else the men on the rope needed to know.

"I'm going to be using pretty close to full power, so there's going to be quite a blast of wind behind the plane. Make sure you stay out of that, but don't come forward of the wing. If you walk into the propeller it will put a real damper on your day."

He walked around the front of plane, automatically checking the snow below the engine for evidence of oil leaks, and levered himself up onto the left float. He pulled open the pilot's door and climbed into the cockpit. It had been less than thirty minutes since he'd landed, so the engine hadn't cooled down completely. He flipped on the master switch, and then the instrument switches. A couple of strokes on the wobble pump to build up some fuel pressure and he was ready to go. Engaging the spring-loaded start switch with the thumb of his left hand, he pumped the throttle a couple of times with his right hand as the big, two-bladed Hamilton-Standard propeller began to swing around. He waited until four blades had blurred past the windscreen and then flipped the magneto switch to BOTH, and was rewarded with a hesitant bark from the exhaust. He held the start switch on for another moment as the rest of the cylinders began firing. Then he let go of the switch and coaxed the engine along with the throttle, expertly walking the fine line between killing it with too little throttle and causing a backfire with too much.

The engine settled into its familiar off-beat idle, and Munro waited until the oil temperature rose to the bottom of the green arc. He scanned the other instruments: oil pressure, fuel pressure, cylinder head temperature, intake air temperature, alternator output. All the needles were where he expected them to be. Reaching for the throttle, he smoothly pushed the lever up, and the staccato rumble of the nine-cylinder radial swelled to a snarling roar.

The plane began to shake and buck as the whirling propeller bit into the air and sent it slamming back against the tail surfaces. Had the plane been on the water it would have been well into its takeoff run, but with its float keels wedged into the snow Six-Six-Zulu simply sat and vibrated. Munro shoved the throttle up a little more, and the propeller tips began to yowl in the frigid air. Still the plane did not move, but Munro was prepared for this. He moved the yoke all the way forward and then all the way back. Behind him, the elevator went from full down to full up. The airstream blasting back from the prop first tried to pick the tail up and then push it down. Munro continued pumping the yoke, alternating the force against the elevator until the plane itself began to rock back and forth.

The rocking broke the floats free of the snow, and the plane began to inch forward. Turning in his seat, Munro waved at the men outside on the rope to start pulling. Slowly the plane began to pivot to the right. Munro shoved the right rudder pedal to the floor in an attempt to help the plane around. The researchers pulled harder and the plane swung faster. The rope pullers began to run forward in order to maintain their ninety degree angle. One man lost his footing and went down, but the other four kept pulling as they ran around with the plane.

When the Beaver was pointing directly downslope, Munro pulled the throttle to idle and waved to the men to stop. Gasping for breath, the researchers dropped the rope and backed away from the plane. Inside, Munro checked the flight controls again for freedom and glanced over the engine instruments. Everything looked fine. He pumped the flaps down to the takeoff position and looked to make sure all the researchers were safely out of the way. Then he eased the throttle back up. This time he went right on up to full power.

The Beaver began to slide forward almost immediately. The noise of the floats was louder than Munro had remembered from his Leduc days. The Leduc had been smoother, too. As in the landing, Six-Six-Zulu began nosing up and down like a boat at sea. The pitching was fairly gentle, but Munro knew the closer he got to the crevasse field, the more violent the up and down movement would become. Unlike a skiplane, a floatplane has no shock absorbers between the floats and the fuselage. Every bump and jolt is transmitted straight up the float struts into the airframe. Exceed the strength of just one bolt, and the whole thing will collapse into a pile of parts with the pilot in the middle.

Munro flicked his eyes between the view out the windshield and the airspeed indicator at the upper left of the instrument panel. Twenty miles per hour, thirty, forty. The floats were skimming across the snow. They made a heck of a racket as they ricocheted off the tops of the bumps, but the plane was accelerating nicely, aided by the gentle slope of the glacier. Fifty miles per hour. Munro began to ease back on the yoke. Sixty.

The hollow scraping and banging from the floats stopped abruptly. The needle in the airspeed indicator zipped past seventy as Six-Six-Zulu climbed smoothly away from the surface. The gaping canyons of the crevasse field flashed below him, and then he was over the smooth, frozen surface of the lake. Munro banked the plane to the left toward the valley that was the first leg on his journey home. Behind him, mere dots in the vastness of the glacial bowl, five tiny figures waved good-bye. Then the researchers picked up their boxes of food and began the slow trek back to their plywood shelter. The beat of the Beaver's engine faded slowly, and then it was gone. The only evidence Munro had been there at all were the parcels in the researchers' arms and two sets of parallel grooves in the snow.

Tangborn was delighted. The ability to fly Beaver-size loads of people and supplies to the glacier year round meant that his team could amass more data, which in the research world translates into greater accuracy in the results. For Munro, the winter glacier flights would be sheer delight, the kind of job he relished most. Every landing and takeoff would challenge his judgment and skills to the maximum, but offsetting the risk was the setting, his beloved mountains where wind-blasted ridges of rock and ice towered over tumbling clearwater creeks and snow-speckled forests. It was creation at its most intense, and Munro found it amazing to contemplate, standing in the snow beside his airplane. He was not one to talk much about religion or the meaning of life, but his reticence was not due to a lack of belief. He found it incomprehensible that anyone could stand where he was standing and not come away believing in something. Science alone couldn't account for the perfection he saw expressed in every spire of rock, in every tongue of ice, in the wind itself.

Although there was work to be done at the glacier during the winter, the level of activity wasn't nearly as high as it was during the summer. Tangborn sent crews up to perform specific tasks and then had them flown out a few days later. This was great for the researchers as it minimized the time they had to spend enduring the grim conditions at the cabin, but it made things harder for Munro. In the summer, the resident glacier crews were almost always able to radio in the weather conditions on the day of a flight, so the pilots knew what to expect. Judging winds and landing conditions was much more difficult in the winter, and the fact that there was often nobody on the ground to communicate the conditions meant Munro had no way of knowing what it was like at the glacier until he got there.

> "We didn't bother putting up a windsock because the storms would have ripped it apart in a week. But not knowing the wind direction wasn't the only problem. Unless you've gone in there yourself you don't realize how hard it can be to see the surface of the glacier itself. Everything's white, and it can become almost impossible to judge your height.
>
> "If someone was up there they'd go out and make some marks in the snow using tarps or whatever. They'd line up about three marks which made it pretty easy to judge your height off the surface. But if there wasn't anyone there, it could get very difficult to get in. We tried dropping fir boughs and smoke bombs and a bunch of other things. The problem was we'd drop the fir boughs and then I'd come around on my approach and I'd see the boughs and I'd figure I've got it, I've got it, and then I'd fly by the boughs and be in the white again."
>
> **BOB MUNRO**

The most effective landing zone marker was red dye. It required someone to be at the glacier to spread it out, but it made a runway outline that could be seen for miles. The researchers tried to keep a stock of it on hand at the cabin during the winter, and they used it whenever they could.

Between the Leduc Glacier airlift, the South Cascade Glacier supply flights, and Kenmore's final glacier project on the Blue Glacier in the Olympic Range, Bob Munro made over a thousand snow landings. In all those landings and takeoffs, he damaged a plane only once.

It was on the South Cascade, on a day of rotten visibility and gusty winds. There was no one at the cabin to mark the snow, and the fir boughs his passengers had shoved out the door had been whirled away out of sight. Nevertheless, Munro felt confident enough to make the landing. He circled down over the glacier until he was at the proper altitude. The cabin on the ridge was almost completely buried in snow, but he knew where it was and he crossed over heading west. Following his approach procedure to the letter, he rolled Six-Six-Zulu into a right turn and reduced the power.

Everything looked fine until he rolled out on final. He could see the surface well enough to judge his height, but he couldn't make out the actual condition of the snow.

Not that he could do anything about it, for by now he'd flown past the point of no return and was committed to land. Whether the culprit was a sudden slackening of the wind or he simply misjudged his height he'll never know, but the plane touched down sooner and harder than he'd intended. There was a tremendous bang and a violent lurch upwards, followed by the familiar sound of the floats sliding and bumping across the snow.

The plane came to a stop and everyone piled out. Munro wasn't sure what he'd find, but the impact had been so hard and loud that he expected to find something broken. At first glance there didn't seem to be anything wrong at all. The diagonal brace wires, usually the first thing to let go in a hard landing, were intact. The two big spreader bars between the floats were straight and securely fastened. It wasn't until Munro walked out in front of the plane that he saw what had happened. The right front strut, one of the streamlined tubes that connect the float to the fuselage, was bent. Not a lot, but it definitely had a kink in it.

Had he discovered this kind of damage on a plane back at the Air Harbor, Munro would have grounded it immediately until the strut was replaced and every other component of the attachment system had been thoroughly inspected. But he wasn't at the Air Harbor, he was sitting more than a mile high on top of a glacier. Getting a new strut flown in was out of the question; Bill Fisk had flown the Leduc airlift with him, but the South Cascade was a different story. Munro was unwilling to expose his other pilots to the potentially deadly consequences of a blown landing on the snow, so once the lake froze he was the only pilot allowed to make the flight. Besides, it would take more than just the delivery of a new strut to fix Six-Six-Zulu. He'd need the proper tools and some way of supporting the fuselage while the strut was changed.

Munro wrapped both hands around the center of the strut and pushed and pulled on it as hard as he could. He couldn't discern any play, and an examination of the fasteners at either end showed them to be undamaged, at least to the eye. He decided the strut would hold up for one takeoff. There was no telling what it might do when he landed at Kenmore, but even if it snapped in two and put Six-Six-Zulu on the bottom of the lake, Munro knew he'd at least have ready access to the equipment he'd need to salvage the plane and fix it.

He helped the researchers unload their equipment, and then he took a walk back down his landing tracks to inspect the surface. At the bottom he found why he'd hit so hard. A ridge of wind-packed snow had built up over some imperfection in the surface, and he'd had the misfortune to touch down just in front of it. Looking around, he noticed this wasn't the only ridge in the area. The last thing he needed was to hit one on the way out when his speed over the ground was the greatest, so he decided he would taxi farther up the glacier before turning the plane around.

He trudged back up the gentle slope to the plane and explained what he was going to do.

"How much farther do you think you need to go?" one of the researchers asked.

"Oh, maybe a couple of hundred yards," Munro answered. "But I'll help you carry this stuff to the cabin first."

It wasn't nearly as easy as it had been in the summer. The trail was slippery, and then it took the better part of an hour to dig enough snow away from the door to get in. It was early afternoon by the time the men got back to the plane. One good thing, Munro noticed, was that the wind had eased off a bit.

"Hop in," he told his helpers. "There's no sense walking when you can ride."

The researchers clambered into the cabin while Munro gave the bent float strut one more examination. He was sure it would hold. He climbed into the cockpit and started the engine. His passengers had flown with Kenmore enough to understand the need to let the engine reach operating temperature, so they talked about the snow measurements they'd be taking over the next few days while Munro watched the oil temperature creep slowly up the dial toward the green arc.

When the engine was warmed up, Munro eased the throttle forward. The floats unstuck quickly in the cold, dry snow, and Six-Six-Zulu began to slide slowly up the glacier. Just before the slope began to slant up toward the summit Munro pulled the power to idle and the Beaver jerked to a stop. The researchers piled out into the snow and grabbed the rope trailing back from the tail. When Munro saw they were ready, he waved at them to start pulling and opened the throttle almost all the way. The men on the rope had a hard time of it as they scrambled to keep abreast of the pivoting airplane. The snow was deep and they kept breaking through the surface crust. Between struggling simply to keep their footing and actually pulling on the rope, the researchers were exhausted by the time they had Six-Six-Zulu pointing back down the glacier. Munro pulled the power back to idle and climbed down from the cockpit.

"Thank you," he said to the panting group of men. "I'd give you a ride back down but you might have a tough time getting off as we went past the cabin. If you have a chance to put some markers in the snow when I come back to pick you up, it would really help a lot if you put the first one just this side of that ridge I hit this morning. That way I'll know where not to land."

"What will happen if that strut breaks during your takeoff run?" one of the researchers asked.

"Oh, I think it will be okay. But if I'm wrong, you'll have to set an extra place for dinner."

Munro levered himself back up onto the float and climbed through the pilot's door. A quick check of the engine instruments showed all was well with the rumbling radial bolted to the firewall in front of him. He settled himself in his seat, checked the flight controls, and tightened his seatbelt. He was confident the strut would hold, but he wasn't absolutely positive. If it does collapse, he told himself, the front of the fuselage will drop down between the floats and hit the snow. It might flip over and it might not. All I can do is pull the power off and shut off the fuel.

Mentally prepared for the worst, he eased the power up and rocked the yoke back and forth to free the floats. The plane began to slide forward and he went to full throttle. The Beaver picked up speed fast, aided by the gentle downward slope of the glacier. He was amazed at how rough the surface was; he hadn't noticed it during his earlier taxi upslope. There was nothing he could do as Six-Six-Zulu lurched from side to side and banged across the wind ridges. The jolts grew more severe and he began to wonder if he'd been overly optimistic in his assessment of the damage. There was no way the weakened strut could hold up much longer under this abuse.

The airspeed indicator hit fifty miles per hour, and Munro turned the yoke all the way to the left hoping to ease the load on the bent strut by picking up the right wing a bit. He didn't feel much difference as the floats continued to pitch and buck across the surface, but any reduction of stress on the damaged strut was better than none.

Suddenly he sensed that Six-Six-Zulu was ready to fly. He eased back on the yoke, and was rewarded with silence. The engine was still thundering away in front of him, but the scraping and banging and grinding of the floats against the snow had disappeared. The strut had held, a tribute to the engineers at EDO and to the mechanics at Kenmore who kept the company's planes in such superb condition.

The term "bush pilot" conjures up an image of a rugged pilot and an equally rugged airplane taking on the challenges of Alaska or the Canadian wilderness. You don't think about bush pilots when you think about a city like Seattle. But for thirty-five years, Bob Munro flew in the same world of remote lakes, isolated bays, rugged mountains, and unpredictable weather as his northern counterparts. And while he readily admitted to making a few errors in judgment over the years, his career at the controls was remarkable for its relative lack of danger and suspense in the Hollywood sense. There were few close calls, no crazy stunts, no hair-raising adventures. In this way, too, Munro's flying career paralleled the bush pilots up north, who, despite the romantic, devil-may-care aura surrounding them, do everything they can to make their flights as pleasant and safe for their passengers as possible.

Munro took up flying more by necessity than by choice, but the fact that he proved to be extremely good at it is due largely to his ability to recognize his own limitations. While some of his flights, particularly the ones to the glaciers, may have seemed hair-raising to everyone else, Munro never took on anything he wasn't confident he could do. Except once.

It was in October 1969. Wendell Tangborn needed to go up to the glacier to take the final measurements for the year and to button things down for the winter. Not knowing if the lake was still open, he decided to hire a helicopter to fly him to the glacier for a few days. Three other men went with him, including a hydrologist named Arne Hansen. The chopper dropped them off on the glacier near the base of the trail leading up to the cabin, and the men got to work. The weather was sunny and clear and was forecast to remain that way for the next few days. Eight hundred feet below the cabin, the lake was still unfrozen, but the sudden chill that settled in when the sun went down made it obvious the lake's days as a liquid were numbered.

Tangborn had volunteered to cook dinner the first night. When shortly after the meal Hansen began complaining of stomach pains, Tangborn became the butt of some rowdy cooking jokes until the men realized Hansen was rapidly getting worse. By ten he was writhing in agony and vomiting constantly. Tangborn tried the Forest Service radio, but at that hour no one was monitoring the frequency. Hiking out was out of the question. The nine-mile trail to the road was difficult enough in the daytime; walking it at night would be almost suicidal, even if Hansen was in a condition to attempt it. And simply reaching the road was no guarantee of assistance. One of them would have to keep walking down it until he found help. The only thing they could do was make Hansen as comfortable as possible and try the radio again in the morning.

Hansen's condition continued to deteriorate. Clearly this was not just a case of food poisoning, as the others had all eaten the same thing with no ill effects. Then, as if the suffering of their co-worker was not enough, the wind kicked up about midnight and got steadily stronger. Between the roar of the wind and Hansen's painful moans, no one got any sleep that night.

By sunup, Tangborn estimated it was blowing fifty miles per hour from the southwest with gusts fifteen to twenty miles per hour higher. The men began broadcasting again on the radio at dawn, but their calls went unanswered until eight o'clock. Upon learning of Hansen's plight, the Forest Service immediately called the Coast Guard station at Bellingham. The station had a helicopter at its disposal, and the flying time from Bellingham to the South Cascade glacier would have been only thirty or forty minutes. But when the Coast Guard officers learned how hard the wind was blowing in the mountains, they refused to let the helicopter fly. It would be madness, they said, to send a chopper into those winds. Between the updrafts and the downdrafts and the swirling currents screaming around the peaks, a helicopter pilot would be lucky to maintain control of his machine, let alone conduct a rescue operation. They would put the helicopter on alert, and take off the moment they heard the winds at the glacier had dropped.

Tangborn took the news with a sense of dread. If the Coast Guard couldn't fly, nobody could, and Tangborn knew the winds could blow fifty-plus for hours if not days. None of the men at the glacier had a clue as to what was twisting Arne's gut into knots of pain, but it didn't require any medical expertise to see that he was still getting worse. Although they dared not discuss it openly, they were beginning to fear for their friend's life.

Tangborn keyed the microphone on the Forest Service radio and asked the person on the other end if they would contact Kenmore Air Harbor.

"Ask for Bob Munro," Tangborn said. "Tell him what's going on up here and ask him if he has any ideas."

Tangborn was grasping at straws. If the Coast Guard couldn't get a helicopter to the glacier, he certainly didn't expect Munro to try it with an airplane. But he'd been flying with the quiet, competent pilot for more than a year, and he'd observed enough to know that if there was anything Munro could do, he'd do it.

Thirty minutes after Tangborn's last transmission, the radio crackled back to life. The message from the Forest Service was short and simple. An airplane was on the way.

As luck would have it, Munro was home when the call came in from the Forest Service. He listened quietly as the caller repeated Tangborn's description of the weather conditions at the glacier, but his mind was racing feverishly. That he didn't want to fly up there was a given. He'd been bashed about in the mountains by winds that were far weaker than the ones howling around the South Cascade today, and he knew how deadly the downdrafts could be. The turbulence could cause a pilot to lose control and fly into a ridge, or if violent enough could cause an airplane to stall. If this occurred as the pilot was attempting to land or takeoff there might not be enough room to recover, and the plane would end up in the rocks as permanently as if the wind had hammered it there itself.

It had been twenty-three years since Munro's first flying lesson with Jack Mines, and everything he'd learned and experienced since then told him the Coast Guard had the right idea: stay on the ground until the winds died down and then go in. But even though Munro hadn't talked to Tangborn directly, he sensed an urgency in the scientist's message that elevated the situation beyond just a need to help a sick man. It sounded like a life or death situation, and Munro couldn't let himself leave a critically ill man suffering in the mountains without trying to do something about it. He asked the Forest Service official to radio a message to the cabin that Kenmore would try to get a plane onto the lake, and that it would be on its way within thirty minutes.

While Six-Six-Zulu was being put into the water, Munro walked across the tiedown area to his house to tell Ruth what he was about to do. If she was upset by the idea of her husband going off to fly in unflyable conditions she didn't show it. She agreed that every effort should be made to get the sick man out of the mountains and into a hospital.

"I shouldn't be gone very long," Munro said reassuringly. "I'll just be up there long enough to pick this fellow up and then I'll be heading back. I should think two hours at the most."

As he walked back to the office, the line boy intercepted him to tell him Six-Six-Zulu was ready to go.

"I've topped off the oil and pumped all the float compartments dry. The front and center tanks are full, the rear and wingtip tanks are empty."

Munro thanked the young man and stepped into the office to find Mildred Hall bustling about.

"I've called the hospital," she announced, "and they said they'll have an ambulance here by the time you get back. But I'm going to get some blankets just in case so we can keep him warm on the couch. And I can send another pilot with you if you think that would be helpful."

"No, I'll go by myself. There's no sense in two of us getting into trouble up there."

Munro genuinely didn't want to extend the risk he was facing to any of his other employees, but an even greater motivation for rejecting Mildred's suggestion was that he knew he'd have a better chance of success if he made the flight alone. Many people prefer tackling a difficult challenge in the company of other people. Two or three or four heads are better than one, they figure. And sharing the danger and responsibility gives at least the illusion that the situation isn't as tough as it seems.

Bob Munro was not one of these people. He preferred flying by himself, particularly if the conditions were bad.

"It's a big responsibility, looking out for another person. I don't want to make it sound like we're unsafe, but you'll do things, gamble a little bit, if it's just you in the plane. If you have someone else in there with you, you might think, 'Well, I'd better not do this because I might scare them.' So you don't go or you turn back, where if you'd been by yourself you'd have pushed on through.

"I had to ferry a new Cessna 206 out from the factory in Wichita once, and a friend of mine really wanted to go. I thought it would be wonderful for him to see the country from the air, so I took him with me. We hadn't been gone from Wichita thirty minutes when we hit turbulence and he began upchucking. You sit there for twelve hours with someone that ill and it's not very pleasant. All the way back I kept offering to land and put him on the airline, but he kept saying, 'Oh, I can make it.' And then he'd double up in the seat again. That's hard on you to have that going on when you're trying to fly."

BOB MUNRO

So Munro took off alone in Six-Six-Zulu to face whatever it was the mountains were going to throw at him. The air was reasonably smooth around Kenmore, but as he approached the foothills, the Beaver began to bobble. Munro let it wander; trying to correct every movement would just tire him out and wouldn't do much to make the flight any smoother. But by the time he reached the Skagit River Valley the bashing was much worse, and he was on the controls constantly, raising the nose, lowering a wing, or adding power to compensate for a downdraft.

The Beaver does not ride turbulence very well. It's strong enough to take almost anything the weather can dish out, but it's slow speed and long wings make it susceptible to the slightest air movement. Where a faster airplane with shorter wings and a higher wing loading will punch through turbulence, a Beaver wallows forward, yawing and rolling in an aerial ballet that's made more than a few passengers paw desperately through the seat pockets in search of a sick sack.

Munro guided his bucking airplane up the South Fork of the Cascade River to the third valley that led to the South Cascade glacier. As he banked around to begin the final leg of the flight to the lake the wind funneling out of the valley seemed to bring his plane to a dead stop. Munro glanced at the fuel gauge. Bucking the wind was eating up a lot more fuel than normal, but he figured that no matter what happened he'd have enough gas to at least get back out of the mountains and land on the Skagit River near the town of Mt. Vernon or across the bay at Anacortes. One thing he had going for him was the visibility, which was unlimited under a virtually cloudless sky. The wind might succeed in taking control of my airplane, he thought as he glanced down at the quivering instrument panel, but at least I'll see whatever it is I crash into.

With a ground speed half its airspeed, Six-Six-Zulu crept up the valley toward the lake. Munro had never experienced such violent turbulence over such a long period. Sure, he'd had the occasional bad jolt on other flights, but nothing like this. It just went on and on. His only weapons of defense were the control column, the throttle, and the strength of the airplane. He couldn't do much about the airframe's integrity at this point, but he fought off the wind's punches as best he could with the yoke and the throttle. One moment he'd be at full power as a downdraft elevatored him toward the valley floor and then he'd have to yank the power off as a swirling updraft sent him rocketing skyward. Horizontal eddies of air would knock one wing up almost vertically, and then as soon as he'd brought it back down with the yoke, slam it right back up again.

His only references to level flight were what he saw out the windshield and the sound of the engine. Even if he'd wanted to use the instruments, they were almost worthless. The airspeed needle jerked back and forth across the dial, dipping below stall speed one second and then jerking around to the never-exceed speed the next. The vertical speed indicator was just a blur as it tried to keep up with the violent changes of altitude. The turn coordinator was useless as well; the only time it showed the plane being coordinated was the brief instant the needle and ball passed through the center of the gauge on their wild swings from one extreme to the other.

If Munro was concerned at the degree of turbulence he was experiencing in the valley, he was downright dismayed when he saw the lake. In fact, he could only see half the lake, the half closest to him with the gauging station and the outlet stream. The far end of the lake was almost invisible. The wind was so strong, and was ricocheting off the cliffs in so many directions, the water was literally being lifted into the air. An angry white haze filled the basin at the foot of the glacier, almost obliterating the maelstrom of muddy water leaping and foaming beneath it.

The near end of the lake wasn't quite so bad. The surface was covered with whitecaps, but here the wind was coming from only one direction as evidenced by the orderly rows of waves marching toward the outlet stream. It took only a glance for Munro to realize that whatever he decided to do, he had less than half the lake to do it on. Peering down from his wildly bucking airplane, he figured he had about one thousand feet of water on which to land and take off. Tangborn, who's practiced eye was more accurate at judging distances, stated later that the length of usable water on the lake, meaning water that wasn't being whipped into an airplane-destroying frenzy, was less than 750 feet.

Seaplane pilots, at least the good ones, figure out their takeoffs before they figure out their landings. There isn't a seaplane pilot alive who hasn't heard the story about the pilot who landed on a lake too small to take off from. And Munro was a good seaplane pilot. It took him only an instant to realize that even if he managed to land without breaking the plane, taking off again would be almost impossible. A downwind takeoff in the gale shrieking off the glacier would be tantamount to suicide. The only way to go was into the wind, which would mean taking off toward the glacier and the rocky ridge that spilled down into the lake.

No one had ever attempted this before, even on a nice day. There simply wasn't room to take off into the basin and turn around with any degree of safety. And today, half the basin was unusable. The filthy, heaving water at the far end of the lake mirrored the violence in the air above it. Munro knew if he allowed the invisible banshees of wind to get a grip on even one of Six-Six-Zulu's wings, the airplane would be ripped from his control in an instant. The only possible way out would be to start the takeoff run at the gauging station, head directly for the rocky ridge, lift off, and bank steeply to the right in an almost 180-degree turn back toward the outlet stream and the valley beyond it. All this in less than 750 feet.

Any floatplane pilot looking at these conditions would say it couldn't be done. The charts in the back of the Beaver's operating manual said it couldn't be done. Munro very much wanted to say it couldn't be done and go home. But he couldn't bring himself to turn his tail to the people on the ground.

He wasn't terribly worried about the landing; he was confident he could maintain control of the airplane through the approach and touchdown. And even if he couldn't, and control was snatched away from him at the last moment, he wasn't particularly afraid of damaging or destroying Six-Six-Zulu. It was just a plane, after all, and he knew how to salvage and fix planes. He wasn't even all that worried about his own life. Loggers, fishermen, pilots, anyone in a risky profession always figures it's the other guy that will have the accident. Besides, Munro thought wryly, the lake is shallow so even if the plane gets blown over, about the worst that will happen to me is that I'll get wet.

No, it was the takeoff that had him scared. There was the very real danger that he simply wouldn't get off the water in time to make the turn. And if he misjudged the liftoff and smeared the plane across the face of the ridge, well, the fellow he'd rescued would be a lot worse off than he'd been before he got in the plane. He knew if he turned around and went home no one would fault him. Even the Coast Guard had refused to attempt the flight. But while no one else would blame him for heading home, he knew he would spend the rest of his life wondering if he could have pulled it off.

In the end, it was an easy decision. I'm here, he said to himself, so I might as well give it a try. After all, what's the worst that can happen? He decided not to think about the answer to that question. He reduced power and banked around to begin his standard approach. The only thing he did differently was to maintain a higher than normal speed. Instead of descending toward the lake at eighty miles per hour, he decided to fly at ninety. This would give him an additional cushion of speed against the gusts, which if they fluctuated wildly enough, could cause Six-Six-Zulu's wing to momentarily stall. And if he was low enough, a momentary stall could put him into the rocks.

The trickiest part of the approach was going to be hitting his touchdown point. With the far end of the lake in turmoil, Munro wanted to touch down as close as possible to the near shore. It wouldn't be easy with the gusts slamming his plane around, but the combination of an empty airplane and a powerful and responsive engine gave him the best chance he could ask for.

The turbulence got worse as he got lower. Downdrafts are the greatest concern during an approach because they can cause a pilot to undershoot his touchdown point, but in this situation, the updrafts were just as frustrating. The last thing Munro wanted to do was coast across the border into the bad part of the lake, but every time Six-Six-Zulu was ballooned upwards he was running the risk of doing just that. But if he still harbored apprehensions about the wisdom of what he was trying to do he no longer had time to think about it as he wrestled with the yoke to keep the wings level and the airspeed constant while his right hand worked the throttle lever back and forth in an attempt to counteract the gusts and maintain his descent path.

It was without question the most difficult piece of flying Munro had ever attempted. There were times as he crossed the valley toward the outlet stream that he was sure he wasn't going to make it, but he refused to submit to the fear. Acting on instinct alone—there wasn't time to reason anything out—he regained control of Six-Six-Zulu again and again until suddenly he swept past the gauging station and hit the water with a thump almost exactly where he'd hoped to.

The gale funneling out of the basin brought the Beaver to a stop almost instantly. In fact, Munro found he needed partial power just to maintain his position in the lake; at idle the plane would have been blown backwards onto the mud. Turning the plane around was out of the question. Even if he'd been able to force the Beaver to turn out of the wind, the gusts ripping across the water would pick up the outside wing and flip the plane before he could react. He decided the only course of action was to taxi straight ahead toward the ridge sticking out into the lake where he might get a little protection from the wind. He remembered Tangborn telling him the bottom was composed almost entirely of mud. If he was right, Six-Six-Zulu should run aground well before reaching the base of the ridge. This would make it more difficult to get the sick man out to the plane, but the wind made it the only option.

Munro increased power until Six-Six-Zulu was moving slowly forward. He hoped there weren't any rocks in front of him, although punching a hole in a float would eliminate the stomach-churning ordeal of the takeoff yet to come. He could see the gusts surging towards him, their strength and speed mirrored by the dark patches of ruffled water that swept across the surface. When they hit, Six-Six-Zulu's wings rocked wildly, but as long as he kept heading directly into them, the gusts wouldn't be able to get the leverage they needed to flip the Beaver over.

The floats hit bottom when he was still fifty feet from shore. Munro pulled the power to idle. He started to shut the engine down, but then decided to leave it running to prevent the wind from blowing him backwards into deeper water. He could see no one on the lakeshore, and he had no way to contact the cabin. So he sat behind the rumbling Pratt & Whitney and stared at the ice-gouged rock face in front of him, hoping someone up on the ridge had heard him arrive.

The news that a plane was on its way was heartening to the men in the cabin, but none of them really expected it to land. Hansen's condition was very bad now, and it seemed pointless to put him through the agony of a trip down the steep trail to the lake only to wait for a plane that might not even show up, let alone land. So they tried to make him comfortable and then sat down to see which would hold out the longest, Hansen's will to survive or the wind.

Between the lack of sleep and the hypnotic shriek of the wind, the scientists sank into an almost comatose state as they stared at the vibrating walls of their plywood cabin. It was Tangborn who suddenly realized a new sound had been added to the yowling cacophony outside the cabin, but it took him almost a minute to realize that the booming roar echoing up from the lake was not the wind, but an engine. An engine he recognized.

"There's a plane on the lake!" he shouted, and he fought the door open against the wind to get a better view. From his vantage point on the ridgetop, he looked down on the white wings and yellow and brown cowl of a Kenmore Beaver. He clawed back through the door into the cabin.

"Arne, the plane made it, but I don't think it can stay here very long. We've got to get you down there right now. Can you walk at all?"

Arne nodded grimly and rolled out of his bunk onto his feet. He stood up, swayed a moment, and then doubled over, clutching his stomach. Tangborn's heart sank; the trail was narrow and steep, and while it might be possible for the three of them to carry Hansen down to the lake, it would take a long time. More time than the pilot had, he was sure. But Hansen had other ideas.

"I can walk like this," he grunted through gritted teeth. "Let's go."

He shuffled to the door and waited while Tangborn fought it open again.

"Do you want us to come, too?" one of the other men asked.

Tangborn shook his head. "Get on the radio and tell the Forest Service the plane got here and was able to land. Tell them we're going down to the plane now, and to have an ambulance ready to pick up Arne at Kenmore. Then keep an eye on us in case we get into trouble on the way down."

The wind tore the door from his hands and slammed it shut with a crash. Tangborn turned to see Hansen, bent over and still clutching his stomach, side-stepping down the steep trail, and he hurried to catch up.

A bit of movement and a tiny splash of color high on the rocks caught Munro's eye, and he peered up through Six-Six-Zulu's windshield to see two figures making their way slowly down the ridge. He'd been up and down the trail enough times to know it by heart, and when the figures reached a particularly steep part he could see one of them helping the other one. As they got closer, he could see one of the men was Tangborn. He didn't recognize the other one, but it was obvious from the way he was walking that he was in considerable pain. Occasionally, he stumbled, and each time he did Munro wondered if he should shut off the engine and wade ashore to help, but he knew if he did, Six-Six-Zulu would probably be blown backwards off the mud and flipped over, so he stayed where he was.

The two men reached the shore and began picking their way through the rocks to the end of the point. Munro wondered how Tangborn was going to get his staggering, doubled-over companion out to the plane, but he didn't have to wonder very long. With rescue so near, Hansen found reserves of willpower he didn't know he had. When he was as close to the plane as he could get on dry land, he waded unhesitatingly into the water and began splashing toward the rumbling Beaver. Tangborn waded in after him, and Munro suddenly realized both men were on a collision course with the propeller. He pulled the mixture to idle-cutoff, and the radial rattled to a stop. The wings rocked and vibrated in the wind that roared around the point as Munro climbed out onto the left float, and he prayed the plane would stay wedged in the mud long enough for him to get the ill scientist aboard and restart the engine.

Gasping in pain, Hansen reached the side of the float but he was too weak to pull himself up. Tangborn splashed up beside him, wrapped his arms around Hansen's legs, and levered him up as Munro lifted him under the arms. They got him seated on the float, and then they repeated the maneuver to move him up onto the middle seat in the cabin where he slumped, moaning, onto his side.

"You'll be all right now," Tangborn shouted over the thunder of the wind. "Bob will have you back at Kenmore in no time."

Hansen nodded weakly as Munro strapped him in as best he could.

"It's going to be pretty bumpy on the way out but I'll do everything I can to make it easy on you."

"Don't worry about that," Hansen said with a weak smile. "I'm just glad you made it in here."

Munro tactfully decided against telling his passenger that making it in had been the easy part. Making it out again was what had his own stomach in knots.

"Okay," he called to Tangborn after he'd finished securing Hansen. "When I give the signal, push me back off the mud and then get back to shore as fast as you can."

Tangborn nodded and splashed around to the front of the float. Munro slammed the cabin door shut and stepped forward over the flap handle to the pilot's seat. He shoved the mixture control to full rich, flipped on the master switch, and pointed at Tangborn. Outside, the scientist bent down, put both hands on the rubber bumper on the front of the float, and shoved as hard as he could. Six-Six-Zulu slid backwards off the mud and began to rock wildly as the wind yanked and tore at the wings.

Munro waited until Tangborn was safely out of the way, and then he hit the start switch. The starter began its characteristic whine and the prop began to turn. Munro pumped the throttle twice as he counted the blades swinging past the windshield. He switched on the magnetos as the third blade went by, and the warm engine fired instantly. The plane was drifting back rapidly now, and Munro fed in power to halt the drift. As he hung there, halfway between the base of the ridge and the muddy shore near the gauging station, he pondered his next move.

Turning the plane around was out of the question. There was no way he could overpower the wind's force with the rudders, and even if he could the Beaver would be flipped the moment he pivoted even slightly out of the wind. His only recourse was to let the plane drift slowly backwards until the floats were almost touching the mud near the outlet stream, and then firewall the throttle and hope for the best. His eyes swept across the instrument panel; temperatures and pressures were all in the green, and he pumped the flaps down to the takeoff position.

Holding the yoke full forward in an attempt to keep the nose down, Munro opened the pilot's door and peered aft as he played the throttle to keep the plane from drifting back too fast. When he judged the tails of the floats were just feet from grounding out in the mud behind him he banged the door shut and opened the throttle all the way.

From his perch on the rocks at the base of the ridge, Tangborn heard the engine go to full power. For a moment, the wind had a rival as the roar of the exhaust and the howl from the long, two bladed propeller filled the basin. The yellow-cowled nose rose high into the air as the plane climbed ponderously onto the step, and then it pitched over to thunder directly at the rock face at Tangborn's back. Closer and closer it came, until Tangborn was sure Munro wasn't going to make it. Suddenly, miraculously, the Beaver blasted off the water and banked steeply to the right. For an instant, Tangborn thought the wingtip was going into the waves, but it remained what seemed mere inches above the whitecaps. The noise was deafening as the plane arced around in front of him, showing the full breadth of its belly. He could see every detail: the wing seams with their rows of rivets, the algae stains on the bottoms of the silver-painted floats, the dark streaks on the paint behind the oil cooler and fuel drains. For a moment the Beaver hung there, its propeller screaming defiantly against the roar of the wind.

And then it was gone, vanished down the slope beyond the gauging station. The engine sound was gone, too. All that was left was the boom of the wind and the hiss of the waves. It was as though the plane had never existed. Tangborn stood at the base of the ridge, stunned. The hurricane streaming off the glacier had won, swatting Six-Six-Zulu out of the air as easily as a man swats down an annoying mosquito. Tangborn didn't know what to do. Should he try to make his way down to the wreckage or should he scramble up the trail to the cabin for help?

He did neither. There was a brilliant flash of white out in the valley, and then he was staring at the cruciform shape of Munro's steeply climbing airplane. The Beaver clawed for altitude in silence, the thunder of its straining engine snatched away by the wind. Tangborn watched as Munro climbed higher and higher into the cloudless sky, his sunlit airplane looking more and more toylike as it was swept along by the wind until it skimmed over the top of a distant ridge and was gone.

The gusts tore at Tangborn's wet clothes and stung his cheek with needles of spray, but he remained motionless, staring across the churning lake at the spot where Munro had begun his takeoff. Tangborn wasn't a pilot, but his scientific mind had little trouble realizing he'd just watched Munro exceed every performance limitation of his airplane and get away with it. Hunching his shoulders against the gale sweeping along the base of the ridge, the scientist began picking his way back to the trail. There was no hurry; the wind showed no sign of abating, which meant the Coast Guard helicopter was still on the ground. But he wanted to make sure they got the word they were no longer needed.

Seventy miles from where Wendell Tangborn was trudging up to his wind-blasted research cabin, Arne Hansen was being loaded into the back of an ambulance. He was operated on within the hour for a severely blocked intestine which the doctors said would have killed him by sunset. Munro's only comment when he heard the news was that he was delighted the man was going to be all right. He'd said little about the flight when he got back other than to describe in minimal detail the conditions on the lake that had forced him to deviate from the normal takeoff procedure.

Thirty years later, he described the incident the same way. "It was pretty windy, but I was able to land and get that fellow out." When pressed by close friends like Reg Collins or Dick Gee, he would give up a little more detail, but he never made himself out to be a hero.

Was it his most dangerous flight? Munro felt his flights along the coast in minimal weather were far more risky. But for a few seconds, as he coaxed Six-Six-Zulu into a takeoff few other pilots would have attempted, he was flying in the same world as Chuck Yeager, Jimmy Doolittle, Roscoe Turner, and all the other test and racing pilots who've pushed the absolute limits of their machines and lived to tell about it. His most spectacular flights were yet to come, but as far as Arne Hansen and Wendell Tangborn were concerned, Bob Munro's flight to the South Cascade Glacier on that windy, October morning was the greatest feat in aviation history.

> "Bob was scared. He was really scared. He was way more worried about making that flight than he let on. But he felt a need to go in there for that man, and he was very proud of the fact that he did. Not proud in the sense that he showed the world that he could do something that no one else could or would do on that day, but proud because he was able to help someone."
>
> **DICK GEE**

Arne Hansen's emergency surgery went well, and by mid-afternoon he was resting comfortably in a recovery room. Up at the glacier, the wind continued to blow unabated into the night.

THE BIG BLUE

THE MORNING BOB MUNRO FLEW Arne Hansen back to the rest of his life, Gregg Munro was lying in a cot near the DMZ in South Vietnam wondering if the North Vietnamese Army would ever run out of rockets. The rocket attacks were actually rather sporadic, but the NVA had mastered the art of psychological timing. Despite the few number of launchings, they had managed to convince the Americans they were under threat of attack pretty much all day, every day. The rockets themselves weren't terribly accurate, but what they lacked in guidance they more than made up for in noise. A direct hit by one could be fatal, but most of the time they screeched harmlessly through camp and exploded with a bang, leaving behind a hazy trail of profanity from the GIs who were scrambling for cover.

Gregg spent a lot of his time thinking about not becoming dead, but when he did allow his mind to wander, he invariably envisioned the dark blue water of Lake Washington and the pale green docks at the Air Harbor. He'd been gone less than a year, but it seemed like forever since he'd last loaded up a planeload of passengers and flown over the sand-colored bluffs and rocky islands of Puget Sound. His father had never pushed him to become a pilot, but after going through the usual cowboy-fireman-locomotive engineer phases, Gregg had eventually decided the most interesting occupation was the one going on in his own backyard.

His aviation experience predated his enthusiasm. He'd started as a lineboy, washing and fueling planes, and mowing the grass in the tie-down area. At age eleven, he wasn't thinking in terms of a career. He needed a way to earn pocket money, and his dad's business seemed a convenient way to do it.

The loss of Vern Wilson and the Staggerwing in October 1955 put a temporary damper on the company's flying activities, but the creation of Kenmore Marina and the Bell Boy boat dealership gave Gregg plenty to do the following summer. He still worked the floatplane docks, but most of his time was spent across the property at the marina, launching and retrieving boats, pumping fuel, and doing whatever odd jobs Bill Peters and the marina staff could think of.

The purchase of a thirty-five horsepower Bell Boy ski boat with his dockboy earnings gave

Gregg a new degree of freedom. Some of his friends also lived near the lake, but closer to Seattle. Now instead of begging his mother to drive him to see his friends he could crank up his little boat and be with his pals in a matter of minutes.

As he started his senior year in high school, he began to think that if a boat was good, a plane would be even better. Having a pilot's license would mean he could fly over to visit his cousins on Lake Sammamish. His friends had always been far more intrigued by the fact that his folks owned a flying service than he had, but when some of his schoolmates began taking flying lessons themselves, Gregg finally decided to take advantage of what had been around him all along.

Once he started taking lessons in the company's Aeronca Champ, he couldn't take them fast enough. He flew with any instructor who had the time to go up with him, but mostly he flew with Bill Fisk. Pilots who've taken lessons from Fisk almost always describe the man's teaching style as "unique." What they generally mean by this is that Fisk was not above hollering at a student when he felt the student needed it. Nor was he adverse to giving a student an occasional whack as a way of drawing attention to something he felt the student needed to observe right away. Gregg might have been the boss's son, but that didn't mean anything in Fisk's book, and the younger Munro enjoyed the same benefits of Fisk's unique style as every other student.

Partway through his course somebody wrecked the Champ, and Gregg's lessons came to an abrupt halt. It was weeks before the plane was replaced, and Gregg began to think he'd never get his license. Fisk finally found a two-place trainer that met his requirements and Bob Munro's budget, and after the company mechanics worked their magic on it, the plane was added to the Air Harbor fleet. Gregg was back in the air again.

It didn't take him long to earn his Private certificate, and his logbook was soon filling with entries that read, "KAH - L. Sam - KAH." The flights to his cousins' place on Lake Sammamish took less than fifteen minutes each way, but the real value was in the takeoffs and landings. When landplane pilots begin or end a flight, most of their decisions are made for them. Runways and taxiways dictate where they will take off and land, and how they will maneuver on the ground. Most airports have traffic controllers who dictate what pilots will do in the air and on the ground. The only variable the average landplane pilot has to contend with at an airport is the wind.

The seaplane pilot's world is much different. Except at the handful of locations around the world with marked takeoff and landing lanes and, in a couple of cases, traffic controllers, seaplane pilots are virtually on their own. It's up to them to figure out which way the wind is blowing, and where on the water they should takeoff or land, and if there are boats or floating logs that might get in the way. On the water, they have to pick their own way to or from shore, and figure out the best way to approach or depart a dock. No one's around to tell them the wind is blowing fifteen knots with gusts to twenty-five, or that in two minutes some idiot's going to blunder through the takeoff area in a forty-foot Bayliner. In a seaplane, every takeoff and every landing is different. The wind's different, the water's different, the visibility's different, the boat traffic's different, the number of planes at the dock is different. Every aspect of every takeoff, landing, and docking is a judgment call on the part of the pilot, and in the course of his countless little flights between Kenmore and Lake Sammamish, Gregg Munro became very, very good at judging takeoffs, landings, and dockings.

He continued working as a lineboy during summer vacations and college holiday breaks. He earned his Commercial certificate, and then his Instrument rating. Finally in the summer of 1968, Bob Munro decided his son was ready to start taking some of the company's charter flights on his own. To Gregg, the day he carried his first paying passenger was a momentous one. It wasn't the Cessna 180 he was flying or the place he was flying to; he'd experienced both many times before. It was the sense of responsibility, the knowledge that he was now a professional pilot in every sense of the word, that made that first charter flight so important to him.

The summer of '68 was Gregg Munro's first and last season of charter flying for awhile. The Vietnam war was using up men at an increasing rate, and as college graduation approached that spring, Gregg realized he was going to have to deal with military service one way or another.

Assured by the local recruiting office that volunteering for the Army would pretty much guarantee him a non-combatant role, Gregg signed up before the draft board was able to issue him one of their infamous "Greetings" notices. But despite his degree in business administration, his volunteer status, and his subsequent graduation from NCO school with the rank of sergeant, he ended up in the 101st Airborne Division, one of the most front-line, ground-pounding outfits around. If he was surprised by his assignment, he was downright dismayed by his posting. His unit was headed for the DMZ, the optimistically-labeled demilitarized zone that separated North and South Vietnam. The only place it was demilitarized was on the map; in the forested hills and steamy valleys that actually comprised the zone, it was militarized as hell.

Fortunately for Gregg and the future of the Air Harbor, the DMZ was such an obvious target that as the war progressed, most of the North Vietnamese infiltration efforts had moved further south, leaving the DMZ to steam and drip in relative quiet. Gregg spent his tour sitting in camp or trudging around on patrol being miserable along with the rest of the unit. The fact that everyone was equally miserable was the only thing that made it bearable. The occasional firefights were just that; flurries of muzzleflashes among the trees followed by an ear-ringing silence.

He bought a portable cassette recorder and read his thoughts and experiences into the microphone and sent the tapes home. On some of them his family could hear the NVA's rockets screeching and banging in the background. Gregg and his fellow sufferers finally came to the conclusion that the North Vietnamese had an unlimited supply of rockets, which of course, they did.

By the late sixties, thanks mainly to Mildred Hall's excellent rapport with the company's customers, the charter business was really starting to blossom. In addition to the growing number of wealthy businessmen who were using Kenmore to fly to their yachts and summer homes in the San Juans and British Columbia, more and more sportsmen were finding their way to the north end of the lake for a flight to the fabled steelhead rivers of British Columbia. The steelhead is, in essence, a seagoing rainbow trout. Like salmon, steelhead hatch in the rivers and make their way to the sea. Unlike salmon, steelhead don't die after returning to spawn in the rivers where they were born, but turn around and go back again to the sea. An adult steelhead may return to spawn in its home river two, three, or even more times during the course of its life. And each time it comes back, it's bigger, stronger, and smarter than the last time.

Rivers like the Kispiox and the Thompson in British Columbia were becoming legendary for the huge steelhead that were being caught in their swift-flowing waters. But the best steelhead river of them all, the river that conjured up images of hour-long battles with the most cunning fish in the system, was the Dean. Emerging from a series of small lakes east of the Coast Mountains in BC's Cariboo region, the Dean flows north and then west to cut through the mountains and meet saltwater at Kimsquit, an old village site seventy miles from the sea at the head of the Dean Channel.

Surrounded by seven-thousand-foot peaks, the Dean is accessible by boat or seaplane, or some really serious walking. Once there, you're on your own. There are no towns along the Dean, no Provincial campgrounds with stacks of pre-cut firewood, picnic tables, and outhouses. You make your camp beside the river and take your chances with the bears. But the fishing more than makes up for the inconvenience of spending your days in a cloud of insects and shooing the occasional grizzly out of the tent. The Dean came to represent the ultimate in fresh water gamefishing, and Kenmore began getting requests to fly there, ferrying guests to the commercial fish camps that sprang up along the river, as well as individuals who wanted to go it alone.

The lower part of the river is wide enough to land on, but getting off again proved to be more challenging than Bob Munro had anticipated.

"It's quite a winding river. Landing isn't difficult, because you land upstream into the current which brings you to a pretty quick stop. You land and get up to the shore to let everybody out, but then what are you going to do? If you just taxi out from shore, the current will grab you and carry you off downstream sideways until you hit something.

"A fellow who ran one of the fish camps there came up with a way of getting us turned around and pointing downstream for the takeoff. He drove a big stake into the bank of the river and piled rocks around it to hold it in place. What we'd do is tie a length of line to the tail of the plane and taxi upriver to where the stake was. A fellow on shore would take the free end of the line and tie it to the stake. Then we'd taxi the plane out into the current. The river would start to carry us down sideways, but then we'd hit the end of the line which would hold the tail and force the plane to start swinging around to point downstream. As soon as we were pointing downstream, the fellow on the bank would cut the line and we'd hit the throttle and take off."

BOB MUNRO

Fifty miles south of the Dean Channel another broad fjord slices east toward the Coast Range. Most people think Rivers Inlet is named for the salmon-spawning streams flowing into it, while in fact, the inlet was named by George Vancouver in August 1792, for a friend back home in England, George Pitt, Baron Rivers of Stratfieldsaye. But it was salmon that put Rivers Inlet on the map. The massive runs of kings and silvers drew commercial trollers and net boats from every harbor between Victoria and Prince Rupert. The inlet's steep, rocky shores are not conducive to construction, so forests of pilings were driven into the mud to support the clattering, steaming cannery that ran day and night during the salmon runs. The tins of pressure-cooked fish were boxed and stacked on pallets which once a week were wheeled aboard the red-and-black funneled ships of the Union Steamship Company and taken to Vancouver, where they went out to the world as premium-packed Pacific salmon.

Ice makers, refrigeration, and larger boats eventually closed the Rivers Inlet cannery, but the salmon runs went on. The commercial boats still circled offshore, but up in the inlet a new kind of fisherman was making an appearance. City dwellers who spent fifty-one weeks each year dreaming of hooking into a monster king were spending the fifty-second week trying to do it. The new fish camps at Rivers Inlet offered an experience unmatched by anything farther south. The looming Coast Range, the brooding, forested shore, and the clear, green water made a spectacular setting for a ninety-minute struggle with a sixty-pound king.

Like the Dean further upcoast, there are two ways to get to Rivers Inlet. Kenmore began getting calls from sportsmen who didn't fancy spending half their vacation riding a slow boat up and down the Inside Passage, but wanted instead to leave Seattle in the morning and be reeling in that sixty-pounder by mid-afternoon. Mildred Hall took every opportunity to promote the Rivers Inlet fish camps to the Air Harbor's regular customers. The flight was four hours up and four hours back plus fueling stops, which meant a plane and pilot were earning money pretty much the whole day.

While charters were keeping the pilots busy, business was booming out in the hangar. Bill Peters was pleased with the new shop and office building that had opened for business in 1963. He and everyone else figured it would accommodate the company's overhaul and repair business for years to come. Two years later, Peters was wishing he'd made the building twice as large. At the November 1965 board of directors meeting, Peters proposed building a new hangar large enough to accommodate eight airplanes plus a paint shop. He calculated the hangar would cost thirty-four thousand dollars. The elimination of lost maintenance time would more than cover the cost of the new building, he argued, and the board eventually gave him the green light to proceed.

The hangar was finished a year later, with eleven bays plus a paint shop at the south end. True to form, Peters not only managed to make the building larger and more useful than his original proposal, but by doing a lot of the work himself and using company employees whenever he could, he came in fourteen thousand dollars under budget.

The new hangar was completed just in time. The company entered 1967 with eleven planes in its own fleet, and a growing number of private planes were calling Kenmore home as well. The company's venture into the Beaver rebuilding business was not far off, and space would soon be at a premium. Having finally convinced management to fix the heating system, Walt Winseman was happy in his new engine shop, the former Kenmore Marina building. The room he vacated, the extension Peters had built against the north wall of the main hangar, was refurbished into a sheet metal shop. For the first time since 1946, Bob Munro could look around the property and feel his company had adequate facilities for the work it was doing.

While Gregg was swatting bugs and dodging rockets in Vietnam, Munro had taken on another glacier project. Many people unfamiliar with Washington don't realize the state has two major mountain ranges, not just one. The Cascades are the middle link in the chain that includes the Coast Mountains in British Columbia and the Sierras in California. The landmark volcanoes—Baker, Rainier, Adams, St. Helens, Hood, and Shasta—are in the Cascades. On clear days passengers on the Alaska Airlines flights between Seattle and San Francisco can see at least four of them at any one time, mammoth watchtowers above the jagged rubble of a lower wall.

Washington's other mountain range is west of Seattle, out on the Olympic Peninsula. The Olympics, barely fifty miles long, don't possess the continuous, knife-edge drama of the Cascades. But rising almost straight out of Hood Canal, they are the mountains most familiar to Seattle residents, who willingly pay thousands of dollars extra for a home with even a peek-a-boo glimpse of the peaks across the Sound.

The line of mountains so beloved by Seattle's real estate agents represents only the leading edge of the Olympics. It's more a circle of mountains than a range, and its largest peak is far to the west, where city residents on the balconies of their million-dollar condominiums can't even see it. At 7,965 feet, Mt. Olympus is not a giant. But it's an impressive pile, rising as it does from the deep, forested valleys that surround it. And it has a glacier. Actually, it has several glaciers, but only one, the Blue, has the mass and volume to sustain a frozen flow that winds from the summit to the mountain's lower slopes.

The Blue Glacier is a fascinating piece of geography. It drapes across the mountain's north ridge like a blanket over the back of a sofa. From its smooth upper level, the Blue spills off the back of the sofa in jagged chunks before reforming on the seat into a curving river of ice that snakes down the mountain to end in a debris field of its own making. The north ridge itself is not straight, but bends to the south halfway along its length. At the bend, a huge chunk of rock protrudes, pyramid-like, from the snow lapping its base. Here a narrow tongue of ice escapes the main flow, a frozen waterfall curving steeply down beside the massive outcropping to disappear into the valley below. On the north ridge above the icefall, between the pyramid and the summit of Mt. Olympus itself, the gently rounded back of the Blue suggested a nickname, at least to the pilots who volunteered to land on it. They called it the Snow Dome.

The Blue oozed undisturbed off the side of Olympus for centuries, its meltwater thundering down the rocky slopes and through the coastal rainforest to the sea. The native tribes who inhabited the coast were certainly aware of the mountain, and it's hard to believe that in all those years not one person ventured high enough to clamber onto the smooth, curved back of the Blue. But official history tends to be white man's history, so regardless of the peninsula's unrecorded native achievements, Olympus wasn't climbed until 1890, when an exploration party under the command of Army lieutenant Joseph O'Neil hiked through the Olympics from east to west, blazing a mule trail as they went. Smaller groups were sent off from the main party to explore side valleys, and one of them managed to clamber up Olympus to the summit.

Everyone who visited the peninsula's interior after that came away impressed, including President Theodore Roosevelt, who in 1909 bestowed national monument status on the mountain. Two and a half decades later, the peninsula was visited by another president, also a Roosevelt. Franklin D. was so impressed with what he saw that he recommended a sizable chunk of the peninsula be turned into a park. This was decades before presidential ideas were subjected to endless hearings and media investigations, so it didn't take long for Roosevelt's recommendation to become a reality. In 1938, the first of an endless stream of visitors entered what had been officially named Olympic National Park.

Few people made the ascent to the upper slopes of the Blue Glacier, but its lower edge became a waypoint for hikers on their trek along the popular trail that bisects the peninsula. Then in 1957, the same year the South Cascade Glacier began attracting the interest of the US Geological Survey, the Blue became a hot topic at the University of Washington.

Blue Glacier, Mt. Olympus. The research huts are at the far end of the rock ridge just above the engine cowl. The planes landed on the broad expanse of snow in the center of the photo. Takeoffs were made over the edge of the steep ice fall to the immediate left of the rock ridge. This photo was taken in late summer, and a huge crevasse has opened across the top of the ice fall. (photo by C. Marin Faure)

The UW places a lot of stock in research. With everything from active volcanoes to the world's largest octopus in its back yard, the university takes the process of finding things out very seriously. To aid its scientific endeavors, the UW has constructed a number of research stations. Some, like the station at Friday Harbor in the San Juans, are devoted to marine studies. Others are situated higher up, where faculty and students can gather data on the social behavior of marmots or the makeup of clouds.

By the mid-1950s, the university decided it needed a field station way up high in the mountains and preferably next to a glacier, where researchers could study mountain weather, air chemistry, and cloud physics, to say nothing of tracking the behavior of the glacier itself. The Blue seemed the perfect choice. Situated far from Seattle's automotive and industrial haze, the Blue sits six thousand feet up in a pristine world where the wind blows in fresh from the Pacific and the snow never turns gray. An aerial survey followed by a twenty-five mile trudge up the mountain convinced a UW field team that the best spot for a field station was on the lower slopes of the pyramid peak at the foot of the Snow Dome.

Lying completely within the boundaries of Olympic National Park, Mt. Olympus is under the jurisdiction of the National Park Service. Today, it would be virtually impossible to build a permanent research station next to a glacier in a designated wilderness area, but in the 1950s, the Park Service was a little more flexible. The university applied for and received a conditional use permit, and the project was up and running.

A design was drawn up for a simple but strong hut that could accommodate four people in passable comfort, or six if they were really good friends. Designing the hut was the easy part. Like the South Cascade cabin under construction across the Sound, the problem was access. The South Cascade site was seven miles from the nearest road. The Blue was twenty-five. The only practical way to move lumber and supplies up to Mt. Olympus was by air. Helicopters were used when necessary, but like the scientists on the South Cascade, the university relied heavily on Bill Fairchild and his ski-equipped Aeronca Champ.

It took awhile, given the limited capacity of Fairchild's little plane, but he eventually ferried enough lumber, plywood, and nails to the Blue to construct the platform and hut. There was an oil stove for cooking, and an oil heater to provide at least a degree of protection against the frigid air. Automated weather observation equipment was installed along with the survey tools the students and researchers would need to track the accumulation of snow and the movement of the ice.

The Park Service was adamant about what could and couldn't be done on their mountain. Only aircraft carrying supplies to the station could land on the glacier; they didn't want a bunch of weekend thrill seekers zooming around daring each other to try a landing on the snow. Another rule was that whatever the researchers took in they had to take out. The Park Service didn't want the surface of the Blue to become a repository for soda bottles, fuel cans, bits of paper, and all the other kinds of rubbish that seem to magically appear whenever humans occupy one spot for more than five minutes.

The death of Bill Fairchild in 1966 did not have as severe an impact on the activities on the Blue as it did on Wendell Tangborn's operation over on the South Cascade. The university's projects were not as intensive, and the volume of core samples, logbooks, equipment, and supplies that had to be transported was much lower. Researchers and students headed for a stint of duty at the station continued the tradition of trekking the twenty-five miles up to the glacier; a helicopter was needed only occasionally to take in food and fuel and haul out the garbage.

Then in the late 1960s, activity at the Blue Glacier began to intensify. The environment was becoming a hot topic, and the university's field station high in the Olympics proved an ideal spot to study things like air quality, atmospheric pollution, and the migration of airborne particulates through snow and into the meltwater. More and more researchers began requesting time at the field station, but after withstanding more than a decade of freezing temperatures and Pacific storms, the hut was no longer up to the job. People who went up to the Blue to study spent as much time patching the building back together as they did making observations. Besides that, there wasn't enough space. If the Blue Glacier station was to continue being useful, it would need some serious upgrading.

The Park Service granted permission to rebuild the hut and construct two small outbuildings, but it was up to the university to get the materials up to the glacier. Helicopters offered one choice, but they were expensive and their load capacity was limited. The other choice was to take the lumber in by plane, but with Bill Fairchild gone, this didn't seem much of an option.

In the spring of 1970, one of the Seattle papers ran a local interest piece about Kenmore Air Harbor, with emphasis on Bob Munro's exploits on the Leduc and South Cascade glaciers. The day after the article appeared, Mildred Hall got a phone call from the University of Washington. Would Mr. Munro be interested in doing the same thing on Mt. Olympus? Mildred allowed that he would.

Once again, Munro found himself poring over aerial photos and contour maps. The only reasonably level section of the Blue was the top of the Snow Dome, south of the research cabin. The landing approach would have to be made straight toward the summit, skimming in over the top of the icefall beside the rock pyramid to touch down on the rounded back of the dome. One thing Munro noticed right away was that the Blue's "top-of-the-world" location meant he'd be able to break off his landing approach if he wasn't happy with the way it was shaping up. The South Cascade in its deep, narrow bowl was exactly the opposite; once he started in there was no turning back.

The only real danger Munro could determine from looking at the maps and photos in front of him was what would happen if he approached too low. A low approach would put him on a collision course with the rounded top of the icefall, and there was no way at that altitude that a heavily loaded Beaver would be able to outclimb the slope at the last minute.

Other than that, the landing looked pretty straightforward. The real challenge of flying onto the Blue was going to be flying off of it. The top of the Snow Dome was considerably shorter than the South Cascade glacier, and it was a lot shorter than the vast expanse of the Leduc. There was no way even an empty Beaver could accelerate to flying speed in the distance available on top of the dome. But Munro saw immediately that it wouldn't have to. The South Cascade had airplane-eating crevasses at its foot, and the Leduc had a sharp drop-off. But the Blue Glacier had that marvelous icefall that curved smoothly down from the Snow Dome and plunged down the side of the valley.

It wouldn't matter how fast Munro was going when he got to the edge of the Snow Dome. He would simply ride the curve until he was sliding down the icefall at a forty-five degree angle. With gravity augmenting the Six-Six-Zulu's radial engine, he calculated that flying speed would be reached long before the snow ran out, and Munro would simply lift off and ease the plane out of its dive into level flight high above the valley floor.

Powering a Beaver into a roller-coaster ride over the edge of a glacier wasn't something Munro could practice beforehand, although his experience together with a careful study of the photographs and snow condition reports told him it should work. But there was only one sure way to find out if his instincts were correct, and that was to go up and try it. He would have preferred to make the first flight alone, but after learning there would be no one at the cabin to help turn the plane around he agreed to take two of the university's researchers with him. It was a good thing he did.

The April day selected for the first flight dawned relatively clear over Seattle, but there were broken clouds sagging down on the Olympics. Knowing that conditions were often better along Juan de Fuca Strait than they were over Puget Sound, Munro decided to make an end run to the north around the mountains and come in from Port Angeles rather than attempt a frontal assault on the wall of peaks facing Seattle. Sure enough, the cloud cover along the strait wasn't nearly as dense as it was over the eastern half of the range, but it still obscured most of the peaks. Munro held his map so the researcher in the seat beside him could see it and leaned closer so the man could hear him.

"I'm going to follow the Elwha River." Munro traced his finger up the narrow ribbon of pale green snaking between the heavily contoured brown patches that represented the six-thousand foot peaks guarding the northern approach to Mt. Olympus.

"Once we get around this mountain here," Munro's finger moved south and around the base of seven-thousand foot Mt. Carrie, "we should be able to see Olympus and the glacier."

The researcher nodded, and Munro banked Six-Six-Zulu left and headed for the Elwha. He was at five thousand feet, three thousand feet lower than he wanted to be, but he planned on climbing as he worked his way up the valley. It wasn't easy. The clouds were scattered all over the place at different altitudes. It was imperative that he stay over the river. Any deviations to the right or left would run him head on into geography that stuck up a lot higher than he was.

Munro dodged his way up the Elwha, coaxing Six-Six-Zulu into a climb whenever he thought he could get away with it, while his passengers peered anxiously to the south trying to catch a glimpse of Olympus through the clouds. The plane cleared the bulk of Mt. Carrie, but where there should have been the broad summit of Mt. Olympus there were only layers of overcast.

Munro began weaving through the clouds in the hope that someone in the plane would catch a glimpse of Olympus though a gap in the white walls that surrounded them. The wind was light so the clouds weren't moving around much. If he could see even the tiniest bit of the mountain, he knew could work his way over to it.

Back and forth Six-Six-Zulu droned, its silhouette a tiny speck against the towering clouds. Occasional shafts of sunlight lit up the cockpit and Munro, shielding his eyes, could see streaky patches of blue high above them. Then the light would wipe away and they'd be back in a gloom of whites and grays, with only the dusty greens and browns of the slopes thousands of feet below to relieve the monotony.

"There!" the backseat passenger shouted. "Right there! There's Olympus!"

Munro snapped his eyes to the end of the pointing finger and then out in the direction it indicated. Down a narrow corridor of cloud was a slab of brilliant white studded with patches of shiny black. Munro threw Six-Six-Zulu into a steep bank to keep the slope of ice and rock in sight. He knew if he lost the corridor he could circle until the tanks ran dry and not find it again.

Whether or not the chunk of mountain gleaming through the clouds was Olympus was anyone's guess as far as Munro was concerned. He was somewhat familiar with the Olympic Range, but with all the turning and twisting they'd been doing, the rock ahead of them could have been any one of several peaks in the area. His expression as he peered ahead must have made his skepticism obvious, because the researcher beside him reached over and tapped him on the shoulder.

"Don't worry," the man shouted above the engine. "We know this area like the back of our hands. That's Olympus, no question."

Munro nodded. They'd find out soon enough.

The feathery walls of the cloud corridor rose high above the plane, at times seeming no farther apart than the Beaver's forty-eight foot wingspan. Munro had managed to wriggle his way up to 7,500 feet while casting back and forth in search of the mountain. The roofless corridor gave him the opportunity to power Six-Six-Zulu up five hundred more. Level at eight thousand, Munro breathed a little easier. He was higher, albeit by only thirty-five feet, than any piece of real estate in the Olympic Range. Even if the corridor collapsed around him and reduced his visibility to zero, as long as he didn't go down he wouldn't hit anything. The fact that Six-Six-Zulu's altimeter could be off by considerably more than thirty-five feet was something he decided not to think about.

The corridor didn't collapse. In fact, it began to get wider, and then Munro flew out from between the walls and found himself face to face with the Blue. It was a startling sight. Unlike the South Cascade with its muddy lake, or the Leduc with its bordering patches of dirty snow and rockslides, the Blue was absolutely, starkly white. Munro wondered for a moment how anyone could possibly have come up with the word "blue" to describe the scene that lay before him. The smooth curve of the Snow Dome lay along the ridge in front him. Below the ridge, the ice was a frozen cauldron of crevasses, their jumbled, gaping mouths a dramatic contrast to the smooth perfection of the Snow Dome up above. The overwhelming whiteness was made even more brilliant by the exposed peaks and pyramids of rock that dotted the summit, their flanks glistening black from the moisture condensing out of the heavy clouds sliding in from the Pacific.

Whoever had named the glacier had not had the benefit of Munro's vantage point. Peering up at the mountain's summit, he would have seen only the underside of glacier's layered edges spilling over the north ridge, the naked ice glowing an eerie blue. The glow is easily explained: blue is the only color in the sunlight spectrum that isn't absorbed by the ice. But to the people who first ventured up the side of the mountain, native or not, the blue mantle spilling off the north ridge must have been an unworldly sight.

But Munro saw only white, not only on the mountain in front of him but in the clouds around him that were threatening to cut off his approach to the glacier. If he was going to land, he had no time to waste sightseeing. He circled the Snow Dome once to make sure the surface was not dimpled with suncups or split by crevasses. The clouds gave him little room to maneuver, but he was able to extend his circle far enough out over a valley to swing around in line with the icefall. Keeping in mind the dangers of flying too low an approach, Munro deliberately kept Six-Six-Zulu high as he closed in on the Snow Dome. The Beaver's effective flap system would make it easy to lose altitude fast if he needed to, but he didn't want to put himself in the position of having to climb back up to the glacier's surface in order to land on it.

He sailed in over the lip of the icefall and closed on the rounded back of the Snow Dome. He was still too high, so he pumped in more flap and pulled the power to idle. He could see the edges of the Snow Dome in his peripheral vision, and this made it easier than he'd anticipated to judge his height from the snow. He eased back on the yoke to keep the float tips from digging in and waited for the touchdown.

It came with a solid thump. The plane bounced once and then there was the familiar hiss of snow against aluminum as the float keels knifed cleanly across the top of the Snow Dome. It was almost like landing on water, the surface was so smooth. Munro pushed the right rudder pedal to the floor in an attempt to steer the Beaver around to face the opposite direction, but the turn had barely begun when the friction of the snow dragged Six-Six-Zulu to a stop. Munro pulled the mixture control back to idle-cutoff, and the heavy, two-bladed propeller pulled the clattering magnetos through a couple of revolutions before it jerked to a stop and there was silence.

"Great landing," his passengers said as they pulled on their mittens and heavy coats. They'd been to the glacier before, so they weren't nearly as impressed by the surroundings as they were by Munro's feat of landing a heavy floatplane on the snow. To Munro, of course, the landing was no big deal. What impressed him was the location. Although clouds blocked much of the surrounding view, Munro could see enough to feel he was truly on top of the world. The gently rounded back of the Snow Dome fell away on three sides into the valleys while in front of him, the surface stretched away on a mild grade before bending steeply upwards toward the row of jagged rock teeth that marked the mountain's summit.

The researchers piled out the doors and jumped down into the snow. Munro opened his door and eased out onto the left float. There was enough of a breeze to send the chill factor below zero, but it wasn't nearly as bad as it could have been, given their altitude. He zipped his heavy coat up all the way and pulled the hood over his head. One of his passengers crunched around the front of the plane and looked up at him.

"If we have the time we'd like to show you the cabin and give you an idea of the kinds of things we'll need you to fly in."

Munro checked his watch and then looked at the sky. He'd checked the weather reports before leaving Kenmore, but the forecasts for Seattle and the Puget Sound region had little relevance for the top of Mt. Olympus. At least he'd learned there wasn't a major pressure change on the way, so what he saw above and around him was what should remain, at least for the next few hours. From his vantage point on the front of the float, he could see the cabin several hundred yards away, a tiny rectangle of gray against the massive slab of wet, black rock behind it.

"Sure, let's take a look," he said.

The three men trudged off across the Snow Dome toward the cabin. The only sound was the crunch of boots in the snow and the soft murmur of the wind that curved over the top of the glacier and polished it smooth. One of the researchers dropped back to walk beside Munro.

"This is actually pretty nice for this time of year. There's hardly any wind. I've been up here when it's really been blowing, and believe me, you don't want to be flying around here then."

"We'll need some way of finding out what the winds are like before we take off from Kenmore," Munro said.

"There's a radio in the cabin that's connected to the Forest Service in Forks. We can radio the weather conditions to them and they can relay them to you on the phone."

Munro nodded. "That's what we do on the South Cascade."

"Just wait 'til you come up here on a sunny day. It's warm enough to wear shorts and you can see all the way to the Pacific Ocean. It's really spectacular."

Munro thought it was pretty spectacular the way it was. The slope was getting steeper as they neared the cabin, and Munro began to realize just what kind of a ride he was in for on the takeoff. The photographs and contour maps, as dramatic as they had been, were nothing in comparison to actually standing at the top of the icefall, the flawless white curve arcing down to end in a harsh scrabble of broken ice and shattered rock thousands of feet above the valley floor.

Munro looked back at the fragile form of Six-Six-Zulu perched on the rounded back of the Snow Dome. Then he turned to the top of the fall and tried to envision the plane pitching over the curve, sliding down at an ever-increasing angle with nothing but rock and the valley floor filling the windscreen. What if the speed didn't build fast enough? What if his calculations were off and he reached the end of the fall before he reached flying speed? Once off the smooth snow, the Beaver would shred itself as it tore down through the rocks and rubble that studded the valley walls. Pulling the throttle back would do nothing. The plane would be propelled to destruction by gravity, and he would be powerless to prevent it.

The floats would fail first, their bottoms slashed open and the struts bent back until the bolts snapped. Stripped of support, the fuselage would smash down to slide on the bare slope. The thin belly skin would disintegrate in seconds, exposing the fuel tanks under the floor. A jagged edge, a sharp splinter of granite, and a gush of pink fuel would spray back to ignite in the sparks streaming from the shattered steel float mounts.

The flaming hulk would tumble down the slope, perhaps all the way to the valley floor, perhaps coming to rest against a ledge somewhere higher up. And there it would lie, hissing and popping as it cooled, nothing worth salvaging and little left to bury. It was an ugly image and Munro didn't hang on to it. He was confident he would be in the air long before reaching the danger point.

The men stepped up into the cabin, kicking the doorframe to knock the snow off their boots.

The wood walls were weather-beaten and worn, with crude plywood patches over the worst of the cracks.

"We need to bring up enough wood to fix the walls and roof properly, and to build two new buildings."

"The same size as this?" As simple as the hut was, Munro could see that the platform, walls, and roof contained a lot of wood. He knew Bill Fairchild had flown most of it in, and he was impressed by the amount of material the man had been able to strap to his little, two-place Aeronca.

"The new buildings will be smaller," the researcher answered. "They'll be mainly used for storage."

One of the other men looked up from his inspection of the cabin's supplies. "We'll also need oil for the stove and heater, and food, depending on how many people are up here at any given time."

"Plus you'll be hauling a lot of stuff out. All the empty fuel cans have to go out, the garbage, everything."

"What about passengers?" Munro asked.

"The only thing that's supposed to come in by air are supplies. They don't want us using airplanes or helicopters to ferry people back and forth. There may be an occasional passenger, but for the most part you'll be carrying only supplies and equipment."

The two men led Munro out onto the rock to show him where the two outbuildings were to be constructed, and then it was time to go. Munro explained the turnaround procedure as they trudged back up the slope to the plane. After regaining their breath in the thin air, the researchers lined up next to the tail and Munro levered himself up onto the left float and pulled the rope out of the baggage compartment.

The two men had their work cut out for them as they pulled hard on the rope while Munro revved the engine and rocked the plane back and forth with the elevator, but eventually Six-Six-Zulu was facing back downslope toward the top of the icefall. The researchers scrambled aboard and fastened their seatbelts as tight as they would go. Munro had explained the takeoff procedure several times before the flight, with assurances that the airplane wouldn't care if they were taking off from level ground or a forty-five degree downward slope. As long as the wing was moving through the air at flying speed, he said, the airplane would fly.

It had all seemed very logical when explained in the safety of the office back at Kenmore, but the reality of sitting in what suddenly seemed a very frail airplane that was about to pitch over the edge of a cliff was a different matter altogether. The men's confidence was ebbing fast, so they tugged on their seatbelts and watched Munro closely for any signs of trouble.

Their pilot may have had some momentary misgivings back at the top of the icefall, but he was all business now. While the cylinder head temperature was coming up to green, he tested the flight controls and pumped the flaps down to the takeoff position. Glancing over his shoulder, he made sure his backseat passenger had his seatbelt on and that the main cabin doors were latched shut. Then he pulled his map from the door pocket beside him and reviewed his route out of the mountains.

The fall would catapult him into a different valley than the one he'd used to approach the mountain. If the clouds permitted, he planned to work his way back around Mt. Carrie to the Elwha valley and north to Port Angeles. If that proved impossible, the only alternative would be to follow the Hoh River off to the west toward the Pacific until he could turn north and fly around the mountains to Port Angeles.

From the top of the Snow Dome, Munro could see the air immediately beyond the icefall was relatively cloud-free, but beyond that only bits and pieces of the surrounding peaks were visible through the patchy overcast. There was only one way to find out which way he could go, and that was to launch himself down the fall and find out. The cylinder head temperature hit green. Munro stuffed the map back into the door pocket and reached for the throttle.

"Everybody ready?" he called over his shoulder.

His passengers nodded and tugged on their seatbelts and grabbed the edges of the seat frames.

"Okay," Munro said. "Here we go."

He smoothly slid the black-knobbed throttle all the way to the front of its slot. At six thousand feet of elevation he didn't have to worry about overboosting the engine. The supercharger ran out of boost at five thousand feet, so even with the throttle all the way forward the engine couldn't develop its maximum power. Not that it needed it. Munro knew all he had to do was get the airplane moving forward. Once he was on the downslope of the Snow Dome, gravity would prove a far more efficient accelerator than Pratt & Whitney.

The nose pitched down as the engine pulled against the grip of the snow and then rose level as the floats began to slide. The scratchy hiss of the snow against the keels grew louder as Six-Six-Zulu began accelerating off the top of the dome. The plane kept trying to veer left, but Munro was able to head it back toward the icefall by stepping hard on the right rudder pedal.

It was a takeoff based on faith. Faith that the icefall actually existed, because from the cockpit it looked as though they were heading for a shear drop-off. Munro knew the fall was there, of course, but it was an unnerving sight nevertheless. He'd heard stories about seaplane pilots who routinely took off from tiny lakes by launching their planes over the edges of waterfalls, but never in his twenty-plus years of flying had he experienced anything even remotely similar.

The Beaver reached the top of the icefall and pitched over the edge. To the passengers, it felt exactly like a rollercoaster, the moment the cars begin their downward plunge from the top of the highest incline. The view through the windscreen was like watching a movie, the camera tilting down rapidly from a panorama of sky and clouds to a much more immediate foreground of rock and snow. The university men weren't sure what to feel, exhilaration or terror as the plane thundered down the slope, engine roaring.

Munro was definitely exhilarated as Six-Six-Zulu continued to pitch over. Thirty degrees, forty, forty-five. It was the most exciting thing he'd ever done in an airplane, but he didn't dare sit back and watch the show because the outcome of the show depended on him. He shifted his eyes constantly between the windscreen and the airspeed indicator. Irregularities in the snow caused the plane to hunt slightly left and right, and Munro constantly had to make tiny corrections with the rudder pedals to keep Six-Six-Zulu headed straight down the fall. He wasn't sure what would happen if the plane got sideways on the slope, and he didn't want to find out.

> "It was a real thrill. You accelerate so fast, it takes you by surprise. On that first takeoff I pulled the yoke back because we were sliding down so fast I instinctively wanted to stop it. Then I really got worried because even though we kept going faster and faster, the plane refused to fly. I could see we were going to be off the good snow and into the rocks pretty quick, but I couldn't get the plane into the air. All of a sudden I realized that by holding the yoke back I was keeping the plane in a full stall. I relaxed the yoke a little bit, and we lifted off immediately.
>
> "I flew off that glacier for years, and every single time I had to fight the tendency to pull back as we went over the edge."
>
> **BOB MUNRO**

Everyone in the plane breathed easier as Munro eased Six-Six-Zulu out of its dive toward the valley floor. A quick glance at the cloud cover told him he'd have no trouble picking his way back around Mt. Carrie to the Elwha valley and Port Angeles. Less than an hour after takeoff the Beaver was on the dock at Kenmore, and the researchers were driving back to the university in silence, mentally struggling to find the words to describe their incredible ride down the side of the Big Blue.

Within weeks of Munro's test flight to the Blue Glacier, Mildred Hall was penciling the first revenue flights onto the schedule. The first loads consisted primarily of lumber, food, and fuel oil. From April through early July, Munro took off for the Snow Dome at least once a week. Some days when the weather was perfect and there was a lot of cargo to haul he made three or even four round trips. But unlike the South Cascade project, where the lake at the foot of the glacier made it possible to conduct flight operations all summer, landings could be made on the Blue only when the snow conditions were right. By mid-July, temperatures at the six-thousand foot level increase enough to permit the formation of suncups, the hard-edged, dish-shaped depressions that can batter a landing airplane to pieces in seconds.

Suncups were not the only danger. Rising temperatures also cause the snow on the icefall to slip. Where one day there is a perfectly smooth surface, the next day can find the fall sliced wide open by huge crevasses. Not until enough new snow fell to bridge the crevasses and fill the suncups could flights resume. But by then it would be winter, and winter weather in the Olympics can be virtually unflyable for weeks on end.

Landing on the Blue was not nearly as dangerous as landing on the South Cascade where the surrounding ridges and peaks prevent a pilot from going around for another try if he miscalculates an approach. Short of coming in too low, there aren't many mistakes a pilot can make on the Blue approach that he can't correct by simply turning away or overflying the Snow Dome and banking off to either side. But Munro was the Air Harbor's acknowledged glacier expert, so at first he was the only pilot Mildred scheduled for the Olympus flights.

Of course, Munro was not the Air Harbor's only pilot with glacier experience. Bill Fisk had flown almost a third of the Leduc airlift flights back in 1953, most of them in the company Seabee. He wasn't allowed to fly the South Cascade flights for the same reason Munro kept all the Kenmore pilots off the valley glacier: he didn't want to subject them to the risk. But from everything Fisk had heard about the Blue, it seemed pretty tame. After all, it was he who, during the Leduc airlift, had landed the Seabee on one side of an un-named saddle glacier and slid up and over the top to take off on the other side. Fisk could see little difference between the little Canadian glacier he'd named for himself and the Blue, other than the Blue's greater size, so he resolved to go up there as soon as he got the chance.

The chance came on a pleasant June Saturday a few weeks after Munro had begun ferrying supplies to the Snow Dome. This particular day the boss was off on a flight up north somewhere. Mildred and Bill Peters had taken the day off, and Bill Whitney and the other pilots were either flying or at home. The parts department was closed, the airframe shop was closed, and the engine shop was closed. No students were scheduled, so there were no instructors about. Fisk was the only one there. It was the day he'd been waiting for.

> "I gassed up a Super Cub, and I jumped in that bugger and headed for the Snow Dome. Forty-five minutes it took me. I got up there and circled around while I looked her over. It was a big patch of snow up there, and I could see that you could make landings and takeoffs in a bunch of different directions. I made a landing and took off, and then I went around and came in again. This time I stopped, and one of the glacier guys came over. I left the engine running and got out and gave him my camera. He took a picture of me standing up there with this Super Cub. Then I took off and came back here. I don't think I told Bob about it for quite awhile. I just took off and went up there. I figure that if nothing happens, well then, you don't have to say anything."

> **BILL FISK**

Munro found out eventually, probably because Fisk couldn't resist showing off the photo the "glacier guy" had taken of him standing beside the Super Cub. Fisk's flight hadn't been authorized, but since no one had expressly forbidden him to go, it hadn't been unauthorized, either. And whatever else Bill Fisk was, he wasn't a careless pilot. In the forty-two years he flew for Kenmore he had only one accident, when a freak wave overtook his taxiing Taylorcraft at Clallam Bay and pitchpoled it onto its back. That's not to say he never had airplane problems; he experienced plenty of them, particularly with the Seabees, whose engines and propeller mechanisms were prone to regular bouts of self-destruction. But the luck that first joined him in the cockpit of his B-24 over Italy never left.

Munro decided if Fisk could land a Super Cub on the Snow Dome he might as well land a Beaver up there, too. Fisk was delighted; he loved doing things that were different. But that is where the similarity between Fisk and his boss ended. Munro enjoyed being on the glacier as much, if not more, than flying up to it. He genuinely liked carting supplies from the plane to the hut, talking with the researchers about their projects, or just gazing at the stunning surroundings. Fisk loved the flying part, but it wasn't in his job description to stagger around in the snow under armloads of groceries and fuel cans, and peering at jars of preserved ice worms left him cold.

By the time the suncups shut down the Blue Glacier flying for the summer of 1970, the flights had become routine, or as routine as a forty-five degree career down the side of a glacier can become.

"You should sell rides up here," the university people told Fisk and Munro. "It's better than Disneyland."

As exhilarating as they were, there was one thing about the flights to the Snow Dome that Munro hated. The stove and heater in the cabin were oil-fired, which meant that Kenmore regularly had to fly in full drums of fuel and bring out the empties. The drums, empty or full, always had their filler plugs screwed down tight, which meant the air pressure inside the drums remained the same no matter what was happening to the pressure outside. On the flight up, the pressure outside the full drums would gradually decrease until the differential suddenly became greater than the resistance of the steel. Then the top of each drum would pop outward with a deafening bang, and Munro's heart would stop as he wondered if the engine had just let go. He didn't have to endure this only once during each flight but as many times as there were drums in the cabin, as each one responded differently to the pressure changes.

Descending into higher pressure on the way home was worse because the ringing bangs as the empty drums flexed inward were ear-shattingly louder. He knew it was going to happen, but he didn't know when, so like a kid waiting for a firecracker to explode, the shock of the actual bang was made far worse by the anticipation that preceded it.

By the start of the second season in 1971, Munro and Fisk had the procedure down pat. The landing conditions were always different on the Snow Dome, and of course there was that roller-coaster ride down the icefall at takeoff. But the pattern never varied. Load the plane, take off, climb to altitude across the Sound, point the nose at Mt. Olympus, circle the glacier, line up on the Snow Dome, land, turn the plane around, unload and load, take off, fly back through the mountains, descend over Puget Sound, land, and unload the plane. The whole thing could be done in less than three hours.

Munro never got tired of it, but Fisk did. Not the flying so much as the routine. They always landed in the same place and they always took off the same way. This was fine with Munro, who had learned early on that flying seaplanes involves enough variables as it is; introducing more merely increases the odds of getting into trouble. Fisk, on the other hand, lived to do things differently. He wondered what it would be like to land a little higher up on the Snow Dome, or lower down, or a bit off to one side. So he did.

It wasn't dangerous, just different. Munro had long since learned to live with Fisk's little deviations, so he didn't worry about them until the day Fisk decided to try taking off down the length of the Blue Glacier instead of over the icefall. He was flying N17598, a Beaver Kenmore had acquired from the Falkland Islands and rebuilt. His reason for going down the length of the ridge, he later stated, was to reduce the need for precise directional control. Instead of having to aim for the top of the narrow fall, he had the whole width of the glacier to slide down.

His theory was good, but the facts did him in. What he failed to realize was that after the ridge curved to the right, the snow became laced with crevasses. Not big ones, but crevasses all the same.

On this day, Fisk had three people to take out in Five-Nine-Eight plus a pile of empty boxes, bottles, and cans, the cabin's weekly accumulation of garbage. Before climbing in himself and firing up the engine, he walked around to where three students stood holding the rope attached to the Beaver's tail.

"I want you to swing me around that way," Fisk ordered, pointing east to where the long back of the Snow Dome curved off down the ridge.

"Huh?" one of the students said in surprise. "You don't want to go down past the hut?"

"No, I'm going that way. I think it will work better."

The students shrugged. The whole flying thing was magic to them, so if a pilot wanted to take off in a different direction, who were they to question it?

Fisk was not big on conversing with his passengers, especially about flying, which he figured they wouldn't understand anyway. He wasn't above discussing other subjects, however, on the rare occasions when the mood struck. Once during a Navy flight, as his Beaver wallowed north through vicious turbulence, rain ricocheting off the windscreen like shotgun pellets while the gray surface of the Strait of Georgia heaved and twisted below them, Fisk scared the life out of the officer beside him by announcing suddenly in a loud voice, "We've got problems!"

The officer turned white and stared wildly around him. Was the engine losing oil pressure? Had the plane experienced a structural failure? Were they about to run out of fuel? He peered down at the clawing waves only a hundred feet below and turned wide-eyed to Fisk. They were going down, the officer was sure of it.

"Gophers!" Fisk yelled over the roar of the engine. "I got gophers in my lawn like you wouldn't believe." He then happily launched into a long discourse on the frustrations of gopher eradication as he nonchalantly guided the wildly bucking Beaver through the screaming wind to a flawless landing at the torpedo test range. He was still ranting on about his plague of lawn rodents as the officers staggered away up the dock.

So Fisk saw little reason to inform his load of "glacier guys" that he was about to take off in an entirely different direction. The fact they might be upset by a change in routine, especially a change they might feel was dangerous, didn't occur to him. They were, after all, only passengers. So he scrambled onto the float, levered himself through the door into his seat, and cranked up the engine. When it was up to temperature he waved at the students on the rope and shoved the throttle up. Heaving back and forth on the yoke, he got the plane rocking, and the students hauled the tail around.

"Where are you going?" his front seat passenger shouted over the snarl of Five-Nine-Eight's engine.

"That way." Fisk pointed ahead out the windscreen, wondering what other direction the man might think the plane was going to go.

"Why aren't we going the regular way?" the passenger asked, but his question was lost in the roar of the engine as Fisk pushed the throttle to the stop.

The Beaver eased forward and then began accelerating down the slope. The view was spectacular, although no one in the plane was relaxed enough to enjoy it. In front of them, the huge expanse of the Blue poured down the ridge toward the valley below the summit, while in the distance the eastern wall of the Olympics sawed into the brilliant blue sky above Puget Sound. At first, the takeoff seemed no different than any of the others off the Snow Dome. The slope was not quite as great so the plane was taking longer to reach flying speed, but otherwise everything seemed fine.

Suddenly the snow ahead didn't seem so smooth. They were entering the upper crevasse zone, but Five-Nine-Eight wasn't ready to fly. Fisk felt a sudden pang of worry. He hadn't realized there were crevasses so high up.

Wham! The plane bounced across the first crack in the snow and Fisk felt the brace wires between the floats begin to vibrate. There was nothing he could do. It was too late to stop, and the crevasses were too long to steer around.

Wham! The floats careened off the edges of the next crevasse. This time the wings began to vibrate. The next crevasse was coming up fast. Fisk glanced at the airspeed indicator. Fifty miles per hour. Close enough, he decided, and he jerked back on the yoke with one hand while pumping the flaps down some more with the other. Five-Nine-Eight staggered off the snow just feet from the next crevasse and mushed through the thin air. Fisk expertly played the yoke and the flap handle, tottering along the fine line between flying and stalling as the airspeed built slowly. He felt the floats touch a couple of times, but he managed to keep the plane from sinking its weight back onto the rough snow.

It was over in seconds, and as Five-Nine-Eight curved smoothly out over the valley, Fisk decided it really hadn't been that bad. Next time he'd make sure to start his takeoff from higher up on the Snow Dome. His passengers sat in silence during the forty-five minute flight home. The ones who'd made the flight before didn't remember Munro ricocheting off cracks in the snow, and they didn't see why they had to run the risk with another pilot.

Munro wasn't in the office when Fisk landed, but a few days later one of the researchers reached him by phone. He and his fellow passengers had not appreciated Fisk's experiment, he said, so in the future would it be possible for them to fly with Munro only? Of course, Munro replied, wondering how he was going to break the news to Fisk.

In the end, he didn't have to. He mentioned the researchers' concerns to Mildred, so she simply made sure the only flights Fisk took from then on were cargo only, in and out. But there were plenty of charter and Navy flights on the schedule, and more and more students were signing up for lessons, so it wasn't long before Fisk had phased out of the Blue Glacier project altogether.

Munro never questioned Fisk's flying abilities, but scaring passengers unnecessarily was bad for business. As for Fisk, the flights he'd taken to the Blue gave him more material for the little instructional booklet he'd written a few years earlier. Titled *Fundamentals of Float Flying*, the booklet had been printed in 1964, and was standard issue to Kenmore's new flight students. Now he could add to it, and he wrote two new chapters, *Seaplanes in the Mountain Lakes*, and *Glacier Flying*. At the end of the second edition, on page forty-five, he put one of his favorite photos. Under a cloudless sky, with snow-streaked peaks stretching to the horizon, Fisk is standing in the sun beside Five-Nine-Eight, the Beaver's blunt nose angled up jauntily as it sits on its heels in the pure snow of the Big Blue.

Starting in the late 1960s, Kenmore's planes have been fitted with company radios, UHF units with a range of perhaps two hundred miles if the conditions are right. A base station transceiver is installed in the office, and a large whip antenna adorns the roof. Pilots report their progress during their flights, and the dispatcher can let them know if last-minute passengers need to be picked up somewhere along the route.

Bob Munro was not used to reporting his whereabouts, but even *he* realized the importance of letting people know things were okay up on the glacier. So he called in when he started his approach to the Snow Dome, and he called in again after the slide down the icefall launched him off the mountain. Gregg Munro, his Vietnam experience a memory he was doing his best to forget, was back in the cockpit again, pushing the company's Cessnas and Beavers up and down the coast of British Columbia.

> "When he was on the glacier and I was flying, we had the UHF radios, so I would know when he was going up there. He'd call as he was going in, and then I'd keep flying and waiting and watching the clock. After about forty-five minutes, I'd figure okay, it's time for him to call off. Sometimes an hour and a half would go by and he wouldn't have called, and then I'd start to worry. Had the plane broken down, or had he had an accident? All sorts of things start going through your mind at that point. Then finally I'd hear 'Six-Six-Zulu off the Snow Dome,' and I'd breathe a big sigh of relief. I don't know how many times I went through that, but I worried all the way through that project."
>
> **GREGG MUNRO**

Had he not got into flying, Gregg may well have made a career for himself in film or television. He's always been interested in movies and movie making, and the films and videos he's shot over the years for the company are proof of his creative abilities. But none of his footage is as dramatic as the single roll he shot on a warm, cloudless day in 1975. It was going to be a busy day at Kenmore. In addition to the scheduled charter and training flights, the UW had sent over a truckload of stuff for the glacier. There were sacks of groceries, stove fuel, and boxes of equipment. There was even more stuff up on the glacier to bring out, and Munro figured it would take two flights to accomplish it all. It was the chance Gregg had been waiting for.

"What I'd like to do," he told his father, "is ride in on the first flight, and then come home on the second flight. That way I can film a takeoff and a landing from outside the plane."

Munro had no objections, so Gregg grabbed his Super-8 movie camera and climbed aboard. What he came back with is a remarkable piece of film, not only because you don't often see floatplanes landing on glaciers, but because Bob Munro makes it all look so easy. But it isn't easy, and in Gregg's footage there are glimpses of why.

He filmed the landing approach, and the view forward over the cowling shows the almost total lack of detail in the snow ahead. Add to this the fact that the plane is going down as the landing surface is going up, and you begin to appreciate the judgment, skill, and even intuition that's required to ease a two-and-a-half-ton floatplane into a touchdown it was never designed to make.

The camera bobbles when Six-Six-Zulu's floats touch the snow, but the runout is suprisingly smooth. Gregg climbed out to film the researchers hauling the plane around by the tail, and then he climbed back in to shoot the short taxi to the unloading area. It's a bit like being on the bridge of a ship in a gentle swell, watching the Beaver's nose pitch up and down as the floats slide across the wind-sculpted waves in the snow.

There were a lot of people up at the glacier that day, and everyone pitched in to help unload the plane. Gregg got a few shots of the growing pile of supplies beside the plane, but he was soon distracted by a pretty young woman in the group. Despite the stark and frigid surroundings, the weather on Mt. Olympus that day must have been downright tropical judging by the young lady's shorts and halter top.

At one point in the film, she trudges up the slope to where Bob Munro is standing near his airplane. Gregg's camera was not equipped for sound, so we'll never know the exchange that took place between the shapely student and the lanky pilot. But by the gestures and expressions, the woman is probably telling Munro what an impressive job he did landing the plane, and Munro is probably waving away her compliments in embarrassment, accompanied by his usual, self-deprecating remarks.

"Oh, it's nothing really," he could be saying. "Anyone could do it."

The woman also solved a mystery that had been puzzling the Kenmore line crew from the moment the glacier cargo had showed up at the dock. In addition to the expected containers of food, fuel, and equipment, there was a piano. Well, sort of a piano. It was a practice keyboard, actually, and it belonged to the girl on the glacier, who was studying music in addition to ice and rocks. She had signed up for a stint at the cabin, but she didn't want her fingering skills to get rusty. The practice keyboard was the answer. Gregg persuaded her to set it up, so in the middle of his movie is an unlikely scene of a tanned young woman sitting on an upended supply crate vigorously playing a piano in the middle of the Blue Glacier.

Gregg didn't have much film with him, so a brief moment of comic relief with the piano was all he could afford. Then it was back to the main plot. As Bob Munro prepared Six-Six-Zulu for takeoff, Gregg worked his way carefully down the bare rock at the edge of the icefall to a position well below the top. From here he would be able to see the Beaver as it crested the top of the fall and accelerated into its downward slide. The liftoff should occur right in front of him.

He adjusted his camera and waited. There was no wind and the mountain was absolutely silent. He thought he'd experienced silence before, crouching in the forest on patrol in Vietnam, but now he realized it hadn't been silence at all. There had been the tiny noises of insects and unseen animals even on the stillest of nights. But here on the mountain there was nothing. It was eerie, to be surrounded by such overpowering objects—the mammoth pyramid of rock at his back, the curving mass of ice at his feet, the looming peaks across the valley—and yet be in such total silence. Gregg looked down the icefall to the valley floor. It was like being in a photograph; the scale was impossible to judge. He could see rocks on the floor of the valley, but how big were they? The size of a dog? The size of a house?

A new element entered the picture below him. A bird, wings outstretched and rigid, was circling silently far below. A hawk perhaps, or a raven. It was too far down to tell. But this single bird, gliding slowly over the rockslides and scrubby trees that littered the base of the mountain, put the picture in a frame. The bird turned its lazy circles, and Gregg felt the immensity of the landscape around him.

There was a faint, pulsing whine from the slope above the icefall, and then the distant bark and offbeat rumble of Six-Six-Zulu's engine as the starter motor kicked it into life. Gregg lifted his camera and practiced following an imaginary plane down the slope a few times. He didn't want to blow the shot. At least the airplane's sudden appearance at the top of the icefall wouldn't take him by surprise; he'd know it was on its way when he heard the engine go to full power.

The engine continued its distant muttering, and Gregg knew his father was waiting for the oil temperature to reach the green. He looked down into the valley again, but the bird had gone. Above him, the muttering swelled to a roar, and the yowl of the accelerating propeller began to sizzle off the surrounding peaks. Gregg braced his legs and peered through the viewfinder at the top of the fall. The banshee wail of the prop grew louder, but Gregg didn't squeeze the trigger. He ignored the waves of sound pulsing over him and tried to envision the yellow and white plane sliding down the side of the Snow Dome. It would move slowly at first, despite all the racket. Then as the slope increased it would slide faster, accelerating toward the rounded lip of the icefall. It should be approaching the fall... NOW!

 Gregg squeezed the trigger on his camera, and an instant later Six-Six-Zulu came into sight. It tipped over the top of the fall and thundered down the slope toward Gregg's position. The roar of the engine and the snarl of the propeller combined and recombined as they bounced between the walls of rock lining the fall until the sound became almost stupefying. Gregg's instinct was to drop the camera and run, but he forced himself to realize he was in no danger. He kept filming, panning with the plane as it pitched over to forty-five degrees. Then the floats lifted from the snow, and Six-Six-Zulu eased out of its rollercoaster plunge and sailed out over the broad valley. The sound faded away almost instantly. Gregg released the trigger, and only then realized he'd been holding his breath the whole time. The silence was back, broken only by the ringing in his ears and the faint, distant drone as Bob Munro headed for home.

Gregg clambered back up to the cabin to wait for his father's return. Two hours later, the distant rumble of a radial engine announced the second flight of the day. Gregg ran to the top of the Snow Dome to capture the landing. Munro's touchdown was as smooth as always, but then he did something he had never been able to do before, and was never able to do again. Keeping the Beaver moving on top of the firm snow, he steered the plane into a sweeping right turn. Normally, the plane would have bogged down and stopped less than a quarter of the way around, but this time Six-Six-Zulu kept moving. Gregg was expecting the plane to stop, too, so he was surprised to watch through the viewfinder as the Beaver taxied all the way around and back toward the cabin.

"This one time I had perfect snow, the time Gregg got the picture, and I was coming in empty. I touched down and came in with rudder right away, and I could tell by the way the plane felt that I'd be able to keep it going around if I kept some power in. So I kept the plane moving and kept the rudder pedal to the floor, and we came on around to where I could head back out again. But that was the only time that worked. Normally, I would land uphill and just start my turn, and then it would stop and we'd get the rope out and pull it around."

BOB MUNRO

Gregg Munro accompanied his father to the Blue at least once more, using the occasion to add to the footage he'd shot on his first visit. He got a great shot of the turnaround procedure, with the researchers stumbling through the snow on the end of their rope, trying desperately to keep the momentum going after they'd gotten the tail moving around. One man gets tangled in the rope and falls, but the others keep plowing ahead, knowing if they stop it will take a Herculean effort in the thin air to get the heavy plane moving again.

Kenmore supplied the Blue Glacier research station for seven years. But the university's research projects at the station were dependent on funding, and in 1977 the money ran out. Munro flew in that spring to haul out the more valuable equipment as well as the unused supplies, and the station was shut down. Munro guided Six-Six-Zulu into one last, triumphant slide down the icefall, and the mountain was alone again. That night, under a sky brilliant with stars, the wind whispering in from the Pacific slowly filled in the parallel grooves Munro had carved down the flank of the Snow Dome. By daybreak, they had disappeared completely.

Munro didn't fly much after that. A field crew wintered over at the South Cascade station in 1977-78, but the weather was so bad Munro was unable to make a single flight. Tangborn's former assistant, Tom Williams, was one of the winter crew, and he remembers going for almost a month with no supply support at all until the weather eased up enough for a helicopter to make it in. Munro made a few flights to the lake after the ice went out, but with the study winding down, the project manager decided the Beaver's one-ton payload was no longer needed.

Munro was sixty-one years old, but his decision to step down from the cockpit had nothing to do with age. He was better fit and more capable than many pilots twenty years younger. But the challenge was gone. Kenmore Air Harbor was becoming an airline, with regularly scheduled flights to the San Juans and British Columbia. Flying to Friday Harbor and back, even in his beloved Six-Six-Zulu, held little interest for the man who had recently been pitching planes off the edge of a glacier and landing on postage-stamp lakes deep in the mountains.

And the business was changing. Every time Jerry Rader came up with a good idea, the FAA wanted more and more paperwork to support it. Munro found himself having to deal with issues he, Reg Collins, and Jack Mines couldn't even have conceived of as they stood in the mud bog beside the shingle mill in 1946. The paint hangar and the fuel pumps had to comply with a growing complexity of environmental regulations. There were noise complaints to deal with. By 1980, the company had almost fifty employees, which brought wage, benefits, and profit-sharing conflicts to resolve.

The Beaver rebuild program was a smashing success thanks to the efforts of Jerry Rader, Greg Gay, Gordy Barnes and the rest of the mechanics. Kenmore had customers all around the world now, most of whom seemed to be needing something all the time. Out in the engine shop, Walt Winseman was thinking about retiring, and when he did, Gordon Holbrook was going to have his hands full meeting the company's engine requirements.

In short, the Air Harbor had succeeded beyond its founders' wildest dreams, but it was requiring more and more of Munro's time to keep it that way. Even Bill Peters was finding less time to fly as he wrote up orders for Beaver rebuilds and juggled the shop's ballooning workload.

It would have been sad if Munro had been forced out of the cockpit while there were still challenges to be met, still glaciers to land on and mountain lakes to explore. But the call for that kind of flying had all but disappeared. Environmental activists succeeded in getting seaplanes banned from the lovely Alpine Lakes region in the Cascade Mountains. Vancouver Island still offered some of the best fishing around, but most of the lakes and streams had become accessible by car, which meant they were more crowded. The days of fabulous fishing were numbered.

In fact, Munro didn't really mind relinquishing the cockpit. He would miss the adventure the last thirty-two years had brought, but he was perfectly happy not to be pushing floatplanes up and down the coast to the same destinations day after day. To Munro, flying had always been about freedom. The freedom to see new places, meet new people, and learn new things. He was as happy listening to a scientist explain the sediment layers on the Snow Dome as he was guiding Six-Six-Zulu through the spectacular mountain passes of the Coast Range.

He was, perhaps, the best floatplane pilot ever. Not because his flying skills were better than everyone else's. One only has to ride with Bill Whitney or Gregg Munro to see what flying skill is all about. But Bob Munro put it all together: the flying, the desire for adventure, the self-reliance, the determination to see every job through, the infectious fascination for the project at hand. His answer was never, "No, I can't," but, "Let me see what I can do."

He enjoyed passing his enthusiasm to his passengers. He wanted them to feel the same excitement he felt every time he lifted off the smooth, blue water of Lake Washington. When his passengers tuned out, when they became more interested in poring over their schedule planners and business magazines than in gazing out at the wondrous world Munro was trying to show them, he lost the incentive to share it.

Bill Peters on top of the world after his one and only landing on the Blue Glacier. (photo courtesy Bill Peters)

It's fitting that he chose to end his flying career with the Blue Glacier project. The invigorating air, the challenge of judging the landing, the mountains marching off to the sea, the exciting plunge down the icefall, the Blue Glacier defined Munro's very soul. He did a lot of things with a lot of airplanes, but the image that will last forever is a picture someone took of him on the Snow Dome. He's standing in the sun, squinting against the glare with Six-Six-Zulu's gleaming radial over his shoulder and the world at his feet.

"I didn't really do it for money. And it wasn't that I wanted to be a hero, landing up there. I don't care if people know about what we did or not. It was a challenge, and I accepted the challenge. It was a wonderful feeling to get out on top of the Snow Dome and look out over the ocean on one side and the Strait with Victoria and Vancouver Island on the other. It was a very rewarding experience to be up on top of that mountain, and having done it to help someone out, not just doing it for the sake of doing it. There was a purpose, it was a job that had to be done. The fact that I accomplished the job was every bit as rewarding to me as being up there."

BOB MUNRO

STINKY THINGS

<h1 style="text-align:center">21</h1>

THERE WAS TENSION IN THE room even before the meeting was called to order. The banquet tables had been pushed together to form a hollow rectangle, and it didn't take long for the opposing parties to choose their positions.

The neighborhood representatives sat stiffly along the north side, facing the windows that looked out onto Lake Union. There was a woman from the Floating Homes Association, a fellow from Freemont, a couple of people from Ballard, and a woman from Sunset Hill. Together, they represented most of the communities bordering Lake Union and the Ship Canal.

The seaplane pilots took the chairs on the south side. There was Lana Kurtzer, now well into his seventies. Lake Union Air Service was represented by owner Clyde Carlson. Jim Chrysler of Chrysler Air Service was there. Kenmore had sent two people, Gregg Munro and Tim Brooks. The area's recreational pilots were represented by Marin Faure, president of the local Seaplane Pilots Association.

The issue that had put all these people in the same room at the same time was noise. The pilots caused it, the residents didn't like it. Noise complaints were nothing new; the Air Harbor got a handful of them every year. But this was the first time they'd been confronted with an organized protest campaign.

One lake over, in his downstairs office beside the basin he'd helped dredge by hand forty years earlier, Bob Munro rubbed his forehead in frustration as he looked at growing pile of correspondence and phone messages on his desk. The noise issue was only the latest shot in the volley of government regulations, public relations hassles, and paperwork that was rapidly taking the enjoyment out of running the business. For the first time in his life, Munro began to wonder if maybe he'd be happier doing something else.

For him, the job had always been about providing great service. Pumping gas, repairing planes, flying supplies to a glacier, it was all the same to Bob Munro and the people who worked for him. Do it right and do it well. Managing the company had been easy. It was just a matter of making sure each customer went away happy. Now it all seemed to be changing. Munro felt he was losing touch with his customers as the business side of the business demanded more and more of his time.

There were internal problems, too. As the company grew, so did the number of employees. Suddenly there were complaints about pay, about benefits, about how the company was being run. Munro was at a loss for a way to deal with them. The problem was not that he didn't want to give his employees more, the problem was that he couldn't. But his attempts to explain this were largely ineffective, and the grumbling continued.

Munro wanted to fix and fly airplanes, not spend his days poring over paperwork and listening to a parade of people who were either telling him what he should be doing or telling him what he wasn't doing right. And now there was this noise thing. "Crisis management" was not a term Munro would have used, but it was rapidly becoming a way of life. The problems were like the waves lapping rhythmically against the pale green dock outside the office. There was always another one on the way.

Back in the meeting room Charles Kleeburg took his seat at the end of the table. He'd been assigned to chair the noise committee, but he didn't really want to be there; he felt the City of Seattle had far bigger problems to deal with than the buzz of departing floatplanes. The number of complainers was actually quite small; most people living near Lake Union and the Ship Canal either liked seaplanes, didn't care, or didn't think they were any noisier than the jackhammers, trucks, buses, piledrivers, and trains that rattled, rumbled, banged, screeched, and hooted most hours of the day.

But the anti-seaplane coalition was persistent. A letter and phone call campaign was launched. A city council member was persuaded to take up the cause. Eventually, the ruckus over seaplane noise grew loud enough that Seattle mayor Charles Royer had little choice but to declare it an Official Issue.

"The problem of seaplane noise on and around Lake Union will be examined with the goal of reaching a solution that will be amicable to all parties concerned," was the statement issued by City Hall, or words to that effect.

The site chosen for the first meeting was the back room of a restaurant. On Kleeburg's right, the row of resident representatives ominously shuffled their stacks of typewritten complaints and demands. On his left, the pilots sat wondering why, amidst the ever-present roar from Interstate 5, the thunder of medivac and TV news helicopters, and the regular rumble of jets coming and going from Boeing Field and Seatac airport, they had been the ones singled out as being too noisy.

The first shot was fired by the woman from the Floating Homes Association. "I've counted up to eighty flights a day from the lake during the summer, and every one of them takes off right in front of our houseboat. It's gotten so we can't sit outside, or even leave the windows open, the noise is so constant."

Lana Kurtzer had a lot of fine qualities, but tact wasn't one of them.

"Listen," he said, leaning forward to glare at the row of homeowners. "I started flying off this lake in 1928. That's before any of you were even born. We've been flying here with no problems and no complaints for all these years, and then you move up from California or someplace and start whining about the noise. What I want to know is, if you don't like seaplane noise, why'd you buy a house near a seaplane base? Seems pretty stupid to me."

The other pilots were impressed. It was the longest thing any of them had ever heard Kurtzer say. The neighborhood representatives were less impressed, particularly by Kurtzer's assessment of their intelligence.

"When we moved here, there were a lot less planes using the lake," the Floating Homes lady retorted testily. "If we'd known there were going to be this many planes using the lake, we wouldn't even have considered living here."

Kurtzer shrugged and sat back in his chair. "There's more flights because there's more customers. We aren't just flying around for fun."

"Times have changed." The man from Ballard had made no secret of his position during the introductions: he wanted planes off the lake, period. "Lake Union might have been a working lake in 1928, but it isn't now. It's a residential area. You and the rest of the seaplane operators will simply have to accept that fact and move on."

This was too much for a woman from the Lake Union Business Owners Association.

"Anyone who thinks Lake Union isn't a working lake hasn't been paying attention," she scolded. "We've got shipyards, commercial fishermen, tug and barge companies, and every kind of marine supplier you can think of based here. Lake Union is a job-creating, revenue-earning hotbed of commercial activity. It's a stated city objective to retain the working nature of Lake Union. The seaplane operators are a major contributor to that objective."

And so it went, for meeting after meeting, month after month. The pilots tried hard to explain the value of the service they provided, and why, in the interest of safety, they flew the traffic patterns they flew, but the neighborhood people would have none of it. They didn't care that that the local seaplane services carried tens of thousands of passengers a year, passengers who contributed one way or another to the city's economy. They didn't care that the seaplane operators provided employment, directly or indirectly, to hundreds of people. All they cared about was the inconvenience to their lives from the shock waves spiraling off the fast-turning propeller tips as the planes accelerated down the lake and climbed out toward Puget Sound.

The anti-seaplane militant from Ballard had been right about one thing: times *had* changed. The seaplane operators knew that ignoring the residents' complaints would cost them in the long run. The environment was a hot topic, and it would just be a matter of time before the noise issue came roaring back. Gradually, under Kleeburg's patient guidance, the pilots and residents began working out a set of voluntary guidelines. The number of daily flights wouldn't be restricted, but takeoff times would be. Departure and arrival routes were drawn up to meet the pilots' safety requirements while at the same time minimizing the noise drumming down on the neighborhoods. A seaplane noise hotline would be set up for residents to report violations to both the city and the offending operator.

It took a long time to hammer out the formal agreement. Some of the neighborhood representatives quit in frustration; others arrived to take their place. Lana Kurtzer lost his medical certificate and could no longer fly. He tried running his business from a desk, but he was a pilot at heart. He sold his dock and buildings to Lake Union Air Service and retired. He professed to enjoy his retirement, but life just wasn't as interesting when viewed from ground level. He'd spent his life pushing seaplanes up and down the northwest raincoast, and he must have figured that if he couldn't fly his old routes anymore he'd try a new one. He died on January 17, 1988. Speculation has it that he's giving rides up and down a beautiful coast in perfect weather in a floatplane that never runs out of gas. But he's probably just as crabby as ever.

Lake Union Air Service itself soon changed hands. The pleasant and community-minded Carlson was replaced at Kleeburg's negotiation table by an ever-changing string of general managers and chief pilots sent over by the new owner. But Jim Chrysler, Gregg Munro, Tim Brooks, and Marin Faure stayed for the duration. The final voluntary agreement was drawn up and signed by the key participants during a ceremony in Mayor Royer's office. It went into force the next day.

The person at Kleeburg's negotiating table who probably best understood the handwriting on the wall was Tim Brooks. Brooks was a relative newcomer to Kenmore, having joined the company in 1976. But if the Air Harbor ever awards a prize to the employee with the most colorful background, Brooks will win it hands down.

His father had been a Corsair pilot in WWII, flying for a time with the famous Pappy Boyington. Exchanging the cockpit for a career in the State Department, he was in South America on assignment when his son entered college in the mid-1960s. Tim Brooks visited his parents on vacations, and after graduation he moved to Bogota, Colombia with the intention of learning Spanish. He supported himself by teaching English three days a week at one of the city's universities. With little to do on the other four days, young Brooks decided to learn to fly.

Soloing is a big event for every student pilot. Weeks of impatience give way to stomach-churning apprehension as the instructor opens the door and steps out of the plane. "Take it around yourself a few times," and the door slams shut, leaving the student sitting alone, palms sweating as he peers at an instrument panel that's gone suddenly blurry. Then the hours of training take over, and the student discovers a confidence he didn't know he had.

It used to be that as the soloist received the congratulations of his fellow students, someone would sneak up with a pair of scissors and cut off his tie and nail it to the flight school wall. As dress became more casual, the tradition was changed to shirttails. A large square is hacked from the back of the soloist's shirt, inscribed with the date and time of the flight, and nailed to the wall. But a sliced-off shirttail is nothing compared to what Brooks had to endure after his colonel hopped out of the Super Cub and ordered him to fly a few circuits by himself.

"Very few people could afford to learn to fly in Colombia, so when someone took lessons and actually soloed, it was a really big deal. When I soloed, they put me through a ritual that was just unbelievable. I've told people about it, and to this day they don't believe me.

"First, they stripped me naked. Then they built a little bonfire and burned all my clothes, including my shoes. They tied my hands behind my back and put me out in the middle of the runway. I had to hop the length of the runway. Then they took me to a barrel of used motor oil and I had to dunk myself in that. I remember it burned like crazy. Then they shaved me all over. I was a teacher, so I managed to convince them to spare some of the hair on top of my head so I wouldn't look totally ridiculous in front of my students. But everything else came off. Then I had to drive home. Everyone was yelling and screaming and popping open champagne bottles while all this was going on. It was wild."

TIM BROOKS

The ordeal of soloing behind him, Brooks went on to get his Private License before returning home to California. He wanted to improve his skills, so he continued his lessons and earned his Commercial License and then his Instrument rating. Intrigued with the idea of living in the coastal cannery town of Monterey, he moved there in the early 1970s and got a job on a sixty-five-foot squid boat. When the local squid fishery took a dive, the Algerian captain decided to try for sardines off the coast of Mexico. Brooks went ashore occasionally in San Diego to rent a plane in an attempt to spot sardines for the boat from the air. The results were marginal, but the experience of flying and navigating over water would eventually pay off.

After a year on the squid boat, Brooks headed back to Colombia where he got a job with an American mining company. Working deep in the jungle near the Peruvian border, his job was to hire and supervise the local labor force that performed the general construction work at the mine. The mine folded a year later, but Brooks had so enjoyed his South American adventures he decided to go back to school for a Masters Degree in international economics and management. Two years later, he had his degree. Now he needed a job.

His brother had met the Munros at a party in Seattle, and he suggested that Brooks contact the Air Harbor to see if they needed a pilot. After two years of classrooms and intense study, flying a plane for awhile sounded pretty good. His letter to Kenmore outlining his flying experiences and inquiring about a job brought the reply that, yes, the company was always on the lookout for qualified pilots, and if he wanted to come to Seattle they would give him a try. Brooks moved north in August 1976. The first thing he had to do was learn to fly floats, so he signed up for lessons. When his instructor thought he was ready, he turned Brooks over to Bill Fisk for a checkride. Fisk passed him, and Brooks worked as a flight instructor for a season before graduating up to the controls of the company's Cessna 180s and Beavers.

He proved to be a skilled pilot with an engaging manner that soon had repeat customers requesting him by name. But Brooks' attitude and personality had a value far beyond the cockpit.

His experiences on the squid boat and at the gold mine had taught him the value of trying to understand the other person's point of view. In Tim Brooks, the Air Harbor had acquired someone who could grasp all sides of a complex issue and then present his company's position in a clear and persuasive manner.

Today, when the press calls with an inquiry about the Air Harbor, or the company is challenged on environmental issues, or communities start talking about imposing restrictive regulations on seaplanes, Tim Brooks is the one who answers the phone or attends the meetings. He is the consummate negotiator, preferring to work out a compromise that benefits everyone rather than trying to maintain an unyielding position by beating down the opposition.

In an era when the trend is to blame someone or something else for every problem, there seems to be no lack of axes for people to grind. "There's too much traffic, there's too much noise, there's too much construction, why do planes have to fly over *my* house?" Companies, particularly those with operations visible to the public, never know where the next complaint, the next restrictive proposal, the next lawsuit, might come from. The Boeing Company has entire departments dedicated to dealing with the public relations and legal problems that crop up on an almost daily basis. Kenmore Air Harbor doesn't need a department; they have Tim Brooks.

Kenmore had successfully reduced the Beaver's noise and vibration by fitting the airplane with a three-bladed propeller. As the issue of seaplane noise heated up in the mid-1980s, Jerry Rader decided the same principle could be applied to the company's Cessna 180s.

Actually, Rader had a lot more planned for the front ends of Kenmore's 180s than just a propeller change. The demise of 80-octane aviation fuel in the early 1980s had forced the engine manufacturers to rework their powerplants to run on 100-octane fuel. Unfortunately, the high-octane version of the Cessna 180's 230-horsepower engine didn't have the reliability of the earlier versions. It didn't take long for Rader to notice that the company's newest Cessnas were spending an inordinate amount of time in the shop instead of earning money in the air. Leafing through the repair logs showed him the primary cause was the high-octane engine. Get rid of the engine, Rader reasoned, and we'll get rid of the downtime.

The ideal substitute, he decided, was the engine from a Cessna 185. Cessna's hot-rod version of the 180, the 185 sports a fuel-injected engine that can crank out 300-horsepower at takeoff. Rader was well aware of the bush pilot's axiom that you can never have too much power in a floatplane, but the real reason he liked the 185's engine was that it had been designed from the outset to run on high-octane fuel. Putting one in a 180 would make the valve problems go away and put an end to the plane's earnings being eaten up by the shop.

Changing the 180's wonderfully simple fuel system to accommodate fuel-injection would be a costly and complicated undertaking, so Rader decided he could take the 180's carburetor, modify it a bit, and mount it in place of the fuel injection system on a 185 engine. It worked like a charm. Rader's new engine didn't develop quite as much power as the injected original, but Kenmore's pilots would still have forty extra horses at their disposal.

The modification and installation of the engine was relatively easy. Satisfying the FAA's paperwork requirements was another story, and there were times when Rader seriously wondered if his idea was worth pursuing. But every time he walked into the shop and saw one of the Air Harbor's 180s sitting there with the engine cowl off he was reminded of why he'd started the project in the first place. After glaring at the offending engine for a moment, he would return to his desk with a renewed determination to conquer the FAA's mountain of paperwork and give his company the reliable airplanes it needed.

Kenmore's four Cessna 180s were fitted with the new engine along with the 185's three-bladed propeller, and the benefits were immediate. Nicknamed Super 180s, they actually cruised faster than a float-equipped 185, which made the passengers happy. The planes got out of the water faster and climbed faster, which made the pilots happy. The three-bladed propeller reduced takeoff noise, which made Tim Brooks and the residents around Lake Union happy. And the number of unscheduled engine overhauls dropped to almost zero, which made Rader, Munro, and the company accountant very happy.

Bob Munro always claimed he had no grand plan for the Air Harbor. There were no fifteen-year plans or five-year plans. To hear him tell it, there was barely a next-week plan. Jack Mines was the one with the vision, he'd say, but of course Jack Mines was long gone. But, in fact, Munro had always had a vision of what he wanted. He wanted satisfied customers and happy employees. He wanted safe airplanes. But whatever else his vision might have included, it's a safe bet a fleet of jet-powered floatplanes wasn't part of it.

As with so many things at Kenmore, it started with a phone call. Harold Hansen had called the company back in 1966 to try to talk them into buying a Beaver. That phone call had changed the course of the company, so when he called twenty years later to pitch another airplane, Bill Peters, who took the call, paid attention.

"You guys should think about a Turbo Beaver," Hansen urged. "Holds more, goes faster. You'd like it."

Sporting an angular, sweptback fin in place of the piston Beaver's aesthetically rounded tail, the Turbo Beaver's cabin was stretched forward of the wing to accommodate another row of seats and a double freight door next to the co-pilot. But the biggest change was bolted to the firewall. Instead of a war-surplus, 450-horsepower radial engine, de Havilland had installed a 550-shaft horsepower Pratt & Whitney gas turbine. The lightweight turbine was mounted backwards in the long, pointy nose, and the output shaft was mated through a reduction gearbox to a huge, paddle-bladed propeller.

"A turbine is just what you guys need," Hansen continued persuasively. "A turbine will give you more power, more speed, more seats, less maintenance, and less noise."

It was a good summary of the benefits of jet power, but Hansen's suggestion was met with skepticism, particularly from Munro. The plane's carrying capacity and speed was appealing, but the thought of operating a turboprop was daunting. Even their exhaust smelled funny. "Stinky things," Munro called them.

The reason for Hansen's call became apparent a short time later when Peters got another call, this time from an operator in Alaska. They had a Turbo Beaver for sale and were wondering if the Air Harbor might be interested.

"We'll make you a good deal," the owner said, which made sense since someone had recently taxied the plane into the side of a truck. The airframe was fine, but the propeller and turbine were toast.

The notion of adding a turbine to the fleet was discussed at length over the next few weeks. Bob Munro found it hard to get excited about the idea. Gregg Munro was almost as skeptical of turbine power as his father, but as manager of the flight department, he had to admit the size of the cabin appealed to him.

"How many times have we had to send a Beaver and a 180 on a flight because there were too many passengers for the Beaver? If we had a Turbo Beaver, we'd only have to send one plane instead of two. That means only one pilot instead of two. Plus the flight would get there faster."

"Turbines are expensive," Bob Munro countered "They use jet fuel, which we don't have. And we've never worked on those stinky things. We wouldn't even know where to start."

This wasn't totally true. Both Greg Gay and Gordon Barnes out in the Beaver shop had worked on stinky-powered aircraft during their stints in the military. Neither one had been an engine specialist, but in the course of their work, both men had learned a fair amount about the care and feeding of turbojet powerplants.

"Don't forget," Jerry Rader said, "if we get this thing and then decide we don't want to run it ourselves, we can always sell it."

Rader's point hit home. Stinky thing or not, Munro knew if there was one thing the Air Harbor truly excelled at it was fixing up damaged airplanes and selling them for a profit. The more they talked about the idea the more they liked it. The Turbo Beaver offered some real speed and payload advantages, but there was also the excitement of taking on something new. Jets were scary, but that was part of the challenge. Munro finally agreed to give it a shot, and the Air Harbor became the proud owner of a severely ground-bound Turbo Beaver.

While the Beaver shop got to work stripping, cleaning, and reassembling the airframe, Rader went in search of an engine to replace the one that had been totaled against the truck. He decided to do the same thing to the Turbo Beaver that he'd done to the Cessna 180: exchange the original, old-technology engine for a newer, more powerful version. He thought he'd found the solution in a Texas company that had a Supplemental Type Certificate (STC) to install a newer engine in the

Turbo Beaver, but after months of frustrating phone calls and broken promises, it became obvious this was a dead end.

"Why can't we do the engine installation ourselves?" Gay wondered. "We don't have much turbine experience, so if we do the installation, we'll learn a lot about maintaining the engine at the same time."

Barnes agreed. "If we buy someone else's conversion, we'll have an airplane, but we won't know any more about maintaining it than we do now."

It made sense to Rader. Several dozen more phone calls convinced him to use an even better engine than the one he'd tried to buy from Texas. The most modern of Pratt & Whitney's PT6A lineup, the Dash-135 turbine was more powerful, generated less noise, and featured a fresh-water flushing system that if used daily would eliminate the threat of power-sapping blade corrosion. The Dash-135 seemed perfect in every respect except price. Brand new, it cost $300,000.

Bob Munro had built Kenmore on the principle of living within the company's means and staying out of debt. Steve Gattis, who'd become the company's accountant in 1975, was impressed by Munro's simple but effective manner of tracking the company's finances.

> "He had his Brown Book. The Brown Book was his cash book. Every day the office would open the mail and take all the checks and make the deposit, and that deposit would go in the Brown Book. So Bob would know exactly how much cash came in, and then he'd find out how many checks had been written that day and that would come out of the total. So he always knew what his cash balance was. Even when the company started phasing in computers, Bob kept his Brown Book.
>
> "He also had a listing of receivables. Usually he let collections happen normally as customers paid their bills. But if an opportunity came up to buy a bunch of Beaver frames or engines and he couldn't do it with the cash he had on hand, he would call certain customers and try to get collections early. He abhorred borrowing money. So he made a point of always knowing the Brown Book balance, because that told him what the company could and couldn't afford."
>
> **STEVE GATTIS**

Three hundred thousand dollars for an engine was way out of line as far as Munro was concerned, and the turbine pro-and-con debate started all over again. Buying a brand new engine meant it would come with a warranty, which was a plus, but in the end, it was the speed argument that carried the day. Where a piston Beaver might make one round trip a day to destinations in Desolation Sound, the Turbo Beaver could make two. The potential to earn twice the revenue with the plane plus the high reliability and low maintenance that were supposed to be the hallmarks of turbine power persuaded Munro to let Rader buy the engine. The money would come from airplane and parts sales; Munro refused to go to the bank for it.

While Gay and Barnes designed the necessary linkages and wiring harnesses to connect the new engine to the controls, Rader ran interference for them, tracking down manufacturers who could make the custom parts they needed. Gradually the plane came together out in the Beaver shop. The porthole rear window was replaced with Rader's rectangle. Sue Peters crawled around the interior with her tape measure and pattern paper, and then returned to her shop to create a complete set of new sidewall panels, headliners, and seats.

Bill Whitney getting ready to give Five-Five-Tango's turbine a fresh-water rinse by replacing one of the igniters with a wash-out fitting. (photo by C. Marin Faure)

And suddenly it was finished. The painters wheeled it into the paint shop and applied a handsome variation of Kenmore's white, yellow, and brown paint scheme. The plane's number was outlined in white over the yellow speed stripe: N1455T. Then they rolled it across to the main shop, where it was lifted into the air and set on a pair of brand new EDO Model 4930 floats. When the last strut bolts had been torqued down, a forklift lifted Five-Five-Tango gently off the shop floor and eased it outside to the pavement between the parts department and the Beaver shop. It sat there, crouched on its silver floats facing the lake, the huge exhaust stacks, streamlined nose, and yawning air intake looking more like a shark than an airplane.

It was time to test the engine. The Pratt & Whitney regional representative was Roy McSwain, and he had been extremely helpful throughout the conversion process, offering suggestions and answering countless questions as Rader, Gay, and Barnes solved one problem only to confront another one. When asked if he'd be willing to come up for the first light-off of the engine, McSwain said he'd be happy to be on hand.

It was a good thing he was. The engine's fuel control unit was defective. The engine would start but it wouldn't develop any power above idle. McSwain helped diagnose the problem, and a new control unit was sent out from the factory. Rader's decision to go with a new engine under warranty had just paid off.

Then it was Chief Pilot Bill Whitney's turn. He and Gay put the plane in the water and prepared it for its first flight. With the exception of a few short hops in a Soloy Turbine 206, Whitney had never flown a turbine-powered aircraft before. But de Havilland had deliberately designed the Turbo Beaver to be as similar as possible to the piston Beaver, so while the view over the slim, pointed nose was certainly different, everything else appeared to Whitney to be about the same.

Until he applied maximum takeoff power. The Super Turbine was off the water almost before it was on the step. To someone used to the piston Beaver's sluggish climb rates and plodding cruise speeds, Five-Five-Tango felt like a fighter. But the flight test program was not just an excuse to zoom around in a hot airplane. There were a whole host of FAA requirements to be met. Whitney flew the plane as slow as he could without falling out of the sky, and as fast as he could without vibrating the tail off to determine the plane's safe operating envelope. He stalled Five-Five-Tango with the flaps up and with the flaps down to determine the handling and stability characteristics. Other tests required him to apply maximum reverse pitch to the propeller blades during cruise flight, something he said afterwards yielded a descent rate he didn't think was physically possible to achieve.

The Kenmore Super Turbine was awarded its STC on April 25, 1988, and Gregg Munro lost no time in adding the plane to the schedule. It was an instant success with the Air Harbor's passengers. The turbine whine, sparkling paint job, and immaculate interior belied the fact the plane itself was well over twenty years old. Some customers began making Five-Five-Tango a requirement in their reservations. "If it ain't the turbine, we ain't flyin'," they'd say. The Air Harbor had entered the jet age.

Five-Five-Tango and the second Super Turbine that would join the fleet a year later would solve the problem of what to do when there were too many passengers for a piston-Beaver, but they wouldn't resolve the problem of what to do when there were ten or twelve passengers signed up for a flight. The obvious solution was to send two Beavers, but this could sometimes entail some serious juggling of the schedule. What Kenmore needed was a really *big* plane.

"What about an Otter?" someone suggested. Designated the DHC-3, the Otter was de Havilland's third in-house design. In essence an enlarged Beaver, the Otter had first flown in December 1951, with deliveries starting a year later. With a gross weight of 8,000 pounds, the DHC-3 was designed to carry ten passengers, although operators have installed as many as thirteen seats in the cabin.

Incredibly rugged, with a reinforced floor and huge double doors in the cabin, the Otter seemed the ideal workhorse for anyone needing a big plane in tough country. Like the Beaver, an Otter can be fitted with wheels, skis, or floats. Many of the 460 that were produced went to the US and Canadian armed forces, but by 1980 most of the military Otters had been sold off as surplus.

For such a large and seemingly useful plane, a used Otter was amazingly cheap. In the 1980s, an Otter complete with floats could be had for less than one hundred thousand dollars. On wheels, the planes were often half that. This at a time when a Kenmore Beaver cost upwards of three hundred thousand dollars.

The reason for the Otter's low resale value was not the airplane, but its engine. De Havilland had fitted a gearbox to Pratt & Whitney's R-1430 Wasp radial in an effort to gain more power, but even 600 horsepower wasn't enough to haul four tons of airplane into the air with any degree of performance. The Otter quickly gained a reputation for blowing cylinder heads on takeoff, and the gearbox was a constant source of problems. There were enough crashes to tarnish the plane's reputation forever, but it did have that spacious cabin and rugged construction...

The notion of buying an Otter was kicked around at Kenmore after the 1987 season. The routes on which Gregg Munro envisioned using the plane were at sea level with plenty of takeoff room. Neither he nor Bill Whitney could imagine any reason why a pilot would need to overtax the engine. The only problem would be at Lake Union, where pilots taking off to the north had to scramble for altitude to clear the high Aurora Avenue bridge that spans the eastern entrance to the Ship Canal.

The idea was kicked into high gear in early 1988 when someone leafing through an aviation magazine noticed an ad for an Otter down in Texas. N3125S had six hundred hours on its current engine, which meant whoever bought it could fly it for six hundred more before the geared radial would have to be rebuilt or replaced. Gregg estimated the Air Harbor would fly it two hundred hours a year, so the company should be able to get three full seasons of work out of it before having to decide whether to overhaul it or sell it.

Bob Munro readily agreed to purchase the plane. It was dirt cheap; even a worn out, beat up Beaver would cost more. And a big, radial-engined plane was something Munro understood. They were part of his world; he'd flown them for thirty years under every condition imaginable. The turbine, with its eerie, impersonal whine and snapping igniters, was from someone else's world, a world he wasn't sure he liked all that much. Oh, he knew how turbines worked, he liked the fact they weren't noisy, and he most definitely understood the potential cost advantages of operating them. He just didn't care for them.

Because Two-Five-Sierra was in Texas, someone had to go get it. None of the Air Harbor's pilots had ever flown an Otter, but there was one who'd flown a lot of funky taildraggers off strange little airstrips in some of the remotest places on earth. Paul Carlson had been in the Navy when in 1956 a friend invited him to tag along while he took a flying lesson. At the end of the session, the instructor asked Carlson if he'd like to have a go. The plane was a Piper J-3 Cub, and the cost was ten dollars for a thirty minute lesson. Carlson had barely strapped himself into the front seat when he knew this was what he wanted to spend his life doing.

After earning his Airframe and Powerplant Certificate he was hired as a mechanic by Kenmore in 1962, but as soon as he could he signed up for flight lessons. He didn't stop until he'd earned his Commercial and Flight Instructor ratings. After a year of instructing at the Air Harbor, he was promoted to charter pilot.

He left Kenmore only twice, to fly Helio Couriers and Cessna 206s as a missionary pilot in the Philippines and New Guinea. But it was safe to say he had the most landplane experience of any of the Air Harbor pilots, and the three years he'd spent coaxing Helio Couriers in and out of remote airstrips had given him a real feel for tailwheel airplanes, which have very different ground-handling characteristics than tricycle-gear planes.

Bill Peters had a Beaver to pick up with the truck, so he, Carlson, and a mechanic named Mike Cummings headed for Texas. Cummings had not only worked on Otters, he'd had some experience flying them on floats. He spent a couple of days servicing and testing Two-Five-Sierra's engine, instruments, and flight controls, and then he gave Carlson a rudimentary flight checkout. Satisfied that Carlson could get the beast home on his own, Peters and Cummings headed east in the truck to collect the Beaver.

Carlson's flight to Renton was easy enough, albeit rather slow; at 120 miles per hour, the view out the windscreen doesn't change very fast. The next step was to get the plane up the lake to Kenmore. The Otter was too large and heavy for the platformed catamaran the company used to ferry wheelplanes up the lake.

"I guess we'll have to hire a barge," Munro said, reaching for the phone. He was not happy when he hung up. "They want two thousand dollars to transport a plane up the lake. I hate paying so much for something we ought to be able to do ourselves, but I guess we don't have a choice."

"I can fly it up if you like," Carlson volunteered. "I can land right over there." He pointed across the channel to the freight yard the Air Harbor had used in the past as a Beaver airstrip.

Munro was skeptical. "You think you can get an Otter in there? It's a pretty big plane."

"Sure. I'll come in over the trees and land toward the lake so if I have to go around there won't be anything in the way. If I remember right, the usable part of that yard is about seven hundred feet long. I've landed Helio Couriers in a lot less space than that."

Munro winced. The Air Harbor had tried a Helio Courier on floats once. Munro hadn't been particularly impressed with the plane, stating that he could get off the water faster in a Cessna 180 despite the Courier's vaunted STOL (short takeoff and landing) design. Carlson, who knew firsthand what a Courier was capable of, took the challenge and proceeded to blast off the water in little more than half the distance Munro used with the 180.

So while Munro may have been skeptical, he knew if Carlson said he could do something with an airplane, he could do it. Besides, landing an Otter on a dirt patch was the sort of thing he would have liked to do himself.

"Okay, if you think it can be done, go ahead and do it. I'll talk to the people with the property over there and let them know what we want to do."

The following Thursday, June 2, someone flew Carlson down the lake to Renton while every-one else who wasn't busy or out flying trooped down the road past the cement plant to the shipping yard. Gregg Munro had grabbed his movie camera, and he took up a position beside the lake on the centerline of Carlson's improvised runway. He figured that would be the best spot for a dramatic shot of the landing.

They heard it first, the slow, rumbling beat of the geared radial echoing off the hills across the lake. Then they saw it, the silver and gray Otter looking increasingly huge as it droned slowly up the lake.

"There's no way he's going to pull this off," one of the pilots said, "The field's not long enough."

"If anyone can land that thing here it's Paul. I think he'll make it."

Speculation ran up and down the line of Kenmore employees as Carlson slowly circled the container yard. Then he straightened the plane out and headed away from the lake.

"Here he comes," someone shouted, and the group fell silent, all eyes following the huge plane as it banked smoothly around to head back toward the yard. The engine note dropped to a mutter and the onlookers could see the flaps coming down. At the far end of the field, Gregg lifted his movie camera and got ready to press the trigger.

Two-Five-Sierra seemed to float as it settled slowly toward the yard, the wings wobbling slightly as Carlson corrected for the air currents spilling off the nearby hill. It was a tricky landing because there was no margin for error. Too short, and the Otter would hit the trees and phone poles that lined the road at the east end of the yard. Too long, and the plane would slam into the huge concrete blocks that had been dumped along the lake shore. Too slow, and Carlson would risk a stall that could drop the plane in on its nose. Too fast, and he'd never get it stopped in time. It was a tight envelope to fly in, and Carlson had already crept outside it. He was a little bit high and a little bit fast.

This was understandable, as low and slow is the most potentially dangerous flying condition there is. But Carlson couldn't afford to be high and fast, either. As soon as he knew he'd made the yard, he chopped the power and the Otter began to settle, but it wasn't settling fast enough. Carlson dropped the flaps all the way down and the sink rate increased, but it still looked like the touchdown point was going to be at least halfway down the yard. No good. Shaking his head, Carlson shoved the power up and retracted the flaps. The engine thundered and Two-Five-Sierra sailed out over the lake. Strike one.

His second approach was better. He started the plane down sooner this time, but the trees and telephone poles were awfully close. Like the Beaver, the Otter carries its fuel in its belly. Carlson had a sudden vision of the bottom of the plane ripping open on a pole, the fuel streaming out to ignite as the plane plunged headlong into the dirt. Forcing that image out of his mind, he concentrated on setting up as steep an approach path as possible. The plane slid over the trees and down toward the dirt. For a moment it looked as if he might make it, but Two-Five-Sierra refused to touch down. It floated along on its huge wings, eating up precious runway. It was too high for Carlson to simply shove the yoke forward and slam the wheels onto the ground, so when the mid-point of the field flashed by, he gave up. Once again the radial blasted to full power and the plane climbed ponderously out over the lake as Carlson retracted the flaps. Strike two.

He was beginning to think he'd bitten off more than he could chew. Seven hundred feet sure didn't look like seven hundred feet from the cockpit of the Otter. It looked more like fifty feet. He wondered if this was how carrier pilots felt as they guided their fighters down an invisible line in the sky toward the postage-stamp deck of their ship. At least the carrier pilots had cables and a hook to get them stopped. All he had were the questionable brakes on Two-Five-Sierra's main wheels. Well, he thought, I'll try it once more. If I don't make it the third time, I'll go back to Renton and Bob can call the barge company.

Once again he swung the plane around and lined up with the patch of dirt. He chopped the power and put in some flap. The plane began to settle toward the line of trees. Carlson gritted his teeth and put in more flap. The trees came up faster. You've done this before, he told himself. Hundreds of times in the Philippines and New Guinea. This isn't any different. Just imagine the line you want to fly and stay on it.

He lowered the flaps all the way, raised the nose, and pulled the power all the way off. The airspeed needle slid down to quiver just above stall speed. He felt the Otter begin to shudder, the unmistakable sign that a plane is about to stop flying.

He half expected to hear the sound of branches hitting the belly as he skimmed over the trees, but he didn't and now he had clear air in front of him. But he had to slow his sink rate or he'd impact the ground like a bug hitting a windshield. He shoved the throttle up to full power. Engine roaring, the Otter settled toward the dirt. This is it, he thought. I'm going to make it! But once again Two-Five-Sierra refused to touch down. The plane floated along, the wheels only feet above the dirt. Carlson was helpless. He needed the brakes to stop the plane, but brakes aren't much good if the wheels aren't rolling on the ground.

Suddenly the Otter dropped onto the dirt, bounced back into the air, and slammed down again. Carlson yanked the power off and stepped on the brakes as hard as he could without tipping the plane up onto its nose. Trailing a billowing cloud of dust, Two-Five-Sierra careened toward the cement blocks where Gregg Munro stood peering through his movie camera.

The landing looked a safe distance away in the tiny viewfinder, but something told Gregg he should open his other eye for a true picture of what was happening. He was stunned to see the Otter bearing down fast, the huge engine and whirling propeller seeming only yards away. He ran for the sidelines, praying that he would at least make it beyond the reach of the propeller and landing gear.

In the cockpit, Carlson was vaguely aware of a figure diving out of the way of the plane, but his attention was riveted on the line of huge blocks that marked the end of the yard. He knew he was going to hit them, and he had a fleeting thought that perhaps the damage wouldn't be too bad and the plane would be repairable. He mashed down on the brakes as hard as he could and waited for the impact.

The Otter jolted to a stop and immediately disappeared in a choking cloud of dust. Carlson sat tensely, waiting for the next thing to happen, and then he realized it was over. In front of him, the Wasp engine settled into the comfortable, offbeat rumble of an idling radial, while the big geared propeller swung lazily past the windscreen. It was several seconds before he realized the significance of the turning propeller; he hadn't hit the blocks after all. Keeping the pressure on the brakes, he reached forward and pulled the mixture back. The engine burbled on for a moment and then clanked to a stop. He reached down and switched off the master and magneto switches, and shoved open the door beside his seat. The dust was almost gone, and he could see people running toward him.

"According to de Havilland, the Otter's minimum landing distance is 810 feet. I'd made it in six hundred. Somebody paced it off later and told me I'd stopped only seventy-five feet from the blocks.

"But the worst thing about the landing was that I got arrested. Somebody had called the police to complain that a plane was buzzing the area. So the next thing I know a cop car shows up and they want to take me into custody for hazardous flying or something. We told them we had permission to land in the yard, and that planes had landed there before, but they wanted to arrest me anyway. They hauled me off to the precinct station where fortunately there was an officer who'd been a military pilot. He saw my pilot's license and called the FAA. The FAA said there was nothing illegal about what I'd done, so the cops let me go."

PAUL CARLSON

Otter Two-Five-Sierra being craned onto the base after Paul Carlson's dramatic landing in the container yard across the channel. (photo courtesy Bill Peters)

Rather than take the plane apart, Bill Peters decided to move it in one piece. He hired a barge-mounted crane, and the Otter soared into the air on the end of a bridle attached to the lift rings. The barge idled across the channel, and Two-Five-Sierra was lowered gently to the pavement in front of the office.

After a thorough going over, Kenmore's new airliner was mounted on a set of Bristol 7170 floats and put into service. Its eleven-passenger capacity was a welcome addition to the schedule, but the plane itself left something to be desired. In short, it was a dog. With a climb rate of barely eighty feet per minute, the company couldn't use it at all on Lake Union. The full-power struggle to clear the Aurora bridge would have blown the engine sooner rather than later, and flying under the bridge was illegal. So Two-Five-Sierra was restricted to flights originating at the main base on Lake Washington.

Disappointed at the Otter's poor performance in Kenmore service, Bob Munro called his operator friends in Alaska to see if any of them might be interested in leasing the plane the following season. He found a taker in Ward Air in Juneau. The plane was sent north the following spring where it worked for two seasons before coming back to Kenmore in 1991. Ward Air had installed an overhauled engine which helped the plane's performance a little, but not enough to allow it to be used off Lake Union.

Bob Munro, meanwhile, was getting more and more worried about the plane. A number of operators up north had added Otters to their fleets for the same reason Kenmore had, to take advantage of the plane's big cabin and high payload. But the engines just weren't up to the task, and as the phone rang in his office with reports of Otter accidents and near-accidents, he became convinced his own pilots and passengers were flying around in a crash waiting to happen. He ordered it pulled off the line at the end of the 1991 season.

The Air Harbor had two choices. They could do what Ward Air had done and install another overhauled, zero-time engine, or they could sell the plane. Gregg and his dispatchers hated the idea of losing the capacity of the plane, but even a fresh engine wouldn't change Munro's feeling they were courting disaster. A few years earlier his decision would have been immediate, and Two-Five-Sierra would have been sold out of the fleet.

But something had occurred a hundred miles north in the town of Bellingham that not only changed the fate of Two-Five-Sierra, it would ultimately change the nature of the Air Harbor itself.

Dara Wilder specialized in the design and manufacture of sophisticated extraction and separation equipment for the gold mining industry. From his base in Bellingham, he traveled the world, visiting mines and figuring out ways to make his equipment better. Many of the companies he visited used de Havilland Otters to transport men and machinery to and from the mine sites. Wilder, a pilot himself, quickly realized why. While not as maneuverable as a helicopter, an Otter can carry a heavy a load for a fraction of what it would cost to do the same job with a chopper.

Wilder was also well aware of the Otter's Achilles heel of an engine. The solution was obvious: replace the unreliable geared radial with a reliable turbine. Wilder wasn't the first person to think of this, nor was he the first person to try it. But he was the first person to make it work.

The engine installation itself was designed by Floyd Perry in Salinas, California. A veteran of turbine conversions from crop dusters to twin-engine commuter planes, Perry selected the same

Super Turbine Four-Four-Tango and the best Beaver modification and rebuild team in the business. From left, Jerry Rader, Gordon Holbrook, Greg Gay, and Gordon Barnes. (photo by C. Marin Faure)

engine Jerry Rader had chosen for the Super Turbine: the Pratt & Whitney PT6A-135. Despite being more powerful, the turbine was much lighter than the hulking radial it was replacing, so to preserve the Otter's center of gravity, Perry hung the new engine way out ahead of the firewall. The long, steel-tube engine mount was sheathed in a graceful cowling that tapered from the cockpit down to the huge, polished prop spinner.

Dara Wilder called his conversion the Vazar Dash-3, a combination of his company's name with the Otter's official designation. The price of the conversion kit, which included everything but the Otter it would be bolted to, was just shy of half a million dollars. After four years of development, testing and, of course, paperwork, Wilder's conversion received the blessing of the FAA in November 1988. Transport Canada followed suit early the following year.

Like the Turbo Beaver project, converting Two-Five-Sierra to turbine power would be a huge gamble for the Air Harbor. The cash outlay was gigantic by Air Harbor standards, and the return on investment was uncertain at best. But Gregg Munro and Tim Brooks know you have to spend money to make money. The potential to grow the passenger business was there, they felt, but to take advantage of it they needed to augment their fleet of seven and nine-passenger Beavers with something larger.

Had it not been for the success of the two Super Turbines, Munro probably would have said, no, we can't afford to convert Two-Five-Sierra, and that would have been the end of it. But the two Turbo Beavers had definitely made a difference. The company's level of service had improved because of them, and so had its image. Even the anti-noise activists in the lakeside neighborhoods grudgingly admitted the whoosh of the turbines was a huge improvement over the snarl of the piston planes.

So Munro sat in the meetings, listening to the arguments pro and con and asking questions. At night he mulled over what he'd heard. Starting in 1946, Kenmore Air Harbor had succeeded by taking advantage of opportunities as they came along. And starting in 1946, the company had succeeded because of Bob and Ruth Munro's fiscal responsibility. So what to do now? The Vazar Dash-3 was certainly an opportunity, but it also looked like a great way to lose a lot of money.

He decided to take the chance. Two-Five-Sierra's worn-out radial was removed, and one of Dara Wilder's Vazar Dash-3 conversion kits was bolted on in it's place. The whole process took only three days, after which the plane was wheeled into the paint hangar. It emerged with an experimental paint job of sorts; the design was similar to the scheme on the Super Turbines, but where the two Beavers used Kenmore's traditional yellow and brown, Two-Five-Sierra sported gold and black. Some people liked it, most didn't, and when the airframe was overhauled a few years later it was repainted in the traditional company colors.

Paul Carlson was the most qualified to render judgment on the success of the conversion. He'd flown Two-Five-Sierra on wheels and on floats under just about every weather and water condition imaginable.

"The conversion expense is high, but the result is really worth it. It's ten times the plane it used to be. It's a dream to fly, with a cruise speed about thirty miles an hour faster than the piston Otter. And it will go even faster if you fly higher. The beta prop gives you all sorts of maneuverability on the water. You can stop, back up, turn around, things you can't even dream of doing in a piston plane.

"Takeoffs are great. The plane pops off the water and then keeps going up. We can fly out of Lake Union with no problems, not only because we can safely clear the bridge, but because the engine's so reliable the chance of an engine failure is just about zero."

PAUL CARLSON

The decision to convert Two-Five-Sierra changed the Air Harbor forever. No one knew it at the time, of course. It just seemed like the right thing to do, a good opportunity to add some much-needed capability to the fleet. But as chief pilot Bill Whitney spooled up the engine and powered Two-Five-Sierra away from the Kenmore docks on its first turbine-powered flight, the Air Harbor grew up. The spray whipped into the air by Whitney's departure erased the quaint floatplane operator at the north end of the lake and replaced it with an airline. Even the name had changed. The square lettering that for decades spelled out "Kenmore Air Harbor" on the sides of the planes had been quietly replaced with a new logo in a rounded, modern font. It said simply, "Kenmore Air."

SUCCESS ON THE STEP 22

OB MUNRO WASN'T MUCH FOR writing things down outside of the figures he entered each day in the Brown Book. But one day he penned four sentences that pretty much defined the path he'd followed every day of his working life.

"Dedicate yourself to achieve success in whatever you do.
Have your priorities in order.
Be willing to take risks and be confident in your ideas.
And don't work necessarily for money but for accomplishment."

No one knows what motivated him to put his guiding principles in writing, if it was something he'd read and liked, or if he'd come up with the words himself. He didn't show them to anyone, and the paper sat in the back of a file folder until his grandson stumbled across it years later. The heavy hitters in commercial aviation—the airlines and airframe manufacturers—spend millions to have consultants draw up inspirationally worded declarations titled, "Our Vision." The permanently precarious state of a good portion of the air transportation industry suggests the high-priced philosophies are either irrelevant or unread. Probably both. Kenmore Air, meanwhile, soldiers on in a direction defined by four simple sentences that cost nothing and came from the heart.

Statistically, the company shouldn't have made it past the 1960s. It's probably safe to say the majority of commercial seaplane operators don't survive twenty years, and many of them miss even that lifespan by a considerable margin. The Air Harbor's remarkable longevity has little to do with the airplanes they fly, the routes they follow, or the services they sell. Kenmore flies on because of the kind of people who work there.

It's easy to espouse lofty business principles when times are good. But when revenue falls off, when the bills overwhelm the checks, when you start wondering if you can make the payroll, the high road can start looking pretty hazardous. It was certainly beginning to look this way to Munro and his employees as the company entered its fourth decade of service.

Lake Union Air Service had been in business as long as Kenmore Air Harbor, although after a string of owners the only resemblance to the original company was the name. But starting in the early 1980s, Clyde Carlson took on the task of turning the company into a serious competitor. He initiated scheduled service to the San Juans and in the process acquired control of the seaplane docks at most of the most popular destinations. Kenmore could continue to use the docks, but if a Lake Union plane was due in or already there the Kenmore pilot had to go in search of another and invariably less convenient place to let off his passengers.

With his scheduled island service off and running, Carlson next set his sights on Victoria. Seat of the BC provincial government, Victoria had grown to become a well-established center of British sophistication and culture when Vancouver over on the mainland was still a handful of shacks sprawled across a mudflat. A two to four hour boat ride from Seattle, Victoria is only twenty minutes away by air. With attractions like the Canadian Pacific Railroad's Empress Hotel, the remarkable Royal Provincial Museum, and quaint rows of "high-street" shops, Victoria was fast becoming as popular a destination as the San Juan Islands. Carlson was convinced a scheduled service between the two cities had even more revenue potential than his popular island service. Even better was the fact that Kenmore wouldn't be able to compete with him.

The only way a US commercial operator can offer regular air service to destinations north of the border is to obtain an operating certificate from the Canadian government. Munro had managed to obtain one back in 1949, although the only paying passengers he envisioned flying into BC were steelhead fishermen and moose hunters. The Air Harbor's certificate was amended from time to time over the years, until by the early 1980s it included a number of destinations along the BC coast.

Victoria wasn't one of them. The Canadians had granted only one operating certificate for air service between Seattle and Victoria, and it belonged to Lake Union Air. Carlson launched his new service, and it wasn't long before his blue and white Cessna 206s were making as many as six flights a day to the bustling harbor in front of the ivy-draped Empress. All the Kenmore pilots could do was watch.

If there was an upside to all this, it was that the Air Harbor's employees had no intention of simply sitting still while Lake Union Air gobbled up the local passenger market. In his office, Bob Munro listened to a continuous stream of suggestions, some good, some bad, and some just silly, but all of them designed to get Kenmore Air back in the game. In the end, he thought about what he'd heard, weighed it against the probable outcome of doing nothing, and decided it was time to take some risks.

Risk number one was to take on Lake Union Air in the San Juans. Not only would Kenmore offer a daily schedule of flights to the islands, but for the first time their service would be based on seat fares instead of charter rates. In the past, people wanting to fly somewhere with Kenmore had to hire the whole plane. Kenmore's new San Juan service would be run like an airline. Passengers would pay a fixed amount for their tickets, regardless of how many people were actually on the plane. If the schedule called for a 10:00 a.m. flight, there would be a 10:00 a.m. flight whether there was one person on the plane or seven. The only thing that would cancel a flight was weather, and it takes a lot of weather to ground a Kenmore pilot.

The initial focus of Kenmore's new service was Friday Harbor. The largest and busiest community in the islands, Friday Harbor not only generates the most traffic, but the publicly owned seaplane dock was beyond the reach of Lake Union Air's dock monopoly. Carlson did agree to let Kenmore use his docks at Roche Harbor and on Orcas and Lopez islands awhile longer, but he made it clear if they expected the privilege to continue indefinitely, they'd have to start paying for it.

Gregg Munro launched his pilots into the new San Juan service in 1985, and it was an immediate success. Island residents were already familiar with the company's yellow, white, and brown floatplanes thanks to decades of charter flights. Now they had regular and affordable air service they could depend on. At least, that's what they were promised.

The good mood at the north end of Lake Washington was short-lived. For over ten years Kenmore Air had been winning the Navy contract for air transportation between the torpedo development facilities in Puget Sound and the open-water test range in the Strait of Georgia north of Nanaimo. No other company had the right combination of Cessnas and Beavers needed to provide the service the Navy required. It was a big contract, and it provided a good chunk of the Air Harbor's revenue.

Then a Kenmore pilot noticed a Beaver at Lake Union Air's dock. A few weeks later there was another one. And then another, and another. The Navy contract was coming up for bid again, and Clyde Carlson had decided it was time Lake Union Air stopped sitting on the bench. Two envelopes went off to the Navy this time, and when they were opened Kenmore was out of the military transportation business.

The successful launch of Lake Union Air's Victoria service had been frustrating to Kenmore because they hadn't been able to do it themselves. But they hadn't lost anything. Lake Union's winning of the Navy contract was something else again. It wasn't just the big loss in revenue that worried Munro; what really bothered him was knowing that he'd probably have to lay off some of his employees. He and Gregg did their best to come up with odd jobs to keep the idle pilots busy, but they both knew they were just staving off the inevitable. An air service doesn't need pilots to man planes that aren't going to fly.

Fortunately the gaping holes in the flight schedule didn't stay empty for long. Carlson soon realized that even with his additional airplanes he didn't have the resources he needed to fly the demanding Navy contract and still meet his profitable San Juan and Victoria schedules. He began asking Kenmore to pick up the Navy flights his pilots couldn't handle, but even this didn't give him the relief he needed. After a few months, he made it known he wanted out, period.

Munro could have let Lake Union Air default on the contract and then gone to the Navy and offered to do the job for the amount Kenmore had originally bid. It's safe to say this is what most business owners would have done, and no one would have faulted them for doing it. But Bob Munro had never used someone else's misfortune to leverage his own advancement, and he wasn't about to start now. Instead of letting Lake Union Air suffer the consequences of defaulting on the contract, Munro informed the Navy that Kenmore Air would be happy to take over the contract for the amount Carlson had bid for it. No matter that Kenmore would probably lose money on the deal. The money wasn't as important as seeing that everyone involved was treated fairly.

It was classic Bob Munro, and some of his business associates thought he was nuts. Every time there's a conflict, they'd say, Bob always settles it in favor of the customer even when the customer is wrong. He's never going to succeed doing that. And they'd shake their heads and never think to ask themselves why Kenmore had been succeeding for forty years and counting. Munro knew, of course, although if asked he may have found it difficult to put into words. But it was simple enough in his mind: happy customers come back. Which is the better formula for success: lose a little money on one job and have a loyal customer for life, or fight to get every penny due you and never see the customer again?

But if Munro's handling of the Navy contract had been a good illustration of his philosophy in practice, there was a far more impressive one on the way.

In 1986, Clyde Carlson received an offer to buy Lake Union Air and he decided to take it. The buyer had first tried to acquire the Air Harbor but the Munros weren't interested in selling. Carlson had been a determined competitor, but his focus had always been on simply making his company a success. The new management had a slightly different agenda. They made it known their intention was to run Kenmore flat out of business, and they lost no time in getting started. Gregg Munro was notified that his planes and pilots would no longer be tolerated at the docks controlled by Lake Union Air.

While Gregg and Tim Brooks tried to figure out how to deal with this setback, Munro began asking for ideas on additional ways to grow the company's passenger business. The obvious answer was to go after the lucrative Victoria traffic, but that could never happen as long as Canada refused to issue another operating certificate. But then someone saw a glimmer of light. It would be risky, more risky than starting the San Juan service, because it meant Munro would have to try something he'd never tried before. For the first time, he'd have to grow his company by acquisition.

The target would be Otter Air. The brainchild of marketing-expert Keith Lashley, Otter Air's sole asset had been a red, white, and black Beaver mounted on a set of old Norseman floats. Lashley's idea was to do by air what the local tour bus companies had been doing by ferry for years, shuttling tourists between Seattle and Victoria for a day of sightseeing and shopping. With no chance of getting a Seattle-Victoria operating certificate, Lashley applied for a certificate to fly between Port Townsend and Victoria. His application probably prompted quite a chuckle in Canada, as it was doubtful Port Townsend could generate a planeload of tourists once a month, let alone several times a day. But if Lashley wanted to give it shot, more power to him, and they granted the certificate.

Of course Lashley had no intention of trying to drum up business in Port Townsend. His only interest in the town was its location, which is directly under the flightpath between Seattle and Victoria. All of Otter Air's flights actually originated on Lake Union. From there they headed to Port Townsend where they made a brief stop, often just a touch-and-go in front of the town, to fulfill the requirement of the operating certificate before heading on to Victoria. Coming back, they did the same thing.

The scheme worked, but Lashley continued to lobby for a genuine Seattle-Victoria certificate until early 1987 when the Canadians finally relented and gave him one. But Lashley simply didn't have the resources he needed to grow his business. He'd managed to acquire a second plane, but even with his new operating certificate he knew he'd never be more than a small-time operator.

So when Tim Brooks and the Munros began making overtures to see if Lashley might be interested in selling, he was all ears. The overtures became full-fledged negotiations, and in the spring of 1987 Otter Air became a division of Kenmore Air. Lashley's two planes were overhauled and sold, and the tiny airline ceased to exist, except on paper. Kenmore's new Otter Air Division immediately began scheduled service between Lashley's dock on the east side of Lake Union and Victoria, using Kenmore's airplanes and the Otter Air operating certificate. The Battle of Victoria had begun.

It was a battle Kenmore was destined to lose. As the 1988 season drew to a close, it became painfully apparent the flight department was losing the struggle to meet the demands of the over-loaded schedule. The dock problem in the islands had been solved when the resort owners realized their own businesses would grow if they provided Kenmore Air with the dock space they needed. But too often planes that were supposed to go to the San Juans were being rescheduled for Victoria, sent north on a fishing resort run, or diverted to support the Navy contract. Instead of two or three flights a day to Friday Harbor, on some days there might be only one or, even worse, none. Island residents began complaining loudly and often that Kenmore's new scheduled service was becoming a lot less than what they'd been promised.

The pilots were tired, the dispatchers were short-tempered, and the mechanics were fed up with pulling all-nighters to make sure the whole fleet was up and running the next morning. Kenmore Air had gone from doing a few things extremely well to doing a bunch of things very badly. It was a far cry from Munro's self-directive to "achieve success in whatever you do."

As Gregg Munro reviewed the season's schedules, it didn't take him long to figure out the big problem was Victoria. Competing head to head with Lake Union Air meant Kenmore Air had to match them flight for flight. There was enough traffic on the route to support one operator, but not two.

"If we drop the Victoria service," Gregg concluded in a strategy meeting, "we'll have enough planes and pilots to cover all our San Juan and fishing resort flights as well as the charters and Navy flights. If we keep the Victoria service, the only way we can do the rest of it reliably is to buy more planes and hire more pilots."

"And the Victoria service," added Brooks, "isn't making any money overall and probably won't as long as Lake Union is flying there, too."

Brooks is an enthusiastic proponent of expansion, and he's always trying to come up with ways Kenmore can improve its business base. But even he knows that expansion at the expense of existing customers is not a route to success.

> "We really let our San Juan customers down. We'd promised them we would be there, day in and day out. Now we were all over the map, schedule-wise. Some days we'd be there and some days we wouldn't. We'd cancel flights at the last minute, or tell someone waiting at Roche Harbor they had to go to Friday Harbor to catch the plane. The loyalty we'd been building up for years was wiped out almost overnight. It doesn't take long for your customers to abandon you when they can't depend on you."
>
> TIM BROOKS

For a company founded on the principles of integrity and customer satisfaction the decision was obvious and Bob Munro didn't waste any time making it. The priority as far as he was concerned was the promise they'd made to their San Juan customers. The Victoria service was out.

"If we can't do it right, we won't do it at all," was his announcement to his staff.

Having won the Battle of Victoria, Lake Union Air lost no time in making the most of the victory. As Gregg Munro and his pilots took on the uphill task of convincing island residents they really could count on Kenmore, there was scarcely a competitive floatplane in sight. Lake Union's planes were all over on the Victoria run.

> "It took us a long, long time to win back the loyalty of the San Juan residents. 'How do we know you're not going to let us down again?' was a question we got a lot in those days. We learned a really valuable lesson. It's a big mistake to think customer loyalty will carry you through if your service starts slipping. Loyalty will keep your customers coming back when your service is good, but if you start letting them down, they aren't going to stick by you very long. We finally got our reputation back in the islands, but we never should have lost it in the first place. I hope it's a lesson we'll always remember."
>
> TIM BROOKS

Where Bob Munro's response to an over-extended schedule had been to pull his operations back to a sustainable level, the management at Lake Union Air took the opposite approach. When Lana

Kurtzer sold out to Clyde Carlson, Carlson had moved Lake Union Air from its little prefab office next door into Kurtzer's larger building. Then when Carlson sold the company, the new management set about remodeling the property with a vengeance. They tore out Kurtzer's floating dock, knocked down his parts shed, and finally demolished his big wooden hangar with its classic, multi-paned windows and unique water-powered airplane elevator. Then they went on a spending spree, adding more Beavers and then a monstrous Twin Otter on floats. They increased the number of flights to Victoria and started service to the remote communities on the west coast of Vancouver Island.

Beavers warming up for the first flight of the day. The two turbines in the lineup don't need a warm-up; they're ready to go as soon as the engines are started. (photo by C. Marin Faure)

Had the times been different, the strategy might have worked. But the combination of high expenses and an economic recession proved too much for the company to weather and by 1991, Lake Union Air was heading down the road to bankruptcy. Bob Munro was well aware of what was going on at the south end of Lake Union, and he undoubtedly realized that all he had to do was wait and the company that had vowed to put him out of business would be gone. As gratifying as that might be, he knew rubbing his hands in glee over the demise of a competitor wouldn't do anything for his own company.

Lake Union Air had a bunch of Beavers, an airplane nobody knew more intimately than Kenmore Air, and they had the best seaplane facility on Lake Union. Munro could sit by while the company was sold as-is or broken up and the assets sold off. Or he could take another risk. As Kenmore Air's accountant, Steve Gattis was a front row witness to the events that followed.

"Munro made a remarkable offer to Lake Union Air's owner. Instead of waiting for Lake Union to go out of business and buying their airplanes for ten cents on the dollar through bankruptcy, he offered to pay fair value for the aircraft.

"To me, that was business ethics at its best. Everything in 'normal business practice' suggested Bob buy the planes for ten cents on the dollar. Instead, Lake Union's owner, who had earlier tried to force Bob out of business, was treated fairly. Bob always saw the human element as being much more important than dollars and cents. If there's ever a classic example of 'do the right thing in business and the money will come' it was Bob Munro's business ethics."

STEVE GATTIS

Three years after Munro had ended his company's scheduled service to Victoria, he'd positioned Kenmore Air to be the only operator on the route. An office staff was hastily put together and dispatched to the Lake Union Air office. The first flight of Kenmore's re-established Victoria service was flown by pilot Jim Kastner in one of Jerry Rader's Super 180s, N2803K.

Bill Peters, Jerry Rader, Greg Gay, and Gordon Barnes picked through the Lake Union Air fleet and selected the planes they felt were worthy of being added to the Kenmore fleet. The others were cleaned up and sold as-is, or became candidates for the Beaver rebuild program.

In an era of mega-mergers, buyouts, and hostile takeovers, Kenmore Air remained true to its family origins. Gregg Munro was running the flight department. Leslie (Munro) Banks had taken over as office manager following Mildred Hall's retirement. And in 1992, parts department manager Eric Johanson hired a young man who'd had enough of the indoor intensity at Microsoft and wanted to do something a little more connected with the real world. He was Leslie and Tim Banks' oldest son, Todd, Bob Munro's grandson.

Todd Banks' first job was to help coax the parts department into the computer age. The departmental distinctions at Kenmore had been casual at best during the company's first twenty years of existence. There were the pilots, there were the mechanics, and whenever Bill Fisk got on his bicycle for the wobbly pedal up to the barn, there was a parts department. As the inventory in the barn grew to include hardware for dozens of different kinds of airplanes, engines, and floats, the parts department became the company nomad, migrating to wherever room could be found for it. By 1970, it had invaded the main office and shop building where it occupied space on both floors. Longtime parts employee Norm Bullen often had a tough time simply getting a part off a shelf.

"Everything was so crammed together, you couldn't bend over when you went down the aisles. You had to walk sideways and if you wanted to turn around you had to come out of the aisle to do it and then go back in.

NORM BULLEN

Banks knew what computers could do, and while it took awhile, he and the vendors who were doing the job finally managed to put together a practical inventory and accounting system. The greatest challenge was convincing his grandfather of the benefits. Bob Munro didn't understand computers and he didn't want to. He eventually ended up with one in his office, but he seldom turned it on. But while he had no interest in the system being wired up in the parts department, he grudgingly admitted he was impressed by the efficiency it promised.

He was far more impressed by the interest his grandson was taking in the business. Years earlier, if anyone had asked young Banks what he'd like to do when he grew up, working at Kenmore wouldn't have even made the list. But sometimes the smallest thing is what prompts the biggest decision.

"I read once that you don't choose the things you believe in, they choose you. When we were younger we'd walk around Ketchikan with my grandpa and you felt like you were with the town hero. He knew everybody and everybody knew him.

"Then I went to Alaska when I was sixteen years old to work at a fishing lodge, Yes Bay, cutting and cleaning fish, and then I started guiding. The lodge had a Beaver and we'd get a chance to fly in it every now and then and help the pilot. And I'd look in and the data plate in the plane said 'Overhauled by Kenmore Air Harbor.' And I felt like I had something to do with that.

"After college I got a job at Microsoft and I'd go outside to lunch and I'd see these float-planes flying overhead and I'd think, 'What the heck am I doing here?' So it's something that gets in your blood, I guess, and I've always wanted to be a part of it."

TODD BANKS

In order to computerize the company's accounting system, Banks had to understand it. He spent hours with his grandfather learning how the Brown Book worked, how the cost of a shop job was calculated, how customers were dealt with, and above all, how to keep earnings ahead of expenditures. It was time they both enjoyed, and Banks emerged from it with a real understanding of how the company worked. It was knowledge that would soon prove critical to Kenmore's very existence.

Even though Bob Munro had been on the scene from day one, he still found it hard to come to grips with what his one-plane, mudhole-based flying service had become in fifty years. He worked every day in his corner office, presiding over a multi-million dollar parts operation, a fleet of jet-powered floatplanes, and a shop that was putting together airplanes for dot-com millionaires and movie stars. He was proud of the way everyone had risen to the challenges brought on by the competition.

A lot of familiar faces were gone, of course. Bill Lund, for years a fixture beside the office water cooler where he told stories of bush flying to anyone who would listen. Walt Winseman, retired to concentrate on catching that elusive monster steelhead. Bill Fisk, spending his last years tinkering happily with his collection of old farm tractors. Mildred Hall, retired and living in southern

California. Sue Peters, helping her father care for the family's property holdings before taking on her next challenge.

Bill Peters had retired, too, but he wasn't really gone. When the docks needed rebuilding, or the railcar needed overhauling, or some other project on the property needed doing, he came back, doing his part to make sure Kenmore Air never disappears back into the bog that still lurks beneath it. Paul Carlson retired as well, but so expert are his skills in the turbine Otter that he continued to be asked back every year to help out during the busy summer season.

Everyone knew Munro would retire eventually, but like a tax audit, nobody wanted to think about it in the hopes that if they didn't, it wouldn't happen. Jerry Rader, when asked ten years earlier who he thought would succeed Munro when the day came, thought for a moment and then said, "I don't know. We all just assume Bob will be here forever."

Bob Munro retired in March 2000. The family had worked together to build a vacation home overlooking the Strait of Juan de Fuca, and Munro and Ruth began spending as much time there as possible, playing with the great-grandkids and enjoying the ever-changing panorama of water and weather. Munro didn't look eighty-three, but he was, and for some time he'd been thinking the pressures of running the complex business Kenmore had become would be better handled by someone younger. The question was, who?

With no one person poised to step into the void, management of the company was taken over by a committee made up of the department heads. Munro's office was converted into a conference room, and the little group held daily meetings to resolve problems and oversee the day to day operations. To a customer or passenger, the company seemed the same, but in fact, its future was very uncertain. The drama didn't play out in the newly converted meeting room but in the family members' homes. Some favored selling, others wanted to keep it. The debate went on for months, but eventually the tide began to turn in the direction of selling.

It hadn't gone out very far before Gregg Munro stopped it in its tracks by declaring his intention to keep the company going. He was immediately seconded by Todd Banks, the grandson who'd absorbed everything his grandfather had taught him about the business. It wasn't right, they said, to risk selling the company to someone who might simply sell off the assets and walk away. It wouldn't be fair to the employees, it wouldn't be fair to the customers, and it wouldn't be fair to the opportunity Bob Munro had worked so hard to give them. Who knows what Kenmore Air could grow into if they kept working at it? Between the two of them, they were determined to find out.

In the end, it was Gregg's passionate determination to carry on and Bank's business vision that carried the day. Banks fired up his computer and figured out a way to keep the company together while meeting the financial needs of the other family members. Bob Munro's office was put back the way it had been, and Banks moved down from his cubbyhole in the upstairs business office to take over the day-to-day management of the company.

If anyone had been expecting dramatic changes as a result of all this, they were sorely disappointed. Banks knows the value of technology—he didn't bat an eye at the notion of investing in a state-of-the-art reservation system, and the company's website is more interesting and user-friendly than the sites of most major airlines—but he'd paid attention to his grandfather's discourses in fiscal responsibility. Even though computer screens now glow on every desk, he still maintains the Brown Book.

Under Gregg Munro's continuing stewardship, the flight department seems to set a new record every year for the number of passengers carried. The company's mix of piston and turbine Beavers and turbine Otters makes it economical to add a new destination to the schedule, service it with a smaller airplane, and then as the route grows more popular, either switch to a larger plane or add more flights with the smaller plane. It's the same strategy employed by every successful airline on the planet.

The Caravan over Elliott Bay and the Seattle waterfront. Although not as large as the de Havilland Otter, the Caravan is much faster. (photo by Ed Turner)

Kenmore acquired its first Beaver in 1966. It was a good plane, but whether or not it would prove useful to the Air Harbor was something only time would tell. History repeated itself in 2003 when a new type of plane showed up at the Kenmore dock. Like the Beaver, it had been flying for almost twenty years before Kenmore got a good look at one. And like the Beaver, its future with Kenmore Air is something only time will tell.

The Cessna Caravan first flew in 1985. In many ways, it's the Beaver all over again, but with a much more modern flair. Designed as a utility plane, the turbine-powered Caravan can carry up

Thirty-plus years in Kenmore colors and still going strong. Six-Six-Zulu fresh from the overhaul shop with (from left) pilots Paul Carlson, Tim Brooks, Bill Whitney, and Gregg Munro. (photo by C. Marin Faure)

to nine passengers at speeds only dreamed of by Beaver pilots. Even on floats, a Caravan is almost fifty miles per hour faster than the de Havilland round-engined classic. True, the Caravan's cabin isn't as roomy as the Beaver's, and the Otter's cabin is a barn by comparison. But the Caravan has wonderful seats and better soundproofing. As soon as Kenmore put the plane into service, passengers began praising its quiet, smooth ride.

It's not just the new airplane itself that repeated history at Kenmore. Bob Munro had benefited from enthusiastic supporters like Harold Nicholas who were willing to help finance the company's growth in the 1940s. Nicholas' modern-day equivalent is Mark Torrance. Torrance's relationship with Kenmore Air started with the purchase of a Cessna 180. He soon moved up to a Beaver, but like Nicholas almost sixty years earlier, Torrance quickly recognized there was more to this remarkable company than the selling and servicing of airplanes. The dedication to customers, the determination to do the job right that had so impressed Nicholas impressed Torrance as well.

And, like Todd Banks and Gregg Munro, Torrance was convinced that what Bob Munro had started could keep going, could expand into new markets and offer new services. But the company's image would have to keep pace, and in the airline industry, few improvements capture the attention and imagination of passengers like the introduction of a brand new airplane.

The best candidate for the job was the Caravan. Powered by the same trouble-free Pratt & Whitney PT6A turbine that's nestled in the noses of the company's turbine Beavers and Otters, the Caravan's capacity and speed would add even more flexibility to the Kenmore Air fleet. Torrance and Banks worked out a partnership arrangement to finance the acquisition of a Caravan and put it on floats. It was an instant hit with passengers.

> "They prefer the Caravan. The people that ride the Caravan and can afford to use any plane they want keep asking for the Caravan. It's a little smaller, yes, but they appreciate the speed and the quiet ride. Boeing uses the Caravan to fly its airline customers to the islands. The people who own Foss Tugs, they ask for the Caravan. On longer routes it does the same mission in almost half the time as the Beaver."
>
> **TODD BANKS**

But the real potential of the Caravan may be in doing things the company has never before considered doing. One of Kenmore Air's biggest challenges has always been figuring out what to do with the planes and pilots during the slow winter season. Airplanes are expensive assets to have sitting around doing nothing, so as the days grow short and the clouds slide into the convergence zone, Todd Banks, Gregg Munro, and Tim Brooks stare out the windows at the rows of gleaming yellow, white and brown floatplanes crouching on their silver floats in the tie-down area and wonder what to do with them.

The answer might lie in taking some of them off their floats. Air travel used to be fun. It used to be an adventure. People used to dress up to go on an airplane trip. Today air travel is mostly an impatient, frustrating hassle in which overtaxed security, overcrowded airports, and outdated air traffic management systems conspire to make an airplane trip little more than an endurance contest for the participants.

Passengers flying from Seattle-Tacoma International Airport south to Portland or north to Vancouver, BC spend far more time getting to and through the airports than sitting on the planes. It's a thirty minute flight that generally requires at least four hours to complete. Would these same passengers be willing to go to a secondary airport like Boeing Field in south Seattle, go straight from their car to their plane, fly for fifty minutes or so, and then go straight to a car or cab ride to their final destination? It's an intriguing possibility.

Drive around the perimeter roads of any northwest airport and you'll see them, the amateur plane spotters, leaning against the hoods of their cars with their notebooks and binoculars. Will they someday be jotting down the tail numbers of Cessna Caravans with "Kenmore Air" written on the sides? Will a teenager working a summer fish camp in southeast Alaska peer into the cockpit of a float-equipped Caravan and read on the data plate, "Overhauled by Kenmore Air Harbor?" Only time will tell.

Kenmore Air serves a unique corner of the world, a landscape of startling contrasts. A landscape where trees cling to solid rock, where swirling channels lead to placid bays, where veiling mists part to reveal brilliant clarity. A landscape which, once seen, is never forgotten. Perhaps more than any other place on earth, the maze of islands and mountains stretching from Puget Sound to Glacier Bay binds all who venture in closer to life itself. It's in the simple genius of the coast Indian's story about Raven's discovery of fire and how he brought it to the First Men. It's in the steam-valve sigh of a gray whale surfacing through the liquid mirror of Blackfish Sound. It's in the darting flash of a kingfisher, the stealthy step of a heron, the lazy circle of an eagle. It's in the distant drone of a solitary floatplane, it's triple silhouette of floats and fuselage sharp against a pewter sky.

Flying with Kenmore Air is an experience not soon forgotten by even the most jaded traveler. There's not much point in dragging a floatplane up to nose-bleed altitudes; it usually makes more sense to stay low, a few thousand feet up at most. For passenger and pilot alike, float flying is like being inside a painting as opposed to peering at one from across the room. It's a perspective seldom seen, and even nervous passengers are soon so engrossed in looking down on houses and yards and cars and cows and beaches and boats that about the time they remember they're supposed to be scared the plane is easing up to the dock at their destination, and they climb out disappointed that it's all over so soon.

Kenmore's pilots have grown used to passenger manifests as varied as the landscape they fly through. Katherine Hepburn, Goldie Hawn, Bill Gates, Neil Armstrong, Jimmy Buffet. Movie stars, software visionaries, astronauts, and platinum-record musicians ride the same planes as boat mechanics and visiting relatives from Iowa. Kenmore supplied the Beaver used in the movie *Six Days and Seven Nights*. Harrison Ford, an accomplished pilot in his own right, grew so enamored of the plane during the filming that he had Kenmore's Beaver shop put one together especially for him.

The immaculate Beavers and turbines Kenmore Air flies today bear little resemblance to the tiny, two-place plane that sputtered to life in 1946 and tentatively lifted the Air Harbor off the water in front of the mud bog the company had chosen to call home. But the view down the lake is no different. It's the same view Jack Mines, Reg Collins, and Bob Munro contemplated as they wondered where their little venture might take them. It's a different generation now, standing on the shore watching the changing moods slide across the water in front of them, wondering where their much bigger venture will take them.

But the possibilities that lie beyond the lake are no fewer today than they were then. Times change, markets change, employees change, but the basic principles for success never change.

Dedicate yourself to achieve success in whatever you do. Have your priorities in order. Be willing to take risks and be confident in your ideas. And don't work necessarily for money but for accomplishment.

These are not guidelines for staying the same, for playing it safe. They are guidelines which, if followed intelligently, lead to new opportunities, new adventures. Kenmore Air tomorrow will be different than Kenmore Air today, just as the company today is different than the company Bob Munro steered to success for fifty-four years.

The Caravan climbs out past the Space Needle after departing Lake Union. Lake Washington is in the distance, with the Cascade Mountains on the horizon. (photo by Ed Turner)

Change is scary only when you don't control it. The people who are Kenmore Air today have a unique opportunity, for they are in a unique position. They stand on an uncompromised foundation of ethics and integrity, of fiscal responsibility, of doing business by doing the right thing. Behind them they have the strength of a respected brand, a loyal customer base, and an unmatched level of skill and ability. Ahead of them...well, ahead of them lies whatever they choose to do with the remarkable legacy they have been given.

Bob Munro never boasted about his accomplishments. To hear him tell it, he was hardly involved in Kenmore at all.

"Oh, the three of us started this little company, and I've kind of kept it going all these years, and here we are."

But in fact he was very proud of the Air Harbor. He was proud of the things he had done, and proud of what his family and employees had done. He'd started out wanting nothing more than a simple repair shop where he could make a living tinkering with airplanes. As he, Reg Collins, and Jack Mines hammered together their little company with its chicken-coop office and car-garage shop, he never in his wildest dreams imagined what it would eventually become. But the future wasn't something Bob Munro spent a lot of time worrying about. He just tried to do the right thing, one day at a time, confident it was the only sure road to success.

"The best thing about this job has been wanting to come to work every day. There's always a challenge. I like being able to do a good job for people. Hearing someone say, 'Kenmore's the best,' or 'That was a wonderful flight.' That's the whole thing of it. It's not about making money, it's not about trying to build up a fortune for myself. It's coming in and feeling good about the business.

"I don't talk to people as much as I probably should, so I think maybe a lot of the people that have worked for us have never known how important they were to me. Every one of them has put their mark on the company, and the only reason we're still here is because of what they've done.

"I can't predict the future, so it's hard to say what the company will be like a few years down the road. But I like to think we've started something that will keep going. I absolutely believe if we take the attitude that we're going to do a good job and deliver what we promise, we'll succeed.

"As long as we have the kind of people working for us that we've had since the beginning, there should be airplanes with 'Kenmore' on the side flying around this part of the world for a long, long time. I sure hope that's what happens, and I hope everyone enjoys the experience as much as I have."

ROBERT B. MUNRO, 1917–2000